ArtScroll Tanach Series®

A traditional commentary on the Books of the Bible

Rabbis Nosson Scherman/Meir Zlotowitz
General Editors

Daniel

Daniel

DANIEL / A NEW TRANSLATION WITH A COMMENTARY ANTHOLOGIZED FROM TALMUDIC, MIDRASHIC AND RABBINIC SOURCES.

Published by

Mesorah Publications, ltd

Translation and Commentary by
Rabbi Hersh Goldwurm

An Overview/

  'Daniel — A Bridge to Eternity'
by Rabbi Nosson Scherman

FIRST EDITION
First Impression . . . February 1979

SECOND EDITION
Revised and Corrected
Six Impressions . . . October 1980 — May 2002

Published and Distributed by
MESORAH PUBLICATIONS, Ltd.
4401 Second Avenue
Brooklyn, New York 11232

Distributed in Europe by
LEHMANNS
Unit E, Viking Industrial Park
Rolling Mill Road
Jarrow, Tyne & Wear NE32 3DP
England

Distributed in Australia & New Zealand by
GOLDS WORLD OF JUDAICA
3-13 William Street
Balaclava, Melbourne 3183
Victoria Australia

Distributed in Israel by
SIFRIATI / A. GITLER — BOOKS
6 Hayarkon Street
Bnei Brak 51127

Distributed in South Africa by
KOLLEL BOOKSHOP
Shop 8A Norwood Hypermarket
Norwood 2196, Johannesburg, South Africa

ISBN
0-89906-079-X (hard cover)
0-89906-080-3 (paperback)

Typography by CompuScribe at ArtScroll Studios, Ltd.
4401 Second Avenue / Brooklyn, N.Y. 11232 / (718) 921-9000

Printed in the United States of America by Moriah Offset
Bound by Sefercraft, Quality Bookbinders, Ltd. Brooklyn, N.Y.

This volume is dedicated

with respect and affection

to

מרביצי תורה ותמכין דאורייתא

the Rabbis and Educators

who spread and teach Torah,

and those who support their efforts.

They are the human treasures

whose devotion has built a new world

of Torah life in America.

Rabbi and Mrs. J. Marcus and family

Irving and Libby Forman and family

Staten Island, New York

Table of Contents

This was the first work of

Rabbi Hersh Goldwurm זצ״ל

one of the treasures of our generation.
His vast knowledge and wisdom
are reflected not only in the large body of
Torah literature he wrote and edited,
but in much of the ArtScroll Series.
He embodied Torah greatness,
piety, kindness, and humility.
His untimely passing on,
at the height of his powers
left a gaping void among his peers
and the Torah world in general.

תנצב״ה

RABBI MOSES FEINSTEIN
455 F. D. R. DRIVE
New York 2, N. Y.
—
OREGON 7-1222

משה פיינשטיין
ר״מ תפארת ירושלים
בנוא יארק

בעה״י

הנה ידידי הרב הגאון מוהר״ר צבי הירש גאלדווארם שליט״א
מחשובי תלמידי בית מדרש עליון אשר הוא ת״ח מפורסם
ומרביץ תורה ברבים הרבה שנים והעמיד תלמידים חשובים
בתורה וביראת ה׳ טהורה נשאו לבו לחבר חיבור חשוב על ספר
דניאל בשפה האנגלית המדוברת ביותר במדינה זו, אשר הוא
חלק מהמפעל הגדול של חברת ,,ארטסקרול״ שמוציאים לאור
קובץ דברים יקרים ופנינים נחמדים מספרי רבותינו נ״ע על כל
ספרי תנ״ך אשר הם מעוררים לאהבת התורה וקיום המצוות
וחזוק האמונה בהשי״ת. וגם אני מברך את ידידי הרה״ג הנכבד
מוהר״ר נתן שערמאן שליט״א אשר הוסיף לבאר תוכן ספר
דניאל לפי דברי חז״ל בפתיחת הספר בדברים המושכים את הלב
לתורה ויראת השי״ת. אשר על כן דבר טוב הוא שחברת
,,ארטסקרול״ בנשיאת ידידי הרב הנכבד מאד **מוהר״ר מאיר
יעקב בן ידידי הרב הגאון ר׳ אהרן זלאטאוויץ שליט״א** מוציאו
לאור עולם להגדיל אהבת השי״ת ותורתו הקדושה ואמונתנו
בגאולה שהובטח לנו מהשי״ת.

וע״ז באתי עה״ח   יום ג׳ צו תשמ״ו

משה פיינשטיין

גדלי׳ הלוי שארר

ר״מ ומנהל במתיבתא תו״ד

ברוקלין, נ. י. יע״א

בס״ד

כ״ב טבת תשל״ט לפ׳ק

למע״כ ידידי הרה״ג החו״ב טובא **הרב צבי גאלדוואַרם שליט״א**
אחדשה״ט באהבה ויקר;

מאוד שמחתי בשמעי כי כבודו קבל על עצמו לקחת חלק
במפעל הגדול בהוצאת כתבי הקודש בתרגום בשפה המדוברת,
ולהוציא לאור ספר דניאל. ומהעלים שהיו בידי ראיתי מעשה ידי
אומן, בסגנונו הבהיר, ובידיעותיו המקיפות בדברי חכז״ל
ובפירושי הראשונים והאחרונים ז״ל, הוציא מתח״י דבר **שלם,** הן
בפירוש המילים, הן בעומק הפשט, וגם בהבנת עומק העניינים,
והעיר עיני המעיינים בה גם בדברים הקשים שבספר דניאל,
והפליא לעשות בזה.

אשר על כן ברכתי אמורה לו שנותן התורה יהא בעזרו, ויזכה
להרביץ תורה מתוך הרחבה ושמחה, ומעינותיו יפוצו חוצה
ורבים יהנו מאורו.

וגם ברכתי אמורה לידידי הנכבד הרה״ג הנעלה **הרב נתן
שערמאַן שליט״א** אשר כבר נודע גדול כוחו בחיבוריו הקודמים,
בסקירותיו הכלליות, אשר בהן השקיע אדני יסוד האמונה של
רבותינו הקדושים זי״ע, וכמעשהו בראשונים כן מעשהו בספר
הזה. ויהא ה׳ עמו שיהא ביכולתו להמשיך במפעלו הגדול, מתוך
הרחבה ושמחה,

כעתירת ידי״נ הדו״ש ואשרו כל הימים,

החותם בברכה והוקרה

[signature]

Preface

With mixed emotions of joy and trepidation, I approach the publication of this volume. I thank Hashem for having granted me the opportunity and endowed me with the ability to bring this work to completion. However, in the words of R' Nechunyah ben Hakanah, I pray יְהִי רָצוֹן שֶׁלֹּא אֶכָּשֵׁל בִּדְבַר הֲלָכָה, May it be God's will that I not err in deciding a matter of halachah. If one must fear the possiblity of an erroneous halachic decision, surely in matters of basic אֱמוּנָה, faith — the foundation of Judaism — one must tremble thousandfold, lest he err.

I pray that, because of the זְכוּת הָרַבִּים, the merit of the wide circle of readership enjoyed by the ARTSCROLL TANACH SERIES, Hashem has led me in the right path that 'I might not err in a matter of halachah.'

The book of Daniel enjoys a special distinction among the Books of the Bible. Nowhere else are the promised redemption, the קֵץ, End, and תְּחִיַת הַמֵּתִים, the resurrection of the dead, so explicitly spelled out. But this is part of the mystery of the Book of Daniel. Because of its very explicitness the Book is sealed to us with many seals. These matters were not meant to be grasped with any degree of clarity, but rather to be accepted and believed with fervent hope. As the angel said to Daniel (12:4): Obscure the matters and ·seal the Book until the time of the End.' However, it was not meant for the Book of Daniel to become a secret hidden book, accessible only to a chosen few. If so it surely would not be part of the Bible, for נְבוּאָה שֶׁנִּצְרְכָה לְדוֹרוֹת נִכְתְּבָה, only that prophecy needed by the generations was written (Megillah 14a). Rather the matter of the קֵץ, End, was meant to be studied with full realization that it remains complex and inaccessible. It was meant to be an 'open' סֵפֶר חָתוּם, sealed Book. As the angel concluded (12:4), 'Let the multitudes muse and the knowledge multiply.' This is all the more true in our generation of עֲקַבְתָּא דִמְשִׁיחָא, when the footsteps of the Messianic king are already reverberating in our ears. Indeed, the Book is the clarion call of the Messiah — as Chazon LaMoed relates, in Greek communities it was read during the three week period of mourning for the Holy Temple.

The Book teaches us another lesson, one that is relevant as long as Jews are in exile. When Daniel and his companions were taken to Nebuchadnezzar's court, they faced unprecedented circumstances.

Never since the giving of the Torah had observant Jews found themselves in an alien and hostile environment. By their example, Daniel, Chananyah, Mishael, and Azaryah demonstrated to countless generations that existence in Galus requires persistent and obstinate perseveranc·. Had Daniel not jeopardized his life to observe such commandments as Kashruth and prayer, he would surely not have been chosen to be the prophet of the קֵץ, End.

Like its predecessors in the ArtScroll Series, this Book presents an anthologized commentary culled from the Talmud, Midrash and classical commentaries. It is designed to make as intelligible as possible, both the פְּשׁוּטוֹ שֶׁל מִקְרָא, the literal sense of Scripture, and philosophical and homiletical interpretations of the Sages and commentators. Among the commentators, we have generally given precedence to Rashi, 'the father of commentators'.

The translation attempts to remain faithful to the sequence and idiom of the original text.

This has been especially difficult in the Aramaic portion of the book where many unusual words pose difficulty. In a few isolated cases involving words of a technical nature, we have transliterated from the original without giving any translation.

The transliteration in this book follows the usage already established by ArtScroll: Consonants are given according to the Ashkenazi tradition and the vowels according to the Sephardi. The Four Letter Name of God is given as HASHEM, while Elohim is translated God. As pointed out by Rabbi Moshe Eisemann in his preface to the ArtScroll Ezekiel, the prefix vav has many meanings besides 'and'. The translation reflects this.

The dates given in this volume are based on the traditional chronology given in the Seder Olam; it dates back to Talmudic times, is based on Biblical and Rabbinic sources, forms the basis for such halachic matters as the determination of Shmittah, and is founded upon an uninterrupted tradition (cf. Rabbi S. Rothenberg, Toldos Am Olam I p. 55; Igros Chazon Ish, no. 302). It differs from the chronology used by secular scholars in that it dates the destruction of the First Temple and the building of the Second Temple 166 years later and assigns, consequently, a much shorter duration to the period of Persian rule over the Jews prior to Alexander the Great. (For efforts to reconcile the differences, see R' S. Schwab, Comparative Jewish Chronology, in the Rabbi Dr. Joseph Breuer Jubilee Volume, N.Y., 1962).

Acknowledgments

I owe a great debt of gratitude to many people who helped make possible, or at least eased, the production of this volume.

I am deeply grateful to my dear friend, RABBI NOSSON SCHERMAN, whose confidence has been an unending source of inspiration. In addition to enhancing this volume with his perceptive and masterful Overview, he has edited numerous passages in the commentary and spent many hours under trying conditions reviewing and redoing the translation. There is hardly a verse which does not bear his imprint.

My profoundest thanks to RABBI YEHOSHUA LEIMAN who has gone far beyond his duties as an editor. Aside from his considerable editorial skills, he has been an incisive critic and has pointed out numerous sources that have enriched the final product. The comments which appear in the book over his name are evidence of his role.

To RABBI MEIR ZLOTOWITZ whose inspiration is the life-giving force in the ArtScroll series, I give special thanks. His pioneering concept of anthologized commentary is now so accepted as to be taken for granted, but it is a product of his discerning eye, critical judgment, and single-minded devotion to illuminating the meaning of the text and the major commentaries. His friendship and advice during this project have been an additional bonus in my association with ArtScroll.

REB SHEA BRANDER has again excelled himself in supervising all areas of production and graphics that resulted in a Book of outstanding beauty. He has spent many long hours of hard work in a labor of love.

RABBI AVIE GOLD has read the galley proofs with his unusual meticulous precision and dedication to the word of Torah. He has brought many important points to my attention and has my deepest thanks to him for this. The finished product reflects his participation in many subtle ways that can be appreciated only by someone who works with him.

To the typesetting staff go my sincerest thanks. They have struggled with a difficult and many times complicated manuscript — and done it with unfailing cooperation and good cheer.

I extend my thanks to MR. SHMUEL KLEIN *of the Mendel Gottesman Library. He translated from the original Arabic all the technical terms taken from R' Saadiah Gaon's* Tafsir *in chapter 2. He also helped in obtaining much rare and out of print material.*

RABBI MOSHE LIPSHITZ, *the librarian of the Central Torah Library of Agudath Israel of Boro Park has placed at my disposal his wealth of knowledge and the resources of that library.* MR. DAVID H. SCHWARTZ *has gone out of his way to obtain copies of rare books and has been a source of support and encouragement. I am grateful to them both.*

I also thank RABBI *and* REBBETZIN JOSEPH B. SOLOVEITCHIK *of Monsey, New York, for lending me a very rare volume needed in my work.*

Finally, אַחֲרוֹן אַחֲרוֹן חָבִיב, MARAN HARAV HAGAON R' YAAKOV KAMINETZKEY שליט״א *was gracious enough to allow me use of one of Jewry's great treasures — his wisdom, judgment, and time. I have been privileged to consult with him about the more sensitive issues in this Book, and have been granted the advantage of his sage advice. My profoundest thanks to him for this. May Hashem grant him* אֲרִיכוּת יָמִים וְשָׁנִים.

In closing I wish to mention those of my family who are no longer with us, and whose memories have been constant sources of inspiration:

לזכר נשמת אבי אבי ר' משה ב״ר צבי הי״ד

נלב״ע בשנות הזעם תש״ג יום הזכרון יח אדר

אשתו אסתר בת ר' שמואל אלימלך ז״ל, ו חשון תשי״ז

אבי אמי ר' ישראל ב״ר דוד הכהן ז״ל, ז חשון תשט״ז

אשתו סימא בת ר' פנחס ז״ל, ו אייר תשכ״א

Rabbi Hersh Goldwurm

Teves, 5739 / January 1979
Monsey, New York

An Overview/
Daniel — A Bridge to Eternity

An Overview /
Daniel — A Bridge to Eternity

לא ירד דניאל לגוב האריות אלא כדי שיעשה לו
הקב״ה נסים וגבורות בשביל לקדש שמו בעולם
*Daniel descended to the lions' pit only so
that the Holy One, Blessed be He, should
perform for him miraculous and mighty
deeds in order to sanctify [God's] Name in
public (Sifre Haazinu 306).*

תנו רבנן בשעה שהפיל נבוכדנצר חנניה משאל
ועזריה לכבשן האש אמר לו הקב״ה ליחזקאל
לך והחיה מתים בבקעת דורא
*The Rabbis taught that at the moment
when Nebuchadnezzar threw Chananyah,
Mishael, and Azaryah into the fiery kiln,
the Holy One, Blessed be He, instructed
Yechezkel, 'Go and resuscitate the dead in
the Valley of Dura' (Sanhedrin 92b).*

... שמא תאמר אנו מחכים והוא אינו מחכה?
ת״ל וְלָכֵן יְחַכֶּה ה׳ לַחֲנַנְכֶם ...
*... Perhaps you will say, 'We await [the
Messiah but [God] does not await [our
redemption]?'*

*Scripture teaches (Isaiah 30:18):
Therefore HASHEM waits to show you
favor (ibid. 97b).*

I. The Historical Background

*The Last
Hope*   The declining years of the Kingdom of Judah were
turbulent and bloody. They marked the end of
the glorious period that began with the crossing of
the Jordan into *Eretz Yisrael* and reached its zenith

with the reigns of David and Solomon. The decline led to the tragedy of the Temple's destruction and Israel's exile to Babylon. There, laying the groundwork for the future rebirth of Jewish national greatness, was a boy being groomed for royal ministry in the academy of Nebuchadnezzar's court. His name was Daniel.

Menashe's Legacy

The notoriously wicked reigns of Menasheh (3228-3283) and his son Ammon (3283-3285) led to the final sealing of God's decree that Israel must suffer an exile and that the Temple had been robbed of its sanctity by the sins of its people. Menasheh implanted, and Ammon nurtured, the festering seeds of idolatry and rebellion against God. The spiritual ravages of Menasheh's reign had so eaten away at the moral fiber of the people that their fate was sealed; they could no longer avoid the exile and suffering that had been foretold by the prophets if their evil ways were to continue (II Kings 21:10-15, 23:26). Even Menasheh's own repentance after the first twenty-two years of his fifty-five year reign (II Chronicles 33:12) could not reverse the inexorable train of events he had set in motion. The corruption had eaten too deeply.

The brief two-year rule of his son, Ammon, exceeded the blasphemy and wickedness even of his father (Sanhedrin 103b). Menasheh, for all his evil, had at least been raised in the righteous ways of his glorious father, Hezekiah (3199-3228), but Ammon had grown up with only Menasheh to guide him.

Menasheh, for all his evil, had at least been raised in the righteous ways of his glorious father, Hezekiah, but Ammon had grown up with only Menasheh to guide him.

True, the sins of the generation and its leaders were measured by standards appropriate to a people steeped in holiness, molded by God's Presence, attuned to the stirring words of the prophets. More was expected of them than of their neighboring nations and of succeeding generations, and they were judged accordingly [see Overview to Ruth, which helps provide perspective for understanding the sins of the ancients]. Nevertheless, Scripture speaks of their evil in the severest terms and categorically

states *(II Kings* 21:10-15) that they caused the *Shechinah* to be banished from the Temple and the Land.

Hope shone brightly for one last period before the darkness closed in finally.

Hope shone brightly for one last period before the darkness closed in finally. Ammon's son, Josiah (3285-3316), was the last truly great and noble scion of the House of David. 'He was like a golden ornament, like precious stones and pearls' *(Eichah Rabbasi* 4:1). Josiah cleansed the land of idols and set about with energy and zeal to bring its people back to their Father *(II Kings* 23:3-20). But though they followed his lead in the streets and on the hilltops, their hearts and homes still belonged to the abominations of Menasheh and Ammon *(Taanis* 22b). Finally, Josiah was killed in battle against Egypt *(II Kings* 23:29). The last hope gone, the Land began a twenty-two year death rattle.

Crossroads of Conquest

Josiah's son, Yehoachaz (3316) reigned for only three months until Pharaoh Necho, the Egyptian conqueror, who killed the father, deposed the son and replaced him with his brother Yehoyakim (3316-3327). The new king was weak and pliant at first. He and his crippled, lowly kingdom were trapped between two giants who contested for domination of the civilized world — Egypt and Babylon (present-day Iraq).

A few years later, Nebuchadnezzar became king of Babylon. He turned his eyes to the southwest and decided to conquer *Eretz Yisrael* and to supplant Egypt as the world's leading power. A year later, Nebuchadnezzar swept across *Eretz Yisrael*, and Yehoyakim acquired a new master; the noose of Babylon began to tighten around the neck of Judah. The spiritual grandeur of Josiah had not outlived him; both Yehoachaz and Yehoyakim were heirs of their grandfather rather than of their father. Spiritually, they failed to uplift their people; temporally they were reduced to pledging allegiance and paying heavy tribute, first to the conqueror from the south and then to the conqueror from the north.

Nebuchadnezzar swept across Eretz Yisrael, and Yehoyakim acquired a new master; the noose of Babylon began to tighten around the neck of Judah.

After three years of submissive vassalage, Yeho-

yakim revolted against Nebuchadnezzar's dominion and proclaimed his freedom. His romantic notion endured only as long as Babylon was willing to tolerate it. After three years, Nebuchadnezzar's army put down the rebellion and strengthened its control of *Eretz Yisrael*. The conquering king took away with him many vessels from the Temple. He took people as well. Some of Judah's finest youth — among them, Daniel, Chananyah, Mishael, and Azaryah — were taken to Babylon to be trained in the ways of the court, so that the legendary wisdom of Jerusalem could be put to the service of Babylon (*Daniel* 1:2-3).

Daniel, Chananyah, Mishael, and Azaryah — were taken to Babylon to be trained in the ways of the court so that the legendary wisdom of Jerusalem could be put to the service of Babylon.

That in itself should have been a harbinger of Israel's end as a nation of God; if its youthful talent were to become assimilated into foreign bureaucracies, Israel might not have survived. In the Book of *Daniel*, we shall see how Jewish integrity survives and rebuilds.

A few years later, in 3327, Nebuchadnezzar returned. He deposed Yehoyakim and led him off in chains to an ignominious death in Babylon. For three months, Yehoyachin (Yechoniah) succeeded his father as king. Then, Nebuchadnezzar swooped down again. He took Yehoyachin to a Babylonian prison, looted the Temple treasury, and carried off its golden vessels. He looted the Land of its human treasures, too. Ten thousand of its best people were taken away, among them, the *Charash* and *Masger* — a thousand of its most distinguished Torah scholars — along with the civil and military leadership (*II Kings* 24:12-16). His plan was simple. By denuding Jerusalem of its most accomplished people, he would ensure that it could never again flout his authority, and by contemptuously demonstrating his mastery over the Temple, he would crush the morale of the downtrodden remnant.

By denuding Jerusalem of its most accomplished people, he would ensure that it could never again flout his authority, and by contemptuously demonstrating his mastery over the Temple, he would crush the morale of the downtrodden remnant.

Nebuchadnezzar appointed Zedekiah, Yehoyachin's uncle, as king (3327) and exacted an oath of allegiance. The end was near, but not because of *Eretz Yisrael's* further reduced political, economic, and military state. For Israel, neither greatness nor

degradation is a function of garrisons or vaults. Israel was created to be God's nation; its fortune rises or wanes depending on how well it follows that calling. Under Zedekiah, the nation's spiritual state continued downhill — so its temporal fortunes followed suit. The end came in 3338 when the Temple was destroyed.

Under Zedekiah, the nation's spiritual state continued downhill — so its temporal fortunes followed.

[For further information and perspective see *Overview* to ArtScroll *Ezekiel.*]

Seeds of the Future

But *the Protector of Israel neither sleeps nor slumbers (Psalms* 121:4). Sinful the nation may be, with exile and degradation as its lot, but God sets the stage for its ultimate survival and rejuvenation.

Jeremiah sent a message to the exiles in Babylon:

כֹּה אָמַר ה׳ צְבָאוֹת אֱלֹהֵי יִשְׂרָאֵל לְכָל הַגּוֹלָה אֲשֶׁר הִגְלֵיתִי מִירוּשָׁלַם בָּבֶלָה. בְּנוּ בָתִּים וְשֵׁבוּ וְנִטְעוּ גַנּוֹת וְאִכְלוּ אֶת פִּרְיָן. קְחוּ נָשִׁים וְהוֹלִידוּ בָּנִים וּבָנוֹת וּקְחוּ לִבְנֵיכֶם נָשִׁים וְאֶת בְּנוֹתֵיכֶם תְּנוּ לַאֲנָשִׁים וְתֵלַדְנָה בָּנִים וּבָנוֹת וּרְבוּ שָׁם וְאַל תִּמְעָטוּ. וְדִרְשׁוּ אֶת שְׁלוֹם הָעִיר אֲשֶׁר הִגְלֵיתִי אֶתְכֶם שָׁמָּה וְהִתְפַּלְלוּ בַעֲדָהּ אֶל ה׳ כִּי בִשְׁלוֹמָהּ יִהְיֶה לָכֶם שָׁלוֹם.

'To the entire exile which I have banished from Jerusalem to Babylon. Build homes and settle; plant orchards and eat their fruit.'

So says HASHEM of hosts, God of Israel, 'To the entire exile which I have banished from Jerusalem to Babylon. Build homes and settle; plant orchards and eat their fruit. Take wives and beget sons and daughters. Take wives for your sons and give your daughters to husbands that they may beget sons and daughters; increase there and do not diminish. Seek the peace of the city to which I have exiled you and pray on its behalf to HASHEM — for through its peace will you have peace' (Jeremiah 29:4-7).

Let us try to find God's mercy amid the fury of the destruction and exile. Let us try to discern the tools of His salvation.

II. Levels of History*

God's purpose is that the universe be perceived by man as a reflection of His absolute mastery and oneness, that evil disappear and that good become man's only course of conduct. Assurance of this goal's fulfillment is a theme that runs through prophecy after prophecy, but His manner of leading to its realization is multi-faceted and varied. There are times when good is openly rewarded, and evil openly punished. There are other times when evil ascends with impunity, and good grovels in humiliated rejection. Even then, His plan is not being thwarted; He merely chooses to conceal His ways until the time when His wisdom decrees that all should be revealed and made comprehensible. Until we see the whole, we cannot understand the parts; when we see the whole — sometimes after generations, sometimes not until the End of Days — we will understand why each ingredient had to enter the picture when it did and as it did.

There are times when good is openly rewarded and evil openly punished. There are other times when evil ascends with impunity and good grovels in humiliated rejection. Even then, His plan is not being thwarted.

If only we could see the world with God's vision! — but we cannot. He created a world that masks His Presence and He created incomplete human beings who can reach their own full potential only after a lifetime of unremitting striving and effort.

For the first two millennia after Creation, the universe was a spiritual wasteland. Our Sages aptly called it שְׁנֵי אֲלָפִים תֹּהוּ, *two thousand years of desolation*, until Abraham brought about the first overt stirrings of holiness that culminated with the giving of the Torah — an event that was like a spiritual sunrise after a night of almost endless blackness. Until then, God gave continued existence to the universe purely out of His goodness and His foreknowledge that, outward appearances notwithstanding, creation *was* moving toward His goals, just

Abraham brought about the first overt stirrings of holiness that culminated with the giving of the Torah — an event that was like a spiritual sunrise after a night of almost endless blackness.

[* This section is based on themes from *Da'as Tevunos*.]

as the churning activity of a volcano goes on beneath the placid crust above.

When the Temple stood in its glory, both God's Presence and the irresistible flow of His plan were more—although not entirely—revealed. People could see and feel the holiness of the Sanctuary. The efficacy of sacrifice and prayer was perceived and felt; not by belief alone did one know that God listened, looked, weighed, and responded, but through the testimony of heavenly fire, a holy pillar of cloud; rain in response to observance of the Torah, and drought as the wages of transgression; universal homage in tribute to spiritual elevation, and foreign harassment and conquest as the outgrowth of sin and idolatry. Even that did not constitute an *absolute*, inner knowledge of God's all-pervasive and all-powerful Being, because it was a knowledge that was based on tangible phenomena. Had the miracles not existed, the conviction would have waned, as it did when sin resulted in the removal of such miracles. As *Rambam* states, Jewish faith reached its peak at Sinai because it was based not on miracles, but on revelation. Israel knew *then* that God exists because they attained a degree of prophecy making it possible for them to 'see and hear' Him, as it were. Not the rumbling and flashing of thunder and lightning, but the perceived reality of God's Presence, made the deepest impression when He revealed Himself to Israel as its God.

But with the destruction of the Temple, even the miracle-based manifestation of God's Presence no longer existed. What was left to prevent Israel — and certainly all the world — from falling again to the utter depths of spiritual impurity and decay, of the sort that very nearly extinguished the final spark of hope during the waning moments of the Egyptian exile?

In Egypt there was not yet a Torah. Egypt was a continuation of the initial two millenia of *desolation*, but in succeeding exiles the nation had the benefit of God's Word and His Law to sustain within it the inextinguishable spark of holiness and aspiration.

When the Temple stood in its glory, both God's Presence and the irresistible flow of His plan were more — although not entirely — revealed.

In Egypt there was not yet a Torah. But in succeeding exiles the nation had the benefit of God's Word and His Law.

*By no means is this
to imply that Israel
in Exile is
equivalent to the
nation with
Temple and Land.
But the world
could never again
be as desolate as it
had been earlier.*

By no means is this to imply that Israel in Exile is equivalent to the nation with Temple and Land. Both history and bitter experience teach otherwise. But the world could never again be as desolate as it had been earlier, because God had chosen and consecrated His nation, and given it the Torah, which allowed His message to be known even if mankind as a whole was not yet ready to accept it.

In Degree, not in Kind

שמואל אמר באו עשרה בני אדם וישבו לפניו
אמר להן חזרו בתשובה אמרו לו עבד שמכרו
רבו ואשה שגרשה בעלה כלום יש לזה על זה
כלום? ...

Shmuel said, 'Ten men came and sat before [Yechezkel]. He told them, "Repent." They said to him, "A slave whose master has sold him or a woman whose husband has divorced her — does either have a claim on the other?" ' (Sanhedrin 105a).

*Such was the state
of demoralization
of Israel after its
expulsion from the
Land and the
destruction of the
Temple that
distinguished
people
seriously asked
whether they were
still bound to
observe the
commandments of
the Torah.*

Such was the state of demoralization of Israel after its expulsion from the Land and the destruction of the Temple that *distinguished* people — according to *Midrash Shir HaShirim,* even Chananyah, Mishael, and Azaryah were among them! — seriously asked the prophet Yechezkel whether they were still bound to observe the commandments of the Torah. If Israel had been considered God's slave, had God not 'sold' it into the bondage of a new master? If Israel had been considered God's bride, had He not expelled her from His Presence? Does a sold slave or a divorced wife owe any allegiance to a former master or husband?

To us, the very question seems impertinent and rhetorical — but that is only because we know the answer. That our perspective of Jewish suffering does not cause us to doubt ח"ו that we are still His people is only because we have absorbed the lessons and precedents of earlier epochs. The teachings of Yechezkel and other prophets and leaders, and the accumulated centuries of steadfast loyalty and faith have established in our minds and hearts that Israel

remains God's servant, firstborn, and love, no matter what the results of its sins, and no matter how inscrutable His ways seem to be. But in the context of those times, the doubts seemed eminently reasonable. From the time it left Egypt, Israel had enjoyed a unique closeness to God. When they grew apart during periods of sinfulness in the course of the nearly nine centuries from the Exodus to the Exile, it was Israel's doing, not God's. Always, He awaited their return. Now, apparently *He* had had His fill of *them* — and perhaps they were expelled from His dominion to that of whichever human master might hold the keys to their shackles. Such was their fear and the basis of their question to Yechezkel.

In the context of those times, the doubts seemed eminently reasonable.

But God was to teach Israel that its condition had changed only in degree, not in kind. It was a principle of His creation that great light always was born in utter darkness: before the Torah was given, there was an Egyptian exile; before the holiness of the Tabernacle was revealed in its fullest glory, there were the sin and death of Nadab and Abihu; before Aaron became High Priest, there were his awesome remorse and repentance at having been instrumental in the sin of the Golden Calf; before Jerusalem was brought under Jewish control and the Temple eventually built, there was the demoralizing tragedy of the Holy Ark's capture by the Philistines. Indeed, the recognition of spiritual eclipse, and the attempt to fight it; the experience of sin and the desire to repent the deed and rise above its degrading effects — these constitute the driving force that often brings holiness and faith into human life (*Resisei Laylah* 24).

But God was to teach Israel that its condition had changed only in degree, not in kind. It was a principle of His creation that great light always was born in utter darkness.

In the same sense, the exile became the vehicle which brought about Babylon's golden era of Torah development. Its product was the flowering of the Oral Torah to an unprecedented degree. [See first *Overview* to ArtScroll *Bereishis*]. And the prime instrument in attaining this result of awesome spiritual proportions was Daniel, along with his comrades Chananyah, Mishael, and Azaryah — and even the kings of Babylon and Media.

And the prime instrument in attaining this result of awesome spiritual proportions was Daniel, along with his comrades Chananyah, Mishael, and Azaryah.

Among the answers given by the *Talmud* (*Sanhedrin* 105a) to the question put to Yechezkel is that God anticipated the quandary when He referred to Israel's future master as נְבוּכַדְרֶאצַר מֶלֶךְ בָּבֶל עַבְדִּי, *Nebuchadnezzar, king of Babylon, My servant* (*Jeremiah* 43:10). This was to make clear to the perplexed Jews of the future, explains the *Talmudic* sage Reish Lakish, that just as everything owned by a slave reverts to his master, so, too, Israel had not changed hands merely by becoming subjects of the Babylonian monarch, for he, too, was the possession of God.

If Nebuchadnezzar was God's slave, then he acted as God's agent in doing what he did to God's people and its land.

There is a further implication in Jeremiah's reference to the king. If Nebuchadnezzar was God's slave, then he acted as God's agent in doing what he did to God's people and its land. So Israel had *not* been expelled or abandoned; it was still God's nation though it had been punished by being denied the privilege of continuing to see His 'Face' — or even His 'Hand.'

God has ways. Israel may not merit that evil be subjugated and good rewarded. It may find itself in a period of spiritual pallor when evil grows and blooms with the trappings of triumph. But things happen. God's hidden hand may manipulate events so that an unplanned and undreamed of outcome emerges from the very deed of the malefactors:

God's hidden hand may manipulate events so that an unplanned and undreamed of outcome emerges from the very deed of the malefactors.

— Joseph's brothers felt justified in going to extreme lengths to frustrate the possibility that he would reign over them — so they sold him into slavery. What slave can become a ruler? Events demonstrated that their challenge to Joseph's dream became the very means of its fulfillment. *Because* he was a slave he was in a position to interpret Pharaoh's dream and become viceroy of Egypt (*Harav Chaim Friedlander*).

— Pharaoh decreed that every boy baby be drowned, because his sorcerers foretold that a boy about to be born would free the Jewish slaves. Thanks to his decree, Moses was placed in the reeds along the Nile, where Pharaoh's own daughter took

pity on him and raised him as part of the very royal family that had tried to destroy him. Not only that, but it was in Pharaoh's own palace that Moses learned the arts of protocol and statecraft that he would later need when he became God's emissary to the royal court *(Rabbi Simcha Zissel Ziev)*.

— Haman was the one who advised Ahasuerus to put Vashti to death for insubordination. Thanks to his advice, Esther became queen, enabling her to thwart his plan to murder the Jews of the Persian Empire. The entire story of Purim illustrates how their own deeds came back to confound those who wished Israel ill *(ibid.)*.

Nebuchadnezzar, too, unwittingly brought about the failure of his own plans.

— Nebuchadnezzar, too, unwittingly brought about the failure of his own plans. By bringing to Babylon the finest youngsters of Jerusalem, he expected to deny Israel the benefit of its finest talents and by draining Jerusalem of its greatest scholars, he thought he was forever stunting Israel's capacity for spiritual growth and independent nationhood.

Daniel and his colleagues, and Mordechai and his colleagues, built the foundations of a flourishing Torah community in exile.

Instead, Daniel and his colleagues, and Mordechai and his colleagues, built the foundations of a flourishing Torah community in exile and of the later generation that would go back home and rebuild the Temple. And they sanctified God's Name publicly so that even Nebuchadnezzar was forced to declare his *own* acknowledgment of God's greatness (2:47; 3:28; 4:34).

III. Israel as Community

Scion of Judah

So it was Daniel's mission to create the underpinnings of future Jewish life in Babylon. He bore a responsibility similar to that carried by his ancestor Judah. When Jacob descended to Egypt with his family, he dispatched Judah:

וְאֶת יְהוּדָה שָׁלַח לְפָנָיו אֶל יוֹסֵף לְהוֹרֹת לְפָנָיו גֹּשְׁנָה

And Judah, he [Jacob] sent before himself

to Joseph to prepare before him to [*settle in*] *Goshen* (Genesis 46:28).

לְהוֹרוֹת לְפָנָיו: לתקן לו בית תלמוד שמשם תצא הוראה

'*To prepare before him*' — *to make ready for him a house of study from which teaching would emanate* (Rashi).

Jacob set a pattern of traveling into exile. Just as he prepared for his private exile in Laban's home by spending fourteen years of uninterrupted study in the Academy of Eber, so, too, he showed his family that it could not conceive of entering Egypt until one of their number had prepared a study hall. Israel's spiritual sustenance requires Torah study, and it dares not enter a hostile environment without making provision for its spiritual survival.

Israel's spiritual sustenance requires Torah study, and it dares not enter a hostile environment without making provision for its spiritual survival.

How fitting that the similar task in Babylon be entrusted to a scion of Judah's Davidic line. For the main task of Jewish royalty is to provide such leadership in the face of adversity: not to rule, but to serve; not to seek personal pomp, but to place oneself at the service of the people. *ARIzal* writes that Judah's very name *Yehudah*, יְהוּדָה, symbolizes this task for it contains within it the Four-Letter Name of HASHEM. *Chiddushei HaRim* goes further and adds that the fifth letter of Judah's name, the *dalet*, literally means *poverty* [=דַּלּוּת], because the true king — the kind epitomized by David and his finest descendants — took absolutely nothing for himself. In his eyes everything is for Israel. He sees even the trappings and wealth of the throne as belonging to the nation because their primary purpose is to lend dignity and honor to the nation, not merely to the individual who wears the crown. [This concept is developed at length in the *Overview* to ArtScroll *Ruth*.]

The names of the angels end with the suffix אֵל, God, to make clear that whatever powers they possess are not theirs, but God's.

Daniel, too, carried his essence in his name. As *Ramban* writes (*Genesis* 34:20) the names of the angels end with the suffix אֵל, *God*, to make clear that whatever powers they possess are not theirs, but God's. They act as His agents in moving the levers of

nature. This concept is embodied in their names: Raphael, the angel of healing, is רְפָא־אֵל, *healing is God's*. Gabriel, the angel of strength, is גַּבְר־אֵל, *strength is God's*. Daniel lived at a time of judgment, but his name expressed the recognition that Israel's fate was not random: דָנִי־אֵל, *my judgment is God's*. Israel's deeds had been weighed in the scales of justice and found wanting. It was to face dispersion, exile, oppression. Other nations have suffered similar fates and attributed them to the vagaries of history, geography, power, politics. But the leader of Israel was Daniel whose name represented the concept that judgments came from God and were not the result of happenstance.

Surely it was a profound act of God's Providence that caused the covetous eye of Nebuchadnezzar's recruiters to fall upon Daniel. The boy chosen to be pressed into training in Babylon had the capacity to become one of the great and pivotal figures in one of Israel's most trying periods. Daniel took the first steps to bring God's Name into the inhospitable atmosphere of Babylon by moving to preserve Israel's identity there. The Sages teach that Daniel forbade the eating by Jews of non-Jewish cooking. Indeed, his first risky act of leadership was to refuse the non-kosher food of the king's own kitchen (ch. 1; see *comm.*). He was the first to employ this device to prevent intermingling and assimilation. The Jews in Egypt had their devices, too. Even after they had fallen to the forty-ninth level of spiritual impurity, when they were *virtually* indistinguishable from the Egyptians, there were still devices that kept them apart, that made it possible to say that the Jews were מְצוּיָנִים שָׁם, *separate* or *identifiable there (Passover Haggadah)*: they maintained their own names, dress, and language.

Like Mordechai, his contemporary who was to assume leadership in the next stage of that exile, Daniel displayed personal courage in showing an example of dedication to God. Mordechai would not bow to the image Haman wore around his neck and Daniel

would not forego his thrice-daily prayers even after royal ministers had duped their king into declaring prayer to be a capital offense.

Michtav MeEliyahu (vol. II), citing *Maharal* and others, shows how Mordechai was not content merely to refuse to bow. He actually sought opportunities to confront Haman and display his refusal to bow. He made the determination that he must sanctify God's Name, and so his deed precipitated Haman's downfall and the miracle of Purim. Was Daniel required to court death by persisting in prayer? Presumably not. Yet according to many views, he refused to alter his pattern of service even to conceal what he was doing (see *comm.* to 6:7). Mordechai stands erect and Daniel prays. And Israel watches — if the nation as a whole does not entirely emulate its great men, at least it absorbs the lesson that Israel is unique, isolated, exalted.

Mordechai stands erect and Daniel prays. And Israel watches — it absorbs the lesson that Israel is unique, isolated, exalted.

Definitions of Life

Israel, the nation and the ideals it represents, is eternal.

In effect, these are manifestations of the concept that Israel, the nation and the ideals it represents, is eternal. That concept finds one of its most eloquent expressions in this *Talmudic* passage:

אמר ר' יוחנן יעקב אבינו לא מת. אמרו ליה וכי בכדי ספדו ספדנייא וחנטו חנטייא וקברו קברייא? אמר להם מקרא אני דורש שנאמר "וְאַתָּה אַל תִּירָא עַבְדִּי יַעֲקֹב נְאֻם ה' וְאַל תֵּחַת יִשְׂרָאֵל כִּי הִנְנִי מוֹשִׁיעֲךָ מֵרָחוֹק וְאֶת זַרְעֲךָ מֵאֶרֶץ שִׁבְיָם." מקיש הוא לזרעו מה זרעו בחיים אף הוא בחיים

R' Yochanan said, 'Our father, Jacob, did not die.'

They said to him, 'Was it in vain that the orators eulogized, the embalmers embalmed, and the buriers buried?'

[R' Yochanan] answered them, 'I expound upon a Scriptural verse: "And as for you, do not fear, My servant, Jacob," says HASHEM, "and do not be broken O Israel, for behold! I shall help you from afar, and your offspring from the land of

their captivity" (Jeremiah 30:10). [*The verse*] *likens him to his offspring. Just as his offspring lives, so he lives'* (*Taanis* 5b).

Inspiring though R' Yochanan's statement may be, it is not easily understood. Indeed, the question put to him seems to be irrefutable. Was Jacob not embalmed, buried, and eulogized? R' Yochanan does not seem to deal with the question at all. He answers only that he expounds upon the verse from *Jeremiah*. But does homiletical exegesis change the fact that Jacob did die?

Sefer HaZechus explains with a piercing analysis of the nature of 'reality.' There are several levels of existence. For example, ask divergent individuals to give a detailed description of their own hypothetical ideal person. The descriptions will be many and varied: a beautiful physical specimen; a brilliant, incisive scholar; a devoted, virtuous *tzaddik*; a wealthy, sophisticated patron of the arts; a bubbling, interesting personality; a moral, ethical man of character; a graceful, powerful athlete; an inspirational, charismatic leader; and the list goes on and on. Each respondent will give a full description of the kind of person that would be precious to *him* or *her*, but the people described are radically different from one another. Moreover, the qualities of life represented by the many choices differ in far more than degree. What one considers the ideal person is a bizarre caricature to another.

Two people can listen to a lecture. One is bored with the presentation but is dazzled by the floodlights and flashbulbs. The other ignores the lights but is deeply moved by the brilliant insight provided by the speaker. When it is all over, both will speak of brightness and illumination and both will be right, but one speaks in praise of the lighting engineer and the other of the profound intellectual. Which one is wrong? Neither. They merely use the same words to describe different concepts.

Similarly, a verse of Scripture has more than one meaning — all of them are true, though they may

There are several levels of existrence. For example, ask divergent individuals to give a detailed description of their own hypothetical ideal person. The description will be many and varied.

Which one is wrong? Neither. They merely use the same words to describe different concepts.

seem to be different or even contradictory. In the vocabulary of *Kabbalah*, Scripture is said to be like a פַּרְדֵּס, *an orchard*, with different sorts of luscious fruits. The word פַּרְדֵּס, *pardes*, is an acrostic of פְּשַׁט, *simple meaning;* רֶמֶז, *allusion;* דְּרוּשׁ, *hermeneutics;* סוֹד, *mystery* of Torah. Each form of interpretation represents a different level — a different spiritual universe — of understanding and interpretation.

It is true, therefore, that Jacob was laid to rest, but it is equally true that, in a higher level of spiritual existence, he never died.

It is true, therefore, that Jacob was laid to rest, but it is equally true that, in a higher level of spiritual existence, he never died. The particular plane of his eternal life is suggested by the verse expounded by R' Yochanan. His exegesis teaches מה זרעו בחיים אף הוא בחיים, *just as his offspring lives, so he lives.* R' Yochanan does not dispute his questioner. The Jacob who lived in the world of flesh-and-blood certainly died. But the Jacob who was the culmination of the Patriarchal epoch did not die.

Is he dead? Is it wrong to define life in terms of eternal influence? Is the end of life better signified by shovelfuls of sand and tearful oratory than by the cutting off of an ideal? If Jacob's accomplishment lives on in his children then is he not more truly 'alive' than billions who breathe but contribute nothing to the historic mission for which heaven and earth were created?

The Living Jacob

His mission — his achievement — was that he raise the embryonic Jewish nation from the level of individuals to that of a family group with an assurance of replenishing and reproducing itself and building a nation. [See *Overviews* to *Bereishis II* and *III* for a fuller discussion of the roles of the Patriarchs and the uniqueness of Jacob.] Jeremiah tells us that Jacob's offspring need not fear because Jacob lives *within them.* Much as it is true that there is a spark of Abraham and a spark of Isaac in every Jew, the lifespark of Jacob is present to an even greater degree (*Michtav MeEliyahu*).

Much as it is true that there is a spark of Abraham and a spark of Isaac in every Jew, the lifespark of Jacob is present to an even greater degree.

When Jacob's standard of perfection spread to embrace a family of seventy, thus constituting a

community, it was ready to be tested and refined in the dark exile of Egypt where it grew to become a *nation*. The concept of community was expressed vividly when, as the *Talmud* relates, Jacob gathered his sons around him before his death and they assured him *as a collective unit* of their devotion to God *(Pesachim 56a)*. The Patriarch as an individual might leave this world, but he would continue to exist in the dedication to God of his children and theirs.

For each individual contributes his own potential to the group thus assuring within the nation as a whole that Jacob continues to live in the most meaningful of 'worlds.'

That the Jewish nation grew to number 600,000 participating adults before it could be redeemed is equally significant. The number 600,000 is not coincidental. *Kabbalists* teach that, esoterically, there are 600,000 letters in the Torah and that each Jewish soul is a living letter. The Torah of ink and parchment was given when the Torah of flesh and blood — the nation — was ready to receive it. But there is a further teaching here. Although the letters of a word, a phrase, a verse, a chapter are written separately, they do not exist in isolation from one another. The total is greater them the sum of its parts because the combinations of letters spell words, laws, concepts.

Scattered letters are meaningless; gathered properly they express the will of God. Similarly, the Jewish *nation* is infinitely greater than the sum total of its individual members because it is the embodiment of God's scheme of creation. This interrelationship between nation and Torah is expressed in the acrostic of the name *Yisrael*, the name shared by the nation and the Patriarch: יֵשׁ שִׁשִּׁים רִבּוֹא אוֹתִיּוֹת לַתּוֹרָה, *there are 600,000 letters to the Torah (ibid.).*

Of all the Patriarchs, therefore, only Jacob is described as never having died because it is his legacy of united nationhood which exists in the eternity of his offspring. This was the quality that Daniel had to safeguard — by keeping the nation separate, as Judah and his successors did in Egypt, and by causing

God's Name to be proclaimed even in the empires of
Babylon and Media.

IV. Prophetic Images

Symbolic Visions

God manifests Himself in the physical creation just as a human monarch demonstrates his ultimate sovereignty by means of his authority over all areas of life in his kingdom.

Daas Tevunos, in discussing the subject of
prophecy, explains the function of symbolic visions that may be shown a prophet. In His attribute
of מַלְכוּת, kingship, God manifests Himself in the
physical creation just as a human monarch demonstrates his ultimate sovereignty by means of his
authority over all areas of life in his kingdom. The
king who controls his personal valet proves little. If
his word is law even in the most insignificant hamlet
of a sprawling kingdom, however, he has indeed
demonstrated majesty. Prophecy is an expression of
kingship because it represents God's unfathomable
wisdom and spiritual nature distilled and distilled,
contracted and contracted, disguised and disguised,
until it can be grasped by the agency of a human
being—the prophet. [This is by no means to suggest
that prophecy was accessible to any human
being—even during times when man was permitted
to enjoy the gift of prophecy. To the contrary, it is so
elevated and sublime that only the greatest people
could receive it and then only after intense preparation. (See *Hilchos Yesodei HaTorah* 7).]

Since prophecy is God's excursion, so to speak, into the material world, it is clothed in the terms and images of creation.

Since prophecy is God's excursion, so to speak,
into the material world, it is clothed in the terms and
images of creation. Thus, the prophet may see a vision of mundane human and animal activity, but his
prophetic vision provides him the divine insight with
which to grasp the underlying meaning of the vision.

Very obvious illustrations of this fundamental can
be seen in the famous dreams of Pharaoh and Nebuchadnezzar. While they were not 'prophecies' in the
strict sense of the word, they were nevertheless
Divine messages. The dreamers and their wise men
had no inkling of the dreams' true meanings. Joseph

and Daniel were given the meanings by God. Thus they were shown that cows and grain represented lean and fat years, or that statues and the substance of which they were made (see ch. 3), or animals (see ch. 7), represented kingdoms and the thousands of years of world history. Although God transmitted His revelation in material images, within the dreams there lay profound meaning that He made known only to his prophets.

Although God transmitted His revelation in material images, within the dreams there lay profound meaning that He made known only to his prophets.

[In all of Scripture, we find only Joseph and Daniel giving interpretations of dreams. A perspective on the deeper meaning of dreams and their interpretation, and the reason why these two people seemed uniquely equipped to interpret them, will be offered in the *Overview* to *Vayeshev* in ArtScroll *Bereishis / Genesis*.]

The True Lion

In the light of the above, we can better understand two of the major events in the Book of *Daniel*. *Daas Tevunos* notes that a lion is the symbol of royalty. The ultimate royalty, however, is God's. The regal bearing and impressive mane of the lion represent in earthly terms the ultimate spiritual truth of God's sovereignty. In this sense, the lion is nothing more than the graphic representation of a truth in the same way that an artist's rendering of two tablets brings to mind the Ten Commandments. Just as no one would even suggest that the message is the drawing and the tablets given to Moses are the symbolism, so too should we understand that *the* King is God, and that the lion is given us merely as a symbolic reminder. Scholarly claims that the lion, no matter how handsome, is not truly the 'king of beasts,' are immaterial. It was created as a symbol, a purpose it serves quite well. When a prophet sees a lion in his prophetic vision, therefore, he knows that he is to interpret it as a revelation of a higher monarchy.

A lion is the symbol of royalty. The ultimate royalty, however, is God's.

When a prophet sees a lion in his prophetic vision, therefore, he knows that he is to interpret it as a revelation of a higher monarchy.

This being so, if we are asked what is the *true* earthly lion, our answer should be the Davidic dynasty. Judah was blessed with monarchy, a status and privilege that were transmitted to the descen-

dants of David. Daniel was one of them. He was from the royal family and, as such, was the *true* lion.

To punish Daniel for his crime of praying to God, Darius had Daniel thrown to the lions' pit (see ch. 6). Surely lions could devour a man, as indeed they later disposed of those who had the temerity to denounce Daniel *(ibid.)* — but God's scheme was to demonstrate that His chosen one was inviolate. *Of course* the lions feared Daniel. They could not harm him because he was the true lion; they were nothing more than the material representation of his spiritual qualities just as the kings of the House of David are but the righteous embodiments on earth of God's sovereignty over all realms of existence.

Of course the lions feared Daniel. They could not harm him because he was the true lion.

Angelic Fire

Angels are everywhere described as 'fiery' beings. This, too, is an attempt to make a spiritual concept comprehensible in human terms. Just as fire's power is awesome and dreaded by people, so are angels in their spiritual untouchability. Chananayah, Mishael, and Azaryah were condemned to death by Nebuchadnezzar for their refusal to bow to the magnificent statue. They were to die by fire and they were placed in a kiln heated to such an extent that its tongues of flame consumed even the officers who stood at its edges (ch. 2). But Chananyah, Mishael, and Azaryah survived. Not only that, but Nebuchadnezzar saw a fourth figure standing with them in the furnace, a figure he recognized as that of an angel.

By miraculously allowing them to survive and by emplacing an angel to stand with them, God was demonstrating the reason for their indestructability. By their bravery and steadfast devotion to God — by demonstrating that the Godly suffixes of their names were not accidental — they became human expressions of the angels' creed that everything is God's. This being so, the three heroes were fire in its higher sense. A blazing inferno was but a metaphor for the reality of the three Jewish youths. How, then, could they and their angelic companion be harmed by a

The three heroes were fire in its higher sense. A blazing inferno was but a metaphor for the reality of the three Jewish youths.

mere fire? Can an angel be burned by fire? [See further for a more extensive treatment of Chananyah, Mishael, and Azaryah.]

לִשְׁנֵי בְּנֵי אָדָם גִּלָּה לָהֶם הקב״ה אֶת הַקֵּץ לְיַעֲקֹב וּלְדָנִיֵּאל

To [only] two people did the Holy One, Blessed be He, reveal the קֵץ, End; to Jacob and to Daniel (Midrash Shocher Tov 31:7).

How fitting, therefore, that Daniel was shown what no one but Jacob was privileged to know. Jacob had created the concept of community that expanded to nationhood. Daniel was called upon to prevent the disintegration of that concept at a time when it faced its most extreme challenge. Never before had Israel's national survival been so endangered. Subsequent responses in future exiles were made possible, and even foreshadowed, by those of Daniel. Thus, what Jacob began, Daniel perpetuated. Thanks to both, the End remained possible, so each was made privy to its mystery. Faith in the eternal truth that God did not 'sell' His slave or 'divorce' His wife was articulated by Yechezkel, but it was put into practice by the Judean lion who reigned in the spiritual jungle of Babylon — Daniel.

What Jacob began, Daniel perpetuated. Thanks to both, the End remained impossible, so each was made privy to its mystery.

V. Chananyah, Mishael, and Azaryah — The Soul responds*

באיזה זכות יצאו בני ישראל ממצרים? בזכות
חנניה משאל ועזריה

Because of which merit did the Jews leave Egypt? In the merit of Chananyah, Mishael, and Azaryah (Midrash Shocher Tov 114:5).

בשעה שהטילם נבוכדנצר לתוך כבשן האש ...
'וְרֵוֵהּ דִּי רְבִיעָיָא דָּמֵה לְבַר אֱלָהִין' זה גבריאל
שהיה מהלך אחריהם כתלמיד ההולך לפני רבו

When Nebuchadnezzar had them cast into the fiery kiln [there was a fourth figure with them]; the form of the fourth is like an angel (3:25). He was Gabriel who followed them as a disciple walks with his master (Pesikta Rabbasi 35).

Chananyah, Mishael, and Azaryah were taken from ther Jerusalemite families when they were children.

Chananyah, Mishael, and Azaryah were taken from their Jerusalemite families when they were children. While we have no certain knowledge of their ages, Scripture calls them יְלָדִים, *children*, and *Ibn Ezra* surmises that they were no older than fifteen (1:4). Nebuchadnezzar knew of the legendary wisdom of Jerusalem's children, and wished to train some of its outstanding sons to serve his empire.

The illustrious, but still youthful, Daniel became the leader of the group and emerged as one of the greatest people of the age, a man who was at the center of Babylonian and Median power for half a century, who was instrumental in forging Israel's response to Exile [see above], and who was granted visions and knowledge of the *End* that were withheld from every man except for Jacob.

*[The following presentation is based primarily upon the formulation of Rabbi Moshe Eisemann who very kindly provided his notes.]

Chananyah, Mishael, and Azaryah were not the equals of Daniel, but they faced an awesome challenge all alone as we shall see, and thereby infused Israel with courage and inspiration. From a previously contemptuous world they wrung impassioned declarations of respect for the God of Israel. Beyond a doubt, the spectacle of three young Jews defying the all-powerful Babylonian king of kings in the presence of the gathered representatives of all his vassal states had a profound effect on their attitudes toward Israel, the recently defeated tributary state that was about to be disgraced and dispersed. The praise of the Sages is the greatest testimony to the distinction of the young trio: Israel was redeemed from Egypt because it had within itself the capacity to produce such a trio, and the angel Gabriel followed them as their humble disciple. Clearly, their response to the challenge was of a proportion that transcended the heroism of three individuals.

Israel was redeemed from Egypt because it had within itself the capacity to produce such a trio.

Israel Upholds the Statue

By means of his statue, Nebuchadnezzar proclaimed that Babylon would endure forever.

Nebuchadnezzar erected a huge statue of gold in the Plain of Dura (ch. 3). It was his response to Daniel's interpretation of the dream that foretold four kingdoms, one succeeding the other, until eventually all would be displaced by the one eternal kingdom — Israel. By means of his statue, Nebuchadnezzar proclaimed that Babylon would endure forever. The statue was the symbol of his might and all must pay obeisance to it. But it kept toppling over. Its height was sixty cubits and its thickness only six; the base could not support a statue of such immensity. What did they do to keep it erect?

ר' חגי בשם ר' יצחק עד שהביאו כל כסף וזהב שהביאו מירושלים ושפכו דימוס על רגליו לקיים מה שנאמר ,,כַּסְפָּם בַּחוּצוֹת יַשְׁלִיכוּ וּזְהָבָם לְנִדָּה יִהְיֶה.''

Rabbi Chaggai said in the name of Rabbi Yitzchak, until they brought all the silver and gold that they looted from Jerusalem and poured it as a base around the statue's feet to fulfill the verse (Ezekiel 7:19):

Their silver they will throw in the streets and their gold will be fit for discarding (*Yalkut Yechezkel* 346 from *Pesikta Rabbasi*).

The greatness of the nations is dependent upon Israel. When Israel lives up to its mission, it is humanity's conduit to God and all the world is subservient to it. Its Temple is a magnet drawing all who lift their eyes above the earthly, and its Torah radiates from Zion to enlighten the world. But when Israel falls, it becomes a vassal. It contributes its wealth to carry out the designs of others. Without Jerusalem's gold and silver, Nebuchadnezzar's statue could not stand. His own kingdom and all others would fall in obedience to God's priestly kingdom. Only when Israel contributes its riches to others — casting into the streets the 'gold and silver' which should be dedicated to God's service — can kings dream of permanent sway. So Nebuchadnezzar shores up his power with the symbols of Jerusalem's fall.

Without Jerusalem's gold and silver, Nebuchadnezzar's statue could not stand. Only when Israel contributes its riches to others — can kings dream of permanent sway.

Then he decrees that representatives of every nation must come and bow to his statue. Amid feasting, festivity, music, and celebration, the king's triumph is heralded by lackeys from around the civilized world. And Chananyah, Mishael, and Azaryah are brought to add their submissiveness to that of the multitudes that grovel in acknowledgment of the undefeatable kingdom of man.

Three children away from family, home, and country! What are they to do?

Three children away from family, home, and country! What are they to do? According to many commentators, the statue was not an idol, but a symbol of the king's sovereignty. If so, they would not be forbidden to bow. But to do so would desecrate the Name! Even if it were an idol, was it fair to expect that three tender boys must carry upon their shoulders the honor of the God of Israel? Older men had not withstood the test of idolatry in idolatrous times—could they? Should they?

Older men had not withstood the test of idolatry in idolatrous times — could they? Should they?

On Their Own

Midrash Shir HaShirim tells how the trio sought guidance from the greatest of the age:

*'Our teacher
Daniel —
Nebuchadnezzar
had set up an idol.
What do you say
— should we bow
or not?*

Chananyah, Mishael, and Azaryah went to Daniel and said to him, 'Our teacher, Daniel—Nebuchadnezzar has set up an idol and has ... selected us from among all Israel [to bow before it]. What do you say—should we bow or not?

He told them, 'The prophet [Ezekiel] is before you. Go to him.'

Immediately, they went to Ezekiel. ... He told them, 'I have a tradition from Isaiah, Hide for a brief moment until the fury has passed' *(Isaiah 26:20). [Ezekiel would not answer their question directly. He urged them to avoid a direct confrontation; insteasd they should go into hiding until the crisis was over. Surely their absence would not be noted among the thronging multitude.]*

*'Do you want all
the nations to
assume that even
Israelites bowed?
... We wish to be
there and
denigrate the
statue.*

They answered, 'Do you want all the nations to assume that even Israelites bowed? ... We wish to be there and denigrate the statue by not bowing so that they will say, 'All bowed to this statue except Israel!' [This public refusal would put them in danger, but it would sanctify God's Name.]

He said, 'If such is your wish, wait while I consult the Holy One, Blessed be He.'

... [God] said to him, 'I will not stand by them' [i.e., they cannot expect miraculous intervention].

[Ezekiel told them that God would not protect them]. They replied, 'Whether or not He protects us, we will offer our lives for the sanctification of His Name!'

As soon as they left Ezekiel, the Holy One, Blessed be He, appeared to him and said, 'Do you think I will not stand by them? Of course I will protect them, but

*you are to let them go without telling them
so that they will go with perfect faith as it
is written,* He that goes with perfect faith
goes securely *(Proverbs* 10:9).

Where was Daniel during their ordeal? He was not
even in the country *(Sanhedrin* 93a). The *Talmud
(ibid.)* states that God had a reason for not wanting
Daniel to witness the ordeal of his disciples:

הקב"ה אמר ילך דניאל מכאן שלא יאמרו
בזכותו הוא ניצל

*[God] said, 'Let Daniel leave here so that
people will not say that they were rescued
in his merit' (ibid.).*

Chananyah,
Mishael, and
Azaryah were not
prophets, were not
people privy to the
intention of God.
Their greatness lay
in their perfect
faith and in their
readiness to give
up everything.

The scenario becomes clearer. Chananyah,
Mishael, and Azaryah were not prophets, were not
people privy to the intention of God. Their greatness
lay in their perfect faith and in their readiness to give
up everything to show the world that Israel remains
loyal to its God.

Who could have blamed them if they had
despaired? They were isolated. *Eretz Yisrael* had lost
its independence. Neither Daniel, nor Ezekiel, nor
even God would promise them safety. God made it
clear that they were totally on their own.

This was His plan.
It was not enough
that only great
men maintain their
devotion to Him.
The ultimate
redemption
required that the
masses recognize
HASHEM.

This was His plan. It was not enough that only
great men maintain their devotion to Him. The
ultimate redemption required that the masses of the
people recognize that HASHEM was still their God
and that they be prepared to defy kings and multitudes to demonstrate their loyalty to Him. What
was required was the awakening of the *pintele yid,*
the sometimes silent, sometimes dormant, sometimes
hidden spark of Jewishness that does not become extinguished. For the symbol of Israel's downfall—the
stability of Nebuchadnezzar's statue—was Jerusalem's gold and silver, Israel's resources that were
serving its oppressors.

*Wind of
Life*

Chananyah, Mishael, and Azaryah prevailed. Having done so, another thing happened: God sent a
wind that threw down the statue. No longer did it

have a strong base because the spiritual decline represented by Nebuchadnezzar's acquisition of Jerusalem's treasure had been arrested and reversed. The true base of the statue had been Jewish despair that was symbolized by Jerusalem's confiscated gold and silver. The three young heroes had transformed Israel's hopelessness into courage and faith in God. That done, the statue could stand no longer. The wind did not stop there. It continued through the Plain of Dura to where Ezekiel had been dispatched by God with the mission of bringing back to life the dry bones of Jews who had fallen there in the course of the exile (Shir HaShirim Rabbah 7:14). Of them, God said to Ezekiel:

הִנֵּה אֹמְרִים יָבְשׁוּ עַצְמוֹתֵינוּ וְאָבְדָה תִקְוָתֵנוּ נִגְזַרְנוּ לָנוּ

Behold! they say, 'Our bones are dry, our hope is lost, we are cut off' (Ezekiel 37:1).

The three young heroes had transformed Israel's hopelessness into courage and faith in God. That done, the statue could stand no longer.

Those dry bones in the plain represented the national despair, the widespread feeling that Israel could never rise from its defeat to a national rejuvenation. But the general despondency was banished when Chananyah, Mishael, and Azaryah proved that even ordinary Jews remain alive to their mission, that they refuse to surrender to the 'inevitable.'

That wind, and the dedication that caused it, was a harbinger of the ultimate תְּחִיַת הַמֵּתִים, Resurrection of the Dead. Winds of life blow not only across valleys, but across centuries.

That wind, and the dedication that caused it, was a harbinger of the ultimate תְּחִיַת הַמֵּתִים, *Resurrection of the Dead.* Winds of life blow not only across valleys, but across centuries. The millennia-long reign of the fourth monarchy that Daniel was shown in such terribly fearsome visions would lead many to shake their heads sadly over the 'dry bones and lost hope' of Israel. But the nation that produced a Chananyah, Mishael, and Azaryah in an earlier era of darkness would continue to do so.

Small wonder that Gabriel became their follower in the flaming kiln. Human beings who rise above circumstances and challenges to serve God are truly higher than angels who have no free will, no evil inclination, no existence other than that of carrying out

the will of God. People are called הוֹלְכִים, *those who move forward*, while angels are called עוֹמְדִים, *those who remain standing in place* (see *Zechariah* 3:7). For man is created with potential that can be realized only through struggle and effort. Angels never change. Great though Gabriel was—and no human being can approach the heavenly prince in *absolute* terms—he is no greater today than he was the moment he was created. But Chananyah, Mishael, and Azaryah? They went far beyond the limitations of the flesh. They overcame the physical and emotional barriers that worked to stunt their spiritual growth. Justly did Gabriel pay them tribute. [See *Overview* to ArtScroll *Bircas Hamazon*.]

They overcame the physical and emotional barriers that worked to stunt their spiritual growth. Justly did Gabriel pay them tribute.

Israel went forth from Egypt as a *nation* dedicated to the Torah's mission, not as a large group of separate individuals [see above p. xxxiv-xxxv]. The greatness of a Moses, an Aaron, a Miriam was not enough to satisfy God's will. With the accomplishment of Jacob, the era of glorious individuals had given way to the primary role of the nation as the eternal servant of God until the universe could be raised to its ultimate level of perfection. That *collective* function of Israel was endangered when destruction and exile raised fear and doubt in Jewish minds. What would have become of the mission Israel accepted at the Exodus if devotion to God had become the exclusive province of the Daniels, Mordechais, and other spiritual elite? Would not the purpose of the Exodus have been frustrated? More—would the Exodus have taken place at all if its effect was to remain a temporary phenomenon?

What would have become of the mission Israel accepted at the Exodus if devotion to God had become the exclusive province of the Daniels, Mordechais, and other spiritual elite?

Midrash Shocher Tov teaches, therefore, that Israel was redeemed from Egypt because of the merit of Chananyah, Mishael, and Azaryah. They accomplished in the dreary, debilitating time of despair what their forefathers had accomplished in the heady, elevating moment of national uplift. When Nebuchadnezzar set his statue above all nations and powers, three young Jews displayed the same faith in God that their ancestors had shown when Pharaoh

was buried under the falling walls of the sea. But the ancestors were faithful after seeing Ten Plagues and experiencing God's benevolence; the offspring were faithful after seeing Jerusalem conquered and experiencing God's wrath. Israel continued its historic mission when even the relatively undistinguished ones rose to the challenge of threatening times. Therefore, the miracles of the Exodus were justified and a wind was set in motion that would topple all the monuments to materialistic disbelief and bring new life to dry bones.

The miracles of the Exodus were justified and a wind was set in motion that would topple all the monuments to materialistic disbelief and bring new life to dry bones.

VI. The Scripture and the 'End'

תרגום של נביאים יונתן בן עוזיאל אמרו ...
יצתה בת קול ואמרה מי הוא זה שגילה סתריי
לבני אדם? עמד ... ואמר ... שלא לכבודי עשיתי
... אלא לכבודך ... ועוד ביקש לגלות תרגום של
כתובים יצתה בת קול ואמרה דייך מאי טעמא
משום דאית ביה קץ משיח

The Targum [*Aramaic interpretive translation*] *of Prophets was said by Yonasan ben Uziel. A heavenly voice went forth saying, 'Who is this who [dared] reveal My mysteries to humans? He arose ... and said ... 'I did it not for my own glory ... but for Your glory ...' He wished to continue and reveal the* Targum *of the* Kesuvim [*Hagiographa lit. Writings*]. *A heavenly voice went forth saying, 'You have done enough! Why? Because [the Kesuvim] contain the End [i.e., the final time by which the Messiah must come]* (Megillah 3a).

No mystery is more heavily shrouded than the time of the קץ, End, when the Messiah will at long last lead Israel with the world in its wake to final redemption.

No mystery is more heavily shrouded than the time of the קץ, *End*, when the Messiah will at long last lead Israel with the world in its wake to final

redemption and perfection. Jacob knew the time. As he lay on his deathbed and his children stood on the threshold of an exile that would plunge them to the lowest of depths, he wished to reveal the secret to them — but God denied him the ability to do so. The closing chapters of *Daniel* reveal visions of the *End*, but Daniel was enjoined by the angel to seal them from human comprehension. Yonasan ben Uziel revealed the mysteries of the prophets in order to increase the manifestation of God's glory. He wanted to do the same for the Writings, but the heavenly voice enjoined him from doing so, for sealed within the entire body of the Writings is the secret of the *End* — it is a secret man may not know.

What is this thing called קץ, *End, and if it is a fixed time, how can we reconcile it with the fundamental tenet of our belief that we must await the possible coming of the Messiah any and every day?*

What is this thing called קץ, *End*, and if it is a fixed time, how can we reconcile it with the fundamental tenet of our belief that we must await the possible coming of the Messiah *any* and *every* day?

Much has been written by the Sages concerning the conditions and timing of the Messiah's coming (see primarily the end of *Sotah* and *Sanhedrin* ch. 11). The closing chapters of *Daniel* as well, with their visions of the various exiles, the Four Kingdoms, and the End of Days, are clearly the vessels within which are contained revelations that plot the course of history from Daniel's day onward until the final promised redemption.

The Messiah will arrive when all are righteous; he will arrive when all are sinful. He will come amid pomp and magnificence; he will come humbly and in poverty. He will come at an appointed time; he can come at any moment. The tribulations preceding his coming will be so frightening that one should hope not to witness them; one should long to greet him — indeed, many great *tzaddikim* had special suits of clothes or composed joyous tunes with which to greet the Messiah. Contradictory and confusing—such are the sources discussing the longed-for climax of history.

Contradictory and confusing—such are the sources discussing the longed-for climax of history.

The Sages strongly warned against attempts to derive from the Scriptural verses a specific time

when the Messiah was to come (see *Sanhedrin* 97b). Generally the strictures have been followed. *Rambam (Iggeres Teman)* explains that the Sages were deeply concerned lest a predicted time come and go without the hoped-for coming. Were that to happen, people of little sophistication and insufficient faith would think that he would *never* come. The reaction might be like that of Yechezkel's ten visitors (see above): 'Perhaps we are like the slave who has been sold or the wife who has been divorced.' People might say that if the Messiah had not come when he was expected, perhaps the Divine bond with Israel had been severed ח״ו and the promises concerning his coming had been annulled. Therefore, *Rambam* continues, the Sages prayed about those who dared predict in violation of the Torah's prohibition, that their predictions be so erroneous that people would forever ignore such attempts to teach the unknowable.

The Sages were deeply concerned lest a predicted time come and go without the hoped-for-coming. Were that to happen, people of little sophistication and insufficient faith would think that he would never come.

Nevertheless, *R' Saadiah Gaon (Emunos V'Deos) did* makes such predictions based on interpretations of Scripture. Lest that great luminary be condemned, *Rambam (ibid.)* points to the historical conditions in which the Gaon lived. Christian and Moslem persecutions and Karaite infiltrations had so succeeded in breaking the spirit of Israel that, had it not been for the leadership and courage of *R' Saadiah*, 'Torah would nearly have been lost.' The *Gaon* brought new life to the nation. As part of his work, he found it necessary 'to gather the broad community on the path of calculating the time of the *End* in order to encourage them and increase their hope. His intention in all that he did was for the sake of heaven — no one may argue against him for having erred in his calculations.'

After explaining forcefully that it is forbidden to make such calculations, both Rambam *and* Ramban *go ahead to do so!*

The striking thing is that, after explaining forcefully that it is forbidden to make such calculations, both *Rambam* and *Ramban* go ahead to do so! Their reasons are clear, however. Both addressed themselves to generations that suffered intense persecution. *Rambam* wrote to the brave but oppres-

sed Jews of Yemen who were beset by a government that demanded conversion, an imposter who claimed to be a Jewish messiah, and renegade Jews who expounded upon Scripture to prove that Mohammed was the new savior. *Ramban* lived in pre-Inquisitional Spain which, even in those days, placed Jews under duress to convert, forced *Ramban* and others to engage in religious debates under the most unfair conditions, and eventually forced *Ramban* into exile because he was too successful in refuting the priests — his life saved only by the personal intervention of his grudging admirer, King James I of Aragon. Their followers needed hope and encouragement. Reluctantly, *Rambam* and *Ramban* provided it, but only after going to great lengths to make it clear that Jewish faith should never be based on such predictions, traditions, or Scriptural expostions, no matter how reliable they appeared to be.

The interpretations were not borne out; the prophecies of Daniel are as hidden as ever. Nevertheless, when such projections have been given by such monumental greats as *R' Saadiah Gaon*, *Rambam*, and *Ramban*, as well as such others as *Rashi* and *R' Bachya* and numerous later commentators, we dare not say that they were all mistaken in the conventional sense of the word. We cannot even begin to fathom their greatness; surely we cannot relegate their words to the scrap heap. The luminaries from whose mouths we live must have had a basis for saying what they did. It is incumbent upon us, therefore, to seek at least a minimal understanding of the concept of קֵץ, *End.*

Two Extremes

אמר רבי אלכסנדרי רבי יהושע בן לוי רמי כתיב "בְּעִתָּה" וכתיב "אֲחִישֶׁנָה"? זכו "אֲחִישֶׁנָה" לא זכו "בְּעִתָּה".

Rabbi Alexandri said that Rabbi Yehoshua ben Levi noted a contradictory passage. Scripture says [that the redemption will occur] בְּעִתָּה, *in its appointed time. Then it says* אֲחִישֶׁנָה, *I will hasten it (Isaiah 60:22).*

[The explanation is] if they are deserving: I will hasten it. *If they are not deserving:* in its appointed time *(Sanhedrin* 98a).

This seminal passage sheds light on the great body ot Messianic literature. There *is* an appointed time, but there can also be ways to hasten his coming.

On that same page, the *Talmud* relates how R' Yehoshua ben Levi was dispatched by the prophet Elijah to inquire directly of the Messiah as to when he would arrive. The holy *Tanna* did so and the Messiah greeted him warmly. In answer to his question, the redeemer said הַיּוֹם, *[I will come] today.* R' Yehoshua complained to Elijah that the Messiah had deceived him — that day was over, but the Exile still endured. Elijah answered that R' Yehoshua had misunderstood. The Messiah had meant to say הַיּוֹם־אִם בְּקוֹלוֹ תִשְׁמָעוּ, *[I will come] today — if you but heed His voice (Psalms* 95:7) [i.e., if Israel would but obey the word of God].

It has been said on behalf of Chassidic masters that we, on earth, have the capacity to rebuild the Holy Temple through the performance of *mitzvos.* Each good deed, they say, creates a vessel in the heavenly Temple, but each sin destroys the entire structure. If only the performance of good deeds could continue uninterrupted — the heavenly Temple would be completed and it would descend to earth. Exile would end and all the glorious prophecies of fulfillment and the End of Days would be realized. Such is the power of good deeds. As the Sages have said: If only all Israel would observe two consecutive Sabbaths perfectly, *that* would bring the Messiah. But, the Chassidic masters continue, a sin destroys the entire heavenly structure, requiring Israel to begin anew.

Difficult though the Exile may be and terrifying though the ordeals of the fourth kingdom have proven, Israel is never without hope. Despair does not belong in our vocabularies, because we can never know how God measures the quality of a good deed. As *Rambam* writes in *Hilchos Teshuvah,* we

There is an appointed time, but there can also be ways to hasten his coming.

It has been said on behalf of Chassidic masters that we, on earth, have the capacity to rebuild the Holy Temple through the performance of mitzvos.

can never know the value of a good deed or the destructiveness of a bad one. In God's scales, one good deed may outweigh many evil ones, and vice versa. The *Chofetz Chaim* wrote during the 1920s — surely a time of spiritual decline and suffering of those who were most committed to God and Torah — a sincere attempt at self-improvement, a successful fight against the tide, a dedicated attempt to help build Torah is considered far more worthy in God's eyes than a similar achievement in more tranquil, more God-fearing times.

But if Israel's spiritual accomplishments do not bring about the Messiah's speedy coming, there is another way: בְּעִתָּהּ, *the appointed time.* The dire, frightful conditions attending the Messiah's coming, the awful calamities and moral decay foretold by the Sages, will envelop that era in suffering and gloom, foreboding and dread.

Those are the two extremes: the joyful coming brought by Israel's merit, and the travail of the קֵץ, End—the appointed time.

Those are the two extremes: the joyful coming brought by Israel's merit, and the travail of the קֵץ, End—the appointed time, beyond which the Messiah can tarry no longer. But there is something in between.

For Each Generation

According to traditions handed down from generation to generation, there come times when it is likely that the Messiah *can* come. These, too, are in the nature of appointed times. They come, and if Israel is receptive and deserving, they achieve their purpose and the *End* will have arrived. To achieve success at such propitious moments does not require the strenuous exertion for holiness that would be needed to hasten the coming at an unappointed moment. Neither do such times constitute the *final deadline* beyond which he *must* arrive. They are simply moments when great events *can* occur — or they can slip through careless, unfeeling fingers if the effort is not made to utilize them.

The Vilna Gaon writes that God treats every generation in a unique manner. He utilized a different atribute for each era.

The *Vilna Gaon* writes that God treats every generation in a unique manner. He utilizes a different attribute for each era. Not only His expecta-

tions for the generation, but even His regulation of nature is predicated on the particular manner in which He has chosen to deal with the generation. Within the parameters of the attribute assigned for them, the members of that generation will exercise their free choice, influence the course of the universe, and be judged on the degree of their success or failure. For example, one generation may be expected to show self-sacrifice, another to intensify Torah study, another to show kindness. Whatever the particular demand upon it, of course, each era must find its way within the boundaries of the Torah, but the form and nature of its leaders, resources, and challenges will vary according to the demand made upon the generation.

Similarly, the Gaon continues, each generation will have its own קֵצִין, appointed Ends, depending upon the unique forms of merit and repentance expected of it.

Similarly, the *Gaon* continues, each generation will have its own קֵצִין, *appointed Ends*, depending upon the unique forms of merit and repentance expected of it. If the people are worthy when the appointed time arrives, the Messiah will come; if not they must await the next possible time — or attain so exalted a spiritual level that they unconditionally earn his arrival. But there is a *final End*, an absolute deadline. If he has not arrived by then, the Messiah will be brought by God's attribute of lovingkindness and the merit of the Patriarchs. Only that final deadline was revealed to the Patriarchs *(Even Shlomo* 11:9).

From this perspective, we must view the Messianic predictions of the great commentators. What they divined were undoubtedly times when the Messiah was at Israel's doorstep.

From this perspective, we must view the Messianic predictions of the great commentators. What they divined, whether from their understanding of the prophecies or through רוּחַ הַקּוֹדֶשׁ, *Divine Inspiration*, were undoubtedly times when the Messiah was at Israel's doorstep, waiting to be allowed in. Our yearly calendar is filled with days which are auspicious moments for particular types of spiritual emanations. Passover is uniquely a time of freedom, Shavuous is uniquely a time to absorb Torah inspiration and knowledge, Yom Kippur is uniquely a time to gain forgiveness, Tishah B'Av is uniquely a time of potential tragedy [see *Overview* to ArtScroll

Eichah]. The same is true of the eternal calendar. There are times which are especially propitious for the coming of the Messiah, and there is an ultimate time when he absolutely *will* come if he has not already done so.

Perhaps they knew one of the intermediate times would be at hand, perhaps they thought that such a propitious time was truly the ultimate End.

When the classic commentators give times for the coming of the Messiah, perhaps they knew one of the intermediate times would be at hand, perhaps they thought that such a propitious time was truly the ultimate *End*. Even if they erred, their error was surely of this nature, but not an absolute one.

Thoughts of Maharal

Maharal in *Netzach Yisrael* (ch. 31 and 44 and *Chiddushei Aggados Sanhedrin* 97-99) has written extensively on the subject. The following is drawn from his works:

Jacob was the logical one to reveal the final appointed time because the final Exile, that which was brought on by the descendants of Esau, would be directed against the high spiritual level of Jacob.

Because he was the climactic Patriarch, Jacob was great enough to pierce the dense layers of concealment that hide the End from the vision of all others. He knew—but he was not permitted to reveal it.

Because he was the climactic Patriarch, the one whose greatness culminated the patriarchal epoch and who succeeded in giving birth to a generation of perfect *tzaddikim*, Jacob was great enough to pierce the dense layers of concealment that hide the *End* from the vision of all others. He knew—but he was not permitted to reveal it.

At the moment when Jacob wished to inform his children of the *End*, God caused him to forget its time. When that happened, Jacob feared that perhaps there was some unknown imperfection in his children. If so, then he would lack the degree of holiness necessary to know and to reveal. His sons reassured him by declaring: *Hear O Israel* [i.e., our father, Israel]—*HASHEM our God, HASHEM is One* (*Pesachim* 56a)

[Indeed, even Daniel, to whom the *End* was directly revealed, was permitted only to formulate the words within which the secret was contained, and which would later be committed to writing by the Men of the Great Assembly. The angel commanded

him to conceal their meaning and never to reveal the interpretation of the visions that had been given him.]

It should be understood, therefore, that no man may know the time of the *End*. The *End* is hidden; there is no knowledge of it. Know, therefore, that when the Sages described dire conditions concerning the era of the Messiah, they did not mean to say that such dire circumstances *must* take place. They meant to say that when such hardship and decay are observed, it should be taken as an indication that the time is propitious for the coming of the Messiah. His coming at the appointed time may well be preceded by intense suffering; therefore the presence of such conditions may well be taken as symptomatic that the *End* is at hand. But they surely did not mean to say that he *must* come at such a time, for no one may reveal the definite time of the Messiah's coming even if he could know it.

When the Sages described dire conditions concerning the era of the Messiah, they did not mean to say that such dire circumstances must take place.

Sin is not of Israel's essence. Though Israel may sin—and sin grievously—its essential nature remains pure. Therefore, even God's Attribute of Justice always maintains that Israel be redeemed and the world fall under the sovereignty of the Messiah at the proper time. This must happen for such was the purpose of Creation and Israel is the vehicle for its fulfillment. Only if Israel's essential nature were to change could its mission change. Such has not happened and cannot happen.

Not only Israel anticipates the Messiah's coming; God, too, awaits it anxiously. God's Own creation is deficient as long as Israel remains subservient to others.

Not only Israel anticipates the Messiah's coming; God, too, awaits it anxiously *(Sanhedrin 97b)*. Since the universe was created in order to be brought to its fulfilment under the spiritual sovereignty of Israel, God's Own creation is deficient as long as Israel remains subservient to others. It is inconceivable, therefore, that the Exile should not come to an end. Why does it still endure? Because מִדַּת הַדִּין, *the Attribute of Justice*, does not permit the Messiah to come while Israel is undeserving *(ibid.)*. Those who predicted the *End* erred because they thought that His mercy was at hand; it was not. But even the At-

tribute of Justice demands that the Messiah must come eventually, otherwise, the purpose of Creation would be disrupted. The exile will not endure forever, and we earn reward by having faith in that principle.

The Exile will not endure forever and we earn reward by having faith in that principle.

Therefore, although we remain without knowledge of the exact time of the *End*, we continue with the unquestioning conviction that we await him and God awaits us. The time will come: 'today — if you heed His call.'

> '*I believe with a perfect belief in the coming of the Messiah. Even though he may delay, I will wait every day for him to come*' (Rambam, Thirteen Principles of Faith).

— *Rabbi Nosson Scherman*

ספר דניאל

א בִּשְׁנַת שָׁלוֹשׁ לְמַלְכוּת יְהוֹיָקִים מֶלֶךְ־
יְהוּדָה בָּא נְבוּכַדְנֶאצַּר מֶלֶךְ־בָּבֶל
ב יְרוּשָׁלַ͏ִם וַיָּצַר עָלֶיהָ: וַיִּתֵּן אֲדֹנָי בְּיָדוֹ
אֶת־יְהוֹיָקִים מֶלֶךְ־יְהוּדָה וּמִקְצָת כְּלֵי

I

1. בִּשְׁנַת שָׁלוֹשׁ — *In the third year.*[1]

The time referred to is *the third year* of his independence which was the eleventh year of his rule (*Rashi; R' Saadiah* from *Seder Olam*, 25; cf. *Megillah* 11b, *Arachin* 12a, *Yalkut, II Kings* 23). For explanation see footnote.

However, *Ibn Ezra* (and *Ralbag, Malbim,* and *Radak* to *II Kings* 24:1; see also *Radak* to *Jeremiah* 25:1) interprets *In the third year* to mean after having ruled for three whole years — i.e., in his fourth year. See *footnote.*

Abarbanel (comm. to *Jeremiah* 25:1) cites and totally rejects a third opinion, that of *Josephus Flavius* (*Antiquities* X, 6, 1-2) who supposes that the third year refers to the third year of Yehoyakim's vassalage to Nebuchadnezzar. The highlights in Yehoyakim's reign, according to him, are: In Yehoyakim's fourth year Nebuchadnezzar becomes king; in Yehoyakim's eighth year Nebuchadnezzar conquers Jerusalem for the first time and Yehoyakim serves Nebuchadnezzar two years; in the third year of his bondage he revolts; Nebuchadnezzar comes to Jerusalem in the same year, conquers it, and takes Yehoyakim captive. This is the event narrated here. *Abarbanel* objects to this opinion because Scripture unequivocally states, *In the third year of the 'reign.'*

וַיָּצַר עָלֶיהָ — *And [he] besieged it.*

Nebuchadnezzar was forced to

---

1. As evidenced by the *commentary*, the dating of the occurrence described in this verse presents a problem. On the surface it would appear that this happened in Yehoyakim's third year — i.e., after having ruled two years. Also it would appear that this event terminated his reign, as is said in *v.* 2: *The Lord gave Yehoyakim, King of Judah, into his hand ...*

Both of these suppositions are contradicted by verses elsewhere. In *Jeremiah* 25:1, we read: *In the fourth year of Yehoyakim ... which was the first year of Nebuchadnezzar.* And in *II Kings* 23:36 we see that Yehoyakim reigned *eleven* years in Jerusalem, not three years as implied here.

In order to understand the solutions to these problems which are advanced by the commentators, it is necessary to know more about Yehoyakim's reign.

In *II Kings* (ch. 23-24; cf. *II Chronicles* ch. 36), Scripture tells us, *And the people took Yehoachaz the son of Yoshiyahu ... and made him king ... And Pharaoh Necho put him in bonds ... that he should not reign in Jerusalem ... And Pharaoh Necho made Elyakim, son of Yoshiyahu, king ... and changed his name to Yehoyakim ... In his days Nebuchadnezzar, King of Babylon, came up, and Yehoyakim became his servant three years; then he turned and rebelled against him.*

It follows from this narrative that the only time Yehoyakim reigned independently was after his revolt against Nebuchadnezzar. At the beginning of his reign he had been subservient to Pharaoh, and subsequently to Nebuchadnezzar.

What is meant here is that *in the third year of the 'reign' of Yehoyakim* — i.e., of his independent rule — *Nebuchadnezzar ... came.* Scripture is telling us that at the end of Yehoyakim's eleven-year rule — i.e., in the third year of his revolt — Nebuchadnezzar

*I*n the third year of the reign of Yehoyakim, King of
Judah, Nebuchadnezzar, King of Babylon, came
to Jerusalem and besieged it. ² The Lord gave Yehoyakim, King of Judah, into his hand with some of the

come in person to quell the revolt
(see *comm.* above). Still Jerusalem
refused to surrender without a
struggle, and he was constrained to
besiege the city. In light of this we
would have expected Nebuchadnezzar to sack the city and massacre
its inhabitants. Instead, all he did
was capture Yehoyakim and take
part of the holy vessels. From this
we can see that Nebuchadnezzar's
conquest of Judah was not the
result of his military prowess, but
an act of *Hashgacha*, God's personal supervision of the universe.
The sins of the Jews did not yet
warrant dire punishment. As Scripture specifies (*v.* 2): *The Lord gave
... into his hand* (*Alshich*).

2. וַיִּתֵּן אֲדֹנָי בְּיָדוֹ אֶת יְהוֹיָקִים
מֶלֶךְ יְהוּדָה — *The Lord gave
Yehoyakim, King of Judah, into his
hand.*

He did not have to tarry in his
conquest, because it was an act of
God (*Malbim*).

וּמִקְצָת כְּלֵי — *With some of the vessels.*

The rest of the vessels remained,
as we read (*Jer.* 27:19-20), *concerning the rest of the vessels which Nebuchadnezzar did not take ...*
(*Rashi*).

The *Mishkan* (Tabernacle) and
its vessels remained. They had been
hidden previously by Yoshiyahu
King of Judah and the prophet
Jeremiah (*R' Saadiah; R'
Yeshayah*).

[In *Sotah* 9a the *Talmud* quotes from
Tosefta 13:1, מִשֶּׁנִּבְנָה בֵּית הַמִּקְדָּשׁ נִגְנַז
אֹהֶל מוֹעֵד, *when the [First] Temple was
built, the Tabernacle was hidden.* It
would seem from this that it was hidden
in the days of King Solomon. However,
from a cryptic remark in *Tosafos*

returned to Jerusalem to put down the revolt. He captured the city and took Yehoyakim into
captivity. Subsequently he put Yehoyakim to death ignominiously as prophesied by Jeremiah
[*Jer.* 22:19]: *He shall be buried with the burial of an ass* [i.e., without proper burial; cf. *comm.*
ad loc.] *drawn and cast forth beyond the gates of Jerusalem* [see *Malbim* to *II Kings* 24:1 for
the particulars of Yehoyakim's death]. This is the viewpoint of the Sages in *Seder Olam*, as
quoted in *comm.* above.

Another viewpoint is advanced by *Ibn Ezra* and other commentators. They hold that the
event referred to here is the same as in *II Kings* 24:1 — i.e., the initial subjugation of
Yehoyakim by Nebuchadnezzar. The conflict between the dates given is explained in a few
ways. E.g., *the third year* could mean after the passage of three years, which is the fourth year.

Ibn Ezra and *Malbim* offer another solution. According to the *Mishnah* (*Rosh Hashanah*
1:1) 'Rosh Chodesh Nissan is the beginning of the year for [the purpose of calculating the
year of] kings.' It follows that a king who ascended his throne in Adar would start his second
year in Nissan, although he had reigned just one month. If we were to take the anniversary of
his accession as the terminus of his first year, it would end only the following Adar. The conquest of Yehoyakim may have taken place some time between Nissan and the anniversary of
his accession, so that while it was the fourth year counting from Nissan, it was only the third
year counting from his *reign* — i.e., his accession.

Accordingly, the capture of Yehoyakim (*v.* 2) did not terminate his reign. He was returned
to his throne and ruled as Nebuchadnezzar's vassal for three years (*II Kings*, 24:1). Then he
revolted (*ibid.*) and ruled independently until the end of his reign — i.e., five more years. His
reign was terminated by the reconquest of Judah and his death.

בֵּית־הָאֱלֹהִים וַיְבִיאֵם אֶרֶץ־שִׁנְעָר בֵּית
אֱלֹהָיו וְאֶת־הַכֵּלִים הֵבִיא בֵּית אוֹצַר
אֱלֹהָיו: וַיֹּאמֶר הַמֶּלֶךְ לְאַשְׁפְּנַז רַב
סָרִיסָיו לְהָבִיא מִבְּנֵי יִשְׂרָאֵל וּמִזֶּרַע
הַמְּלוּכָה וּמִן־הַפַּרְתְּמִים: יְלָדִים אֲשֶׁר
אֵין־בָּהֶם כָּל־מאום וְטוֹבֵי מַרְאֶה

Shantz (Sotah 9a) it would seem that it was hidden in the days of Yoshiyahu. The word מִשֶּׁנִּבְנָה can be construed to mean *after* the First Temple was built without a specific date being given. When the *Tosefta* goes on to say (paragraph 2): *When the Holy Ark was hidden, the flask with the Manna was hidden with it* ... it can be taken to mean the Holy Ark with all its accessories — i.e., the Tabernacle and its vessels. The Tabernacle is called מִשְׁכָּן הָעֵדוּת, a resting place for the עֵדוּת — i.e., the stone tablets on which God etched the Ten Commandments, and which were deposited in the Holy Ark (cf. *Exod.* 25:16). The *Tosefta* goes on to say (see also *Yoma* 52b) that Yoshiyahu hid the Holy Ark. See also *II Hasmoneans* 2:5, where the hiding of the Tabernacle is attributed to Jeremiah, who was a contemporary of Yoshiyahu.]

וַיְבִיאֵם — *He brought them.*
He brought both the vessels and the people to the temple of his god to give thanks (*Rashi*).

שִׁנְעָר — *Shinar.*
Another name for Babylon. The Talmud (*Shabbos* 113b; cf. comm. to *Gen.* 6:17 s.v. הַמַּבּוּל) explains that it was called Shinar because the dead of the Flood were deposited there on account of the low-lying terrain. Shinar is derived from שֶׁנִּנְעֲרוּ, lit. *that they were shaken out* (*Rashi*; *R' Saadiah*).

בֵּית אֱלֹהָיו — *To the house of his god.*

He should have realized that his victory was a consequence of God's punishment of the Jews. But he chose to ignore this and attributed his victory to his idol. This verse is written here to explain the misfortunes that befell Nebuchadnezzar and his successors because of the vessels, as related later in this book. Even though it had been decreed by the Almighty that the vessels be brought to Babylon (*Jeremiah* 27:22), Nebuchadnezzar brought destruction upon himself when he brought them to his temple (*Alshich; Malbim*).

R' Saadiah maintains that אֱלֹהָיו is used here to mean *his judges* (cf. *Onkelos* to *Exodus* 22:8). Thus, he brought the captives to his courthouse — lit. *to the house of his judges.* He brought the captives to court to have sentence pronounced upon them. There was no purpose in doing so with the vessels.

וְאֶת הַכֵּלִים — *And the vessels he brought into the treasure-house of his god.*
Only the vessels were brought to the treasure house. Whereas, in the previous phrase, *he brought 'them'* — i.e., the vessels and the captives — to the temple of his god (*Rashi*, see comm. above).

According to *R' Saadiah*, who interprets that the prisoners were brought to the courthouse, only the

vessels of the House of God. He brought them to the land of Shinar to the house of his god, and the vessels he brought into the treasure-house of his god.

³ The king told Ashpenaz, the chief of his officers, to bring — from the children of Israel, from the royal seed, and from the nobles — ⁴ youths in whom there was no blemish; good-looking, skillful in all wisdom,

vessels were brought to his temple. He put the vessels in the treasure house of his god. The previous phrase meant that *he brought 'them'* [the captives] *to his courthouse,* whereas here it is said that the vessels were *brought to the treasure house of his god.*

3. Quest for Courtiers.

רַב סָרִיסָיו — *The chief of his officers.*

The noun סָרִיס refers primarily to a eunuch. The rulers of antiquity used to employ eunuchs to administer their courts. Accordingly רַב סָרִיסָיו is to be rendered *the chief of his eunuchs* (Ibn Ezra; cf. *Sanhedrin* 93b).

Other commentators maintain that סָרִיס, in its secondary meaning, means *a servant* or *official.* Therefore, רַב סָרִיסָיו is *the chief of his officials* (Metzudos). Onkelos (*Genesis* 39:1) and Yonasan (*Isaiah* 39:7) also prefer this interpretation (cf. *Sanhedrin* 93b, Maharsha, s.v. וְהָיוּ סריסים).

מִבְּנֵי יִשְׂרָאֵל וּמִזֶּרַע הַמְּלוּכָה וּמִן הַפַּרְתְּמִים — *From the children of Israel, from the royal seed, and from the nobles.*

Alshich understands the phrases *from the royal seed, and from the nobles,* to be an explanation of the phrase *from the children of Israel.*

From among the Jewish population the king picked members of the nobility. Nebuchadnezzar's primary interest in the nobility was because of their Jewish descent. He had heard about the fabulous wisdom of the Jews and wished to utilize it.

Malbim, however, views each phrase as standing by itself. He picked from *the children of Israel* — i.e., the common population — and also *from the royal seed, and from the nobles.* The commoners were to be used as servants, and the royal descendants as officials and advisers.

הַפַּרְתְּמִים — *The nobles.*

R' Saadiah derives הַפַּרְתְּמִים from פְּרִי תָמִים, lit. *a fruit without blemish* — i.e., the most perfect of people. However, most of the commentators define it as a foreign word — probably of Persian or Chaldaic origin — meaning *nobles.*

4. כָּל מאוּם — *No blemish* [lit. *not any blemish*].

They did not even have scratch marks (*Sanhedrin* 93).

Malbim remarks on the unusual spelling מאוּם instead of the usual מוּם. The word מאוּם can be derived from מְאוּמָה, *anything.* Thus, youths who did not have anything [*wrong*], not even the slightest imperfection.

וּמַשְׂכִּלִים בְּכָל־חָכְמָה וְיֹדְעֵי דַעַת
וּמְבִינֵי מַדָּע וַאֲשֶׁר כֹּחַ בָּהֶם לַעֲמֹד
בְּהֵיכַל הַמֶּלֶךְ וּלְלַמְּדָם סֵפֶר וּלְשׁוֹן
כַּשְׂדִּים: וַיְמַן לָהֶם הַמֶּלֶךְ דְּבַר־יוֹם בְּיוֹמוֹ
מִפַּת־בַּג הַמֶּלֶךְ וּמִיֵּין מִשְׁתָּיו וּלְגַדְּלָם
שָׁנִים שָׁלוֹשׁ וּמִקְצָתָם יַעַמְדוּ לִפְנֵי

ה

וּמַשְׂכִּלִים — *Skillful in all wisdom.*

The translation follows *Rambam* in *Moreh Nevuchim* (3:54) who interprets חָכְמָה as that which encompasses all pursuits of the mind — i.e., *the native power of the mind* — whereas דַעַת is *accumulated knowledge.*

Malbim understands חָכְמָה to be knowledge not arrived at by reasoning — e.g., *the knowledge of good and bad.* It is arrived at through basic human intuition or through a higher mental consciousness such as רוּחַ הַקֹּדֶשׁ, *holy spirit,* or revelation in the form of נְבוּאָה, *prophecy.* Therefore, we never find the expression בִּינוּ חָכְמָה, *understand* חָכְמָה, because חָכְמָה by its very nature is not to be understood rationally. דַעַת is that knowledge which is arrived at through reasoning.

וְיֹדְעֵי דַעַת — *Discriminating in knowledge.*

The translation follows *Malbim* (see above). *Ibn Ezra* renders it literally, *knowers of thought* — i.e., of such dexterity of mind that they knew from the beginning of a sentence what the speaker intended to say.

וּמְבִינֵי מַדָּע — *Perceptive in learning.*

The translation follows *Malbim* who explains מַדָּע — in contradistinction to דַעַת — to be a systematic body of knowledge. Individual bits of information, not worthy of the name מַדָּע, are called דַעַת.

Ibn Ezra regards מְבִינֵי as a transitive verb — i.e., people who can articulate their knowledge and transmit it to others. He remarks pithily that 'there are wise men who despair of bringing to their tongue what is in their mind.'

וַאֲשֶׁר כֹּחַ בָּהֶם — *And who had the stamina to stand in the king's palace.*

He asked for people who had the power to restrain themselves from smiling, talking, and sleeping in the royal presence, and also had control over their bodily functions while in the presence of the king (*Rashi* from *Sanhedrin* 93).

וּלְלַמְּדָם — *And to teach them.*

Metzudos explains this phrase as referring back to the previous verse, as if it said לְהָבִיא מִבְּנֵי יִשְׂרָאֵל וּלְלַמְּדָם. The translation reflects this viewpoint.

Rashi however regards this as a continuation of וַאֲשֶׁר כֹּחַ בָּהֶם, *those who have the ability to learn* (*Rashi*).

סֵפֶר — *The script* (*R' Saadiah* from *Chulin* 24).

5. וַיְמַן לָהֶם הַמֶּלֶךְ — *And the king provided for them.*

1
5

discriminating in knowledge, and perceptive in learn-
ing, and who had the stamina to stand in the king's
palace; and to teach them the script and language of
the Chaldeans. 5 *And the king provided for them a*
daily portion from the king's food and from his
drinking-wine to nurture them for three years, after
which they should stand before the king.

[I.e., the king gave instructions concerning their diet.]

The translation follows *Rashi* and *R' Saadiah. Ibn Ezra,* however, derives the word from the noun מָנָה, *portion.* He renders וַיְמַן, *he apportioned.*

The upbringing of these children concerned Nebuchadnezzar so much that he personally saw to their needs *(Malbim).*

דְּבַר־יוֹם בְּיוֹמוֹ — *A daily portion* [lit. *each day's item in its day*].

The king ordered that their diet be monitored daily by his doctors and dieticians, who adjusted the diet to the changing seasons. He wanted to keep them in perfect physical and mental health *(Malbim).*

מִפַּת־בַּג הַמֶּלֶךְ — *From the king's food.*

The translation rollows most commentators *(Ibn Janach; Rashi; Ibn Ezra). R' Saadiah,* however, translates פַּת in its traditional usage *bread* and renders בַּג as similar to בַּר, *wheat;* thus, פַּת בַּג is *wheat bread.*

[R' Saadiah's interpretation is based on the rule that certain sets of letters in Hebrew are occasionally interchanged. Among these interchangeable letters are ג'ר, ב'ש, א'ת, etc; i.e., the first and last letters of the alphabet, *aleph* and *tav,* are paired; the second and the twenty-first, *beis* and *shin;* the third and twentieth, *gimel* and *resh.* The letters of each pair may be interchanged; thus the *gimel* of בַּג in our verse may be exchanged with a *resh.*]

Ibn Ezra adds that the food referred to may have been cooked meat. This would explain why Daniel refused to eat it (see *v.*8).

שָׁנִים שָׁלוֹשׁ — [For] *three years.*

The purpose of all this preparation was *to teach them the script and language of the Chaldeans. Alshich* explains that Nebuchadnezzar supplied the youths with three things which are conducive to the attainment of excellence in studies: peace of mind, proper food, and an extended period of time for study. To guarantee the youths peace of mind, *the king provided for them,* thus freeing them from the burden of seeking their own sustenance. To insure that the youths would have the proper food, the king sent provisions *from the king's food and from his drinking-wine* — i.e., the best food available for strengthening both the body and the mind. To allow sufficient time for the accumulation of knowledge, the king supported the youths in this manner *for three years (Alshich).*

From this waiting period, the Sages derived the dictum that a student who has not succeeded after three years of study will surely not succeed thereafter *(Chullin 24a).*

וֹ הַמֶּלֶךְ: וַיְהִי בָהֶם מִבְּנֵי יְהוּדָה דָּנִיֵּאל
ז חֲנַנְיָה מִישָׁאֵל וַעֲזַרְיָה: וַיָּשֶׂם לָהֶם שַׂר
הַסָּרִיסִים שֵׁמוֹת וַיָּשֶׂם לְדָנִיֵּאל

וּמִקְצָתָם — *After which* [lit. *at their conclusion*].

I.e., at the end of these three years.

The translation follows *Ibn Ezra* and *R' Sa'adiah*. Alternately, according to *R' Saadiah* and *Ibn Ezra*, וּמִקְצָתָם means *some of them*, referring to the Jewish children. Thus, the king's hope was that *some of them should* [be worthy to] *stand before the king*.

All of the above mentioned preparations would not necessarily assure total success. Nebuchadnezzar would have been content if only a few of the children had lived up to his expectations. וּמִקְצָתָם יַעֲמְדוּ, *'and some of them would stand'* before the king (*Alshich*).

6. New Names.

מִבְּנֵי יְהוּדָה — *From the children of Judah.*

I.e., from the descendants of Hezekiah, King of Judah.

By drawing from Hezekiah's descendants, Nebuchadnezzar fulfilled the prophecy of Isaiah (39:7): *And of your sons that will issue from you ... they will take away and they will be officials in the palace of the king of Babylon* (*R' Saadiah; Mayenei Hayeshuah* 5:2). *Ralbag*, however, is of the opinion that since they are referred to only as *from the children of Judah*, they must have been neither *from the royal seed*, nor *from the nobles* (cf. v. 3). They were only *from the children of Judah*, rather than from the Judean aristocracy.

Abarbanel vigorously rejects *Ralbag's* opinion because Isaiah's prophecy points to its fulfillment through Daniel. Furthermore, the Sages (*Sanhedrin* 93b) are unquestionably of the opinion that Daniel, at least, was of the royal seed. He also points to the prophetic blessing given Judah by Jacob (*Genesis* 49:10): *The scepter will not depart from Judah, nor the ruler's staff from between his feet until the Messiah will come.* This is understood by the Sages (*Sanhedrin* 5a) to indicate that even in exile the leaders of the Jews will come from the royal seed. In keeping with Jacob's prophecy, Daniel, as the main Jewish representative at the Babylonian court, must have been of royal lineage (*Mayenei HaYeshuah* 5:2).

[Scripture, in ascribing royalty to Daniel, describes him not as a descendant of David, but of Judah — an obvious allusion to Jacob's blessing.]

R' Elazar said that all of them were from the children of Judah. R' Shmuel bar Nachmani said [only] Daniel was from Judah, but Chananyah, Mishael, and Azaryah were from other tribes (*Sanhedrin* 93b).

The other three should have been mentioned before Daniel, since they were considered prophets, whereas Daniel was not. Since Daniel was given precedence over the others, he must have been of royal descent (*Chidushei Aggadoth Maharal*).[1]

[It is possible that R' Shmuel bar Nachmani interpreted v. 3 as meaning to bring children from each category separately (cf. *comm.*) — i.e., Nebuchadnezzar wanted *youths from the children of Israel* in addition to children *from the royal seed*. In v. 19 it is clear that only these four people were

*6 Among them, from the children of Judah, were
Daniel, Chananyah, Mishael, and Azaryah. 7 The
chief officer assigned them names: to Daniel he as-*

chosen. It therefore follows that all four could not have been *from the children of Judah.* The only one certainly from Judah would be Daniel, who is mentioned first.

The cantillation, however, seems to point to R' Elazar's view. The *esnachta* (which serves as a comma or semicolon) is placed under מִבְּנֵי יְהוּדָה, *from the children of Judah,* followed by the four names without indication that they are of different status. According to R' Shmuel bar Nachmani, however, the pause should have followed Daniel's name, in order to set off his ancestry from that of his three companions.]

דָּנִיֵּאל — *Daniel.*

[Since the *tzeirei* (ֵ) is under the *yud,* the proper pronunciation is *Daniyel.* We have, however, retained the spelling *Daniel* since it is so well known.]

7. וַיָּשֶׂם לָהֶם שַׂר הַסָּרִיסִים שֵׁמוֹת — *The chief officer assigned them names.*

It was customary to change the names of people who were elevated to the royal staff — Pharaoh

changed Joseph's name to Zofnas Paaneach; Nebuchadnezzar changed Matanyah's name to Zedekiah *(Ibn Ezra).* [This was done by the chief official at the king's request. In 5:12 it is stated explicitly that the king renamed Daniel.]

Toras Chessed advances another view. Since the chief officer was a eunuch (cf. *comm.* 1:3), he had no hope of having his own offspring. By giving names to the youths in his charge, he would consider them as his own children, thereby perpetuating his name. Scripture stresses that it was the שַׂר הַסָּרִיסִים, *the chief eunuch,* who conferred the names, thus implying that just because he was a eunuch he gave them names.

[It is also possible that since their own names had the name of the One true God suffixed to them (יָה and אֵל =God), they could not be tolerated by Nebuchadnezzar. He therefore substituted names of an idolatrous or secular nature.]

1. The passage *(Sanhedrin 93b)* to which *Maharal* refers does not specifically identify Chananyah, Mishael, and Azaryah as prophets. *Maharal* interpolates that fact from an interpretation cited later in the same *Talmudic* passage. There, a verse from 10:7 is quoted. *And I, Daniel, alone saw the vision, and the men who were with me did not see the vision.* Who were the [unnamed] men? R' Yirmiyah, and some say R' Chiya bar Abba, commented that the men were Chaggai, Zachariah, and Malachi, who were greater than Daniel because they were prophets while he was not, yet they did not see the vision which was revealed to him.

Maharal clearly assumes that the unnamed men of 10:7 were the same people who were Daniel's constant companions: Chananyah, Mishael, and Azaryah. Thus, if the men of 10:7 are identified as the three acknowledged prophets — Chaggai, Zechariah, and Malachi — we must infer that they and Daniel's three companions are one and the same. If so, their standing as prophets made them spiritually superior to Daniel and this should have been acknowledged by listing them before Daniel in our verse. As a result, *Maharal* gives the above interpretation that the listing of Daniel prior to them could be based only on his royal descent; otherwise, their status as prophets would have given them precedence over him.

That *Maharal* so identifies Daniel's three companions is indicated by his explanations of two passages in *Sanhedrin 93b:* those expounding both 1:6 and 10:7.

א
ח

בֶּלְטְשַׁאצַּר וְלַחֲנַנְיָה שַׁדְרַךְ וּלְמִישָׁאֵל
מֵישַׁךְ וְלַעֲזַרְיָה עֲבֵד נְגוֹ: וַיָּשֶׂם דָּנִיֵּאל ח
עַל־לִבּוֹ אֲשֶׁר לֹא־יִתְגָּאַל בְּפַת־בַּג הַמֶּלֶךְ

בֶּלְטְשַׁאצַּר — *Belteshazzar.*

The name of a Babylonian idol, as we see later (4:5), *whose name is Belteshazzar like the name of my god* (Rashi; Ibn Ezra).

R' Saadiah analyzes this further. בֵּל is the name of a Babylonian idol (cf. *Jeremiah* 51:44). טֵשׁ is from טַשׁ, *hiding* (cf. *Shabbos* 33b). אצַּר is a treasure; thus, *'Bel' who guards (hides) the treasure of Babylon.*

שַׁדְרַךְ ... מֵישַׁךְ ... עֲבֵד נְגוֹ — *Shadrach ... Meshach ... Abed Nego.*

These are Aramaic names (Ibn Ezra).

R' Saadiah Gaon (cited in *Ibn Ezra*) sees a similarity between Nego and Nebo — a Babylonian idol (cf. *Isaiah* 46:1); thus, *Abed Nego — the servant of Nebo.*

It is possible that the other names, too, are of idolatrous nature. They may however be names of famous Babylonians (Ralbag).

The fact that Nebuchadnezzar singled out Daniel to be named after his own god shows that Nebuchadnezzar had a premonition of Daniel's greatness. He must have sensed in Daniel the man of the spirit, one who was imbued with the gift of prophecy (*Ralbag; Malbim; Mayenei HaYeshuah* 5:3). This also explains the recurrence of the word וַיָּשֶׂם, *and he assigned*, in this verse. The first time refers to the namegiving in general. The second stresses that Daniel was especially chosen for the name Belteshazzar (*Toras Chessed*).

An interesting point is made by *Toras Chessed.* The prophecy of Isaiah (39:7) that Hezekiah's offspring would be officers at the palace of the Babylonian king was fulfilled through Daniel (cf. *comm.* 1:6). When Isaiah (56:4-5) says, *Concerning the officers who keep my Sabbaths, and hold fast in my covenant ... I will give them an everlasting name that shall not be cut off*, he alludes to Daniel and his companions. This is clearly the view of the Sages (*Sanhedrin* 93b). Thus, when Nebuchadnezzar names him Belteshazzar, he is assured by the prophet that this Babylonian name is only transitory, but his name for posterity, the *everlasting name that shall not be cut off*, remains Daniel.

[It is noteworthy that throughout the narrative, Daniel is never referred to as Belteshazzar, but always as *Daniel whose name is Belteshazzar*, except where Nebuchadnezzar himself is speaking (4:15,16)].

The above quotation from *Isaiah: I will give him an everlasting name* is understood by the *Talmud* (*Sanhedrin* 93b) as referring to the Book of *Daniel*, which is called by his name.

Chida comments that the numerical value of סֵפֶר, *book*, is the same as שֵׁם, *name* (*Pesach Ainayim* to *Sanhedrin*).

8. Daniel's Resolution

וַיָּשֶׂם דָּנִיֵּאל עַל לִבּוֹ — *Daniel resolved* [lit. *placed upon his heart*].

Daniel, fearing the effects of the

signed *Belteshazzar;* to *Chananyah, Shadrach;* to
Mishael, Meshach; and to *Azaryah, Abed Nego.*
   ⁸ *Daniel resolved not to be defiled by the king's*

food produced by his idolatrous masters, sought to avoid the use of such food. The *Talmud* cites a dispute concerning the measures taken by Daniel: Rav said he *placed upon 'his heart'* and also decreed it for all Jews. Shmuel said he took it only upon himself but did not decree it for all Jews *(Avodah Zarah* 36a).

[The above controversy in the *Talmud* is basically about oil bought from a gentile. The *Mishnah (Avodah Zarah* 35b) mentions oil among the items a Jew may not buy from a gentile. This prohibition was lifted in the days of Rabbi Yehudah Nessiah. The question arose whether the original prohibition had been promulgated by Daniel or by the academies of Shamai and Hillel. The *Talmud* assumes that the plural form מִשְׁתָּיו, *his drinks,* instead of the singular מִשְׁתּוֹ, *his drink,* clearly indicates that Daniel abstained from both wine and oil. The only unanswered question is whether his abstention was a private act, or whether it was meant as a decree incumbent upon all Jews.

Ramban (Chidushim, ibid.) holds that this controversy concerns only the ban on oil, which was lifted later. However, foods cooked by a gentile (בִּישׁוּל עַכּוּ''ם) and wine bought from him were surely prohibited by Daniel. In *Pirkei d'Rabbi Eliezer* (Ch. 47), we find that a ban had already been pronounced by Phineas, who lived many centuries earlier. *Rabad* (quoted by *Ramban*), however holds that the controversy about oil also includes both cooked food and wine. All commentators agree that Daniel himself abstained from the king's food and wine for the same reason that these things were prohibited to all Jews, namely to avoid the temptation of חִתּוּן, [*inter*]-

marriage. Mingling with non-Jews in an eating and drinking relationship strengthens social bonds, and may ultimately lead to intermarriage. The significance of this problem at the time of the Babylonian captivity can readily by seen from *Ezra* ch. 9-10.]

Daniel's voluntary decision to abstain from the delicacies of the king's table was not shared initially by his friends. To Daniel, eating was merely a measure to sustain the body for a higher purpose — the worship of God. This could be accomplished by eating the plainest and most essential foods. There was no need for royal delicacies. Once Daniel set the the example, the others followed suit *(Mayenei Ha-Yeshuah* 5:3).

Since Daniel alone had been named for a Babylonian idol, he suspected that he was being consecrated to this idol and that his food consisted of animals sacrificed to the idol, including wine used for libations. Since the Torah enjoins total abstention from objects used in the worship of idols, it would be incumbent on Daniel to suffer death rather than submit. The *Halachah* requires that יֵהָרֵג וְאַל יַעֲבֹר, *one submit to death rather than transgress,* in a situation where there is intent to estrange a Jew from his religion (לְהַעֲבִיר עַל הַדָּת) *(Malbim;* cf. *Sanhedrin 74b).*

[According to some authorities, the mere eating of idolatrous sacrifices would fall under the category of idol worship which requires that יֵהָרֵג וְאַל יַעֲבוֹר, *one be killed rather than transgress,* even if there is no intent to wean

וּבְיֵין מִשְׁתָּיו וַיְבַקֵּשׁ מִשַּׂר הַסָּרִיסִים
אֲשֶׁר לֹא־יִתְגָּאָל: וַיִּתֵּן הָאֱלֹהִים אֶת־
דָּנִיֵּאל לְחֶסֶד וּלְרַחֲמִים לִפְנֵי שַׂר
הַסָּרִיסִים: וַיֹּאמֶר שַׂר הַסָּרִיסִים לְדָנִיֵּאל
יָרֵא אֲנִי אֶת־אֲדֹנִי הַמֶּלֶךְ אֲשֶׁר מִנָּה אֶת־
מַאֲכַלְכֶם וְאֶת־מִשְׁתֵּיכֶם אֲשֶׁר לָמָּה
יִרְאֶה אֶת־פְּנֵיכֶם זֹעֲפִים מִן־הַיְלָדִים
אֲשֶׁר כְּגִילְכֶם וְחִיַּבְתֶּם אֶת־רֹאשִׁי לַמֶּלֶךְ:
וַיֹּאמֶר דָּנִיֵּאל אֶל־הַמֶּלְצַר אֲשֶׁר מִנָּה
שַׂר הַסָּרִיסִים עַל־דָּנִיֵּאל חֲנַנְיָה מִישָׁאֵל
וַעֲזַרְיָה: נַס־נָא אֶת־עֲבָדֶיךָ יָמִים עֲשָׂרָה

him from his Jewish religion. Any transgression linked with idol worship is in the category of אֲבִיזְרֵיהוּ דַעֲבוֹדָה זָרָה, *secondary forms of idolatry*, which have the same *halachic* requirements as idol worship itself (cf. *Ran, Pesachim* 25a; *Tosafos* there s.v. חוּץ).]

אֲשֶׁר לֹא יִתְגָּאָל — *That he not be defiled.*

I.e., that he not be coerced into defiling himself. The translation follows *Rashi* and *R' Saadiah.*

Ralbag cites the interpretation of his father, *R' Gershon,* who derives יִתְגָּאָל from וְאִם אֵין לָאִישׁ גֹּאֵל, *if the man has no redeemer* [i.e., close kin] (*Numbers* 5:8). However, like other words in Hebrew, יִתְגָּאָל is a verb that can be used for opposite meanings: to have kin or to be left without kin (cf. *Rashi Exodus* 27:3 s.v. לְדַשְּׁנוֹ). Thus אֲשֶׁר לֹא יִתְגָּאָל means that he should not be left without kin — i.e., heirless. The eating of the king's food could lead to intermarriage (cf. *comm.* above), in which case Daniel's offspring would not be considered his according to *Halachah.*

Ralbag adds that according to the more generally accepted translation, which relates יִתְגָּאָל to defilement, it should be understood as follows: By eating of the king's food he would establish closer social contacts with the gentiles, and would thereby *defile himself,* becoming influenced by their attitudes and mores.

Ibn Ezra attributes Daniel's refusal to eat to the fact that he was being served non-kosher meat (cf. *comm.* to 1:5 s.v. מִפַּת בַּג).

The wine was probably from idolatrous libations which were very prevalent among the Babylonians. Since the food was forbidden, it would defile Daniel.

9. לְחֶסֶד וּלְרַחֲמִים — *Favor and mercy.*

Even though the chief officer would not be the one to fulfill Daniel's request, Daniel still needed his mercy. For had he informed Nebuchadnezzar of the request, it might have cost Daniel his life, for his request indicated a brazen refusal to submit to Nebuchadnez-

1
9-12
food nor by his drinking-wine, and he asked the chief officer that he not be defiled. ⁹ *God granted Daniel favor and mercy before the chief officer,* ¹⁰ *and the chief officer said to Daniel, 'I fear my lord the king, who has provided your food and your drinks. For why should he see your faces more depressed than the youths like yourselves, and you will forfeit my head to the king?'*

¹¹ *So Daniel said to the steward whom the chief officer had assigned to Daniel, Chananyah, Mishael, and Azaryah,* ¹² *'Please test your servants for ten*

---

zar's authority (*R' Saadiah Gaon,* quoted by *Ibn Ezra*).

Though he was an important official and Daniel a mere youth, he displayed *favor* toward him and condescended to discuss the matter with him (*Mayenei HaYeshuah* 5:3; *Malbim*).

10. אֲשֶׁר מִנָּה אֶת־מַאֲכַלְכֶם — *Who has provided your food.*

I fear the king's wrath should he learn of your request. The matter of the food served to you concerns him so much that he himself *has provided your food.* Would I acquiesce to your demand, I fear that he will *see your faces ... depressed* and thereby learn of our changes in his plan (*Malbim*).

אֲשֶׁר כְּגִילְכֶם — [*Who are*] *like yourselves.*

The translation follows *Rashi, Ibn Ezra,* and *Radak* in *Sefer Hashorashim.*

[This is the only place in Scripture where this word is used. We find it in the *Talmud* occasionally with similar connotations. The modern usage of the word גיל to denote age is probably of recent origin.]

11. Daniel's Proposal

אֶל־הַמֶּלְצַר — *To the steward.*

Daniel did not broach his plan to the steward before he had spoken to *the chief officer* and found favor and mercy in his eyes, lest he be discovered by the chief officer and suffer dire consequences. Having won the chief officer's heart, Daniel was confident he would turn a blind eye to whatever he saw. He had hinted as much when he said, *'Why should "he" see your faces more depressed?'* Daniel was confident that his appearance would not suffer from this test, thus removing the chief officer's sole objection (*Alshich; Malbim*).

12. נַס־נָא — *Please test your servants.*

Daniel did not suggest his plan to the chief officer, because he felt it inappropriate for so important an official to bother with such detail. Nor did he ask him to command the steward to conduct this test; — just in case Daniel's plan was discovered by the king, the chief officer, himself uninvolved, could always plead for the exoneration of his underling (*Alshich*).

וְיִתְּנוּ־לָנוּ מִן־הַזֵּרְעִים וְנֹאכְלָה וּמַיִם

יג וְנִשְׁתֶּה: וְיֵרָאוּ לְפָנֶיךָ מַרְאֵינוּ וּמַרְאֵה

הַיְלָדִים הָאֹכְלִים אֵת פַּת־בַּג הַמֶּלֶךְ

יד וְכַאֲשֶׁר תִּרְאֵה עֲשֵׂה עִם־עֲבָדֶיךָ: וַיִּשְׁמַע

לָהֶם לַדָּבָר הַזֶּה וַיְנַסֵּם יָמִים עֲשָׂרָה:

טו וּמִקְצָת יָמִים עֲשָׂרָה נִרְאָה מַרְאֵיהֶם טוֹב

וּבְרִיאֵי בָּשָׂר מִן־כָּל־הַיְלָדִים הָאֹכְלִים

טז אֵת פַּת־בַּג הַמֶּלֶךְ: וַיְהִי הַמֶּלְצַר נֹשֵׂא

אֶת־פַּת־בָּגָם וְיֵין מִשְׁתֵּיהֶם וְנֹתֵן לָהֶם

יז זֵרְעֹנִים: וְהַיְלָדִים הָאֵלֶּה אַרְבַּעְתָּם נָתַן

יָמִים עֲשָׂרָה — *[For] ten days.*

If their diet were insufficient, symptoms would surely show up within ten days (*Ralbag; Mayenei HaYeshuah* 5:3).

הַזֵּרְעִים — *[The] pulse* [i.e., raw seeds; e.g. rice, peas, beans, etc.].

... So as to be sure they had not been cooked in the king's utensils and thereby rendered non-kosher. Had they asked for cooked pulse, they would have said מַאֲכַל זֵרְעִים (*Alshich*).

13. וְיֵרָאוּ לְפָנֶיךָ מַרְאֵינוּ — *Then let our appearance ... be seen by you* [lit., *may there appear before you our appearance.*]

Daniel did not tell the steward that the real intent of his request was so as *not to be defiled by the king's food* (v. 8). The steward would not go along with this, because it would be interpreted as an insult to the king and if discovered, it would carry the penalty of death. Instead, he pretended that his purpose was to achieve the king's will in a better way. The pulse would enhance their ap-

pearance over that of the other youths *who eat the king's food* (*Alshich*).

Daniel was confident that his simple fare would go further to achieve the king's purpose than the delicacies of the king's table. The latter, though more pleasant to the palate, do not necessarily provide better nourishment (*Mayenei HaYeshuah* 5:3; *Malbim*; see *comm.* to v. 15).

Abarbanel comments that before the Deluge, when Adam and his descendants were not permitted to eat meat (cf. *Sanhedrin* 59b; *Rashi* to *Genesis* 9:3) people lived to an average of nine hundred years. After meat was permitted to Noah, life expectancy dropped drastically (*ibid.*).

14. The Test

וַיִּשְׁמַע לָהֶם — *He heeded them.*

He was confident he would not be found out in case the test was a failure, for the king was not scheduled to see the youths until the end of three years (*Malbim*).

He was motivated by the prospect that he would be able to keep

1

13-17

days, and let them give us pulse to eat and water to drink. ¹³ Then let our appearance and the appearance of the youths who eat the king's food be seen by you; in accord with what you will see, act toward your servants.'

¹⁴ He heeded them in this matter, and tested them for ten days. ¹⁵ At the end of ten days they looked better and fatter than all the youths eating the king's food. ¹⁶ The steward would take their food and drinking-wine, and give them pulse.

¹⁷ God gave these four youths learning and skill in

the youth's portions for himself (*Mayenei HaYeshuah* 5:3).

לַדָּבָר הַזֶּה — *In this matter.*
Daniel requested two things: 1) to conduct a test for ten days, 2) that the purveyors of the king's food (the steward's job was just to distribute) should supply the pulse (cf. *v.* 12 *and let 'them' give us pulse*). But the steward did not stand to gain anything by the second request. He therefore listened to them only in '*this*' matter, i.e., to conduct the test. He supplied the pulse on his own without informing the purveyors of any change and took the youths' portions of the king's food for himself (*Alshich*; cf. *v.* 16).

15. נִרְאָה מַרְאֵיהֶם טוֹב — *They looked better* [lit. *their appearances appeared good*].

Good appearance is the result of both diet and spirit. The inner peace and feeling of satisfaction resulting from the fulfillment of God's will radiated outward and enhanced their appearance. As for fattening the flesh, that could naturally be better achieved by eating the king's food, which contained meat and

other fattening food. Daniel promised the steward only that *our 'appearance'* will be seen... However, because of their earnestness (*v.* 13) and fervor, God miraculously caused them to also be *fatter* (*Alshich*).

16. וַיְהִי הַמֶּלְצַר נֹשֵׂא אֶת פַּת בָּגָם — *The steward would take their food.*

He took it for himself (*Rashi*; cf. *comm.* to *v.* 14).

17. וְהַיְלָדִים הָאֵלֶּה אַרְבַּעְתָּם נָתַן לָהֶם הָאֱלֹהִים — *God gave these four youths* [lit., *These youths, the four of them, God gave to them*].

All four abstained from the king's food, so they were all equally endowed with God-given learning and wisdom. But since Daniel had taken the initiative and risked his life, he merited a greater reward. Therefore: *and Daniel understood all visions and dreams* (*Alshich*; *Malbim*).

[The others, not risking their lives, had done a natural thing and they were rewarded with excellence in natural things. Daniel, who sacrificed himself for God and rose above nature, merited a reward of a supernatural nature. Therefore *Daniel understood all dreams*

לָהֶם הָאֱלֹהִים מַדָּע וְהַשְׂכֵּל בְּכָל־סֵפֶר
יְחָכְמָה וְדָנִיֵּאל הֵבִין בְּכָל־חָזוֹן וַחֲלֹמוֹת:
יח וּלְמִקְצָת הַיָּמִים אֲשֶׁר־אָמַר הַמֶּלֶךְ
לַהֲבִיאָם וַיְבִיאֵם שַׂר הַסָּרִיסִים לִפְנֵי
יט נְבֻכַדְנֶצַּר: וַיְדַבֵּר אִתָּם הַמֶּלֶךְ וְלֹא נִמְצָא
מִכֻּלָּם כְּדָנִיֵּאל חֲנַנְיָה מִישָׁאֵל וַעֲזַרְיָה
כ וַיַּעַמְדוּ לִפְנֵי הַמֶּלֶךְ: וְכֹל דְּבַר חָכְמַת
בִּינָה אֲשֶׁר־בִּקֵּשׁ מֵהֶם הַמֶּלֶךְ וַיִּמְצָאֵם
עֶשֶׂר יָדוֹת עַל כָּל־הַחַרְטֻמִּים הָאַשָּׁפִים
כא אֲשֶׁר בְּכָל־מַלְכוּתוֹ: וַיְהִי דָּנִיֵּאל עַד־
א שְׁנַת אַחַת לְכוֹרֶשׁ הַמֶּלֶךְ: וּבִשְׁנַת

and visions — a supernatural gift. As Joseph said (*Genesis* 40:8): *Do not interpretations belong to God?*]

בְּכָל־סֵפֶר — *In all scripts.*
[Cf. *comm.* to *v.* 4.]

בְּכָל־חָזוֹן וַחֲלֹמוֹת — *(In) all visions and dreams.*

Other interpreters could interpret visions and dreams only in a general sense, without going into detail. Daniel, however, since his understanding was God-given and prophetic, understood 'entire' visions and dreams (*Mayenei HaYeshuah* 5:4; *Malbim*).

It is possible that this refers to the visions Daniel saw, as narrated later in this book (*Mayenei HaYeshuah,* ibid.).

19. Incomparable Foursome

וַיְדַבֵּר — *The king conversed* [lit., spoke] *with them.*

Their excellence was so apparent, that merely by speaking with them — without testing them — the king was able to realize their superiority (*Alshich*).

20. וְכֹל דְּבַר — *In every matter* of the art of reasoning.

He was able to recognize their superiority merely by speaking to them (cf. *comm. v.* 19), because *in every matter ... he found them ten times better than all the necromancers and astrologers,* let alone than their peers.

הַחַרְטֻמִּים — *The necromancers.*

The translation follows *Midrash Tanchuma (Miketz): those who inquire of the bones of the dead* (see *Rashi* and *Mizrachi* to *Genesis* 41:8 and *Rashi* here).

[*Onkelos* (*ibid.*). translates it חַרְשַׁיָּא, which is also the translation of מְכַשֵּׁף, *magician* (see *Exodus* 22:17). This does not contradict our translation, because necromancy, being a branch of witchcraft, can also be called by the more general term, witchcraft. *Ibn Ezra* suggests that חַרְטוֹם could be an Egyptian word. This has been verified in modern times. It would seem that the

1
18-21
all scripts and wisdom, and Daniel understood all visions and dreams.

18 At the end of the years after which the king had
said to bring them, the chief officer brought them
before Nebuchadnezzar. 19 The king conversed with
them, and of them all, none compared to Daniel,
Chananyah, Mishael, and Azaryah; so they stood
before the king. 20 In every matter of the art of
reasoning that the king asked of them, he found them
ten times better than all the necromancers and
astrologers throughout his kingdom. 21 And Daniel
remained until the first year of King Cyrus.

Hebrew and Aramaic languages had no word to denote this specific kind of magic. That חַרְטֻמִּים here does not mean magic in general is clear from the mention of מְכַשְׁפִים in 2:2 together with חַרְטֻמִּים.]

הָאַשָּׁפִים — [The] astrologers.
The translation here follows Midrash Tanchuma (Miketz), those who stress [interpretation of] the constellations.

21. וַיְהִי דָּנִיֵּאל — And Daniel remained [lit. was].
He remained in Babylon until the

first year of King Cyrus (Ibn Ezra; Ralbag).
I.e., he remained in his high position at the royal court until the first year of King Cyrus (Rashi; Metzudos; Malbim).[1]

At this time Cyrus proclaimed throughout his kingdom: Whoever there is among you ... let him go up to Jerusalem (Ezra 1:3; cf. there 1:1, In the first year of Cyrus King of Persia ...). Daniel took advantage of this opportunity and went to Jerusalem (Ralbag).

1. According to Chazal in Seder Olam, four monarchs of the Perso-Median empire are mentioned in Scripture (cf. Seder Olam ch. 28 and Rashi to Daniel 11:2; Ibn Ezra ibid.).
A) Daryavesh (Darius) ben Ahasuerus the Mede (Daniel 9:1, 6:1, 11:1).
B) Koresh (Cyrus the great) the Persian, son-in-law of Darius. Cyrus, together with his father-in-law, Darius, conquered Babylon (Rashi to Daniel 6:29 from Yossippon 3; Josephus Flavius in Antiquities 10,11,4 says, he was Darius' kinsman). After a year Darius died (Seder Olam 28) and Cyrus ruled alone. During Darius' rule Daniel was thrown into the lion's pit (Daniel ch. 6). Cyrus, in the first year of his rule, proclaimed, whoever there is among you ... let him go up to Jerusalem (Ezra 1:3; II Chron. 36:23).
C) Achashverosh (Ahasuerus the husband of Esther), King of Persia.
D) Daryavesh (Darius) son of Achashverosh, the Persian. During his rule of the Temple was rebuilt (Ezra 6).
The Sages (Rosh Hashanah 3b) say that this latter Darius is also called Cyrus and Artachshasta.
In light of this, the Cyrus mentioned here can be either the first Cyrus or Darius/Cyrus. Rashi brings the opinion of Rav and Shmuel (Megillah 15a) that Hasach (in Esther ch. 4) is identical with Daniel. Rav holds he was called Hasach from חָתַךְ, (lit. cut down) because he was demoted from his greatness. According to this, the Cyrus referred to here is Cyrus the

שְׁתַּיִם לְמַלְכוּת נְבֻכַדְנֶצַּר חָלַם נְבֻכַדְנֶצַּר א ב
חֲלֹמוֹת וַתִּתְפָּעֶם רוּחוֹ וּשְׁנָתוֹ נִהְיְתָה עָלָיו

II

1. The Dream of the Four Kingdoms.

וּבִשְׁנַת שְׁתַּיִם — *In the second year.*

This refers to the second year after the destruction of the Temple (*Seder Olam* ch. 28 quoted by *Rashi*).

The difficulty in placing the occurrence of Nebuchadnezzar's dreams in the second year of his reign (as *Ralbag* and *R' Saadiah* do), lies in the fact that we find Daniel interpreting this dream. As narrated in the previous chapter, Daniel did not stand before the king till the end of the third year of training. According to *Seder Olam* this event actually occurred in Nebuchadnezzar's twenty-first year (cf. *comm.* to 11:1; *Seder Olam* Ch. 27; *Megillah* 11b with *Rashi* s.v. שניה).

Accordingly, *In the second year of Nebuchadnezzar's reign* means the second year of his direct reign over Judah and Jerusalem. Previously he had ruled Judah through regents, e.g., Yehoyakim.

Great who reigned before Ahasuerus. Therefore, by the time Esther became queen, Daniel had already been demoted.

Shmuel holds that he was called Hasach because all the matters of state were decided (lit. *cut by his mouth*) by him. According to him, Cyrus in this verse must mean Darius/Cyrus because Daniel was still a powerful figure in Esther's time (*Rashi*).

[According to the latter view, Daniel was extremely old. According to the Sages (*Megillah*; *Seder Olam* 28), the time lapse between the conquest of Yehoyakim — when Daniel was taken captive — and the reign of Darius/Cyrus was eighty-seven years. Add to that Daniel's age at captivity and we get a minimum of one hundred years.

Even according to the first view he was about eighty-five years of age.]

Abarbanel (*Mayenei HaYeshuah* 5:4) relates in the name of *Joseph ben Gorion* (*Yossipon* 3) that Daniel, after his miraculous escape from the den of lions (ch. 6), asked the king to be excused from his service, because of the jealousy of the nobles and his advanced age. The king refused to accept his resignation unless he would find a suitable replacement for himself. Daniel recommended Zerubabel ben Shealtiel, grandson of King Yehoyachin (see *I Chron.* 3:17). Daniel then retired to Shushan, where he spent the rest of his days in the service of God and in the service of his brethren, to whom he gave most of the salary he received from the king's court. *Abarbanel* comments that though Daniel's resignation was tendered to Darius, Daniel did not leave Babylon immediately. In the short time he tarried in Babylon, Darius died and Cyrus became king, so Daniel remained till the first year of King Cyrus. He later returned to Babylon, as we see in 10:1.

Abarbanel attributes this to the hindering of the building of the Temple by the foes of the Jews in the days of *Cyrus* as related in *Ezra* (4:5). Daniel returned to Babylon to intercede on behalf of his brothers and, while in Babylon, saw the vision described in ch. 10.

Josephus Flavius knows nothing of this appointment of Zerubabel instead of Daniel. He speaks of him only as governor of Judah, as is known also from *Haggai* 1:1. The story which *Yossipon* tells about Zerubabel at the court of Darius the Mede, Josephus tells as happening during the rule of Darius the Persian (*Antiquities II* 3). It should also be noted that the tradition of the Persian Jews is in agreement with *Yossipon's* account. Daniel's grave is by local tradition on the banks of the Tigris in the vicinity of Shushan, as narrated by *R' Benjamin* of Tudela and *R' Pesachiah* of Regensburg in their itineraries (second half of 12th century). In modern times the location of this grave has been forgotten.

According to the *Midrash* (*Shir HaShirim Rabbah* 5:5), Daniel went to the Holy Land when Cyrus allowed all the Jews in his kingdom to return (see *Yefeh Kol, ibid.*; *Ralbag* cited in *comm.* here).

דניאל [74]

2

1-2

*I*n *the second year of Nebuchadnezzar's reign, Nebuchadnezzar dreamed dreams. His spirit was agitated and his sleep was interrupted.* ² *Then the*

Abarbanel adds that until the year of the destruction of the Temple, Nebuchadnezzar was not a king on a global scale. In that year he also conquered many other nations, as prophesied by Jeremiah (27:1-9, cf. *Megillah* 11a). Thus: *In the second year of the* [global] *reign of Nebuchadnezzar ...* (*Mayenei HaYeshuah* 6:1; *Malbim; Alshich*).

R' Saadiah, however, understands this date in its literal sense. He explains that the dream kept on recurring to Nebuchadnezzar after he originally saw it *in the second year of ... reign.* By the time Nebuchadnezzar was sufficiently alarmed to convene all his wise men, Daniel had already been accepted to stand before the king.

חֲלֹמוֹת — *Dreams.*

The plural form חֲלֹמוֹת is used instead of the singular חֲלוֹם. Because Nebuchadnezzar's dream was composed of many different parts, each having its own meaning (e.g., the head of gold, the breast and arms of silver, the stone that was thrown at the statue), this one dream is considered as containing many dreams (*Mayenei HaYeshuah* 6:1; *Malbim; R' Saadiah*).

Nebuchadnezzar saw this dream several times, like Pharaoh in Joseph's time (*Ralbag*).

[Joseph interpreted the doubling of Pharaoh's dream as a sign that *God will shortly bring it to pass* (*Gen.* 42:32). This interpretation surely does not apply here. Nebuchadnezzar's dream anticipated the establishment of the kingdoms that would influence the history of mankind until the coming of

the Messiah. Nevertheless, since part of the dream, at least, alluded to Nebuchadnezzar's as the first of these kingdoms, it was clearly beginning to come to pass immediately.]

According to the *Midrash* (*Bereishis Rabbah* 89:5 quoted later in *comm.*), Nebuchadnezzar really asked for the interpretation of two separate dreams, the dream of the statue, and that of the tree (ch. 4).

וַתִּתְפָּעֶם רוּחוֹ — *His spirit was agitated* [lit. *and his spirit pounded itself*].

I.e., he was frightened and disquieted.

This signified to Nebuchadnezzar that this was not an idle dream but a premonition of things to come (*Malbim*).

[In describing Pharaoh's reaction to his dreams (*Gen.* 41:8), this word is spelled וַתִּפָּעֶם. The extra ת, *tav*, gives the word a stronger connotation (*Mizrachi* to *Gen.* 41; cf. *Gur Aryeh ibid.*).

R' Yehudah said that Pharaoh knew the dream and only wanted to be told the interpretation; however Nebuchadnezzar wanted to know the dream and the interpretation (*Bereishis Rabbah* ch. 89:5, quoted by *Rashi*).

R' Nechemiah said the doubling of the letter ת, indicates that Nebuchadnezzar asked for the dream of the statue and the dream of the tree (*Bereishis Rabbah ibid*; see *comm.* above).

Abarbanel comments that according to R' Nechemiah it is possible that he really remembered his dream. We find that he remembered the dream of the tree on his own. He pretended to have forgotten the dream in order to test the wise men, for had he told them the dream they would have had no dif-

ב עָלָיו: וַיֹּאמֶר הַמֶּלֶךְ לִקְרֹא לַחַרְטֻמִּים
וְלָאַשָּׁפִים וְלַמְכַשְּׁפִים וְלַכַּשְׂדִּים לְהַגִּיד
לַמֶּלֶךְ חֲלֹמֹתָיו וַיָּבֹאוּ וַיַּעַמְדוּ לִפְנֵי
ג הַמֶּלֶךְ: וַיֹּאמֶר לָהֶם הַמֶּלֶךְ חֲלוֹם חָלָמְתִּי

ficulty in concocting an interpretation (see *comm.* to *v.* 3). This would also explain the plural form of חֲלֹמֹת (see *comm.* above). After testing Daniel he found it unnecessary to resort to this subterfuge any more, so he told him the dream of the tree and asked just for the interpretation (*Mayenei HaYeshuah* 6:1; cf. *Yefeh Toar* to *Bereishis Rabbah, ibid.*).

The Sages said that וַתִּתְפָּעֶם (denoting a strong pounding) is used because the purpose of the dream and Nebuchadnezzar's disquietude was to give greatness to four people (Daniel and his friends), while וַתִּפָּעֶם (denoting a weaker pounding) is used for Pharaoh's reaction to his dreams because its purpose was to give greatness to only one person [Joseph] (*Bereishis Rabbah, ibid.*).

[The elevations of Joseph and Daniel are viewed not as consequences of the dreams but as the cause of their occurrence. In the search for the hidden ways of Providence, the roles of cause and effect are sometimes the reverse of what they appear to be to the observer who is guided solely by his senses.]

נִהְיְתָה עָלָיו — *Was interrupted.*

The translation follows *Rashi* and *Ibn Ezra* citing *Ezekiel* 7:26, הִנֵּה עַל הִנֵּה תָּבוֹא.

[*Malbim* renders it *and his sleep was with him* (in the regular sense of הָיָה) — i.e., he did not wake up. This was to Nebuchadnezzar a sign of the prophetic nature of his

dream. Had it been an ordinary nightmare, he would have awakened as a result of the physiological effect of the fright. His continuing to sleep showed that the fright was of an inner, spiritual nature.]

2. לַחַרְטֻמִּים וְלָאַשָּׁפִים — *The necromancers, [and] the astrologers.*

See *commentary* to 1:20 for explanation of the translation.

וְלַמְכַשְּׁפִים — *[And] the sorcerers.*

Those who change (or make it appear as if they change) the nature of things (*Ibn Ezra*). This corroborates the view of the Sages[1] (cf. *Sanhedrin* 67a,b).

וְלַכַּשְׂדִּים — *And the Chaldeans.*

Chaldeans is the Latin and Greek version of כַּשְׂדִּים (cf. *R' B. Mossafia* to *Aruch s.v.* כלדאי and *Ramban* in *Teshuvos HaRashba Hameyuchasos LaRamban* 283).

The *Talmud* uses the term *Chaldeans* (e.g., *Pesachim* 113b). Although כַּשְׂדִּים is the name of a particular nation which practiced astrology, it seems that with the passage of time this appellation was applied to astrologers in general — the sense in which it is used in the *Talmud* (cf. *Shabbos* 156 and *Tosafos s.v.* כלדאי; *Aruch, ibid.*).

In this verse, though, *Chaldeans*

---

1. There are variant views on whether apparent change brought about by deception is included in the Torah's ban on magic. [See *Sefer Hamitzvos* by *Rambam* (*Lo Sa'asseh* 32, 34; *Mishneh Torah, Hilchos Avodah Zarah* 11:15-16; and *Kessef Mishneh*). For further references see *Darkei Teshuvah* to *Yoreh Deah* 179:15].

2
3

king had the necromancers, the astrologers, the sorcerers, and the Chaldeans called to tell the king his dreams. They came and stood before the king. ³ The king said to them, 'I have dreamed a dream and my

is not merely an alternative term denoting astrologers, since אַשָּׁפִים already denotes astrologers. In *v.* 4, the statement, *the Chaldeans spoke to the king in Aramaic,* clearly refers to Chaldeans in a national sense. Nevertheless the term cannot be taken here to mean that he called on the whole Chaldean nation. It would seem that in Nebuchadnezzar's time (since Nebuchadnezzar was known as king of Babylon) his native tribe, the Chaldeans, was no longer known as a separate national entity, but had been absorbed by the Babylonians. The appellation כַּשְׂדִּים, however, remained in use for the Chaldean astrologers, since astrology had been the main branch of knowledge among the ancient Chaldeans, who had greatly furthered the related sciences of astronomy and astrology. Modern archeology has unearthed considerable evidence that points to their proficiency in both of these disciplines. Therefore, *the Chaldeans=the Chaldean astrologers.*

The king felt that his team of wizards, all claiming knowledge of the future through their sundry powers, should surely be able to relate what had already taken place. Their inability to do so proved to the king that their whole art was built upon deceit, for which he ordered them executed.

The verse does not mention whether Daniel and his companions were called. From Daniel's question to Aryoch in *v.* 14 it seems that Daniel did not know

what Nebuchadnezzar had requested of the sages. Implicitly he was not called and was not present. This seems strange after the king had tested them and found them *ten times better than all the necromancers* (1:20). *Ralbag* explains that this episode took place before the end of the three-year learning period allotted for them. *Ralbag* here is consistent with his opinion that this story took place in the second or third year of Nebuchadnezzar's reign (see *comm.* to *v.* 1).

According to the accepted view of *Seder Olam* (above *v.* 1), when this episode took place Daniel had already been recognized as excelling over all the other sages. *Alshich* advances two possible reasons why Daniel and his companions were not called with the sages. The king called only those sages who had already proven themselves by experience. Daniel and his companions, in spite of their demonstrated brilliance, lacked practical experience. Also, Daniel and his companions had demonstrated their superiority only in matters of *the art of reasoning* (*v.* 20), which would be of no use in telling the king his forgotten dream.

[The statement in *v.* 17 that *Daniel understood all visions and dreams* is Scripture's statement of fact. It does not mean that this was known to Nebuchadnezzar.] *R' Yeshayah* mentions (see *comm.* to *v.* 13) that Daniel and his companions had also been requested to tell the king his dream. [The implication of *v.* 14 that Daniel knew nothing of the happenings at the court may mean only that he was unaware of the dialogue between Nebuchadnezzar and his sages, but he *did know* that the king had demanded to be told the content and explanation of his dream.]

ב
ד

ד וַתִּתְפָּעֶם רוּחִי לָדַעַת אֶת־הַחֲלוֹם: וַיְדַבְּרוּ
הַכַּשְׂדִּים לַמֶּלֶךְ אֲרָמִית מַלְכָּא לְעָלְמִין

3. רוּחִי וַתִּתְפָּעֶם — *And my spirit is agitated.*

Here the spelling is with only one ת, *tav*, unlike v. 1, where the spelling is וַתִּתְפָּעֶם [see *comm.* there]. Since Nebuchadnezzar only asked the assembled sages to tell him the dream — *to know the dream* — one *tav* is sufficient (*Mayenei HaYeshuah* 6:1).

Nebuchadnezzar hinted that though he did not remember the dream, his amnesia was not total. He would recognize his dream when it was told to him. Therefore, the spelling is with one *tav*, thus containing the hint that only one thing *really* disquieted Nebuchadnezzar — the mystery of the dream's meaning. Thus the sages were forewarned against fabricating a spurious version of the dream, since this might be recognized by the king (*Alshich*).

According to R' Nechemiah [see *comm.* to v. 1], since only the dream about the image is referred to in this verse, one *tav* is sufficient (*Mayenei HaYeshuah* 6:1).

The *Midrash* ascribes an interesting motive to Nebuchadnezzar's seemingly strange request. Nebuchadnezzar said [to himself]: I know the dream. But if I will tell them the dream they will surely in-

vent a [deceitful] interpretation (*Midrash Tanchuma*, ed. Buber, *Parsha Miketz*).

Nebuchadnezzar was only testing their vaunted 'supernatural powers,' a test which they failed miserably.

4. הַכַּשְׂדִּים וַיְדַבְּרוּ — *The Chaldeans spoke.*

Out of the whole assembly of assorted sages, only they had the courage to speak up and demand that the king change his request. As the king's fellow nationals who spoke the king's language — Aramaic — fluently, they felt safe in assuming this risky prerogative. The other sages, of different nationalities and other languages, had no grounds for harboring such illusions (*Malbim*).

The Chaldeans thought it was incumbent upon them to answer the king, since their professed skill was the reading of people's minds (*Ralbag*; see *comm.* to v. 2).

They felt that the obligation to answer the king fell upon them, since their profession was the divination of the future (*Ibn Yachya*).

אֲרָמִית — *In Aramaic.*[1]

Scripture does not note that the king's words in v. 3 were in Ara-

1. Aramaic enjoys a special distinction in Scripture. 'Do not consider Aramaic insignificant, for it is used in the Torah, the Prophets, and the Writings' (*Yerushalmi Sotah* 7:2). The *Talmud* (*Sanhedrin* 21b) relates that the Torah was rewritten by Ezra in Aramaic. R' Yehudah Halevi (*Kuzari* 2:68) asserts that Abraham's native language was Aramaic (cf. Laban's use of Aramaic in *Genesis* 31:47), which he used for secular purposes while reserving Hebrew for his spiritual needs. *Ibn Ezra* (*Safah Berurah* p. 2) contends that Hebrew and Aramaic (as well as Arabic) are closely enough related to be considered one language. R' Shmuel Yehudah Katzenellenbogen (*Teshuvas HaRama* 126-8) explains that this is the reason why a גט, *bill of divorce*, is written in a mixture of these two languages in spite of the prohibition against writing a bill of divorce in two languages. *Rama (ibid.)* contends that Aramaic has a special

spirit is agitated to know the dream.'

⁴ The Chaldeans spoke to the king in Aramaic, 'O
king, live forever! Tell your servants the dream and

maic. *Ramban* (to *Genesis* 45:12)
takes this as an indication that the
king spoke in Hebrew. He contends
that Hebrew was understood and
spoken in governmental circles of
those days [like English in modern
times]. See *II Kings* 18:28 and *Isaiah*
36:13, *and Ravshakeh stood and
cried with a loud voice in the Jewish
language.*

Perhaps the king addressed the
sages in some other language, and
his remarks in *v.* 3 have been
translated into Hebrew. This would
indicate that only those statements
originally made in Aramaic have
been preserved here in their original
form. Therefore the mention of the
language the Chaldeans spoke explains why the following dialogue is
given in Aramaic.]

מַלְכָּא לְעָלְמִין חֱיִי — *O king, live
forever!*

[This form of address is used
again by the Chaldeans slanderers
(3:9), and in 6:22 by Daniel
himself. Curiously, however, Daniel never addresses Nebuchadnezzar with this salutation. Perhaps the
reason for this is that he did not
want to greet the idolatrous king
with the same formula which was
used (*I Kings* 1:31) as a benediction
for his ancestor King David.]

The Chaldeans surmised that the
king really remembered his dream
but was reluctant to disclose it for
fear of the obvious, ominous interpretation. Since all dreams follow
the interpretation (*Berachos* 55b),
the king was reticent to disclose his
dream for fear of a bad interpretation. Only a supernaturally inspired
interpretation would do. Hence the
king's strange request. The Chaldeans then tried to calm the king by
assuring him of their good intentions toward him. *O king, live
forever!* — i.e., we bear only good
will toward you. As the king's
countrymen who spoke his mother
tongue, they felt the king would
trust them and reveal his dream
(*Mayenei HaYeshuah* 6:1; *Malbim*).

sanctity, since the Torah was given to Moses in Hebrew together with the Aramaic *Targum.*
All this explains why Aramaic is the only language other than Hebrew that is retained in its
original form in Scripture.

So much of the book of *Daniel* is written in Aramaic because the Jews in the Babylonian exile
used Aramaic sas their vernacular, as evidenced in this book. However, the written word,
especially when used for sacred purposes, remained לְשׁוֹן הַקֹּדֶשׁ, *the holy language* — i.e., Hebrew.
Therefore, the book begins in Hebrew. When we get to the dialogue between Nebuchadnezzar
and his sages, we are given their dialogue untranslated. The same holds true for the
conversations between Daniel, Aryoch, and Nebuchadnezzar. Since most of the chapter is
dialogue, the narrative which binds it together is also given in Aramaic. The same applies to
chapters 3-6. Chapter 7 tells us what Daniel *related* about his vision. (See 7:2, *Daniel exclaimed I
watched* . . ., and *comm.* to 7:1-2). Again, because we have the *spoken* Aramaic word, the original
language is retained. The visions recounted in chapters 8-12, on the other hand, are not a record
of spoken words. The first appearance of these words is when they are put in writing. Hence
they are written in Hebrew. See *prefatory notes* to ch. 8.

חֱיִי אֱמַר חֶלְמָא °לְעַבְדָּיךְ וּפִשְׁרָא נְחַוֵּא: ה

עָנֵא מַלְכָּא וְאָמַר °לְכַשְׂדָּיֵא מִלְּתָה מִנִּי

אַזְדָּא הֵן לָא תְהוֹדְעוּנַּנִי חֶלְמָא וּפִשְׁרֵה

הַדָּמִין תִּתְעַבְדוּן וּבָתֵּיכוֹן נְוָלִי יִתְשָׂמוּן: ו

וְהֵן חֶלְמָא וּפִשְׁרֵה תְּהַחֲוֹן מַתְּנָן וּנְבִזְבָּה

וִיקָר שַׂגִּיא תְּקַבְּלוּן מִן־קֳדָמָי לָהֵן חֶלְמָא ז

וּפִשְׁרֵה הַחֲוֹנִי: עֲנוֹ תִנְיָנוּת וְאָמְרִין

אֲמַר חֶלְמָא לְעַבְדָּךְ — *Tell your servants the dream.*

We can only employ our skills for divining the future from material presented to us. Therefore you must at least tell us the dream, before we can attempt to foretell the future (*Ibn Yachya*).

If it is an ominous dream, our advice to you is: *tell your servants* — i.e., your trusted confidants who wish you only good — *the dream.* The Sages tell us (*Berachos* 55b): One who sees a dream which troubles him should go to three friends and tell them, 'I've seen a good dream.' They should answer, 'It is good and it will be good.' By answering the king in this manner (*O king, live forever!*) they were actually nullifying the evil the dream portended (*Toras Chesed*).

Tell the dream to your [personal] *servants* (i.e., other than the sages). The sages believed that something existing just in the mind of a person is unknown even to the angels. It was therefore impossible for them to find out the dream. Once the king's dream had been revealed on earth, it would no longer be in the realm of the mind alone and could be known to the angels and consequently, also to the sages (*Lechem Sesarim*).

[Cf. *Tosafos* to *Shabbos* 12b s.v. שאין and *Chida* in *Pesach Einayim* on whether angels know the thoughts of people.]

5. The Missing Dream

מִלְּתָה מִנִּי אַזְדָּא — *The thing has escaped me!*

The translation follows *Rashi* (and *Malbim*). The king now assured them that he had really forgotten his dream (cf. *Aruch* s.v. אזדא).

Ibn Ezra interprets: *This much is certain* (lit. *this word from me is certain*): *If you do not* ...

Previously (*v.* 3) Nebuchadnezzar had not been this explicit. He had merely said, 'My spirit is agitated to know the dream.' Therefore the sages misunderstood him (or pretended to) to mean the *interpretation* rather than the dream itself. Thus, they said (*v.* 4), 'Tell your servants the dream and we will relate an interpretation.' Now the king made the matter crystal clear. He was not interested only in an interpretation: 'The thing has escaped me' — They would have to tell him the dream (*Alshich*).

הֵן לָא תְהוֹדְעוּנַּנִי — *If you do not make ... known to me.*

Nebuchadnezzar did not say 'tell me,' but *make known to me* or *cause me to recognize.* If they

we will relate the interpretation.'

⁵ *The king exclaimed to the Chaldeans: 'The thing has escaped me! If you do not make the dream and its interpretation known to me, you will be cut to bits, and your houses will be made a dunghill.* ⁶ *But if you relate the dream and its interpretation, gifts, rewards, and great honor will you receive from me; only tell me the dream and its interpretation.'*

would tell him the true dream, he would surely recognize it *(Alshich)*.

וּפִשְׁרֵהּ — *And its interpretation.*

The sages had promised to furnish 'an' interpretation. Nebuchadnezzar now notified them that not only would they have to tell him the dream, but they would have to interpret it in such a way that he would be convinced that this was 'its' interpretation — i.e., the only one that fit it perfectly *(Alshich)*.

הַדָּמִין תִּתְעַבְדוּן וּבָתֵּיכוֹן נְוָלִי יִתְּשָׂמוּן — *You will be cut to [lit. made into] bits, and your houses will be made a dunghill.*

The palace left over by a renowned man stands as a monument and memorial to his name. As punishment, even this remembrance of them would not be allowed to remain *(Ibn Yachya)*.

6. מַתְּנָן וּנְבִזְבָּה — *Gifts [and] rewards.*

From its use together with מַתְּנָן, we can infer that נְבִזְבָּה is a type of present. However it is difficult to establish the exact meaning. *Targum Yonasan* to *Jeremiah* (40:5) gives מַתְּנָן וּנְבִזְבָּה as the translation of אֲרֻחָה וּמַשְׂאֵת. But here the exact definition of the Hebrew terms is unclear. *Radak* (ad loc.) comments

that these are two different types of presents.

Chazon LaMoed suggests that נְבִזְבָּה is the Aramaic equivalent of מִנְחָה. This is reinforced by *Rashi* and *Ibn Ezra*, who give דּוֹרוֹן as the translation of נְבִזְבָּה. דּוֹרוֹן is used by *Targum Yonasan (Genesis 32:14)* for מִנְחָה. See also *Targum* to *Psalms* (20:4, 141:2). *Chazon LaMoed* differentiates between מַתָּנָה and מִנְחָה in the following way: מִנְחָה is a present given in repayment of a favor or any other obligation [following this we have translated נְבִזְבָּה as *rewards*]; מַתָּנָה is what is given without any previous consideration. Therefore an offering to God is called a מִנְחָה. *Radak's* suggestion that the root of מִנְחָה may be נָחֹה, *to rest* — i.e., a present whose intent is to assuage and put the recipient to rest — fits in with this. To those of the sages whose function it was to interpret dreams, Nebuchadnezzar did not owe any remuneration, since it was their job to do so. Therefore, any present given them would be מַתְּנָן, *gifts*. To those of the sages who did not specialize in dream interpretation, Nebuchadnezzar promised נְבִזְבָּה, *rewards* — i.e., gifts earned with the extra service they would give the king.

מַלְכָּא חֶלְמָא יֵאמַר לְעַבְדוֹהִי וּפִשְׁרָה
נְהַחֲוֵה: עֲנֵה מַלְכָּא וְאָמַר מִן־יַצִּיב יָדַע ח
אֲנָה דִּי עִדָּנָא אַנְתּוּן זָבְנִין כָּל־קֳבֵל דִּי
חֲזֵיתוֹן דִּי־אַזְדָּא מִנִּי מִלְּתָא: דִּי הֵן־ ט
חֶלְמָא לָא תְהוֹדְעֻנַּנִי חֲדָה־הִיא דָתְכוֹן
וּמִלָּה כִדְבָה וּשְׁחִיתָה °הַזְמִנְתּוּן לְמֵאמַר

R' Saadiah interprets מַתְּנָן as goods of enduring value — i.e., gold, silver, and clothing. נְבִזְבָּה are presents which are consumed, such as food.

7. מַלְכָּא חֶלְמָא יֵאמַר לְעַבְדוֹהִי — *Let the king tell his servants the dream.*

They now changed their request slightly. The king should tell *his servants* the dream in the future — in secret — whenever he would remind himself. The sages would then give the interpretation (*Malbim*).

8. 'You Are Doomed'

מִן־יַצִּיב יָדַע אֲנָה — *I know for a certainty.*

I know that your repeated requests that I tell you the dream are only a ruse. Afraid that my refusal to tell you the dream is in order to test you, you want to be sure that I will not ultimately contradict your version of my dream. So you have repeatedly asked me to tell you the dream, thus forcing me to declare time and again that I have forgotten it, so that I will not be able to say later that I really remember it (*Alshich*).

דִּי עִדָּנָא אַנְתּוּן זָבְנִין — *That at this time you are doomed* [lit. *sold*.]

The translation follows *Rashi* and *Radak*. *Ibn Ezra* and *Malbim* render it: *that you are buying time*

— i.e., you are stalling for time [see *comm.* to *v.* 9].

כָּל־קֳבֵל דִּי חֲזֵיתוֹן דִּי־אַזְדָּא מִנִּי מִלְּתָא — *Because you have seen that the thing has escaped me.*

[I.e., since you know how annoyed I am by the obvious fact that I have forgotten the dream, it should be clear to you that I must be told what it was. If you cannot reveal to me a matter of such great importance, then you deserve to be put to death.]

Rashi adds to this verse: The sages were being sentenced not for their inability to tell Nebuchadnezzar the dream, but for their insistence that he reveal the dream to them. Had they initially told the king that they were unable to fulfill his demand, they might have been excused; but they angered him by repeating their demand.

[Perhaps the crafty king realized that the sages did not trust him, feeling that his request was a ruse to trap them when they failed to divine the contents of the dream (see *Alshich* cited above).]

[The sequence of the verse is as follows: *I know ... that ... you are doomed because you 'wish to see' that the thing has escaped me* — i.e., I recognize that your repeated requests that I tell you this dream are meant to ascertain whether I have truly forgotten

⁷ *They answered again, 'Let the king tell his ser-vants the dream, and we will relate the interpreta-tion.'*

⁸ *The king exclaimed, 'I know for a certainty that at this time you are doomed — because you have seen that the thing has escaped me — * ⁹ *If you do not make the dream known to me there is only one sentence for you; and if you have prepared lying and corrupt*

---

the dream. For this attempt to 'see' and ascertain whether *the thing has escaped me,* I sentence you to death.]

Ibn Ezra interprets this verse in the following way: *I know* for a fact *that you are buying time because you have seen that the decree* [lit. *the word] has gone forth (issued) from me: That if you do not tell me the dream ...*

Since you know that I really have forgotten the dream, your request that I tell the dream to my servants whenever I recall it in the future (see *comm.* to v. 7) is just a subterfuge to gain time (*Malbim*).

9. דִּי הֵן־חֶלְמָא לָא תְהוֹדְעֻנַּנִי — *If you do not make the dream known to me.*

Do not expect any clemency because of your proposal to tell me the interpretation without the dream. *If you do not make the 'dream' known to me, there is only one sentence ... (Malbim).*

חֲדָה־הִיא דָתְכוֹן — *There is* [only] *one sentence for you* [lit. *Your law is one*].

[A similar expression is found in *Esther* (4:11). No exception will be made to the rule and no clemency will be granted.]

וּמִלָּה כִדְבָה וּשְׁחִיתָה הִזְדַּמִנְתּוּן — *And*

[if] *you have prepared lying and corrupt words.*

The translation reflects the comments of *Rashi.* This phrase is part of the sentence being pronounced upon the sages. Whether they desist from telling the dream at all, or they manufacture a false version, the sentence is the same — a horrible death.

The *if* in the translation has no corresponding word in the text [e.g. הֵן]. According to *Rashi,* וּמִלָּה, *and words,* parallels חֶלְמָא, *the dream,* and both are introduced by דִּי הֵן, *if.*

Ibn Ezra and others understand this phrase to be a new accusation. Thus: *And you have prepared lying and corrupt words to speak before me until the time changes.* You have prepared to talk and stall, *until the time changes* and I occupy myself with other matters and forget about the dream.

R' Saadiah, Ralbag, and *Alshich,* understand *lying and corrupt words* to refer to the sages' proposal to interpret the dream after it would be told to them. To this Nebuchadnezzar replies that such an interpretation would in his eyes be *lying and corrupt words,* since that interpretation could in no way be corroborated. Only if they tell him the dream will he know that they

ב
י״-יא

קַדְמֵי עַד דִּי עִדָּנָא יִשְׁתַּנֵּא לָהֵן חֶלְמָא
אֱמַרוּ לִי וְאֶנְדַּ֫ע דִּי פִשְׁרֵהּ תְּהַחֲוֻנַּנִי: עֲנֹו
° כַשְׂדָּאֵי קֳ כַשְׂדִּיאָ קֳדָם־מַלְכָּא וְאָמְרִין לָא־אִיתַי
אֱנָשׁ עַל־יַבֶּשְׁתָּא דִּי מִלַּת מַלְכָּא יוּכַל
לְהַחֲוָיָה כָּל־קֳבֵל דִּי כָּל־מֶלֶךְ רַב וְשַׁלִּיט
מִלָּה כִדְנָה לָא שְׁאֵל לְכָל־חַרְטֹם וְאָשַׁף
יא וְכַשְׂדָּי: וּמִלְּתָא דִי־מַלְכָּה שָׁאֵל יַקִּירָה
וְאָחֳרָן לָא אִיתַי דִּי יְחַוּנַּהּ קֳדָם מַלְכָּא
לָהֵן אֱלָהִין דִּי מְדָרְהוֹן עִם־בִּשְׂרָא לָא

can *relate 'its'* (i..e, the truthful) *interpretation.*

עַד דִּי עִדָּנָא יִשְׁתַּנֵּא — *[Wait] until the time changes* [lit. *will change*].

I.e., when morning changes to afternoon. Nebuchadnezzar did not have to clarify the meaning of the threat. He had done that in *v. 8* (*Rashi*).

Ibn Ezra and others who understand the previous phrase as an accusation, do not add *wait* to the text.

R' Saadiah, Ralbag, and *Alshich,* following their commentary to the previous phrase (see s.v. וּמִלָּה), have this phrase refer to the events which would be foretold in the sages' interpretation. The king thus accused the sages of planning to devise an interpretation in such a manner that it could be fulfilled only *after the time changes* — i.e., in the distant future, when the whole episode of the king's dream will have been forgotten.

10. לָא אִיתַי אֱנָשׁ — *There is no man.*

Our refusal to answer your request is not rooted in any evil intent on our part. Your request is inherently impossible to fulfill (*Alshich*).

11. וְאָחֳרָן לָא אִיתַי — *And there is no other.*

What the king asks is beyond human capacity to grasp and requires the gift of prophecy, which we have never claimed to possess.

The seeming redundancy of this phrase (in *v. 10* we have: *There is no man on earth who can relate what the king wishes*) indicates that more is hinted at in this verse than the apparent meaning.

In *Midrash Tanchuma* (*Mikeitz* 2, quoted by *Rashi*) we learn: [They said,] 'And Aaron[1] is not here. There is now no high priest wearing the *Urim* and the *Tumim*[2] to tell you your dream.'

1. The *Midrash* reads אַהֲרֹן instead of אָחֳרָן by substituting *he* for *ches*. The letters אהחע are sometimes interchangeable.

Minchas Shai tells us that some manuscripts give אַהֲרֹן as the *k'siv* here. He attributes this to a scribe's error, due to faulty understanding of the *Tanchuma.*

2. *Urim Ve Tumim* is the שֵׁם הַמְפוֹרָשׁ, *explicit Name of HASHEM,* inserted in the חֹשֶׁן הַמִּשְׁפָּט *high priest's breastplate,* which caused the letters engraved on the precious stones to light up and foretell the future (see *Rashi* to Exodus 28:30).

דניאל [84]

2

10-11

words to speak before me, wait until the time changes! Only tell me the dream, and I will know that you can relate its intepretation to me.'

¹⁰ The Chaldeans exclaimed to the king: 'There is no man on earth who can relate what the king wishes. That is why no king, leader, or ruler has ever requested such a thing of any necromancer, astrologer, or Chaldean. ¹¹ The king's request is difficult and there is no other who can relate it to the king, except the angels, whose dwelling is not with people!'

In *Tanchuma* (ed. Buber, p. 191), there is an addition to this: The Chaldeans said, 'Only when God dwells among people is it possible to fulfill your request (obviously rendering לָהֵן אֱלָהִין, *only God*; see *comm.* below).'

Nebuchadnezzar said, 'Ask of Him (now).'

They answered, 'His *dwelling is not with people* (now). Since His Temple was destroyed, His Presence does not rest among us' (cf. *Yalkut ad loc.*).

Then the king said to them: 'So great was the power of that Temple; yet you advised me to destroy it.' With this the king flew into a rage and had them put to death.

אֱלָהִין — *The angels.*

The translation follows *Rashi* and all the other commentators.

[To render אֱלָהִין *God* would conflict with the plural ending of the phrase (דִּי מְדָרְהוֹן), unless this can be attributed to the idolatrous beliefs of the Chaldeans. Thus, *Midrash Tanchuma* (cited above), which seemingly translates אֱלָהִין as *God* probably means it in the midrashic sense, not as the literal meaning. *Tanchuma* could, however, find precedent for the Deity being referred to in the plural in *Genesis* (1:26), *Let Us make a man* ... (see *Rashi* and ArtScroll *comm. ad loc.*) and in *Joshua* (24:19), *For He is a holy God*

(קְדֹשִׁים, *holy*, is in the plural). See *Sanhedrin* 38b and *Bereishis Rabbah* 8:9.]

אֱלֹהִים means *angels* elsewhere, too. *Rambam* (*Yesodei HaTorah* 2:7) lists *elohim* as the seventh of ten categories of angels. כִּי ה' הוּא אֱלֹהֵי הָאֱלֹהִים ... [*Deut.* 10:17, usually translated, *For HASHEM ... is the God of gods*; cf. *Menachos* 110a, דקרן ליה אלקא וְאלקיא] is defined, *For HASHEM ... is the God of the angels* (*Moreh Nevuchim* 2:6; see *Ramban's comm.* to Torah *ad loc.*; cf. *Onkelos*, אֱלָהָא דַיָּנִין. See also *R' Avraham ben HaRambam* to *Exodus* 7:1 quoting *Rambam* and *R' Sa'adiah*).

It is *Rambam's* opinion (*Moreh Nevuchim* 2:6) that the primary meaning of אֱלֹהִים is *judge*. Its application to God (and to angels) is only a secondary and acquired meaning. *Abarbanel* (*Genesis* 1:1) objects vigorously, maintaining that this word applies primarily to God, and its usage to denote angels and judges is secondary.

דִּי מְדָרְהוֹן עִם־בִּשְׂרָא לָא אִיתוֹהִי — *Whose dwelling is not with people!* [lit. *whose dwelling with flesh does not exist.*]

The Babylonians believed that there were two categories of angels. Those who mingled with men, whose dwelling *is* with people, constituted the lower category. To know thoughts present in a

ב
יב-יד

יב אִיתוֹהִי: כָּל־קָבֵל דְּנָה מַלְכָּא בְּנַס וּקְצַף
שַׂגִּיא וַאֲמַר לְהוֹבָדָה לְכֹל חַכִּימֵי בָבֶל:
יג וְדָתָא נֶפְקַת וְחַכִּימַיָּא מִתְקַטְּלִין וּבְעוֹ
יד דָּנִיֵּאל וְחַבְרוֹהִי לְהִתְקְטָלָה: בֵּאדַיִן
דָּנִיֵּאל הֲתִיב עֵטָא וּטְעֵם לְאַרְיוֹךְ רַב־

person's mind, albeit beyond the scope of humans, would not be too difficult for these celestial beings (cf. *Tosafos Shabbos* cited in *comm.* to *v. 4*), but to relate a dream of which no human has any recollection would be impossible for these angels. This would require the power of angels *whose dwelling is not with people* (Malbim; cf. Ibn Ezra).

[*Rambam* (*Yesodei HaTorah* 2:7) enumerates ten categories of angels. The lowest category are the *ishim*, who have contact with mankind and through whom prophecy is revealed (אִישִׁים from אִישׁ, *man*). The category of angels called *elohim* (seventh in descending order) do not communicate with men. Thus אֱלָהִין in this sentence may refer to angels not in the broad sense, but in the specific sense to those called *elohim*, whose *dwelling* (unlike the *ishim*) *is not with people*. Thus the belief attributed above by *Malbim* to the Babylonians is rooted in truth — i.e., that this category of angels possesses greater power than those angels which communicate with men.]

12. The King Orders Sages Killed

בְּנַס וּקְצַף שַׂגִּיא — *Greatly upset and angry.*

Rashi accepts the view of *Donash ben Lavrat* that נַס and קְצַף are nouns meaning *upset* and *anger*. With the prepositional prefix בְּ, *into*, the literal meaning of the verse would be [went] *into great upset and anger*. Our translation follows this line of thought.

Toras Chesed comments that *upset* and *anger* refer to two different facets of the king's disturbed feelings. He was grieved and frustrated at his failure to remember the dream which he understood conclusively to be of great significance for himself and his kingdom. Because he understood it to be so consequential he insisted that his court sages devise some means to determine what he had dreamt. Their deviousness in attempting to free themselves of an obligation they could not discharge angered him further. Thus he was *upset* over the dream and *angry* over their deceitfullness.

לְכֹל חַכִּימֵי בָבֶל — *All the sages of Babylon.*

In his great anger he failed to differentiate between the necromancers and company, on the one hand, and other sages who had nothing to do with dream interpretation (e.g., doctors, lawyers). Thus, Daniel and his companions were to be killed, even though they had not had a chance to tell the king his dream (Malbim).

The Chaldeans had admitted that the king's request required the power of prophecy, which had been curtailed as a consequence of the destruction of the Temple (see *comm.* to *v. 11*). Therefore the king held *all the sages of Babylon* accountable. All of them had approved the destruction of the Temple, some overtly by counseling the

דניאל [86]

¹² *In response to this the king grew greatly upset and angry, and he ordered the destruction of all the sages of Babylon. ¹³ As the decree was being implemented and the wise men slain, Daniel and his companions were sought for slaying.*

¹⁴ *Then Daniel gave counsel and advice to Aryoch,*

king to do so, and the others covertly by not advising the king against this step (*Alshich*). [See footnote 2 to v. 11.]

13. וּבְעוֹ דָנִיֵּאל וְחַבְרוֹהִי לְהִתְקְטָלָה — *Daniel and his companions were sought for slaying.*

Since the king had angrily ordered the execution of *all the sages of Babylon*, he had not had the presence of mind to exclude the few innocent ones. Therefore even Daniel and his companions could not escape death at the hands of the king's executioners (*Malbim*).

The Babylonians knew that once all their sages were killed, Daniel and his companions, as the only wise men left after the killings, would attain positions of power and influence at court. The Babylonians' national pride and jealousy did not allow for such a turn of events. Therefore they sought even *Daniel and his companions ... for slaying,* though they knew that they should not be included under the king's decree. They felt they could exonerate themselves later by pleading that they had been following orders and had not been told to differentiate between the innocent and the guilty (*Alshich; Toras Chesed*).

R' Yeshayah of Trani comments that Daniel and his companions had also been requested to tell the king his dream. [See *comm.,* end of v. 2.]

[They were surely not present when the Chaldeans tried to remonstrate with the king, thus, angering him into issuing an order for their execution. Otherwise they could not have asked Aryoch (v. 14), *Why is the king's decree so preemptory?*]

Alshich (see *comm.* to v. 14) holds that Nebuchadnezzar's order had been to kill only the *sages of Babylon* (v. 12). Thus Daniel and his companions were excluded. The executioners, however, failed to make this distinction. [See *comm.* to vs. 14-16 for alternative views.]

14. עֵטָא וּטְעֵם — *Counsel and advice.*

He advised Aryoch how to evade the king's order till Daniel would be able to tell the king his dream and terminate the executions. Aryoch, no doubt, had misgivings about the king's barbaric order to execute all the sages of his nation, and was therefore receptive to this plan which offered hope. Scripture does not tell us what this advice was. Daniel's conversation with Aryoch in v. 15 gives us no clue (*Metzudos*).

[This *counsel and advice* was apparently given after the conversation in v. 15.]

לְאַרְיוֹךְ רַב טַבָּחַיָּא — *To Aryoch the ... chief executioner.*

The *Midrash (Eichah Rabasi 5:5)*

טַבָּחַיָּא דִּי מַלְכָּא דִי נְפַק לְקַטָּלָה
לְחַכִּימֵי בָבֶל: עָנֵה וְאָמַר לְאַרְיוֹךְ טו
שַׁלִּיטָא דִּי־מַלְכָּא עַל־מָה דָתָא
מְהַחְצְפָה מִן־קֳדָם מַלְכָּא אֱדַיִן מִלְּתָא
הוֹדַע אַרְיוֹךְ לְדָנִיֵּאל: וְדָנִיֵּאל עַל וּבְעָא טז
מִן־מַלְכָּא דִי זְמַן יִנְתֶּן־לֵהּ וּפִשְׁרָא
לְהַחֲוָיָה לְמַלְכָּא: אֱדַיִן דָּנִיֵּאל יז

---

identifies *Aryoch* with Nebuzeradan who was directly responsible
for the destruction of the Temple (*II
Kings* 25:8-11). He is there called
*Nebuzeradan, the chief execution-
er.* He is called *Aryoch* from אַרְיֵה,
lion, because he growled like a lion
at the exiles of Jerusalem till he
drove them over the Euphrates.[1]

דִּי נְפַק לְקַטָּלָה לְחַכִּימֵי בָבֶל — *Who
had gone to slay the sages of Babylon.*

The king's order had been to kill
only the *sages of Babylon* (see *Alshich* to v. 13). Therefore Daniel
wisely presented himself to Aryoch,
fully aware that his orders had been
to *slay the sages of Babylon.* Daniel
made it appear that it was not his
own life he was concerned with,
but rather the lives of the wise men
of Babylon. He calculated that by
this he would gain the confidence of
Aryoch, who would be sympathetic
to an attempt to save his countrymen (*Alshich*).

15. שַׁלִּיטָא דִּי־מַלְכָּא — *The king's
official.*

Not the *chief executioner* as in v.
14. Daniel wanted to emphasize
that he thought of *Aryoch* as one of
the king's inner circle, who would
be privy to what had brought on
this terrible decree (*Malbim*).

עַל מָה דָתָא מְהַחְצְפָה — *Why is the
king's decree so peremptory?*

The translation follows *Rashi*
and *R' Yeshayah,* who seem to understand that Daniel was inquiring
about the executions themselves,
not knowing (or pretending not to
know) what had transpired at the
court (see below s.v. אֱדַיִן). חֲצִיפוּת is
understood as meaning firmness or
severity (*R' Shmuel Masnuth* cites a
parallel in *Targum* to *Ezekiel* 2:4
which is not found in our editions).

Daniel knew what had happened.
His question was only a way to start
a conversation with Aryoch about
this matter (*R' Yeshayah*).

Daniel's feigned ignorance was
cleverly calculated. Until now Daniel had not attempted to fulfill the
king's command, knowing it was
humanly impossible. Only now,
when his life was threatened, did he

---

1. The *Talmud* (*Gittin* 57b) relates that Nebuzeradan became a Jewish proselyte. His
respect for the prophet Jeremiah was extraordinary (*Jeremiah* 40) and bespeaks nobility of
character greater than our own usual image of an executioner. Knowing these facts, we can
speculate that a man of this caliber would not willingly carry out the king's order. Probably
Aryoch, knowing Daniel's great sagacity, solicited his advice, otherwise Daniel would not
have proffered unsolicited advice. *Then Daniel 'returned'* (התיב) corresponds to הֵשִׁיב, *returned
or responded*) with *counsel and advice* (Rabbi Y. Leiman).

2
15-16

the king's chief executioner, who had gone to slay the sages of Babylon. [15] *He exclaimed to Aryoch, the king's official: 'Why is the king's decree so peremptory?' Then Aryoch told Daniel the story.* [16] *Daniel went and requested of the king that he be given time to tell the interpretation to the king.*

hope that God would answer his fervent prayer and reveal to him the king's secret. In order to gain the king's ear, he would need to explain why he had kept quiet till now. Therefore Daniel feigned ignorance about the whole affair to make it appear as if he had just learned about the king's dream and was using the first available opportunity to answer his request (*Malbim*).

Ibn Ezra translates מְהַחְצְפָה, *hasty*. [Daniel did not feign ignorance about the affair of the dream. He only inquired as to the reason that the edict was being so speedily executed.]

אֱדַיִן מִלְּתָא הוֹדַע — *Then Aryoch told Daniel the story* [lit. *the matter*].

He told him that the king had become enraged because no one could tell him his dream (*Rashi*).

Ibn Ezra (following his comments on עַל מָה דָתָא מְהַחְצְפָה) understands מִלְּתָא to refer to *the matter* that follows in the next verse. Aryoch advised Daniel to petition the king for more time in order to enable Daniel to tell the king the interpretation.

Alshich and *Metzudos* (following *Ibn Ezra*) say that Aryoch explained to Daniel that the king's haste was due to the fact that the sages had categorically refused the king's request on the grounds that it was impossible, but had not asked for more time. Hearing this, Daniel im-

mediately went to the king to petition him for more time.

16. וּפִשְׁרָא לְהַחֲוָיָה לְמַלְכָּא — *To tell the interpretation to the king.*

Though the king had demanded to know the dream, his primary interest was in the interpretation. The recital of the dream interested him only as a means to assure the veracity of the interpretation. Therefore Daniel stressed that he would *tell the interpretation 'to the king'* — i.e., his interpretation would convince and please the king (*Mayenei HaYeshuah* 6:1).

Since the king's executioners had begun to execute the sages immediately without giving them time to find out the dream, it would be embarrassing for the king to grant Daniel time to do so now. Therefore Daniel diplomatically hinted to the king that he needed time only for the interpretation, thus giving the king an opening to save face. Now he could say that had the sages indicated a similar readiness to tell the dream, they too would have been given time (*Malbim*).

Though Daniel did not know whether he would be able to fulfill the king's request, he put his trust in God to save him (*R' Shmuel Masnuth*).

Midrash Tanchuma (Mikeitz 2) indicates that Daniel felt assured that his prayer would be answered.

לְבַיְתֵהּ אֲזַל וְלַחֲנַנְיָה מִישָׁאֵל וַעֲזַרְיָה
יח חַבְרוֹהִי מִלְּתָא הוֹדַע: וְרַחֲמִין לְמִבְעֵא
מִן־קֳדָם אֱלָהּ שְׁמַיָּא עַל־רָזָא דְּנָה דִּי לָא
יְהוֹבְדוּן דָּנִיֵּאל וְחַבְרוֹהִי עִם־שְׁאָר
יט חַכִּימֵי בָבֶל: אֱדַיִן לְדָנִיֵּאל בְּחֶזְוָא דִי־
לֵילְיָא רָזָא גֲּלִי אֱדַיִן דָּנִיֵּאל בָּרֵךְ לֶאֱלָהּ

[The *Talmud (Berachos* 10a) quotes King Hezekiah of Judah, 'I have a tradition from my forefather (David) that: Even if a sharp sword is already lying on one's neck, he should not despair of being saved.' Daniel, as a scion of that same dynasty (see *comm.* to 1:6), also abided by that tradition.]

17. Revelation to Daniel

לְבַיְתֵהּ אֲזַל — *Went home.*

In order to seclude himself (*Ibn Ezra*).

Since Daniel was praying for a revelation, he had to seclude himself in order to prepare himself to receive the prophecy. 'All the prophets (other than Moses) do not prophesy whenever they wish to. Rather they concentrate their minds and wait, attaining [an appropriate] state of mind in seclusion' (*Rambam* in *Yesodei HaTorah* 7:4).

[*Rashi* to *Exodus* 9:29 comments that Moses would not pray in Pharaoh's palace because it was full of idols. Perhaps, in our case, Daniel *went home* to pray for the same reason.]

וּלְחֲנַנְיָה מִישָׁאֵל וַעֲזַרְיָה חַבְרוֹהִי מִלְּתָא הוֹדַע — *And told his companions, Chananyah, Mishael, and Azaryah, the story* [lit. *the matter*].

In order that they too should pray, because the power of collective prayer transcends individual pray-

er. The prayer of the many is sometimes answered immediately as it is written (*Deut.* 4:7), *Who is like HASHEM our God in all 'our' calling to him* (R' Shmuel Masnuth).

They too should seclude themselves and prepare for prophecy (*Malbim*).

18. וְרַחֲמִין לְמִבְעֵא — *And to pray ... for mercy.*

[The ו, *vav,* would seem to be superfluous since the apparent meaning [פְּשָׁט] of this verse is that Daniel *told his companions ... the story* so that they should *pray.* For other instances of *vavim* superfluous in פְּשָׁט, see *Rashi* to v. 12 (s.v. בְּנָס) and to *Genesis* 36:24. According to *Malbim's* comment (v. 17) that Daniel's companions also prepared themselves for prophecy, the sequence may be understood as follows: *Daniel went home* to prepare himself *and told his companions ... the story* so that they should do likewise. Another purpose for his telling them was that they should *pray ... for mercy.* The *vav* can then be translated *and* as it usually is.]

מִן קֳדָם אֱלָהּ שְׁמַיָּא — *To the God of heaven.*

In the books of *Daniel* and *Ezra,* God is referred to as 'the God of heaven.' Before Abraham came, God was called 'the God of heaven,' as in *Genesis* 24:7, *HASHEM the God of heaven Who has taken me from my father's house.* This is because God's Presence was not

¹⁷ Daniel then went home and told his compa-nions, Chananyah, Mishael, and Azaryah, the story, ¹⁸ and to pray to the God of heaven for mercy con-cerning this secret, so that Daniel and his compa-nions should not be destroyed with the rest of the sages of Babylon. ¹⁹ Then in a nocturnal vision, He revealed the secret to Daniel. Daniel then blessed the God of heaven.

acknowledged by the entire world (see *Rashi* to *Genesis* loc. cit.). After Abraham spread the true belief in God through the world, He was cal-led *The God of heaven and earth* (loc. cit. *v.* 3). When Israel sinned and was exiled from its land, God said, *Let Me return to My original place* (Hosea 5:15). Since then, He is called *the God of heaven* (R' Shmuel Masnuth).

עַל־רָזָא דְנָה — *Concerning this secret.*

The Sages (*Taanis* 8b) note that the phrase, prayed *for mercy con-cerning 'this' secret*, hints that there were other pressing matters which warranted Daniel's prayer at this time. Nevertheless, they prayed only *concerning 'this' secret.* We learn from this that one should not pray (specifically) for more than one thing at a time.

[According to those who hold (*comm.* to *v.* 1) that at this time Nebuchadnez-zar also wanted to know the interpreta-tion of the dream of the tree (ch. 4), the other object of Daniel's prayers might have been the interpretation of the se-cond dream.]

עִם־שְׁאָר חַכִּימֵי בָבֶל — *With the rest of the sages of Babylon.*

Rabbi Yochanan said: We find that the *tzaddikim* beg of God that they should not be interred together with רְשָׁעִים, *evildoers.* To pray ...

that *Daniel and his companions should not perish 'with the rest of the sages of Babylon'* (Midrash Tehillim; Yalkut here and loc. cit.).

[The words *that Daniel and his companions should not perish* would have sufficed. The additional phrase *with the sages of Babylon* in-dicates that in addition to their con-cern that *they should not perish*, they prayed that if it was their lot to die now, it should at least not be *with the rest of the sages of Babylon.* This concept finds its ex-pression in *halachah.* It is not per-missible to bury a *tzaddik* near an evil-doer (Yoreh Deah 362:5 from Sanhedrin 46a).]

19. רָזָא גְלִי — *He revealed the secret.*

He refers to the angel Gabriel (*Zohar* to *Parshas Mikeitz*).

The *gematria*, numerical value, of רָזָא גְלִי is the same as that of בְּבָא גַבְרִיאֵל, *when Gabriel came —* i.e., at that time the secret was re-vealed (Chomas Anach).

[Gabriel is named in 8:16 and 9:21 as the angel who spoke to Daniel in those chapters. *Rashi* in 11:1 names him as the angel who conveyed the visions of chapters 10-12. Thus it appears that Gabriel had a close connection to Daniel as mentioned by *Zohar* above.]

כ שְׁמַיָּא: עָנֵה דָנִיֵּאל וְאָמַר לֶהֱוֵא שְׁמֵהּ
דִּי־אֱלָהָא מְבָרַךְ מִן־עָלְמָא וְעַד־עָלְמָא
כא דִּי חָכְמְתָא וּגְבוּרְתָא דִּי־לֵהּ הִיא: וְהוּא
מְהַשְׁנֵא עִדָּנַיָּא וְזִמְנַיָּא מְהַעְדֵּה מַלְכִין

בָּרַךְ — *Blessed.*

Abarbanel (Gen. 27) points out that בְּרָכָה, *blessing,* has two meanings: 1) to cause to be fruitful and to multiply, as in: *and He will bless your bread and your water (Exod.* 23:25); 2) to thank, as in: *And David blessed HASHEM (I Chron.* 29:10). When we offer בְּרָכָה to the omnipotent God, it is untenable in the former sense. It can only be construed as giving thanks. However, *R' Bachya (Deut.* 8:10), after alluding to the difficulty of rendering בְּרָכָה in the first sense, allows it to be rendered this way עַל פִּי סוֹד, *according to the mystical tradition of Torah.*

Thus, in the tradition of *Ramban* and most of the early Kabbalists not to divulge the secrets of the *Kabbalah* to the wide masses (cf. *Ramban's* introduction to his *comm.* on *Torah),* he leaves this difficulty unresolved. [1]

R' S.R. Hirsch (Psalms 113:2; cf. *ibid.* 41:14), explains יְהִי שֵׁם ה' מְבֹרָךְ, *Let the Name of HASHEM be blessed,* thus: We make our contribution to the advancement and realization of God's purposes on earth by proclaiming the ways in which He has revealed Himself through His mighty acts. Thus, he approximates to *R' Bachya's* con-

cept of בָּרוּךְ, without resorting to Kabbalah.

The translation uses the verb *bless* which includes both meanings instead of the less inclusive 'praise' so as to allow for both interpretations.

20. Daniel Thanks God

מִן עָלְמָא וְעַד עָלְמָא — *Forever and ever* [lit. *from forever to forever*].

Ibn Ezra (Psalms 41:4), *Radak (ibid.* and 106:48), and *Hirsch* render עוֹלָם as referring to time, *from time past throughout the future.* This approximates the intent of *Targum* and *Rashi (ibid.),* who render *from this world to the world to come. Metzudos* (ad. loc.) has, *from the highest world to the lowest world.*

It may very well be that these two definitions of the noun עוֹלָם are related etymologically. *S.R. Hirsch (Genesis* 21:33) sees an affinity between עוֹלָם, *eternal time,* and הֶעְלֵם, *hiding.* עוֹלָם refers to the hidden times i.e., that which has not yet been revealed to us — the future — and that which has already passed and is no longer before us — the past.

In line with his identification of עוֹלָם, *eternity,* with הֶעְלֵם, *hiding, Hirsch* derives a further implication from the phrase. The future is surely hidden, but so is much of the past. Nevertheless, all

---

1. It is not within the scope of the *commentary* to discuss this at length. Those wishing to pursue this further are directed to *Likutei Torah* by R' Shneur Zalman of Liady to *Shir Hashirim* p. 56, *Devarim* p. 16, and sources quoted there. Cf. *Derech Mitzvosecha,* by R' Menachem Mendel of Lubavitch, p. 178 s.v. ואולם; *Nefesh Hachaim,* by R' Chaim of Volozhin, *Sha'ar* 2:1-5. See also *Overview* to ArtScroll *Bircas Hamazon.*

2

20-21

²⁰ *Daniel exclaimed: 'Let the Name of God be bles-*
sed forever and ever, for wisdom and might are His.
²¹ *He alters times and seasons; deposes kings and es-*

that has occurred and that will occur is part of the inexorable movement of the universe toward the goal ordained for it by God.

Similarly many commentators explain that the world is given a name with the connotation of hiddenness, because it is the vehicle chosen by God in which to camouflage His Omnipresence. The purpose of presenting man with a world in which Godliness exists but where it can be overlooked, is to present him with the challenge of being master of his destiny by exercising his God-given freedom of choice, to find the truth amid the concealment.

It may also be that time, itself a creation, (cf. *Derech Mitzvosecha* by *R' Menachem Mendel* of Lubavitch p. 57), is part of the great עֶלֶם of creation. Thus both these forms, עוֹלָם and הֶעְלֵם, rest upon the same philosophical foundation.

A third meaning of עוֹלָם — *people of the world* — is found in Talmudic literature. It is evidently an offshoot of עוֹלָם, world. Since the הֶעְלֵם, *hiddenness,* of the world was created for, and is evident only to man, whose primary mission is to pierce with his gifts of perception and wisdom this veil obscuring God's Presence, it is very fitting to apply the appellation הֶעְלֵם־עוֹלָם to man himself. These three renditions of עוֹלָם correspond to the well known division of the whole of creation into three: 1) עוֹלָם — *world, universe, space;* 2) שָׁנָה — *year, time;* 3) נֶפֶשׁ — *soul, life (Sefer Yetzirah* 6:2).

דִּי חָכְמְתָא וּגְבוּרְתָא דִּי לֵהּ הִיא — *For wisdom and might are His.*

The *wisdom and might* of men are basically God's. The human equivalents of these Godly attributes are mere earthly forms taken by these Godly emanations

after going through extensive transformations in mystical ways understood only by the creator Himself. Our wisdom and might are in the final analysis really God's wisdom and might *(Malbim).*

Wisdom — because He has revealed the dream and its interpretation to me ...

And might — because of the might He will show in the end of the days when he will uplift the downtrodden as was revealed in the king's dream *(Ibn Yachia).*

21. וְהוּא מְהַשְׁנֵא עִדָּנַיָּא וְזִמְנַיָּא — *(And) He alters times and seasons.*

He changes day into night *(Metzudos).*

According to *Metzudos,* this part of the verse is just the first in a list of things that Daniel credits to God's omnipotence. It is placed here only because of its similarity to the praises that follow. According to the *Vilna Gaon's* perception of the words עֵת and זְמַן (see *comm.* below), it is possible to put this phrase into clearer context. He changes the עִדָּנַיָּא, *the dates* in history, e.g., the exodus from Egypt was supposed to have happened later than it did. He also changes the זְמַנִים, *the epochs* of history. As related to Nebuchadnezzar *(vs.* 39-44), each of the great kingdoms has its epoch in which it will hold sway. The change from one epoch to another is not a random one but is guided by the everpresent hand of God. This may also mean that the time span allotted for a certain epoch is flexible in God's hand. It lies in His power to shorten the time allotted any of these great kingdoms. The next phrase מְהַעְדֵּה מַלְכִין is referring to individual kings, not to kingdoms. (Cf. *R' Yisroel of Kozhnitz,*

וּמְהַקֵּים מַלְכִין יָהֵב חָכְמְתָא לְחַכִּימִין
כב וּמַנְדְּעָא לְיָדְעֵי בִינָה: הוּא גָּלֵא עֲמִיקָתָא
וּמְסַתְּרָתָא יָדַע מָה בַחֲשׁוֹכָא °וּנהִירָא

° וּנְהוֹרָא ק׳

מְהַעֲדֵה מַלְכִין וּמְהָקֵים מַלְכִין — [He]
deposes kings and establishes kings.

He deposes them while they are
still kings — i.e., in their full
powers. And He *establishes kings* —
i.e., he takes an unknown, and with
phenomenal speed, sets him up as a
king with all the accompanying
regal grandeur. These abrupt
changes in the history of the nations
point to the guiding hand of God in
human history (*Alshich*).

יָהֵב חָכְמְתָא לְחַכִּימִין — [He] gives
wisdom to sages.

I.e., he bequeathes the gift of
wisdom to those who are mentally
prepared to receive it. חַכִּימִין here
does not refer to the already wise,
but to the potentially wise (*Ibn
Yachia; Malbim*).

[The word לְחַכִּימִין would
otherwise be superfluous, since it is
understood that as a result of the acquisition of wisdom, they become
wise.]

In connection with this it is
worthwhile to quote the *Midrash
Tanchuma* (*Vayakhel* 2; cf. *Koheles
Rabbah* 1:7): A noble lady asked R'
Yosef ben Chalafta what is [meant by]
that which is written, *He gives wisdom
to the wise*. It should have said, 'to the
stupid.'

He said to her: My daughter, if two
people, one poor and one rich, should
come to you to borrow money, to whom
would you lend?'

She answered him, 'To the rich man.'

He said to her, 'Why'?

She said, 'So that if he has a loss he
should have money to pay. But if a poor
man has a loss, from where would he
take money to pay?'

---

notes to *Be'er Hagolah* by *Maharal of
Prague*, London 5724, p. 154).

Since Nebuchadnezzar's dream
foretold the great upheavals that
were to occur in world history,
Daniel's prefatory remarks acknowledge God's guiding hand in
these changes (*Ibn Yachia*).

עִדָּנַיָּא וְזִמְנַיָּא — *Times and seasons.*

These are the Aramaic equivalents of עֵת וּזְמַן. The *Gaon of Vilna*
(*comm.* to *Isaiah* 5:19) distinguishes
between these synonyms. עֵת refers
to the exact point in time when an
event occurred, i.e., its date. זְמַן
refers to the time consumed by the
action itself — i.e., its duration. This
is similar to the distinction given by
R' Almosnino (ArtScroll *comm.* to
Ecclesiastes 3:1).

[*Iyun Tefillah* in *Sidur Otzar Hatefillos*
p.543 comes to an opposite conclusion! Cf.
editor's note *ibid.*]

S.R. Hirsch (*comm.* to *Siddur*, p.
256) in explanation of מְשַׁנֶּה
עִתִּים וּמַחֲלִיף אֶת הַזְּמַנִים, a paraphrase of this verse in Daniel, differentiates between the nouns thus:
זְמָן is time itself, while עֵת refers to
specific times, such as seasons of
the year, hours, minutes, etc.

עִדָּנַיָּא, *times*, refers to the time of
Sodom, and וְזִמְנַיָּא, [*and*] *seasons*,
refers to the season of Jerusalem
(*Seder Olam Rabbah* 30).

עִדָּן is a definite time, and refers to
the gentile empires which have their
set time. זְמַן is an undefined time,
and refers to Israel, which does not
have a set time for its reign, as
described below in *v.* 44 (*Gaon of
Vilna, comm.* to *Seder Olam*).

2
22

tablishes kings; gives wisdom to wise and knowl-
edge to those who know how to reason. ²² *He reveals*
the deep and the mysterious, knows what is in the

He said to her, 'Let your ears hear what your mouth is saying. If the Holy One, Blessed be He, would have given wisdom to the stupid, they would sit in unclean places and in the theaters and use it. So he gave wisdom to the wise, so that they should sit in the synagogues and the *Batei Midrashos* (houses for Torah study) and use it.'

וּמַנְדְּעָא לְיָדְעֵי בִינָה — *And knowledge to those who know how to reason.*

חָכְמָה is the mental capacity to distinguish between good and bad, wise and foolish (see *comm.* to 1:4). This distinction is based not on purely rational and logical considerations, but rather upon the laws and rules established by the Creator so that His creation may be governed by them. Hence, חָכְמָה is primarily wisdom revealed through prophecy. That חָכְמָה, *wisdom,* which is not perceived through revelation is achieved through the emulation of God's ways, thus fulfilling God's will and purpose in the world. Even in this type of חָכְמָה the underlying principle has been revealed, and only the adaptation of the principle to reality has been left to human reason. Our Sages interpret the command וְהָלַכְתָּ בְּכָל דְּרָכָיו, *and to go in all His ways (Deut. 11:22):* Just as He is merciful so be you merciful (quoted by *Rashi* loc. cit., cf. *Sifrei* loc. cit.; cf. *Rambam* in *Sefer Hamitzvos, Mitzvas Asseh 8, Hilchos Deos 1:6* who derives this from a different source.)

On a third level, חָכְמָה, *wisdom,* is the ability to absorb and comprehend the transmitted wisdom and to adapt it to life. Therefore, one cannot say that he 'knows' wisdom, for knowledge implies a clarity and exactness similar to that which is transmitted by the senses. Such exact knowledge of abstract concepts is possible only in concert with בִּינָה, the intellectual capacity to compare and differentiate, and to derive the unknown

from the known; by means of בִּינָה, *reason,* one can develop *wisdom* until it becomes *known* with utmost clarity. Thus, חָכְמָה, *wisdom,* is 'given' to the *wise,* but מַנְדְּעָה, *knowledge,* of this חָכְמָה, *wisdom,* is only for *those who know* [how to apply] *understanding* (from *Malbim* here and to *Prov.* 1:1).

22. הוּא גָּלֵא עֲמִיקָתָא וּמְסַתְּרָתָא — *He reveals the deep and the mysterious* [lit. *hidden*].

Only He can and does reveal matters that are עֲמִיקָתָא, so *deep* and complex that they are inaccessible to the human mind; וּמְסַתְּרָתָא, and things so *mysterious* that they are unknowable to man because of their secrecy (*Malbim*).

Seder Olam (ch. 30) interprets עֲמִיקָתָא, *the deep,* as the profundities of *the Merkavah* (See *Ezekiel* chs.1,2,10 and ArtScroll introduction); and מְסַתְּרָתָא, the *mysterious,* as the mysteries of מַעֲשֵׂה בְרֵאשִׁית, God's *act of creation.*

Be'ur HaGra explains *Seder Olam's* interpretation: Because it is prohibited to teach the *Merkavah* to others (see *Chagigah* 2:1), the *Merkavah* can only be contemplated in the 'depth' of one's heart.

The mysteries of the creation may be taught to others (see *Chagigah* 2:1) on condition that it is done secretly. Therefore these mysteries are referred to as the hidden.

יָדַע מָה בַחֲשׁוֹכָא — *(He) knows what is in the dark.*

God's knowledge — unlike human knowledge — is not acquired from outside Himself. One of the ways humans acquire knowledge is

כג עִמֵּהּ שְׁרֵא: לָךְ | אֱלָהּ אֲבָהָתִי מְהוֹדֵא
וּמְשַׁבַּח אֲנָה דִּי חָכְמְתָא וּגְבוּרְתָא יְהַבְתְּ
לִי וּכְעַן הוֹדַעְתַּנִי דִּי־בְעֵינָא מִנָּךְ דִּי־
כד מִלַּת מַלְכָּא הוֹדַעְתֶּנָא: כָּל־קֳבֵל דְּנָה
דָּנִיֵּאל עַל עַל־אַרְיוֹךְ דִּי מַנִּי מַלְכָּא
לְהוֹבָדָא לְחַכִּימֵי בָבֶל אֲזַל | וְכֵן אֲמַר־לֵהּ
לְחַכִּימֵי בָבֶל אַל־תְּהוֹבֵד הַעֵלְנִי קֳדָם
מַלְכָּא וּפִשְׁרָא לְמַלְכָּא אַחַוֵּא:

through the sense of sight. This sense, since it depends on external stimuli, i.e., the reaction of the eye in conjunction with the brain to the rays reflected to it from an object, cannot perceive what is in the dark. God's knowledge, however, is an innate attribute. In the words of *Rambam (Yesodei Hatorah* 2:10), 'And He does not know through knowledge which is outside of Him as we know ... He is the knower and He is that which is known and He is knowledge itself; everything is one. This concept is not within the power of the mouth to say, nor of the ear to hear, nor of the heart of a person to understand clearly ...' (cf. *Gevuros Hashem* by Maharal, Second preface; *Derech Mitzvosecha* by R' Menachem Mendel of Lubavitch pp. 92-99).

Therefore there can be no darkness, no external obstruction to God's knowledge. יָדַע מָה בַחֲשׁוֹכָא, [He] *knows what is in the dark*, because וּנְהוֹרָא עִמֵּהּ שְׁרֵא, *the light dwells with Him* (From *Alshich, Malbim*).

[This interpretation is consistent with the parable of our Sages on the verse וַיַּבְדֵּל אֱלֹהִים בֵּין הָאוֹר וּבֵין הַחֹשֶׁךְ, *And God separated the light from the darkness* (Genesis 1:4): A king saw a nice portion, so he said, 'This is mine'.

When the Holy One, Blessed is He, created His world and He created a great light, He said, 'No created being may use this, only I.' And so it is written: *And light dwells with Him (Bereshis Rabbah* 3:1). *Ralbag (comm.* to *Genesis* 1:4) comments that the Sages clearly understood the light created on the first day to be, not physical illumination, but spiritual and intellectual illumination. *Abarbanel* (loc. cit.) agrees that this was the intent of the *midrash.*]

וּנְהוֹרָא עִמֵּהּ שְׁרֵא — *And light dwells with Him.*

'Nehira is the Messiah's name as it is written וּנְהוֹרָא עִמֵּהּ שְׁרֵא, *Nehira dwells with Him:* the *kesiv* (spelling) is נהירא *(Midrash Eichah Rabbah* 1:51, amended according to *Minchas Shai;* cf. *Sanhedrin* 98b).

[This *Midrash* is illuminated by the homiletical interpretation of the Sages: וּנְהוֹרָא עִמֵּהּ שְׁרֵא refers to the giving of reward to the righteous (apparently because the proper reward for good deeds 'illuminates' God's process of dealing with mankind) [Seder Olam 30; *Bereshis Rabbah* 1:6)]. In this vein, the Sages see a special significance in a spelling which draws attention to the word. It is taken as a רֶמֶז, *hint*, of a specific reward for the righteous — namely the Messiah, because the coming of the Messiah will be the ultimate proof that the events of history are not haphazard and unconnected.]

2
23-24

dark, and light dwells with Him. ²³ *To You, O God of my forefathers, I give thanks and praise, Who has given me wisdom and might, and now You have made known to me what we prayed of You — that the matter of the king have You made known to us.'*

²⁴ *Consequently, Daniel came to Aryoch, whom the king had appointed to destroy the sages of Babylon. He went and said thus to him: 'Do not destroy the sages of Babylon. Bring me before the king, and I will tell the king the interpretation.'*

---

23. לָךְ אֱלָהּ אֲבָהָתִי — *To You, O God of my forefathers.*

I dare not assume that I have been given more *wisdom and might* than my companions on my own account. It must be in the merit of my ancestors who were Your servants and prophets (*Alshich*).

דִּי חָכְמְתָא וּגְבוּרְתָא יְהַבְתְּ לִי — *Who has given me wisdom and might.*

You gave me the *wisdom* to inquire of Aryoch about the haste of the decree (*v.* 15), and the *might* and courage to ask the king to extend the time to fulfill his request (*Alshich*).

וּכְעַן הוֹדַעְתַּנִי דִּי בְעֵינָא מִנָּךְ — *And now You have made known to me what we prayed of You.*

That *now You have made known to me* the king's dream is also not exclusively to my credit. It was in response to the prayers that *'we' prayed of you* that I was answered (*Ibn Ezra; Alshich*).

דִּי־מִלַּת מַלְכָּא הוֹדַעְתֶּנָא — *That the matter of the king have you made known to us.*

Daniel specifies what he meant in the preceding, vague phrase, *You have made known to me what we prayed of you.*

הוֹדַעְתֶּנָא — *Have You made known to us.*

The translation follows *Ibn Ezra*, who explains that though the dream was revealed only to Daniel, God revealed the secret to him only in the merit of דִּי בְעֵינָא מִנָּךְ, *what 'we' prayed of You.* The collective merit and prayer of Daniel and his companions earned him the revelation, which he proceeded to share with them.

Rashi translates הוֹדַעְתֶּנָא, *You have made known to me,* although the suffix נָא usually indicates the plural.

24. דִּי מַנִּי מַלְכָּא לְהוֹבָדָא לְחַכִּימֵי בָבֶל — *Whom the king had appointed to destroy the sages of Babylon.*

Since Nebuchadnezzar had ordered Aryoch to arrange the execution of all the sages of Babylon, he had to proceed with this task even while Daniel was negotiating with the king. Daniel, however, sought to save as many of the sages as possible. So he said to Aryoch, 'Do not destroy the sages of Babylon. I have found a way to excuse you from this gruesome duty. *Bring me before the king.* Thus employed, you will be free of discharging your assignment. During my talk with

כה אֱדַיִן אַרְיוֹךְ בְּהִתְבְּהָלָה הַנְעֵל לְדָנִיֵּאל
קֳדָם מַלְכָּא וְכֵן אֲמַר־לֵהּ דִּי־הַשְׁכַּחַת
גְּבַר מִן־בְּנֵי גָלוּתָא דִּי יְהוּד דִּי פִשְׁרָא
כו לְמַלְכָּא יְהוֹדַע: עָנֵה מַלְכָּא וְאָמַר
לְדָנִיֵּאל דִּי שְׁמֵהּ בֵּלְטְשַׁאצַּר °הַאִיתַיְךְ °הַאִיתָךְ ק׳
כָּהֵל לְהוֹדָעֻתַנִי חֶלְמָא דִי־חֲזֵית וּפִשְׁרֵהּ:
כז עָנֵה דָנִיֵּאל קֳדָם מַלְכָּא וְאָמַר רָזָא דִּי־
מַלְכָּא שָׁאֵל לָא חַכִּימִין אָשְׁפִין חַרְטֻמִּין
כח גָּזְרִין יָכְלִין לְהַחֲוָיָה לְמַלְכָּא: בְּרַם אִיתַי
אֱלָהּ בִּשְׁמַיָּא גָּלֵא רָזִין וְהוֹדַע לְמַלְכָּא
נְבוּכַדְנֶצַּר מָה דִּי לֶהֱוֵא בְּאַחֲרִית יוֹמַיָּא
חֶלְמָךְ וְחֶזְוֵי רֵאשָׁךְ עַל־מִשְׁכְּבָךְ דְּנָה
הוּא: °אַנְתְּה מַלְכָּא °רַעְיוֹנִיךְ °אַנְתְּ ק׳ °רַעְיוֹנָךְ ק׳
כט עַל־מִשְׁכְּבָךְ סְלִקוּ מָה דִּי לֶהֱוֵא אַחֲרֵי

the king I will soften his anger against the wise men, and the death decree will be lifted' (Alshich; Malbim).

25. Daniel Before the King

בְּהִתְבְּהָלָה — In haste.

He thus gave the impression that having adjusted his busy schedule to allow for this unforeseen turn of events, he was hurrying to return to his duties (Alshich; Malbim).

דִּי־הַשְׁכַּחַת גְּבַר — I have found a man.

It seems that Aryoch had not been informed by Daniel about the talk he had had with the king (v. 16). Aryoch could therefore, in good conscience, say to Nebuchadnezzar that he had found a man of the exiles of Judah who will make known the interpretation to the king. This is consistent with Alshich

and Malbim's comment that Daniel did not need Aryoch to gain entry to the king, but merely used Aryoch to divert him from executing the Babylonian sages.

26. דִּי שְׁמֵהּ בֵּלְטְשַׁאצַּר — Whose name is Belteshazzar.

Even though Nebuchadnezzar doubted that Daniel could tell him the dream, he had a feeling that Daniel might possess this power because he had been named Belteshazzar for Nebuchadnezzar's idol (4:5), and had thus received supernatural powers from this god (Alshich; Malbim).

27. רָזָא דִּי מַלְכָּא שָׁאֵל לָא חַכִּימִין ... — The secret the king requests no sages ... can tell the king.

Daniel, wishing to save the sages of Babylon, emphatically declared

2
25-29
²⁵ *Then Aryoch brought Daniel before the king in haste and said thus to him: 'I have found a man from the exiles of Judah who will make known the interpretation to the king.'*

²⁶ *The king exclaimed to Daniel whose name is Belteshazzar: 'Are you capable of making known to me the dream I saw and its interpretation?'*

²⁷ *Daniel answered the king, and he said, 'The secret the king requests no sages, astrologers, necromancers, or demonists can tell the king. ²⁸ But there is a God in heaven Who reveals secrets and He has informed King Nebuchadnezzar what will be at the end of days. Your dream, and the visions in your mind on your bed, are the following:*

²⁹ *'You, O king — your thoughts came while on your bed about what would happen in the future,*

---

to the king that he had asked the impossible of the sages. Had he told the king his dream without preamble, he would only have established that the king's request was really answerable (*Alshich*).

גָּזְרִין — *Demonists.*

The translation follows *Rashi* and *R' Shmuel Masnuth.* R' Saadiah declares *Gazrin* to be the name of a people.

28. רֵאשָׁךְ — *In your mind* [lit. *in your head*].

29. רַעְיוֹנָךְ עַל מִשְׁכְּבָךְ סְלִקוּ — *Your thoughts came while on your bed.*

During the day you had been wondering what would happen to your empire after your demise. As you retired for the night, this worry was still on your mind. Literally, your thoughts *came up* [with you] *upon your bed* (*Rashi*; cf. *Ibn Ezra*).

R' Shmuel bar Nachmani said in the name of R' Yonasan: A person

is only shown [in his dreams] from the thoughts of his heart [what he thinks about during the day — *Rashi*] as it has been said: *You — O king, your thoughts came while on your bed* (*Berachos* 55b).

Even in truthful dreams which are revealed from above, as in the case of Nebuchadnezzar, a person is shown only that to which he has already given thought (*Chidushei Agados Maharsha* loc. cit.).

A multitude of information is continuously being transmitted to this world from above, but it is only received by those who make some preparation to receive it. The king, in his preoccupation with the worry of what would happen after him, had been in the right frame of mind to receive this dream (*Mayenei HaYeshuah* 6:1).

[It seems from the above passage of the Talmud that even true divinely revealed dreams appear only within the framework of the person's own

דְּנָה וְגָלֵא רָזַיָּא הוֹדְעָךְ מָה־דִי לֶהֱוֵא:

וַאֲנָה לָא בְחָכְמָה דִּי־אִיתַי בִּי מִן־כָּל־ ל

חַיַּיָּא רָזָא דְנָה גֱּלִי לִי לָהֵן עַל־דִּבְרַת דִּי

פִשְׁרָא לְמַלְכָּא יְהוֹדְעוּן וְרַעְיוֹנֵי לִבְבָךְ

תִּנְדַּע: °אַנְתְּ ק׳ °אַנְתְּה מַלְכָּא חָזֵה לא

הֲוַיְתָ וַאֲלוּ צְלֵם חַד שַׂגִּיא צַלְמָא דִּכֵּן רַב

וְזִיוֵהּ יַתִּיר קָאֵם לְקָבְלָךְ וְרֵוֵהּ דְּחִיל:

הוּא צַלְמָא רֵאשֵׁהּ דִּי־דְהַב טָב חֲדוֹהִי לב

וּדְרָעוֹהִי דִּי כְסַף מְעוֹהִי וְיַרְכָתֵהּ דִּי

נְחָשׁ: שָׁקוֹהִי דִּי פַרְזֶל רַגְלוֹהִי °מנהון ק׳ °מִנְּהֵן לג

פַּרְזֶל °ומנהון ק׳ °וּמִנְּהֵן דִּי חֲסַף: חָזֵה הֲוַיְתָ עַד דִּי לד

הִתְגְּזֶרֶת אֶבֶן דִּי־לָא בִידַיִן וּמְחָת

לְצַלְמָא עַל־רַגְלוֹהִי דִּי פַרְזְלָא וְחַסְפָּא

thoughts. Just as the visual side of the dream is a combination of images already present in the mind, (cf. *Rambam* in *Shmoneh Perakim* ch. 1) so are the underlying ideas — i.e., the interpretation — of the dream composed of ideas already present in the mind. The novelty lies in the particular combination of images and ideas as arranged in the dream. The *Talmud* (*ibid.*) cites a proof for R' Shmuel bar Nachmani's statement: Rava said, 'A proof of this is that they neither show a person a golden tree nor an elephant going through the eye of a needle.' Dreams such as Nebuchadnezzar's can thus serve as vehicles for transmission of messages from above, but the materials used to spell out the message are the images and ideas already present in the receiver's mind.]

30. לָא בְחָכְמָה דִּי־אִיתַי בִּי מִן־כָּל־חַיַּיָּא — *Not because I possess more wisdom than any other being.*

There is no reason for you to be angry at the sages for their inability to tell your dream whereas I was

able to. God chose to reveal the future to you and I was chosen at random to decipher this divine message (*Malbim*).

עַל דִּבְרַת — *So that.*

The translation follows *Metzudos.*

[We find similar use of this phrase in *Ecc.* 7:14, עַל דִּבְרַת שֶׁלֹּא יִמְצָא הָאָדָם אַחֲרָיו מְאוּמָה, *so that man should find nothing after him.*]

דִּבְרַת is probably the feminine counterpart of דָּבָר, which when used בִּסְמִיכוּת, *in the construct form*, becomes דְּבַר. Similarly, דִּבְרָה, the feminine form of דָּבָר, would become דִּבְרַת in סְמִיכוּת. עַל דְּבַר in the sense our verse uses עַל דִּבְרַת is common, e.g. וַהֲרָגוּנִי עַל דְּבַר אִשְׁתִּי, *they will slay me because of my wife* (*Gen.* 20:11). See *Radak Shorashim* s.v. דבר; cf. *Rashi* to *Genesis* 49:22 s.v. בנות.]

31. This is the Dream

דְּכֵּן — *This.*

The translation follows *Ibn Ezra, Metzudos,* and *Malbim. Rashi* renders it, *with a base,* כֵּן being the

and the Revealer of secrets informed you what will happen. ³⁰ As for me, this secret was revealed to me not because I possess more wisdom than any other being, but rather to make the interpretation known to the king, so that you may know what has occupied your thoughts.

³¹ 'You, O king were watching and behold! a huge image; this image which was immense, and whose brightness was excessive, stood facing you, and its form was fearsome. ³² This image — its head was of fine gold, its breast and arms of silver, its belly and thighs of copper, ³³ its legs of iron, and its feet partly of iron and partly of earthenware. ³⁴ As you watched, a stone was hewn without hands and struck the image on its feet of iron and earthenware and

---

root of the word. Thus, *an image with a great base.*

וְזִיוֵהּ יַתִּיר — *Whose brightness was excessive.*

Its brightness was much greater than the brightness warranted by the precious metals (*R' Saadiah*).

וְרֵוֵהּ — *And its form.*

The translation follows *Ibn Ezra.* *Rashi* and *Radak* render it *form,* but *R' Saadiah* seems to accept both תּוֹאַר, *form,* and מַרְאֶה, *appearance,* as synonymous translations. [This is puzzling in view of *Genesis* 29:17. See ArtScroll *comm.* to *Gen.* 12:11.]

32. הוּא צַלְמָא — *This* [lit. *he, the*] *image.*]

וְיַרְכָתֵהּ — *And [its] thighs.*
See *comm.* to v. 33.

33. שָׁקוֹהִי ... רַגְלוֹהִי — *Its legs ... its feet.*

שׁוֹק in Scripture and *Talmud* is used to denote the leg — i.e., from

the knee down to the ankle. The thigh — from the knee up — is called יָרֵךְ (see *Metzudos*).

[This is the majority opinion. Cf. *Mishnah Oholos* 1:7 with *comm.* of *Rav, Eliyahu Rabbah,* and *Tifereth Yisrael.* This also seems to be the opinion of *Rash, Rosh,* and *Rambam.* Cf. *Tosafos* to *Menachos* 37a s.v. קבורת. *Tosafos Yom Tov,* assuming that שׁוֹק is *the thigh,* found difficulty in understanding the definition of קַרְסוֹל in *Rav* and *Rash.* The *Mishnah* itself, however, allows no room for this definition, as is pointed out by *Chazon Ish* to *Orach Chaim* 16:8. Nevertheless, *Pri Megadim* (in *Mishbetzos Orach Chaim* 75:1) seems to be of the same opinion as *Tosafos Yom Tov. Chazon Ish* (ibid.) thinks that the meaning of שׁוֹק is flexible, primarily meaning the thighs, but also denoting the legs, too, as in the above cited *Mishnah.* Since the previous verse mentions יַרְכָתֵהּ, which according to the context of the verse almost certainly means the thigh, the translation *legs* for שׁוֹק, is almost certain. *Tiferes Yisroel's* argument (*cit loc. Boaz* 14) is easily refuted. For better understanding of this topic see the above sources and *Sidrei Taharos* to *Oholos* 24b s.v. קרסול.]

מִנְּהֵן דִי פַרְזֶל וּמִנְּהֵן דִי חֲסַף — *Partly of iron and partly of earthenware.*

Each of its feet was made partly

וְהַדְּקֶת הִמּוֹן: בֵּאדַיִן דָּקוּ כַחֲדָה פַּרְזְלָא
חַסְפָּא נְחָשָׁא כַּסְפָּא וְדַהֲבָא וַהֲווֹ כְּעוּר
מִן־אִדְּרֵי־קַיִט וּנְשָׂא הִמּוֹן רוּחָא וְכָל־
אֲתַר לָא־הִשְׁתְּכַח לְהוֹן | וְאַבְנָא דִי־מְחָת
לְצַלְמָא הֲוַת לְטוּר רַב וּמְלָאת כָּל־
אַרְעָא: דְּנָה חֶלְמָא וּפִשְׁרֵה נֵאמַר קֳדָם־
מַלְכָּא: °אנתה

לה

לו
לז   ° אַנְתְּ ק׳

מַלְכָּא מֶלֶךְ מַלְכַיָּא דִּי אֱלָהּ שְׁמַיָּא
מַלְכוּתָא חִסְנָא וְתָקְפָּא וִיקָרָא יְהַב־לָךְ:
וּבְכָל־דִּי °דארין בְּנֵי־אֲנָשָׁא חֵיוַת בָּרָא
וְעוֹף־שְׁמַיָּא יְהַב בִּידָךְ וְהַשְׁלְטָךְ בְּכָלְּהוֹן
°אנתה הוּא רֵאשָׁה דִּי דַהֲבָא: וּבַתְרָךְ

לח   ° דָּיְרִין ק׳

לט   ° אַנְתְּ ק׳

of iron and partly of earthenware (Metzudos).

35. וְכָל־אֲתַר לָא־הִשְׁתְּכַח לְהוֹן — And no trace of them could be found [lit. And no place was found for them].

I.e. they were to be found no place, and no trace remained. (Rashi).

Metzudos renders this verse in a contrary fashion: The rubble of the image was so great that no place could be found for it.

36. וּפִשְׁרֵה נֵאמַר קֳדָם מַלְכָּא — And we will tell its interpretation before the king.

The telling of the dream was done openly in the king's court. The interpretation, since it foretold the fall of the Babylonian empire, would cause distress and chagrin to the king. In deference to the king's sensitivities, Daniel chose to reveal the interpretation in private, only be-

fore the king (Mayenei HaYeshuah; Malbim).

וּפִשְׁרֵה — Its interpretation.

Not וּפִשְׁרָא, 'an' interpretation, (as it is spelled in the words of the Sages vs. 4,7), but וּפִשְׁרֵה, 'its' interpretation (as Nebuchadnezzar consistently said in vs. 5,7,9,26), the only true interpretation of this dream (Alshich).

37. The Four Kingdoms

מֶלֶךְ מַלְכַיָּא — The King of kings, Who is the God of heaven.

Wherever מֶלֶךְ is mentioned in Daniel, the reference is to a secular king except here, where Daniel is referring to the Holy King, God (Shevuos 35b quoted by Rashi).

[Cf. Kessef Mishneh to Yesodei HaTorah 5:9 quoted by Minchas Shai that what is meant here is whenever מֶלֶךְ is mentioned by Daniel. For another instance in this book where מֶלֶךְ is sacred, see Sefer Kovetz to Rambam, ibid. and Minchas Shai.]

Metzudos renders this phrase thus; You,

2

35-39

crumbled them. ³⁵ Then the iron, the earthenware, the copper, the silver, and the gold were crumbled together. They became like chaff from summer threshing floors, and the wind carried them away, and no trace of them could be found. And the stone that struck the image became a great mountain and filled the whole earth. ³⁶ This is the dream, and we will tell its interpretation before the king.

³⁷ 'You, O king — whom the King of kings, Who is the God of heaven, has given a strong kingdom, power, and honor; ³⁸ and wherever people, wild beasts, and birds of the sky dwell, He has subjugated them to you, and made you ruler over them all — you are the head of gold. ³⁹ After you will arise another

---

O king, king of kings, whom the God of heaven has given …

The cantillation *(trop) esnachta* under מַלְכַיָּא, which separates מַלְכַיָּא from דִּי, favors this interpretation. [Cf. *Gilyon Hashas to Shabbos* 55b for similar contradictions between the *Talmud* and the *Mesorah*].

The question of this interpretation has its halachic ramifications. See *Rambam, Yesodei HaTorah* 6:9; *Kessef Mishneh*, there.

מַלְכוּתָא חִסְנָא — *A strong kingdom.*

The translation follows *Rashi* and others, making חִסְנָא an adjective describing מַלְכוּתָא, *kingdom*, while וְתָקְפָּא וִיקָרָא, *power and honor*, are nouns.

Malbim seems to render מַלְכוּתָא חִסְנָא וְתָקְפָּא וִיקָרָא as nouns. Thus: *Whom the King of kings has given kingship, strength, power, and honor.*

[The punctuation חִסְנָא instead of חֲסִינָא (cf. תַּקִּיפָא in *vs.* 40 and 42) points to this rendition.]

וְתָקְפָּא — *[And] power.*

תַּקִּיפוּת suggests *overpowering strength* as in the *Talmudic* expression תָּקַף לֵיהּ עַלְמָא. This is also suggested by *Koheles* (4:12) וְאִם יִתְקְפוּ

הָאֶחָד הַשְּׁנַיִם יַעַמְדוּ נֶגְדּוֹ. See also *Rashi* to *Job* 14:20. The *Vilna Gaon* in his commentary to *Esther* 10:2 defines תַּקִּיפוּת as the quality of making others subordinate their will to one's own.

38. חֵיוַת בָּרָא — *Wild beasts* [lit. *beasts of the outside*].

אַנְתְּ הוּא — *You are.*

[This phrase is a continuation of the preceding verse. After saying אַנְתְּ מַלְכָּא, *You, O king*, and then going into a long parenthetical description of the king, Daniel reiterates אַנְתְּ הוּא…, *You are the head of gold*, omitting the title מַלְכָּא, *king*, since the preceding parenthetical phrase has been a lengthy description of Nebuchadnezzar's awesome power. It is as if he were saying, '*You, O king … are the head of gold.* It is also possible that אַנְתְּ הוּא is not a repetition, but that it is added for additional emphasis. Thus: *You, O king, 'you' are the head of gold.*]

ב °אֲרַע ק׳ תְּקוּם מַלְכוּ אָחֳרִי °אַרְעָא מִנָּךְ וּמַלְכוּ
מ °תְּלִיתָאָה ק׳ °תְּלִיתִיָא אָחֳרִי°° דִּי נְחָשָׁא דִּי תִשְׁלַט
°רְבִיעָאָה ק׳ מ בְּכָל־אַרְעָא: וּמַלְכוּ °רְבִיעָיָה תֶּהֱוֵא

39. אֲרַע מִנָּךְ — *Inferior to you.*

Just as silver is inferior to gold, and the chest lower than the head, so will the kingdom that follows Babylon — that of the Persians and the Medes — be inferior and lower (*Rashi*).

דִּי נְחָשָׁא — *Of copper.*

Strong like copper (*Rashi*).

This refers to the rule of Alexander the Great and his successors (*Rashi* and other commentators. See v. 40).

דִּי תִשְׁלַט בְּכָל־אַרְעָא — *Which will rule the whole earth.*

This is indicated by the symbol used for this kingdom, copper, which is among the most resonant metals. The sound of the third kingdom will reverberate throughout the whole world (*Mayenei HaYeshuah* 6:1).

⇥§**Prefatory Note to v. 40**

The identity of the fourth kingdom is the topic of a great controversy which transcends the interpretation of this verse. For the theme of the four kingdoms recurs not only in the Book of *Daniel* (ch. 7), but in other prophets as well (e.g., *Zechariah*, ch. 6). The understanding of many other passages of this book is influenced by this controversy.

The *Midrashim* (see, e.g., *Avodah Zarah* 2b זו רוֹמִי חַיֶּיבֶת and many other places) consistently list יָוָן, *Greece*, as the third kingdom and רוֹמִי, *Rome*, as the fourth kingdom. (Rome is sometimes referred to as מַלְכוּת הָרְשָׁעָה, *the wicked kingdom*. In many places, deletions and changes of Christian censors in the *Talmudic* and *Midrashic* texts have made the original text unintelligible.) This is followed by almost all the commentators, starting with *R' Saadiah Gaon* (cited by *Ibn Ezra* 2:40) and including *Rambam (Iggeres Teiman)* and *Ramban (Sefer HaGeulah* 3, and *comm.* to *Genesis* 36:23 and *Numbers* 24:20 [ed. Chavel]).

A notable exception is *Ibn Ezra*, who is followed by *Metzudos* (the view of the *commentary* attributed to *R' Saadiah* is very unclear; he seems to lean toward *Ibn Ezra's* interpretation). This view holds that Rome is included in the third kingdom as relatives of the Greeks. The Romans are considered to be the Kittim mentioned in *Numbers* (24:24) and in this book (11:30; see *comm.* there). In *Genesis* (10:4) *Kittim* are the sons of *Yavan* (Greece).

The fourth kingdom, according to *Ibn Ezra*, is the Arab kingdom.

Ibn Ezra argues that according to the traditional interpretation, the mighty and extensive kingdom of the Arabs is left unmentioned in Daniel's visions of things to come, an omission which surely warrants an explanation, for then there should have been five kingdoms in the vision.

Ramban (ibid.) counters this argument with the idea that the four kingdoms are not meant to embrace all of mankind's history, but are to include, in outline form, the history of the Jewish exile. Therefore only the kingdoms considered responsible for the exile are mentioned. Other kingdoms, no matter how great their might, are not named. The era of the second Temple is considered part of the exile since most of the Jews did not return to the Holy Land, the Temple was not rebuilt to perfection, the presence of the *Shechinah* was missing, and for the greater part of this period the Jews were not autonomous (see *Ramban* to *Leviticus* 26:23). Babylon, responsible for the first exile, is named. Persia, successor in its totality to the Babylonian empire is considered the second kingdom; and Greece the third for the same reason. Rome is identified as the fourth kingdom for two reasons: 1) Its conquests included *Eretz Yisrael*, the center of Jewry; 2) It was directly responsible for the subsequent exile from the Holy Land. So long as no new empire arises which, by its conquests, can be considered successor *in toto* of Rome's power, we are still in the 'Roman' exile. The Arabic empire did not succeed Rome in the scope of its conquests.

kingdom inferior to you, and another — a third kingdom — of copper, which will rule the whole earth. ⁴⁰ *The fourth kingdom will be as strong as*

The influence of Rome in the formation of Arab and Turkish empires also allows one to consider them extensions or outgrowths of the Roman empire. *Abarbanel (Mashmia Yeshuah* 3:7) points to the influence of Christianity in the formation of Islam.

According to the commentators, Rome, in the heavenly vision (7:8) seen by Daniel and explained by the angel, undergoes a metamorphosis from the secular power of the old empire into the religious power, Christianity. The powerless orphan adopted by the mighty empire, originally by Emperor Constantine I and later by his successors, grew up to utilize its unique position as state religion of the great empire and moved on to a period of unprecedented growth. Its power, whether temporal or spiritual, eclipses that of kingdoms and empires. Thus throughout our exile, the fourth kingdom is represented by the Christian church, conceived of, despite all its diverse forms, as one unit.

The coming of the Messiah, about whom the prophet Zephaniah prophesied (3:9): *Then I will turn to the nations a pure language, that they shall all call upon the name of HASHEM, to serve Him in unison,* is contingent upon and parallels the demise of the most powerful religion challenging the tenet of pure monotheism which is the cornerstone of our religion.

In the words of *Rambam (Hilchos Melachim* ch. 11 appendix to *Mishneh Torah,* ed. Pardes, compiled by *Rabbi K. Kahane* from the relatively uncensored Rome edition, 1480, and others; our editions of this chapter in *Mishneh Torah* have had all this material excised by the censors): 'And all these matters — that of Yeshu the Nazarene and that of this Ishmaelite who arose after him — are only to prepare the way for the Messianic king and to perfect the whole world to serve God together, as it is written *(Zeph. 3:9): Then I will turn to the nations a pure language, that they shall all call upon the Name of HASHEM to serve him in unison.*

How? The world has already been filled (כְּבָר נִתְמַלֵּא הָעוֹלָם) with the subject of the Messiah, the subject of the Torah, and the subject of the commandments. These matters have already spread to the far isles and to many unrefined nations, who discuss these things and the commandments of the Torah. Some say that these commandments were true, but have been abrogated in our times and they are not binding for [all] the generations. Others say that the commandments have mystical meanings, and are not to be taken literally, and that the Messiah has already come and revealed their mysteries. But when the true Messianic king will come and succeed and be elevated and exalted, they will immediately recant and they will know that they have inherited falsehood from their ancestors and that their prophets and ancestors have misled them.'

As put forth in the comment of the Sages on the prophecy given to our mother, Rebecca, וּלְאֹם מִלְאֹם יֶאֱמָץ, *and the one people shall be stronger than the other ...* (Genesis 25:23), when one stands up the other must fall (see *Rashi loc. cit.*). Jacob's redemption must bring with it the fall of Esau. The Rabbinical tradition linking *Edom* (Esau) with Rome is well known. See *commentary.*

40. וּמַלְכוּ רְבִיעָאָה תֶּהֱוֵא — *[And] the fourth kingdom will be.*

Here he does not mention אָחֳרִי, *another,* as for the second and third kingdoms. Rome, the fourth kingdom, is considered by the Sages to be מַלְכוּת אֱדוֹם, *the kingdom of Edom* (see *Ramban* and *Ibn Ezra* to Genesis 46:43).

Edom is not considered אָחֳרִי, *another,* for he is Israel's brother, Esau, who was called Edom (Gen. 25:30; see *Yalkut* to 7:7).

That the Sages consider Rome to be *Edom* is unquestionable. References to the present exile as *Galus Edom* are too numerous to need mention. *Ramban (Sefer Geulah* ch. 3, p. 284, ed. Chavel) believes that because the Edomites were the first to accept the Nazarene's creed and they brought the cult to Rome, where it later became the state religion, Rome (representing Christianity; see

תַּקִּיפָה כְּפַרְזְלָא כָּל־קֳבֵל דִּי פַרְזְלָא
מְהַדֵּק וְחָשֵׁל כֹּלָּא וּכְפַרְזְלָא דִּי־מְרָעַע
מא כָּל־אִלֵּין תַּדִּק וְתֵרֹעַ: וְדִי־חֲזַיְתָה רַגְלַיָּא
וְאֶצְבְּעָתָא °מִנְּהוֹן חֲסַף דִּי־פֶחָר
°וּמִנְּהוֹן פַּרְזֶל מַלְכוּ פְלִיגָה תֶּהֱוֵה וּמִן־
נִצְבְּתָא דִי־פַרְזְלָא לֶהֱוֵא־בַהּ כָּל־קֳבֵל דִּי
חֲזַיְתָה פַּרְזְלָא מְעָרַב בַּחֲסַף טִינָא:

prefatory notes to this verse) is called Edom. Abarbanel (Mashmia Yeshuah 3:7), though admitting that he can find no source for his statement, champions **Ramban's** assertion. *Ramban's* reputation is assurance enough that he had good sources for his statement though these have been lost to us.

Yossipon (ch. 3) relates that Zepho (son of Elifaz son of Esau; *Genesis* 36:11) came to Italy and was crowned king by its inhabitants. *Abarbanel* (ibid.) surmises that Zepho may be the mythological Janus who, according to Roman legend, came from the East just after the deaths of Jacob and Esau. *Abarbanel* contends that we have no evidence that the ancient Romans were not themselves descendants of Esau since Roman beginnings are shrouded in mystery. It may very well be that the original settlers of Italy were the *Kittim* (see *prefatory notes* to this verse) and that the Edomites arrived later and absorbed the original ethnic stock through intermarriage. Finally, *Abarbanel* argues that Rome, as representative of Christianity, is the spiritual heir of Edom. Just as Isaac had two sons, Jacob and Esau, so does the true belief in one God figuratively have two sons — Jacob, the Jewish faith, and Edom, representing variants of monotheism. *Abarbanel* cites many other parallels between Christianity and Edom.

Ibn Ezra believes that the Edomite exile (גָּלוּת אֱדוֹם) is a misnomer, and that Rome has no intrinsic tie to Edom. Because the Edomites, age-old sworn enemies of the Jews, were the first to rejoice at Israel's destruction, the exile is called *Galus Edom*.

This controversy has halachic ramifications. *R' Yaakov Emden* (Sh'eilos Yavetz 1:46) discusses the permissibility of marrying Italian proselytes upon their conversion, since an Edomite is permitted to *enter the assembly of HASHEM* (Deut. 23:10) only after three generations. (See *Chazon Ish, Even HaEzer* 5:8.)

מְהַדֵּק — *Crumbles.*

See *Radak Shorashim* s.v. דקק and *M'turgeman* s.v. דקק.

וְחָשֵׁל — *And flattens.*

The translation follows *Rashi* and *Radak (commentary). Radak (Shorashim* s.v. חשל) and R' *Shmuel Masnuth* relate this word to the Hebrew נֶחֱשָׁלִים, *weak* (Deut. 25:18). Hence here *like iron which . . . and weakens.*

The metals crumbled and flattened by iron are ready to be refashioned into other forms for the benefit of their owners. The Roman empire, where practicable, will not destroy the nations it conquers; rather it will remold them for Roman exploitation (*Malbim*).

מְרָעַע — *Shatters.*

In some cases iron is used in a purely destructive manner. It breaks in a way that renders the

2
41

iron. Just as iron crumbles and flattens everything and as iron shatters all these, will it crumble and shatter. ⁴¹ *The feet and the toes that you saw, partly of potter's earthenware and partly of iron — it will be a divided kingdom, and it will have some of the firmness of iron — just as you saw iron mixed with*

fragments unusable in their present form. Likewise the Romans will in some instances physically destroy the nations they vanquish [as they intended to in the case of Israel].

41. חֲסַף — דִי־פֶחָר — *Potter's earthenware.*

[This seemingly redundant phrase reflects the Aramaic idiom. The same is true about חֲסַף טִינָא, *clayish earthenware.*

The commentators do not explain these strangely redundant phrases, nor why the description changes from *potter's earthenware* to *clayish earthenware.* The answer may lie in Nebuchadnezzar's changing perception of the earthenware during the dream. At first he saw the earthenware as *potter's earthenware,* i.e., fully baked and hardened, and as such unfit to mix with and adhere to the iron. This symbolized the division of the empire,.thus: *The feet and the toes that you saw, partly of potter's earthenware and partly of iron — it will be a divided kingdom.* Then the king saw the earthenware in a soft clayish form, readily blending with the iron. This symbolized that even the weak part of the kingdom represented by the earthenware *will have some of the firmness of iron — just as you saw iron mixed with earthenware.* The same can be said in v. 43 where the fact of iron mixing with the earthenware is interpreted by Daniel to show that: *they will mingle with the*

seed of men.]

מַלְכוּ פְלִיגָה תֶּהֱוֵה — *It will a divided kingdom.*

The area occupied by the Roman empire came to be dominated by two religions, Christianity and Islam. Both together comprise the latter day *fourth kingdom.* One is as strong as iron, the other as weak as pottery (*Mayenei HaYeshuah* 6:1; *Malbim*).

[The division of the kingdom may also refer to the split of the Roman empire into the Eastern (Byzantine) Empire, and the Western (Roman) Empire.]

Only the feet and toes were pictured as being of pottery and iron. The legs, though, were made only of iron. The division of its empire occured late in the history of the fourth kingdom. At its outset, as pictured, it was strong and mighty throughout (*Malbim*).

וּמִן נִצְבְּתָא דִי־פַרְזְלָא — *Of the firmness of iron.*

Even the weak part of pottery will have some of the strength of iron. Its weakness is only in comparison with the part of pure iron. Similarly, the weaker parts of the kingdom will be weak only in comparison to their stronger counterparts. The nation will still be strong compared to others (*Rashi*).

פַרְזְלָא מְעָרַב בַּחֲסַף טִינָא — *Iron mixed with clayish earthenware.*

This detail was not mentioned by

מב וְאֶצְבְּעָת רַגְלַיָּא °מִנְּהֵן פַּרְזֶל °וּמִנְּהֵן
חֲסַף מִן־קְצָת מַלְכוּתָא תֶּהֱוֵה תַקִּיפָה
ומִנַּהּ תֶּהֱוֵא תְבִירָה: °דִּי חֲזַיְתָ פַּרְזְלָא
מֵעָרַב בַּחֲסַף טִינָא מִתְעָרְבִין לֶהֱוֹן בִּזְרַע
אֲנָשָׁא וְלָא־לֶהֱוֹן דָּבְקִין דְּנָה עִם־דְּנָה
הֵא־כְדִי פַרְזְלָא לָא מִתְעָרַב עִם־חַסְפָּא:
מד וּבְיוֹמֵיהוֹן דִּי מַלְכַיָּא אִנּוּן יְקִים אֱלָהּ
שְׁמַיָּא מַלְכוּ דִּי לְעָלְמִין לָא תִתְחַבַּל
וּמַלְכוּתָה לְעַם אָחֳרָן לָא תִשְׁתְּבִק
תַּדִּק וְתָסֵיף כָּל־אִלֵּין מַלְכְוָתָא וְהִיא
מה תְּקוּם לְעָלְמַיָּא: כָּל־קֳבֵל דִּי־חֲזַיְתָ דִּי
מִטּוּרָא אִתְגְּזֶרֶת אֶבֶן דִּי־לָא בִידַיִן
וְהַדֵּקֶת פַּרְזְלָא נְחָשָׁא חַסְפָּא כַּסְפָּא

Daniel in his recountal of the dream (v. 33). A similar filling in of detail is found in the next verse.

42. מִנְּהֵן פַּרְזֶל וּמִנְּהֵן חֲסַף — *Partly of iron and partly of earthenware.*

This refers to the distant end of the divided kingdom, just like the toes are the ends of the feet. The ten *toes*, corresponding to the horns of the *fourth beast* (7:7, 24) are interpreted to correspond to ten major powers, all together comprising the *fourth kingdom* (see *comm.* to 7:7). Both in the foot of iron and in the foot of pottery there will be iron toes and toes of pottery. Both camps will include strong nations and weak nations. Hence: *part of the* [i.e., *either*] *kingdom will be powerful and part* [*of it*] *will be broken* (Malbim).

Ibn Ezra, holding to his view that the fourth kingdom is Islam, interprets the toes to refer to the dif-

ferent Islamic powers (*v. 39*). *Part of the kingdom* does not refer to a geographical part, but rather to chronological parts — i.e., at times they will be strong and victorious (over the European powers) and at other times they will be defeated. In his *Perush HaKatzar, Ibn Ezra* sees this as a reference to Jerusalem, which will sometimes be ruled by Islam and at other times by Christianity.

43. פַּרְזְלָא מְעָרַב בַּחֲסַף טִינָא — *Iron mixed with clayish earthenware.*

In *v.* 41, Daniel had explained the existence of pottery alongside iron as showing the strength of even the pottery. Here it seems that the toes of pottery had iron mixed in with them. The previous interpretation will not do here, since Daniel said in *v.* 42 that the toes of pottery showed that *part of it* [will be] *broken.*

clayish earthenware. ⁴² The toes, partly of iron and partly of earthenware — part of the kingdom will be powerful and part of it will be broken. ⁴³ That you saw iron mixed with clayish earthenware — they will mingle with the offspring of men, but they will not cling to one another; this is like iron, which does not blend with earthenware. ⁴⁴ In the days of these kingdoms the God of heaven will establish a kingdom that will never be harmed nor will its sovereignty be left to another people; it will crumble and consume all these kingdoms, and it will stand forever. ⁴⁵ Just as you saw that a stone was hewn from the mountain not by human hands, and it crumbled the iron, the copper, the earthenware, the

---

מִתְעָרְבִין לֶהֱוֹן בִּזְרַע אֲנָשָׁא — *They will mingle with the offspring of men.*

The different nations will intermarry with each other, but these intermarriages will not bring about a blending of the different ethnic, racial, and religious divisions. Each group will retain its distinctive features, just *like iron, which does not blend with earthenware* (Rashi; Ibn Ezra).

Though they will intermarry, this will not cause them to love one another. There will still be hatred and strife among these nations (R' Saadiah).

44. וּבְיוֹמֵיהוֹן דִּי מַלְכַיָּא אִנּוּן — *In the days of these kingdoms.*

Rashi comments on this phrase: 'While the fourth kingdom will still be in existence.' [Evidently *Rashi* takes מַלְכַיָּא to mean *kings*. Thus: in the days of the kings (of the fourth kingdom)].

In the days of the two rival kingdoms represented in the dream by the iron and copper — i.e., the Roman and the Arabic empires (*Ibn Ezra;* see *prefatory note* to *v.* 40 for *Ibn Ezra's* interpretation of the four kingdoms).

Ramban (Sefer HaGeulah ch. 3) contends that all four kingdoms are meant here. Though the supremacy of the three previous kingdoms had by now been replaced by the fourth kingdom, they had nevertheless retained some form of existence as nations. Now they would be totally destroyed together with the fourth kingdom. This is clearly indicated by the dream which, though it envisions the stone as striking only the feet (*v.* 34), goes on to say, *Then the iron, the earthenware, the copper, the silver and the gold were crumbled together ... (v.* 35). With the demise of the fourth kingdom the three preceding ones ceased to exist.

מַלְכוּ — *A kingdom.*

The kingdom of God which will be ruled by the Messiah (*Rashi*).

וְדַהֲבָא אֱלָה רַב הוֹדַע לְמַלְכָּא מָה דִּי
לֶהֱוֵא אַחֲרֵי דְנָה וְיַצִּיב חֶלְמָא וּמְהֵימַן
מו פִּשְׁרֵהּ:   בֵּאדַיִן מַלְכָּא נְבוּכַדְנֶצַּר
נְפַל עַל־אַנְפּוֹהִי וּלְדָנִיֵּאל סְגִד וּמִנְחָה
מז וְנִיחֹחִין אֲמַר לְנַסָּכָה לֵהּ: עָנֵה מַלְכָּא
לְדָנִיֵּאל וְאָמַר מִן־קְשֹׁט דִּי אֱלָהֲכוֹן הוּא
אֱלָהּ אֱלָהִין וּמָרֵא מַלְכִין וְגָלֵה רָזִין דִּי
מח יְכֵלְתָּ לְמִגְלֵא רָזָא דְנָה: אֱדַיִן מַלְכָּא
לְדָנִיֵּאל רַבִּי וּמַתְּנָן רַבְרְבָן שַׂגִּיאָן יְהַב־
לֵהּ וְהַשְׁלְטֵהּ עַל כָּל־מְדִינַת בָּבֶל וְרַב־
מט סִגְנִין עַל כָּל־חַכִּימֵי בָבֶל: וְדָנִיֵּאל בְּעָא
מִן־מַלְכָּא וּמַנִּי עַל עֲבִידְתָּא דִּי מְדִינַת

46. The King [Nebuchadnezzar] Exalts Daniel

וּמִנְחָה — *And with sacrifice.*

The translation follows *Rashi, Ibn Ezra,* and others who understand that Nebuchadnezzar intended to deify Daniel.

וְנִיחֹחִין — *And incense.*

The translation follows *R' Shmuel Masnuth*; it derives from רֵיחַ נִחוֹחַ.

R' Saadiah (and *Metzudos*) translate *libations,* apparently because לְנַסָּכָה is easily translated, *to pour* (e.g., וַיַּסֵּךְ עָלֶיהָ נֶסֶךְ, *Genesis* 35:14). This poses a difficulty because only libations can be poured, not sacrifices.

אֲמַר לְנַסָּכָה לֵהּ — *He wished* [lit. *he said*] *to exalt him.*

From וַאֲנִי נָסַכְתִּי מַלְכִּי, *I exalted My king* [*Psalms* 2:7, see commentaries there and *Sefer HaShorashim, s.v.* נסך] (*R' Yeshayah of Trani*; cf. *R' Saadiah*).

R' Yeshayah of Trani, *R' Saadiah,* and *R' Shmuel Masnuth* suggest that Nebuchadnezzar intended only to honor Daniel, not to deify him. Therefore מִנְחָה is translated *gift(s)* (cf. מִנְחָה לְעֵשָׂו אָחִיו, *Genesis* 32:14). נִיחֹחִין may then be objects that would please Daniel [from נַחַת רוּחַ] (cf. *Rashi* to *Exodus* 29:18).

[The *talmudic* and *midrashic* sources clearly understand that Nebuchadnezzar deified Daniel. The *Talmud* (*Sanhedrin* 93a) explains Daniel's absence during the episode of the golden image (ch. 3) by saying that he left Babylon because he feared Divine punishment for being worshiped as an idol.

R' Shmuel Masnuth suggests that since Daniel seemingly protested only against sacrifices being offered to him, but not when Nebuchadnezzar prostrated himself before him,[1] he was punished (ch. 6) by being thrown into the lions' pit (cf. *Bamidbar Rabbah* 13:5).

47. מִן־קְשֹׁט — *In truth.*

When the king saw that Daniel

silver, and the gold, so has the great God made known to the king what will happen in the future. The dream is true and its interpretation is reliable.'

46 Then King Nebuchadnezzar fell upon his face and prostrated himself before Daniel; and with sacrifice and incense he wished to exalt him. 47 The king exclaimed to Daniel, 'In truth I know that your God is the God over gods, Lord of kings, and the Revealer of secrets, since you were able to reveal this secret.' 48 Then the king promoted Daniel, and gave him many great gifts. He empowered him ruler over the entire land of Babylon, and chief official over all the sages of Babylon. 49 Daniel asked the king and he appointed Shadrach, Meshach, and Abed Nego over

refused to be worshiped as a god, he realized that the God of Daniel was not just one more deity to be added to his pantheon, but rather the only true God (R' Saadiah; cf. Malbim cited below).

הוּא אֱלָהּ אֱלָהִין — *Is the God over gods.*

Nebuchadnezzar rationalized his worshiping Daniel, by claiming that it did not in anyway constitute an affront to Daniel's God. Daniel's God is the Supreme God, the God over gods. This did not — to Nebuchadnezzar's mind — preclude the existence of secondary gods. It would therefore be no sin to worship Daniel (Malbim; see Menachos 110a דקרן ליה אלקא דאלקיא).

48. אֱדַיִן — *Then.*

When Daniel refused to let himself be worshiped, Nebuchadnezzar found a different manner in which to express his gratitude to Daniel. He *promoted Daniel and gave him ... gifts* (Malbim).

מְדִינַת בְּבֶל — *The ... land of Babylon.*

Ibn Ezra expresses his opinion that מְדִינָה here refers to the capital city Babylon: 'If מְדִינָה means a province, how could Ahasuerus reign over 127 provinces? A king who rules over ten is already considered a great king'. However, it is apparent from the words of the Sages (Megillah 11a) that מְדִינָה means a province. They consider Ahasuerus to have ruled over almost the entire known world. See comm. to 7:2.

49. וְדָנִיֵּאל בְּעָא — *[And] Daniel asked.*

Daniel asked that his companions be allowed to share the burden of his office, so that he would be free

1. The *Midrash* also notes that Daniel protested (*Tanchuma* to *Miketz* 3; *Bereishis Rabbah* 96:5). This is indicated by the words *he wished to*, which imply that he was hindered from actually doing so. [Since, however, the words *he wished* are used only for the sacrifices, it would seem that Daniel did not protest when Nebuchadnezzar prostrated himself before him.]

בָּבֶל לְשַׁדְרַךְ מֵישַׁךְ וַעֲבֵד נְגוֹ וְדָנִיֵּאל
בִּתְרַע מַלְכָּא: א נְבוּכַדְנֶצַּר מַלְכָּא
עֲבַד צְלֵם דִּי־דְהַב רוּמֵהּ אַמִּין שִׁתִּין
פְּתָיֵהּ אַמִּין שֵׁת אֲקִימֵהּ בְּבִקְעַת דּוּרָא

to act as the king's personal advisor (Malbim).

וְדָנִיֵּאל בִּתְרַע מַלְכָּא — And Daniel was at the king's gate.

Ibn Ezra takes this to mean that he was appointed to the king's (judicial) court. There are other instances in Scripture where the court is called the gate such as Deut. 21:19 where שַׁעַר מְקֹמוֹ is translated by Onkelos as the court of his place.

Rav Shmuel Masnuth cites the opinion that Daniel became one of the king's personal bodyguards, a post highly esteemed in those days (cf. Esther 2:21 מִשֹּׁמְרֵי הַסַּף).

Daniel became the king's personal advisor (Malbim). [Cf. the statement of the Sages in Megillah 15a. 'Hasach (Esther Ch. 4) is Daniel.' He was called Hasach from חָתַךְ, to cut, because all matters of state were cut by his mouth (i.e., decided by him).]

III

◄§Nebuchadnezzar's Golden Image

Chapter III tells the story of Nebuchadnezzar's construction of an enormous golden statue and his attempt to force Chananyah, Mishael, and Azaryah to bow to it, or face death in a flaming kiln. Their refusal to obey and the miraculous salvation which followed it have become synonymous with Jewish courage and devotion to God. [See Overview.]

Concerning the underlying meaning of Nebuchadnezzar's golden image there are basically two opinions.

One school of thought (R' Saadiah, Ri HaZaken in Tosafos to Pesachim 53b s.v. מה) maintains that this image was idolatrous. When Chananyah, Mishael,and Azaryah defied the king, they were only acting according to the dictum of the Torah that in case of forced idol worship יֵהָרֵג וְאַל יַעֲבֹר, one should submit to martyrdom rather than transgress (Sanhedrin 74a).

Thus Chananyah, Mishael, and Azaryah were one more link in the glorious chain of martyrdom stretching from our forefather Abraham to present times. Their resolute and heroic bearing demonstrated to Nebuchadnezzar and the world that the essence of life is not this temporal existence; that there are beliefs and values which transcend it.

The motives for Nebuchadnezzar's action are perhaps not worth seeking, because Jewish history is sadly replete with similar instances of religious intolerance. Yet R' Saadiah supplies a strong motive for the king's despotic behavior. Nebuchadnezzar knew (from his dream and Daniel's prophetic interpretation) of the limited role his empire was to play in the arena of world history, and that the final, most glorious chapter,would be written by the Jewish nation. He also knew that the uniqueness of the Jewish nation lies in their belief in the one true God and their acceptance of His Torah. He reasoned that if he could coerce the Jews into rejecting their beliefs, the covenant between God and His people would be broken and the status of the Jewish people would be reduced to that of other nations. Having robbed God's master plan of its ultimate purpose — i.e., the establishment of the fifth kingdom, which shall never be destroyed (2:44), — he aspired to prevent God's involvement in the downfall of Babylon and hoped for the perpetuation of his empire.

Another view, proposed at first by R' Tam (Tosafos, ibid.) and later adopted by Abarbanel, Alshich, and Malbim, holds that the image was not an idol but a statue put up for the glory of the king. The purpose of the image was intertwined with Daniel's interpretation of Nebuchadnezzar's dream. In the dream, Babylon was represented by the golden head. Thus gold

the affairs of the land of Babylon; and Daniel was at the king's gate.

K ing Nebuchadnezzar made an image of gold, its height sixty cubits, its width six cubits; he set it

was the symbol for Babylon. By constructing an image identical to the one in his dream, but made entirely of gold, he symbolized the substitution of Babylon — the kingdom of all gold — for the kingdoms represented by the other materials.

The worship of this image by all the nations implied the symbolic submission of all the nations destined to succeed the Babylonian empire to Nebuchadnezzar's version of the world's future.

[This seemingly strange reliance on symbolism, although misplaced, has its roots in a truth. Ramban (Genesis 12:6) lists many instances where symbolism plays a role. However, it is only when the symbolism is inspired by God that it is endowed with any real power. Otherwise, it is just an empty display devoid of any meaning. Thus Nebuchadnezzar's elaborately staged spectacle, no matter how successful, could never have changed the course of history. This is just another instance where a belief, though founded on a true premise, becomes so distorted that it loses all the meaning and truth it may have had.]

In this second view, the Jewish nation, though not represented by the statue, would also meet its symbolic defeat. In the dream, a stone — representing the Jewish nation — struck the feet of iron and earthenware and broke them. This implied to Nebuchadnezzar that only because the feet were weakened by the mixture of earthenware could they be broken by a stone. If the feet had been of pure metal they would not have been broken by the throwing of the stone.

A further interpretation may be offered for the fact that the statue's base was made of gold from Jerusalem (see comm. to 3:2). Nebuchadnezzar may have intended this to symbolize that he would build his all-conquering and eternal kingdom upon the never-to-rise ruins of Israel's nationhood (Rabbi Yehoshua Leiman).

The statements of the Talmudic and Midrashic Sages on this matter seem to point conclusively to the first point of view, as argued at length by R' Shlomo Alkavetz (Menos Halevi, Preface, p. 6), R' Achai Gaon (Sheiltos 42), and Bahag (Hilchos Avodah Zarah). The numerous allusions to the story of Chananyah, Mishael, and Azaryah in the Midrashim consistently refer to their refusal to worship an idol.

1. רוּמֵהּ אַמִּין שִׁתִּין — Its height sixty cubits.

Alshich understands the sixty cubits to symbolize the primary epochs in the history of mankind, beginning with Nebuchadnezzar's kingdom and ending with the kingdom of God which will come at the End of Days. In Nebuchadnezzar's dream (ch.2), the history of mankind was divided into four periods, each represented by a section of the image, and composed of a different material. Because the fourth kingdom in his dream was composed of two different substances, iron and earthenware, it represented two different kingdoms within the same period. Thus there was a total of five kingdoms. They would be followed by a sixth. After all these epochs and monarchies there would be the final, everlasting kingdom that the God of heaven will set up (24:44). Including this final step of God's master plan for the world into his vision of an everlasting Babylonian hegemony over the world, Nebuchadnezzar made the image sixty cubits high, each ten cubits representing one of the six epochs in world history (Alshich).

פְּתָיֵהּ אַמִּין שֵׁת — Its width six cubits.
If its width was only six cubits,

ב בִּמְדִינַת בָּבֶל: וּנְבוּכַדְנֶצַּר מַלְכָּא שְׁלַח
לְמִכְנַשׁ | לַאֲחַשְׁדַּרְפְּנַיָּא סִגְנַיָּא וּפַחֲוָתָא
אֲדַרְגָּזְרַיָּא גְדָבְרַיָּא דְּתָבְרַיָּא תִּפְתָּיֵא וְכֹל
שִׁלְטֹנֵי מְדִינָתָא לְמֵתֵא לַחֲנֻכַּת צַלְמָא
ג דִּי הֲקֵים נְבוּכַדְנֶצַּר מַלְכָּא: בֵּאדַיִן
מִתְכַּנְשִׁין אֲחַשְׁדַּרְפְּנַיָּא סִגְנַיָּא וּפַחֲוָתָא
אֲדַרְגָּזְרַיָּא גְדָבְרַיָּא דְּתָבְרַיָּא תִּפְתָּיֵא

---

how could it support a height of sixty cubits? Said R' Bevai, 'They put it up and it kept falling, until they brought all the gold of Jerusalem and poured a base for its feet, to fulfill the prophecy (*Ezekiel 7:19*), *Their gold will be for an object of disgust*'. [According to *Rashi's* interpretation of 2:31 (See *comm.*) this base could have been patterned on the base Nebuchadnezzar saw in his dream] (*Rashi* from *Pesichta* of *Eichah Rabbah 23*).

[Our sages (*Mishnah Shabbos* 9:1; 82a) infer from *Isaiah* (30:22), where in reference to idolatrous images it is said, '*You shall put them far away as* דָּוֶה — *one unclean*,' that a parallel is being drawn between דָּוֶה (the Aramaic equivalent of זָבָה) and idolatrous images. Therefore when Ezekiel foretells that *their gold will be* לְנִדָּה, *for an object of disgust*, this prophecy is considered fulfilled by having the gold used for an idol; זָבָה and נִדָּה are practically synonymous (the difference is a technical one; cf. *Shabbos, ibid*). We may therefore conclude that the above *Midrash* considers Nebuchadnezzar's image an idol.]

אֲקִימֵהּ בְּבִקְעַת דּוּרָא — *He set it up in the plain of Dura.*

Radak (*Shorashim* s.v. בקע) gives two possible translations for בִּקְעָה, either *valley* or *plain*. However, he considers בִּקְעַת דּוּרָא to be a plain.

Alshich has it on the authority of the *Zohar*[1] that Dura was the place where the tower of Babylon was built. Nebuchadnezzar's choice of the plain of Dura to be the stage for his spectacle was significant, if not ominous. No doubt he felt that this location possessed magical powers with which he could defy Divine will. He was confident he would succeed where his predecessors had failed.

דּוּרָא — *Dura.*

[Local tradition points to a site near the famous ruins of Babylon (southwest of Baghdad and north of Hilla) as the place where Chananyah, Mishael, and Azaryah were thrown to the flames. Tradition places the lions' pit into which Daniel was thrown (ch. 6) near this area.]

2. [The exact translations of the various titles listed in this verse are difficult, if not impossible, to arrive

---

1. *Zohar* to *Parshas Noach* (p. 75a). *R' Bachya* (*Genesis 11:4*) mentions this without ascribing it to the *Zohar*. See *Shikchas Leket* s.v. *Bavel*. Interestingly, *Ibn Ezra* (here), indicates the very same idea. He says, *And they settled there* (*Genesis 11:4*) — that was the Dura Valley.

3
2-3
up in the plain of Dura in the land of Babylon.
² Then King Nebuchadnezzar sent to assemble the satraps, the nobles, and the governors; the Adargaz-raya, the Gedavraya, the Desavraya, the Tiftaye, and all the provincial officials to come to the dedication of the image which King Nebuchadnezzar had set up.

³ Then there gathered together the satraps, the nobles, and the governors, the Adargazraya, the Gedavraya, the Desavraya, the Tiftaye, and all the

---

at with any degree of certainty. *Midrash Shir HaShirim* (7:9) gives us translations of each of these words, but they are in Latin and Greek. *Ibn Ezra, Radak,* and *R' Yeshayah* content themselves with commenting that these are terms for differing ranks in the Persian nobility, listed in descending order of their standing. We have translated the first three terms, because these appear in other places in Scripture and have more or less traditional translations. The last four terms have been transliterated only, with some of the possible translations given in the *commentary.*

לַאֲחַשְׁדַּרְפְּנַיָּא — [*To*] *the satraps.*
This is similar to dukes, the translation given by *Rashi.* (See *Tishbi* s.v. דוכס cf. *Mosaf HeAruch* s.v. דוכס).
R' Saadiah Gaon (all translations attributed to *R' Saadiah Gaon* in this chapter are taken from his *Tafsir*) translates *the generals. Targum to Esther* (3,12) renders אֲחַשְׁדַּרְפְּנִים אִסְטְרַטְלוּסֵי. According to *R' Benyamin Mosaphia* (*Mosaf He'Aruch* s.v. דוכס) these are field marshals. This approximates the *R' Saadiah Gaon's* translation (as does the

Syrian Targum cited by *R' Shmuel Masnuth*).

סְגְנַיָּא — *The nobles.*
The translation follows *Radak, Shorashim* (s.v. סגן). *Radak* adds that the use of סְגָן for deputy, as in סְגָן הַכֹּהֲנִים, *deputy High Priest,* is a *Mishnaic* usage.
R' Saadiah Gaon translates *commanders.*

וּפַחֲוָתָא — *And the governors.*
As in פַּחַת יְהוּדָה, *governor of Judah* (*Chaggai* 1:1).
Most commentators translate the last four terms· as names of various government officials. *Rashi,* although he acknowledges the first three to be names of officials, takes אֲדַרְגָּזְרַיָּא גְדָבְרַיָּא דְּתָבְרַיָּא תִּפְתָּיֵא to be names of nations. This is based upon the *Talmud* (*Sanhedrin* 92a; cf. *comm.* to *v.* 27). Support for this view can be found in the way Scripture positions the conjunctive *vav* with פַּחֲוָתָא, thereby separating the latter four categories from the following three.
They would represent their nations in submission to the image (*Malbim*).
R' Saadiah Gaon translates: אֲדַרְגָּזְרַיָּא, *judges,* גְדָבְרַיָּא, *scribes,* דְּתָבְרַיָּא, *governors,* and תִּפְתָּיֵא. *policemen.*

וְכֹל שִׁלְטֹנֵי מְדִינָתָא לַחֲנֻכַּת צַלְמָא דִּי
הֲקֵים נְבוּכַדְנֶצַּר מַלְכָּא °וְקָאֲמִין לָקֳבֵל
צַלְמָא דִּי הֲקֵים נְבֻכַדְנֶצַּר: וְכָרוֹזָא קָרֵא
בְחָיִל לְכוֹן אָמְרִין עַמְמַיָּא אֻמַּיָּא
וְלִשָּׁנַיָּא: בְּעִדָּנָא דִּי־תִשְׁמְעוּן קָל קַרְנָא
מַשְׁרוֹקִיתָא °קִיתְרֹס סַבְּכָא פְּסַנְתֵּרִין
סוּמְפֹּנְיָה וְכֹל זְנֵי זְמָרָא תִּפְּלוּן וְתִסְגְּדוּן
לְצֶלֶם דַּהֲבָא דִּי הֲקֵים נְבוּכַדְנֶצַּר מַלְכָּא:
וּמַן־דִּי־לָא יִפֵּל וְיִסְגֻּד בַּהּ־שַׁעֲתָא
יִתְרְמֵא לְגוֹא־אַתּוּן נוּרָא יָקִדְתָּא: כָּל־
קֳבֵל דְּנָה בֵּהּ זִמְנָא כְּדִי שָׁמְעִין כָּל־
עַמְמַיָּא קָל קַרְנָא מַשְׁרוֹקִיתָא °קִיתְרַס
שַׂבְּכָא פְּסַנְטֵרִין וְכֹל זְנֵי זְמָרָא נָפְלִין כָּל־

3. The King's Command

וְקָאֲמִין לָקֳבֵל צַלְמָא — *And they stood facing the image.*

They had not been told that they would have to prostrate themselves before the image. Nebuchadnezzar feared the reaction of the nations under his rule if they would guess the purpose of this spectacle. Therefore his edict calling together all the officials of his kingdom omitted any mention of what was to occur in the plain of Dura. They were blandly invited *to come to the dedication of the image.* Once the representatives of the nations were standing in front of the image, none had the courage to defy Nebuchadnezzar's order. To do so would have meant instant death (*Alshich*).

In *Malbim's* view, just the opposite happened. The representatives, aware they were going to the dedication of the image, went with a clear understanding of what it represented. They went with the knowledge and assent of their constituents, so their actions would be representative of their entire nation. Thus Nebuchadnezzar gained the symbolic submission of all the nations.

4. לְכוֹן אָמְרִין עַמְמַיָּא — *To you it is commanded, O peoples.*

These prefatory remarks to the proclamation served to underline the king's wish that all the nations be represented at the dedication. Although the proclamation reached only the ears of the officials, it was addressed to them in their capacity as representatives of the people (*Malbim*).

עַמְמַיָּא אֻמַּיָּא וְלִשָּׁנַיָּא — *Peoples, nations, and languages.*

Malbim differentiates between these synonyms: עַם designates a

3
4-7

provincial officials for the dedication of the image that King Nebuchadnezzar had set up, and they stood facing the image that Nebuchadnezzar had set up. ⁴ A herald cried aloud, 'To you it is commanded, O peoples, nations, and languages: ⁵ When you hear the sound of the horn, the whistle, the tambourine, the drum, the cymbals, the flute, and all kinds of music, you shall fall and prostrate yourselves before the golden image that King Nebuchadnezzar set up. ⁶ And whoever does not fall and prostrate himself will be thrown instantly into a flaming kiln.'

⁷ Therefore, as soon as all the peoples heard the sound of the horn, the whistle, the tambourine, the drum, the cymbals, and all kinds of music, all the

group of people having a common political system — i.e., those living under one government (cf. *Perush HaGra* to *Isaiah* 2:4).

אום is the term for a group of people united by one common religion.

לָשׁוֹן is a group of people sharing the same language. (Cf. *Beur LeShemos HaNirdafim* by *R' S.A. Wertheimer*).

5. בְּעִדָּנָא דִּי־תִשְׁמְעוּן — *When you hear.*

Music is a usual part of coronation ceremonies. Therefore this music was played to symbolize the acceptance of Nebuchadnezzar's perpetual kingdom (*Malbim*).

[The translations given for the musical instruments are taken from *R' Saadiah Gaon's Tafsir.*]

לְצֶלֶם דַּהֲבָא דִּי הֲקֵים נְבוּכַדְנֶצַּר — *Before the golden image that King Nebuchadnezzar set up.*

Scripture, throughout this chap-

ter, hints at the purpose of the image by continuously reiterating that the image was set up by 'King' Nebuchadnezzar, i.e., in order to perpetuate his kingdom. The symbolism underlying the use of gold is similarly underlined (*Alshich; Malbim*).

6. יִתְרְמֵא לְגוֹא־אַתּוּן נוּרָא — *Will be thrown ... into a flaming kiln* [lit. *a kiln of burning fire*].

This was a traditional mode of execution in Babylon. Abraham had faced this type of death (See *Pesachim* 118a and *Sefer HaYashar*) when he refused to bow to Nimrod's idols (*Alshich*).

The burning of any would-be recalcitrant, besides serving as a deterrent, would also serve a symbolic purpose. Just as the burning would leave no trace of the unfortunate rebel, so would there remain no trace of insurrection against Nebuchadnezzar's regime (*Malbim*).

עַמְמַיָּא אֻמַּיָּא וְלִשָּׁנַיָּא סָגְדִין לְצֶלֶם
הַדַּהֲבָא דִּי הֲקֵים נְבוּכַדְנֶצַּר מַלְכָּא: כָּל־ ח
קֳבֵל דְּנָה בֵּהּ זִמְנָא קְרִבוּ גֻּבְרִין כַּשְׂדָּאִין
וַאֲכַלוּ קַרְצֵיהוֹן דִּי יְהוּדָיֵא: עֲנוֹ וְאָמְרִין ט
לִנְבוּכַדְנֶצַּר מַלְכָּא מַלְכָּא לְעָלְמִין חֱיִי:
°אַנְתָּה מַלְכָּא שָׂמְתָּ טְעֵם דִּי כָל־אֱנָשׁ י
דִּי־יִשְׁמַע קָל קַרְנָא מַשְׁרוֹקִיתָא °קִיתָרֹס
שַׂבְּכָא פְסַנְתֵּרִין °וְסוּפֹנְיָה וְכֹל זְנֵי זְמָרָא
יִפֵּל וְיִסְגֻּד לְצֶלֶם דַּהֲבָא: וּמַן־דִּי־לָא יִפֵּל יא
וְיִסְגֻּד יִתְרְמֵא לְגוֹא־אַתּוּן נוּרָא יָקִדְתָּא:
אִיתַי גֻּבְרִין יְהוּדָאִין דִּי־מַנִּיתָ יָתְהוֹן עַל־ יב
עֲבִידַת מְדִינַת בָּבֶל שַׁדְרַךְ מֵישַׁךְ וַעֲבֵד
נְגוֹ גֻּבְרַיָּא אִלֵּךְ לָא־שָׂמוּ °עֲלַיִךְ מַלְכָּא

---

7. כָּל־עַמְמַיָּא — *All the peoples.*

Since all the nations had sent delegates to represent them at the ceremony, it was considered as though all the nations had prostrated themselves before the image (see *comm.* to *v.* 2).

8. Slander

וַאֲכַלוּ קַרְצֵיהוֹן — *And defamed.* [lit. *they ate their winks*].

Rashi explains the idiom thus: It was customary for gossip to be conveyed at a meal; the partaking of food was considered a sign that the gossip had been accepted. Therefore this repast was called קַרְצִין, *a cue* or *sign*, from קוֹרֵץ בְּעֵינָיו, *he winks with his eyes* (*Proverbs* 6:13).

Ramban (*Leviticus* 19:16) points out that אֲכַלוּ in the *Talmud* means *they made noise.* Therefore אֲכַלוּ

קַרְצֵהוֹן literally means *they made hinting noises.*

דִּי יְהוּדָיֵא — *The Jews.*

Since Chananyah, Mishael, and Azaryah refused to heed the king's order because of their Jewishness, their refusal to bow down could be interpreted as representative of the whole Jewish People (*Malbim*).

[All the officials present at the ceremony were there as representatives of their people, therefore any action taken by them could be taken as the action of that entire nation. Besides, the fine distinction between the single Jew and the whole Jewish People has always eluded antisemites.]

12. גֻּבְרִין יְהוּדָאִין — *Jewish men.*

The defamers wanted to underline the gravity of the three Jews' defiance by stressing their nationality. Nebuchadnezzar understood

peoples, the nations, and the languages fell and prostrated themselves before the golden image that King Nebuchadnezzar had set up.

⁸ Thereupon, at that very time, Chaldean men came forth and defamed the Jews. ⁹ They exclaimed to King Nebuchadnezzar: 'O King, live forever! ¹⁰ You, O king, issued a decree that every person who hears the sound of the horn, the whistle, the tambourine, the drum, the cymbals, the flute, and all kinds of music is to fall and prostrate himself before the golden image, ¹¹ and whoever does not fall and prostrate himself is to be thrown into a flaming kiln. ¹² There are Jewish men whom you have appointed over the affairs of the land of Babylon — Shadrach, Meshach, and Abed Nego. These men have not accepted upon themselves, O king, your decree; your

that the kingdom that the *God of heaven will set up* (2:44) would be the Jewish People. Thus, if the Jews did not humble themselves before his image, his plan would be thwarted. *(Alshich).*

דִּי־מַנִּיתָ יָתְהוֹן — *Whom you have appointed.*

Because of their ingratitude, the most severe punishment should be meted out to them (*Alshich*).

Since *you have appointed* them to positions of power, they were included in the king's order that *all*

the provincial officials (v. 3) should humble themselve before the image *(Malbim).*[1]

לָא שָׂמוּ עֲלָךְ מַלְכָּא טְעֵם — *Have not accepted upon themselves, O King, your decree.*

The translation follows *R' Saadiah* and *R' Shmuel Masnuth,* who apparently render טְעֵם as *decree* (cf. *v.* 10 שָׂמְתָּ טְעֵם).

Rashi evidently renders טְעֵם as *counsel* (cf. עֵטָא וּטְעֵם 2:14). Thus, *they have not taken counsel on account of you, O king* (to heed your

1. The commentators ask why Daniel is not mentioned in this story. It is inconceivable that he was among those who bowed to the image.

This question is touched upon in the *Talmud (Sanhedrin* 93a). The consensus is that Daniel was not in Babylon when this occurred (see *comm.* to 2:46). Some maintain that Nebuchadnezzar's high regard for Daniel precluded them from accusing Daniel (*Ibn Ezra*). Others maintain that since Nebuchadnezzar invited the officials of his realm to participate in his spectacle, only Chananyah, Mishael, and Azaryah, who were *appointed over the affairs of the land of Babylon (v.* 12; 2:49), were invited. Daniel, notwithstanding the king's high regard for him, and although he was a private advisor to the king, did not serve in an official capacity, and therefore was not included in the king's edict (*Malbim;* see also *Malbim* cited in *comm.* to 2:48, 49).

טְעֵם °לֵאלָהָיךְ לָא פָלְחִין וּלְצֶלֶם דַּהֲבָא
דִּי הֲקֵימְתָּ לָא סָגְדִין: בֵּאדַיִן
נְבוּכַדְנֶצַּר בִּרְגַז וַחֲמָא אֲמַר לְהַיְתָיָה
לְשַׁדְרַךְ מֵישַׁךְ וַעֲבֵד נְגוֹ בֵּאדַיִן גֻּבְרַיָּא
אִלֵּךְ הֵיתָיוּ קֳדָם מַלְכָּא: עָנֵה נְבוּכַדְנֶצַּר
וְאָמַר לְהוֹן הַצְדָּא שַׁדְרַךְ מֵישַׁךְ וַעֲבֵד
נְגוֹ לֵאלָהַי לָא אִיתֵיכוֹן פָּלְחִין וּלְצֶלֶם
דַּהֲבָא דִּי הֲקֵימֶת לָא סָגְדִין: כְּעַן הֵן
אִיתֵיכוֹן עֲתִידִין דִּי בְעִדָּנָא דִּי־תִשְׁמְעוּן
קָל קַרְנָא מַשְׁרוֹקִיתָא °קִיתְרֹס שַׂבְּכָא
פְּסַנְתֵּרִין וְסוּמְפֹּנְיָה וְכֹל | זְנֵי זְמָרָא
תִּפְּלוּן וְתִסְגְּדוּן לְצַלְמָא דִּי־עַבְדֵת וְהֵן

decree). We have chosen R' Saadiah's translation here because it is the simpler of the two.

[Difficulties with both these renditions are evident. According to Rashi, part of the intended meaning of the verse is left unsaid and has to be added parenthetically. R' Saadiah's rendition leaves open the question why עֲלָךְ, upon yourself, is used where עֲלֵיהוֹן upon themselves, is meant.

[The context of this passage seems to point to a rendition of טְעֵם — importance. Thus; They have not placed upon you, O king, any importance. A parallel can be found in בִּטְעֵם חַמְרָא (5:2), where the context suggests, under the influence of wine. The concepts of importance and influence are related closely enough for them to be identified by a common noun in Aramaic (cf. R' Shmuel Masnuth).

[Accordingly רְחוּם בְּעֵל טְעֵם (Ezra 4:8) can easily be rendered, R'chum, a man of influence or power (cf. comm. ad loc.). Even the use of טְעֵם for decree could be related in concept. Laws and decrees, by their very nature, are but the stated intentions of the State, accompanied by covert or overt assurances that these will be enforced. A law that depends on the individual to freely make his choice whether to obey or not is surely no law. Thus laws are a way of wielding power and influence. The only use of טְעֵם which

probably could not be included in this concept is where we render טְעֵם as counsel. The well known Talmudical expression מַאי טַעְמָא, what is the reason, also falls into this category. These are probably related to the Hebrew טַעַם, taste, as in כְּטַעַם לְשַׁד הַשָּׁמֶן (Numbers 11:8). Interestingly, in Hebrew we also find טַעַם with the meaning reason, as in טָעַם זְקֵנִים יִקָּח (Job 12:20). (Cf. טַעֲמוּ וּרְאוּ Psalms 34:9.)]

לֵאלָהָךְ לָא פָלְחִין וּלְצֶלֶם דַּהֲבָא דִּי הֲקֵימְתָּא לָא סָגְדִין — Your god they do not worship, nor before the golden image that you set up do they prostrate themselves.

The superfluous remark, 'Your god they do not worship' served a a hint as to the reason that they do not prostrate themselves before the golden image. Their beliefs, which hinder them from paying homage to your gods, also preclude their aquiescing to your wish in the matter of the golden image. Thus their defiance reflects on all their coreligionists (Malbim).

Tosafos (Kesuvos 33b, s.v. אילמלי) quotes the contention of R'

3
13-15

gods they do not worship, nor before the golden image that you set up do they prostrate themselves.'

13 Then King Nebuchadnezzar, in anger and fury, commanded to bring Shadrach, Meshach, and Abed Nego; these men were then brought before the king. 14 Nebuchadnezzar shouted at them: 'Is it true, O Shadrach, Meshach, and Abed Nego, that my god you do not worship and that before the golden image I set up you do not prostrate yourselves? 15 Now, be ready, when you hear the sound of the horn, the whistle, the tambourine, the drum, the cymbals, the flute, and all kinds of music, to fall and prostrate yourselves before the image I made. And if you do

---

Tam that this verse supports the view that the golden image was not an idol. Otherwise the second phrase would be redundant, since the golden image would already have been included in, *Your god they do not worship.* Thus the defamers, in order to magnify the crime, added that in addition to refusing to bow to the golden image, the three Jews had also abstained from, worshipping the king's god (see introduction to this chapter).

13. Nebuchadnezzar's Fury

אֲמַר — *Commanded* [lit. *said*].
[I.e., his servants.]

14. הַצְדָּא — *Is it true ...?*
... An unusual word. *Rashi* relates it to צְדְיָא, *desolate* (cf. *Onkelos* to *Genesis* 1:2 תֹהוּ). *Is then my decree meaningless* (=*desolate*) *in your eyes?*
R' *Hai Gaon* (quoted by *Radak*) compares this word to וַאֲשֶׁר לֹא צָדָה, *and one who did not lie in wait,* i.e.,

did not intend to murder *(Exodus* 21:13). *Is it with intent, Shadrach, Meshach, and Abed Nego that my gods you do not worship ... ?* This is the view of R' *Yosei bar Chanina (Vayikra Rabbah* 33:6).

A third view, cited by *Radak* and shared by *Ibn Ezra,* is הַצְדָּא =*true. Is it true, Shadrach ... ?* This is the view of R' *Abba bar Kahana. (Vayikra Rabbah, ibid.).* The translation follows this view because it blends best into the context.

15. כְּעַן הֵן אִיתֵיכוֹן עֲתִידִין — *Now, be ready.*
The translation follows R' *Shmuel Masnuth* (cf. *Rashi; Ibn Ezra*) who renders this phrase a command, *'Be ready ... to.' Metzudos* understands הֵן to represent the conditional *if* (as in וְהֵן לָא, *and if not). If you are ready to ...* The consequence of this acquiescence to the king's will is not spelled out, it being understood that in this case all would end well. A similar instance is found in *Genesis* (4:15) where the threat, *therefore whoever slays*

לָא תִסְגְּדוּן בַּהּ־שַׁעֲתָא תִתְרְמוֹן לְגוֹא־
אַתּוּן נוּרָא יָקֵדְתָּא וּמַן־הוּא אֱלָהּ דִּי
טז יְשֵׁיזְבִנְכוֹן מִן־יְדָי: עֲנוֹ שַׁדְרַךְ מֵישַׁךְ
וַעֲבֵד נְגוֹ וְאָמְרִין לְמַלְכָּא נְבוּכַדְנֶצַּר
לָא־חַשְׁחִין אֲנַחְנָא עַל־דְּנָה פִּתְגָם
יז לַהֲתָבוּתָךְ: הֵן אִיתַי אֱלָהַנָא דִּי־אֲנַחְנָא
פָלְחִין יָכִל לְשֵׁיזָבוּתַנָא מִן־אַתּוּן נוּרָא

Cain...is not completed (see *Rashi, ibid.*).

The king gave them another opportunity to submit to his decree, contrary to his proclaimed determination that *whoever does not fall and prostrate himself will be thrown instantly into a flaming kiln.* He did so out of deference to their friend Daniel and to their high rank (*Ibn Ezra; Ralbag*).

Because the defamers had attributed the trio's refusal to fall before the image to their religion (cf. *comm. v.* 12), they were not guilty of non-compliance with Nebuchadnezzar's edict. Since freedom of religion was allowed in the king's realm, refusal to obey any specific law on religious grounds would be automatically exempt under the law. Now that the king had been made aware of this matter, he ruled specifically that in this case the death sentence should apply in spite of religious objections. This would overrule the king's general policy of religious freedom. Any freedom granted under Nebuchadnezzar's autocratic rule was, after all, given at the king's pleasure and could be revoked any time at his whim (*Malbim*).

וּמַן הוּא אֱלָהּ ... — *And who is the*

god Who will save you from my hands?

[A transparent hint that he was aware of, and insensitive to, the religious nature of their objection.]

This vain boast of Nebuchadnezzar directly contradicts his humble recognition of God's omnipotence in his declaration, *In truth ... your God is the God of gods and the Lord of kings* (2:47).

Alshich cites the view of the *Zohar* (*Parshas VaYeshev s.v.* לְמַעַן הַצִּיל אֹתוֹ מִיָּדָם [37:22]) that even though God intercedes to save someone endangered by the forces of nature — e.g., drowning or wild animals — he does not interfere if the person is threatened by another human being. To do so is to tamper with the principle of בְּחִירָה, *free determination*, the cornerstone of God's purpose for this world; it is His intention that humans, with their gift of their own בְּחִירָה, *free determination*, should recognize His Presence in the world and submit to His will. Thus, Nebuchadnezzar was saying correctly, that even though God's intercession could save them from the fire, *who ... will save you from 'my hands'?*

[Clearly, though, the *Zohar* does not place it beyond God's omnipotence to hamper a rational be-

not prostrate yourselves, you will instantly be thrown into a flaming kiln, and who is the god who will save you from my hands?'

¹⁶ *Shadrach, Meshach, and Abed Nego answered the king: 'O Nebuchadnezzar, we are not concerned to reply to you about this matter.* ¹⁷ *Behold there is our God Whom we worship — He is able to save us;*

ing. It is evident from the words of the *Zohar* that it would constitute a serious breach in the intended order of the universe for God to interfere with a man's freedom of choice. Only a high degree of merit on the part of the intended victim could justify God's interference with the free will of the attacker. This is indicated by Nebuchadnezzar's own boastful words. He did not say וּמַן ... דִּי יָכֵל לְשֵׁיזְבִנְכוֹן, *who ... is able to save you ...* rather he said, וּמַן הוּא ... דִּי יְשֵׁיזְבִנְכוֹן , *who ... 'will' save you.*]

16⁻18 'He is able to save us.'

16. לְמַלְכָּא נְבוּכַדְנֶצַּר — *(To) the king: 'O Nebuchadnezzar'.*

'If [Scripture honors him with the title] *king* why [did they address him by his personal name] *Nebuchadnezzar*, and if [it was proper to call him] *Nebuchadnezzar* why [does Scripture honor him with the title] *king?* They said thus to him, 'If it is to pay taxes you are king. But for this thing that you order us to do you are just Nebuchadnezzar' (*Vayikra Rabbah* 33:6 quoted by *Rashi*).

The name of Nebuchadnezzar in conjunction with his title occurs many times (e.g., *v.* 9). The objection of the *Midrash* to this form here is because the cantillation mark under לְמַלְכָּא is an *esnachta* which

indicates a pause, as a semi-colon does in English. Therefore the word *Nebuchadnezzar* is the beginning of the quotation. Thus, Chananyah, Mishael, and Azaryah addressed the king and said to him, '...*Nebuchadnezzar! We are not ... '* (*Kad HaKemach* cited by *Minchas Shai*).

לָא חַשְׁחִין — *We are not concerned.*

We do not care to confer in order to find a suitable way to answer you (*Rashi*).

Without the words added by *Rashi* the verse does not make sense since in fact they did answer the king.

Ibn Ezra and *R' Saadiah* translate: *We do not need.* There is no need to answer since the answer is clear: *Our God ... is able to rescue us ... from your hand, O king. But if He does not ...* This rendition has been chosen because of its relative simplicity.

[We find חשש in the *Mishnah* meaning *fear*. In *Pesachim* (9a) we have אֵין חוֹשְׁשִׁין שֶׁמָּא גֵּירְרָה חוּלְדָה, *We do not fear* [the possibility] *that a weasel dragged ...* Thus we could translate: *We do not fear to answer you.*].

17. יָכֵל לְשֵׁיזָבוּתַנָא ... יְשֵׁיזִב — *He is able to save us; ... He can rescue.*

The punctuation follows *Rashi* (and the cantillation): *He is able to save us,* from any misfortune [in general. Specifically,] *from the flaming kiln and from your hand, O king, He can rescue.*

יח   יְקִדְתָּא וּמִן־יְדָךְ מַלְכָּא יְשֵׁיזִב: וְהֵן לָא

יְדִיעַ לֶהֱוֵא־לָךְ מַלְכָּא דִּי °לֵאלָהָיךְ לָא־

אִיתַנָא פָלְחִין וּלְצֶלֶם דַּהֲבָא דִּי הֲקֵימְתָּ

יט   לָא נִסְגֻּד: בֵּאדַיִן   נְבוּכַדְנֶצַּר

הִתְמְלִי חֱמָא וּצְלֵם אַנְפּוֹהִי °אֶשְׁתַּנּוּ

עַל־שַׁדְרַךְ מֵישַׁךְ וַעֲבֵד נְגוֹ עָנֵה וְאָמַר

לְמֵזֵא לְאַתּוּנָא חַד־שִׁבְעָה עַל דִּי חֲזֵה

כ   לְמֶזְיֵהּ: וּלְגֻבְרִין גִּבָּרֵי־חַיִל דִּי בְחַיְלֵהּ

אֲמַר לְכַפָּתָה לְשַׁדְרַךְ מֵישַׁךְ וַעֲבֵד נְגוֹ

כא   לְמִרְמֵא לְאַתּוּן נוּרָא יָקִדְתָּא: בֵּאדַיִן

גֻּבְרַיָּא אִלֵּךְ   כְּפִתוּ   בְּסַרְבָּלֵיהוֹן

°פַּטִּישֵׁיהוֹן   וְכַרְבְּלָתְהוֹן   וּלְבֻשֵׁיהוֹן

Metzudos, however, punctuates differently. *He is able to save us from the flaming kiln; and from your hand, O King, He can rescue.*

מִן־אַתּוּן נוּרָא יָקִדְתָּא וּמִן־יְדָךְ מַלְכָּא יְשֵׁיזִב — *From the flaming kiln and from your hand, O king, He can rescue.*

Not only from the *flaming kiln* which does not act by its own determination can He rescue us, but even *from your hand, O king.* Although you act with free will, He can rescue us if He wishes (*Alshich; Malbim* cf. *v.* 15).

19‑23. Into the Flaming Kiln

19. עַל־שַׁדְרַךְ —*At Shadrach.*

[This refers back to הִתְמְלִי חֱמָא, *was filled with fury. Nebuchadnezzar was filled with fury ... at Shadrach.* עַל may also be rendered *because.* Thus: *Nebuchadnezzar was filled with fury because of Shadrach...*

עָנֵה וְאָמַר — *He loudly commanded.* He commanded his servants.

לְמֵזֵא לְאַתּוּנָא חַד־שִׁבְעָה ... — *To heat the kiln to seven times ...*

Nebuchadnezzar thought — as did many others in his day — that Hashem's power to subjugate the forces of nature to His will did not arise from His being the source of all life. They thought of the forces of nature as independent of Him, and even acting contrary to His will. God, in their conception, was only the greatest among powers, and therefore under favorable conditions one might combine great forces to temporarily overcome even the power of God. Therefore — so thought the king — even if God could easily save them from an ordinary fire, His task would be compounded if the fire was seven times as hot. In addition the king ordered that the death sentence be carried out in haste and that the executioners be picked from the

3
18-21
from the flaming kiln and from your hand, O king,
He can rescue. ¹⁸ *But if he does not, let it be known to*
you, O king, that we do not worship your god, and
before the golden image you set up we shall not
prostrate ourselves.'

¹⁹ *Then Nebuchadnezzar was filled with fury at*
Shadrach, Meshach, and Abed Nego, and the form of
his face was contorted; he loudly commanded to heat
the kiln to seven times more than it was normally
heated. ²⁰ *And he commanded strong men of his*
guard to bind Shadrach, Meshach, and Abed Nego
and to throw them into the flaming kiln. ²¹ *Then*
these men were bound in their cloaks, their pants,
their robes, and their clothing, and were thrown into

---

strongest men (*v.* 20-22). With this combination of safeguards, the king imagined he could thwart God (*Malbim*).

21. כְּפִתוּ בְּסַרְבָּלֵיהוֹן — *Were bound in their cloaks.*

They went to the king arrayed in their official vestments. Though they knew that sentence was to be pronounced upon themselves, they did not change their clothing in order not to demean their noble standing. From this our Sages learn: Even in the time of danger a person should not change from [the garb of] his high office (*Sanhedrin* 92). By not appearing afraid and confused, he will shame his enemies (*Rashi, ibid.*).

Ralbag comments that this teaches us that when confronted with martyrdom, one should emulate the example of Chananyah, Mishael, and Azaryah, and offer one's life gracefully and cheerfully. Chananyah and his companions did not don sackcloth when they went

to the king, rather they went arrayed in their best (*Toaliyos*).

בְּסַרְבָּלֵיהוֹן — *In their cloaks.*

Ibn Ezra describes this as the outer apparel. The same description emerges from *Rashi* and *Radak*. Other translations offered include:
— *stockings, or shoes (R' Sa'adiah);*
— *turbans (Bereishis Rabbah 36:6);*
— *pants (Mosaf He'Aruch).*

פַּטְשֵׁיהוֹן — *Their pants.*

This translation from *Yelamdenu* (cited in *Aruch*) is adopted by *Radak, R' Saadiah* (as an alternate translation), and *Ibn Ezra.*

וְכַרְבְּלָתְהוֹן — [*And*] *their robes.*

Rashi, Ibn Ezra, and *R' Shmuel Masnuth* from וְדָוִיד מְכֻרְבָּל בִּמְעִיל בּוּץ (*I Chronicles* 15:27).

Other translations are *hats* (*Aruch* citing *Yelamdenu; Radak; R' Saadiah*), *wraps, cloaks,* or *shirts (R' Saadiah).*

וּלְבוּשֵׁיהוֹן — *And their clothing.*

I.e., the rest of their clothing (*Rashi*).

כב וּרְמִיו לְגוֹא-אַתּוּן נוּרָא יָקִדְתָּא: כָּל-קֳבֵל
דְּנָה מִן-דִּי מִלַּת מַלְכָּא מַחְצְפָה וְאַתּוּנָא
אֵזֵה יַתִּירָה גֻּבְרַיָּא אִלֵּךְ דִּי הַסִּקוּ
לְשַׁדְרַךְ מֵישַׁךְ וַעֲבֵד נְגוֹ קַטִּל הִמּוֹן
כג שְׁבִיבָא דִּי נוּרָא: וְגֻבְרַיָּא אִלֵּךְ תְּלָתֵּהוֹן
שַׁדְרַךְ מֵישַׁךְ וַעֲבֵד נְגוֹ נְפַלוּ לְגוֹא-אַתּוּן-
כד נוּרָא יָקִדְתָּא מְכַפְּתִין: אֱדַיִן
נְבוּכַדְנֶצַּר מַלְכָּא תְּוַהּ וְקָם בְּהִתְבְּהָלָה
עָנֵה וְאָמַר לְהַדָּבְרוֹהִי הֲלָא גֻבְרִין
תְּלָתָה רְמֵינָא לְגוֹא-נוּרָא מְכַפְּתִין עָנַיִן
כה וְאָמְרִין לְמַלְכָּא יַצִּיבָא מַלְכָּא: עָנֵה
וְאָמַר הָא-אֲנָה חָזֵה גֻּבְרִין אַרְבְּעָה
שְׁרַיִן מַהְלְכִין בְּגוֹא-נוּרָא וַחֲבָל לָא-
אִיתַי בְּהוֹן וְרֵוֵהּ דִּי °רְבִיעָיא דָּמֵה לְבַר-

° רְבִיעָאָה ק'

---

22. כָּל-קֳבֵל דְּנָה...קַטִּל הִמּוֹן שְׁבִיבָא
דִּי נוּרָא — *Because of ... were killed
by a tongue of flames.*

Their lack of caution because of
their haste and the extraordinary
heat of the oven combined to bring
about their deaths (*Malbim; Metzudos*).

23. נְפַלוּ — *Fell.*

Our verse indicates that the three
Jews were not thrown or pushed
into the flames, rather they *fell*. It
seems that the executioners were
killed as soon as they brought them
to the opening of the oven, for in *v.*
22 we read דִּי הַסִּקוּ, *who carried up,*
not דִּי הַפִּלוּ, *who threw in.* As the
Jews were already over the opening

of the kiln, they fell in by
themselves as soon as the executioners lost consciousness
(*Malbim*).[1]

24-25. Four Unbound Men

25. הָא-אֲנָה חָזֵה — *Lo, I see.*

[Since the kiln was below ground
level (see note to *v.* 22) and Nebuchadnezzar did not approach it until
later (see *v.* 26), it is difficult to understand how he was able to look
into the pit. The *Talmud* (*Sanhedrin* 92b) declares that this was a
miracle. Six miracles happened on
that day: the [floor of the] kiln rose
[to ground level], the walls of the
kiln were breached, its plaster was

---

1. From *Rashi* to *Sanhedrin* (92b s.v. צף and נפרץ) we see that the *kiln* was a pit dug into
the earth with masonry walls. Probably these walls rose above ground level. Therefore
Chananyah, Mishael, and Azaryah had to be *carried up*. Thus, when the *men who carried
them up* were killed, Chananyah, Mishael, and Azaryah had not yet been thrown into the pit,
but were on top of its walls. They fell in later by themselves (*v.* 22).

the flaming kiln. 22 Thereupon, because of the king's preemptory command and because the kiln was so overheated, these men who carried up Shadrach, Meshach, and Abed Nego were killed by a tongue of flame. 23 And these three men, Shadrach, Meshach and Abed Nego, fell bound into the flaming kiln.

24 Then King Nebuchadnezzar, bewildered, stood up in haste. He exclaimed to his ministers, 'Did we not throw three bound men into the fire?'

They answered the king, 'True, O King.'

25 He exclaimed, 'Lo, I see four unbound men, walking in the fire, and there is no wound on them;

---

dissolved (see *Rashi ad. loc.*), the image was overturned on its face, four nations were consumed by the fire (see *comm. v.* 27), and the prophet Ezekiel resurrected the dead in the plain of Dura (see *Ezekiel ch.37*). *Midrash Shir HaShirim* (7:9) and *Tanchuma (Tzav 3)* add that Nebuchadnezzar himself was partly burned by the fire. [See prefatory notes to *vs. 31-33*.]

וַחֲבָל לָא־אִיתַי בְּהוֹן — *And there is no wound on them.*

'When wicked Nebuchadnezzar threw Chananyah, Mishael, and Azaryah into the fiery furnace, Yurkami the [angel appointed as] heavenly prince of hail stood before the Holy One, Blessed be He, and said, 'Lord of the World! I will go down and cool the furnace and save these righteous men from the fiery furnace.'

Then Gabriel said to him, 'The might of the Holy One, Blessed be He, is not [best displayed] in this [manner], because you are the heavenly prince of hail and everyone knows that water extinguishes fire. I am the heavenly prince of fire; I will go down and cool [the kiln] from inside and heat it from outside, and [thus] I will perform נֵס בְּתוֹךְ נֵס, *a miracle within a miracle' (Pesachim* 118a; see *Rashbam).*

One way to accomplish this miracle would have been to miraculously effect the quenching of the fire (the heavenly prince of hail); but an even greater miracle happened. The fire not only retained its full power, it even multiplied in intensity and killed the people surrounding the furnace. It melted off the fetters binding Chananyah, Mishael, and Azaryah. Yet did them [and their clothing] no harm *(Mayenei HaYeshuah* 6:4).

[*Rav Zadok haKohen of Lublin* explains the expression נֵס בְּתוֹךְ נֵס this way; Had the fire been quenched suddenly by some phenomenon of nature (e.g., a flood, rainstorm) the coincidence would have been נֵס בְּתוֹךְ הַטֶבַע, *a miracle within the bounds of nature;* but to leave the fire with its power of destruction intact and still save Chananyah and friends is a miracle which alters the forces of nature and is therefore נֵס בְּתוֹךְ נֵס, *a miracle within a miracle.* It is a miracle by the very coincide of its occurence, in addition to being a miracle by its peculiar nature (*Sichos Malachei haShareis* p. 67).]

כו אֱלָהִין: בֵּאדַיִן קְרֵב נְבוּכַדְנֶצַּר
לִתְרַע אַתּוּן נוּרָא יָקֵדְתָּא עָנֵה וְאָמַר
שַׁדְרַךְ מֵישַׁךְ וַעֲבֵד־נְגוֹ עַבְדוֹהִי דִּי־
אֱלָהָא °עִלָּאָה פֻּקוּ וֶאֱתוֹ בֵּאדַיִן נָפְקִין
שַׁדְרַךְ מֵישַׁךְ וַעֲבֵד נְגוֹ מִן־גּוֹא נוּרָא:
כז וּמִתְכַּנְּשִׁין אֲחַשְׁדַּרְפְּנַיָּא סִגְנַיָּא וּפַחֲוָתָא
וְהַדָּבְרֵי מַלְכָּא חָזַיִן לְגֻבְרַיָּא אִלֵּךְ דִּי לָא־
שְׁלֵט נוּרָא °בְגֶשְׁמְהוֹן וּשְׂעַר רֵאשְׁהוֹן
לָא הִתְחָרַךְ וְסָרְבָּלֵיהוֹן לָא שְׁנוֹ וְרֵיחַ

°עִלָּאָה ק׳

°בְּגֶשְׁמְהוֹן ק׳

דָּמֵה לְבַר־אֱלָהִין — *Is like an angel's.*

When Sennacherib's army was miraculously wiped out by the angel of God on the outskirts of Jerusalem (*Isaiah* 37:36), Nebuchadnezzar was among the few survivors and was privileged to see the angel. Otherwise how did he know that *the form of the fourth is like an angel?* (*Rashi* from *Sanhedrin* 95b; cf. *Pesikta Rabbasi* 36).

לְבַר־אֱלָהִין — *An angel's.*

This is not the only place where angels are called בְּנֵי אֱלֹהִים. The בְּנֵי אֱלֹהִים in *Job* (1:6) are also clearly angels. *Rambam* (*Yesodei HaTorah* 2:7) lists בְּנֵי אֱלֹהִים among the ten categories of angels. [See

commentary end of 2:11.] *Metzudos* suggests that this title is accorded them because we view them as if they were part of the Divine household.[1]

26-27. Ineffective Fire

27. וּמִתְכַּנְּשִׁין אֲחַשְׁדַּרְפְּנַיָּא — *[And] the satraps ... assembled.*

Of the seven different categories enumerated in *v.* 2-3, only the first three are mentioned here. 'Four nations were consumed in the fire' (*Sanhedrin* 92b quoted by *Rashi;* see *comm.* to *v.* 2).

Rashi comments that they were consumed by the *tongue of flame* (*v.* 22) that destroyed the men who

1. The existence of angels is an indisputable fact according to the Torah. 'That angels exist does not need proof from the Torah, because the Torah mentions this explicitly in many places' (*Moreh Nevuchim* 2:4). *Abarbanel* (*Genesis*) states emphatically that to deny the existence of the angels is equal to questioning the validity of the Torah itself.

But there is controversy about the form these angels take. *Rambam* (*Yesodei HaTorah* 2:4; *Moreh Nevuchim* 2:42; cf. *Ma'aseh HaShem* to *Vayera*) is of the opinion that since the angels are spirits (intellectual beings) without bodies, they cannot be perceived by the senses. Thus it follows that wherever mention is made of seeing an angel, this is part of a prophetic vision. Since Nebuchadnezzar surely did not aspire to the lofty heights of prophecy, *Rambam* and his school of thought have to interpret this verse allegorically. *Abarbanel* suggests that Nebuchadnezzar's reference to a fourth man means that he was attributing the miracle of the trio's deliverance from the fire to Daniel's credit, and it is Daniel who in the king's eyes is דָּמֵה לְבַר אֱלָהִין, *like an angel.*

Ramban (*Genesis* 18:1) and *Abarbanel* (*ibid.*) object strenuously to *Rambam's* opinion. The words of the Sages quoted above also stand in apparent contradiction to *Rambam*.

Ramban believes that though the angels are spiritual and as such cannot be perceived by the senses, they can nevertheless be perceived by spiritual means (בְּעֵינֵי הַשֵּׂכֶל). Moreover,

3

26-27

and the form of the fourth is like an angel's.'
²⁶ Then Nebuchadnezzar approached the opening
of the flaming kiln. He exclaimed: 'Shadrach, Me-
shach, and Abed Nego, servants of the Supreme God,
step out and come here!' Then Shadrach, Meshach,
and Abed Nego stepped out of the fire. ²⁷ The
satraps, nobles, governors, and ministers of the king
assembled, saw these men over whose bodies the fire
had had no effect, the hair of whose heads was not
singed, whose cloaks were unaltered, and who had

were to throw Chananyah, Mishael, and Azaryah into the fire.

[Taken literally, the above passage of the *Talmud* seems to say clearly that these four latter categories were nations. However, *Rashi* (*Sanhedrin* 92b) comments that the verse refers to the rulers (of these four nations) and their henchmen who participated in the attempt to burn Chananyah, Mishael, and Azaryah. Perhaps he understood the expression to mean four governments [i.e., the leaders] rather than four entire nations. However, since Nebuchadnezzar had assembled the leaders of *all* nations to witness the execution, it remains unclear why only these four were singled out. Possibly these four were the only ones who volunteered to help in the burning. If so, we may conjecture that the King's call went out equally to *all* nations. These four, because they would later stand out as participants in the burning, were specified as having been called to witness the spectacle.

Midrash Tanchuma (*Tzav* 3 cf. Buber ed. p.14) substitutes אומות, *nations*, for the *Talmudic* reading of מַלְכֵיוֹת, *kingdoms*, the implication being that their *populations* attended.

[*Rashi* (*v.* 2) comments עבומי'ז, *idol worshipers*. This is clearly a version inserted at the insistence of gentile censors, since the

idolatry of the audience is immaterial to the context. Presumably, *Rashi's* own version was גויִם, *nations*, a usage which the censors found offensive. Even according to this version, the four leading participants are singled out for mention.

Still unclear is why these four nations participated so eagerly. Perhaps they wished to impress the King with their outstanding loyalty to his will.]

Midrash Tanchuma (ibid.) holds all the categories listed to be names of nations: 'In the beginning there were eight nations, as it is written ...' (The difficulty raised by the number *eight* is discussed by *Anaf Yosef*, ibid., and *Matnos Kehunah* to *Shir HaShirim Rabbah* 7:9).

[*Shir HaShirim Rabbah* (7:9) is puzzling because, after referring to *the nations* that were burned, it goes on to translate all seven terms as different types of government officials.]

Malbim conjectures that these four categories were priests of the fire cult which was widespread in Persia. Their death in the fire is taken figuratively — i.e., the embarrassment brought upon them by the miracle of the fire caused them to destroy themselves.

whenever the angels are spoken about in human terms — e.g., when the angels visited Abraham (*Genesis* 18) — it is because the angels have in this instance temporarily adopted a human form (just as the soul, which is also spiritual and has existence without the body, comes to rest within a corporeal body). This adopted body of the angels is however not of the same substance as a human body — being of an ethereal nature — and is therefore only visible to the eyes of the chosen few. Thus it was possible that Nebuchadnezzar — although he certainly did not deserve to see angels in their human form of his own merit — was allowed to see the angel since it so suited the purpose of God. He did not have to ascend to the heights of prophecy to do so. [For other opinions about this topic see *Abarbanel* and *Ma'aseh Hashem* to *Genesis* 18:1.]

כח נּוּר לָא עֲדָת בְּהוֹן: עֲנֵה נְבוּכַדְנֶצַּר וְאָמַר
בְּרִיךְ אֱלָהֲהוֹן דִּי־שַׁדְרַךְ מֵישַׁךְ וַעֲבֵד נְגוֹ
דִּי־שְׁלַח מַלְאֲכֵהּ וְשֵׁיזִב לְעַבְדוֹהִי דִּי
הִתְרְחִצוּ עֲלוֹהִי וּמִלַּת מַלְכָּא שַׁנִּיו וִיהַבוּ
°גֶשְׁמֵיהוֹן דִּי לָא־יִפְלְחוּן וְלָא־יִסְגְּדוּן   ° גֶשְׁמְהוֹן ק׳
כט לְכָל־אֱלָהּ לָהֵן לֵאלָהֲהוֹן: וּמִנִּ֫י שִׂים
טְעֵם דִּי כָל־עַם אֻמָּה וְלִשָּׁן דִּי־יֵאמַר
°שָׁלָה עַל־אֱלָהֲהוֹן דִּי־שַׁדְרַךְ מֵישַׁךְ   ° שָׁלוּ ק׳
וַעֲבֵד נְגוֹא הַדָּמִין יִתְעֲבֵד וּבַיְתֵהּ נְוָלִי
יִשְׁתַּוֵּה כָּל־קֳבֵל דִּי לָא אִיתַי אֱלָהּ אָחֳרָן
ל דִּי־יִכֻּל לְהַצָּלָה כִּדְנָה: בֵּאדַיִן מַלְכָּא
הַצְלַח לְשַׁדְרַךְ מֵישַׁךְ וַעֲבֵד נְגוֹ בִּמְדִינַת

וְרֵיחַ נוּר לָא עֲדָת בְּהוֹן — *And who
had not absorbed the smell of fire.*

Even if they had found some way
to protect themselves by natural (or
supernatural) means, the smell of
fire would have remained with
them. Even the most hardened
skeptic would have to be convinced
God's hand had intervened here
(*Malbim*).

**28⁻29. "There is no other god
able to rescue so."**

28. דִּי־שְׁלַח מַלְאֲכֵהּ — *Who sent His
angel.*

Nebuchadnezzar here changes
his wording when he uses מַלְאֲכֵהּ
instead of בַּר־אֱלָהִין (*v.25*). Note of
this is made in the *Talmud.*

'At that moment [when the king
said דָּמֵהּ לְבַר אֱלָהִין] an angel came
down and smote that evildoer on his
mouth and said to him: 'Correct
your words. Does He then have a
son?'

Then he said, 'Blessed ... Who
sent His angel'; it does not say
Who sent His son' (*Yerushalmi
Shabbos* 6:9

[We find other places where angels
are referred to as בְּנֵי אֱלֹהִים. In *Job* (1:6)
we find this phrase; angels are clearly
indicated. *Rambam* (*Yesodei HaTorah*
2:7) counts בְּנֵי אֱלֹהִים among the ten
categories of angels. Another instance is
the famous prayer בְּרִיךְ שְׁמֵיהּ derived
from the *Zohar.*]

It is obvious that בְּנֵי in this phrase is
not to be translated *sons*, but as
denoting members if a certain group
(perhaps similar to the Arabic *ibn*). Examples of this usage abound, e.g., בֶּן
שְׁלֹשָׁה עֶשֵׂר, *a thirteen-year old,* or בֶּן
מָוֶת, *one who is liable to the death penalty* (cf. *Sefer HaShorashim* by *Radak*
s.v. בנה). This would explain the usage
בְּנֵי אֱלֹהִים.

In Nebuchadnezzar's case, however,
his intended meaning of the word בַּר
was *son*, as evidenced by the change in
language from בַּר אֱלָהִין to מַלְאֲכֵה. That
Nebuchadnezzar intended the heretical
meaning that God had a son ח״ו, may be

3

28-30

not absorbed the smell of fire.

²⁸ Nebuchadnezzar exclaimed: 'Blessed is the God of Shadrach, Meshach, and Abed Nego, Who sent His angel and saved His servants who relied on Him and disobeyed the king's order and offered their bodies in order not to worship or prostrate themselves to any god, other than their God. ²⁹ I issue a decree that any people, nation, and language who will speak amiss about the God of Shadrach, Meshach, and Abed Nego, will be cut to bits, and his house will be turned into a dunghill, because there is no other god able to rescue so.' ³⁰ Then the king promoted Shadrach, Meshach, and Abed Nego in the land of Babylon.

further defended in light of *Rambam's* view that an evildoer's actions should always be held suspect to the highest degree. The dictum הֱוֵה דָן אֶת כָּל הָאָדָם לְכַף זְכוּת, *judge everyone favorably*, applies only to a person whose character is yet unknown to you (*Avos* 1:6; see *Rambam's comm.* there). Thus, Nebuchadnezzar's characterization of the fourth one as similar to a בַּר־אֱלָהִין would be strongly suspect (*Salman Mul Eder, R' S. Zahlen*, part I, p.5, ed. Prague; Cf. *Nitzutzei HaZohar* by *R' Reuven Margolies* on *Zohar Vayakhel*, p.205 בְּרִיךְ שְׁמֵיהּ and *Siddur Tzelosa D'Avraham* by R' Verdiger).

דִּי הִתְרְחִצוּ עֲלוֹהִי — *Who relied on Him.*

[Their trust in God was so deep that it transcended their natural concern for their temporal life. They accepted the fulfillment of God's will as the best possible way for themselves, regardless of the physical consequences they might suffer. In their own words; *Our God Whom we worship. He is able to save us ... If ... not, let it be*

known to you ... that we do not worship your gods (vs. 17-18). This is truly the ultimate degree of trust in God (cf. *Chazon Ish; Inyanei Emunah uBitachon Ve'od* ch. 2).]

שַׁנִּיו — *Disobeyed* [lit. *altered*].

וִיהַבוּ גֶשְׁמְהוֹן — *And offered their bodies.*

This refers back to דִּי הִתְרְחִצוּ עֲלוֹהִי, *who relied on Him,* — i.e., their trust in God was so great as to enable them to give their bodies in order to comply with His will. The strength of their resolve had its roots in the knowledge that only their bodies were in danger. The center of their being, the soul, was inviolate (*Alshich*).

29. כָּל עַם — *Any people.*

[Any member of *any people, nation,* or *language.* Thus the sentence ends in singular — (he) will ... and his house.]

הַדָּמִין — [*To*] *bits.* [See commentary to 2:5.]

לא בָּבֶל: נְבוּכַדְנֶצַּר מַלְכָּא לְכָל־
עַמְמַיָּא אֻמַּיָּא וְלִשָׁנַיָּא דִּי־°דָארִין בְּכָל־
לב אַרְעָא שְׁלָמְכוֹן יִשְׂגֵּא: אָתַיָּא וְתִמְהַיָּא דִּי

❧Epilogue

From here on we find no mention of Chananyah, Mishael and Azaryah. In the *Talmud* (*Sanhedrin* 93a) several opinions about this are cited.

One view holds that they died soon after this episode. Another view maintains that they emigrated to the Holy Land and lived out their lives there. According to this view, when Scripture mentions the friends of Yehoshua the high-priest and calls them אַנְשֵׁי מוֹפֵת, *men of miracle* (Zechariah 3:8), Chananyah, Mishael, and Azaryah are meant.

Abarbanel (*Mayenei HaYeshuah* 6:3) conjectures that since they had been victimized by Nebuchadnezzar's cruelty and despotism in the affair of the golden image they did not feel safe in his proximity.

[This seemingly contradicts the view of the Sages (*Yoma* 54a) that up to the reign of the Persians no Jews were living in *Eretz Yisrael* (see *Rashi*, ibid s.v. נ'ב שָׁנָה). However, *Rambam* (*Sefer HaMitzvos, Mitzvas Asseh* 153) also seems to contradict this (see *HaSagos HaRamban*, ad loc). The solution that suggests itself is that since the language of the above passage of the *Talmud* is that 'No person passed through *Yehudah*,' it is possible that *Yehudah* is used in its narrower sense — i.e., the portion of *Eretz Yisrael* occupied by the kingdom of Yehudah. Or perhaps the term *Yehudah* is used the way it was understood in the time of the *Mishnah* when *Eretz Yisrael* was comprised of the three provinces — Yehudah, Galilee, and Trans-Jordan (see *Sheviis* 9:2 and *Bava Basra* 38a). Although in four other places where this passage occurs in the *Midrashim* and *Yerushalmi* the reading is *Eretz Yisrael* where the Babylonian *Talmud* has *Yehudah*, a strong argument can be made for the greater accuracy of the Babylonian *Talmud* where this passage occurs twice.]

Another compelling argument is that we do find evidence in Scripture of the occupation of *Eretz Yisrael* at the time. In Ezra (4,1) we find *the enemies of Yehudah and Binyamin* trying to hinder the rebuilding of the Temple soon after the first exodus from Babylon. These enemies are clearly the Kuthim so well known from the *Mishnah*, as seen in vs.9-10 (ibid. cf. *Rashi*, ad.loc.). Further impetus is given to this argument by the passage in *Yerushalmi* (*Kilayim* 9:3 42b) which clearly says that the Kuthim were in *Eretz Yisrael* during the period it lay desolate. This passage is repeated in three other places. The known habitat of the Kuthim was in the part of *Eretz Yisrael* occupied by the kingdom of the ten tribes (*II Kings* 17:24).

S. Buber's suggested emendation of the text (*Pesikta D'Rav Kahana* p. 114, note 77) is unacceptable for various reasons.]

In conclusion, *Abarbanel* suggests that the underlying idea of the story is the parallel that we can draw from it to the Jewish nation's condition in the exile. Even at times of the greatest adversity we should not forget that God's הַשְׁגָחָה, *Providence*, is always with us. This is the lesson taught to us by the conduct of Chananyah, Mishael, and Azaryah in their hour of trial.

❧Prefatory Note to verses 3:31-4:34
Nebuchadnezzar's Letter

At first glance Nebuchadnezzar's letter appears to be the sequel to the miracle of Chananyah, Mishael, and Azaryah s rescue from the fire. In response to his recognition of omnipotence, Nebuchadnezzar sent a proclamation of his newly found faith throughout his lands. This seems to have been R' Saadiah's understanding.

Support for this view can be found in *Shir HaShirim Rabbah* (7:9) and *Yalkut* (Daniel 3). I* raises a few questions. Why does Nebuchadnezzar say, *The signs and the wonders ... performed with 'me'* ... (*Shir HaShirim Rabbah* nevertheless explains that Nebuchadnezzar's own deliverance from the fire is meant [See commmentary to v.25] but since this episode is not

3
31-32

³¹ **F**rom King Nebuchadnezzar,
*To all the peoples, nations, and languages
that dwell throughout the earth:
May your peace be multiplied!*
³² *The signs and the wonders*

mentioned explicitly in Scripture, it is probable that the *Midrash* does not mean for us to accept this as the literal interpretation but rather as a homiletical exegesis.)

Another difficulty is the style of Chapter 4. This chapter is a departure from the first three chapters, all related in the third person. Here Nebuchadnezzar himself recounts the story of his suffering.

All this suggests that *vs.*31-33 are connected to Chapter 4 comprising together with it the whole text of Nebuchadnezzar's letter. Thus the letter started in verse 31 of chapter 3 ends only with the conclusion of Chapter 4. Verses 25-31 in Chapter 4, which depart in style from the rest of the letter, are probably an addition to Nebuchadnezzar's own words by the divinely inspired authors [1] of this book to fill in historical data not supplied by the letter. These facts were too well known to the people to whom the letter was addressed to have needed mentioning in it, or were·too embarrassing for Nebuchadnezzar to write.

This is probably the reason why the consensus of the commentators (*Ralbag, Ibn Yachya, Abarbanel, Metzudos, Malbim, R' Yeshaya*) connects these verses to the following chapter. Even the *Midrash* mentioned before may agree with the literal interpretation. Only the redundancy of אָתַיָּא, *signs*, and וְתִמְהַיָּא, *wonders*, and their plural form, leads the *Midrash* to feel that the rescue from the fire was also alluded to in the king's letter.

[The chapter division, which makes it appear that *vs.* 31-33 are part of the story of the golden image and that 4:1 starts a new narrative, does not carry any authority. Such division is not of masoretic origin, nor from any other Jewish source, but was introduced by gentile Bible scholars. These chapter divisions were first introduced into Jewish Scripture by *Ya'akov ibn Adoniyahu* in his edition of Scripture (Venice 1524) for practical reasons (see his introduction to the Scripture and the *Mesorah* reprinted in *Mikraos Gedolos* [Warsaw 1894] toward the end, s.v. וּבְהִיוֹת). *Ibn Adoniyahu* went even further and divided *Samuel, Kings,* and *Chronicles,* each into two parts, and made the last thirteen chapters of *Ezra* into a separate book, *Nechemiah*. This has no basis in the *Mesorah* and the *Talmud* (Cf. *Bava Basra* 14 and *Sanhedrin* 93b from where it is clear that no separate book of *Nechemiah* ever existed).

31. נְבוּכַדְנֶצַּר מַלְכָּא — *[From] King Nebuchadnezzar.*

The following verses, through the end of chapter 4, are the transcript of a letter Nebuchadnezzar sent out throughout his dominions (see *prefatory note* above). This verse is the heading of the letter.

32. אָתַיָּא וְתִמְהַיָּא — *The signs and the wonders.*

Malbim perceives a difference between the apparent synonyms אָתַיָּא, *signs*, and תִמְהַיָּא, *wonders*. An אוֹת is an event, whether natural or supernatural, which is a *sign*, a

proof of Divine intervention in the affairs of humans. The warning given to Nebuchadnezzar in his dream, as interpreted by Daniel, and the subsequent fulfillment of this interpretation, would be an אוֹת, *sign*, whether the event itself were natural or supernatural. A מוֹפֵת (the Hebrew counterpart of תִמְהַיָּא), *wonder*, however, is a miracle, the supernatural juggling of the forces of nature.

Here the transformation of Nebuchadnezzar into something resembling an animal (Chapter 4) is the מוֹפֵת, *wonder*.

---

1. The אַנְשֵׁי כְּנֶסֶת הַגְּדוֹלָה, *Men of the Great Assembly* (see *Bava Basra* 15a).

ג ק׳ °עֲבַד עִמִּי אֱלָהָא °עִלָּאָא שְׁפַר קֳדָמַי
לג לְהַחֲוָיָה: אָתוֹהִי כְּמָה רַבְרְבִין וְתִמְהוֹהִי
כְּמָה תַּקִּיפִין מַלְכוּתֵהּ מַלְכוּת עָלַם

ד א וְשָׁלְטָנֵהּ עִם־דָּר וְדָר: אֲנָה נְבוּכַדְנֶצַּר
א-ב ב שְׁלֵה הֲוֵית בְּבֵיתִי וְרַעְנַן בְּהֵיכְלִי: חֵלֶם

דִּי עֲבַד עִמִּי — *That ... has performed with me.*

Nebuchadnezzar perceived that he was not himself worthy to be the recipient of miracles. He had only served as the undeserving tool used by God to proclaim His presence to the world (*Malbim*).

שְׁפַר קֳדָמַי לְהַחֲוָיָה — *It behooves me to relate.*

[For even to be just the instrument for the revelation of God's presence upon earth is a privilege to give thanks and praise for. This could be the intent of the Sages (*Pesachim* 118b) who interpret the verse (*Ps.* 117:1) הַלְלוּ אֶת ד׳ כָּל גּוֹיִם, *praise HASHEM, all you nations,* as referring to *the miracles that He did with them.* They are to praise God for having been chosen to be the tools with which God helps His people and thereby proclaims His presence. This fits very well with the following verse that begins כִּי גָּבַר עָלֵינוּ חַסְדּוֹ [the nations should praise HASHEM], *for His kindness is mighty over us*' ... (from *Kedushas Levi to Sidra Shemos* s.v. לכה).

33. אָתוֹהִי כְּמָה רַבְרְבִין וְתִמְהוֹהִי כְּמָה תַּקִּיפִין — *How great are His signs! And how mighty His wonders!*

The *signs* attest to the greatness of a Creator, Who after creating the universe, does not relinquish the mundane management of the daily affairs of the world to lower powers.

His ability to overcome and change the established laws and forces of nature and to alter them to conform to His will attest to His might (*Malbim*).

מַלְכוּתֵהּ...וְשָׁלְטָנֵהּ עִם דָּר וְדָר — *His kingdom ... His dominion is with every generation* [lit. *generation and generation*].

מַלְכוּת is government with the consent of the governed. שָׁלְטוֹן, in contrast, embraces even rule by force (*Malbim; cf. Perush HaGra to Proverbs* 27:27)

By מַלְכוּתֵהּ, *His kingdom,* we can understand God's regular conduct of the affairs of the world as effected through His management of the forces of nature without upsetting these created forces. This הַנְהָגָה, *conduct,* can be viewed as one unbroken continuous unit of time; for the upsetting of the natural order of the world is always just temporary and the event confined to an isolated miraculous revelation. The rest of the world goes on. Therefore this מַלְכוּת conduct is לְעָלַם, *forever,* unbroken.

But שָׁלְטָנֵהּ, *dominion,* here refers to God's power to supercede the forces of nature and to allow for miracles. Although it is also potentially infinite, it is limited in practice and is revealed עִם דָּר וְדָר, *with generation and generation*

In order to preserve the delicate balance needed to insure בְּחִירָה,

דניאל [134]

3
33

that the Supreme God has performed with me. It behooves me to relate.[33] How great are His signs!

And how mighty His wonders!

His kingdom is an everlasting kingdom,

And His dominion is with every generation.

4
1-2

¹ I, Nebuchadnezzar, was tranquil in my house and vigorous in my palace. ² I saw a dream which

---

freedom of choice, God in His infinite wisdom saw fit to conduct His world in a way that would hide His presence from the disinterested viewer. To insure, however, that the world not be led astray with arguments proving His absence from the world, God forbid, He saw fit to

light up the darkness induced by this conduct by revealing *the light of His countenance* from time to time in the form of super-natural miracles so as to restore the balance between dark and light needed to insure בְּחִירָה, *self-determination,* (Malbim).

IV

[See Appendix: *Nebuchadnezzar's Arrogance and Punishment*]

1. A Frightening Dream

שְׁלֵה הֲוֵית בְּבֵיתִי — *I ... was tranquil in my house.*

Nebuchadnezzar's dream could not be attributed to his uneasiness about his future (cf. *Berachos* 55b 'A person is shown [in his dreams] only that which he has thought about during the day'). *I ... was tranquil in my house,* i.e., completely at ease; nothing was disturbing my peace of mind. Still I had this disturbing dream *(Alshich).*

Nebuchadnezzar's subsequent madness, as narrated in this chapter, did not have its origin in circumstances usually associated with mental illness, such as personal misfortune, distress, or hardship. *I ... was tranquil in my house,* i.e., there was nothing in my life to which to attribute my illness. In light of this plus the fact that he

had been forewarned of his impending misfortune by Daniel's interpretation of the dream, Nebuchadnezzar had to accept that his fate was directed by Divine providence and that his illness was punishment for his misdeeds and arrogance. He admitted as much when he exclaimed at the conclusion of his illness *(v. 34), those who walk proudly He is able to humble* (Malbim).

וְרַעְנַן בְּהֵיכְלִי — *And vigorous in my palace.*

My personal life was in perfect order; *I ... was tranquil in my house.* My political fortune too was at the apex of its success; *I ... was ... vigorous in my palace,* i.e., at the height of my vigor *(Toras Chesed).*

Nebuchadnezzar's phenomenal success — both personal and political — led him to indulge exces-

חֲזֵית וִידַחֲלֻנַּנִי וְהַרְהֹרִין עַל־מִשְׁכְּבִי

ג וְחֶזְוֵי רֵאשִׁי יְבַהֲלֻנַּנִי: וּמִנִּי שִׂים טְעֵם

לְהַנְעָלָה קָדָמַי לְכֹל חַכִּימֵי בָבֶל דִּי־פְשַׁר

ד חֶלְמָא יְהוֹדְעֻנַּנִי: בֵּאדַיִן °עללין °עָלִין ק׳

חַרְטֻמַיָּא אָשְׁפַיָּא °כשדיא וְגָזְרַיָּא °כַּשְׂדָּאֵי ק׳

וְחֶלְמָא אָמַר אֲנָה קָדָמֵיהוֹן וּפִשְׁרֵהּ לָא־

ה מְהוֹדְעִין לִי: וְעַד אָחֳרֵין עַל קָדָמַי דָּנִיֵּאל

דִּי־שְׁמֵהּ בֵּלְטְשַׁאצַּר כְּשֻׁם אֱלָהִי וְדִי

רוּחַ־אֱלָהִין קַדִּישִׁין בֵּהּ וְחֶלְמָא קָדָמוֹהִי

---

sively in pleasure under the delusion that his own brilliance and capability were the cause of his success (כֹּחִי וְעֹצֶם יָדִי). Therefore God used him as an example to mankind that the consequence of pride is downfall. As Scripture teaches (*Proverbs* 16:18), לִפְנֵי שֶׁבֶר גָּאוֹן, *before destruction goes pride* (Ibn Yachya).

Nebuchadnezzar's prefatory remarks highlight the frail nature of human achievement. In one instant a person can descend from the pinnacle of success to the lowest abyss of despair and destitution. God's eternal providence is the ruler of a person's future, and no man — no matter how powerful he may seem to be — is the master of his destiny. This is the central theme of this story.

The commentators derive the word שלה, *tranquil*, from the Hebrew שָׁלֵיו. *R' Shmuel Masnuth* renders this word שׁוֹקֵט וּבוֹטֵחַ, *tranquil and secure*. Similarly, *Radak* and *R' Yonah Ibn Janach* (*Sefer HaShorashim* s.v. שלה) seem to understand even the Hebrew שָׁלֵוה in this manner. Furthermore *Targum* (*Jeremiah* 48:11) renders שַׁאֲנַן מוֹאָב, *Moab has been tranquil*, שְׁלַן מוֹאֲבָאֵי. *Targum to Proverbs* (1:33), וְשַׁאֲנַן מִפַּחַד רָעָה, *and tranquil without fear of evil*, renders by וְנִשְׁלֵה מִן דְּלוּחָא בִישָׁתָא. (This is

the reading given by *R' Eliya HaBachur* in *Meturgeman* s.v. שלה). Likewise *Rashi* (ibid.) couples שָׁלֵיו with שָׁקֵט, *tranquil*, as synonyms of שַׁאֲנָן. Thus it seems that a strong case can be made for rendering שְׁלֵוָה as *tranquility*.

[*R' Shmuel Masnuth* renders רַעֲנָן, *vigorous* [lit. *fresh*], as tranquil. However, wherever רַעֲנָן occurs in Scripture it is understood as moistness — i.e. freshness — in plant life. By extension, as a metaphor applied to a person it would signify freshness and vigor.]

2. וְחֶזְוֵי רֵאשִׁי יְבַהֲלֻנַּנִי — *And the visions of my mind bewildered me.*

Not only was I frightened during the dream, but even upon awakening, the dream disquieted me with *thoughts while in my bed.* Also the fear I had felt during the dream did not leave me upon awakening as is usual after a nightmare. *The visions of my mind,* i.e., the memory of the dream, *bewildered me* (Ibn Yachya).

3. דִּי־פְשַׁר חֶלְמָא יְהוֹדְעֻנַּנִי — *So that the interpretation of the dream they should make known to me.*

Since I was only asking for the interpretation of the dream, not the recital of the dream itself, I felt it was not necessary to call for Daniel. The Babylonian sages would suffice in this instance (Alshich).

4

3-5

frightened me; and thoughts while upon my bed, and the visions of my mind bewildered me. ³ I issued a command to bring before me all the sages of Babylon, so that the interpretation of the dream they should make known to me. ⁴ Then came the necromancers, the astrologers, the Chaldeans, and the demonists; and I related the dream before them, but its interpretation they did not make known to me.

⁵ At last there came before me Daniel — whose name is Belteshazzar like the name of my god, and in whom is the spirit of the Holy God — and I related

---

4. וּפִשְׁרֵה לָא־מְהוֹדְעִין לִי — *But its interpretation they did not make known to me.*

It seems they were able to come up with various interpretations, but none of these impressed Nebuchadnezzar as 'its' interpretation. (Had they not found any interpretation, he would have said וּפִשְׁרָא, *the interpretation.*) He sensed that 'its' interpretation, the message the dream had been meant to convey, had eluded them *(Alshich).* [Cf. *Rashi* to *Genesis* 41:8, s.v. וְאֵין פּוֹתֵר אוֹתָם לְפַרְעֹה.]

5. וְעַד אָחֳרֵין — *At last.*

When the king realized that the necromancers and their ilk were of no avail, he summoned Daniel. Now he knew that he needed someone *in whom is the spirit of the Holy God (Malbim).*

דִּי־שְׁמֵהּ בֵּלְטְשַׁאצַּר כְּשֻׁם אֱלָהִי וְדִי רוּחַ אֱלָהִין קַדִּישִׁין בֵּהּ — *Whose name is Belteshazzar like the name of my god, and in whom is the spirit of the Holy God.*

[From these remarks by Nebuchadnezzar we see that though he acknowledged the existence of a supreme God, this — in his mind — did not negate the existence of other, subordinate gods. Indeed, judging from his professed amazement at the misfortune that befell him, it seems he believed that the Supreme Deity did not concern Himself with matters of this world but left these matters to his subordinates. As our Sages say, 'They call him אֱלָקָא דְאֱלָקַיָא, *the God of gods (Menachos* 110; cf. *Chidushei Agados Maharsha* there and *Derashos HaRan* 9).

To his thinking, the affairs of each nation were administered by their local diety, who was supreme in his sphere of influence. Thus the miraculous rescue of Chananyah, Mishael, and Azaryah proved to Nebuchadnezzar only that the Jewish God — who was in his mind just another local deity — was a very powerful God, *because there is no other god able to rescue in this manner (3:29).* His amazement was probably heightened because to his way of thinking, the interference of a strange god in the matters of a country not directly under his jurisdiction proved the great power of that god (similar to the intervention of one country in the affairs of another). When Nebuchadnezzar was confronted with Daniel's superior power in interpreting dreams, he attributed this power to Daniel's relationship with his Jewish God (2:47). In his conception

אָמְרֵת: בֵּלְטְשַׁאצַר֙ רַב חַרְטֻמַיָּא דִּי | אֲנָה ‏ו
יִדְעֵת דִּי רוּחַ אֱלָהִין קַדִּישִׁין֙ בָּךְ וְכָל־רָז
לָא־אָנֵס לָךְ חֶזְוֵי חֶלְמִי דִי־חֲזֵית וּפִשְׁרֵהּ
אֱמַר: וְחֶזְוֵי רֵאשִׁי עַל־מִשְׁכְּבִי חָזֵה הֲוֵית ‏ז
וַאֲלוּ אִילָן בְּגוֹא אַרְעָא וְרוּמֵהּ שַׂגִּיא:
רְבָה אִילָנָא וּתְקִף וְרוּמֵהּ֙ יִמְטֵא לִשְׁמַיָּא ‏ח
וַחֲזוֹתֵהּ לְסוֹף כָּל־אַרְעָא: עָפְיֵהּ שַׁפִּיר֙ ‏ט

---

this *God of gods*, though he left the management of the affairs of the world to his subordinates, was nevertheless all-knowing. He was therefore called *the Holy God*, whose holiness removed him from interest in the mundane matters of the world. The sages of Babylon, though they also undoubtedly claimed spiritual powers, could not know Nebuchadnezzar's dream, because such information was not available to the local deity by its very nature (see *comm.* to 3:19), or because the dream contained predictions pertinent to the whole of mankind.

When Daniel interpreted the king's dream to mean that Nebuchadnezzar would go mad as punishment for his self-aggrandizement and *so that the living may know that the Supreme One rules in the kingdom of man (v. 14)*, the king refused to believe him, since in his mind this would be an unprecedented act of interference by the *Supreme One* in the mundane affairs of this world.]

6. רַב חַרְטֻמַיָּא דִּי אֲנָה יִדְעֵת — *Chief of the necromancers, since I know.*

You are known popularly as the *chief of the necromancers,* i.e., the greatest expert in the art of the occult. As such I really should no place too much hope in obtaining from you a better interpretation of my dream than from the rest of the sages. But *I know* that your power is of an entirely different nature; in you is *the spirit of the holy God.*

Therefore I expect that you will tell me *its interpretation (Alshich).*

קַדִּישִׁין — *Holy.*

The plural form (equivalent to the Hebrew קְדוֹשִׁים) is found elsewhere in Scripture to describe God (*Joshua* 24:9; cf. *Bereishis Rabbah* 8:9). This may be due to the plural form of אֱלֹהִים (ים־ is the usual form used to indicate plurality). See *Abarbanel (Genesis* 1:1 s.v. אלהים) for a lengthy discussion of this. The meaning here may be *holy angels.* This seems to be *R' Saadiah's* understanding.

חֶזְוֵי חֶלְמִי דִי חֲזֵית — *[This is] the vision of the dream which I saw.*

I.e., what follows in *vs.* 7-15 is *the vision of the dream which I saw.*

וּפִשְׁרֵהּ אֱמַר — *Tell its interpretation.*

I will tell the dream, and I command you to render *its interpretation (R' Saadiah; Ralbag; Metzudos).*

[At first glance, the king seems to be saying that Daniel is to tell him the dream also. This is untenable, since in *vs.* 7-15 we have the king himself reciting his dream to Daniel.]

Malbim connects this phrase with the beginning of the verse *Belteshazzar ... since I know that the spirit of the Holy God is in you*

4

6-9

the dream to him. ⁶ 'Belteshazzar, chief of the necromancers, since I know that the spirit of the Holy God is in you, and no secret is hidden from you: this is the vision of the dream which I saw; tell its interpretation. ⁷ The visions of my mind while upon my bed:

I was watching and behold! a tree in the midst of the earth, its height, tremendous. ⁸ The tree grew and became powerful, its height reaching the sky; and it was visible to the end of the whole earth. ⁹ Its branches were beautiful, its fruit plentiful, and food

---

... tell me the dream which I saw and its interpretation. I know your power to be so great as not to need me to tell you the dream. Nevertheless, *The visions of my mind ...* (v. 7).

Alshich, noting the use of חֶזְוֵי רֵאשִׁי, *the visions of my mind*, in vs. 2 and 7 and חֶזְוֵי חֶלְמִי, *the visions of my dream*, here, comments that the latter refers not to the dream itself but to the message the dream was meant to convey. This underlines the basic difference between Daniel and the conventional dream interpreters. The sages of Babylon derived their interpretation from the dream itself, i.e., through translating the imagery of the dream into the realities of life, thereby making the interpretation and the *vision* of the dream one and the same. Daniel, however, because *the spirit of the Holy God* was in him and therefore *no secret ... hidden from him*, could go to the source of the dream and relate the *vision* of the dream without resorting to its interpretation. Therefore, Nebuchadnezzar says, 'Tell me *the vision of the dream which I saw* and then tell me *its interpretation*' — i.e., the reconcilia-

tion of the vision with the imagery of the dream.

7⁻15. The Dream of the Tree

8. וּתְקִף — *And became powerful.*
I.e., its trunk thickened.

וַחֲזוֹתֵהּ לְסוֹף כָּל־אַרְעָא — *And it was visible to the end of the whole earth.*

Because of the trunk's thickness the tree was visible to the end of the earth *(Malbim)*. Malbim's comment follows the translation of *R' Saadiah, R' Yeshayah*, and *Metzudos*.

Ibn Ezra and *R' Shmuel Masnuth* render וַחֲזוֹתֵהּ, *its branches*.

When a tree grows to excessive height, it generally tilts to one side. But although this tree grew till *its height reached the sky*, it kept upright because *it grew and* simultaneously *became powerful (Alshich)*.

[Interpolated into the interpretation of the dream, this would probably mean that though the Babylonian Empire expanded tremendously, its strength was not dissipated by the process.]

9. עָפְיֵהּ שַׁפִּיר — *Its branches were beautiful.*

The translation follows *Rashi, Ibn Ezra* (quoting *Yefes*), and *R' Shmuel Masnuth.*

ד

וְאִנְבֵּהּ שַׂגִּיא וּמָזוֹן לְכֹלָּא־בֵהּ תְּחֹתוֹהִי

תַּטְלֵל | חֵיוַת בָּרָא וּבְעַנְפּוֹהִי °יְדוּרָן ק׳ י״ב

תִּשְׁכְּנָן צִפֲּרֵי שְׁמַיָּא וּמִנֵּהּ יִתְּזִין כָּל־בִּשְׂרָא: חָזֵה י

הֲוֵית בְּחֶזְוֵי רֵאשִׁי עַל־מִשְׁכְּבִי וַאֲלוּ עִיר

וְקַדִּישׁ מִן־שְׁמַיָּא נָחִת: קָרֵא בְחַיִל וְכֵן יא

אָמַר גֹּדּוּ אִילָנָא וְקַצִּצוּ עַנְפוֹהִי אַתַּרוּ

עָפְיֵהּ וּבַדַּרוּ אִנְבֵּהּ תְּנֻד חֵיוְתָא מִן־

תְּחֹתוֹהִי וְצִפֲּרַיָּא מִן־עַנְפוֹהִי: בְּרַם עִקַּר יב

שָׁרְשׁוֹהִי בְּאַרְעָא שְׁבֻקוּ וּבֶאֱסוּר דִּי־

פַרְזֶל וּנְחָשׁ בְּדִתְאָא דִּי בָרָא וּבְטַל שְׁמַיָּא

Another translation (cited by *Ibn Ezra* and *R' Shmuel Masnuth* and adopted by *Radak* and *Metzudos*) is *its leaves* or *foliage*. If one renders וַחֲזוֹתֵהּ, (v. 8) *branches*, then עָפְיֵהּ means *its foliage* or *leaves*.

This part of the dream was not interpreted by Daniel (see *comm.* to v. 19). Various interpretations are given.

Abarbanel has חֲזוֹתֵהּ, *its branches*, representing Nebuchadnezzar's relatives — i.e., the nobles whom he appointed to rule over various parts of his domain. עָפְיֵהּ, *its leaves*, represent the armies, whose shade acts as a protective cover for their countrymen.

According to *R' Saadiah*, עָפְיֵהּ, *its branches*, represent the governors. וַחֲזוֹתֵהּ, *and it was visible to the end of the whole earth* (v. 8), refers to Nebuchadnezzar's legions, which occupied his vast domain. Thus the tree represents the total governmental structure — the military and administrative branches under whose protective shade everyone lives.

וְאִנְבֵּהּ — *Its fruit.*

According to *R' Saadiah* this refers to the general population. *Abarbanel* has it referring to Nebuchadnezzar's rule — i.e., the fruit of the governmental structure represented by the tree.

[וְאִנְבֵּהּ may possibly represent the economic benefits of Nebuchadnezzar's great rule.]

חֵיוַת בָּרָא — *Wild beasts.*

[See *comm.* to 3:28.]

These represent the nations of the world.

צִפֲּרֵי שְׁמַיָּא — *The birds of heaven.*

These represent the Jewish People (*R' Saadiah;* cf. *Rashi* to *Genesis* 15:10).

10. עִיר — *A wakeful ... one.*

From the context we infer that עִיר וְקַדִּישׁ refers to an angel. *Rashi, Ibn Ezra,* and *R' Shmuel Masnuth* derive עִיר from עֵר, *awake.* The angels, constantly awake and alert, are therefore called עִירִין, *wakeful ones.*

R' Saadiah renders עִיר, *a destructive angel* (as in עָרוּ עַד הַיְסוֹד בָּהּ, *Psalms* 137:7).

דניאל [140]

4
10-12   for all in it; under it wild beasts found shade, in its branches nested the birds of heaven, and from it all flesh was fed. ¹⁰ In the visions of my mind while upon my bed I was watching and, behold! a wakeful holy one came down from heaven.¹¹ He cried out loudly, and said the following: "Chop down the tree and cut off its branches, cast down its branches, and scatter its fruit; let the animals move away from under it, and the birds from its branches. ¹² However, its major roots leave in the ground, and with a bond of iron and copper in the herbage of the field, and by the dew of heaven he will be washed, and with the

---

[For additional insight into the matter of עִירִין and the intent of the sentence see *Ramban* to *Vayikra* 18:25].

11⁻14. A Holy One Speaks

11. אַתַּרוּ עָפְיֵהּ — *Cast down its branches.*

The translation follows the commentators who translate עָפְיֵהּ, *branches* (see above v. 9). Although the branches had already been *cut off*, they were still entangled with each other and attached to the tree's trunk. Now, they were cast down to the ground.

12. וּבֶאֱסוּר דִּי־פַרְזֶל — *And with a bond of iron.*

I.e., he shall be bound *with a bond of iron.*

The tree is here abruptly metamorphosed into a person, as if the dream were interpreting itself by identifying the tree as a person who, having gone berserk, must be bound in chains (*Alshich; Malbim*).

בְּדִתְאָא דִּי בָרָא — *In the herbage of the field.*

I.e., he shall be bound and forced to remain in the field among the

herbage. The translation follows *Rashi, Ibn Ezra,* and *Metzudos.*

This represents another stage of madness. After the person has been bound in chains, he refuses all food except the *herbage of the field;* thus: [he will be fed] the herbage of the field. Later on he will advance to a more extreme degree of madness where he will refuse to even stay among humans: *and with the wild beasts he will share*(*Malbim*).

וּבְטַל שְׁמַיָּא יִצְטַבַּע — *And by the dew of heaven he will be washed.*

Still another development: he will refuse to stay indoors, preferring to live under the open sky and to be *washed* — i.e., drenched — with the *dew of the heavens* (*Malbim*).

Rashi and *Radak* string all these developments together. Thus, he will be bound *with a bond of iron and copper* (בְּדִתְאָא דִּי בָרָא) *in the herbage of the field* — i.e., he will not be allowed to move from his place. Therefore *by the dew of heaven he will be washed, and with the wild beasts he will share in the grass of the earth.*

יְצַטַּבַּע וְעִם־חֵיוְתָא חֲלָקֵהּ בְּעֵשַׂב אַרְעָא:

יג לִבְבֵהּ מִן־°אֲנָשָׁא יְשַׁנּוֹן וּלְבַב חֵיוָא
°אֲנָשָׁא ק'

יִתְיְהִב לֵהּ וְשִׁבְעָה עִדָּנִין יַחְלְפוּן עֲלוֹהִי:

יד בִּגְזֵרַת עִירִין פִּתְגָמָא וּמֵאמַר קַדִּישִׁין
שְׁאֶלְתָּא עַד־דִּבְרַת דִּי יִנְדְּעוּן חַיַּיָּא דִּי־
שַׁלִּיט °עִלָּיָא בְּמַלְכוּת °אֲנָשָׁא וּלְמַן־דִּי
°עִלָּאָה ק'
°אֲנָשָׁא ק'

יִצְבֵּא יִתְּנִנַּהּ וּשְׁפַל אֲנָשִׁים יְקִים °עֲלַהּ:
°עֲלַהּ ק'

טו דְּנָה חֶלְמָא חֲזֵית אֲנָה מַלְכָּא נְבוּכַדְנֶצַּר
°וְאַנְתְּ בֵּלְטְשַׁאצַּר °פִּשְׁרֵא אֱמַר כָּל־
°וְאַנְתְּ ק'
°פִּשְׁרֵהּ ק'

קֳבֵל דִּי | כָּל־חַכִּימֵי מַלְכוּתִי לָא־יָכְלִין
פִּשְׁרָא לְהוֹדָעוּתַנִי °וְאַנְתְּ כָּהֵל דִּי
°וְאַנְתְּ ק'

רוּחַ־אֱלָהִין קַדִּישִׁין בָּךְ: טז אֱדַיִן דָּנִיֵּאל דִּי־
שְׁמֵהּ בֵּלְטְשַׁאצַּר אֶשְׁתּוֹמַם כְּשָׁעָה חֲדָה

וְעִם־חֵיוְתָא חֲלָקֵהּ — *And with the wild beasts he will share.*

This is the last stage of Nebuchadnezzar's madness. Refusing to dwell among people, he will flee to the woods and jungles to live with *the wild beasts (Malbim).* [Malbim translates חֲלָקֵהּ, *his lot.*]

13. לִבְבֵהּ מִן אֲנָשָׁא יְשַׁנּוֹן — *They will change his heart from a man's.*

I.e., his emotions will be changed so that he will not fear to live among the animals *(Malbim).*

וְשִׁבְעָה עִדָּנִין — *And seven periods.*
The length of each period is not clear. It could be a day, month, season, or year. *Ralbag* points out that Nebuchadnezzar's madness must have covered a long span of time since *his hair grew like eagles'* [feathers] *and his nails like birds'* [claws] *(v. 30).* He therefore favors the view that these *periods* were

years, as do *Rashi, Ibn Ezra,* and *R' Saadiah.*

Abarbanel (Mayenei Hayeshuah 6:4), however, is inclined to consider these *periods* as seasons, since this would also be sufficient to explain Nebuchadnezzar's animal-like appearance at the end of his suffering.

Malbim suggests that Nebuchadnezzar's madness passed through seven different stages which here are called *periods.*

14. וּמֵאמַר קַדִּישִׁין שְׁאֶלְתָּא — *And by word of the holy ones is the sentence.*

Since the angels hand down their verdict only after consulting with God Himself, their verdict is called שְׁאֶלְתָּא, *a query (Rashi from Midrash Tanchuma Shemos 18).*

Ibn Ezra separates שְׁאֶלְתָּא from the preceding words. He thus renders the first five words as a single phrase: *By decree of the wakeful ones is the matter* (verdict) *and by word of the holy ones;* שְׁאֶלְתָּא [as to] *the*

4

13-16

wild beasts he will share in the grass of the earth. ¹³ They will change his heart from a man's, and a beast's heart will be given to him, and seven periods will pass over him. ¹⁴ By decree of the wakeful ones is the matter, and by word of the holy ones is the sentence; so that the living may know that the Supreme One rules in the kingdom of man and to whomever He wishes He gives it, and the lowest of men He will raise up over it." ¹⁵ This dream I saw — I, King Nebuchadnezzar. And you, Belteshazzar, tell its interpretation, since all the sages of my kingdom are unable to make the interpretation known to me; but you are able, because the spirit of Holy God is in you.'

¹⁶ Then Daniel, whose name was Belteshazzar, was confounded for a moment, and his thoughts bewildered him.

---

question [why?]: So that ... However, the position of the esnachta under שְׁאֵלְתָּא contradicts this interpretation.

וּלְמַן־דִּי יִצְבֵּא יִתְּנִנַּהּ — And to whomever He wishes He gives it.

Having established the principle that the Supreme One rules (present tense) in the kingdom of man — i.e., the empire ruled by Nebuchadnezzar — the corollary is that to whomever He pleases He will give it (יִתְּנִנַּהּ — future tense) follows naturally. This obviously refers to the three empires that will follow the Babylonian empire in spite of the king's machinations. (Mayenei HaYeshuah 6:5).

וּשְׁפַל אֲנָשִׁים יְקִים עֲלַהּ — And the lowest of men He will raise up over it.

The Sages understand this phrase as referring to Nebuchadnezzar. His being characterized as שְׁפַל אֲנָשִׁים,

the lowest of men, is due to his extremely short stature (R' Saadiah from a passage quoted in Yalkut Shimoni — probably from Moed Katan 18; cf. Tanchuma to Shemos, ed. Buber, p. 90 note 20).

Mulbim and Abarbanel (Mayenei HaYeshuah 6:4) interpret this phrase as an allusion to the ultimate triumph of the kingdom of God. Israel, the lowest among nations in the גָּלוּת, exile, will ultimately assume its rightful role and rule the world.

15. וְאַנְתְּ כָּהֵל — But you are able.

[Here Nebuchadnezzar reaffirms his conviction that Daniel's superiority is due not to greater skill, but to the spirit of the Holy God in him. Even though ᶜl the sages of my kingdom are unable to tell me a (plausible) פִּשְׁרָא, interpretation, I am sure you are able to give me פִּשְׁרֵהּ, 'its' interpretation.]

ד

יז-כ ׳וּפִשְׁרֵהּ ק׳ וְרַעְיֹנָי יְבַהֲלֻנַּנִי עָנֵה מַלְכָּא וְאָמַר

בֵּלְטְשַׁאצַּר חֶלְמָא ׳וּפִשְׁרֵא אַל־יְבַהֲלָךְ

יז ׳לְשָׂנְאָךְ ק׳ עָנֵה בֵלְטְשַׁאצַּר וְאָמַר מָרִאי חֶלְמָא

׳לְעָרָךְ ק׳ ׳לְשָׂנְאָיךְ וּפִשְׁרֵהּ ׳לְעָרָיךְ: אִילָנָא דִּי

חֲזַיְתָ דִּי רְבָה וּתְקִף וְרוּמֵהּ יִמְטֵא

יח לִשְׁמַיָּא וַחֲזוֹתֵהּ לְכָל־אַרְעָא: וְעָפְיֵהּ

שַׁפִּיר וְאִנְבֵּהּ שַׂגִּיא וּמָזוֹן לְכֹלָּא־בֵהּ

תְּחֹתוֹהִי תְּדוּר חֵיוַת בָּרָא וּבְעַנְפוֹהִי

יט ׳אַנְתְּ ק׳ יִשְׁכְּנָן צִפֲּרֵי שְׁמַיָּא: ׳אַנְתָּה־הוּא מַלְכָּא

׳רְבַת ק׳ דִּי ׳רְבִית וּתְקֵפְתְּ וּרְבוּתָךְ רְבָת וּמְטַת

כ לִשְׁמַיָּא וְשָׁלְטָנָךְ לְסוֹף אַרְעָא: וְדִי חֲזָה

מַלְכָּא עִיר וְקַדִּישׁ נָחִת | מִן־שְׁמַיָּא וְאָמַר

גֹּדּוּ אִילָנָא וְחַבְּלוּהִי בְּרַם עִקַּר שָׁרְשׁוֹהִי

בְּאַרְעָא שְׁבֻקוּ וּבֶאֱסוּר דִּי־פַרְזֶל וּנְחָשׁ

בְּדִתְאָא דִּי בָרָא וּבְטַל שְׁמַיָּא יִצְטַבַּע

16. Daniel Interprets and Advises

חֶלְמָא וּפִשְׁרֵהּ אַל־יְבַהֲלָךְ — *Let not the dream and its interpretation bewilder you.*

Nebuchadnezzar had a foreboding of the ominous message his dream contained. Observing Daniel's bewilderment at hearing the dream, the king reassured Daniel that he need not fear to reveal to him the unpleasant truth (*Mayenei HaYeshuah* 6:4).

חֶלְמָא לְשָׂנְאָךְ וּפִשְׁרֵהּ לְעָרָךְ — *Let the dream be upon your foes, and its interpretation on your enemies.*

Malbim explains that עָרָךְ, *your enemies,* are those whose enmity is greater than that of שָׂנְאָךְ, *your foes.* Thus *the dream* — i.e., the fright and distress caused you by the

dream — wish upon those you hate; *and its interpretation* — i.e., the actual disaster — wish upon your worst enemies.

19. וּרְבוּתָךְ רְבָת — *And your greatness has grown.*

Daniel stresses that the allegory of the tree was not — as it implied — referring to the king's person, but to the greatness of his rule. Thus the chopping down of the tree refers not to his physical destruction, but to the temporary cessation of his rule. Daniel thereby resolved the apparent contradiction between the imagery of the dream, which suggests that Nebuchadnezzar, represented by the tree, would be destroyed, and the words of the angel to the effect that he would only lose his sanity (*Alshich*).

4
17-20   The king exclaimed, 'Belteshazzar! Let not the dream and its interpretation bewilder you.'

Belteshazzar replied, 'My lord, let the dream be upon your foes, and its interpretation on your enemies! ¹⁷ The tree that you saw, which grew and became powerful, whose height has reached the sky and is visible to the whole earth, ¹⁸ whose branches were beautiful, whose fruit is plentiful, and food for everyone is in it; under it dwelt the wild beasts, and in its branches nested the birds of the heaven — ¹⁹ it is you, O king, who has grown and become powerful, and your greatness has grown and reached the sky, and your dominion to the end of the earth. ²⁰ That the king saw a wakeful holy one who came down from heaven and said: "Chop down the tree and destroy it, but leave its major roots in the ground, and with a band of iron and copper in the herbage of the earth; and by the dew of heaven it will be washed and

---

וּמְטָת לִשְׁמַיָּא — *And reached the heaven.*

Your power is derived from heaven. According to the Sages each nation of the seventy principal nations mentioned in chapter ten of *Genesis* (cf. *Pirkei d'Rabbi Eliezer* 24) has an angel who represents that nation in the heavenly council (פְּמַלְיָא שֶׁל מַעֲלָה). *Ramban*, in his commentary to *Leviticus* 18:25, derives this from many passages in Scripture. Thus when a nation is elevated to a leading position, this elevation is equal to and dependent on the corresponding elevation of its שַׂר, *angelic representative*, in heaven (*Malbim*).

It would have been perfectly normal for Nebuchadnezzar to dream about the downfall of another king. The sages, unable to imagine the downfall of Nebuchadnezzar (see

Appendix: Nebuchadnezzar's Arrogance and Punishment), may have interpreted the dream this way. But Daniel, pointing to the detailed description of the tree, showed that the total picture suggested a monarch whose powerful rule encompassed all mankind. There was only one king who fit this description — Nebuchadnezzar. Thus the tree (v. 17) and its branches (v.18) all point to the only true interpretation: *it is you, O king* (*Alshich*).

[Daniel did not interpret the details of part of the dream (vs. 9 and 18). His expertise was not needed for the interpretation of these details. He was needed to reconcile the contradiction between the vision of the tree and the words of the angel (see v. 21). Daniel repeated all the details describing

---

וְעִם־חֵיוַת בָּרָא חֲלָקֵהּ עַד דִּי־שִׁבְעָה

כא עִדָּנִין יַחְלְפוּן עֲלוֹהִי: דְּנָה פִשְׁרָא מַלְכָּא

°עֶלָאָה ק׳ וּגְזֵרַת °עֶלָיָא הִיא דִּי מְטָת עַל־מָרְאִי

כב מַלְכָּא: וְלָךְ טָרְדִין מִן־אֲנָשָׁא וְעִם־חֵיוַת

בָּרָא לֶהֱוֵה מְדֹרָךְ וְעִשְׂבָּא כְתוֹרִין | לָךְ

יְטַעֲמוּן וּמִטַּל שְׁמַיָּא לָךְ מְצַבְּעִין וְשִׁבְעָה

°עֲלָךְ ק׳ עִדָּנִין יַחְלְפוּן °עֲלַיִךְ עַד דִּי־תִנְדַּע דִּי־

°עֶלָאָה ק׳ שַׁלִּיט °עֶלָיָא בְּמַלְכוּת אֲנָשָׁא וּלְמַן־דִּי

כג יִצְבֵּא יִתְּנִנַּהּ: וְדִי אֲמַרוּ לְמִשְׁבַּק עִקַּר

---

the tree without commenting on their meaning in order to highlight the correctness of his interpretation that the words of the angel referred to Nebuchadnezzar.]

21. דְּנָה פִשְׁרָא — *This is the interpretation.*

The part of the dream in which the tree is metamorphosed into a person is not another allegory requiring interpretation; it is rather the interpretation of the dream of the tree. Hence the tree does not represent Nebuchadnezzar himself but his greatness, which, as a result of his madness, is temporarily lost (*Alshich; Malbim*).

וּגְזֵרַת עֶלָאָה הִיא — *It is the decree of the Supreme One.*

The insertion of the interpretation into the dream is proof that this is no idle dream but *the decree of the Supreme One* (*Alshich*).

Daniel did not explain the angel's decree to chop down the tree. The lengthy description of the destruction of the tree (*v.* 11) is glossed over with one single phrase, *chop down the tree*. After explaining that

the tree represented not the Babylonian empire but Nebuchadnezzar himself so that his empire would not collapse (*v.* 23), it was self-explanatory that these details represented Nebuchadnezzar's loss of whatever these symbols stood for (*Malbim;* cf. *comm.* to *v.* 9).

דִּי מְטָת — *Which befalls*[lit. *which it has reached*].

[The present perfect tense is used here in the prophetic sense, with the future viewed as though it were happening in the present.

[However, this verse may be understood differently: *This* — i.e., *v.* 19 which likens Nebuchadnezzar to the tree — *is the interpretation* of the dream ... *it* [i.e., this greatness of yours] *is the decree of the Supreme One*, and not, as you vainly believe the result of your personal qualities.]

22. וְלָךְ טָרְדִין — *They will drive you from mankind.*

Do not entertain thoughts that this dream refers to your empire. It is *you* personally whom *they will drive from mankind* (*Alshich*).

4
21-23
with the wild beasts will his portion be, till seven periods pass over him" — 21 this is the interpretation, O king: It is the decree of the Supreme One which befalls my lord the king. 22 They will drive you from mankind, and among wild beasts will be your dwelling; grass, like oxen, they will feed you, and with the dew of heaven they will wash you, and seven periods will pass over you; (till) you recognize that the Supreme One rules in the kingdom of man and to whomever He wishes He gives it. 23 As to their saying

וְעִשְׂבָּא כְתוֹרִין לָךְ יְטַעֲמוּן — *Grass, like oxen, they will feed you.*

The translation follows *Ralbag, Ibn Yachya,* and *Metzudos.*

[An alternative is to translate יְטַעֲמוּן from טַעַם, *taste.* Thus: *They will make grass flavorful to you like to oxen,* i.e., you will eat grass because it will taste good to you. This would be a fulfillment of the angel's prediction (*v.* 13) *They will change his heart from a man's, and a beast's heart will be given to him.*]

כְתוֹרִין — *Like oxen.*

This comparison was not mentioned in the dream. *Abarbanel* thinks Daniel derived it from: *with the wild beasts he will share in the grass of the earth* (*v.* 12). This excludes all the carnivorous animals, whose food is not grass. Among the grass-eating animals, Daniel thought it most fitting to liken the king to an ox, who, because of his great power, is considered king of the herbivores. He also points out (as does *Ibn Ezra* to *v.* 28) that it is a mistake to think Nebuchadnezzar was actually changed into an ox. This can clearly be seen from *v.* 30 where Nebuchadnezzar's hair and

nails grew to extraordinary length while he was going through his punishment. This can only be understood if he retained his human form but lost his sanity (*Mayenei HaYeshuah* 6:5-6).

The language of this verse itself seems to say as much: *like oxen, they will feed you.*

וּלְמַן־דִּי יִצְבֵּא יִתְּנִנַּהּ — *And to whomever He wishes He gives it.*

The end of the angel's words in *v.* 14, *and the lowest of men He will raise up over it,* is conspicuously omitted here. According to the Sages who interpret this last phrase as a disparaging remark directed at the king (*comm.* to *v.* 14), this omission is understandable. Daniel had no reason to repeat this insult to the king, since it was not an integral part of the message the dream conveyed. Out of deference to the king he omitted it.

According to *Malbim* and *Abarbanel,* who interpret this phrase as referring to the impending kingship of God, Daniel did not want to enlighten the king about the meaning of these words so as not to throw suspicion on his interpreta-

שָׁרְשׁוֹהִי דִּי אִילָנָא מַלְכוּתָךְ לָךְ קַיָּמָה
מִן־דִּי תִנְדַּע דִּי שַׁלִּטִן שְׁמַיָּא: לָהֵן מַלְכָּא
מִלְכִּי יִשְׁפַּר °עֲלָיךְ וחטיך בְּצִדְקָה פְּרֻק
וַעֲוָיָתָךְ בְּמִחַן עֲנָיִן הֵן תֶּהֱוֵה אַרְכָה
לִשְׁלֵוְתָךְ: כֹּלָּא מְטָא עַל־נְבוּכַדְנֶצַּר

כד

° עֲלָךְ וַחֲטָאָךְ ק׳

כה

---

tion, lest the king think that Daniel's Jewishness had led him to interpret this passage in a way favorable to his people.

The purpose of Nebuchadnezzar's punishment was to get him to acknowledge that he could not tamper with God's master plan for the world in the manner he had attempted (see *Appendix: Nebuchadnezzar's Arrogance and Punishment*). This would be accomplished as soon as the king knew that *the Supreme One rules in the kingdom of man*. The details of God's master plan are not integral parts of this lesson. Daniel made sure not to incite the king against the Jews unnecessarily (*Malbim*).

23. קַיָּמָה לָךְ מַלְכוּתָךְ — *Your kingdom will remain for you.*

I.e., the interpretation of *its major roots leave in the ground* (v. 12) is *your kingdom will remain for you*. After Nebuchadnezzar recognizes *that Heaven rules*, his throne will revert to him (*Rashi*).

The allegory of the roots remaining in the earth so as to allow the tree to grow again does not refer to the inheritance of the kingdom by Nebuchadnezzar's heirs. *Your kingdom will remain for 'you'.* Since Daniel had by now refuted the apparent interpretation of the allegory, which suggests that Nebuchadnezzar would be destroyed, the way was open to interpret this

passage of the dream in this manner. That is why he left this part till the end of his interpretation, instead of placing it at the beginning of his explanation of the angel's words (v. 21), where it rightfully belongs (*Alshich*).

24. עֲלָךְ יִשְׁפַּר מִלְכִּי — *Let my advice be agreeable to you.*

The Sages (*Bava Basra* 4a) fault Daniel for advising an idolator and blasphemer like Nebuchadnezzar how to escape retribution. (Cf. *Rambam Hilchos Rotzeach* 12:15). According to one view, Daniel was punished by being demoted from his high post at the royal court during the reign of the Persians. This view identifies הֲתָךְ, *Hassach*, mentioned in *Esther* (4:5, see ArtScroll comm.), as Daniel. This name is derived from חֲתָךְ, *cut down*, because he was demoted *(cut down)* from his greatness. According to another view, his ordeal in the lions' den was the punishment for his advice (*Bava Basra* 4a; cf. *Rambam*, ibid.).

Midrash Tanchuma (*Mishpatim* 4, quoted by *Rashi*) gives a worthy motive for Daniel's apparent sin. He saw that the exiled remnant of the Jewish nation was destitute, suffering from hunger and deprivation. Daniel thought that because his intention was to help his people, he had committed no sin even though his advice was helpful to

4

24-25

to leave the major roots of the tree: your kingdom will remain for you — (after) you know that Heaven rules. ²⁴ Nevertheless, O king, let my advice be agreeable to you. Redeem your error with charity, and your sin through kindness to the poor — there will be an extension to your tranquility.'

²⁵ All this befell King Nebuchadnezzar.

Nebuchadnezzar. Eventually, Daniel was convinced, Nebuchadnezzar would get his punishment anyway, since he would not be able to persevere in this philanthropic way of life which was so foreign to his nature.

Maharsha (Chiddushei Aggados Sotah 21a *s.v.* הֵן) comments that in spite of Daniel's good intentions, his actions were wrong (cf. *Rav Shmuel Masnuth).*

Malbim explains that Daniel's seemingly unsolicited advice was really part of his interpretation. The phrase used by the king וּמִנֵּהּ יִתְּזִין כָּל־בִּשְׂרָא, *and from it all flesh was fed (v.* 9), seems to imply that the tree, exemplifying the empire, would actively administer the feeding of the multitudes. This phrase is curiously missing from Daniel's *verbatim* recital of the king's dream. The phrase וּמָזוֹן לְכֹלָּא־בֵהּ, *and food for everyone is in it (v.* 18), with which Daniel apparently replaces it, is placed after וְאִנְבֵּהּ שַׂגִּיא, *whose fruit is plentiful,* possibly suggesting that the former is an elaboration on the latter, i.e., Babylon's *fruit* (its economic rewards) was plentiful enough to supply *food for everyone.*

וַחֲטָאָךְ — *And your sin.*

His sin, arrogance, could only be redeemed by *charity* — an act of

humility and identification with the lowly and the poor *(Mayenei Ha-Yeshuah* 6:4).

Malbim explains that חֵטְא means a sinful deed; therefore the deed of almsgiving would suffice to atone for it. עָוֹן (the singular form of עֲוָיָתָךְ), however, is the corruption of morals and principles, and therefore demands more than a deed for atonement. Showing kindness to the poor — i.e., changing his frame of mind — would suffice to deter the king's punishment.

According to our Sages, who define חֵטְא as שׁוֹגֵג, *inadvertent sin,* and עָוֹן as מֵזִיד, *intentional sin,* for his inadvertent sins mere almsgiving would suffice. But for his עֲוֹנוֹת, *intentional sins,* he would have to change his frame of mind to show mercy to the poor.

[The *Vilna Gaon (Adereth Eliyahū* to *Isaiah* 8:18) defines חֵטְא as the transgression of a מִצְוַת עֲשֵׂה, *positive commandment,* and עָוֹן as a transgression of a לֹא תַעֲשֶׂה, *negative commandment.* Since transgression of a negative commandment is generally a graver infraction than that of a positive commandment, this definition too would fit into this sentence.]

25. כֹּלָּא מְטָא — *All this befell.*

Since Daniel's advice — which

כו מַלְכָּא: לִקְצָת יַרְחִין
תְּרֵי־עֲשַׂר עַל־הֵיכַל מַלְכוּתָא דִּי בָבֶל
כז מְהַלֵּךְ הֲוָה: עָנֵה מַלְכָּא וְאָמַר הֲלָא
דָא־הִיא בָּבֶל רַבְּתָא דִּי־אֲנָה בֱּנַיְתַהּ
לְבֵית מַלְכוּ בִּתְקָף חִסְנִי וְלִיקָר הַדְרִי:
כח עוֹד מִלְּתָא בְּפֻם מַלְכָּא קָל מִן־שְׁמַיָּא

---

was also part of his interpretation of the king's dream — was heeded, the king's punishment was deferred for one year. Then it finally took place in full detail (Malbim).

From here to verse 31 the narrative is in the third person. Ibn Ezra, R' Saadiah, Metzudos, and others believe that in spite of the change in person, these sentences are part of Nebuchadnezzar's letter. Ibn Ezra cites other passages in Scripture where people refer to themselves in the third person.

Malbim cites the opinion of some commentators that these sentences are not part of Nebuchadnezzar's letter. They are rather the divinely inspired parenthetical comments of the אַנְשֵׁי כְּנֶסֶת הַגְּדוֹלָה, Men of the Great Assembly,[1] filling in pertinent information. [It may be that the audience the king's letter was addressed to knew these facts only too well and did not need them.]

26. The Dream is Fulfilled

יַרְחִין תְּרֵי־עֲשַׂר — Twelve months.

Merit (זְכוּת) can defer impending punishment for a [maximum of one] year. We see this from Nebu-

chadnezzar, whose philanthrophy deferred his punishment twelve months (Yerushalmi Sotah 3:4; cf. Bavli ibid. 20b).

[Scripture seems to imply that had Nebuchadnezzar kept up his philanthropy, he would have escaped his doom indefinitely. Perhaps the Talmud's sensitivity is that the mention of the exact period of time elapsed between the dream and the implementation of the punishment is superfluous, since Scripture is not so explicit about the duration of the punishment when it says (v. 31) וְלִקְצָת יוֹמַיָּא, at the end of the years. This implies that these twelve months, in addition to being the arbitrary and incidental span of time Nebuchadnezzar kept up his philanthropy, were also the definite maximum of time allowed for this deferment of divine retribution.

This interpretation opens for consideration the possibility that Nebuchadnezzar's regression to his old arrogant self was not a voluntary act, but orchestrated from Above. The merit of his philanthropy had lost its efficacy, and the time had come for the king to receive his deserved punishment. In order that this lesson should not be lost upon mankind, Nebuchadnezzar had to be manipulated into a declaration of his arrogance in order to dramatize the visitation of the Divine punishment upon him. Otherwise his madness would have been ascribed to natural causes. Nebuchadnezzar's punishment was of course due not to this involuntary outburst of arrogance, but rather to his misdeeds of the past. A similar instance is found in

---

1. See Bava Basra 15a: 'Who wrote the Scriptures? The Men of the Great Assembly wrote ... Ezekiel ... and Daniel.'

Rashi there suggests that Ezekiel did not author his own Book since he prophesied in the Diaspora and perhaps prophecy may not be written outside of Eretz Yisrael. Subsequently, they [i.e., the Men of the Great Assembly] committed it to when they returned to the Land. The same applies to Daniel who was in exile [in Babylon], as well as to Megillas Esther [which took place in Persia].

4
26-28

²⁶ At the end of twelve months he was walking atop the royal palace of Babylon. ²⁷ The king exclaimed, 'Is this not the great Babylon which I have built up into a royal house with my powerful strength and for glorification of my splendor?'

²⁸ While the word was still in the king's mouth, a voice fell from heaven: 'To you, King Nebuchad-

---

God's declaration to Moses concerning Pharaoh: *And I will harden Pharaoh's heart, and multiply My signs and My wonders in the land of Egypt* (Exodus 7:3; see *Rashi* and *Ramban* there; cf. *Mishneh Torah, Hilchos Teshuvah* 6:3).

Since the explicitly stated purpose of the extreme punishment foretold by the dream was to force Nebuchadnezzar to declare his submission to God's will, we would have expected the contrite king to make such an acknowledgment immediately. Nevertheless, although he freely gave charity to ward off the punishment, he made no such declaration until after the year of travail.

Perhaps this is a classic demonstration of Rabbi Shimon ben Lakish's famous saying; 'The wicked do not repent even at the gates of Gehinnom' (*Eruvin* 19a).

Nebuchadnezzar's strange behavior could possibly also be explained through the principle enunciated by *Rambam* (*Hilchos Teshuva* 6:3): 'It is possible for a person to commit a great sin ... so that it is warranted ... that the punishment of this sinner ... should (also) be that they prevent him from repentance ... so that he will die and be destroyed through his sin.'

Since the purpose of Nebuchadnezzar's punishment was to demonstrate that *the Most Supreme One rules in the kingdom of man* (v. 14), the king could not be allowed to repent.]

עַל — *Atop.*

He was walking on the roof of his palace (*R' Shmuel Masnuth*).

27. הֲלָא דָא־הִיא — *Is this not?*

He heard the cries of the poor at his portals. He asked, 'What is this turmoil that I hear?'

His attendants answered, 'These are the poor for whom you have designated a time to collect their stipends.'

Nebuchadnezzar responded, 'If I had [always] squandered my treasuries for the support of the poor, how would I have funded the construction of all these palaces?' (*Rashi* from *Midrash Tanchuma Va'era* 17).

'This is [still] the same *Babylon which I have built*, and no sign of deterioration is discernible.' From this Nebuchadnezzar reasoned that the doom forecast for him had been cancelled. If the threat of punishment were still hanging over his head, some indication of this impending doom would have appeared by now. In the absence of any such symptoms he concluded that his punishment had been rescinded and that he could revert to his old arrogant self (*Alshich; Malbim*).

דִי־אֲנָה בֱנַיְתַהּ — *Which I have built up.*

Here he forgot the lesson he was supposed to have learned: *the Supreme One rules in the kingdom of men and to whomever He wishes He gives it.*

28. קָל מִן־שְׁמַיָּא נְפַל — *A voice fell from heaven.*

Rabbi Yossi ben Chalafta said: 'The Holy One, blessed be He, does not depose a nation before first

נְפַל לָךְ אָמְרִין נְבוּכַדְנֶצַּר מַלְכָּא

כט מַלְכוּתָא עֲדָת מִנָּךְ: וּמִן־אֲנָשָׁא לָךְ
טָרְדִין וְעִם־חֵיוַת בָּרָא מְדֹרָךְ עִשְׂבָּא
כְתוֹרִין לָךְ יְטַעֲמוּן וְשִׁבְעָה עִדָּנִין יַחְלְפוּן
°עֲלָיךְ עַד דִּי־תִנְדַּע דִּי־שַׁלִּיט °עִלָּיא

° עֲלָךְ ק׳
° עִלָּאָה ק׳

בְּמַלְכוּת אֲנָשָׁא וּלְמַן־דִּי יִצְבֵּא יִתְּנִנַּהּ:
ל בַּהּ־שַׁעֲתָא מִלְּתָא סָפַת עַל־נְבוּכַדְנֶצַּר
וּמִן־אֲנָשָׁא טְרִיד וְעִשְׂבָּא כְתוֹרִין יֵאכֻל
וּמִטַּל שְׁמַיָּא גִּשְׁמֵהּ יִצְטַבַּע עַד דִּי שַׂעְרֵהּ
לא כְּנִשְׁרִין רְבָה וְטִפְרוֹהִי כְצִפְּרִין: וְלִקְצָת
יוֹמַיָּא אֲנָה נְבוּכַדְנֶצַּר עַיְנַי | לִשְׁמַיָּא
נִטְלֵת וּמַנְדְּעִי עֲלַי יְתוּב °וּלְעִלָּיא בָּרְכֵת

° וּלְעִלָּאָה ק׳

וּלְחַי עָלְמָא שַׁבְּחֵת וְהַדְּרֵת דִּי שָׁלְטָנֵהּ
לב שָׁלְטָן עָלַם וּמַלְכוּתֵהּ עִם־דָּר וְדָר: וְכָל־

---

deposing its heavenly representative (שַׂר שֶׁלָּהּ). We find that when the Holy One, Blessed be He, deposed Nebuchadnezzar, he first deposed his guardian angel, as it is said: קָל מִן־שְׁמַיָּא נְפַל, "Kol" fell from heaven.' Rabbi Yehoshua ben Avin said: 'The name of the guardian angel of Babylon is Kol!' (Shemos Rabbah 21:5; cf. Ramban to Leviticus 18:7, Exodus 20:3, and comm. to v. 19 s.v. מטת).

31. My Intelligence Returns

עַיְנַי לִשְׁמַיָּא נִטְלֵת — Raised my eyes to heaven.

Prior to this he walked on all four like an animal. When the time came for him to be rehabilitated, he stood upright on his two feet like a human and looked up to heaven (Malbim).

וּמַנְדְּעִי עֲלַי יְתוּב — And my intelligence returned to me.

He regained his sanity gradually. He understood what he had gone through and that he was not an animal but a human. He still had not progressed to the point of regaining his original faculties and brilliance. This occurred (v. 33) only after he had acknowledged the supremacy of God and given thanks to Him (Malbim).

וּלְעִלָּאָה בָּרְכֵת — (And) the Supreme One I blessed.

The concept of בְּרָכָה, blessing, represents man's ability to make himself worthy of God's blessing and, thereby, to enable God to fulfill His desire to confer benefits upon mankind (see comm. to 2:19). Previously, Nebuchadnezzar had conceived of God only as עִלָּאָה, the

nezzar, we say: the kingdom has departed from you; ²⁹ and we are driving you from mankind, and with wild beasts will be your dwelling; grass, like oxen, they will feed you; and seven periods will pass over you; till you recognize that the Supreme One rules in the kingdom of man and to whomever He wishes He gives it.' ³⁰ At that moment the decree befell Nebuchadnezzar: From mankind he was driven; to eat grass, like oxen; and with the dew of heaven to wash his body, till his hair grew like eagles' and his nails like birds'.

³¹ 'At the end of the years, I, Nebuchadnezzar, raised my eyes to heaven, and my intelligence returned to me; the Supreme One I blessed and the Eternal One I praised and glorified, Whose rule is eternal rule and Whose kingship is with every generation. ³² All the inhabitants of the earth are

---

Supreme One, who was too exalted to concern Himself with the mundane affairs of earth. The task of guiding earthly affairs, Nebuchadnezzar thought, had been assigned by God to the angels. This being his understanding, the king could not 'bless' God, for according to his reasoning God was not the one who brought beneficence to earth. During his travail, however, the king came to realize that God was indeed the One who was חֵי עָלְמָא, *the 'enlivener' of the world.* Therefore, he finally came to bless God (*Malbim*).

דִּי שָׁלְטָנֵהּ שָׁלְטָן עָלַם — *Whose rule is eternal rule.*

This is in contradistinction to his previous declaration (3:33) where he had said: *His dominion is in every generation (see comm. ibid.).*

As explained previously (3:33), שָׁלְטָן refers to the power of God to supersede the rules of nature He has instituted to govern this world. This power, however, is used only occasionally; therefore שָׁלְטָנֵהּ, *his rule,* is distinguished from מַלְכוּתֵהּ, *his kingship,* which refers to God's rule of the world through the powers of nature created by Him. His *kingship* is therefore לְעָלַם, *everlasting,* whereas His שָׁלְטָן, *rule,* is only עִם־דָּר וְדָר, *with every generation,* i.e., occasional and temporary.

Now Nebuchadnezzar realized that even His *rule* — i.e., His interference with the powers of nature to make them conform to the higher purpose of His creation — is also לְעָלַם, *incessant* and *forever.* As *Ramban* so aptly puts it (in reference to the purpose of

°דָּיְרֵי ק׳ °דָאֲרֵי אַרְעָא כְּלָה חֲשִׁיבִין וּכְמִצְבְּיֵהּ
°וְדָיְרֵי ק׳ עָבֵד בְּחֵיל שְׁמַיָּא °וְדָאֲרֵי אַרְעָא וְלָא
אִיתַי דִּי־יְמַחֵא בִידֵהּ וְיֵאמַר לֵהּ מָה
לג עֲבַדְתְּ: בֵּהּ־זִמְנָא מַנְדְּעִי | יְתוּב עֲלַי
וְלִיקַר מַלְכוּתִי הַדְרִי וְזִיוִי יְתוּב עֲלַי וְלִי
הַדָּבְרַי וְרַבְרְבָנַי יְבַעוֹן וְעַל־מַלְכוּתִי
לד הָתְקְנַת וּרְבוּ יַתִּירָא הוּסְפַת לִי: כְּעַן
אֲנָה נְבֻכַדְנֶצַּר מְשַׁבַּח וּמְרוֹמֵם וּמְהַדַּר
לְמֶלֶךְ שְׁמַיָּא דִּי כָל־מַעֲבָדוֹהִי קְשׁוֹט
וְאֹרְחָתֵהּ דִּין וְדִי מַהְלְכִין בְּגֵוָה יָכִל
לְהַשְׁפָּלָה:

miracles): 'From the great and manifest miracles a person comes to acknowledge the hidden miracles, נִסִּים נִסְתָּרִים, which are the basis of the whole Torah' (Exodus 13:16). And as he explains elsewhere (Genesis 27:1): 'It is not attributable to nature that the rains should come in their time when we serve God.' This belief in hidden miracles is a necessary corollary to the principles of הַשְׁגָּחָה, God's Providence, and שָׂכָר וָעוֹנֶשׁ, His reward and punishment, the very cornerstones of Judaism. These hidden miracles, skillfully hidden and interwoven in the tapestry of nature are also לְעֹלָם, unceasing and everlasting. We attest to this in our daily prayers when we say 'וְעַל נִסֶּיךָ שֶׁבְּכָל יוֹם עִמָּנוּ, and for Your miracles which are with us every day' (Shemoneh Esrai). Nebuchadnezzar's madness was not an occurrence that transcended nature. Only the circumstances surrounding it — i.e., the dream foretelling it, its sudden appearance, and its remarkable coincidence with the king's arrogant words (v. 28) — elevated it to the rank of a miracle. This demonstrated to the king that the hand of God directs all the other occurrences of this kind — i.e., the miracles not apparent to the eye of the nonbeliever (Malbim).

32. כְּלָה — For nothing.

The word לָא, nothing, is usually spelled with an א, aleph, and not the ה, he, used here. However, a Masoretic note on this verse reads, 'ה, he, in place of א, aleph.' Thus, the translation follows this substitution.

בְּחֵיל שְׁמַיָּא — With the host of heaven.

The fortunes of kings and their empires are tied to what transpires to their representatives in heaven (see comm. to v. 28).

וְלָא אִיתַי דִּי־יְמַחֵא בִידֵהּ — (And) there is no one who can stay His hand.

4

33-34

reckoned for nothing, and according to His will does He do with the host of heaven and the inhabitants of the earth; there is no one who can stay His hand or say to him, "What have You done?"

³³ At that time, my intelligence returned to me and to the glory of my kingdom I returned, my appearance came back to me, and my ministers and nobles asked for me; over my kingdom I was established, and additional greatness was given to me. ³⁴ Now, I, Nebuchadnezzar, praise and extol and glorify the King of heaven, all of Whose works are truth, and His path justice, and those who walk proudly He is able to humble.'

Our sages interpret this remark as a reproach by Nebuchadnezzar. In a manner reminiscent of Job, he realized the helplessness of man vis-a-vis God and gave vent to his feeling that man was but a plaything in the hand of God, who does as He pleases with man because He has to answer to no one for His actions (עפ״ל). One hears an echo of Job's complaint: 'If the scourge slay suddenly He will mock at the calamity of the guiltless' (Job 9:23). As his perception of God's rule of the world deepened, he repented from his hasty criticism of God's ways and exclaimed: 'All of [His] works are truth, and His path justice' (From Shemos Rabbah 20:10).

33. מַנְדְּעִי יְתוּב עֲלַי — My intelligence returned to me.

His former brilliance of mind and the acuteness of his senses returned fully. He was again fit to rule his empire (Malbim).

34. אֲנָה נְבֻכַדְנֶצַּר — I, Nebuchadnezzar.

Alshich points out the curiosity that throughout the whole letter the king titles himself King Nebuchadnezzar, whereas here, at the pinnacle of his glory, after additional greatness was given to me, he calls himself simply Nebuchadnezzar. This demonstrates how well Nebuchadnezzar had learned the lesson about the evils of arrogance.

The Talmud (Berachos 34a) rules, regarding a Jewish king, 'from the time he bows down he does not raise his head until he finishes his prayer' (Rambam, Hilchos Tefillah 5:10), unlike all other Jews who bow only at four points during prayer. This illustrates that the king has a greater obligation to guard against the evil of arrogance. Therefore, as Nebuchadnezzar's glory reached new heights, he recognized the need for a greater show of humility and self-depreciation.

בֵּלְשַׁאצַּר מַלְכָּא עֲבַד לְחֶם רַב א

לְרַבְרְבָנוֹהִי אֲלַף וְלָקֳבֵל אַלְפָּא חַמְרָא

שָׁתֵה: בֵּלְשַׁאצַּר אֲמַר | בִּטְעֵם חַמְרָא ב

לְהַיְתָיָה לְמָאנֵי דַּהֲבָא וְכַסְפָּא דִּי הַנְפֵּק

נְבוּכַדְנֶצַּר אֲבוּהִי מִן־הֵיכְלָא דִּי

V.

Belshazzar's Great Feast

1. בֵּלְשַׁאצַּר — *Belshazzar.*

There is disagreement about who this Belshazzar was. *Rashi,* probably relying on verses 18 ('*Nebuchadnezzar, your father*') and 22 ('*But you, his son Belshazzar*') assumes that both Belshazzar and Evil Merodach, who reigned before him (*II Kings* 25:27; *Jeremiah* 52:31), were sons of Nebuchadnezzar (cf. *Midrash Asarah M'lachim* in *Otzar Midrashim* p.463; *Tanchuma,* ed. *Buber, Bereishis* p.96; *Yalkut Esther* 1049).

The consensus of the commentators is that Belshazzar was Evil Merodach's son. This is based on the verse in *Jeremiah* (27:7), *And all the nations shall serve him (Nebuchadnezzar) and his son and his son's son.* Since Belshazzar was the last ruler of the Babylonian empire (see *vs.* 5:28-6:1), he must have been Nebuchadnezzar's grandson. This also seems to be the view of *Seder Olam Rabbah* (ch. 28). Indeed *Rashi* concurs in his commentary to *Jeremiah* (loc. cit.). The references to Nebuchadnezzar as Belshazzar's 'father' are explained with proof from other passages in Scripture where grandfathers are referred to as אָב, *father* (see *Rashi* to *Numbers* 10:29).

The *Midrash* (*Bereishis Rabbah* 85:2) asks, And where is Evil Merodach [i.e., why is no mention made of him here? Did nothing noteworthy pertaining to the Jews take place during his reign of twenty-three years?]. Rabbi Elazar said: ['This is] in order to place the matters of an evildoer next to the matters of another evildoer.' [Nebuchadnezzar and Belshazzar were both wicked, but Evil Merodach nullified some of his father's evil decrees'] (*Rashi;* see *II Kings* 25:27; *Seder Olam Rabbah,* ch. 28; *Yalkut Isaiah* 418). Rav Huna bar Acha said, '[The events are not listed in direct chronological sequence] so that they should not say it is [narrative] poetry, so that all should know that he [the author of the book] wrote it *under the influence of the Holy Spirit.*' Scripture is not a chronological record of events. All of it, even the parts dealing on their surface with historical events, are revelations from God to man carrying His message, whether in their פְּשַׁט, *apparent meaning,* in their רֶמֶז, *implications,* or in allusions so hidden as to be esoteric (סוֹד). Chronology is adhered to only where it does not interfere with the transmission of the underlying message. This is the principle behind the well known dictum: אֵין מוּקְדָם

5

1-2

King Belshazzar made a great feast for his thousand nobles and drank wine before the thousand. ² Belshazzar gave orders, while under the influence of the wine, to bring the gold and silver vessels which Nebuchadnezzar, his father, had removed from the

וּמְאוּחָר בַּתּוֹרָה, *the Torah does not necessarily follow chronological sequence (Pesachim 6b; Rashi to Numbers 9:1).*

לְחֶם — *Feast.*

לְחֶם, lit. *bread,* here means סְעוּדָה, *feast,* as evidenced from the context (*Rashi; Metzudos;* cf. *Rashi to Leviticus 21:21*).

Radak (Shorashim s.v. לחם) assumes that the opposite is true. לְחֶם is a generic term for food, but because bread is the mainstay of most diets, this term most often means bread alone (cf. *Genesis 43:32*).

לְחֶם רַב — *A great feast.*

The purpose of this celebration is not given here. *Rashi,* citing *Yosippon* (ch. 3), relates that Belshazzar had battled Darius and Cyrus that day and had been victorious. But in the middle of the festivities the Persians and Medes returned and conquered Babylon. Another purpose can be found in the calculations mentioned in *v. 2.*

וְלָקֳבֵל אַלְפָּא — *[And] before the thousand.*

I.e., in their presence — contrary to the custom of kings. The *Talmud* (*Megillah* 11b) interprets that in his drunken orgy, Belshazzar drank as much as a thousand people normally would.

2. בִּטְעֵם — *While under the influence.*

Rashi and *Ibn Ezra* derive this verb from עֵטָא וּטְעֵם, *counsel and advice* (2:14). Thus, literally, the king acted *on the advice of the wine* — i.e., under its influence. He was intoxicated (see *comm.* to 3:12).

דִּי הַנְפֵּק נְבוּכַדְנֶצַּר אֲבוּהִי — *Which Nebuchadnezzar, his father, had removed.*

The *Talmud* (*Megillah* 11b; cf. *Seder Olam Rabbah* 28), sees this seemingly casual act of desecration as a meticulously calculated and premeditated act on the part of Belshazzar. The prophetic words of Jeremiah in his letter to the Babylonian exiles: *For thus says HASHEM: 'After seventy years are complete for Babylon, I will remember ... and return you to this place' (Jeremiah 29:10),* were known to the Babylonian monarchs. As long as they feared the fulfillment of this prophecy, the Babylonian kings left the vessels of the holy Temple untouched in the treasure house of their gods (see 1:3). But as soon as his calculations proved to Belshazzar that the seventy years had passed without the divinely promised return of the Jews to *Eretz Yisrael* taking place, he felt that the Chaldean royal house had finally triumphed over the God of the Jews, and therefore proceeded to desecrate the vessels of the temple without fear of retribution.

Belshazzar calculated the seventy years from Nebuchadnezzar's ac-

בִּירוּשְׁלֶם וְיִשְׁתּוֹן בְּהוֹן מַלְכָּא

ג וְרַבְרְבָנוֹהִי שֵׁגְלָתֵהּ וּלְחֵנָתֵהּ: בֵּאדַיִן

הַיְתִיו מָאנֵי דַהֲבָא דִּי הַנְפִּקוּ מִן־הֵיכְלָא

דִּי־בֵית אֱלָהָא דִּי בִירוּשְׁלֶם וְאִשְׁתִּיו

בְּהוֹן מַלְכָּא וְרַבְרְבָנוֹהִי שֵׁגְלָתֵהּ

ד וּלְחֵנָתֵהּ: אִשְׁתִּיו חַמְרָא וְשַׁבַּחוּ לֵאלָהֵי

דַהֲבָא וְכַסְפָּא נְחָשָׁא פַרְזְלָא אָעָא

---

cession to the throne. Nebuchadnezzar reigned forty-five years. [Yehoyachin (Yechonyah) was taken into captivity in the eighth year of Nebuchadnezzar's reign (*II Kings* 24:12). Scripture tells us that Evil Merodach's reign started in the thirty-seventh year of Yehoyachin's captivity (*II Kings* 25:27; *Jeremiah* 52:31). This gives us a total of forty-five. All the years are assumed to be full years — i.e., Nebuchadnezzar is considered to have exiled Yehoyachin toward the end of his eighth year, so we can count this as a full year in Nebuchadnezzar's reign. In the case of Yehoyachin's thirty-seven year prison term, Scripture tells us that it ended toward the end of the twelfth month.] Evil Merodach's reign lasted twenty-three years. For this there is no Scriptural evidence; the Sages had it through Oral Tradition. [*Zemach David*, (1:364) notes that the years of his reign can be approximated by combining the years of Nebuchadnezzar and Belshazzar and subtracting the total from the seventy years of Babylon. The remaining years must be Evil Merodach's. This however is not a fool-proof method since we have no Scriptural evidence for the number of years Belshazzar reigned. We

know that his reign extended to a third year (8:4; cf. *comm.* to 1:1 and *Overview* to ArtScroll *Esther* p. 23), and so must rely on the tradition of the Sages (that this third year was the last year of his reign).] Add to this two years of Belshazzar's rule, and you have seventy years. Therefore the third year of his reign (the seventy-first from Nebuchadnezzar's accession) was, by this computation, after the deadline given by Jeremiah for the return of the Jewish exiles.

Belshazzar's calculation had one flaw. The seventy years mentioned by Jeremiah did not commence with the beginning of Nebuchadnezzar's reign. The period could not have begun until at least a year later, with the beginning of Babylon's subjugation of Judah. Consequently, at least another year had to elapse for this deadline to be reached. That year was filled out with the reign of Darius the Mede. We find reference to his reign in *Daniel* (8:1): *In the first year of Darius ben Ahasuerus the Mede* (cf. 6:1). Since this is the only date mentioned in connection with Darius, our Sages conclude that his reign lasted no longer than this one year (*Seder Olam* 28; see *Megillah* 11b and *Rashi*). Darius the Mede was

5

3-4 *Temple in Jerusalem; for the king and his nobles, his queen, and his concubines, to drink from them.* ³ *Then they brought the gold vessels that they had removed from the Temple of the house of God in Jerusalem, and the king, his nobles, his queen, and his concubines drank from them.* ⁴ *They drank wine and praised gods of gold and silver, copper, iron, wood, and stone.*

---

succeeded by Cyrus [the Great] about whom it is written, *And in the first year of Cyrus, King of Persia, when the word of God by the mouth of Jeremiah had been concluded,* HASHEM *stirred up the spirit of Cyrus, King of Persia, so that he made a proclamation throughout his kingdom, '... Whoever there is among you of all His people ... let him go up to Jerusalem.'* The prophecy had been fulfilled exactly as foretold. [It seems that had Belshazzar not sinned so grievously, he would have filled out this year himself.]

מִן־הֵיכְלָא דִּי בִירוּשְׁלֶם — *From the Temple in Jerusalem.*

He failed to make note of the fact that it was *the Temple 'of God'* which is *in Jerusalem.* This omission accurately mirrored the derision he displayed toward God when he desecrated the vessels of His Temple in so flagrant a manner *(Malbim).*

שֵׁגְלָתֵהּ וּלְחֵנָתֵהּ — *His queen and his concubines.*

Protocol in that period of history did not have women taking part in revels of this kind, as evidenced by Vashti's separate party for the women in Ahasuerus' time *(Esther* 1:9). The inclusion of women in Belshazzar's drunken feast was calculated to add an air of licentiousness to the revel. This was part of Belshazzar's plan to turn this celebration into a demonstration of disrespect toward God *(Malbim).*

שֵׁגְלָתֵהּ — *His queen.*

The translation follows *Rashi* and the *Talmud (Rosh Hashanah* 4a). Some commentators maintain that שֵׁגְלָתֵהּ refers to one of his wives, and that the queen was not present (see *comm.* to *v.* 10).

3. מָאנֵי דַהֲבָא — *Gold vessels.*

In contrast to the king's order (*v.* 2) *to bring the gold and silver vessels,* only *gold vessels* were actually brought. The gold vessels were so numerous that the silver vessels were not needed *(Alshich).*

מִן־הֵיכְלָא דִּי־בֵית אֱלָהָא — *From the Temple of the house of God.*

Even though the king had displayed his derision by failing to mention that the vessels had belonged to God's temple, the servants whose obligation it was to carry out the king's order did their duty with full awareness of the holy nature of these vessels *(Malbim).*

4. אִשְׁתִּיו חַמְרָא וְשַׁבַּחוּ — *They drank wine and praised.*

At first they were content to simply drink wine from these holy vessels. But, as the party went on,

ה וְאַבְנָא: בֵּהּ שַׁעֲתָה °נְפַקוּ אֶצְבְּעָן דִּי יַד־
אֱנָשׁ וְכָתְבָן לָקֳבֵל נֶבְרַשְׁתָּא עַל־גִּירָא
דִּי־כְתַל הֵיכְלָא דִּי מַלְכָּא וּמַלְכָּא חָזֵה
ו פַּס יְדָא דִּי כָתְבָה: אֱדַיִן מַלְכָּא זִיוֹהִי
שְׁנוֹהִי וְרַעְיֹנֹהִי יְבַהֲלוּנֵּהּ וְקִטְרֵי חַרְצֵהּ
ז מִשְׁתָּרַיִן וְאַרְכֻבָּתֵהּ דָּא לְדָא נָקְשָׁן: קָרֵא
מַלְכָּא בְּחַיִל לְהֶעָלָה לְאָשְׁפַיָּא °כַּשְׂדָּיֵא ק׳
וְגָזְרַיָּא עָנֵה מַלְכָּא וְאָמַר | לְחַכִּימֵי בָבֶל
דִּי כָל־אֱנָשׁ דִּי־יִקְרֵה כְּתָבָה דְנָה וּפִשְׁרֵהּ

the king felt that the ultimate in desecration had not been reached yet. He bade them drink wine out of the vessels and at the same time praise *gods of gold and silver* (Malbim).

5. The Handwriting

בֵּהּ־שַׁעֲתָה — *Just then.*

The dramatic effect of this exquisite timing was needed in order to teach that Belshazzar's temporal success was no gauge for foretelling the future. At the height of his prosperity and power, his imminent downfall was announced. Prosperity and power, which were taken as indications of longevity and security, were only a facade camouflaging an empty core. Babylon, despite outward appearances, had already ceased to exist as an empire from the celestial point of view. The writing was already on the wall (Alshich).

נְפַקָה אֶצְבְּעָן דִּי יַד־אֱנָשׁ — *Fingers of a man's hand came forth.*

The appearance of the hand was needed to remove the suspicion that a prank was being played. Someone might have slipped in unseen and put the writing on the wall. The sight of the unattached hand dispelled all such doubts (Malbim).

לָקֳבֵל נֶבְרַשְׁתָּא — *Facing the candelabrum.*

I.e., the area best lit, so that everyone should see the writing.

Most commentators agree that a *candelabrum* is meant here. *R' Shmuel Masnuth* gives lamp as an alternate interpretation. *R' Saadiah,* according to his conception of a word used in *Yerushalmi* (Yoma 3:8, 19a) renders it *lantern.* All these translations find their expression in *Talmud Yerushalmi Yoma (ibid.)* where we find the *Amoraim* disagreeing about the meaning of נֶבְרַשְׁתָּא mentioned in the *Mishnah.* The first opinion is that it is a מְנוֹרָה, *candelabrum;* the second opinion — depending on the translation of the Greek and Aramaic words used in the text — a *lamp (Korban Ha'edah, P'nei Moshe,* cf. *R' Chananel* to Yoma 37b) or a *lantern (R' Saadiah; M'leches Shlomo* to Mishnah Yoma 3:10).

Still another view cited by *R' Saadiah* renders it *window.* This seems to be also the view of *Rambam* who renders נֶבְרַשְׁתָּא in the Mishnah (Yoma 3:10) as *window-pane.* [According to this view, the feast took place by day.]

5

5-7

⁵ *Just then the fingers of a man's hand came forth and wrote on the plaster of the wall of the king's palace facing the candelabrum; and the king saw a hand that was writing.* ⁶ *Then the king's appearance changed and he was bewildered; the belt around his waist opened and his knees knocked one against the other.*

⁷ *The king cried aloud to bring in the astrologers, the Chaldeans, and the demonists. The king exclaimed, to the sages of Babylon, that whoever will read this writing and tell its interpretation will wear*

עַל־גִּירָא — *On the plaster.*

[The color contrast between the writing and the white plaster would make the writing clearly visible to everyone present.]

וּמַלְכָּא חֲזֵה — *And the king saw.*

Only the king saw the hand actually *writing*. The others only saw *the fingers of a man's hand* without witnessing the actual act of writing. This was to indicate to the king that the message was addressed to him. To keep the king from thinking that what he had seen was just an alcoholic illusion, the others were also permitted to see this unusual sight in order to attest to its authenticity to the king (*Alshich*).

פַּס יְדָא — *A hand* [lit. *palm of a hand*].

[יַד and its Aramaic counterpart יְדָא refer not only to the hand but to the whole arm (see *Tosafos* to *Menachos* 37a, s.v. קבורת). Here, where only the hand is meant, יְדָא is modified by the addition of פַּס. The Hebrew counterpart would be כַּף יַד.]

6. מַלְכָּא זִיוֹהִי שְׁנוֹהִי וְרַעְיֹנֹהִי יְבַהֲלוּנֵּהּ

— *Then the king's appearance changed and he was bewildered* [lit. *his thoughts bewildered him*].

I.e. he turned pale.

Only the king was frightened to this degree. He understood that the message was specifically directed at him, and from the timing, that this was due to his desecration of the Temple vessels. He sensed that the message boded no good for him and his reign (*Alshich*).

וְקִטְרֵי חַרְצֵהּ מִשְׁתָּרַיִן — *(And) the belt(s) around his waist opened.*

The translation follows *Rashi* (cf. *Onkelos, Deuteronomy* 6:8). The plural form קִטְרֵי indicates that the king wore several belts, or that he had several fasteners or knots in a single belt. Because of the extreme fright that befell the king, his loins constricted, causing the belt(s) to open.

Metzudos, following *Ibn Ezra* and *R' Saadiah*, renders: *and the joints of his loins loosened* [i.e., his bones became unfastened]. *Metzudos* remarks that this is not meant literally.

ה ° וְהַמְנִיכָא ק׳ יְחַוְּנַנִי אַרְגְּוָנָא יִלְבַּשׁ °וְהַמוֹנְכָא דִי־
ח־י דַהֲבָא עַל־צַוְּארֵהּ וְתַלְתִּי בְּמַלְכוּתָא
° עֲלִין ק׳ ח יִשְׁלַט: אֱדַיִן °עֲלִלִין כֹּל
חַכִּימֵי מַלְכָּא וְלָא־כָהֲלִין כְּתָבָא לְמִקְרֵא
° וּפִשְׁרֵהּ ק׳ ט °וּפִשְׁרָא לְהוֹדָעָה לְמַלְכָּא: אֱדַיִן מַלְכָּא
בֵּלְשַׁאצַּר שַׂגִּיא מִתְבָּהַל וְזִיוֹהִי שָׁנַיִן
י עֲלוֹהִי וְרַבְרְבָנוֹהִי מִשְׁתַּבְּשִׁין: מַלְכְּתָא

7. Bewilderment and Consternation

אַרְגְּוָנָא יִלְבַּשׁ וְהַמְנִיכָא דִי־דַהֲבָא עַל־
צַוְּארֵהּ — *Will wear purple and [have] a golden chain on his neck.*

These were symbols of nobility (*Rashi; R' Saadiah;* cf. *Genesis 41:42*).

וְתַלְתִּי בְּמַלְכוּתָא יִשְׁלַט — *And will rule one third of the kingdom.*

The translation follows *Rashi* and *Ibn Ezra. R' Saadiah* renders, *and will rule third in the kingdom. Abarbanel (Mayenei HaYeshuah 7:1)* suggests that Babylon was ruled by a triumvirate of great princes subordinate only to Belshazaar. Whoever interpreted the writing would rule as one of the triumvirate. Thus when Scripture mentions (*6:3*), *and over them three ministers of whom Daniel was one,* it means that Darius merely maintained the *status quo.*

8. וְלָא־כָהֲלִין כְּתָבָא לְמִקְרֵא — *But could not read the writing.*

Several reasons are given in the *Talmud (Sanhedrin 22a)* to explain their inability to read the writing. Even if it was written in Hebrew script, it is hardly imaginable that among all the sages of Babylon there were none who could read the

Hebrew script (cf. *Yossipon ch. 3; Mayenei HaYeshuah 7:1*).

One school of thought holds that the writing was in כְּתָב אַשּׁוּרִי, *the Hebrew square script*, used today for Torah scrolls, which was unknown up to that time. Rabbi Yossi holds that originally the Torah was written in the *Ivry* script (כְּתָב עִבְרִי, כְּתָב לִיבוֹנָאָה). *Ramban* (in a note added at the end of his commentary to Torah) identifies this script as the old script used (with variations) by the Samaritans in their Torah scrolls and by the Jews at the time of the Second Temple on their coins (cf. *Rashi ibid.* 21b s.v. ליבונאה; *Chiddushei HaRan ibid.*).

[For the reader interested in pursuing further the change in Hebrew scripts, the following references will give some insight into this delicate subject. *Ritva* and *Rashba* to *Megillah* 2b; *Ikarim* 3:16; *HaKosev* to *Ein Yaakov* on *Megillah* 2b; *Radvaz Responsum* 883; *Pesach Eynayim* (Chida) to *Megillah* 2b; *Toras Haneviim* (R' Hirsh Chayes) 1:13.]

The other school of thought follows Rabbi Elazar HaModai, who holds that the script we use today in Torah scrolls was never changed. Therefore the difficulty the Babylonian sages had in reading the writing could not have been with the script but was in some other area. *Rav* holds that the words מְנֵא

דניאל [162]

purple and have a golden chain on his neck and will rule one third of the kingdom.

⁸ *Then all the king's sages came in, but could not read the writing and make its interpretation known to the king.* ⁹ *Then King Belshazzar was greatly bewildered and his appearance changed, and his nobles were thrown into consternation.*

מְנֵא מְנֵא תְּקֵל וּפַרְסִין, MENEI MENEI TEKEIL UFARSIN, were written in code, each letter in the alphabet substituted for a counterpart from the other end of the alphabet, e.g., *Alef* replaces *Tav*, *Bes* replaces *Shin*, and so on (א״ת ב״ש ג״ר ד״ק; cf. *Shabbos* 104a). Accordingly the words were written, יטת יטם אדך פוגחמט. Thus the sages, though able to read the script, could not decipher the words.

Shmuel holds that the letters forming the words were not arranged in their normal sequence, but the message read, ממתוס ננקפי אאלרן.

Maharsha explains that the letters were written as three five-letter words one atop the other:

מ מ ת ו ס

נ נ ק פ י

ו א ל ר ן

The message can thus be read clearly when it is read from top to bottom instead of the customary right to left.

Maharshal understands Shmuel to mean that there were five groups of three letters each, arranged one above the other. The message could only be understood by reading every fifth letter. The first word was formed by letters 1, 6, 11; the second by letters 2, 7, 12; the third by letters 3, 8, 13; the fourth by let-ters 4, 9, 14, 5, 10, 15.

3	2	1
ת	מ	מ

6	5	4
נ	ס	ו

9	8	7
פ	ק	נ

12	11	10
א	א	י

15	14	13
ו	ר	ל

Rav Yochanan says the words were simply written backwards (from left to right). Thus, אנמ אנמ לקת ניסרפו. *Rav Ashi* holds the first two letters in each word were transposed thus נמא נמא קתל פורסין.

וּפִשְׁרֵהּ לְהוֹדָעָה — *And make its interpretation known.*

Since they could not even read the words, they surely could not interpret them.

If the difficulty the sages had in deciphering the message stemmed from the arrangement of the letters, rather than from any difficulty in reading the script, this phrase takes on the meaning, they *could not read the writing* in such a manner as to be able to *make its interpretation known* (Alshich).

9. שַׂגִּיא מִתְבָּהַל — *Was greatly bewildered.*

His fright grew even greater.

לְקַבֵּל מִלֵּי מַלְכָּא וְרַבְרְבָנוֹהִי לְבֵית
מִשְׁתְּיָא °עַלַּת עֲנָת מַלְכְּתָא וַאֲמֶרֶת
מַלְכָּא לְעָלְמִין חֱיִי אַל־יְבַהֲלוּךְ רַעְיוֹנָךְ
°וְזִיוָיךְ אַל־יִשְׁתַּנּוֹ: אִיתַי גְּבַר בְּמַלְכוּתָךְ
דִּי רוּחַ אֱלָהִין קַדִּישִׁין בֵּהּ וּבְיוֹמֵי אֲבוּךְ
נַהִירוּ וְשָׂכְלְתָנוּ וְחָכְמָה כְּחָכְמַת־אֱלָהִין
הִשְׁתְּכַחַת בֵּהּ וּמַלְכָּא נְבֻכַדְנֶצַּר אֲבוּךְ
רַב חַרְטֻמִּין אָשְׁפִין כַּשְׂדָּאִין גָּזְרִין
הֲקִימֵהּ אֲבוּךְ מַלְכָּא: כָּל־קֳבֵל דִּי רוּחַ |
יַתִּירָה וּמַנְדַּע וְשָׂכְלְתָנוּ מְפַשַּׁר חֶלְמִין
וַאַחֲוָיַת אֲחִידָן וּמְשָׁרֵא קִטְרִין הִשְׁתְּכַחַת
בֵּהּ בְּדָנִיֵּאל דִּי־מַלְכָּא שָׂם־שְׁמֵהּ
בֵּלְטְשַׁאצַּר כְּעַן דָּנִיֵּאל יִתְקְרֵי וּפִשְׁרָה

יא־יב °עַלַּת ק'

°וְזִיוָךְ ק'

יא

יב

וְזִיוֹהִי שָׁנַיִן עֲלוֹהִי — *And his ap-pearance changed* [lit. *upon him*].

I.e., the paleness that had appeared on his face initially, when he saw the hand, now intensified (*Me-tzudos*).

10. 'Let Daniel be called.'

מַלְכְּתָא — *The queen.*

Upon hearing the commotion which had been caused by the writing on the wall, she entered the banquet hall (*Rashi*).

Even though the king's wife and concubine had been present at the time the writing appeared on the wall (*v.* 2), this did not include the queen. Among his many wives, there was one who bore the title queen and was entitled to the special honor and privilege that went with it. Her lofty status excused her from taking part in the king's drunken revel (*Mayenei HaYeshuah* 7:1).

Ibn Ezra quotes an opinion that

this *queen* is the wife of Nebu-chadnezzar — i.e., the queen mother. This is also how *Josephus Flavius (Antiquities* 10, 11:3) relates the story.

[Although *Rashi* interprets שֶׁגְלָתֵהּ in *v.* 2 as מַלְכְּתָא, *the queen*, indicating that the queen was there during the foregoing events, it seems that during the commotion follow-ing the appearance of the writing, she and the concubine left the room. They were not present when the king conferred with the sages. After the sages' endeavors failed, the queen reentered to offer her advice.]

אַל־יְבַהֲלוּךְ רַעְיוֹנָךְ — *Do not be bewildered* [lit. *do not let your thoughts bewilder you*].

The king's fright had doubled when he saw that he could expect no interpretation from the sages (*v.* 9). He may have sensed that the absence of an interpretation signal-ed that there was no escape from the evil fate which hung over his head, for he was not to know his fate to assure that he would not attempt to

¹⁰ *The queen, as a consequence of the words of the king and his nobles, came into the banquet hall. The queen exclaimed: 'O king live forever! Do not be bewildered, nor let your appearance be changed.* ¹¹ *There is a man in your kingdom in whom is the spirit of the Holy God; and in your father's days, illumination, understanding, and wisdom like the wisdom of God were found in him; and King Nebuchadnezzar, your father, made him chief of the necromancers, astrologers, Chaldeans, and demonists — your father, the king.* ¹² *Since extraordinary spirit, intelligence, understanding, interpreting of dreams, solving of riddles, and loosing of knots, are found in Daniel, whom the king named Belteshazzar, let Daniel now be called and he will tell the interpretation.'*

escape it. Thus the queen's assurance that *there is a man* who could interpret the king's dream should serve to mitigate his fright (Alshich; Malbim).

11. רוּחַ — *Spirit.*

The inability of the greatest sages of Babylon to decipher the writing did not indicate that the message was impossible for Daniel to decipher. Daniel, because *the spirit of the Holy God* is within him, could succeed where all the sages had failed (Malbim).

נַהִירוּ — *Illumination.*

He is endowed with the power to shed light upon the most mysterious things (R' Shmuel Masnuth).

וְשָׂכְלְתָנוּ — *(And) understanding.*

The Aramaic וְשָׂכְלְתָנוּ is the equivalent of the Hebrew בִּינָה. See *Onkelos* to וּבִתְבוּנָה וּבְדַעַת (*Exodus* 31:3) (R' Shmuel Masnuth). See

comm. to 1:20 for the difference between חָכְמָה and בִּינָה.

12. דִּי־מַלְכָּא שָׂם־שְׁמֵהּ בֵּלְטְשַׁאצַּר — *Whom the king named Belteshazzar.*

Except for this reference to Daniel's Babylonian name, he is called Daniel throughout this chapter. It seems that name had been all but forgotten and he was generally known as Daniel. See *comm.* 1:7.

The queen mentioned this as part of her unstinting praise of Daniel. Nebuchadnezzar had named him Belteshazzar *like the name of my god* (4:5), because he had sensed that Daniel's extraordinary qualities were due to a supernatural spirit he was endowed with. Thus, *since extraordinary spirit ... are found in Daniel*, the king found it fitting to name him *Belteshazzar* [like his god] (Alshich).

[Daniel's Babylonian name had

בֵּאדַ֫יִן   יְהַחֲוֵֽה: יג

דָּנִיֵּאל֙ הֻעַל֙ קֳדָ֣ם מַלְכָּ֔א עָנֵ֥ה מַלְכָּ֖א

וְאָמַ֣ר לְדָנִיֵּ֔אל °אנתה־הוּא דָ֣נִיֵּ֔אל דִּי־   ° אַנְתְּ ק׳

מִן־בְּנֵ֤י גָלוּתָא֙ דִּ֣י יְה֔וּד דִּ֥י הַיְתִ֖י מַלְכָּ֥א

אַבִ֖י מִן־יְהֽוּד: וְשִׁמְעֵ֣ת °עליך דִּ֣י ר֤וּחַ   יד   ° עֲלָךְ ק׳

אֱלָהִין֙ בָּ֔ךְ וְנַהִיר֧וּ וְשָׂכְלְתָנ֛וּ וְחָכְמָ֥ה

יַתִּירָ֖ה הִשְׁתְּכַ֥חַת בָּֽךְ:   וּכְעַ֣ן הֻעַ֣לּוּ קֳדָמַ֗י   טו

חַכִּֽימַיָּא֙ אָֽשְׁפַיָּ֔א דִּֽי־כְתָבָ֤ה דְנָה֙ יִקְר֔וֹן

וּפִשְׁרֵ֖הּ לְהֽוֹדָעֻתַ֑נִי וְלָֽא־כָהֲלִ֥ין פְּשַׁר־

מִלְּתָ֖א לְהַחֲוָיָֽה: וַאֲנָה֙ שִׁמְעֵ֣ת °עליך דִּֽי־   טז   ° עֲלָךְ

°תוּכַל פִּשְׁרִ֥ין לְמִפְשַׁ֖ר וְקִטְרִ֣ין לְמִשְׁרֵ֑א   ° תכּל ק׳

כְּעַ֣ן הֵ֣ן °תוּכַל֩ כְּתָבָ֨א לְמִקְרֵ֜א וּפִשְׁרֵ֣הּ   ° תכּל ק׳

לְהֽוֹדָעֻתַ֗נִי אַרְגְּוָנָ֤א תִלְבַּשׁ֙ °והמונכא   ° וְהַמְנִיכָא ק׳

דִֽי־דַהֲבָ֣א עַֽל־צַוְּארָ֔ךְ וְתַלְתָּ֥א בְמַלְכוּתָ֖א

תִּשְׁלַֽט: בֵּאדַ֫יִן עָנֵ֤ה דָֽנִיֵּאל֙   יז

וְאָמַ֣ר קֳדָ֣ם מַלְכָּ֔א מַתְּנָתָךְ֙ לָ֣ךְ לֶֽהֶוְיָ֔ן

וּנְבָ֥זְבְּיָתָ֖ךְ לְאָחֳרָ֣ן הַ֑ב בְּרַ֗ם כְּתָבָא֙ אֶקְרֵ֣א

לְמַלְכָּ֔א וּפִשְׁרָ֖א אֲהוֹדְעִנֵּֽהּ:   °אנתה   יח   ° אַנְתְּ ק׳

---

been given him not by the king, but by an officer (1:7). Nevertheless, because Nebuchadnezzar had ratified and praised the use of the name (4:5), the queen's comment was justified.]

13. 'Read, interpret, and rule.'

אַנְתְּ־הוּא דָנִיֵּאל — *You are Daniel.*

Malbim understands this phrase not as a query but as a statement. The king's words were meant in praise of Daniel. The exile that had been brought to Babylon by Nebuchadnezzar had been the elite and the aristocracy. As much is ex-

pressed in Esther where Scripture, after listing Mordechai's pedigree, adds, *who had been exiled from Jerusalem with the exiles who had been exiled with Yechoniah King of Judah, whom Nebuchadnezzar King of Babylon had exiled* (Esther 2:6). Thus it was a mark of distinction to have been of Nebuchadnezzar's exile. The second exile, which was carried out by Nebuzeradan, consisted mainly of the lower strata of Jewish society.

R' Shmuel Masnuth, R' Saadiah, and *R' Yeshaye,* quoting from *Midrash Tanchuma (Mekeitz* ed.

5
13-17

¹³ *Then Daniel was brought before the king. The king exclaimed to Daniel, 'You are Daniel, from among the exiles of Judah, whom the king my father brought from Judah.* ¹⁴ *I have heard about you that the spirit of God is in you, and that illumination, understanding, and extraordinary wisdom are found in you.* ¹⁵ *Now the sages, the astrologers, were brought before me to read this writing and make its interpretation known to me, but they could not relate the interpretation of the matter.* ¹⁶ *But I have heard about you that you are able to provide interpretations and to loosen knots. Now if you will be able to read the writing, and to make its interpretation known to me, you will wear purple, and have a golden chain on your neck, and you will rule one third of the kingdom.'*

¹⁷ *Then Daniel exclaimed before the king, 'Let your presents remain yours, and give your rewards to others. However, I will read the writing for the king and make its interpretation known to him.*

Buber p.191; cf. other editions), understand these words to be a question: *Are you Daniel?* They sense an undercurrent of condescension in the king's query. The king could not have meant this question seriously, since it is inconceivable that he did not know the famous Daniel.

16. פִּשְׁרִין לְמִפְשַׁר — *To provide* [lit. *to interpret*] *interpretations.*

17. Keep Your Presents.

מַתְּנָתָךְ לָךְ לֶהֱוְיָן — *Let your presents remain yours.*

Referring to the gifts of the purple and of the gold chain, and the rulership of a third of the empire, Daniel said to the king, 'Let these

presents remain yours' — i.e., let your dominion not be diminished (*Malbim*).

וּנְבָזְבְּיָתָךְ לְאָחֳרָן הַב — *And give your rewards to others.*

Should you think to reward me with money, I beg you give it to others. Daniel did not think that reading the writing and translating it merited a reward (*Malbim*).

18-24. The uninvited lecture by Daniel in *vs.* 18-25 was in response to the king's belittling remarks in *v.* 13 [see *comm.* there] (*R' Shmuel Masnuth*).

Alshich and *Malbim* consider the following verses a prologue to Daniel's interpretation of the

מַלְכָּא אֱלָהָא °עִלָּיָא מַלְכוּתָא וּרְבוּתָא
וִיקָרָא וְהַדְרָא יְהַב לִנְבֻכַדְנֶצַּר אֲבוּךְ:
וּמִן־רְבוּתָא דִּי יְהַב־לֵהּ כֹּל עַמְמַיָּא
אֻמַּיָּא וְלִשָׁנַיָּא הֲווֹ °זָאֲעִין וְדָחֲלִין מִן־
קָדָמוֹהִי דִּי־הֲוָא צָבֵא הֲוָה קָטֵל וְדִי־הֲוָה
צָבֵא הֲוָה מַחֵא וְדִי־הֲוָה צָבֵא הֲוָה מָרִים
וְדִי־הֲוָא צָבֵא הֲוָא מַשְׁפִּל: וּכְדִי רִם
לִבְבֵהּ וְרוּחֵהּ תִּקְפַת לַהֲזָדָה הָנְחַת מִן־
כָּרְסֵא מַלְכוּתֵהּ וִיקָרָה הֶעְדִּיו מִנֵּהּ: וּמִן־
בְּנֵי אֲנָשָׁא טְרִיד וְלִבְבֵהּ | עִם־חֵיוְתָא
°שַׁוִּי וְעִם־עֲרָדַיָּא מְדוֹרֵהּ עִשְׂבָּא כְתוֹרִין

יט

כ

כא

---

writing. He felt an explanation of the nature of the king's sin was appropriate and necessary.

18. אַנְתְּ מַלְכָּא — *You, O king!*
Since Daniel was about to lecture the king about his sins, he wanted to assure the king this was not due to any irreverence on his part. Thus: 'I declare you are the king! But ...' (*Alshich*).

מַלְכוּתָא — *Kingship.*
This refers to assumption of the throne of Babylon (*Malbim*).

וּרְבוּתָא — *Greatness.*
This was fulfilled when he extended the borders of his kingdom far beyond the borders of Babylon (*Malbim*).

וִיקָרָא וְהַדְרָא — *Honor and glory.*
[The Aramaic noun יְקָרָא is used consistently in the Aramaic translations of Scripture for כָּבוֹד. E.g., see *Onkelos* to וְהוּא נִכְבַּד מִכָּל בֵּית אָבִיו, *And he was honored above all the house of his father* (Genesis 34:19; cf. *Meturgeman* s.v. יְקַר). We find

this use of יְקַר even in Scriptural Hebrew, e.g., *and all the wives will give honor* (יְקָר) *to their husbands* (Esther 1:20). Many other less obvious instances of the root יְקָר could possibly be rendered this way.]

וְהַדְרָא — *And glory.*
[הֲדָר refers to beautiful form — i.e., external beauty, as in זֶה הָדוּר בִּלְבוּשׁוֹ, *this one is glorious in his apparel* (Isaiah 63:1; *Beur Shemos HaNirdofim.* p. 123). However, the synonymous הוֹד refers to inner beauty (*Vilna Gaon, comm.* to *Proverbs* 5:9). The choice of the word הַדְרָא to describe Nebuchadnezzar instead of זִיוָא, the Aramaic form of הוֹד (see *M'turgeman*, s.v. זיו), shows that the outstanding radiance of Nebuchadnezzar, which was a gift of God, was only skin deep. His inner qualities did not exceed the ordinary.]

19. וּמִן־רְבוּתָא דִּי יְהַב־לֵהּ — *And because of the greatness that He gave him.*
This was said in anticipation of

5

18-21

¹⁸ 'You, O king! The Supreme God gave kingship, greatness, honor, and glory to Nebuchadnezzar, your father. ¹⁹ And because of the greatness that he gave him, all the peoples, nations, and languages trembled and were frightened before him; whomever he wished, he killed, and whomever he wished, he kept alive; whomever he wished, he raised up, and whomever he wished, he put down.

²⁰ 'But when his heart grew proud and his spirit was toughened to rebel, he was deposed from his royal throne, and honor was taken from him. ²¹ He was driven from mankind, and his heart was made like a beast's; his dwelling was with wild asses, and grass like oxen, they fed him; and with the dew of

---

Belshazzar's unspoken reproach against God's harsh judgment of him. No doubt Belshazzar felt that his grandfather (or father), Nebuchadnezzar, had sinned much more than he himself had. For Nebuchadnezzar, in the course of his long and despotic rule, had killed many people, whether in the conduct of war or in peace. Therefore Daniel explained that the terror Nebuchadnezzar had thrown into the hearts of his opponents had been the result of God's gift of *kingship, greatness,* etc. Therefore, when, *whomever he wanted to, he killed,* he was only exercising the mandate given him by the One *in whose hand is the soul of all the living* (Job 12:10; *Alshich;* cf. *Ramban* to *Genesis* 15:14).

וְדִי־הֲוָה צָבֵא הֲוָה מָחֵא — *And whomever he wished , he kept alive.*

The translation follows *Rashi* and *R' Saadiah. R' Shmuel Masnuth* cites *Onkelos* (אֲנָא מֵמִית וּמָחֵי)

to אֲנִי אָמִית וַאֲחַיֶּה, *I kill and I make live* (*Deuteronomy* 32:39), as proof for this unusual rendering of the Aramaic מָחֵא. *Radak* renders מָחֵא in its usual sense — *and whomever he wished, he smote.* R' *Eliyah Bachur* ingeniously links מָחֵא to (4:32) יְמָחֵא, *restrain* (*M'turgeman* s.v. מחא). Thus, *whomever he wished, he restrained.*

20. Nebuchadnezzar Knew that God Rules

וּכְדִי רִם לִבְבֵהּ — *But when his heart grew proud.*

Daniel now cited proof to his contention that Nebuchadnezzar's actions were, in general, divinely inspired. For *when his heart grew proud and his spirit was toughened,* he was removed from his kingdom and he met his deserved punishment (*Alshich*).

לַהֲזָדָה — *To rebel.*

לְהָזִיד usually means to sin intentionally. [See *Exodus* 21:14, וְכִי יָזִד אִישׁ.]

[169]   *Daniel*

ה

כב-כז ° עֶלָאָה ק'

יְטַעֲמוּנֵּהּ וּמִטַּל שְׁמַיָּא גִּשְׁמֵהּ יִצְטַבַּע עַד
דִּי־יִדַּע דִּי־שַׁלִּיט אֱלָהָא °עליא בְּמַלְכוּת
אֲנָשָׁא וּלְמַן־דִּי יִצְבֵּא יְהָקֵים °עליה:

° עֲלָהּ ק'

° וְאַנְתְּ ק'

כב °וְאנתה בְּרֵהּ בֵּלְשַׁאצַּר לָא הַשְׁפֵּלְתְּ
לִבְבָךְ כָּל־קֳבֵל דִּי כָל־דְּנָה יְדַעְתָּ: כג וְעַל
מָרֵא־שְׁמַיָּא | הִתְרוֹמַמְתָּ וּלְמָאנַיָּא דִי־
בַיְתֵהּ הַיְתִיו °קדמיך °ואנתה

° קֳדָמָךְ ק'
° וְאַנְתְּ ק'
° וְרַבְרְבָנָךְ ק'

°ורברבניך שֵׁגְלָתָךְ וּלְחֵנָתָךְ חַמְרָא
שָׁתַיִן בְּהוֹן וְלֵאלָהֵי כַסְפָּא־וְדַהֲבָא
נְחָשָׁא פַרְזְלָא אָעָא וְאַבְנָא דִּי לָא־חָזַיִן
וְלָא־שָׁמְעִין וְלָא יָדְעִין שַׁבַּחְתָּ וְלֵאלָהָא
דִּי־נִשְׁמְתָךְ בִּידֵהּ וְכָל־אֹרְחָתָךְ לֵהּ לָא
הַדַּרְתָּ: כד בֵּאדַיִן מִן־קֳדָמוֹהִי שְׁלִיחַ פַּסָּא
דִי־יְדָא וּכְתָבָא דְּנָה רְשִׁים: כה וּדְנָה כְתָבָא
דִּי רְשִׁים מְנֵא מְנֵא תְּקֵל וּפַרְסִין: כו דְּנָה
פְּשַׁר מִלְּתָא מְנֵא מְנָה־אֱלָהָא מַלְכוּתָךְ
וְהַשְׁלְמַהּ: כז תְּקֵל תְּקִילְתָּא בְמֹאזַנְיָא

22. 'But you exalted yourself.'

וְאַנְתְּ בְּרֵהּ — But you, his son.

As Nebuchadnezzar's son, there is no question you were privy to the cause of his temporary madness. Yet, this did not deter you.

כָּל־קֳבֵל דִּי כָל־דְּנָה יְדַעְתָּ — Although you knew all this.

Even though you knew all this, you haughtily disregarded it. This compounds your sin, and your punishment must therefore be that much more severe (Rashi; Alshich; Malbim).

23. נִשְׁמְתָךְ — Your soul.

נְשָׁמָה is used in the Bible for breath as in מִנִּשְׁמַת רוּחַ אַפּוֹ (II Samuel 22:16), and ror soul as in לֹא תְחַיֶּה כָּל נְשָׁמָה (Deut. 20:16). Soul is more fitting to this context (see Radak in Shorashim s.v. נשם).

וְכָל־אֹרְחָתָךְ לֵהּ — And to Whom all your ways [belong].

Your actions are directed by Him so as to lead you to the goal He has designated (Ibn Ezra; R' Shmuel Masnuth).

Your way — i.e., your life — ultimately leads to Him. At the end of your path your soul will surely find itself in His hands (Yeffes quoted by Ibn Ezra).

heaven, his body was washed, until he knew that the Supreme God rules in the kingdom of men, and whomever He wishes, He appoints over it.

²² 'But you, his son Belshazzar, did not humble your heart although you knew all this. ²³ Above the Master of heaven, you exalted yourself, and the vessels of His house they have brought before you, and you, your nobles, your queen, and your concubine drank wine from them and praised gods of silver and gold, copper, iron, wood, and stone which do not see nor hear nor know; and the God in Whose hand is your soul, and to Whom all your ways belong, you did not glorify. ²⁴ Then a hand was sent from before Him, and inscribed this writing.

²⁵ 'This is the writing that was inscribed:
MENEI MENEI TEKEIL UFARSIN.
²⁶ 'This is the interpretation of the matter:
MENEI — God has counted your kingship and terminated it.
²⁷ TEKEIL — you were weighed in the scales and

---

25. 'Your kingship is broken.'

מְנָא... — *MENEI* ...
See *comm.* to verse 8.

26. מְנָה ... וְהַשְׁלְמַהּ — *Has counted ... and terminated* [lit. *completed*] *it.*

God has counted the years of the Babylonian empire and they have been completed now. Belshazzar's reckoning (see *comm.* to *v.* 2), which used the beginning of Nebuchadnezzar's reign as the starting-point, had been correct concerning the duration of the House of Nebuchadnezzar (*Ralbag* in *Toaliyos*).

Daniel only explained one מְנָא. The first מְנָא, which is left unexplained, refers to the king's reckon-

ing. Thus, *you, O king,* מְנָא, *counted, but God also* מְנָא, *counted* (*Alshich*).

מַלְכוּתָךְ וְהַשְׁלְמַהּ — *Your kingship ... terminated.*

The king had been mistaken in his calculation (see *v.* 2). Still God had found the time right to terminate Belshazzar's reign — *Your kingship ... terminated* — although the Babylonian kingdom still had one year left to complete, according to Jeremiah's prophecy. This year was completed with the one year reign of Darius the Mede (see *Rashi* to *Megillah* 11b s.v. שנים, *Seder Olam Rabbah* ch. 28, that his reign lasted only one year).

[The apparent contradiction between Da-

כח וְהִשְׁתַּכַּחַתְּ חַסִּיר: פְּרֵס פְּרִיסַת מַלְכוּתָךְ
כט וִיהִיבַת לְמָדַי וּפָרָס: בֵּאדַיִן | אֲמַר
בֵּלְשַׁאצַּר וְהַלְבִּשׁוּ לְדָנִיֵּאל אַרְגְּוָנָא
°וַהֲמוֹנְכָא דִי־דַהֲבָא עַל־צַוְּארֵהּ וְהַכְרִזוּ
עֲלוֹהִי דִּי־לֶהֱוֵא שַׁלִּיט תַּלְתָּא
ל בְּמַלְכוּתָא: בַּהּ בְּלֵילְיָא קְטִיל בֵּלְאשַׁצַּר
מַלְכָּא °כַשְׂדָּיָא:

° וְהַמְנִכָא ק'

° כַשְׂדָּאָה ק'

niel's prophecy that Belshazzar's reign had been completed, and the tradition of the sages that the seventy years had not yet been completed, needs to be answered. In explanation we may postulate that the verses in *Jeremiah* indicate that there are two separate seventy-year periods which overlap, but are not identical. One period refers to the reign of the Babylonian royal line which began with the ascension to the throne of Nebuchadnezzar. The other refers to Jerusalem's captivity which began with its conquest by Nebuchadnezzar in the second year of his reign. *Jeremiah* 25:12 refers to the duration of Babylonian kingship: *when seventy years are completed I will punish* (אֶפְקֹד) *the king of Babylon.* Belshazzar had now reached that milestone. *Jeremiah* 29:10 refers to seventy years from the conquest: *after seventy years are accomplished at Babylon* [i.e., from the conquest] *I will take note of you* (אֶפְקֹד אֶתְכֶם) i.e., God will remember Israel. That moment arrived a year after Belshazzar's death.

However, the language of the Sages (*Megillah* 12a; *Seder Olam Rabbah*, ibid.), עוֹד שָׁנָה לְבָבֶל בָּא דָרְיָוֶשׁ וְהִשְׁלִימָהּ, *there was one more year due to Babylon so Darius came and completed it,* seems to hint that this year really belonged to the reign of Babylon. It can perhaps be said that some prophecies are purposely left open to interpretation so as to allow for different ways of fulfillment. A prominent example of this is God's promise to Abraham: *and they will enslave and afflict them four hundred years* (Genesis 15:13). We have it from tradition that the Egyptian exile lasted only two hundred ten years. The number four hundred is explained as beginning from Isaac's birth (see *Rashi* and ArtScroll *comm. ibid.*). Still we find the Sages in *Midrash* (*Shir HaShirim* 2:8; *Rashi;*

ArtScroll *comm. ibid.*) referring to this 'reduction' of the exile from 400 to 210 years as a concession to the Jews. This is in no way contradictory. The starting date of the 400 years was deliberately left vague and open to interpretation by Divine wisdom. If the circumstances would warrant it, the Jews would serve out their full four hundred years. If this had happened, the face of history would have changed completely. (See ArtScroll *Haggadah, comm.* p. 97.)

Since the circumstances necessitated another course of action, the interpretation indicating 210 years of exile was implemented, with its mandated consequences.

Similarly here, the seventy years of Babylon could be interpreted in two ways. They could be full years, in which case Belshazzar should have finished this, his seventieth year. Or they could be seventy just in number, so having entered his seventieth year, this could already be counted as the final year. Had Belshazzar not sinned, the former interpretation would have been adopted. Since he did sin, he forfeited the privilege to have the favorable interpretation applied to him, and the latter interpretation was adopted. Thus, it can be said that this was *a year due Babylon* without contradicting the tradition accepted by the sages that Belshazzar was mistaken in his calculation (see *comm.* to *v.* 30).

Malbim explains the double מְנָא as follows: Belshazzar's term as king of Babylon can be viewed through either of two prophecies by Jeremiah. One prophecy (*Jer.* 25:11-12) is *And these nations will serve the king of Babylon seventy*

found wanting.

²⁸ PEREIS — *your kingship is broken and given to Media and Persia.'*

²⁹ *Then Belshazzar commanded. And they clothed Daniel in purple, with a golden chain on his neck, and they proclaimed about him that he would rule one third of the kingdom.* ³⁰ *That night, Belshazzar, the Chaldean king, was slain.*

years. When the seventy years are completed, I will punish the king of Babylon. This prophecy had already reached a terminus. However, from the viewpoint of the second prophecy (*Jer.* 27:7): *And they shall serve him* (Nebuchadnezzar) *and his son and his son's son,* the time was still open. But that depended on Belshazzar's personal merit. Now Daniel tells him: מְנֵא — God has the option of *reckoning* according to the 70 years and consequently your reign is terminated, or מְנֵא — He can *reckon* according to your merits and extend your life and, along with it, your reign. For this another type of measurement had to be resorted to. *You were weighed in the scales and were found wanting.* Had Belshazzar not sinned, his right to live and rule would have held back the destruction of Babylon.

28. פְּרֵס — *PEREIS.*

וּפַרְסִין, UFARSIN is interpreted as the plural of פְּרֵס, *pereis,* as if it had said פְּרֵס פְּרֵס. The first פְּרֵס means to *divide,* break (see *Isaiah* in *Radak* to *Shorashim s.v.* פרס). The second פְּרֵס is interpreted as the name of a nation, Persia. Thus, *your kingship is broken and given to Media and Persia* (*Rashi; Ibn Ezra*).

Abarbanel (*Mayenei HaYeshuah*

7:1) perceives in the first פְּרֵס not only the prophesied destruction of the Babylonian empire, but also the division of the conquered empire between Darius the Mede and Cyrus the Persian. as related in *Yossipon* (Ch. 3). They agreed that after jointly conquering Babylon, Darius would rule Babylon and Cyrus would take the rest of the empire. Daniel indicated that Darius, the senior member of this partnership, would be the first to reign in Babylon proper, when he mentioned Media first.

לְמָדַי — *To Media.*

Alshich sees a hint to the rule of Media in the conjunctive *vav* of וּפַרְסִין, UFARSIN. Since UFARSIN is interpreted to represent פְּרֵס twice, it is as if it said פְּרֵס וּפְרֵס, indicating that besides Persia, another nation would be given hegemony over Babylon.

30. בֵּהּ בְּלֵילְיָא — *That night.*

[God] sees to it that no nation should infringe on [the time granted] another, nor that any kingdom should infringe on another, for even as much as a hair's breadth (*Yalkut; Seder Olam Rabbah* ch. 28; see *Yoma* 38b, *Rashi s.v.* ואין).

[The *Midrash* seems to say that that night had been destined for the

וְדָרְיָ֫וֶשׁ °מְדִיא °מְדָאָה ק׳ א קַבֵּל מַלְכוּתָ֫א כְּבַר שְׁנִ֫ין א ב שִׁתִּ֫ין וְתַרְתֵּ֫ין: שְׁפַר֩ קֳדָ֨ם דָּרְיָ֫וֶשׁ וַהֲקֵ֣ים עַל־מַלְכוּתָ֗א לַאֲחַשְׁדַּרְפְּנַיָּ֫א מְאָ֑ה

start of the Persian empire and the demise of the Babylonian empire. This seems to uphold the view (comm. to v. 26) that the downfall of the Babylonian empire on that night had been foreordained, in spite of the fact that the sources cited hold that עוֹד שָׁנָה לְבָבֶל, *there was one more year due to Babylon.* Hence, Belshazzar's sin was a contributing factor in his death, but in itself was not sufficient to cause it. However, according to the theory (ibid.) that the seventieth year could possibly have been ended under Belshazzar's rule, the explanation given that he had to die that night in order not to infringe on the Persian's rule, is not understandable.]

קְטִיל בֵּלְאשַׁצַּר — *Belshazzar ... was slain.*

Several accounts are given of this. *Yossipon* (ch. 3) (substantiated by *Yalkut* to *Isaiah,* 420; cf. *Shir HaShirim Rabbah* 3:4, *Yefeh Kol ad. loc., s.v.* הָיָה דָרְיָוֶשׁ) relates that members of Belshazzar's entourage, knowing that Daniel's prophecy was sure to be fulfilled, killed Belshazzar and brought his severed head to the Persian camp (see *R' Saadiah*).

Rashi, citing *Yossipon* relates another account. The Persians and Medes, regrouping after suffering defeat at the hands of Belshazzar, returned at night and, catching the Babylonians by surprise, succeeded in conquering Babylon and killing Belshazzar [cf. *Josephus, Antiquities X,* 11, 4.]

VI.

⋙Daniel in the Lions' Pit

1. וְדָרְיָוֶשׁ מָדָאָה — *And Darius the Mede.*

This Darius is identified by the Sages (*Megillah* 11b; *Seder Olam Rabbah* 28) as *Darius son of Ahasuerus* (9:1). The phrasing *Darius son of Ahasuerus of the seed of the Medes who was made king over the kingdom of the Chaldeans,* bears this out. The Sages (ibid.) say that his rule endured for only one

year, after which the reins of monarchy passed to the Persians.

Yossipon (ch.3) relates that Cyrus was Darius' son-in-law. *Josephus (Antiquities X,* 11,4) also mentions that they were kinsmen. However *Josephus* calls him Darius son of Astyages. [*Josephus'* report 440 years later cannot be considered a contradiction of the Scriptural text.][1]

1. [It is however, possible that Ahasuerus the Mede is not the father but the grandfather of Darius. See comm. to 5:1 that even though Scripture refers to Nebuchadnezzar as Belshazzar's father, he was really his grandfather. Since Astyages was the son of Cyaxeres, it may well be that Achashverosh is the Aramaic form of the original Median name that the Greeks rendered Cyaxeres. Just as Achashverosh was turned by the Greeks into Artaxerxes, it is perfectly reasonable to speculate that Cyaxeres was derived from the Median version of Achashverosh. Perhaps the Median version was slightly different from the Persian, so that the Persian Ahasuerus became Artaxerxes in Greek, and the Median turned into Cyaxeres.]

And Darius the Mede received the kingship at the age of sixty-two years. ² It pleased Darius and he appointed over the kingdom one hundred and twenty

כְּבַר שְׁנִין שִׁתִּין וְתַרְתֵּין — *At the age of sixty-two years.*

'Why are we given his age? To tell us that on the day Nebuchadnezzar entered the Temple in the days of Yehoyachin his adversary (Darius) was born.' The Sages inform us that the exile of Yehoyachin took place in the eighth year of Nebuchadnezzar's reign (*Megillah* 11b; see *comm.* to 5:26). We also know that the downfall of Babylon came 70 years after Nebuchadnezzar's accession to the throne. If you subtract the 8 years of his rule until he exiled Yehoyachin, the remainder is 62 (*Rashi* from *Seder Olam Rabba* ch. 28).[1]

This is the reading given in our versions of *Seder Olam. Rashi* here has Yehoyakim. This does not affect the calculation because Yehoyachin reigned only three months (*II Kings* 24:8). Thus the emendation given in

the standard editions of *Rashi* is not really necessary.

[*Minchas Shai* notes in the name of *R' Menachem Lunzano* that even though the *vowel mark* under the *dalet* is *kametz*, it should be read as though it were a *pasach*. Thus Daryovesh, not Doryovesh. The same holds true for the *kametz* under the *samech* in סָרְכַיָּא (*v.* 5). He also notes that the rules for *Sh'va na* do not apply consistently in Aramaic.]

2. וַהֲקֵים עַל-מַלְכוּתָא — *And he appointed over the kingdom.*

Because he was already advanced in age, he felt he needed assistance in order to rule his huge empire (*Mayenei HaYeshua*: 7:2; *Malbim*).

לַאֲחַשְׁדַּרְפְּנַיָּא מְאָה וְעֶשְׂרִין — *One hundred and twenty satraps.*

These were to rule over the 120 states in his empire. The *Talmud* (*Megillah* 11b) uses this verse to prove that Ahasuerus' empire was larger because it contained 127 states (*Esther* 1:1).

1. The tradition given here that Nebuchadnezzar entered the Temple when he exiled Yehoyachin is (as far as this writer can determine) not mentioned elsewhere in Rabbinic literature. *Meir .Ay.n* (to *Seder Olam Rabbah* 28:9) even sees a contradiction to this in the passage of *Vayikra Rabbah* (19:6; see *Yerushalmi Shekalim* 6:2) which narrates that he stayed in the vicinity of Antioch, from where he sent a request to the Sanhedrin to give Yehoyachin up to him.

Antioch, however, is mentioned only as the place from where Nebuchadnezzar sent his request to the Sanhedrin. Perhaps, after his request had been answered, Nebuchadnezzar proceeded to Jerusalem and entered the Temple. This is borne out by *II Kings* (24:10-13) which states concerning the exile of Yehoyachin, *At that time the 'servants' of Nebuchadnezzar came up to Jerusalem ... And Nebuchadnezzar, king of Babylon, came into the city, while his servants were besieging it ... And he carried out from there all the treasures of the house of God ...* The apparent contradiction to *II Chronicles* (36:10) is·easily resolved by *Malbim* (*ibid.*). The attempt by the king to enter the Temple sheds light on well known tradition transmitted by the Sages (*Vayikra Rabbah; Yerushalmi Shekalim, ibid.*) and echoed in the *Kinos* for Tisha B'Av (s.v. אצבעותי שפלו) that Yehoyachin, when confronted with his imminent exile, took the keys of the Temple and threw them skyward, and a hand came out of the sky and took them (or, according to an alternate version they never fell back down). Yehoyachin, when confronted with the probability of the Babylonian king's entrance into the Temple, threw the keys skyward rather than surrender them to Nebuchadnezzar.

ג. וְעֶשְׂרִין דִּי לֶהֱוֹן בְּכָל־מַלְכוּתָא: וְעֵלָּא
מִנְּהוֹן סָרְכִין תְּלָתָה דִּי דָנִיֵּאל חַד מִנְּהוֹן
דִּי־לֶהֱוֹן אֲחַשְׁדַּרְפְּנַיָּא אִלֵּין יָהֲבִין לְהוֹן
ד. טַעְמָא וּמַלְכָּא לָא־לֶהֱוֵא נָזִק: אֱדַיִן
דָּנִיֵּאל דְּנָה הֲוָא מִתְנַצַּח עַל־סָרְכַיָּא
וַאֲחַשְׁדַּרְפְּנַיָּא כָּל־קֳבֵל דִּי רוּחַ יַתִּירָא
בֵּהּ וּמַלְכָּא עֲשִׁית לַהֲקָמוּתֵהּ עַל־כָּל־
ה. מַלְכוּתָא: אֱדַיִן סָרְכַיָּא וַאֲחַשְׁדַּרְפְּנַיָּא
הֲווֹ בָעַיִן עִלָּה לְהַשְׁכָּחָה לְדָנִיֵּאל מִצַּד
מַלְכוּתָא וְכָל־עִלָּה וּשְׁחִיתָה לָא־יָכְלִין
לְהַשְׁכָּחָה כָּל־קֳבֵל דִּי־מְהֵימַן הוּא וְכָל־
שָׁלוּ וּשְׁחִיתָה לָא הִשְׁתְּכַחַת עֲלוֹהִי:
ו. אֱדַיִן גֻּבְרַיָּא אִלֵּךְ אָמְרִין דִּי לָא נְהַשְׁכַּח
לְדָנִיֵּאל דְּנָה כָּל־עִלָּא לָהֵן הַשְׁכַּחְנָא

---

3. סָרְכִין — *Viziers.*

R' *Saadiah, Radak,* and *R' Sh-*
muel Masnuth point out that סָרְכִין
is the Aramaic equivalent of the
Hebrew שׁוֹטֵר(see *Onkelos* to *Deut.*
16:18). However, שׁוֹטֵר in its
traditional meaning is an *officer,*
more specifically a *police officer,* a
meaning which does not fit our context. Perhaps this is why *Metzudos*
simply renders סָרְכִין, *a type of*
ruler. This also seems to be the view
of *Ibn Ezra.* Possibly, since it was
the duty of these three to oversee —
i.e., to police — the governing of the
120 states by the 120 satraps — the
rendering of סָרְכִין as שׁוֹטֵר could
apply here too.

The translation *vizier* is used by
R' *Saadiah Gaon* in his *Tafsir,* and
it seems to fit the context.

דִּי־לְהֱוֹן אֲחַשְׁדַּרְפְּנַיָּא אִלֵּין יָהֲבִין לְהוֹן
טַעְמָא — *So that these satraps should*
give them counsel.

The 120 would advise these
viziers so that they would be fully
aware of all developments in the
huge empire. With all these advisors, the king would suffer no
damage (*Rashi*).

Malbim and *R' Shmuel Masnuth*
(citing other translators) render
טַעְמָא, *accounting* (חֶשְׁבּוֹן); thus,
that these ... should give account to
them. This translation fits smoothly
into the context, but they offer no
other example of this usage.

R' *Shmuel Masnuth* explains that
אֲחַשְׁדַּרְפְּנַיָּא here refers to these three
viziers who, in addition to their
elevated rank, were also אֲחַשְׁדַּרְפְּנַיָּא.
[Perhaps the 120 satraps were

*satraps to be throughout the kingdom, ³ and over
them three viziers of whom Daniel was one, so that
these satraps should give them counsel and the king
should suffer no damage. ⁴ Then this Daniel
predominated over the viziers and satraps as a result
of the extraordinary spirit in him; and the king
thought to appoint him over the whole kingdom.*

*⁵ Then the viziers and the satraps tried to find a
libel against Daniel with regard to the kingdom; but
they could find neither fault nor corruption because
he was faithful; and there was found neither error
nor corruption in him. ⁶ Then these men said, 'We
shall not find any fault with this Daniel, but we will*

organized into three groups, each
being responsible to one of the three
viziers. Thus, in addition to advising the king, each vizier also administered one third of the empire
(see *comm.* to 5:16).] Thus, *these*
[three viziers, who were also]
satraps should give them [i.e., the
other 117 satraps] *counsel.* (See
commentary to 2:14 s.v. טעם).

5. Quest for a Libel

עֲלָה —*Libel.*

The translation follows *Rashi,
Radak,* and *R' Saadiah* who relate
the word to עֲלִילָה, *libelous slander*
(cf. *Deut.* 22:14).

R' Shmuel Masnuth offers *fault*
as an alternative rendering.

[Later in the verse, we are told that
they could not find an עֲלָה. There, the
translation is clearly not libel, but *fault.*
It would appear that they were fully
aware that there were no significant
flaws in Daniel's behavior. They hoped
to find some minor עֲלָה, *fault,* which
they could blow out of proportion and
turn into a major accusation against
Daniel. This would account for the

translation, *libel,* which is used by the
above commentators.]

מִצַּד מַלְכוּתָא — *With regard to the
kingdom.*

They wanted to find a flaw in
Daniel's conduct of the government, such as acceptance of bribes
or misappropriation of public
funds. Yet, no matter how hard
they searched they could find
nothing of this sort *because he was
faithful. However* ...

וְכָל־עֲלָה וּשְׁחִיתָה לָא־יָכְלִין לְהַשְׁכָּחָה —
*But they could find neither fault nor
corruption* [lit. *any fault and corruption they were unable to find.*]

They then proceeded to search
for any evidence of misconduct or
crime in Daniel's private life. But,
וְכָל־שָׁלוּ וּשְׁחִיתָה לָא הִשְׁתְּכַחַת עֲלוֹהִי,
*there was found neither error nor
corruption in him (Malbim).*

וְכָל־שָׁלוּ וּשְׁחִיתָה לָא הִשְׁתְּכַחַת עֲלוֹהִי
— *And there was found neither
error nor corruption in him* [lit. *any
error and corruption could not be
found in him*].

זַ עֲלוֹהִי בְּדָת אֱלָהֵהּ: אֱדַ֫יִן
סָרְכַיָּא וַאֲחַשְׁדַּרְפְּנַיָּא אִלֵּ֣ן הַרְגִּ֫שׁוּ עַל־
מַלְכָּ֑א וְכֵ֣ן אָמְרִ֣ין לֵ֔הּ דָּרְיָ֥וֶשׁ מַלְכָּ֖א
חַ לְעָֽלְמִ֣ין חֱיִֽי: אִתְיָעַ֩טוּ כֹּ֣ל | סָרְכֵ֣י
מַלְכוּתָא֩ סִגְנַיָּ֨א וַאֲחַשְׁדַּרְפְּנַיָּ֜א הַדָּבְרַיָּ֣א
וּפַחֲוָתָ֗א לְקַיָּמָ֤ה קְיָם֙ מַלְכָּא֙ וּלְתַקָּפָ֣ה
אֱסָ֔ר דִּ֣י כָל־דִּֽי־יִבְעֵ֣א בָ֠עוּ מִן־כָּל־אֱלָ֨הּ
וֶֽאֱנָ֜שׁ עַד־יוֹמִ֣ין תְּלָתִ֗ין לָהֵן֙ מִנָּ֣ךְ מַלְכָּ֔א
יִתְרְמֵ֕א לְגֹ֖ב אַרְיָוָתָֽא: כְּעַ֣ן מַלְכָּ֔א תְּקִ֖ים ט
אֱסָרָ֑א וְתִרְשֻׁ֣ם כְּתָבָ֔א דִּ֛י לָ֥א לְהַשְׁנָיָ֖ה

---

6. לָהֵן הִשְׁכַּחְנָא עֲלוֹהִי — *But we will find it in him.*

We will ask the king to promulgate a decree which will interfere with Daniel's religion. Since his loyalty to his religion will surely keep him from obeying the king's decree, we will succeed in causing his downfall and death (*Rashi*).

7. The King's Prohibition

סָרְכַיָּא וַאֲחַשְׁדַּרְפְּנַיָּא אִלֵּן — *These viziers and satraps.*

They came together in a crowd so as not to make Daniel's absence conspicuous. The presence of such a crowd of petitioners would also have the effect of influencing the king to sign the decree immediately without seeking counsel. Had the king given himself time to think things over, he would have, no doubt, consulted Daniel, and the plot would have been uncovered (*Alshich*).

הַרְגִּשׁוּ — *Assembled.*

R' Saadiah, Ibn Ezra, Radak, and *Metzudos* render it *assembled* (from

לָמָה רָגְשׁוּ גוֹיִם, *Psalms* 2:1). *Rashi* to *Psalms* (64:3) seems to concur. The translation follows this consensus.

Here, *Rashi* renders, *they felt out the king* — i.e., they assessed the probability of gaining the king's assent to their proposal. *Rashi* gives no source for this rendering.

R' Shmuel Masnuth (on the basis of *Psalms* 2:1) renders: *they gathered in counsel and came to the king.*

[A strong argument can also be made to translate הַרְגִּשׁוּ as *they thronged tumultuously* — i.e., they came to the king loudly demanding that he accede to their demands. *Targum Yonasan* renders מְהוּמָה, *uproar,* אִתְרְגוּשָׁא (*Ezek.* 7:7, *Isaiah* 22:5). The same is true of *Targum* to *Ruth* 1:19 who renders וַתֵּהֹם כָּל הָעִיר, *and the whole city was tumultuous* — וְאִרְגִּישׁוּ (cf. *Targum* to *Psalms* 55:3 וְאָהִימָה.]

8. כֹּל סָרְכֵי מַלְכוּתָא — *All the viziers of the kingdom.*

Even though only two of the viziers had given their assent [the third, Daniel, was obviously not

6   *find it in him through the law of his God."*

7-9   *⁷ Then these viziers and satraps assembled about the king, and said thus to him: 'King Darius, live forever! ⁸ All the viziers of the kingdom, the nobles and the satraps, the advisors and the governors have conferred to affirm the king's law, and to strengthen his prohibition: that whoever shall make a request of any god or man for the next thirty days, other than of you, O king, will be thrown into the lions' pit. ⁹ Now, O king, establish a prohibition and inscribe the writing so that it cannot be changed, according to the*

consulted] in their petition to the king, the satraps made it appear that the decision had been unanimous. This was necessary in order not to arouse the king's suspicion about Daniel's absence. The presence of such a great multitude of high officials of his realm, and their assertion that *all* the viziers — i.e., including Daniel — had given their assent to the proposal, was enough to allay any misgivings the king may have had about this scheme for his glorification (*Alshich*).

וּלְתַקָּפָה אֱסָר — *And to strengthen his prohibition.*

I.e., to demand more stringent punishment for its transgression as if it were treason and punishable by death (*Malbim*).

[The stated purpose of this decree was to strengthen the new king's rule in the empire. In the thirty days of the decree he would personally answer all requests from his subjects. This extended even to personal matters as seen from the prohibition to pray to *any god.* Had the governors or the king wished to

deify Darius, the decree would not have been limited to thirty days. Through the king's personal and beneficial intervention in his subjects' lives, strong bonds of friendship and devotion would be forged, thus strengthening his rule over his large empire.]

Alshich suggests that the prohibition not to pray to any god meant that Darius would be the sole intermediary between his subjects and their gods. Any petition to any god was to be brought to him, and he would intercede with that god on behalf of the petitioner. This, of course, is only the outer shell of the proposal. Their true objective was to entrap Daniel, as clearly stated in *vs. 5-8* (*Mayenei Hayeshuah* 7:2; *Alshich; Malbim*).

9. כְּעַן — *Now.*

Without delay. They did not want the king to think things over, for fear that their plot would be uncovered. Besides, they wanted Daniel out of the way as soon as possible (*Alshich;* see *comm.* to *v.* 7).

ו ·
י-יא

י כְּדָת־מָדַי וּפָרַס דִּי־לָא תֶעְדֵּא: כָּל־קֳבֵל
דְּנָה מַלְכָּא דָּרְיָוֶשׁ רְשַׁם כְּתָבָא וֶאֱסָרָא:
יא וְדָנִיֵּאל כְּדִי יְדַע דִּי־רְשִׁים כְּתָבָא עַל
לְבַיְתֵהּ וְכַוִּין פְּתִיחָן לֵהּ בְּעִלִּיתֵהּ נֶגֶד
יְרוּשְׁלֶם וְזִמְנִין תְּלָתָה בְיוֹמָא הוּא | בָּרֵךְ

כְּדָת־מָדַי וּפָרַס — *According to the law of Media and Persia.*

The Persian tradition that even the king could not change a law once it had been signed by him, is well known from *Esther* (8:8).

[Throughout this book when פָּרַס, *Persia*, is mentioned together with מָדַי, *Media*, Media is placed first (see 5:28, 6:9, 13, 16, and 8:20), whereas in *Esther* the opposite is true (see 1:3, 14, 18, 19). (The only exception in *Esther*, 10:2, deals with the chronological history of the empire, and as explained below, the Medians were first to occupy the throne). In this chapter, as the Medians had one of their countrymen as king, they were the primary nation in their partnership with the Persians. According to the citation from *Yossipon* (comm. to v. 1) that Darius was Cyrus' father-in-law, this is perfectly natural. By the days of Esther, however, the Persians had taken the dominant role in the empire. The tradition of the Sages (*Bava Basra* 15a) ascribes both *Esther* and *Daniel* to the אַנְשֵׁי כְּנֶסֶת הַגְּדוֹלָה, *the Men of the Great Assembly* (see footnote to 4:25). This precision attests to the great accuracy and the spirit of prophecy which hovered over these unnamed spiritual giants when they permanently set these words in writing.]

11. Daniel Prays as Usual

וְדָנִיֵּאל כְּדִי יְדַע — *When Daniel learned.*

Even though he knew about the decree he did not try to have himself exempted from it. Since the decree had been scheduled to terminate

after the short period of thirty days, and had as its ostensible objective the glorification of the king and the strengthening of his reign, Daniel did not want to give the appearance of nonparticipation in this goal. He felt he could evade the decree by praying in secret (*Mayenei HaYeshuah* 7:2).

עַל לְבַיְתֵהּ — *He went home* [lit. *to his house*].

He did not pray publicly in the synagogue, where he had no doubt prayed up to now. In order not to anger the king, he chose to ostensibly abide by the king's decree, while furtively upholding his obligation to God in every manner possible (*Alshich*).

[This was not a case where יֵהָרֵג וְאַל יַעֲבֹר, *one must let oneself be killed rather than transgress.* This rule applies at all times only to three cardinal sins, *idolatry, immorality, and murder.* However, where coercion is aimed at *conversion*, one must sacrifice his life for קִידּוּשׁ הַשֵּׁם, *sanctification of the Name,* for any Jewish custom at all.

Lacking these conditions, it is obligatory to transgress, since it is written concerning the Torah's laws, *which a man shall do* וָחַי בָּהֶם, *and live by them,* (*Lev.* 18:5). The words וְחַי בָּהֶם teach us that he is not to die because of them. If he died and did not transgress *he* is responsible for the loss of his life (*Mishneh Torah, Hilchos Yesodei HaTorah* 5:1).

If one allows himself to be killed when he should have transgressed, he can be considered a suicide, with all the sanctions imposed on a suicide (*R' Yeruchom,* quoted in *Bais Yosef* to *Yoreh Deah* 157). Since the king's intent here was for הֲנָאַת עַצְמוֹ, *his*

law of Media and Persia, which will not expire.' [10] *As a result of this, King Darius inscribed the writing and the prohibition.*

[11] *When Daniel learned that the writing had been inscribed, he went home. He had windows open toward Jerusalem in his upper chamber — and three times a day he fell to his knees, and prayed and gave*

own glory, without intent to convert Jews, and this was not a case of transgressing the three cardinal sins, Daniel was not obligated or even permitted to jeopardize his life. Therefore Daniel's courageous disregard for his life in light of the royal decree is explained by the commentators (see *Malbim's* explanation below) not as a conscious act of martyrdom, but as a miscalculation as to the danger of his actions. (See *Tiferes Yisrael* to *Berachos* 1:3 citing *Pischei Teshuva* to *Yoreh Deah* 157:3 that where the danger is not clearly apparent, one is permitted to endanger himself for the sake of a *mitzvah*, since the *mitzvah will guard him*.)

There is, however, another school of thought which permitted martyrdom for *Mitzvos* in some (or all) cases (see *Bais Yosef*, *loc. cit.; Shach* there 1:2; *Chinuch* 296). Some authorities refer to Daniel's actions as proof of the principle permitting martyrdom even where the *halachah* does not require it (see *Ran; 49b Ramban; Rashba; Rivta*, and *Ritva ed. Reichman* to *Shabbos* 49b; *Beur HaGra* to *Yoreh Deah* 157:2; cf. *Milchamos* to *Sanhedrin* toward end of *perek Ben Sorer Umoreh*). These authorities evidently understand Daniel's actions to have been an overt act of martyrdom in the absence of *halachic* requirement to do so.]

וְכַוִּין פְּתִיחָן לֵהּ בְּעִלִּיתֵהּ — *He had windows open ... in his upper chamber.*

R' Chiya bar Abba said in R' Yochanan's name: A person should only pray in a house which has windows because it is said, *and he had windows open in his upper chamber ...* (*Berachos* 34b). The reason for these windows is ...

— so that he should be able to see the sky and thereby (through the

association of the sky with God) arouse his devotion (*Rashi, ibid.*).

— because the light creates a pleasant atmosphere, and so enables one to pray with devotion (*R' Yonah, ibid.*).

— So that one should pray toward Jerusalem. Thus, there is a need to open windows or doors toward Jerusalem in order to pray facing them (*Rambam, Hilchos Tefillah* 5:6).

בְּעִלִּיתֵהּ — *In his upper chamber.*

He did not pray in his lower chambers where he could readily be observed (*Mayenei HaYeshuah*).

נֶגֶד יְרוּשְׁלֵם — *Toward Jerusalem.*

He prayed in the direction of the Holy Temple even though it was destroyed, as King Solomon said, *and they shall pray to You toward their land* (I *Kings* 8:48; *Berachos* 30a).

וְזִמְנִין תְּלָתָא בְּיוֹמָא — *And three times a day.*

[The practice of praying three times a day, though not a Torah obligation, had already been instituted in Daniel's time (see below). Otherwise it is inconceivable that Daniel would have endangered himself for the purpose of prayer. *Rambam* (*Hilchos Tefillah* 1:1) states that though the Torah obligates one to pray every day, the number of prayers is מִדְּרַבָּנָן, a rabbinical ordinance. *Ramban* (*Sefer Hamitzvos asseh* 5) disagrees; he maintains that prayer is obligatory only in time of need. Though no authority holds the view that praying three times a day is a

עַל־בִּרְכוֹהִי וּמְצַלֵּא וּמוֹדֵא קֳדָם אֱלָהֵהּ
כָּל־קֳבֵל דִּי־הֲוָא עָבֵד מִן־קַדְמַת דְּנָה׃
יב אֱדַיִן גֻּבְרַיָּא אִלֵּךְ הַרְגִּשׁוּ וְהַשְׁכַּחוּ
לְדָנִיֵּאל בָּעֵה וּמִתְחַנַּן קֳדָם אֱלָהֵהּ׃

Torah obligation, the institution of praying three times a day has its roots in ancient times.

The *Talmud (Berachos* 26b) has two views as to who instituted the practice of prayer three times a day.

R' Yossi bar Chanina said: The Patriarchs (Abraham, Isaac, and Jacob) instituted the prayers. This is the view adopted by *R' Achai Gaon (Sheiltos* 42) and *Halachos Gedolos* (see *Haamek She'eloh* loc. cit.).

R' Yehoshua ben Levi said: They instituted them כְּנֶגֶד תְּמִידִים, *corresponding to the daily* tamid *sacrifices.* Who instituted the prayers and when, is left unsaid according to this view.

R' Avraham ben Yitzchak of Narbonne seems to hold that even according to this view the Patriarchs instituted the practice of praying three times a day. The specific times for prayer were instituted later by the Rabbis to correspond to the sacrifices.

Midrash Tanchuma (KiSavo 1) states that Moses mandated the practice of praying three times a day.

The *Talmud (Berachos* 31a, citing *Tosefta* 3:8) says (in reference to Daniel's praying three times a day): We would think that it [the institution of daily prayer] was started when he went into exile; therefore it is said *(Daniel* 6:11), **as he had been doing before** — i.e., before the exile took place, he had already adopted the practice of daily prayer.

The passage in *Megillah* (17b) referring to the אַנְשֵׁי כְּנֶסֶת הַגְּדוֹלָה, *Men of the Great Assembly*, as the authors of the institution of prayer, is referring to the practice of saying שְׁמוֹנֶה עֶשְׂרֵה, *Eighteen Benedictions*, in prayer. (see *Rambam, Hilchos Tefillah* 1:4) *R' Zidkiah ben Avraham (Shibolei Haleket*, 18, quoted in *Bais Yosef* to *Orach Chaim* 112) quotes a *midrash* to the effect that the Eighteen Benedictions preceded the Great Assembly. The Great Assembly only established the sequence of the benedictions.

Rambam (ibid. 1:5) implies that Ezra and his rabbinical court (=The Great Assembly) mandated the number of prayers to be said daily (see *Kesef Mishneh, ibid.* cf. *Mirkeves HaMishneh, ibid.* 3:1). According to this

view, Daniel's practice of praying three times a day must have been a private custom of his own. The *Talmud (Berachos*, quoted above) intends only to tell us that this custom was not meant as a substitute for the sacrifices, rather it had been his custom *before this* — i.e., from before the destruction of the Temple. In light of this, it is difficult to understand Daniel's risking his life. We must assume that Daniel was not planning martyrdom, but that there was no question in his mind that he was *not* transgressing the king's decree (see *Malbim* below). Perhaps it can be said that Daniel's acceptance of the custom of prayer three times per day gave it the force of a halachic obligation. A parallel to this can be found in the *halachah* which says that even though the evening prayer is not obligatory, since it is customary to pray it, it is considered an obligation (*Rif* to *perek Tefillas Hashachar; Rambam, Hilchos Tefillah* 1:6). Therefore Scripture finds it necessary to inform us that Daniel did so because *he had been doing so before this.*]

בָּרֵךְ עַל־בִּרְכוֹהִי — *He fell to* [lit. *knelt on*] *his knees.*

[King Solomon (*II Kings* 8:54) and Ezra (*Ezra* 9:5), too, knelt while praying, but the custom has been discontinued throughout Jewry. Perhaps the reason given by *R' Yissachar Eilenberg (T'shuvas Be'er Sheva* 73 p. 221) for the discontinuation of another custom found in Scripture pertaining to prayer, that of holding the hands together in an upright position (see verses cited above), applies here too. He maintains that Jews discontinued the practice after it became the universal Christian custom.]

וּמְצַלֵּא וּמוֹדֵא — *And prayed and gave thanks.*

... In accordance with the

6
12

thanks before his God, exactly as he had been doing before this. ¹² *Then these men assembled and found Daniel praying and supplicating before his God.*

halachah that the first three berachos should be praise to God and the last three should contain words of thanks. (*Ralbag* in *To'aliyos;* see *Rambam, Hilchos Tefillah* 1:4).

דִּי־הֲוָא עָבֵד מִן־קַדְמַת דְּנָה — *As he had been doing before this.*

He prayed three times, including עַרְבִית, *the night prayer,* even though according to *halachah* this prayer is not obligatory (*Berachos* 21b; *Hilchos Tefillah* 1:6). Nevertheless he did not exempt himself from even this prayer because this is what *he had [always] been doing before this.* When one commits himself to the custom of praying the night prayer, it becomes obligatory for him (*Alshich;* cf. *Rif* to *Berachos, perek Tefillos Hashachar, Rambam, ibid.*).

[*Rif* and *Rambam (ibid.)* add that in our days, since the entire Jewish community has accepted the obligation of praying the night prayer, it has become incumbent on every individual. The *halachah* is clear on this. See *Tur Orach Chaim* 235. Cf. *Rambam Hilchos Tefillah* 9:9.]

Malbim interpret Daniel's seeming defiance of the king's decree in a very different manner. The king's decree had been that *whoever shall make a request ... (v. 8)* — i.e., whoever asks for something specific. Since his prayers were of a general nature, Daniel understood them not to be covered by the king's decree. Therefore Daniel innocently continued to pray and to give thanks before his God, since he was not making a request, rather he was

doing just as he *had been doing before* (cf. *Toras Chesed, Haamek She'elah* 42:2).

12. הַרְגִּשׁוּ — *Assembled.*
The translation follows the consensus of commentators to v. 7. *Rashi's* interpretation (*ibid.*) also fits this context: they *'felt out'* Daniel — i.e., they spied on him. *R' Shmuel Masnuth* points out that his interpretation in *v. 7 (gathered in counsel)* could not apply here, since their attempt to spy on Daniel would have been done stealthily, lest they forewarn Daniel. [The same applies to our bracketed comment above: *they gathered tumultuously.*] He renders הַרְגִּישׁוּ similar to the *Talmudic* הרגיש בו, *he felt his presence (Shabbos* 115b) — i.e., they lay in wait for him.

בָּעֵה — *Praying* [lit. *requesting*].
Because of their determination to find Daniel guilty of transgressing the king's decree, they interpreted his prayer as a specific petition (*Malbim*).

וּמִתְחַנַּן — *And supplicating.*
We learn from this that a person's prayer should not be a burden and chore, rather it should be said in the manner of supplication and pleading (*R' Shmuel Masnuth;* cf. *Berachos* 28b and 29b). One should pray supplicatingly like a beggar at the door (*Orach Chaim* 98:3). One should not pray like someone carrying a burden, who then throws it down and goes away (*Rambam, Hilchos Tefillah* 4:16).

בֵּאדַיִן קְרִבוּ וְאָמְרִין קֳדָם־מַלְכָּא עַל־
אֱסָר מַלְכָּא הֲלָא אֱסָר רְשַׁמְתָּ דִּי כָל־
אֱנָשׁ דִּי־יִבְעֵא מִן־כָּל־אֱלָהּ וֶאֱנָשׁ עַד־
יוֹמִין תְּלָתִין לָהֵן מִנָּךְ מַלְכָּא יִתְרְמֵא
לְגוֹב אַרְיָוָתָא עָנֵה מַלְכָּא וְאָמַר יַצִּיבָא
מִלְּתָא כְּדָת־מָדַי וּפָרַס דִּי־לָא תֶעְדֵּא:
בֵּאדַיִן עֲנוֹ וְאָמְרִין קֳדָם מַלְכָּא דִּי דָנִיֵּאל
דִּי מִן־בְּנֵי גָלוּתָא דִּי יְהוּד לָא־שָׂם °עֲלַיִךְ
מַלְכָּא טְעֵם וְעַל־אֱסָרָא דִּי רְשַׁמְתָּ וְזִמְנִין
תְּלָתָה בְּיוֹמָא בָּעֵא בָּעוּתֵהּ: אֱדַיִן מַלְכָּא
כְּדִי מִלְּתָא שְׁמַע שַׂגִּיא בְּאֵשׁ עֲלוֹהִי וְעַל
דָּנִיֵּאל שָׂם בָּל לְשֵׁיזָבוּתֵהּ וְעַד מֶעָלֵי
שִׁמְשָׁא הֲוָה מִשְׁתַּדַּר לְהַצָּלוּתֵהּ: בֵּאדַיִן

יג

יד

°עֲלָךְ ק'

טו

טז

---

13. עַל־אֱסָר מַלְכָּא — *About the king's prohibition.*

I.e., about the transgression (by Daniel) of the king's decree (*Rashi*).

They only pretended to be inquiring about the decree because they were afraid that the decree might not be irrevocable. Only when the king affirmed its irrevocability did they tell him about Daniel's transgression. Had they told the king immediately, he might have denied that the decree had already been signed (*Alshich*).

14. לָא־שָׂם עֲלָךְ מַלְכָּא טְעֵם — *Has not accepted your decree, O king.*

[See *comm.* to 3:12].

בָּעֵא בָּעוּתֵהּ — *He prays his prayer* [lit. *he makes his request*].

Here again they were careful to describe Daniel's prayer as petitioning, and as such covered by the king's decree (*Malbim*).

15. Darius Struggles to Save Daniel

שַׂגִּיא בְּאֵשׁ עֲלוֹהִי — *Was deeply grieved.*

This matter perturbed him very much, because he was very fond of Daniel (*Rashi*).

בָּל — *Mind.*

The commentators are unsure of the meaning of this word. *Radak* proposes three possible interpretations.

A. בָּל, *heart*=לֵב — the letters are transposed (similarly we find כשב-כבש) — i.e., he set his heart to save him;

B. *Mind* — *his thoughts*. He finds evidence for this interpretation in Arabic;

C. בָּל — like בַּל in Hebrew (e.g., בַּל־אִמּוֹט, *Psalms* 10:6), *he applied denial to save him*, — i.e., he argued persistently. According to *Rashi*,

6

13-15

¹³ *Then they approached and said before the king,* *'About the king's prohibition: have you not in-* *scribed a prohibition that any person who will re-* *quest of any god or person for the next thirty days,* *other than of you, O king, will be thrown into the* *lions' pit?*

The king exclaimed, 'The statement is true, ac- *cording to the law of Media and Persia, which will* *not expire.'*

¹⁴ *Then they exclaimed before the king, that* *'Daniel, who is one of the exiles of Judah, has not ac-* *cepted your decree, O King, nor the prohibition* *which you have inscribed. Three times a day he prays* *his prayer.'*

¹⁵ *Then the king, when he heard this statement,* *was deeply grieved, and set his mind on Daniel to* *save him, and till sundown he struggled to rescue* *him.*

---

who translates *delay*, the verse would read, *he applied delay to save him* — i.e., he stalled as long as possible. *R' Sa'adiah* (in the name of *R' Mattisyahu Gaon*) proposes still another translation: *ransom*, from בְּלוֹ, *a head tax*, (*Ezra* 4:13; see *Rashi* there).

The translation follows the second given by *Radak* because, in addition to fitting the context smoothly, it is supported with a linguistic proof.

וְעַד מֶעָלֵי שִׁמְשָׁא — *And till sundown.*

When sundown came and it was time for מִנְחָה, *the afternoon prayer*, Daniel fell to his knees before God and prayed, thus destroying the king's defense (*Rashi* from *Midrash Shocher Tov* 64).

[On the surface it seems that Daniel did not realize he was being spied upon. Therefore when the time came, he

prayed, thus playing into the hands of his enemies. But on examination of *Rashi's* source it is clearly evident that Daniel was aware that he was being watched, and consciously chose the path of martyrdom. For a lengthier explanation of this, see *comm.* to *v.11.*]

מִשְׁתַּדַּר — *He struggled.*

Like מִשְׁתַּדֵּל, which is found quite often in the *Talmud* (e.g., *Avos* 2:5). The substitution of *resh* for *lamed* is found elsewhere in Aramaic (e.g., וָארוּ=וָאלוּ [2:31] [7:2]). This word also carries a tone of militancy with it: וַיֵּאָבֵק אִישׁ עִמּוֹ, *and a man wrestled with him* (*Genesis* 32:25) is translated by *Onkelos,* וְאִשְׁתַּדֵּל. Thus, מִשְׁתַּדַּר can mean *he fought for him* (*R' Saadiah* and *R' Shmuel Masnuth*).

He refused to believe them (*Rashi; R' Shmuel Masnuth* from *Midrash Shocher Tov* 64).

גֻּבְרַיָּא אִלֵּךְ הַרְגִּשׁוּ עַל־מַלְכָּא וְאָמְרִין
לְמַלְכָּא דַּע מַלְכָּא דִּי־דָת לְמָדַי וּפָרַס
דִּי־כָל־אֱסָר וּקְיָם דִּי־מַלְכָּא יְהָקֵים לָא
לְהַשְׁנָיָה: בֵּאדַיִן מַלְכָּא אֲמַר וְהַיְתִיו יז
לְדָנִיֵּאל וּרְמוֹ לְגֻבָּא דִּי אַרְיָוָתָא עָנֵה
מַלְכָּא וְאָמַר לְדָנִיֵּאל אֱלָהָךְ דִּי °אַנְתָּה   °אַנְתְּ ק׳
פָּלַח־לֵהּ בִּתְדִירָא הוּא יְשֵׁיזְבִנָּךְ: וְהֵיתָיִת יח
אֶבֶן חֲדָה וְשֻׂמַת עַל־פֻּם גֻּבָּא וְחַתְמַהּ
מַלְכָּא בְּעִזְקְתֵהּ וּבְעִזְקָת רַבְרְבָנוֹהִי דִּי

He advanced the argument that the decree did not cover prayer of Daniel's kind, since his prayer was of a general nature and could not be considered *making a request* (Malbim; comm. to v.1).

16. לָא לְהַשְׁנָיָה — *Cannot be altered.*

They argued that once a decree had been signed, it could not be altered even by the king. The king's argument that Daniel's kind of prayer did not fall within the restrictions of this decree would, if accepted, be considered an alteration. Hence Daniel had to die (*Malbim*).

17. דִּי אַנְתְּ פָּלַח־לֵהּ בִּתְדִירָא — *Whom you serve continually.*

Sifre (Deut. 11:13) asks; 'Is there [sacrificial] service (פְּלְחָן) in Babylon?' (The Aramaic פָּלְחָן and its Hebrew counterpart עֲבוֹדָה contain a nuance of the idea of physical, hence sacrificial, worship.) *Sifre* concludes that there is also עֲבוֹדָה שֶׁבַּלֵּב, *worship in the heart,* i.e., prayer — which is alluded to here and in *Deuteronomy,* respectively, as עֲבוֹדָה and פָּלְחָן.

In *Avos D'Rabbi Nassan* (4:5;

see emendations by *Gaon of Vilna*) we find another perception of this verse. It is narrated that, R' Yehoshua and R' Yochanan ben Zakkai were walking in the vicinity of the ruined Holy Temple. Said R' Yehoshua, 'Woe to us that this place in which they were wont to atone for our sins is in ruins!'

He answered him, 'My son! Let your heart not be saddened. We have a form of atonement (כַּפָּרָה) which is its equivalent — acts of loving-kindness (גְּמִילַת חֲסָדִים), as is written, *Your God Whom You serve continually.* In what kind of service was Daniel engaged in Babylon? Could you say [he offered] burnt-offerings and peace-offerings? But what was [the service attributed to Daniel]? Acts of loving-kindness in which Daniel was engaged. He was wont to prepare brides and gladden them, escort the dead, give alms to the poor, and pray three times a day.'

[R' David Luria explains that though *Avos D'Rabbi Nosson* includes prayer with the term עֲבוֹדָה־פָּלְחָן, it cannot be the sole meaning of the term. Since prayer has specific times it cannot be described as בִּתְדִירָא, continuous. This description only fits acts of loving-kindness, which, though each may be

6

16-18

¹⁶ *Then these men assembled around the king, and said to the king, 'Know, O king, that the law of Media and Persia is that any prohibition or statute that the king establishes cannot be altered.'*

¹⁷ *Then the king commanded and they brought Daniel and threw him into the lions' pit.* <u>*The king exclaimed to Daniel, 'Your God, Whom you serve continually, He will save you.'*</u> ¹⁸ *And a stone was brought and was placed over the opening of the pit, and the king sealed it with his signet ring and with the signet rings of his nobles, so that his will*

---

a one-time act, are considered continuous since their effects are felt continuously (e.g., the effect of clothing the poor outlives the mere act of clothing him). The *Talmud* (*Kesubos* 50a) explains in the same vein that the verse ... *who performs righteousness at all times* must refer to someone who rears an orphan (Glosses to *Pirkei D'Rabbi Eliezer* 16:2).]

הוּא יְשֵׁיזְבִנָּךְ — *He will save you.*

Rabbi Elazar said in Rabbi Chanina's name, let not the blessing of a commoner be slight in your eyes, because Daniel was blessed by Darius, as it is written, *Your God, Whom you serve* ... (*Megillah* 15a).

One feels a note of certainty in Darius' words. The king felt that since Daniel's death sentence was the result of his loyalty to God, God would have to reciprocate with a miraculous deliverance: Since your travail is due to *God Whom you serve continually*, there remains no recourse but that *He will save you* (*Alshich*).

18. וְהֵיתָיִת אֶבֶן חֲדָה — *And a stone was brought.*

In all of Babylon there are no [large] stones, as it is said (*Genesis* 11:3; in reference to the tower of Babylon), *let us make bricks ... And the brick served them as stone ...*

From this we learn that there is no stone in Babylon. But angels brought [the stone] momentarily from *Eretz Yisrael* (*Rashi* from *Bamidbar Rabbah* 14:3).

The commentators on the *Midrash* suggest that this is the reason for the passive term וְהֵיתָיִת (corresponding to the Hebrew נפעל), *the stone was brought*, rather than *they brought the stone*.

וְחַתְמַהּ מַלְכָּא — *And the king sealed it.*

Now, the nobles could not move the stone and kill Daniel themselves. Even if God should order nature suspended so that the lions not harm Daniel, this would not preclude the nobles killing him with their own hands (*Rashi*).

Alshich remarks that from this we can derive the principle that even a miracle does not (usually) interfere with man's בְּחִירָה, *free determination*. [For elaboration on this theme, see *comm.* to 13:15.]

וּבְעִזְקַת רַבְרְבָנוֹהִי — *And with the signet rings of his nobles.*

The nobles, knowing Darius' partiality to Daniel, suspected that the king might remove Daniel from

יט לָא־תִשְׁנֵא צְבוּ בְדָנִיֵּאל: אֱדַיִן אֲזַל מַלְכָּא
לְהֵיכְלֵהּ וּבָת טְוָת וְדַחֲוָן לָא־הַנְעֵל
כ קָדָמוֹהִי וְשִׁנְתֵּהּ נַדַּת עֲלוֹהִי: בֵּאדַיִן
מַלְכָּא בִּשְׁפַּרְפָּרָא יְקוּם בְּנָגְהָא
וּבְהִתְבְּהָלָה לְגֻבָּא דִי־אַרְיָוָתָא אֲזַל:
כא וּכְמִקְרְבֵהּ לְגֻבָּא לְדָנִיֵּאל בְּקָל עֲצִיב זְעִק
עָנֵה מַלְכָּא וְאָמַר לְדָנִיֵּאל דָּנִיֵּאל עֲבֵד
אֱלָהָא חַיָּא אֱלָהָךְ דִּי °אַנְתָּה פָּלַח־לֵהּ
בִּתְדִירָא הַיְכִל לְשֵׁיזָבוּתָךְ מִן־אַרְיָוָתָא:
כב אֱדַיִן דָּנִיֵּאל עִם־מַלְכָּא מַלִּל מַלְכָּא
כג לְעָלְמִין חֱיִי: אֱלָהִי שְׁלַח מַלְאֲכֵהּ וּסֲגַר
פֻּם אַרְיָוָתָא וְלָא חַבְּלוּנִי כָּל־קֳבֵל דִּי

the pit after they had left, or devise some other means to save him (Metzudos.)

19. The King's Concern

וּבָת טְוָת — *And went to bed hungry.*

The translation is the one followed by most commentators. The same expression is used in *Pesachim* (107a) with the same meaning.

Menachem ben Saruk (*Machberes s.v.* טות) connects טות to טוי, *roast* (see *Onkelos* to *Exodus* 12:9). Thus, *the king ... went burning* [with rage].

וְדַחֲוָן — *Table* (i.e., meal).

Rashi, quoting *Donash*, translates *table*. *Radak* cites evidence from an edition of *Tosefta* (*Kelim, Bava Metzia* 5:1) which reads דַחֲוָנוּת instead of חֶזְיוֹנוֹת as in our versions. A small table, unlike our tables, was used like a tray. Thus the food was set upon a table in the kitchen, which was then brought to the dining room with the

food upon it. This custom is found many times in the *Talmud* (e.g., *Pesachim* 114a; cf. *Tosafos s.v.* הביאו לפניו מצה; also *ibid.* 100 s.v. שאין, לאו, and מפסיקין).

R' Saadiah, interchanges the first two letters of the word and relates it to חֶדְוָה, *happiness*. He then translates the word דַחֲוָן as *music*. This is also the opinion of *Aruch* (*s.v.* דחון) and *Ibn Ezra*. *Radak*, in an alternate interpretation, understands דַחֲוָן as a composite of דִי יְחַוֹן, *those who tell* — i.e., readers (cf. *Esther* 6:1) and singers.

20. בִּשְׁפַּרְפָּרָא יְקוּם בְּנָגְהָא — *Arose in the darkness before dawn* [lit., At dawn, arose in the darkness].

בִּשְׁפַּרְפָּרָא, *at dawn*, בְּנָגְהָא, *in the darkness* before it became light (*R' Saadiah; R' Shmuel Masnuth; R' Yeshayah*).

Rashi and *Metzudos* render בְּנָגְהָא, *when it became light.* The *Talmud* (*Pesachim* 3a) relates that נָגְהֵי has both those conflicting

¹⁹ *Then the king went to his palace and went to bed hungry, and had no table brought before him; and his sleep fled from him.*

²⁰ *Then the king arose in the darkness before dawn, and in haste went to the lions' pit.* ²¹ *When he drew near to the pit, to Daniel, he cried in a sad voice. The king exclaimed to Daniel, 'Daniel, servant of the living God, your God whom you serve continually, was He able to save you from the lions?'*

²² *Then Daniel spoke to the king, 'O king, live forever!* ²³ *My God sent His angel and shut the lions' mouths, and they did not wound me, because merit*

meanings in different places in Babylon; hence both these translations are correct. However, since the context of the verse indicates the earliness of the king's return to the pit, it stands to reason that the king rose when it was still dark.

According to the *Mesorah*, the first פ of the word בִּשְׁפַרְפָּרָא, *at dawn*, is written smaller than the rest of the word, while the second פ is written larger — בשפרפרא. *Minchas Shai* finds an allusion to Darius' conduct in this odd calligraphy. The name of the letter פ, *peh*, also means *mouth*. When it came to defending Daniel, Darius had a small פ, *peh*, *mouth* — i.e., he was not able to find words to defend Daniel. Later, however, when he had to pass sentence on Daniel's accusers, he had a large פ, *peh*, *mouth* — i.e., he immediately had the right words to declare their punishment.

21. בְּקָל עֲצִיב זְעִק — *He cried in a sad voice.*

Daniel did not answer the king's cries, because he did not realize that it was the king who was addressing

him. Only when the king started to talk to him in his regular voice did Daniel respond (*Malbim*).

[This interpretation understands the following phrase, עֲנֵה מַלְכָּא וְאָמַר לְדָנִיֵּאל, *the king exclaimed to Daniel* to be unconnected with this phrase. Thus, *The king cried to Daniel in a sad voice* — i.e., he called his name. When he did not receive an answer, the king *exclaimed to Daniel* ... It is simpler however to understand *the king exclaimed* as an elaboration on the previous *he cried in a sad voice* ...]

22-23. 'They did not wound me.'

23. שְׁלַח מַלְאֲכֵהּ — *Sent His angel.*

The *Midrash* (*Shir Hashirim Rabbah* 1:1 and elsewhere) relates that an angel came down and assumed the form of a fearsome lion which so terrified the other lions that they could not even open their mouths. *R' Saadiah* cites a similar opinion.

R' Saadiah goes on to cite another *Midrash* which describes an additional miracle (also cited in *Yos-*

קָֽדָמ֣וֹהִי זָכוּ֮ הִשְׁתְּכַחַת֮ לִ֒י וְאַ֣ף °קדמיך ° קֳדָמָ֣ךְ ק' כד-כז

מַלְכָּ֗א חֲבוּלָ֖ה לָ֣א עַבְדֵ֑ת בֵּאדַ֙יִן֙ מַלְכָּ֔א כד

שַׂגִּ֣יא טְאֵ֣ב עֲל֑וֹהִי וּלְדָֽנִיֵּ֕אל אֲמַ֖ר

לְהַנְסָקָ֥ה מִן־גֻּבָּ֑א וְהֻסַּ֨ק דָּֽנִיֵּ֜אל מִן־גֻּבָּ֗א

וְכָל־חֲבָל֙ לָֽא־הִשְׁתְּכַ֣ח בֵּ֔הּ דִּ֖י הֵימִ֥ן

בֵּֽאלָהֵֽהּ׃ וַאֲמַ֣ר מַלְכָּ֗א וְהַיְתִ֜יו גֻּבְרַיָּ֣א כה

אִלֵּךְ֩ דִּֽי־אֲכַ֨לוּ קַרְצ֣וֹהִי דִּ֤י דָֽנִיֵּאל֙ וּלְגֹ֣ב

אַרְיָוָתָ֣א רְמ֔וֹ אִנּ֖וּן בְּנֵיה֣וֹן וּנְשֵׁיה֑וֹן וְלָֽא־

מְטוֹ֙ לְאַרְעִ֣ית גֻּבָּ֔א עַ֛ד דִּֽי־שְׁלִ֥טֽוּ בְה֖וֹן

אַרְיָ֣וָתָ֗א וְכָל־גַּרְמֵיה֖וֹן הַדִּֽקוּ׃ בֵּאדַ֙יִן֙ כו

דָּֽרְיָ֣וֶשׁ מַלְכָּ֗א כְּתַ֞ב לְֽכָל־עַֽמְמַיָּ֤א אֻמַּיָּא֙

וְלִשָּֽׁנַיָּ֗א דִּֽי־°דארין בְּכָל־אַרְעָ֖א שְׁלָֽמְכ֥וֹן ° דָּיְרִ֥ין ק'

יִשְׂגֵּֽא׃ מִן־קֳדָמַ֗י֒ שִׂים֙ טְעֵ֔ם דִּ֣י | בְּכָל־ כז

שָׁלְטָ֣ן מַלְכוּתִ֔י לֶהֱוֺ֣ן °זאעין וְדָֽחֲלִ֔ין מִן־ ° זָיְעִ֥ין ק'

קֳדָ֖ם אֱלָהֵ֣הּ דִּֽי־דָֽנִיֵּ֑אל דִּי־ה֣וּא | אֱלָהָ֣א

חַיָּ֗א וְקַיָּם֙ לְעָ֣לְמִ֔ין וּמַלְכוּתֵהּ֙ דִּֽי־לָ֣א

---

sipon ch. 3): *An angel brought the prophet Habakkuk from the land of Judah*[1] *together with his workmen and their food, and together they ate and drank with Daniel in the pit and gave thanks to God for the great miracle.*

חֲבוּלָה לָא עַבְדֵת — *I have done no harm.*

My thrice daily prayers were not a transgression of the decree (*Malbim;* see *comm.* to v. 11).

24. דִּי הֵימִן — *Who had trusted.*

His deliverance was due to his great trust in God. Even when things were at their bleakest, he did not refrain from praying to God (*Metzudos*).

25. The Defamers' End

וְהַיְתִיו גֻּבְרַיָּא אִלֵּךְ — *And they brought these men.*

The Midrash (*Shocher Tov* 64, *Yalkut* to *Psalms* 64) relates that when the king confronted the defamers with the fact of Daniel's deliverance, they responded with the argument that the lions had not been hungry. So Darius had them thrown to the lions and the lions, ravenous from their overnight fast,

---

1. See above (*Epilogue* to 3:30) whether anyone was living in Eretz Yisrael in the 52 years following the destruction of the Temple. Since Darius reigned before Cyrus, who allowed the Jews to return from exile, his rule falls within these 52 years.

6
24-27
was found for me before Him; and also before you, O king, I have done no harm.'

²⁴ *Then the king was very pleased, and he commanded that Daniel be brought up from the pit. Daniel was brought up from the pit, and no wound was found on him who had trusted in his God.*

²⁵ *The king commanded and they brought these men who had defamed Daniel, and they threw them into the lions' pit — then their children, and their wives; they did not reach the bottom of the pit, when the lions overpowered them and crushed all their bones.*

²⁶ *Then King Darius wrote,*

'To all the peoples, nations, and languages that live in all the earth; your peace should multiply! ²⁷ I hereby issue a decree that: throughout the extent of my kingdom let them tremble before, and fear, the God of Daniel — Who is the living God and everlasting; His kingdom is that which

---

destroyed the defamers before they reached the ground. This, in addition to being a punishment, also served to highlight the greatness of the miracle. The lions, though ravenous, had refrained from harming Daniel. Thus the death of these skeptics, ironically, served to demonstrate the genuineness of the miracle they had scoffed at.

דִּי־אֲכַלוּ קַרְצוֹהִי — *Who had defamed.* [See comm. to 3:8].

26. Darius' Letter

27. לֶהֱוֹן זָיְעִין וְדָחֲלִין — *Let them tremble before, and fear.*

The king did not decree that all his subjects must relinquish their idols and worship the one and true

God. He only decreed that the God of Daniel should be feared (*Alshich*).

חַיָּא — *The living.*
Unlike the idols of gold and silver who have no life ...

וְקַיָּם לְעָלְמִין — *And everlasting.*
Unlike the elements and the sun, moon, and stars. Even these are not eternal and cannot be compared to God ...

וּמַלְכוּתֵה דִּי־לָא תִתְחַבַּל — *His kingdom [is that] which will not be destroyed.* Not even the great angels who act as the patrons of the nations (see 4:19) are worthy of being worshiped. The fortunes of even the loftiest angels fall and rise

ו
כח־כט

כח תִּתְחַבַּל וְשָׁלְטָנֵהּ עַד־סוֹפָא: מְשֵׁיזִב
וּמַצִּל וְעָבֵד אָתִין וְתִמְהִין בִּשְׁמַיָּא
וּבְאַרְעָא דִּי שֵׁיזִב לְדָנִיֵּאל מִן־יַד
כט אַרְיָוָתָא: וְדָנִיֵּאל דְּנָה הַצְלַח בְּמַלְכוּת
דָּרְיָוֶשׁ וּבְמַלְכוּת כּוֹרֶשׁ °פָּרְסָיָא:

° פַּרְסָאָה ק'

ז
א־ב

א בִּשְׁנַת חֲדָה לְבֵלְאשַׁצַּר מֶלֶךְ בָּבֶל דָּנִיֵּאל
חֵלֶם חֲזָה וְחֶזְוֵי רֵאשֵׁהּ עַל־מִשְׁכְּבֵהּ
ב בֵּאדַיִן חֶלְמָא כְתַב רֵאשׁ מִלִּין אֲמַר: עָנֵה

with the fortunes of the nations
they represent ...

וְשָׁלְטָנֵהּ עַד־סוֹפָא — *And His rule [is]
till eternity.*

Even before the ultimate triumph
of His kingdom, even when Israel is
still subjugated by the nations, still
His rule is to the end — i.e., even
before and up to *the end*, the end of
days alluded to by our forefather
Jacob (*Genesis* 49:1), God reigns
supreme (*Alshich*).

29. וְדָנִיֵּאל דְּנָה — *(And) this Daniel*
[See 1:21.]

וּבְמַלְכוּת כּוֹרֶשׁ — *And in the reign of
Cyrus.*

Rashi relates (from *Yossipon* [our
copies of *Yossipon* do not contain
this]) that Darius was killed in war,
and the armies crowned his son-in-
law, Cyrus, king (see *comm.* to *v.*
1). [This interpretation follows the
view that the Cyrus mentioned here
reigned immediately after Darius
the Mede. (See *comm.* to 1:21).]

VII.

⇛§Daniel's Vision of the Four Beasts

1. בִּשְׁנַת חֲדָה — *In the first year.*
This happened before the events
in chapters 5 and 6. Till here we
have the history of Daniel in perfect
sequence. From here on we are
given Daniel's visions, also in sequence.

Chapters 7-12, unlike the first six
chapters, are written in the first
person since they are Daniel's
original words as he wrote them
himself (see below s.v. רֵאשׁ מִלִּין

אֲמַר). The only exception is this
verse and the first words of v. 2,
which were supplied by the אַנְשֵׁי
כְּנֶסֶת הַגְּדוֹלָה, *Men of the Great Assembly,* who edited this sacred book
(*Bava Basra* 15a). [See *footnote* to
4:25.]The first six chapters, the account of what happened to Daniel
at the courts of three kings, were
written by the Men of the Great Assembly and are therefore narrated in
the third person (*Malbim*).

6

28-29

will not be destroyed, and His rule is till eternity; ²⁸ He saves and rescues, and performs signs and wonders in heaven and on earth — Who has saved Daniel from the lions.'

²⁹ This Daniel was successful in the reign of Darius and in the reign of Cyrus the Persian.

7

1-2

In the first year of Belshazzar King of Babylon, Daniel saw a dream and visions in his mind while upon his bed; he then wrote the dream, relating the major parts. ² Daniel exclaimed:

לְבֵלְאשַׁצַּר מֶלֶךְ בָּבֶל — Of Belshazzar, King of Babylon.

The vision was appropriate at this moment. Jeremiah (27:7) had prophesied; And all the nations shall serve him (Nebuchadnezzar) and his son, and his son's son ...

When Belshazzar, Nebuchadnezzar's grandson (see comm. 5:1), ascended the Babylonian throne, there was a need to reassure Daniel that Jeremiah's prophecy would indeed be fulfilled. Nevertheless, the fall of Babylon would not be followed by the hoped for גְּאוּלָה שְׁלֵמָה, total redemption, but by the advent of three more mighty kingdoms. Only upon the fall of the fourth and last of these kingdoms would there be lasting redemption (Mayenei HaYeshuah 8:1; Malbim).

בֵּאדַיִן חֶלְמָא כְתַב — He then wrote the dream.

So that nothing should be forgotten, he wrote the dream immediately (Mayenei HaYeshuah 8:1; Malbim).

רֵאשׁ מִלִּין אֲמַר — Relating the major

parts [lit. he told the head of the words].

[I.e., he abbreviated and summarized the dream.]

The dream contained some matters which are not told to us (Rav Saadiah Gaon, quoted by Mayenei HaYeshuah 8:1).

He wrote the dream in its entirety but did not tell the whole dream to others (Metzudos).

רֵאשׁ may also mean first. Malbim points out that when Daniel wrote his dream he was writing Scripture. A scribe, when copying Scripture, is required to vocalize every word before putting it into writing (Yoreh Deah 274:2; see Beur HaGra to Orach Chayim 691:16). Therefore, when Daniel wrote the dream, רֵאשׁ, first, מִלִּין אֲמַר, he said the words.

[According to the other commentators cited above, Daniel's written account of this dream has not come down to us. What we have here is only the outline which he told to others. Nevertheless, even in this view, the account given here (from v. 2 onward) is given in Daniel's own words. Therefore, the whole

דָּנִיֵּאל וְאָמַר חָזֵה הֲוֵית בְּחֶזְוִי עִם־לֵילְיָא
וַאֲרוּ אַרְבַּע רוּחֵי שְׁמַיָּא מְגִיחָן לְיַמָּא
רַבָּא: וְאַרְבַּע חֵיוָן רַבְרְבָן סָלְקָן מִן־יַמָּא ג
שָׁנְיָן דָּא מִן־דָּא: קַדְמָיְתָא כְאַרְיֵה וְגַפִּין ד
דִּי־נְשַׁר לַהּ חָזֵה הֲוֵית עַד דִּי־מְּרִיטוּ
°גַפַּיהּ וּנְטִילַת מִן־אַרְעָא וְעַל־רַגְלַיִן
כֶּאֱנָשׁ הָקִימַת וּלְבַב אֱנָשׁ יְהִיב לַהּ: וַאֲרוּ ה

chapter is written in the first person.]

2. עֲנֵה דָנִיֵּאל וְאָמַר — *Daniel exclaimed.*

[This phrase continues the previous verse: *he told the major part of the matter* (i.e., in this manner), *Daniel exclaimed.*]

חָזֵה הֲוֵית — *I was watching.*

From here the narrative begins in the first person. These are Daniel's actual words (*Malbim*).

עִם לֵילְיָא — *At night.*

Even in his dream he saw it was night. Since the vision pertained to the exile, which is likened to night, Daniel was shown night in the vision. I.e., at night I was watching ... (*Malbim*).

Ibn Ezra renders it as if it were בְּחֶזְוִי לֵילְיָא: *I saw in my night vision.*

אַרְבַּע רוּחֵי שְׁמַיָּא — *The four winds of the heaven.*

These *four winds* represent the higher, spiritual forces that correspond to the four kingdoms [in chapter 2 and in the rest of this book] (*Abarbanel* 8:1).

Each of the four kingdoms has its base of power at another corner of the earth (*Malbim*).

מְגִיחָן — *Stir up.*

The translation follows *Rashi* who derives this verb from יָגַּח, *goring*, as in כִּי יִגַּח שׁוֹר, *if an ox will gore* (Exodus 21:28). *Onkelos* renders וַיִּלָּחֶם עִם יִשְׂרָאֵל, *and he warred with Israel* (Exodus 17:8): וְאָגַח קְרָבָא, *he stirred up a war.*

לְיַמָּא רַבָּא — *(To) the great sea.*

The sea is representative of the world because of its great changeability and the severe dangers and terrible storms one encounters while traversing it (*Abarbanel* 8:1).

3. וְאַרְבַּע חֵיוָן רַבְרְבָן — *And four immense beasts.*

The beasts represent the four kingdoms, which are stirred up and influenced by their spiritual counterparts, represented in this vision by the four winds (*Mayenei HaYeshuah* 8:1).

רַבְרְבָן — *Immense.*

Contemporary with these great kingdoms there will be smaller, less conspicuous kingdoms. These four kingdoms were represented only by the biggest, greatest animals (*Malbim*).

שָׁנְיָן דָּא מִן־דָּא — *Different from one another.*

Each of these kingdoms had its own style and nature (*Malbim*).

The manner of oppression dif-

7
3-4
In my vision at night I was watching when, behold! the four winds of heaven stir up the great sea. ³ And four immense beasts come up from the sea, different from one another. ⁴ The first is like a lion with eagle's wings. I was watching till its wings were plucked and it was removed from the earth, and stood upon two feet like a man, and it was given a

fered under each kingdom. Nebuchadnezzar ordered the people to bow down before his statue, Ahasuerus oppressed the Jews through Haman, etc. (R' Saadiah). The same idea is expressed in *Midrash Shir HaShirim Rabbah* (3:4), which comments on this phrase, their blows are *different from one another.*

4. אַרְיֵה כְּאַרְיֵה קַדְמָיְתָא — *The first is like a lion.*

This represents Babylon (*Vayikra Rabbah* 13:5).

[*Jeremiah* (4:7) says in reference to Nebuchadnezzar, עָלָה אַרְיֵה מִסֻּבְּכוֹ, *a lion is gone up from his thicket ...* .]

וְגַפִּין דִּי־נְשַׁר לַהּ — *With eagle's wings.*

Daniel's vision here combined elements from the prophecies of Moses and Jeremiah. Moses said, HASHEM *will bring a nation against you ... as the 'eagle' swoops down* (*Deut.* 28:49). Jeremiah (4:6-7) said, *For I will bring an evil from the north ... A 'lion' is gone up from his thicket ...* (4:6-7) (*VaYikra Rabbah* 13:5 quoted in *Rashi*).

[Our interpretation of *Deuteronomy* 28:49 as a reference to the 'eagle' which destroyed the First Temple follows *Abarbanel*. *Ramban*, however, interprets the chastisement of *Deuteronomy* as a reference to the Second Temple, and the chastisement of *Leviticus* as a reference to the First Temple.

See *Ramban* and *Abarbanel* to *Deut.* 28:42 and *Lev.* 26:16.]

The Babylonian empire was represented as a lion to indicate its great power. The high-flying eagle symbolizes the great arrogance and pride of the Babylonians. The prophet Isaiah (14:12-14), foreseeing the downfall of the haughty Babylonian king, exclaims, *How you are fallen from heaven ... And you said in your heart I will ascend into heaven ... I will be like the Supreme One.* The eagle's wings represent the great speed and energy which were the Baylonian's hallmark (*Mayenei HaYeshuah* 8:2; *Malbim*).

The two wings represent Nebuchadnezzar's two successors, Evil-Merodach and Belshazzar (*Ibn Ezra* to v. 14).

עַד דִּי־מְרִיטוּ גַפַּהּ — *Till its wings were plucked.*

This symbolizes the downfall of Babylon (*Rashi*).

In Belshazzar's reign, Babylon's power was no longer sufficient to subdue the rebellious Persians and Medes. The once proud nation had lost the grandeur and agility symbolized by its eagle's wings (*Mayenei HaYeshuah* 8:2; *Malbim*).

וּנְטִילַת מִן־אַרְעָא — *And it was removed from the earth.*

This indicates the destruction of the Babylonian kingdom (*Rashi*).

The Persians and Medes destroyed the city of Babylon when they conquered it (*Mayenei HaYeshuah* 8:2).

וְעַל־רַגְלַיִן כֶּאֱנָשׁ הֳקִימַת — *It was ... stood upon [two] feet like a man.*

It could no longer fly like an

ז
ו

חֵיוָה אָחֳרִי תִנְיָנָה דָמְיָה לְדֹב וְלִשְׂטַר־
חַד הֲקִמַת וּתְלָת עִלְעִין בְּפֻמַּהּ בֵּין
שִׁנַּיהּ וְכֵן אָמְרִין לַהּ קוּמִי אֲכֻלִי בְּשַׂר
שַׂגִּיא: בָּאתַר דְּנָה חָזֵה הֲוֵית וַאֲרוּ אָחֳרִי

° שָׁנָה ק'

eagle, nor did it have the power of a lion (*Metzudos; Malbim*).

The downfall of Babylon was due not only to the power of the Persians, but to the weakness of Babylon (*Mayenei HaYeshuah* 8:2).

וְלִבַב אֱנָשׁ יְהִיב לַהּ — *And it was given a human heart.*

The loss of morale so weakened Babylon that it fell almost without a fight (*ibid.*).

R' Saadiah Gaon (cited by *Ibn Ezra* to v. 14) interprets this whole verse in reference to Nebuchadnezzar: *with eagle's wings* probably refers to Nebuchadnezzar's madness when *his hair grew like eagles'* [feathers] *and his nails like birds'* [talons] (4:30). *Its wings were plucked off*, i.e., he lost his animal-like appearance — *and stood upon* [two] *feet like a man, and was given a human heart*, i.e., human intelligence.

[The *Midrash* (*Bereishis Rabbah* 92:2) notes that Babylon's downfall was caused appropriately by Daniel (through his prayers — *Radal*) who came from the tribe of Judah, which is also likened to a lion (*Genesis* 49:9).]

5. תִּנְיָנָה — [A] *second* [one].

It came out of the sea second (*Rashi*).

דָמְיָה לְדֹב — *Similar to a bear.*

These are the Persians, who eat and drink [ravenously] like a bear and are corpulent מְסוּרְבָּלִין בָּשָׂר,

like a bear, (*Kiddushin* 72a, cited by *Rashi*).

They did not possess great power like the Babylonians, nor did they have their agility. Likened to the bear — a powerful, corpulent animal not noted for speed — they lacked the eagle's wings and never attained the regal power of the lion (*Mayenei HaYeshuah* 8:2; *Malbim*).

The word לְדֹב is written without a *vav*. Therefore it can be read לְדֵב, similar to the Aramaic word for דֵיבָא, *wolf*, (see *Onkelos* to *Genesis* 49:27). The Persians are also likened to the wolf, probably on account of its voraciousness. [Cf. *Jeremiah* 5:6 with *Rashi*.] Their kingdom fell (i.e., their suppression of the Jews was foiled) through Mordechai and Esther, who were descended from the tribe of Benjamin (see *Esther* 2:5), which is also likened to a wolf (*Genesis* 49:27; *Bereishis Rabbah* 92:2, cited partially by *Rashi*).

וְלִשְׂטַר־חַד הֲקִמַת — (And) *it was stood to one side.*

After the fall of Babylon, the Persians *stood to one side* temporarily — they did not take over the reins of their empire during the year that Darius the Mede reigned (*Rashi*).

The animal represented two separate, though ethnically related peoples: the Persians and the Medes. Therefore, it was first envisioned standing simultaneously on both sides. Then the animal was

דניאל [196]

human heart ⁵ And behold! another beast, a second one, similar to a bear; it was stood to one side, three ribs were in its mouth between its teeth; and thus they said to it, 'Arise, devour much flesh.' ⁶ After this

stood to one side to symbolize that only one nation at a time would be dominant — first Media under Darius, and then Persia *(Malbim)*.

The Persian empire was not as extensive as the Babylonian. Therefore it is depicted as if it stood to the side of the space occupied by the previous animal *(Mayenei Ha-Yeshuah* 8:2).

וּתְלָת עִלְעִין בְּפֻמַהּ בֵּין שַׁנַּהּ — *(And) three ribs were in its mouth between its teeth.*

These are three provinces [1] which were continuously in a state of revolt. Sometimes they were swallowed — i.e., incorporated into the Persian empire — as depicted by the ribs being *in its mouth*, and sometimes they were spit out — i.e.,

separated from the empire — as depicted by the ribs appearing *between its teeth* — not inside the mouth *(Kiddushin* 72a, cited by *Rashi).*

The three ribs can be said to represent the three Persian kings — Cyrus, Ahasuerus, and Darius (11:2; cf. *Rashi).*

The Persian kingdom was divided into three parts: Assyria, which included Babylon; Media; and Persia. Darius therefore appointed three officials to help him govern the divisions (cf. 6:3; *Malbim).*

וְכֵן אָמְרִין לַהּ — *And thus they said to it.*

The bear, not a carnivorous animal, had to be commanded to eat

1. Positive identification of these districts is difficult. Our versions of the *Talmud* give their names as Chalazon, Hadayab, and Netzivin. Netzivin is by all indications Nusaybin (previously called Nesibin) in the northeastern corner of Turkey and includes the country surrounding it. *Targum Yonasan* and *Yerushalmi* (to *Genesis* 10:10) identify the Biblical Akkad with Netzivin. The *Talmud (Pesachim* 3b) mentions Netzivin as the home of the famous *tanna* R' Yehudah ben B'seira. Travelers in the previous century report that in the vicinity of Nusaybin, there is a grave considered by local Jews to be the grave of the revered *tanna.*

Hadayab is probably Adiabene, immediately to the east of Nusaybin (south of Lake Van). *R' Benjamin Musaffiah*, in his glosses to *Aruch* (s.v. חדיב; see s.v. הדיב), identifies Hadayeb as the country of the proselyte king Munbaz *(Bava Basra* 11a). *Josephus (Ant.* XX, 2, 1) relates that Monabaseus, the king of Adiabene, and his mother, Helene (see *Yoma* 37a), converted to Judaism. *Targum* to *Jeremiah* (51:27) uses הדיב to translate *Ashkenaz,* mentioned there as one of the kingdoms of Ararat (Kurdistan). We find הדיב mentioned together with Netzivin and Charan (in Assyria; see *Ramban* to *Genesis* 11:28) in *Ezekiel* (27:23) where חָרָן וְכַנֵּה וָעֶדֶן is translated חַרְנָן וּנְצִיבִין וְהָדַיְב.

The name of the third province is given in our editions of the *Talmud* as חֲלָזוֹן, Chalazon. However in *Yalkut* (ad. loc.) the spelling is חרון. In *Ezekiel* (27:23) חָרָן is transliterated in *Targum* as חָרְנָן. One could contend that this חָרָן is חֲרַיִית, identified by *Targum Yerushalmi (Genesis* 10:10) as כַּלַח (also in northern Assyria near Nineveh). It is also logical to reason that since Netzivin and Hadayab have been identified as places in northern Assyria (near and in Kurdistan), the third province should also be found in that vicinity. (Cf. *Tiferes Yisrael Yoma* 3:10, who erroneously places Adiabene in Arabia.) Possibly חָרָן — חָרְנָן — חֲרַיִית is Haran on the river Beldik (a tributary of the Euphrates) in Turkey near the Syrian border. In *Talmudic* times it was called Carrhae.]

° גֵּבַהּ ק׳   כִּנְמַר וְלַהּ גַּפִּין אַרְבַּע דִּי־עוֹף עַל־°גַבַּיהּ
וְאַרְבְּעָה רֵאשִׁין לְחֵיוְתָא וְשָׁלְטָן יְהִיב
ז   לַהּ: בָּאתַר דְּנָה חָזֵה הֲוֵית בְּחֶזְוֵי לֵילְיָא
° רְבִיעָאָה ק׳   וַאֲרוּ חֵיוָה °רְבִיעָיָא דְּחִילָה וְאֵימְתָנִי

meat. Similarly the Persians, unlike their predecessors, the Assyrians and the Babylonians, were benevolent rulers over the countries they conquered; they did not wreak wholesale destruction upon them. Nevertheless, when they conquered Babylon, they destroyed the city and killed its inhabitants. This deviation from their usual conduct was in fulfillment of God's will (*Malbim*).

The demise of the bear is not as dramatic as that of the lion. He is not *stood upon* [*two*] *feet like a man*; neither is he *given a human heart.* The Persians, unlike the Babylonians, did not lose their empire as a result of drastic weakness from within. Persepolis did not fall without a fight. The hour of the Greeks had come, and Alexander's armies vanquished the Persians in bitter fighting (*Mayenei HaYeshuah* 8:2).

R' Saadiah Gaon (cited by *Ibn Ezra, v.* 14) takes this phrase as a reference to Ahasuerus. The bear (Ahasuerus) was told (incited by Haman) to *devour much flesh* (to destroy the Jewish people). The *Talmud* (*Megillah* 11a), which finds the symbol of the bear fitting for Ahasuerus in particular (though no doubt it refers to the Persians in general, as seen from the same passage of the *Talmud*) seems to support this view (see *Mayenei HaYeshuah* 8:2).

6. כִּנְמַר — *Like a leopard.*

This animal represents Greece (*Vayikra Rabbah* 13:5).

The leopard is distinguished for its ferocity and impudence. This feature distinguished the brilliant reign of Alexander when he conquered most of Asia in one continuous swoop (*Mayenei HaYeshuah* 8:3; *Malbim*).

[Alexander in his conquests can also be compared to the leopard in agility and speed.]

וְלַהּ גַּפִּין אַרְבַּע־דִּי עוֹף — *With four bird's wings.*

The wings symbolize Alexander's speed in making great conquests in all four points of the compass (*Abarbanel* 8:3 and *Ibn Yachya*).

וְאַרְבְּעָה רֵאשִׁין לְחֵיוְתָא — *The beast had four heads.*

Alexander's entire reign had lasted only twelve years; he died prematurely at the age of thirty-two (see *Seder Olam*, ch. 28).

After Alexander's untimely death, his empire was split up among four of his generals. Ptolemy took Egypt; Seleucas, Assyria and Babylon; Antigonas, Persia and Asia Minor; Phillip (Alexander's brother), Macedonia (*Mayenei HaYeshuah* 8:3).

וְשָׁלְטָן יְהִיב לַהּ — *And it was given dominion.*

Only the animal itself — i.e., Alexander himself— had been given total dominion. At his death, when

7
7

I was watching and behold! another, like a leopard, with four bird's wings on its back; the beast had four heads, and it was given dominion.

⁷ After this I was watching in night visions, and behold! a fourth beast excessively terrifying,

his four generals carved up the empire among themselves, no single part of the empire ever attained to the glory that had been Alexander's. The Persian kingdom had passed more or less intact from king to king, but not the Greek kingdom (*Mayenei HaYeshuah* 8:3; *Malbim*).

Ibn Ezra (above 2:39) is of the opinion that the Greek kingdom represented by the leopard includes the Roman empire, for ethnically the Romans were related to the Greeks. The Kittim, identified as the Romans (see below 11:30), were descendants of *Yavan* (Greece): *And the sons of Yavan ... Kittim and Dodanim* (*Genesis* 10:4). The fourth animal then represents the rule of the Arabs (see later). However, all the other commentators (including *R' Saadiah Gaon*, cited by *Ibn Ezra*) reject this interpretation. The *midrashim* consistently lists the four kingdoms as Babylon, Persia, Greece, and Rome. More discussion about this is found above (2:40).

7. The Fourth Beast

בְּחֶזְוֵי לֵילְיָא — *In night visions.*
The vision of the first three beasts he saw in one night, but this last beast he saw the next night in a separate vision. The *exile* represented by this beast would be equivalent to all three previous ones (*Rashi* from *Vayikra Rabba* 13:5).

חֵיוָה רְבִיעָאָה — *A fourth beast.*
As discussed at length above (2:40), the fourth kingdom, represented here by a fearsome unspecified beast, different from all the other beasts, is that of the Roman empire with all of its metamorphoses. This is the view of almost all the commentators and clearly that of our Sages in the *Talmud* and numerous *midrashim*.

Here the word אָחֳרִי, *another*, is not used as it was in *vs.* 5,6 for the second and third beasts. For here we are speaking about *exile* under the descendants of Esau the Edomite, brother to Jacob, and as such cannot be referred to as 'another.' See *comm.* to 2:40.

דְּחִילָה וְאֵמְתָנִי וְתַקִּיפָא יַתִּירָה — *Excessively terrifying, awesome, and strong.*
[דְּחִיל is the Aramaic counterpart of יִרְאָה; therefore דְּחִילָא=נוֹרָא. In *Gen.* 28:17 מַה נּוֹרָא is translated by *Onkelos* מַה דְּחִילָא. It is also found in translation of פַּחַד, as in וַתְּפַחֵד תָּמִיד (*Isaiah* 51:13), which is rendered וּדְחִילַת תְּדִירָא.]

אֵמְתָנִי is the Aramaic form of the Hebrew אָיוֹם (See *Habbakuk* 1:7). The *Gaon of Vilna* (*Aderes Eliyahu* to *Hab.* 1:7) differentiates between these synonyms. אֵימָה is the awe one feels in the presence of one vastly superior. יִרְאָה is the fear of being harmed and punished.

The three attributes given this beast correspond to three charac-

וְתַקִּיפָא יַתִּירָה וְשַׁנַּיִן דִּי־פַרְזֶל לַהּ
רַבְרְבָן אָכְלָה וּמַדְּקָה וּשְׁאָרָא °בְּרַגְלַיהּ
רָפְסָה וְהִיא מְשַׁנְּיָה מִן־כָּל־חֵיוָתָא דִּי
°קׇדָמַיהּ וְקַרְנַיִן עֲשַׂר לַהּ: מִשְׂתַּכַּל הֲוֵית

teristics possessed by the Romans:
1) great brutality — therefore
דְּחִילָא, *terrifying*; 2) meticulous
planning of strategy and great
foresight — therefore אֵימְתָנִי (as in
[*Avos* 1:1] הֱווּ מְתוּנִים בַּדִּין, *be
cautious in judgment*), *cautious*;
and 3) overwhelming power —
therefore תַּקִּיפָא, *strong*. Though
the previous kingdoms had also
possessed these qualifications to
some degree, Rome possessed them
to a greater degree than any power
before it — therefore יַתִּירָה, *excessively* (*Mayenei HaYeshuah* 8:5,
Malbim).

דְּחִילָה וְאֵימְתָנִי — *Terrifying, awesome.*

The seeming redundancy corresponds to the double nature of the
fourth kingdom, which is divided
into two parts: Christianity and
Islam (*R' Saadiah*). [See *prefatory
notes* to 2:40.]

וְשַׁנַּיִן דִּי־פַרְזֶל לַהּ רַבְרְבָן — *With immense iron teeth.*

[The fourth kingdom in Nebuchadnezzar's dream had been represented by iron (2:40).]

The iron teeth symbolize the
rulers of Rome — its consuls, and
later its emperors — who, with
determination and power of iron,
crushed many nations for the glory
and well-being of Rome, just as the
teeth devour food for the well-being
of the body (*Mayenei HaYeshuah*
8:5).

אָכְלָה וּמַדְּקָה — *It was eating and
crumbling.*

During its long history, many
conquered states were absorbed by
Rome and became provinces of the
empire, just as food which is
chewed up and eaten becomes part
of the beast's body (*Malbim*).

וּשְׁאָרָא בְּרַגְלַהּ רָפְסָה — *And trampling the rest with its feet.*

Those nations which were not
absorbed into the empire were
brutally beaten into submission and
exploited for the good of the empire
(*Malbim*).

וְהִיא מְשַׁנְּיָה מִן־כָּל־חֵיוָתָא דִּי קׇדָמַהּ —
*It was different from all the beasts
that preceded it.*

Though each of the beasts was
unique in some way, they were
nevertheless similar in certain ways,
if only in that they were all known
animals. Similarly the kingdoms
they represented were powerful and
talented in a magnitude which had
been known before. The fourth
beast, however, did not resemble
any known beast; it is not given a
name in Daniel's vision. The
Roman Empire dwarfed every nation known to history. Rome's military power, its genius in administration, and its cleverness in
dealing brooked no comparison.
Never had an empire held sway
over so much foreign territory for
so long a time (*Mayenei HaYeshuah*
8:5).

awesome, and strong; with immense iron teeth, it was
eating and crumbling, and trampling the rest with its
feet; it was different from all the beasts that preceded
it, and it had ten horns. ⁸ I was studying the horns,

וְקַרְנַיִן עֲשַׂר לַהּ — *And it had ten horns.*

These ten horns were later (v. 24) identified by the angel as ten kings who would rule Rome before the destruction of the Holy Temple (*Rashi*).

The ten emperors are:
Julius Caesar
    49-44 B.C.E.   3711-3716 A.M.
Augustus
    31 B.C.E.-14 C.E. 3729-3774 A.M.
Tiberius
    14-37 C.E.   3774-3797 A.M.
Caligula
    37-41 C.E.   3797-3801 A.M.
Claudius
    41-54 C.E.   3801-3814 A.M.
Nero
    54-68 C.E.   3814-3828 A.M.
Galba
    68-69 C.E.   3828-3829 A.M.
Otho
    69- C.E.   3829- A.M.
Vitellius
    69- C.E.   3829- A.M.
Vespasian
    69-79 C.E.   3829-3839 A.M.
During his father's reign, Titus, son of Vespasian (אַסְפַּסְיָנוּת), destroyed the Holy Temple (*Mayenei HaYeshuah* 8:5).

[Before Julius, Rome had been ruled by the Senate and two elected consuls. Julius may thus be considered the first emperor of the Roman Empire.]

Malbim advances the possibility that מַלְכִין in v. 24 are kingdoms; thus the Roman Empire would disintegrate and split into smaller un-

its, of which ten countries would be considered the major powers. He does not elaborate on this.

According to *R' Saadiah Gaon*, the Roman Empire is composed of ten governments or monarchies:
1) the Roman emperor in Constantinople (the ruler of the Byzantine Empire);
2) the king of Armenia;
3) the king of Hungary;
4) the king of Germany (Emperor of the Holy Roman Empire);
5) the king of Bulgaria;
6) the king of Canaan, כְּנַעַן (i.e., the western Slavic countries — Bohemia, Moravia, Slovakia. See *Rashi* ed. *A. Berliner* p. 427 and 465, Preface to ערוך השלם p. VII);
7) the king of France;
8) the king of Spain;
9) the king of Russia; and,
10) the king of Ishmael (the Arabic empire) who is included among the rulers of the Roman Empire (*R. Yeshayah*; see *prefatory notes* to 2:40).

Ibn Ezra (comm. to v. 14), holding to his view that the fourth beast represents the Arab Empire, explains the ten horns as ten separate kingdoms — which he names — carved out of the original Arab Empire.

8. מִשְׁתַּבַּל הֲוֵית — *I was studying.*

מִשְׁתַּבַּל is to look with a purpose, — i.e., to scrutinize and examine. *Radak (Shorashim* s.v. שכל) derives it from שֵׂכֶל, *understanding. R' Yonah (Berachos* 25b s.v. ערוה), quoting *R' Hai Gaon*, differentiates between רְאִיָה, which includes all types of sight whether inadvertent or intentional, and הִסְתַּבְּלוּת, which means to look intentionally. *Bach (to Orach Chaim* 75), though he

בְּקַרְנַיָּא וַאֲלוּ קֶרֶן אָחֳרִי זְעֵירָה סְלְקָת **ז**
°בֵּינֵיהוֹן וּתְלָת מִן־קַרְנַיָּא קַדְמָיָתָא **ט**
°אֶתְעֲקַרוּ מִן־°קֳדָמַיה וַאֲלוּ עַיְנִין כְּעַיְנֵי
אֲנָשָׁא בְּקַרְנָא־דָא וּפֻם מְמַלִּל רַבְרְבָן:
ט חָזֵה הֲוֵית עַד דִּי כָרְסָוָן רְמִיו וְעַתִּיק

° בֵּינֵיהֵן ק'
° אִתְעֲקַרֵה ק'
° קֳדָמַה ק'

---

disagrees with *R' Yonah* about the halachic implications of this definition, nevertheless accepts it as valid. The same is true of *Sefer haEshkol (Hilchos Tefillah 7)*. See *Ibn Ezra* and *R' Shmuel Masnuth*.]

קֶרֶן אָחֳרִי זְעֵירָה — *Another horn, a small one.*

This refers to Titus *(Rashi)*.

[Vespasian's son and eventual successor was in command of the Roman armies in the Holy Land and was responsible for the destruction of the Temple. He is referred to as *another horn, a small one*, probably because he was not yet emperor at this time.]

Abarbanel (Mayenei HaYeshuah 8:5), followed by *Malbim*, understands this as referring to the institution of the papacy. [Therefore this is prefaced by: *As I was studying ...* At its inception the papacy was not an institution which made its presence felt. Indeed much time passed until the bishop of Rome could consider himself the head of the Christian church. However, the power of the Roman church grew until the popes of the middle ages were able to challenge Europe's most powerful rulers.]

Ibn Ezra suggests that this part of the vision has not yet come true. The small horn is a nation which will convert to Islam (the religion of *the ten horns), coming up among them ...*

Another interpretation offered by *Malbim* is that the small horn represents the new religion of Islam, small at its inception, which would grow swiftly into a mighty power.

וּתְלָת מִן־קַרְנַיָּא קַדְמָיָתָא — *And three of the previous horns.*

[The commentators offer many interpretations of this, none of which satisfy the text fully.]

Abarbanel (Mayenei HaYeshuah 8:6) offers two interpretations.

Rome had already had three different types of government before the popes gained temporal power in the city. In hoary antiquity Rome had been ruled by kings. This was followed by the Republic (500 B.C.E.). With Julius Caesar (48 B.C.E., 3722 A.M.) the era of the emperors begins.

Abarbanel's second interpretation is: The beginning of the Christian church dates from the reign of the third emperor, Tiberius, who died in 37 C.E.

Malbim suggests that the three horns uprooted here are three kingdoms originally included in the Roman empire which later broke away from it.

[*Malbim* does not elaborate on this. He may be referring to three schisms within Christianity which led to the secession of three regions from the church. The Eastern churches — the Armenian, Syrian, Coptic (Egypt) and Abyssinian churches which seceded in 451 C.E. The secession of the Byzantine

7
9

and behold! another horn, a small one, came up among them, and three of the previous horns were uprooted before it; and behold! eyes like human eyes were in this horn and a mouth speaking haughty words.

⁹ I watched till thrones were set up, and the An-

church — the Balkans, Russia, and neighboring countries — took place in 1054 C.E. The Protestant reformation (which began in 1517) left England and Germany outside of the Roman church.]

Another possibility advanced by *Malbim* and *Metzudos* is that the small horn represents Islam which conquered three of the four kingdoms founded by Alexander's successors.

[This interpretation is already found in Rambam's *Epistle to Yemen:* 'Till he saw that the horn had *human eyes and a mouth speaking big things,* that is to say that this upstart would conjure up a religion similar to the Godly religion. He will say that he is a prophet and say many things.] Daniel here explains that his interest will be to hinder and destroy the true religion *And shall think to change the times and the law (v. 25).'*

עֵינִין כְּעַיְנֵי אֲנָשָׁא — *Human eyes.*

In contrast to the previous *horns* — *powers* — which had been characterized as brute force, this horn did not gain its victories by the might of the sword. This power had *human eyes* symbolizing the force of reason, and a mouth speaking *haughty words* — i.e., the force of persuasion (*Mayenei HaYeshuah* 8:5).

וּפֻם מְמַלִּל רַבְרְבָן — *And a mouth speaking haughty* [lit. big] *words.*

Titus spoke and acted with great arrogance in the inner sanctum of the Holy Temple as recounted in *Gittin* 56b (*Rashi*).

[See below v. 25].

רַבְרְבָן — *Haughty* [*words*].

[Although the verse uses the adjective רַבְרְבָן, *haughty,* without referring it to any specific noun, the word *words* has been interpolated as the tacitly understood noun. This is evident from the use of מְלַיָּא רַבְרְבָתָא, *haughty words,* in *v.* 11.]

9. The Judgment

בָּרְסָוָן רְמִיו — *Thrones were set up.*

The translation follows *Rashi* and *R' Shmuel Masnuth.* רְמִיו from רוּם, *height.* The thrones were elevated, i.e. *set up.* This translation is indicated in *Sanhedrin* 38a. *Ibn Ezra* and others translate *thrones were thrown down,* as in רָמָה בַיָּם, *He threw into the sea (Ex.* 15:2). בָּרְסָוָן, *thrones,* indicates more than one. One is for judgment and one for charity (*Rashi* from *Sanhedrin* 38b).

The thrones representing the kings symbolized by the four beasts and the horns were thrown down. Instead one throne was set up; *and the Ancient of days sat ...* (*Mayenei HaYeshuah* 8:7; *Metzudos. Malbim* cites from *Tanchuma K'doshim* 1, which brings two opinions concerning the interpretation of this verses: one like *Rashi's* and the one quoted here).

יוֹמִין יְתִב לְבוּשֵׁהּ | כִּתְלַג חִוָּר וּשְׂעַר
רֵאשֵׁהּ כַּעֲמַר נְקֵא כָּרְסְיֵהּ שְׁבִיבִין דִּי־
נוּר גַּלְגִּלּוֹהִי נוּר דָּלִק: נְהַר דִּי־נוּר נָגֵד י
וְנָפֵק מִן־קֳדָמוֹהִי אֶלֶף °אַלְפִים
יְשַׁמְּשׁוּנֵהּ וְרִבּוֹ °רִבְוָן קָדָמוֹהִי יְקוּמוּן
דִּינָא יְתִב וְסִפְרִין פְּתִיחוּ: חָזֵה הֲוֵית יא
בֵּאדַיִן מִן־קָל מִלַּיָּא רַבְרְבָתָא דִּי קַרְנָא
מְמַלֱּלָא חָזֵה הֲוֵית עַד דִּי קְטִילַת חֵיוְתָא
וְהוּבַד גִּשְׁמַהּ וִיהִיבַת לִיקֵדַת אֶשָּׁא:
וּשְׁאָר חֵיוָתָא הֶעְדִּיו שָׁלְטָנְהוֹן וְאַרְכָה יב
בְחַיִּין יְהִיבַת לְהוֹן עַד־זְמַן וְעִדָּן: חָזֵה יג

° אַלְפִין ק'

° רִבְבָן ק'

וְעַתִּיק יוֹמִין — *And the Ancient of Days.*

This obviously refers to God Himself sitting in judgment. *Ibn Ezra* alone among the commentaries (v.14; 12:1) interprets it to mean the archangel Michael, the great prince who will rise up *at that time* (12:1).

חִוָּר — *White.*

White symbolizes purity from sin (see *Rashi*). It is also the color that symbolizes kindness and charity (see *Tanchuma*, ed. Buber, Bereishis p. 58).

10. דִּינָא יְתִב — *The judgment was set.*

The translation follows *Rashi*. R' Shmuel Masnuth and *Metzudos* render it *the heavenly tribunal sat in judgment.*

וְסִפְרִין פְּתִיחוּ — *And the books were opened.*

The books where the sins [and merits] of men are written (*Rashi*).[1]

11. מִן־קָל מִלַּיָּא רַבְרְבָתָא — *Because of the sound of the haughty words.*

The wrath of the Ancient of Days was aroused by the blasphemous words of *the small horn* (*Rashi*).

The final judgment upon the fourth kingdom will not take place solely on account of its evil deeds.

1. *Abarbanel* (*Mayenei HaYeshuah* 8:7) finds this the appropriate place to expound on an important cornerstone of Jewish belief.

Many passages in Scripture allude to a great day of judgment in the end of days. This theme recurs below (12:2) and in many passages elsewhere e.g. *before the great and terrible day of HASHEM* ... (*Malachi* 3:23).

Rashi (*Rosh HaShanah* 16b s.v. ליום הדין), and, with greater elaboration, *Ramban* in his *Sha'ar ha Gemul*, derive from this that every person comes before the heavenly tribunal at three stages of his existence: 1. every Rosh HaShanah, when man's material fortunes are decided according to his deeds during the preceding year; 2. at death the soul of every man is judged and accordingly his eternal portions in *Gan Eden* and *Gehinom* are fixed; 3. the *Yom haDin haGadol*, the day of the great judgment, when all men are judged to decide whether they are worthy of resurrection.

Abarbanel argues that the third judgment is superfluous. The judgment at death would

cient of Days sat — His garment white as snow, and the hair of His head like clean wool; His throne fiery flames, its wheels blazing fire; [10] *a stream of fire flowing forth from before Him, a thousand thousands serving him and myriad myriads standing before Him — the judgment was set, and the books were opened.*

[11] *I was watching. Then because of the sound of the haughty words which the horn spoke, I watched till the beast was slain and its body destroyed, and consigned to the fire's burning.* [12] *As for the rest of the beasts — their dominion was taken away, yet a prolongation of life was given them until a season and a time.*

Its ultimate downfall shall come as a consequence of the falsehoods perpetuated by the religions represented by *the small horn (Mayenei HaYeshuah* 8:8; *Malbim).*

וְהוֹבַד גִּשְׁמָהּ — *And its body destroyed —* in this world ...

וִיהִיבַת לִיקָדַת אֶשָּׁא — *And consigned to the fire's burning ...*

... In the world to come — Gehinom *(Mayenei HaYeshuah* 8:8).

אֶשָּׁא, *fire,* refers to the flame of Jacob: *And it shall come to pass that the house of Jacob shall be a fire ... (Obadiah* 1:18; *Rashi).*

12. וְאַרְכָה בְחַיִּין יְהִיבַת לְהוֹן — *Yet a prolongation of life was given them.*

The fourth kingdom only assumed dominion over the previous kingdoms; they were not destroyed. They continued to exist, albeit in a powerless state *(Rashi* and other comm.).

עַד־זְמַן וְעִדָּן — *Until a season and a time.*

Till the war of Gog and Magog which will take place at the appointed time [מוֹעֵד from עִדָּן] *(Rashi* and other comm.).

Abarbanel (Mayenei HaYeshuah 8:8) renders this *for the length of a*

---

seem to have taken everything in account. He points out that the great day of judgment mentioned so many times is really a day of reckoning. The *books* will be opened only to read the sentence before implementation. The nations that have oppressed Israel will receive their just reward. The verse in chapter 12:2 then speaks of another matter. The evildoers shall be resurrected not in order to be judged, but to witness in person the glory which will be awarded the righteous. See comm. to 12:2.

Harav Aharon Kotler suggested another approach to this problem. At the time of death every person is judged by the heavenly tribunal for his deeds during his life-span. However, the influence of a person's actions do not terminate with his demise. For example, Moses' influence is felt by us to this day; therefore, his final judgment must include his effect on subsequent generations as well as the deeds he performed while living. Thus, the final judgment takes into account the sum total of every person's accomplishment and influence up to the last day of history *(Rabbi Y. Leiman).*

הֲוֵית בְּחֶזְוֵי לֵילְיָא וַאֲרוּ עִם־עֲנָנֵי שְׁמַיָּא

כְּבַר אֱנָשׁ אָתֵה הֲוָא וְעַד־עַתִּיק יוֹמַיָּא

יד מְטָה וּקְדָמוֹהִי הַקְרְבוּהִי: וְלֵהּ יְהָב

שָׁלְטָן וִיקָר וּמַלְכוּ וְכֹל עַמְמַיָּא אֻמַּיָּא

וְלִשָּׁנַיָּא לֵהּ יִפְלְחוּן שָׁלְטָנֵהּ שָׁלְטָן

עָלַם דִּי־לָא יֶעְדֵּה וּמַלְכוּתֵהּ דִּי־לָא

טו תִתְחַבַּל: אֶתְכְּרִיַּת רוּחִי אֲנָה

דָנִיֵּאל בְּגוֹא נִדְנֶה וְחֶזְוֵי רֵאשִׁי יְבַהֲלֻנַּנִי:

טז קִרְבֵת עַל־חַד מִן־קָאֲמַיָּא וְיַצִּיבָא

---

lifetime [i.e., a lifespan] *had been given them till a specified time.* The rest of the beast had their dominion ... taken away because a length ... had been given them till a specified time. Once their alloted time had been used up *their dominion* had to cease.

13. One Like a Man

עִם־עֲנָנֵי שְׁמַיָּא — *With the clouds of heaven (i.e., suddenly and swiftly).*

Unlike the earlier beasts which came from the depths of the stormy sea, here we have *one in human likeness coming with the clouds of heaven.* He will have conquered earthliness and will float on clouds formed of his *Torah* and *Mitzvos* which, like the clouds, soar high above this world (*Malbim*).

R' Yehoshua ben Levi asked, Here is written, *with the clouds of heaven* (implying the swift arrival of the Messianic King).[*Elsewhere*] is written *a poor man and riding upon an ass* (*Zechariah* 9:9), (implying sluggishness on the part of Messiah).

[And he replied,] 'If they merit it [he will come] *with the clouds.* But if they do not merit it [he will surely come but sluggishly] *like a poor*

man upon an ass' (*Sanhedrin* 98a; parentheses *Rashi* ibid.).

A similar contradiction is resolved (ibid.) in the same manner: R' Yehoshua ben Levi asked, 'It is written (*Isaiah* 60:22) בְּעִתָּהּ, *in its time* and [in the same verse] is written אֲחִישֶׁנָּה, *I shall hasten it.* [He answered] 'If they merit it, *I will hasten it* (אֲחִישֶׁנָּה). [i.e. HASHEM will bring the promised redeemer before the appointed time]. But if they do not merit it, he will nevertheless come in the appointed time בְּעִתָּהּ.

כְּבַר אֱנָשׁ אָתֵה הֲוָא — *One like a man came.*

This is the *King Messiah* (*Rashi*).

Unlike the previous kingdoms which had been represented by beasts, this kingdom would come about not through brute force, but through the power of intellect and good deeds, with which the Creator endowed that which He created in His form and likeness — man (*Malbim*).

Israel is likened to a man because 'they are humble and wholehearted עֲנוְתָנִים וּתְמִימִים' (*Rashi*).

וּקְדָמוֹהִי הַקְרְבוּהִי — *And they brought him before Him.*

Ibn Yachia understands this to refer to Eliyahu, the angel of the redemption. Eliyahu leads the Messianic King before the Divine throne.

*13 I was watching in night visions and behold!
With the clouds of heaven, one like a man came; he
came up to the Ancient of Days, and they brought
him before Him. 14 He gave him dominion, honor, and
kingship; peoples, nations, and languages will serve
him; his dominion is everlasting dominion such as
will not pass, and his kingship such as will not be
destroyed.*

*15 As for me, Daniel, my spirit was uneasy in its
sheath, and the visions of my mind bewildered
me. 16 I approached one of the standing ones, and I*

There is a lesson to be learned from this. First man has to elevate himself to the heavens and reach toward the Ancient of Days. Then God holds out a helping hand and draws him to Himself (*Malbim*).

14. שָׁלְטָן וִיקָר וּמַלְכוּ — *Dominion, glory and kingship.*

Three things lost to the Jewish People during the exile will be returned to them: 1) courage — as foretold in the Torah: *HASHEM will give you there a trembling heart (Deut.* 28:65). In compensation they will be given שָׁלְטָן, *stronghearted dominion;* 2) *glory* — during the *Exile* they had always been despised and downtrodden — in compensation they will be given וִיקָר, *honor;* 3) kingship — till now they have been ruled by others — now, in compensation, they will be given מַלְכוּ, *kingship,* and will become rulers (*Mayenei HaYeshuah* 8:9).

15. אֶתְכְּרִיַּת רוּחִי — *My spirit was uneasy.*

[We have adopted *Radak's* and *R' Shmuel Masnuth's* translation because their rendition of this idiomatic expression lends itself to translation more easily. They derive this from the *Targum* to וּקְצַר רוּחַ (*Proverbs* 14:29). *Rashi* there explains that קוֹצֶר רוּחַ [lit. *shortness of spirit*] describes a person who is troubled and therefore his spirit and breath are short (i.e. he is impatient). *Rashi* here derives אֶתְכְּרִיַּת from כִּי יִכְרֶה אִישׁ, *when a man digs* (*Exodus* 21:33), i.e. his spirit sank (he was frightened).

בְּגוֹא נִדְנֶה — *In its sheath.*

In the body which is the sheath for the spirit (*Rashi*).

[By using this particular simile to express his tellings, Daniel reveals much about his personal view of the body's purpose.]

16. An Angel Interprets

קָאֲמַיָּא — *The standing [ones].*

The angels are called *standers* as is written, *And I will give you [access] to walk between these standers (Zechariah* 3:7), for the angels have no joints which is why they can only stand (see *Ezekiel* 1:7 וְרַגְלֵיהֶם רֶגֶל יְשָׁרָה, *their legs a straight leg;*

אֶבְעֵא-מִנֵּהּ עַל-כָּל-דְּנָה וַאֲמַר-לִי וּפְשַׁר

מִלַּיָּא יְהוֹדְעִנַּנִי: אִלֵּין חֵיוָתָא רַבְרְבָתָא יז

דִּי אִנִּין אַרְבַּע אַרְבְּעָה מַלְכִין יְקוּמוּן מִן-

אַרְעָא: וִיקַבְּלוּן מַלְכוּתָא קַדִּישֵׁי עֶלְיוֹנִין יח

וְיַחְסְנוּן מַלְכוּתָא עַד-עָלְמָא וְעַד עָלַם

עָלְמַיָּא: אֱדַיִן צְבִית לְיַצָּבָא עַל-חֵיוָתָא יט

רְבִיעָיְתָא דִּי-הֲוָת שָׁנְיָה מִן-°כָּלְּהוֹן

דְּחִילָה יַתִּירָה °שִׁנַּיהּ דִּי-פַרְזֶל °וְטִפְרַיהּ

דִּי-נְחָשׁ אָכְלָה מַדְּקָה וּשְׁאָרָא °בְּרַגְלַיהּ

רָפְסָה: וְעַל-קַרְנַיָּא עֲשַׂר דִּי בְרֵאשַׁהּ כ

וְאָחֳרִי דִּי סִלְקַת °וּנְפַלוּ °מִן-°קָדָמַיהּ

°כָּלְּהֵן ק'

°שִׁנַּהּ ° וְטִפְרַהּ ק'

°בְּרַגְלַהּ ק'

°וּנְפַלָה °קָדָמַהּ ק'

Rashi from *Yerushalmi Berachos* 1:1 and *Bereishis Rabbah* 65:21).

[A very prevalent interpretation is that the angels do not have freedom of determination in their acts, rather they are directed by God. In contrast to humans, they remain standing in one place, whereas humans can elevate themselves through their good deeds.]

וַאֲמַר לִי וּפְשַׁר מִלַּיָּא יְהוֹדְעִנַּנִי — *So he spoke to me making the interpretation of the matters known to me.*

I.e., he spoke to me in such a manner that I should understand the *interpretation of the matters* (*Malbim*).

17. מַלְכִין — *Kingdoms* [lit. *kings*].

The word is used here in its broader sense (*Rashi*).

יְקוּמוּן מִן-אַרְעָא — *Will rise up from the earth.*

Malbim points out that the verb יְקוּם followed by a *mem* or מִן usually carries the connotation of getting up, i.e., leaving. The angel ex-

plained to Daniel that the purpose of the vision was not to show him the greatness of these four kingdoms, but their demise. Therefore he was shown even the first animal, representing Babylon, whose time of grandeur had already passed.

18. קַדִּישֵׁי עֶלְיוֹנִין — *The holy high ones.*

I.e. Israel (*Rashi* and all commentators).

Israel is called holy in *Exodus* (19:6), *You will be for Me ... a holy people*, and in *Deuteronomy* (26:19) *and that you be a holy people* (*R' Shmuel Masnuth; Metzudos*).

[The plural form עֶלְיוֹנִין eliminates the translation *the holy ones of the Most High*; to mean this it would have said קַדִּישֵׁי עֶלְיוֹן.]

This verse explains verses 13-14 (*Ibn Ezra*).

וְיַחְסְנוּן מַלְכוּתָא — *And they will inherit the kingship.*

The term וְיַחְסְנוּן, *and they will*

7

17-20 asked him for the truth concerning all this. So he spoke to me making the interpretation of the matters known to me. ¹⁷ 'These immense beasts, which are four — four kingdoms will rise up from the earth. ¹⁸ And the holy high ones will receive the kingship and they will inherit the kingship forever, and forever and ever.

¹⁹ Then I desired the truth about the fourth beast which was different from them all: excessively terrifying, with teeth of iron and claws of copper, it devoured, crumbled, and trampled the rest with its feet; ²⁰ and about the ten horns that were on its head, and the other one which came up and three fell before

---

inherit, is used in contrast to the word יְקוּמוּן, will rise up, which is used for the four beasts (v. 17) and which has the connotation of departure (Malbim).

וְעַד עָלַם עָלְמַיָּא — And forever and ever.

עָלַם itself could be interpreted as a finite period [as in וַעֲבָדוֹ לְעֹלָם (Exodus 21:7) which is interpreted to mean the Jubilee year. See Rashi ibid.]. The angel reiterated and stressed forever and ever so as not to leave room for misunderstanding (Metzudos).

Malbim renders עָלַם here, world. Thus, they will inherit not only עָלְמָא, this world, but also עָלַם עָלְמַיָּא, the everlasting world, which follows this world (Malbim).

19. More About the Fourth Beast

לְיַצָּבָא — The truth [lit. to stand; to create a foundation].

[I.e., to find out the truth about. In Hebrew, too, we find the expres-

sion לַעֲמוֹד עַל הָאֱמֶת, to stand on the truth [i.e., to find out the truth] (see Rashi). The Aramaic word for truth, יַצִּיב (see v. 16), is derived from this, i.e., something which can stand on its feet, which has foundation. One is reminded of the expression of the Sages שֶׁקֶר אֵין לוֹ רַגְלַיִם, falsehood has no feet.]

עַל חֵיוְתָא רְבִיעָיְתָא — About the fourth beast.

From here through v. 22 we have Daniel's description of the part of the vision for which he sought an explanation from the angel. The angel's reply is given in verses 23-27.

דְּחִילָה יַתִּירָה — Excessively terrifying.

I.e., Daniel desired to find out about the fourth beast, about its terribleness, etc.

וְטִפְרַהּ דִּי־נְחָשׁ — And (its) claws of copper.

This particular had not been mentioned before. It seems that

תְּלָת וְקַרְנָא דְכֵן וְעַיְנִין לַהּ וּפֻם מְמַלִּל

כא רַבְרְבָן וְחֶזְוַהּ רַב מִן־חַבְרָתַהּ: חָזֵה הֲוֵית
וְקַרְנָא דִכֵּן עָבְדָא קְרָב עִם־קַדִּישִׁין
כב וְיָכְלָה לְהֹן: עַד דִּי־אֲתָה עַתִּיק יוֹמַיָּא
וְדִינָא יְהִב לְקַדִּישֵׁי עֶלְיוֹנִין וְזִמְנָא מְטָה
כג וּמַלְכוּתָא הֶחֱסִנוּ קַדִּישִׁין: כֵּן אֲמַר
חֵיוְתָא רְבִיעָיְתָא מַלְכוּ °רביעיה תֶהֱוֵא

בְאַרְעָא דִּי תִשְׁנֵא מִן־כָּל־מַלְכְוָתָא
וְתֵאכֻל כָּל־אַרְעָא וּתְדוּשִׁנַּהּ וְתַדְּקִנַּהּ:
כד וְקַרְנַיָּא עֲשַׂר מִנַּהּ מַלְכוּתָא עַשְׂרָה
מַלְכִין יְקֻמוּן וְאָחֳרָן יְקוּם אַחֲרֵיהֹן וְהוּא
יִשְׁנֵא מִן־קַדְמָיֵא וּתְלָתָה מַלְכִין יְהַשְׁפִּל:

---

after the initial vision certain details changed. The beast grew more awesome and its nails were changed to copper (*R' Shmuel Masnuth*).

20. וְחֶזְוַהּ רַב מִן חַבְרָתַהּ — *And its appearance greater than that of its fellows.*

This too is a detail not mentioned before. Previously when this horn had started to come *up among them* (*v.* 8) it had been a small horn. *Metzudos* understands וְחֶזְוַה here to refer not to the size of the horn, but to its wondrous appearance. *The [wonder] in its appearance was greater than [that] of its fellows.*

21. עָבְדָא קְרָב — *Waged war.*

This, too, was not mentioned in the telling of the initial vision although Daniel had seen it earlier, which is why he prefaces this with חָזֵה הֲוֵית, *as I watched,* i.e., in my first vision (see above *v.* 19; *Rashi*).

War includes the religious debates that Jews were forced to take part in and the persecutions

they had to endure (*Malbim*).

22. וְדִינָא יְהִב — *And granted ... vengeance.*

He punished the *fourth beast* for the harm he had done to the *holy high ones* (*Rashi*).

[דִין is Aramaic for מִשְׁפָּט. See *Rashi* to *Ex.* 28:15 and *Deut.* 32:41 that מִשְׁפָּט is also used to denote the *implementation* of the punishment determined by the judgment.]

לְקַדִּישֵׁי עֶלְיוֹנִין — *To the holy high ones.*

[See above *v.*18.]

The Sages (*Sanhedrin* 98a based on *Isaiah* 60:22) tell us that the redemption (בב"א) can come in one of two ways:

1. זָכוּ אֲחִישֶׁנָּה, if the merits of Jewry are sufficient, then the Messianic king can come before the appointed time;

2. לֹא זָכוּ בְּעִתָּהּ, even if Israel does not repent, the Messiah will not be delayed after the appointed time. [See *Overview*.]

Here the vision foresees the first

7

21-25

it, and this horn had eyes and a mouth speaking haughty words, and its appearance greater than that of its fellows. ²¹ I watched, and this horn waged war with the holy ones and was prevailing over them ²² until the Ancient of Days came, and granted the holy high ones vengeance. And the time came and the holy ones inherited the kingship.

²³ Thus he spoke, 'The fourth beast — there will be a fourth kingdom on the earth which will be different from all kingdoms; it will devour the whole earth, trample and crumble it. ²⁴ And the ten horns — from that kingdom ten kings will arise, and another will rise up after them and he will be different from the former, and he will humble three kings. ²⁵ And he

---

possibility. The redemption is given in *judgment* (Malbim renders דִּינָא, *judgment*) i.e., Israel is found to be worthy, since they are considered קַדִּישֵׁי עֶלְיוֹנִין, *holy high ones* (Malbim).

וְזִמְנָא מְטָה — *And the time came.*

Should Jewry not be worthy of redemption, the Messiah will come at the last moment because *the time came.* This is solely because: *the holy ones* (without the adjective *high* as before) *have inherited the kingdom* [קָדוֹשִׁים is a generic term used to describe Israel in general, regardless of individual merit] (Malbim).

23. The Angel Explains the Fourth Beast

וְתֵאכֻל כָּל־אַרְעָא — *(And) it will devour the whole earth.*

This explains the significance of the great iron teeth (v. 7).

וּתְדוּשְׁנַּהּ וְתַדְּקִנַּהּ — *(And will) trample and crumble it.*

This is in explanation of *and the rest it trampled under its feet* (v. 7);

[*the rest* refers to the nations of the world] (Malbim).

וּתְדוּשְׁנַּהּ — *(And) trample it.*

[There are other instances where the root דוש which usually denotes *threshing,* is rendered *trampling.* וְנָדוֹשׁ מוֹאָב (Isaiah 25:10) surely means that *Moab will be trampled.* Accordingly וְדַשְׁתִּי אֶת בְּשַׂרְכֶם (Judges 8:7) should be translated, *and I will trample your flesh.*

Targum Yonasan (II Kings 7:20) renders וַיִּרְמְסוּ אֹתוֹ הָעָם, *the people trampled him,* וְדָשׁוּ יָתֵיהּ עַמָּא (see M'turgeman s.v. שׁ, *thresh,* and דושׁ, *trample*). The association of דִּישָׁה, *threshing,* with trampling is due to the fact that in ancient times threshing was done by having animals trample upon the grain.]

24. וְאָחֳרָן — *And another.*

This is the small horn (v. 8).

וְהוּא יִשְׁנֵא — *And he will be different.*

In that he will abolish the worship of idols which had till now been prevalent (Malbim).

וּמִלִּין לְצַד °עִלָּיָא יְמַלִּל וּלְקַדִּישֵׁי
עֶלְיוֹנִין יְבַלֵּא וְיִסְבַּר לְהַשְׁנָיָה זִמְנִין וְדָת
וְיִתְיַהֲבוּן בִּידֵהּ עַד־עִדָּן וְעִדָּנִין וּפְלַג

עִדָּן: וְדִינָא יִתָּב וְשָׁלְטָנֵהּ יְהַעְדּוֹן
לְהַשְׁמָדָה וּלְהוֹבָדָה עַד־סוֹפָא:

וּמַלְכוּתָא וְשָׁלְטָנָא וּרְבוּתָא דִּי מַלְכְוָת
תְּחוֹת כָּל־שְׁמַיָּא יְהִיבַת לְעַם קַדִּישֵׁי

◆§ The קֵץ / End — Daniel's prophetic allusion to the Final Redemption

The word *keitz*, literally *End*, is a short word that is replete with meaning. On the surface, it
would seem to refer only to the *end* of the Exile. Its meaning, however, is far deeper, for
tradition teaches that with the end of the current Exile, and the arrival of the Messiah, will
come the ultimate perfection of mankind, and the attainment of the lofty spiritual goals for
which God created the universe.

The date of the *End* as is hinted in *Daniel,* is veiled and obscured to the point where it appears
futile to even attempt to interpret the verses dealing with it. The *End* (as it appears in *v.* 26, and
again in 12:7) is doubly sealed in mystery. Not only do we not know from which point to start
our calculation, but we do not even know how much time an עִדָּן is.

Our Sages warn strongly against trying to foretell the *End:* תִּפַּח עַצְמָן שֶׁל מְחַשְּׁבֵי קִצִּים, *a curse
upon those who calculate the appointed Ends* (Sanhedrin 97b; see *Hilchos Melachim* 12:2). Indeed
Rambam is hard put to explain R' *Saadiah Gaon's* calculation of the *End*. The only justification
he finds is that in the Gaon's generation there was a need to strengthen the faith in the coming
of the Messiah and so he offered a possible *End* in the near future.

Rambam aptly points out (*ibid*) that the end of the Egyptian exile was spelled out in
Abraham's visions, *they will enslave and oppress them four hundred years* (see *Overview* to
ArtScroll *Esther*). Still members of the tribe of Ephraim miscalculated the *End*, left Egypt
thirty years too soon, and were killed by the people of Gath (*PdRE* ch.I; *I Chronicles* 7:21;
Psalms 78:9). They had used the date of the vision as a starting point rather than the birth of
Isaac, thirty years later.

Daniel himself was enjoined by the angel, Obscure, *Obscure the matters and seal the book*
(12:4). Daniel himself indeed transmits the *End* in shrouded and mysterious form. *Ibn Ezra* (8:25)
suggests that Daniel himself did not know the *keitz* (8:25). The *Midrash* (*Bereishis Rabban* 98:2)
states that two people knew the *End* — Jacob and Daniel — but it was later hidden even from
them. *Rambam* (*Sefer HaGeulah* ch.4) interprets a passage in *Sanhdrin* (97b, הַמִּקְרָה הַזֶּה נוֹקֵר וְיוֹרֵד)
to mean that even the *tannaim* and *amoraim* of the *Talmud* erred when they attempted to
unravel the secret of the *End*.

Nevertheless, interpretations to these verses and exact computations abound. *Ramban*
(*Sefer HaGeulah*) and *Mayenei HaYeshuah* (1:2) justify the search for the *End*. The prohibi
tion aginst the calculation, they maintain, is meant only for those who fix firm dates based on
their research and are in danger of losing their faith and even of leading others astray if they
are proved wrong. Indeed the *Talmud,* after expressing the stringent prohibition against
calculation of the *keitz* cited above adds, in explanation: For they say since the *End* came and
he [the Messiah] did not come he will not come anymore. Rather wait for him as it has been
said! If he shall be delayed, hope for him … (*ibid*).

Therefore if one advances an interpretation of these verse only as a possible meaning, not as
a conclusion, it is permitted. (This view is not shared by *Rambam* in *Iggeres Teman,* who
seemingly views this as an unconditional prohibition. See *comm.* to 12:10). This seems to have
been *Rashi's* view. After giving his explanation of a passage dealing with the *End* (8:14), *Rashi*
concludes, 'But we shall hope for the promise of our King [to be fulfilled] *End* after *End*.

will speak words against the Supreme One, and he will exhaust the holy high ones, and he will plan to change the seasons and the law; and they will be given into his hand until a time, and times, and half a time. ²⁶ *But judgment will be set, and they will take away his dominion to be annihilated and destroyed completely.*

²⁷ *'And the kingship, the dominion, and the grandeur of the kingdoms anywhere under the sun, will be*

If the *End* interpreted by a commentator passes, then we know that he erred, and whoever comes after him should search and interpret otherwise.'

Ramban (Sefer HaGeulah) suggests that the Sages, being close to the destruction of the Temple, knew that the redemption was still far off. Therefore they forbade all investigation of the End so as not to discourage the people with the length of the bitter exile. This, he maintains, is no longer applicable in his times, 1200 years into the exile.

At this later date (seven hundred years after *Ramban*), we must exclaim in the words of the *Talmud (Sanhedrin* 97a), בַּעֲוֹנוֹתֵינוּ הָרַבִּים, *'Because of our many sins,* there have passed of them (the years otherwise destined for the Messianic era) what has passed.'

In this commentary we will not present the many diverse calculations advanced by the various commentators, since virtually all of these dates have passed. In this we will be following the lead of *Rashi* who says (8:14) 'I have seen an interpretation in the name of *R' Saadiah* but it has already passed,' and *Rashi* omits the calculation. In order not to leave these verses without any interpretation, we will bring *Rashi's* interpretation and reconciliation of the verses [see *Overview VI*.].

25. עַד־עִדָּן וְעִדָּנִין וּפְלַג עִדָּן — *Until a time, and times, and half a time.*

'This *End* is a sealed *End* as it was said to Daniel, *'Obscure the matters and seal ...'*(12:4). The early Sages, interpreted this verse, each according to his understanding, but their קִצִּים, *Ends,* have already passed. There is yet another way to interpret this in the manner which I have seen written in the name of *R' Saadiah (Rashi;* see *Emunos Vedeos* 8).'

Rashi explains that וְעִדָּנִין וּפְלַג עִדָּן, *times and a half a time,* is an elaboration of עַד־עִדָּן, *till a time.* Thus *till a time* [which is] [two] *times (the plural form indicates at least two)* and *half* [that] *time.* The *vav* is superfluous; [see *Metzudos*].

The two times are the two clearly known periods of pre-Babylonian

Jewish history. The 480 years from the exodus till the building of the First Temple (see *I Kings* 6:1) is the first period. The 410 years that the First Temple stood (*Yoma* 9a) is the second period giving us a total of 890 years. *Half* [that] *time* is 445 years. Adding this to 890 we get a total of 1335 years. This corresponds exactly to the years until the *End* in 12:12 (*Rashi*).

26. וְשָׁלְטָנֵהּ יְהַעְדּוֹן — *And they will take away his dominion.*

This is the interpretation of *till the beast was slain (v.* 11; *Malbim).*

27. The Everlasting Kingdom

וּמַלְכוּתָא — *And the kingship.*

This is the explanation of *He gave him dominion (v.* 14).

עֶלְיוֹנִין מַלְכוּתֵהּ מַלְכוּת עָלַם וְכֹל `

כח שָׁלְטָנַיָּא לֵהּ יִפְלְחוּן וְיִשְׁתַּמְּעוּן: עַד־כָּה

סוֹפָא דִּי־מִלְּתָא אֲנָה דָנִיֵּאל שַׂגִּיא |

רַעְיוֹנַי יְבַהֲלֻנַּנִי וְזִיוַי יִשְׁתַּנּוֹן עֲלַי וּמִלְּתָא

בְּלִבִּי נִטְרֵת:

א בִּשְׁנַת שָׁלוֹשׁ לְמַלְכוּת בֵּלְאשַׁצַּר הַמֶּלֶךְ

חָזוֹן נִרְאָה אֵלַי אֲנִי דָנִיֵּאל אַחֲרֵי הַנִּרְאָה

ב אֵלַי בַּתְּחִלָּה: וָאֶרְאֶה בֶּחָזוֹן וַיְהִי בִּרְאֹתִי

וַאֲנִי בְּשׁוּשַׁן הַבִּירָה אֲשֶׁר בְּעֵילָם

---

28. וּמִלְּתָא בְּלִבִּי נִטְרֵת — *But I guarded the matter in my heart.*

At the beginning of this chapter (v. 1) we were told, *he wrote the* dream relating the major parts. Daniel kept the rest of the vision to himself (*Metzudos*).

[See *comm.* to v. 1.]

VIII
◆§Prefatory Note to Chapter 8

From here on the Book is written in Hebrew. This should not need any explanation, since Hebrew is the language of Divine prophecy. It is specifically fitted for this, as attested by its name, לְשׁוֹן הַקֹּדֶשׁ, *the Holy Tongue* (see *Ramban* to *Exodus* 30:13)

What requires explanation is why the first part of *Daniel* is primarily in Aramaic. This Book begins in Hebrew and continues thus until 2:4, where the beginning of the verse, *the Chaldeans spoke to the king in Aramaic* is in Hebrew, but the rest of the verse, the beginning of a long, direct quotation,is in Aramaic. From there on, most of chapters 2-7 are filled with quotations from Daniel, the kings, and others, and, as such, are also in Aramaic. Since so much of the text consists of direct Aramaic quotations, the connective and narrative verses are also in Aramaic. Consequently, chapter 6, describing events taking place during the rule of the Medes, is in Aramaic, which was still the official language of the kingdom, as seen in *Ezra* (4:19-22 and 7:12-16). But, as pointed out before (7:1), from chapter 7 to the end we have only Daniel's visions. Why is chapter 7 in Aramaic, while the following chapters are in Hebrew?

It must be borne in mind that not only is chapter 7 written in Aramaic, but the vision itself, Daniel's question in *v.* 16 and the angel's answer (*v.* 17-27) are in Aramaic; clearly Daniel questioned the angel, and was answered, in Aramaic. In chapter 8, however, the words of the angels (*vs.* 13-14; 16-17; 19-26) are in Hebrew.

Abarbanel (9:2) suggests that the revelation in chapter 8, which occured in the last year of Belshazzar's reign, was heard in Hebrew to symbolize the downfall of Babylon. Though the Persians, too, used Aramaic as an official language, it was not their native tongue. Therefore the use of Hebrew denotes the fall of the Babylonian language and nation. Conversely, in chapter 7, because Belshazzar still had his whole reign before him, the use of Aramaic was a clue to Daniel that though the fall of Babylon had already been shown to him prophetically, it would not take place immediately. See note to 2:4.

7

28

given to the holy high ones. Its kingdom will be an everlasting kingdom, and all rulers will serve and obey it.'

²⁸ Up to here is the end of the matter. I, Daniel, my thoughts frightened me greatly, and my countenance changed; but I guarded the matter in my heart.

8

1-2

In the third year of King Belshazzar's reign, a vision appeared to me — I , Daniel — after that which had appeared to me at first. ² And I observed the vision. As I watched, I was in Shushan, the capital,

1. Another Vision

אֵלַי אֲנִי דָנִיֵּאל — To me — I, Daniel.

The seemingly unnecessary stress here tells us that though Nebuchadnezzar (in his dream, ch. 2), and Zechariah (ch. 2 and 6) had foreseen the four kingdoms, none had seen them with such clarity and detail as Daniel (Malbim).

אַחֲרֵי הַנִּרְאָה אֵלַי בַּתְּחִלָּה — After that which had appeared to me at first.

I.e., after the vision described in chapter 7. (Rashi)

Even after the seemingly more inclusive vision in chapter 7, there were four areas which had not been made clear to Daniel until this new vision:

1. Daniel had previously known the identity of only the first animal, which he naturally understood to be the kingdom under which he lived, Babylon; he had inquired about the fourth kingdom, (v. 19-22) which was elaborated upon by the angel in vs. 23-27. The second and third kingdoms had not been elaborated upon.

2. The downfall of the first and fourth kingdoms had been spelled out in the previous vision, but not those of the two other kingdoms.

3. The fate of the Jews, under the first and fourth kingdoms had been clear to Daniel. To their fate under Babylon he was an eyewitness, and their fate under the fourth kingdom was foretold by the angel in v. 25.

4. Further elaboration was needed to clarify (to Daniel) the קֵץ, End, given in v. 25: till a time, times, and half a time.

2. וַאֲנִי בְּשׁוּשַׁן הַבִּירָה — I was in Shushan, the capital.

Ralbag explains that Daniel was not as close to Belshazzar as he had been to Nebuchadnezzar. Therefore he was not in Babylon but in Shushan, which is in Elam. This also explains why Belshazzar did not consult Daniel concerning the handwriting on the wall until after the Queen recommended that he do so (5:10-12),

וַאֲנִי, I was, is connecte to וַיְהִי בִּרְאוֹתִי, as I watched. Daniel was in Babylon, but in his vision it appeared as if he were in Shushan (Ibn Ezra).

The purpose of this part of the

הַמְּדִינָה וָאֶרְאֶה בֶחָזוֹן וַאֲנִי הָיִיתִי עַל־
אוּבַל אוּלָי: וָאֶשָּׂא עֵינַי וָאֶרְאֶה וְהִנֵּה | ג
אַיִל אֶחָד עֹמֵד לִפְנֵי הָאֻבָל וְלוֹ קְרָנַיִם
וְהַקְּרָנַיִם גְּבֹהוֹת וְהָאַחַת גְּבֹהָה מִן־
הַשֵּׁנִית וְהַגְּבֹהָה עֹלָה בָּאַחֲרֹנָה: רָאִיתִי ד

vision was to point out to Daniel the identity of the ram standing before Shushan. It would be understood to represent the Persian kingdom (*Mayenei HaYeshuah* 9:3). Daniel foresaw that Shushan would become בִּירָה, *the capital*, an event which occured only after the fall of Babylon. Seeing the ram *in the 'capital' Shushan* foretold the downfall of the Babylonian empire even though Darius had his seat of government in Babylon during his one-year reign (*Malbim*). [בִּירָה is popularly translated *a capital*. However *Ibn Ezra* (*Esther* 1:2) and *Radak* (*Shorashim s.v.* בִּיר) render it אַרְמוֹן, *palace*. The *Vilna Gaon* (*Esther* 1:2) describes it as the strongly fortified part of the city. This view is close to that of *Ibn Ezra* and *Radak*, since an ancient royal palace would no doubt be built in the form of a fortress. See ArtScroll comm. to *Esther* 1:2.] אֲשֶׁר בְּעֵילָם הַמְּדִינָה — *Which is in the province of Elam.*	The province of Khuzistan (*R' Saadiah* in *Tafsir*). [The province which still retains this name is in the southwest corner of Iran. Susa — Shushan — is in the northern part of this province. The province to the north, Ilam, was probably part of this province is ancient times.] עַל־אוּבַל אוּלָי — *At the Ulai River.* אוּבַל is like יוּבַל, which is rendered *stream*, as in יִבְלֵי מָיִם, *streams of water* (*Isaiah* 30:25). *Radak* (*Shorashim s.v.* אבל and יבל), *Rashi*, and *Metzudos* concur with this rendering. *R' Saadiah* rejects this translation with the argument that there is no river in Shushan. He renders it *the gate of Ulai* [as in אָבּוּלֵי דִנְהַרְדְעָא in *Eruvin* 6b]. This was probably a city gate which carried a name, as do many such gates[1]. Other translations are: *the banks of the river Ulai* (*R' Saadiah* in his *Tafsir, R' Shmuel Masnuth*); or *the plain of the Ulai* (*R' Shmuel Masnuth*) as in אָבֵל הַשִּׁטִּים

---

1. *R' Saadiah Gaon* (*Tafsir Daniel*) renders Shushan as *Guss*=Shush, which is Susa in the southeastern Iranian province Khuzistan. Two rivers flow near the town, the Karua, a few miles to the east, and the Karkheh, a few miles to the west. Hence *R' Saadiah's* objection that Shushan is not situated on a river bank. However, archeological excavation has shown that ancient Shushan was situated west of the town and on the bank of a river (the Shaur, a very small tributary of the Karkheh). Writers of antiquity mention Shushan on the river Elaeus.

The Jewish travelers, *R' Benjamin of Tudela* and *Rav Pesachiah of Regensburg* (12th century), both recount the local tradition (of both Jews and Gentiles) that Daniel's remains are contained in a glass coffin suspended in the river. *R' Pesachiah* identifies the site positively as Shushan. In *R' Benjamin's* itinerary this is less clear. The seeming identification of the river as the Tigris is untenable, though it is possible that *R' Benjamin* called the Karkheh 'Tigris'

which is in the province of Elam. And I saw in the vision that I was at the Ulai River. ³ *I raised my eyes and saw, and behold! a ram is standing before the river, and it has horns; and the horns are high, but one is higher than the other, and the higher one is coming up last.* ⁴ *I saw the ram goring westward, and*

(Numbers 33:49). Cf. *Rashi* to *Gen.* 14:10). *Josephus* (Ant. X:20,7) mentions the plain of Susa as the site of the vision.

Abarbanel (Mayenei HaYeshuah 9:3), holding to the view that Daniel only seemed to be in Shushan during the vision, interprets that the river, running so close to the king's palace, symbolized the washing away of the Persian kingdom.

Our Sages (*Mechilta* to *Exodus* 12:1) say that God revealed himself to the prophets in the exile only in a pure place, such as near water, which purifies. Hence, God revealed prophecy to Daniel by the river Ulai.

[In line with *Ibn Ezra* and *Abarbanel's* interpretation that Daniel only envisioned himself as being in Shushan, perhaps he was at some river other than the Ulai, but, as pointed out in the *Mechilta*, the vision was described as being on a river bank in order to allude to the principle that prophecy outside of *Eretz Yisrael* occurs only in a place of purity. It may also be that the extra word הָיִיתִי, *I was*, with regard to the river, would tend to indicate that he was literally at the Ulai River. Thus, Daniel explains that he envisioned himself being in Shushan, when actually he was at the Ulai River

which is in Babylon according to this.]

3. אַיִל אֶחָד — *A ram.*

The ram is later (v. 20) identified as Persia. In the previous vision Persia had been represented by the bear, a wild beast.

As the purpose of that vision had been to give a general picture of the kingdoms and their might, the bear was an appropriate symbol. Here however, the primary object was to prophesy the conduct of these kingdoms vis-a-vis the Jews. Here their conduct was generally gentle and benevolent, as seen in *Ezra-Nechemiah* (See *Yossipon* end of ch. 4; *Mayenei HaYeshuah* 9:3; *Malbim*).

וְלוֹ קְרָנָיִם — *And it has horns.*

The horns represent the partnership of the Persians and the Medes (*Rashi; Ibn Ezra*). [Throughout Scripture, פָּרָס, *Persia*, is mentioned together with מָדַי, *Media*.]

וְהַגְּבֹהָה עֹלָה בָאַחֲרֹנָה — *And the higher one is coming up last.*

The Persians were the dominant partner in the Perso-Median empire. However, Darius the Mede was the first ruler of the empire (6:1), followed by Cyrus the Persian (*Rashi, Ibn Ezra*).

because it was a tributary of the Tigris. The same is attested to by Arabic writers in the 9th century.

R' Saadiah Gaon in his *Tafsir* translates אוּבַל אוּלָי, *the banks of the Ulai.* Since the *Gaon* lived in Babylon, it is probable that he was acquainted with the geographical situation of Shushan.

אֶת־הָאַיִל מְנַגֵּחַ יָמָּה וְצָפוֹנָה וָנֶגְבָּה וְכָל־
חַיּוֹת לֹא־יַעַמְדוּ לְפָנָיו וְאֵין מַצִּיל מִיָּדוֹ
ה וְעָשָׂה כִרְצֹנוֹ וְהִגְדִּיל: וַאֲנִי | הָיִיתִי מֵבִין
וְהִנֵּה צְפִיר־הָעִזִּים בָּא מִן־הַמַּעֲרָב עַל־
פְּנֵי כָל־הָאָרֶץ וְאֵין נוֹגֵעַ בָּאָרֶץ וְהַצָּפִיר
ו קֶרֶן חָזוּת בֵּין עֵינָיו: וַיָּבֹא עַד־הָאַיִל בַּעַל
הַקְּרָנַיִם אֲשֶׁר רָאִיתִי עֹמֵד לִפְנֵי הָאֻבָל
ז וַיָּרָץ אֵלָיו בַּחֲמַת כֹּחוֹ: וּרְאִיתִיו מַגִּיעַ |
אֵצֶל הָאַיִל וַיִּתְמַרְמַר אֵלָיו וַיַּךְ אֶת־

4. מְנַגֵּחַ יָמָּה וְצָפוֹנָה וָנֶגְבָּה — *Goring westward, and northward and southward.*

The Persians expanded to the west, conquering the Middle East to the Mediterranean; to the north, conquering Asia Minor, and crossing the Dardanelles into Europe; and to the south, conquering Egypt (*Malbim*).

וְכָל־חַיּוֹת לֹא־יַעַמְדוּ לְפָנָיו — *And no beasts could stand before it.*

All the nations had to submit to Persian rule (*Malbim*).

5. It Smote the Ram

צְפִיר־הָעִזִּים — *The he-goat.*

[The Aramaic form of שָׂעִיר is צָפִיר, as in *Onkelos* to *Lev.* 16:10. שָׂעִיר is from שֵׂעָר, *hair* (see *Radak* in *Shorashim* s.v. שער). The goat is probably given this appellation on account of its hair. Perhaps a specific kind of goat known for its abundant hair is meant, if so, it might be better rendered as *a hairy he-goat*.]

The he-goat is later (*v.* 21) identified with Greece. The goat, a domestic animal, is substituted for the wild and ferocious leopard which symbolizes Greece in chapter 7. The Greeks, too, were tolerant rulers at the beginning. Only under Antiochus Epiphanes did the Jews suffer religious persecution, and then only in the last four years of his reign. Although Antiochus IV's successors, too, warred with Judea, they did not seek the cultural assimilation of the Jews. When Demetrius I and Antiochus VII retook Jerusalem, they left the Temple worship intact. Their objective was mainly political *(from Malbim)*.

[Later the he-goat will represent Greece and its successors. In the first phase of the vision [*vs.* 5-8], however, it refers to Alexander.]

בָּא מִן־הַמַּעֲרָב — *Comes from the west.*

This represents Alexander the Great (*Pirkei D'Rabbi Eliezer*, ch. 11 and *comm.*).

וְאֵין נוֹגֵעַ בָּאָרֶץ — *Not touching the ground.*

It seemed to be skipping above the earth (*Rashi*).

Alexander's conquests proceeded with astounding speed. It seemed as though nothing could delay or obstruct his march eastward. He

*northward and southward, and no beasts could stand
before it, nor could anyone rescue from it. It did as it
pleased and grew.*

*⁵ I was observing, and behold! the he-goat comes
from the west, across the surface of the whole earth,
not touching the ground. And the he-goat had a conspicuous horn between its eyes. ⁶ It came up to the
horned ram I had seen standing before the river, and
ran at it with the fury of its might. ⁷ I saw it reach the
ram. It fought bitterly with it, and smote the ram and*

ascended to the Macedonian throne at the young age of about 20, and when he died suddenly in Persia twelve years later he had conquered the whole of Asia Minor, the Middle East, Egypt, Persia, and had penetrated India (*Mayenei HaYeshuah* 9:4; *Malbim*).

קֶרֶן חָזוּת בֵּין עֵינָיו — *[Had] a conspicuous horn between its eyes.*

A *horn* is a symbol of strength (e.g., *I Samuel 2:10*, וְיָרֵם קֶרֶן מְשִׁיחוֹ, *and he will uplift the horn of His anointed*). Eyes are symbols of sober understanding (as in מִצְוַת ה' בָּרָה מְאִירַת עֵינַיִם *the commandment of HASHEM is pure, illuminating the eyes* [*Psalms* 19:9]). Alexander's astounding victories were not due solely to his great courage and energy, but also to his brilliant strategy and leadership (*Malbim*).

Ibn Ezra and *Radak* (*Shorashim* s.v. חזה) render חָזוּת, *intricate*. The horn was not straight, but branched off in an involved and intricate way.

6. וַיָּבֹא עַד־הָאַיִל — *It came up to the horned ram.*

Alexander did not await provocation from Darius. He crossed the Dardanelles and penetrated Asia

Minor, Darius' territory (*Ralbag; Mayenei HaYeshuah* 9:4)

וַיָּרָץ אֵלָיו בַּחֲמַת כֹּחוֹ — *And ran at it with the fury of its might.*

[In his initial engagement with Darius, at the battle of Issus in Asia Minor, Alexander won a decisive victory. Darius barely escaped with his life and reorganized his defense much further east.]

7. מַגִּיעַ אֵצֶל הָאַיִל — *Reach the ram.*

[Darius's next line of defense was at Arbela (Erbil), east of the Tigris in Iraq, near Persia proper (*Malbim*)].

וַיִּתְמַרְמַר אֵלָיו — *It fought bitterly* [lit. *became embittered*] *with it.*

[The he-goat will fight bitterly. *Radak* (*Shorashim* s.v. מרר and *R' Shmuel Masnuth* raise the possibility of translating וַיִּתְמַרְמַר as *and he attained superiority over him* (cf. the *Talmudical* title of respect: מַר, *sir*).]

Darius attempted to appease Alexander with concessions [offering to cede all his dominions east of the Euphrates], but was refused (*Mayenei HaYeshuah* 9:4; *Malbim*).

וַיַּךְ אֶת־הָאַיִל — *And smote the ram.*

הָאַיִל וַיְשַׁבֵּר אֶת־שְׁתֵּי קַרְנָיו וְלֹא־הָיָה
כֹחַ בָּאַיִל לַעֲמֹד לְפָנָיו וַיַּשְׁלִיכֵהוּ אַרְצָה
וַיִּרְמְסֵהוּ וְלֹא־הָיָה מַצִּיל לָאַיִל מִיָּדוֹ:
וּצְפִיר הָעִזִּים הִגְדִּיל עַד־מְאֹד וּכְעָצְמוֹ
נִשְׁבְּרָה הַקֶּרֶן הַגְּדֹלָה וַתַּעֲלֶנָה חָזוּת
אַרְבַּע תַּחְתֶּיהָ לְאַרְבַּע רוּחוֹת הַשָּׁמָיִם:
וּמִן־הָאַחַת מֵהֶם יָצָא קֶרֶן־אַחַת

ח

ט

Alexander defeated the armies of Persia and Media (*Mayenei HaYeshuah* 9:4; *Malbim*).

וַיַּשְׁלִיכֵהוּ אַרְצָה — *It threw it to the ground.*

[The might of Persia was humbled.]

וְלֹא־הָיָה מַצִּיל לָאַיִל — *And there was no one to rescue the ram.*

Darius fled into Persia. There he was captured by some of his own satraps, who betrayed him and put him to death (*Ralbag; Mayenei HaYeshuah* 9;4).

8. הִגְדִּיל עַד־מְאֹד — *Grew exceedingly.*

Alexander's Macedonian empire was greatly enlarged (see *v.* 5).

וּכְעָצְמוֹ — *At its mightiest.*

[Alexander had suffered no significant reverses up to his death. His whole career had been an unbroken chain of successes.]

נִשְׁבְּרָה — *Was broken.*

Alexander died suddenly in Persia. His death is shrouded in mystery. There is suspicion that he was poisoned, or he may have died of a fever. At any rate he was not defeated (*Ralbag; Mayenei HaYeshuah* 9:4).

חָזוּת אַרְבַּע — *A semblance of four [i.e., horns].*

The translation follows *Rashi* and *Metzudos*, who render חָזוּת in *v.* 5 *conspicuous* and חָזוּת here merely *what appeared like.* Both renditions are derived from חָזָה *seeing.* Possibly the use of חָזוּת as an adjective for קֶרֶן in *v.* 5 — i.e., a 'visible' horn — suggests a big, conspicuous horn. Here קֶרֶן is not mentioned at all. Therefore, חָזוּת is a noun — *a semblance of Metzudos* renders it here, too, as *conspicuous.*

לְאַרְבַּע רוּחוֹת הַשָּׁמָיִם — *Toward the four directions of the sky.*

The division of Alexander's empire into four (major) parts corresponded roughly to the four points of the compass. See above 7:6 and 11:4 (*Ibn Ezra; Mayenei HaYeshuah* 9:4).

◈§ Prefatory note to verses 9-11

In the interpretation of the following three verses, 9-11, we have two divergent approaches. The first, proposed by *Ibn Ezra* and adopted by *R' Yeshayah, Ralbag, Ibn Yachya, Abarbanel,* and *Malbim* see these verses as referring to the persecutions of Antiochus IV (Epiphanes), under whose rule the miracle of Chanukah occurred. This interpretation will be given first in the commentary since it is the view adopted by most commentators. The second

broke its two horns. The ram lacked the strength to stand before it. It threw it to the ground and trampled it, and there was no one to rescue the ram from it.

⁸ *And the he-goat grew exceedingly. At its mightiest the great horn was broken, and a semblance of four came up in its place toward the four directions of the sky.*

⁹ *Out of the one of them came forth one little horn,*

approach is that of *Rashi, Ramban (Sefer HaGeulah,* 3, ed. *Chavel,* p. 286; his *commentary to Numbers* 24:24), and *R' Shmuel Masnuth.*

9. One Little Horn

וּמִן־הָאַחַת מֵהֶם — *Out of the one of them.*

I.e., the Seleucid kingdom (see below). Alternatively, according to *Rashi,* the *horn* emerged from the Roman Empire.

[*Ibn Ezra,* cited below, understands the *one little horn* to refer to the Seleucid kingdom in general (not only to Antiochus IV specifically). Thus when the *little horn* [i.e., the Seleucid kingdom] is depicted as emerging *out of the one of them* [i.e., from one of Alexander's successors], we are forced to conclude that the Seleucid kingdom became the successor of some other entity. Perhaps the division of Alexander's empire into four parts does not refer to four clearly defined geographic subdivisions. In the turmoil following Alexander's death, boundaries were often drastically shifted as his four successors fought over the spoils. Therefore it can be said that *out of the one of* the four kingdoms the Seleucid kingdom emerged.]

קֶרֶן־אַחַת־מִצְּעִירָה — *One little horn.*

[The *horn* is a symbol of strength (see *v.* 5). A power emerged from one of the four kingdoms represented by the four horns (see *v.* 22).]

The *horn,* representing the Seleucid kingdom, is envisioned as a *little horn.* [Initially] the Seleucid was the smallest of the four kingdoms *(Ibn Ezra* in his *Perush Hakatzar).*

Malbim and *Mayenei HaYeshuah* 9:5 interpret that Antiochus IV is symbolically represented by the *small horn* because he came from the younger branch of the dynasty (see *comm.* below that *young* is an alternative rendering of מִצְּעִירָה).

[Antiochus III (the Great) was the younger son of Seleucus II. When Seleucus III, heir to the throne, was assassinated after ruling for four years, his younger brother Antiochus III, who succeeded him in 3537 (223 B.C.E.), was a mere youth of eighteen. Antiochus III was succeeded by his son Seleucus IV (Philopator) in 3573 (187 B.C.E). When he was assassinated in 3584 (176 B.C.E.), his younger brother Antiochus IV (Epiphanes) seized the throne even though the legitimate heir was Seleucus's son, Demetrius I. Thus Antiochus IV was doubly considered *younger*: a younger brother, son of a younger brother.]

According to *Rashi's* school of thought, the *little horn* refers to Titus' (and Vespasian's) rule over the Roman empire. The epithet

מִצְּעִירָה וַתִּגְדַּל־יֶתֶר אֶל־הַנֶּגֶב וְאֶל־
הַמִּזְרָח וְאֶל־הַצֶּבִי: וַתִּגְדַּל עַד־צְבָא
הַשָּׁמָיִם וַתַּפֵּל אַרְצָה מִן־הַצָּבָא וּמִן־
הַכּוֹכָבִים וַתִּרְמְסֵם: וְעַד שַׂר־הַצָּבָא

small (evidently) does not refer to size, but to quality. The verse in Obadiah (1:2) concerning Edom: You are greatly despised is understood to mean Rome, which Talmudic tradition considers to be Edom (see comm. to 2:40 and Avodah Zarah 10a).

[How the Romans can be considered to have come out of the one of them is not explained. Perhaps the Romans can be considered successors to the Seleucid kingdom because when Pompey invaded the Middle East (64 B.C.E., 3696 A.M.), he abolished the Seleucid dynasty and established Syria as a Roman province. When Agrippa I died (44 C.E., 3804 A.M.), Eretz Yisrael was placed under the dominion of the Roman governor of Syria, the nucleus of the former Seleucid empire. Possibly those in Rashi's school of thought understand Rome to be an offshoot of one of the four parts of Alexander's divided empire. Perhaps the Romans are considered ethnically a Grecian people (see prefatory notes to 2:40), and as such are included in Greece. Thus one of them can refer to Rome itself, and the small horn emerging from the one of them, Rome, refers to the rule of Titus (and Vespasian).

The translation of מִצְּעִירָה as small follows Genesis 19:20: וְהִיא מִצְעָר, it is small. See Rashi loc. cit.; Radak, Shorashim s.v. צער; Ibn Ezra; Metzudos.

R' Shmuel Masnuth derives it from צָעִיר, young, as in וְהַצָּעִיר בִּצְעָרָתוֹ, the youngest in order (Genesis 43:33). A horn emerged from (the מ, mem, is used to mean from) the youngest kingdom. Abarbanel and Malbim follow this translation.

Thus, R' Shmuel Masnuth, who along with Rashi, understands these verses to refer to the Romans, apparently interprets that the

characterization of the horn as young refers to the relative youth of the Roman empire compared to the older Greek powers.

וַתִּגְדַּל־יֶתֶר אֶל־הַנֶּגֶב — Which grew excessively southward.

Antiochus IV attacked and conquered Egypt (168 B.C.E., 3592 A.M.) and would have added it permanently to his domain, had not the Romans intervened, as related at length in 11:22-31.

וְאֶל־הַמִּזְרָח — And eastward.

[Antiochus IV also recovered parts of Persia which had broken away from his dominion at the end of Antiochus III's reign.]

וְאֶל־הַצֶּבִי — And toward the coveted one.

I.e., toward the coveted land of Eretz Yisrael [see comm. to 11:6.]

Antiochus consolidated his grip on Eretz Yisrael, which had been wrenched from the Ptolemys of Egypt by his father, Antiochus III (see 11:17-21; Mayenei HaYeshuah 9,5, Malbim).

[Some historians maintain that when Antiochus III gave his daughter Cleopatra in marriage to Ptolemy V as part of a peace settlement with Egypt (see 11:17), he gave her his income from Eretz Yisrael as her dowry. This was undoubtedly not paid to her by Antiochus IV, and may thus be alluded to in this verse. The verse may also be alluding to Antiochus IV's excessive assertion of his power in Eretz Yisrael, especially by use of the superlative יֶתֶר, excessively. Antiochus IV attempted to become not only its political ruler, but its spiritual ruler, imposing idol worship

which grew excessively southward and eastward and toward the coveted one. ¹⁰ And it grew up to the host of heaven; and it threw to the earth some of the host and some of the stars, and trampled them. ¹¹ It exalted itself even up to the Prince of the legion, and

and his personal cult on the Jews of *Eretz Yisrael.*]

Rashi, as mentioned before, interprets these verses as referring to the Romans.

The Romans expanded *southward* — i.e., to Egypt; *eastward* (where they conquered all of southern Europe and Asia Minor), *and toward the coveted [one]* — Eretz Yisrael — which fell into their sphere of influence during the internecine war of Hyrkanos and Aristobulus *(Avodah Zarah* 10a; *Josephus Ant.* XIV, 3-4, *Yossipon* 38-9), and was under their direct rule after the death of Agrippa I (44 C.E. — 3804).

10. וַתִּגְדַּל עַד־צְבָא הַשָּׁמָיִם — *And it grew up to the host of heaven.*

Ibn Ezra comments that the following three verses are the words of the angel Gabriel, who explained the vision to Daniel (v. 16).

שָׁמַיִם, *heaven*, is a symbol for God. We find in *Avos* (2:2): וְכָל הָעוֹסְקִים עִם הַצִּבּוּר יִהְיוּ עוֹסְקִים עִמָּהֶם לְשֵׁם שָׁמַיִם, *all those who occupy themselves with the community should do so for the sake of heaven.* Thus, the Jewish People, who fulfill God's purpose in this world, are *the host of heaven.* The previous verse tells us about Antiochus' political dominance of *Eretz Yisrael.* Here it tells of his attempt to dominate Jewry in its role as *the host of heaven*, his attempt to suppress Jewish observance, and to substitue for it Greek culture and religion

(Mayenei HaYeshuah 9:5; *Malbim).*

וַתַּפֵּל אַרְצָה מִן־הַצָּבָא — *And it threw to the earth some of the host*

Some of the Jews were led astray under Antiochus' programs, and were hurled down from their honored position as members of the heaven host by joining the pagan multitudes whose lives are devoid of heavenly influence *(Malbim).*

וּמִן־הַכּוֹכָבִים — *And some of the stars.*

These are the pious ones (חֲסִידִים) who kept their faith in these difficult times. See later (12:3) where the faithful are again described as כּוֹכָבִים, *stars (Mayenei HaYeshuah* 9:5; *Malbim).*

וַתִּרְמְסֵם — *And trampled them.*

Many faithful Jews were martyred in this period *(Mayenei HaYeshuah* 9:5; *Malbim).*

Rashi interprets this verse too, as referring to the period of the destruction of the Second Temple.

11. וְעַד שַׂר־הַצָּבָא הִגְדִּיל — *It exalted itself even up to the Prince of the legions.*

God Himself is called *Prince of the legion.* The *legion* here is the legion of angels, as in the sacred Name ה׳ צְבָאוֹת, *HASHEM of legions.* Antiochus dared defy God himself. The nature of his defiance is spelled out in the continuation of this verse, *and through it ... (Ralbag; Mayenei HaYeshuah* 9:5).

הַגְדִּיל וּמִמֶּנּוּ °הֻרַם הַתָּמִיד וְהֻשְׁלַךְ °הורם ק'
יב מְכוֹן מִקְדָּשׁוֹ: וְצָבָא תִּנָּתֵן עַל־הַתָּמִיד
בְּפָשַׁע וְתַשְׁלֵךְ אֱמֶת אַרְצָה וְעָשְׂתָה
יג וְהִצְלִיחָה: וָאֶשְׁמְעָה אֶחָד־קָדוֹשׁ מְדַבֵּר

Michael, the *heavenly prince* of the Jewish nation (see *comm.* to 10:13), is called the *prince of the heavenly legion* — i.e., the prince of the angels — or *the great heavenly prince* (12:1). Antiochus will attempt to impose his will contrary to the interest of Michael *the prince of the legion*, who is at the same time the *prince* of the Jewish nation (*Ibn Ezra*).

וּמִמֶּנּוּ הוּרַם הַתָּמִיד — *And through it the daily sacrifice was removed.*

הוּרַם is used many times in the sense of removing and throwing down (see *Radak* in *Shorashim* s.v. רָמָה) as in וְהָרֵים הָעֲטָרָה, *and remove the crown* (*Ezekiel* 21:31). Antiochus stopped the daily sacrifice for three years (3593-6 A.M. 168-165 B.C.E.) until it was reinstituted by the Hasmoneans (See *Josephus*, *Ant.* XII, 7,6).

Malbim translates הוּרַם, *it was exalted* [from רָם, *high*]. The Prince of the legion is Mattisyahu the Hasmonean, and his sons who succeeded him in the leadership of the revolt, who again *elevated the daily sacrifice* to its proper position.

וְהֻשְׁלַךְ מְכוֹן מִקְדָּשׁוֹ — *And the foundation of His Sanctuary was thrown down.*

מָכוֹן means *foundation* (*Metzudos*). The foundation and purpose of the Temple is the presence of the *Shechinah*. Antiochus transformed the Holy Temple into a temple for idolatry. Thus the Temple was *thrown down* in a spiritual sense (*Mayenei HaYeshuah* 9:5).

As the *Talmud* (*Avodah Zarah* 52b) comments, the Syrian-Greeks defiled the Altar stones. *Milchamos Hashem* (loc. cit.) interprets this desecration to have resulted in בֵּית הַמִּקְדָּשׁ עַצְמוֹ יָצָא מִקְדֻשָּׁתוֹ, *the Temple itself lost its holiness.*

[*Josephus* (*Ant.* XII,7,6) relates that when Yehudah the Hasmonean and his men entered the Temple, they wept upon seeing its (physical) desolation. *The foundation ... was thrown down* could be construed to refer to the physical desolation of the Temple.

Malbim separates this last phrase from the rest of the verse. Till now, the angel was speaking about the Greeks. This part of the verse begins the next topic in the prophecy, — the destruction of the Second Temple.

Rashi interprets this verse, like the previous one, as referring to the destruction of the Second Temple. The *Prince of the legion* is God Himself, Who was defied when *His Sanctuary* was destroyed. During the siege of Jerusalem *the daily sacrifice was removed* (see *Yerushalmi Ta'anis* 4:5 and *comm.* to 9:27).

◆§ Prefatory Note to verse 12

In this verse some of the commentators who interpret the previous verses as referring to Antiochus break ranks with the rest. *Abarbanel* and *Malbim* here join the view of *Rashi* and

8

12-13

through it the daily sacrifice was removed and the foundation of His Sanctuary was thrown down.
¹² And a set time will be allotted for the daily sacrifice because of sin; and it will throw truth to the earth, and it will act and succeed.
¹³ I heard a holy one speaking. And the holy one

Ramban and interpret this verse about the destruction of the Second Temple. This view will therefore be given first. Afterwards, we will present the view of *Ibn Ezra, Ralbag,* and *Ibn Yachya.*

12. וְצָבָא — *And a set time.*

The daily sacrifice is destined to be taken away for a specific span of time (*Rashi; Metzudos*).

צָבָא — *set time.*

As in *Job 7:1* הֲלֹא צָבָא לֶאֱנוֹשׁ, *is there not time for man?* (*Rashi; Radak in Shorashim s.v.* צבא: *R' Shmuel Masnuth*).

Abarbanel renders the word more conventionally as an enemy *army* (*Mayenei HaYeshuah 9:5*).

תִּנָּתֵן עַל־הַתָּמִיד — *Will be allotted for the daily sacrifice.*

The translation follows *Rashi's* interpretation. According to *Abarbanel's* view, תִּנָּתֵן עַל should be translated *will be set upon* — i.e., the armies of the enemy will attack the institution of the daily sacrifice.

Malbim interprets צָבָא as in the previous verses, the *host of the heaven* — the Jewish nation — who *will be given over* (תִּנָּתֵן) to the enemy, עַל־הַתָּמִיד, together *with the daily sacrifice.*

בְּפָשַׁע — *Because of sin.*

The sins of the Jews caused the downfall of the Temple (*Rashi; Mayenei HaYeshuah 9:5*).

וְתַשְׁלֵךְ אֱמֶת אַרְצָה — *And it will throw truth to the earth.*

True faith and Torah will be denigrated (*Rashi; Mayenei HaYeshuah 9:5*).

וְצָבָא means the [heathen] kingdoms ... הַתָּמִיד [lit. *the constant one*] refers to the Jews [who have been commanded to study the Torah day and night (*Radak*)]. בְּפָשַׁע — because of the sin [of not studying the Torah.] אֱמֶת—וְתַשְׁלֵךְ אֱמֶת אַרְצָה can only mean Torah as it is written אֱמֶת קְנֵה, *acquire truth,* (*Proverbs* 23:23). This government legislates edicts [against Israel; וְהִצְלִיחָה] and is successful (*Pesichta to Eichah Rabbah* 2; cf. in *Yerushalmi, Rosh Hashanah* 3:8).

וְעָשְׂתָה — *And it will act.*

The he-goat accomplished whatever it wanted to do (*Metzudos*).

Ralbag and *Ibn Ezra* interpret this verse (like the ones preceding it) to refer to Antiochus.

R' Saadiah understands verses 9-12 to refer to the Arab empire — to its treatment of its Jewish population and to the wars it waged with Rome (Christian Europe).

13. וָאֶשְׁמְעָה אֶחָד־קָדוֹשׁ — *I heard a holy one* [lit. *one holy one*].

I heard one of the angels (*Rashi*).

Transpose and read קָדוֹשׁ אֶחָד. There are other examples of this (*Ibn Ezra*).

This refers to verses 11-13.

וַיֹּאמֶר אֶחָד קָדוֹשׁ לַפַּלְמוֹנִי הַמְדַבֵּר עַד־
מָתַי הֶחָזוֹן הַתָּמִיד וְהַפֶּשַׁע שֹׁמֵם תֵּת
יד וְקֹדֶשׁ וְצָבָא מִרְמָס: וַיֹּאמֶר אֵלַי עַד עֶרֶב

Verses 1-10 describe the vision Daniel saw, while verses 11-13 are the words of the angel to Daniel (*Malbim*, see *comm.* to *v.* 11).

וַיֹּאמֶר אֶחָד קָדוֹשׁ — *And the holy one* [lit. *one holy one*] *said.*

Gabriel was the angel who revealed himself to Daniel in the form of a man (*vs.* 15-16) and explained parts of the vision to Daniel. It was his voice that Daniel now heard addressing this question, obviously meant for Daniel's ears, to the anonymous angel.

פַּלְמוֹנִי is a combination form for פְּלוֹנִי אַלְמוֹנִי (*Ruth* 4:1) which is translated by *Targum Yonasan* כְּסִי וְטָמַר, *covered and hidden.* The angel who was asked the question remains anonymous (*Rashi*).

Abarbanel (*Mayenei HaYeshuah* 9:6) explains that the *holy one* who asked, revealed himself later to Daniel in the form of a man and is identified as Gabriel. The angel to whom the question was addressed is Michael, Gabriel's superior in the heavenly hierarchy. (See 10:13 where Michael is titled *one of the foremost heavenly princes*).

Daniel did not have the זְכוּת, *privilege,* of having Michael revealed to him. He was only able to hear his voice. Hence Michael remained *the anonymous one.*

Abarbanel cites *Midrash Tanchuma* (ed. *Buber, Genesis* p. 17) where R' Yochanan is quoted as identifying פַּלְמוֹנִי, *anonymous one,* as Michael.

הַמְדַבֵּר — *Who was speaking.*

The anonymous one was the angel who had been speaking till now (*Malbim*).

According to *Abarbanel* this would be Michael. According to *Ibn Ezra* (*v.* 10) this was Gabriel.

עַד מָתַי — *For how long* [lit. *till when*].

How long will the miserable situation described in *this vision concerning the daily sacrifice* last?

וְהַפֶּשַׁע שֹׁמֵם — *And the mute abomination.*

An idol, which is mute as a rock, will replace the daily sacrifice in the Temple (*Rashi*).

[In 12:11, there is an essentially identical phrase except that the word שִׁקּוּץ is substituted for פֶּשַׁע. Both have the same meaning, *abomination,* though שִׁקּוּץ connotes *an idol.* The reference is to the idolatrous temple erected by Hadrian on the site of the Holy Temple. Perhaps the change in language can be ascribed to the fact that Hadrian's temple did not last, but was later supplanted by the Moslem mosque which is presently on the Temple site. Although a mosque cannot be called שִׁקּוּץ, *an idol,* because Islam is a monotheistic religion (see *Teshuvas HaRambam,* ed. Freiman 319, ed. Shlesinger 19), nevertheless, the more inclusive פֶּשַׁע, which embraces all kinds of sin and abomination, would include this occupation of the Temple site also in the sense that it is sacrilegious for the sacred Temple Mount to be used for alien worship. Accordingly, פֶּשַׁע and שִׁקּוּץ would indicate two separate matters; the former, in our verse, indicates the whole period of the occupation of the Temple site up to our time, whereas שִׁקּוּץ specifically would refer to Hadrian's temple.]

said to the anonymous one who was speaking, 'For how long, this vision concerning the daily sacrifice and the mute abomination, permitting the trampling of the holy and the host?'

תֵת וְקֹדֶשׁ — *Permitting ... of the ho-ly.*

The translation treats the וֹ, *vav*, as superfluous; thus *permitting the holy ... to be trampled. The holy* refers to the Temple. Superfluous prefixes are often found in Scripture *(Rashi)*.

Sometimes the *vav* is used as a substitute for a שׁ, *shin*. Thus our phrase would be rendered like תֵת שֶׁקֹּדֶשׁ, *to permit that the holy ... be trampled* (*Mayenei HaYeshuah* 9:7 in the name of R' Yonah Ibn Janach).

According to most of the commentators, it is clear that the question is about the time before גְּאוּלָה הַשְּׁלֵימָה, *the ultimate complete redemption.*

Ibn Ezra, as a consequence of his interpretation of the previous verses, interprets the question of the angel to be about the length of the oppression under Antiochus.

However, he is alone in this view. *Ralbag* and *Ibn Yachya* agree with the other commentators that the angel wished to know the length of the long and bitter exile, not of the transitory oppression under Antiochus.

In the *Midrashim* we find two interesting renditions of this verse:

'Who is פַּלְמוֹנִי, *the anonymous one?* R' Yochanan said: This is Michael who stands innermost [i.e., closest to the Holy Presence; see *Bereishis Rabbah* 21:1 where פַּלְמוֹנִי is rendered as if it were פְּנִימִי, and *Rashi* there).] R' Chaninah said: הַמְדַבֵּר, *who was speaking,* ... is Gabriel — he had spoken

about the Jews.(cf. *Malbim's* interpretation *v.* 13 s.v. (המדבר) עַד מָתַי הֶחָזוֹן הַתָּמִיד, *till when will the voice of prophecy be stilled?* [Prophecy stopped in the beginning of the Second Temple period; see *Seder Olam* ch. 30; הַתָּמִיד is probably interpreted as a rhetorical question — *is it then forever?*] תֵת וְקֹדֶשׁ, *permitting the holy,* can only mean Jewry [as is written] *(Jer.* 2:3), יִשְׂרָאֵל לַה', קֹדֶשׁ, *Jewry is sacred to HASHEM.* וְצָבָא מִרְמָס, *till when will Jewry [the host]* *be tramped upon* by the nations of the world? [The angel answered (*v.* 14)], עַד עֶרֶב בֹּקֶר, the oppression will continue till *Jewry's night* [i.e., exile] *will be transformed into morning.* At that time וְנִצְדַּק קֹדֶשׁ, *the holy will be found righteous* (*Tanchuma*, ed. Buber).

Another Midrashic rendition of this verse is found in *Bereishis Rabbah* 21:2 (partially in *Tanchuma*, ibid.): וָאֶשְׁמְעָה אֶחָד, *I heard One*—this means the Holy One, Blessed be He, as is written שְׁמַע יִשְׂרָאֵל ה' אֱלֹהֵינוּ ה' אֶחָד *(Deut.* 6:4). קָדוֹשׁ [He is called קָדוֹשׁ, *holy*] because all say, 'קָדוֹשׁ קָדוֹשׁ קָדוֹשׁ — *holy, holy,] holy'* before him. מְדַבֵּר, *speaking* [harshly] HASHEM has decreed harsh decrees upon his creatures [such as] *thorns and thistles shall it bring forth for you (Genesis* 3:18) ... לְפַלְמוֹנִי, הַמְדַבֵּר, *to the anonymous one who was speaking* — R' Huna said [it means] לִפְלַנְיָא, *to the unspecified one. Aquila* (who translated the Scripture into Greek) translated פַּלְמוֹנִי *to the inner-most one,* לִפְנִימִי [because it should have been written לִפְלוֹנִי *(Rashi).*] This refers to Adam whose place had been [before his sin] closer to the divine Presence than the angels. [The verse is thus construed: וַיֹּאמֶר אֶחָד קָדוֹשׁ לְפַלְמוֹנִי הַמְדַבֵּר, *HASHEM said to Adam who had said ...* עַד מָתַי, *how much longer?* HASHEM's

בֹּקֶר אַלְפַּיִם וּשְׁלֹשׁ מֵאוֹת וְנִצְדַּק קֹדֶשׁ:
טו וַיְהִי בִרְאֹתִי אֲנִי דָנִיֵּאל אֶת־הֶחָזוֹן
וָאֲבַקְשָׁה בִינָה וְהִנֵּה עֹמֵד לְנֶגְדִּי
טז כְּמַרְאֵה־גָבֶר: וָאֶשְׁמַע קוֹל־אָדָם בֵּין

---

answer follows in v. 14 (Rashi).] עַד מָתַי הֶחָזוֹן הַתָּמִיד, Was the decree decreed on Adam meant to continue forever? הַתָּמִיד is meant as a question — is it permanent? (see Rashash). וְהַפֶּשַׁע שֹׁמֵם, Will the sin of Adam cause eternal desolation in their graves [for the generations? (see Rashi)] תֵּת וְקֹדֶשׁ וְצָבָא מִרְמָס, will he [Adam, whom the angels wanted to call קֹדֶשׁ (Bereishis Rabbah 8:10; Rashash)] and his progeny be subjected to trampled upon by the angel of death?

וְצָבָא — And the host.

The host of heaven, as in verse 10, the Jewish nation (Rashi; et al.).

14. עַד עֶרֶב בֹּקֶר — Till nightfall, morning.

Till that night about which it is written (Zechariah 14:7) and it shall come to pass that at nightfall there will be light (Rashi in the name of R' Saadiah Gaon), [i.e., till the final redemption.]

Rashi continues to say that עֶרֶב בֹּקֶר here is meant as a gematria [i.e., the main intent of these words is not for their literal meaning, but for their numerical value, which is 574. This total will be added to that given later in the verse.] Rashi explains that two things support this argument: 1. This calculation equals the number of years given at the end of this book (12:11): and from when the daily sacrifice was removed ... 'one thousand two hundred ninety years' [See Emunos

Vedeos 8:3 where, according to R' Saadiah's interpretation, the two figures do not coincide]; 2. If the calculation were not put cryptically why did the angel have to reiterate (v. 26) and the vision of the night-fall and the morning ... is true?

אַלְפַּיִם וּשְׁלֹשׁ מֵאוֹת — Two thousand and three hundred.

[See 7:25 s.v. The End.]

To these 2300 years, add 574 (the numerical value of עֶרֶב בֹּקֶר) for a total of 2874. These years begin from the first exile in Egypt. If we try to synchronize this with the End given in 12:11 which counts 1290 years from the time the daily sacrifice was removed (ibid.), we find them both ending at the same time. The breakdown is as follows:

Israel's sojourn in Egypt	210 years.
From the Exodus to the building of the first Temple (1 Kings 6:1)	480 years
The First Temple (Yoma 9a and many other places)	410 years
The Babylonian captivity (Jeremiah 19:10; see below 9:2)	70 years
The Second Temple until the removal of the daily sacrifice[1]	414 years
From the removal of the daily sacrifice to the End (12:11)	1290 years
Total	2874 years

14 *And he said to me, 'Till nightfall, morning two thousand and three hundred, and the holy will be rectified.'*

15 *When I, Daniel, had seen the vision and I sought understanding, then, behold! there stood before me the likeness of a man.* 16 *And I heard a human voice*

וְנִצְדַּק קֹדֶשׁ — *And the holy will be rectified.*

[This is the response to the question in *v. 13, For how long ... permitting the trampling ... of the holy?*]

Then Jewry's sin will have been atoned for [making them צַדִּיקִים, *righteous*], and the suffering decreed for them completed (Rashi).

[Rashi interprets וְקֹדֶשׁ in *v. 13 the Temple*. Perhaps he holds that קֹדֶשׁ implies both the Temple and Jewry.]

15. 'Gabriel, Explain the Vision'

אֶת־הֶחָזוֹן — *The vision.*

The *words* of the angels (v. 11-14) were clearly understood by Daniel. But the *vision* — i.e., what happened to the ram and the he-goat — was unintelligible to him. He did not know with certainty

what these animals and their story meant (Malbim).

וָאֲבַקְשָׁה בִינָה — *I sought understanding.*

He wished that an explanation be given him from heaven (Rashi).

כְּמַרְאֵה גָבֶר — *The likeness of a man.*

[The word גָּבֶר, *a man*, evidently alludes to גַּבְרִיאֵל, *Gabriel* (lit. *man of God*). Gabriel is mentioned by name in the next verse.]

16. קוֹל־אָדָם — *A human voice.*

This is the voice of the *anonymous one* in *vs*. 13-14, which he had heard up to now (*vs*. 11-12).

This was Michael (see *comm.* above). Daniel was not allowed to see the speaker; he was only allowed to hear the voice. The voice commanded Gabriel to reveal himself to Daniel, which he did, as related in verses 17-26 *(Malbim)*.

---

1. *Rashi's* calculation is as follows: The Second Temple stood 420 years (*Yoma* 9a and many other places). However, the removal of the daily sacrifice preceded the destruction of the Temple by six years. Although we are later (9:7) told, *and for half a week he will abolish the daily sacrifice*, we have no proof of how long this lasted. The *half a week* in the prophecy need not mean an exact half [three and a half years], rather a fraction of a week (see *comm.* to 9:25). It cannot have been a full seven years, but it may have lasted six years. Since the Second Temple stood 420 years, the abolition of the daily sacrifice would have taken place 414 years after its erection. (See *comm.* to 9:27 for a lengthy discussion of this topic.)

Ibn Ezra (v. 25) understands that 2300 *days* are meant. This adds up to approximately six years (365 × 6= 2190). The oppression of Jewry under Antiochus lasted approximately six years according to the Greek historians. [Antiochus's campaign against Egypt in 170 B.C.E., 3590 A.M. may be considered the beginning of the oppression. Antiochus died six years later. See *comm.* to 11:28.] *Ibn Ezra* understands *vs*. 11-14 to refer to Antiochus.

In another version of *Ibn Ezra* (*Pirush Hakatzar*), the 2300 are not days but half-days, two thousand three hundred evenings and mornings.

אוּלָי וַיִּקְרָא וַיֹּאמַר גַּבְרִיאֵל הָבֵן לְהַלָּז
אֶת־הַמַּרְאֶה: וַיָּבֹא אֵצֶל עָמְדִי וּבְבֹאוֹ יז
נִבְעַתִּי וָאֶפְּלָה עַל־פָּנָי וַיֹּאמֶר אֵלַי הָבֵן
בֶּן־אָדָם כִּי לְעֶת־קֵץ הֶחָזוֹן: וּבְדַבְּרוֹ עִמִּי יח
נִרְדַּמְתִּי עַל־פָּנַי אָרְצָה וַיִּגַּע־בִּי וַיַּעֲמִידֵנִי
עַל־עָמְדִי: וַיֹּאמֶר הִנְנִי מוֹדִיעֲךָ אֵת אֲשֶׁר יט
יִהְיֶה בְּאַחֲרִית הַזָּעַם כִּי לְמוֹעֵד קֵץ:

בֵּין אוּלָי — *In mid-Ulai.*
The voice seemed to be coming from the middle of the river (*Metzudos*).

וַיֹּאמַר גַּבְרִיאֵל — *And said, 'Gabriel!'*
The *voice* of Michael called to Gabriel and said to him, *'Gabriel, explain the vision to this one* (*Metzudos*).
R' Yudan said, 'Great is the power of the prophets in that they can compare the form to its Creator [מְדַמִּין צוּרָה לְיוֹצְרָה], they are able to reveal the Godly potential in man and therefore can visualize God, as it were, as the exalted source of spirituality which serves as man's inspiration] as has been said, *and I heard the voice of a man ...*' [Evidently this is interpreted to mean that Daniel heard God's voice. See v. 13, where the *Midrash* interprets וָאֶשְׁמְעָה אֶחָד־קָדוֹשׁ in a similar vein.]
R' Yehudah bar Simon said: There is a verse that is [even] more explicit (*Ezekiel* 1:26), *And on the throne a likeness like the appearance of a man* [lit. *son of man*] (*Bereishis Rabbah* 27:1).

17. וּבְבֹאוֹ נִבְעַתִּי — *And when he came I was terrified.*
[See 10:7-11 and 10:15-19.]

בֶּן אָדָם — *Ben Adam* [lit. *Son of Man*].
This appellation is found for the first time in *Ezekiel* and is the title by which Ezekiel is addressed throughout the book. This is the only other time in scripture where someone is so called. The term *Adam, man,* alludes to man's highest mission on earth. *Ben Adam,* therefore, implies that the bearer of the title is charged with the responsibility to fulfill an exalted mission (*Overview* to ArtScroll *Ezekiel*).

לְעֶת־קֵץ הֶחָזוֹן — *The vision concerns the time of the End.*
The events foretold in the vision will not [all] come true till the distant future. This makes them difficult to envision and grasp. Thus, you must try very hard to **understand** the vision, because *the vision concerns the time of the End* (*Malbim*).
Abarbanel (*Mayenei HaYeshuah* 9:8) understands that the exhortation of the angel to *understand* refers to the קֵץ, *End,* foretold in verse 14, which had been nebulous to Daniel. The angel said to Daniel, *Understand that you are Ben Adam* — consider your station, for you are a mere son of man, and the vision

8
17-19

in mid-Ulai; he called and said, 'Gabriel, explain the vision to this one.'

¹⁷ So he came to where I was standing, and when he came I was terrified and fell face down. He said to me, 'Understand Ben Adam, that the vision concerns the time of the End.'

¹⁸ As he spoke to me, I fell asleep with my face earthward; but he touched me and stood me up in my place. ¹⁹ He said, 'I am ready to inform you what will be after the wrath, for at the appointed time is the

---

you inquire about *concerns the time of the End.* Therefore, what you ask is very difficult to reveal clearly to you.

18. וּבְדַבְּרוֹ עִמִּי — *As he spoke to me.*

The very appearance of the angel was awesome. In 10:7-8, the very sight of the angel was sufficient to frighten Daniel to a point where *there was no strength left in me ...* Now when Daniel heard the voice of the angel his awe was doubled, for *the sound of his words like the sound of a multitude* (10:6). The description of this wondrous vision and the awesome effect it had upon Daniel proves that these angels were actually seen and heard by Daniel with his eyes and ears, unlike the view held by *Rambam et al.* that the angels cannot be perceived with human senses. According to *Rambam* all visions of angels are seen in prophetic dreams (*Mayenei HaYeshuah* 8:7. See *Moreh Nevuchim* 1:49, cf. *Yesodei HaTorah* 2:3-4 and *Ramban* to *Genesis* 18:1).

[The parallels between this vision and the vision described in chapter 10 (v. 7-10) are striking. Here Daniel, upon seeing the angel next to

himself was frightened and fell face down-as if all his strength had left him. The same is found later (10:8), *And [I] saw this great vision. No strength remained in me...* Here when the angel spoke to Daniel his fright was increased to the point where *I fell asleep with my face earthward.* In chapter 10 (v. 9) his hearing the voice of the angel is described in almost the same words. In both places the angel has to touch Daniel and stand him up. See *Rambam* quoted in 10:8.]

נִרְדַּמְתִּי — *I fell asleep.*

Because of the great fear that befell him, his strength left him and he was left in a slumberlike condition (From *Rashi* and *Metzudos*).

19. אֵת אֲשֶׁר־יִהְיֶה בְּאַחֲרִית הַזָּעַם — *What will be after the wrath.*

What will be after the exile which is a time of *wrath* (*Metzudos*).

The time of wrath is the persecution under Antiochus (*Ibn Ezra*).

[This is in keeping with *Ibn Ezra's* view that this chapter deals only with the persecution under Antiochus and the deliverance from him. See above *vs.* 9-12.]

כ הָאַיִל אֲשֶׁר־רָאִיתָ בַּעַל הַקְּרָנָיִם מַלְכֵי
כא מָדַי וּפָרָס: וְהַצָּפִיר הַשָּׂעִיר מֶלֶךְ יָוָן
וְהַקֶּרֶן הַגְּדוֹלָה אֲשֶׁר בֵּין־עֵינָיו הוּא
כב הַמֶּלֶךְ הָרִאשׁוֹן: וְהַנִּשְׁבֶּרֶת וַתַּעֲמֹדְנָה
אַרְבַּע תַּחְתֶּיהָ אַרְבַּע מַלְכֻיוֹת מִגּוֹי

Abarbanel (Mayenei HaYeshuah 9:8) points out that we do not find the angel elaborating on *what will be after the wrath.* He concludes that these words were meant only to strengthen Daniel in his fright. His fervent desire to find out the time of the redemption would buoy him up and enable him to listen to the angel's words. Similarly Jacob, who assembled his sons before his death and promised to tell them *that which will befall you in the End of days (Gen. 49:1;cf. Rashi* there), did not, in fact, reveal to them what would befall them. It was meant only to heighten his son's attentiveness to what he was saying.

[*Abarbanel's* solution is puzzling for the Sages say that Jacob wanted to reveal the קֵץ, *End* to his sons (*Pesachim* 56a) but was not allowed to. Perhaps the angel did elaborate on the precise time of the *End,* but his words are not recorded here in the spirit of the angel's exhortation (*v.* 26) to *obscure the vision.*

The Sages (*Bereishis Rabbah* 98:2) say that Jacob and Daniel both knew when the *End* would be, but were not permitted to reveal it. (See *Overview* VI).]

כִּי לְמוֹעֵד קֵץ — *For at the appointed time is the End.*

The time appointed for the exile will have an end (*Metzudos*).

Previously (*v.* 17) the angel had used the word עֵת, *time,* in conjunction with the קֵץ, *End.* עֵת, *time,* refers to the natural flow of time — i.e., the Creator has incorporated the End into the natural order of things so that the קֵץ, *End,* will follow the exile naturally just as spring naturally follows winter. Nevertheless the order of nature can be upset by the Almighty Author of this order. Here the angel substitutes the word מוֹעֵד, *appointed time* — i.e., that which is inserted into the cosmic calendar whether or not it follows the preordained itinerary. Thus the קֵץ, *End,* is guaranteed not to be cancelled. The גְּאוּלָה, *redemption,* has both the qualifications of עֵת, *time,* because it is in the natural order of things; and of מוֹעֵד, *appointed time,* because it is decreed to be superimposed upon this order (*Malbim*).

[The suggestion brought forward above that the angel did reveal the End to Daniel but that the words pertaining to this were not transmitted to us, can help to explain this phrase slightly differently. כִּי לְמוֹעֵד קֵץ — *for in the time of the End* ... In this rendition this phrase sounds like an unfinished sentence. We are given the words of the angel verbatim with the exception of those words which were withheld from the public. The angel started his description of *what will be after the wrath* with the words, *for in the*

8

20-22

End. ²⁰ *The horned ram that you saw — the kings of Media and Persia.* ²¹ *And the he-goat — the kingdom of Greece; and the big horn which is between its eyes is the first king.* ²² *And as for the broken one in whose place four arose — four kingdoms will arise from a nation, but lacking its strength.*

time of the End ... The end of his statement was left out by Daniel on the angel's orders. The beginning phrase was left in to let us know that something is indeed missing.]

20. מַלְכֵי מָדַי וּפָרָס — *The kings of Media and Persia.*

The two horns symbolize two powers — Media and Persia (*Rashi*).

21. הַצָּפִיר הַשָּׂעִיר — *The he-goat.*

[צְפִיר הָעִזִּים is here shortened to הַצָּפִיר, as in *Lev.* (16) where שְׂעִירֵי עִזִּים in *v.* 5 is shortened to שְׂעִירִים and שָׂעִיר throughout the chapter, and as הַצָּפִיר is used here in *v.* 5. הַשָּׂעִיר is an explanation of the less common הַצָּפִיר. An example of this is קֵדְמָה מִזְרָחָה (*Exodus* 27:13) where both words mean east, and מִזְרָחָה explains קֵדְמָה, which by strict definition means *to the front* (cf. *Rashi* to *Numbers* 39:15; *R' Shmuel Masnuth* and *Metzudos*).

הַשָּׂעִיר can also be derived from שַׂעַר, storm, as in וַיִּשְׂתָּעֵר עָלָיו מֶלֶךְ הַצָּפוֹן (11:40). Thus, *the wild* (=stormy) *he-goat* (*R' Shmuel Masnuth*). [See also *comm.* to *v.* 5.]

מֶלֶךְ יָוָן — *The kingdom of Greece.*

[The context of the verse clearly indicates that מֶלֶךְ should be rendered *kingdom:* first, because Greece had more than one king, and second, because the verse ends with a reference *to the first king,* implying that there were others as well. For a similar usage, see 7:17.]

[233] *Daniel*

הַמֶּלֶךְ הָרִאשׁוֹן — *The first king.*

This is Alexander (the Great) who conquered Persia and killed Darius, as related in *Yossipon* ch. 9 (*Rashi*).

[*Yossipon* (ch. 5) relates that when Alexander was greeted by the High Priest in his priestly vestments, accompanied by a multitude, he prostrated himself before him. He explained that he had seen the High Priest in a vision in the form of an angel and had been warned to show him this deference (*Yoma* 39a). He then was brought to the Temple, there the priests showed him the Book of *Daniel* and pointed to this chapter, where his future victory over Darius is clearly prophesied.]

Alexander was the first Greek king to wield power on a global scale. Before him, Greece was divided into small city-states, none of them a major power (*Mayenei HaYeshuah* 9:8; *Malbim*).

22. וְהַנִּשְׁבֶּרֶת — *And as for the broken one.*

The angel now reverts to the part of the vision (*v.* 8) that showed the horn being broken and four horns taking its place (*Rashi*).

מִגּוֹי — *From a nation.*

The four kingdoms that will be carved out of Alexander's empire will be ruled by people of the same nationality as Alexander, by Greeks (*Metzudos*).

כג יַעֲמְדֶנָּה וְלֹא בְכֹחוֹ: וּבְאַחֲרִית מַלְכוּתָם
כְּהָתֵם הַפֹּשְׁעִים יַעֲמֹד מֶלֶךְ עַז־פָּנִים
כד וּמֵבִין חִידוֹת: וְעָצַם כֹּחוֹ וְלֹא בְכֹחוֹ
וְנִפְלָאוֹת יַשְׁחִית וְהִצְלִיחַ וְעָשָׂה
וְהִשְׁחִית עֲצוּמִים וְעַם־קְדֹשִׁים:
כה וְעַל־שִׂכְלוֹ וְהִצְלִיחַ מִרְמָה בְּיָדוֹ וּבִלְבָבוֹ

וְלֹא בְכֹחוֹ — *But lacking (its) strength.*

None of Alexander's successors attained the power he had possessed (*Rashi; Ibn Ezra*).

[See below 11:4.]

◄§ Prefatory note to verses 23-25

Here again we have two divergent interpretations. First we will give the interpretation offered by *Rashi, Abarbanel* (second version), and *Malbim* that these verses refer to the rule of the Romans. At the end of each verse we will give the view of *Ibn Ezra, Ralbag, Abarbanel* (first version), and *Ibn Yachia* that these verses refer to the persecutions of Antiochus IV. *R' Saadiah* views these verses (like 9-12) as referring to the rule of the Arabs. These three verses are then an elaboration on verses 9-12.

23. A Brazen-Faced King

וּבְאַחֲרִית מַלְכוּתָם — *At the end of their kingdom.*

[— When the four Greek empires shall have been subjugated by the Romans.]

כְּהָתֵם הַפֹּשְׁעִים — *When the sinners will have been finished.*

[כְּהָתֵם from תָּם, *complete=finished*. It is here used in the sense of destruction — when the sinners will have been destroyed.]

— When the time comes to destroy the Jewish sinners — i.e., in the era of the destruction of the second Temple (*Rashi*).

— When the sinners, the Seleucid kings — Antiochus IV and his successors — have met their end (*Mayenei HaYeshuah* 8:9). [Pompey made Syria a Roman province in 68 B.C.E., 3692 A.M.]

יַעֲמֹד מֶלֶךְ עַז־פָּנִים — *A brazen-faced king will arise.*

I.e., an *arrogant* king will arise. This refers to [Vespasian and] Titus (*Rashi*).

Mayenei HaYeshuah suggests that this refers to the Roman *kingdom* rather than to a *specific king.* The Romans, in their audacity, subdued regions and countries outside their real sphere of influence. רוֹמִי [Rome] has the numerical value 256, whereas עַז פָּנִים [*arrogant*] adds up to 257. This intimates that Rome almost reached the apogee of עֲזוּת פָּנִים, *arrogance* (*Mayenei HaYeshuah* 9:8).

וּמֵבִין חִידוֹת — *An understander of riddles.*

Malbim and *Abarbanel* see this as referring to the influence of the Roman church. Its *kings* (the popes), are said to be understanders of riddles. They have the ability to 'solve' the problems the Bible poses for their religion.

Ibn Ezra's school understands *At*

8

23-25

²³ *At the end of their kingdom, when the sinners have been finished, a brazen-faced king, an understander of riddles, will arise.* ²⁴ *His might will grow, but not through his might, and he will destroy amazingly. He will succeed and accomplish, and will destroy mighty ones and the nation of holy ones.* ²⁵ *Because of his cunning, deceit will succeed in his*

---

the end of their kingdom to refer to the period during and preceding the end of the Seleucid kingdom. [With Antiochus's death (164 B.C.E., 3596 A.M.) his empire started to disintegrate. He was followed by a long line of successors fighting each other for the crown.]

כְּהָתֵם הַפּשְׁעִים — *When the sinners will have been finished.*

The Jewish Hellenism was very influential. In punishment God caused them to be conquered militarily by the Greeks.

24. וְלֹא בְכֹחוֹ — *But not through his might.*

The Romans will not rely only on their military strength, but will also resort to treachery as told in 11:23 (*Rashi*). See also *Rashi* to 11:23.

The church's power will be based mainly on its power of persuasion (*Mayenei HaYeshuah*).

וְנִפְלָאוֹת יַשְׁחִית — *And he will destroy amazingly* [lit., *wonders*].

The translation follows *Rashi* and *Metzudos*, who take this as a reference to the spectacular military victories of the Romans.

Abarbanel and *Malbim* translate וְנִפְלָאוֹת in its strict sense *and wonders*. The Roman church will *destroy the wonders* of the Torah — i.e, attempt to denigrate them — by recounting wonders for the saints of their faith.

עֲצוּמִים — *Mighty ones.*

Many [mighty] nations (*Rashi*).

וְעַם־קְדֹשִׁים — *And the nation of holy ones.*

This refers to the Jewish People, who believes in the Torah (*Rashi*).

Ibn Ezra and his school interpret this verse as referring to Antiochus IV. *His might will grow powerful but not by his [own] might,* rather because HASHEM will use him to punish His people. He *will destroy the wonders* of the Torah — i.e., he will deny their truth, *and [he] will (partially) destroy* — the spiritually mighty and brave Jewish People.

25. וְעַל שִׂכְלוֹ — *(And) because of his cunning.*

The translation follows *Metzudos. Because of his cunning* he will succeed in his attempts at *deceit.* We have chosen to translate in accord with *Metzudos* since his interpretation fits the context more smoothly.

Rashi translates, *And because of his success* [as in וַיְהִי דָוִד בְּכָל דְּרָכָיו מַשְׂכִּיל (*I Samuel* 14:18], he will persevere in his deceit.

Abarbanel and *Malbim* here too interpret this concerning the Roman church, which will succeed not because of any Divine revelation, rather *because of its cunning;* human inventiveness will be its mainstay.

יַגְדִּיל וּבְשַׁלְוָה יַשְׁחִית רַבִּים וְעַל שַׂר־
כו שָׂרִים יַעֲמֹד וּבְאֶפֶס יָד יִשָּׁבֵר: וּמַרְאֵה
הָעֶרֶב וְהַבֹּקֶר אֲשֶׁר נֶאֱמַר אֱמֶת הוּא
כז וְאַתָּה סְתֹם הֶחָזוֹן כִּי לְיָמִים רַבִּים: וַאֲנִי
דָנִיֵּאל נִהְיֵיתִי וְנֶחֱלֵיתִי יָמִים וָאָקוּם
וָאֶעֱשֶׂה אֶת־מְלֶאכֶת הַמֶּלֶךְ וָאֶשְׁתּוֹמֵם

R' Shmuel Masnuth suggests that שִׂכְלוֹ could have its root in סָכָל foolishness [as in הֶחָכָם יִהְיֶה הַסָּכָל Koheles 2:19.] With—i.e., in spite of—his foolishness he will succeed.

וּבְשַׁלְוָה יַשְׁחִית רַבִּים — In peace he will destroy many.

With treachery he will suddenly destroy many unwary nations who had covenants with him (Rashi).

The conquests of the church will not come about solely through armed conflict, but also peacefully through persuasion (Malbim).

וְעַל שַׂר־שָׂרִים יַעֲמֹד — He will stand up against the Prince of princes.

The Roman conqueror, Titus, will arrogantly defy God, Who is the Prince of the heavenly princes (see 10:13). Titus's insolent behavior in the Holy Temple is recorded in Gittin 57b. This is the interpretation of verse 11 (Rashi).

This refers to the church which tampered with the doctrine of monotheism (Abarbanel).

וּבְאֶפֶס יָד יִשָּׁבֵר — And without a hand will he be broken.

Titus died a wondrous death in Rome during his reign (see Gittin 56b). He was broken, but not by armed force, rather through the Prince of of princes Himself (Rashi).

The downfall of the church will

not come through armed conflict, rather it will come of itself. The same was foretold in Nebuchadnezzar's dream (2:34 and 45; Abarbanel; Malbim).

Ibn Ezra comments here that it is known that Antiochus died not in battle, but of an unnatural death. [Yossipon (ch. 20) relates that he fell off an elephant and was mortally wounded. Ibn Ezra says he fell off a roof. His flesh then started to rot while he was still alive so that his attendants were not able to go near him. Historians generally concede that Antiochus died of a mysterious ailment while he was on a plundering mission in Elimais (Elam).]

26. אֲשֶׁר נֶאֱמַר — Which was spoken.

Till now, the angel was elaborating upon the vision which Daniel had seen. Now the angel referred not to what had been seen, but to what had been spoken (Malbim).

אֱמֶת הוּא — (It) is true.

It is not to be interpreted allegorically like the rest of the vision (Malbim).

סְתֹם הֶחָזוֹן — Obscure [lit. seal] the vision.

Do not make it public, rather conceal it in your heart (Rashi).

employ; and he will grow proud in his heart. In peace he will destroy many; he will stand up against the Prince of princes; and without a hand will he be broken. ²⁶ <u>And the vision of the nightfall and the morning which was spoken is true.</u> As for you — obscure the vision for it is for a long time.'

²⁷ And I, Daniel, was broken up and ill for days; then I arose and did the king's business. I was con-

---

[Daniel was commanded to relate his vision without clarity. He would delete enough words to obscure its message, in effect, 'sealing' it. See *comm.* to 12:4.]

[It is quite clear from the words of *Rashi* (and *Metzudos* who echoes him) that Daniel did not make public what the angel had told him. It must then follow that what we have here in this Book is only part of the words of the angel. The parts dealing explictly with the קֵץ, *End*, have been deleted by Daniel as he was told to do by the angel. See *comm.* to *v.* 19.

Write down the vision in a manner that will *obscure* the exact meaning *(R' Shmuel Masnuth).*

כִּי לְיָמִים רַבִּים — *For it is for a long time.*

Since the redemption is a long time off, the knowledge of its date would tend to discourage the faithful *(Malbim).*

Metzudos renders כִּי like אֲשֶׁר *which.* Thus, *obscure the vision which is for a long time.* The parts of the vision pertaining to the distant redemption *obscure* in your heart and do not reveal them.

27. נִהְיֵיתִי וְנֶחֱלֵיתִי — *Was broken up and ill.*

— Because of the suffering which was about to come *(Rashi).*

— From his great fright during the vision *(Malbim).*

וָאָקוּם — *Then I arose.*

Daniel had to force himself to overcome his weakness because of the urgency of his work for the king *(R' Shmuel Masnuth).*

אֶת־מְלֶאכֶת הַמֶּלֶךְ — *The king's business.*

Nebuchadnezzar had appointed Daniel a ruler over the land of Babylon (2:48), an appointment he still held *(Rashi).*

[Even according to the view cited above (loc. cit.) that Daniel resigned from this appointment, he still retained other responsibilities which had been entrusted to him by Nebuchadnezzar. He was *chief officer over the sages of Babylon* (2:48), and *was at the king's gate* (2:49) as his adviser.]

Daniel was called by Belshazzar to decipher the writing which had appeared on the wall during his banquet (see ch. 5) [Both that event and this vision took place *in the third year of ... Belshazzar*] *(Malbim).* [See above *comm.* to *v.* 2 whether Daniel was in Babylon or in Elam at the time of the vision.]

Pesikta Rabbasi (ch. 6) interprets מֶלֶךְ, *king,* as figuratively referring to HASHEM, the King of kings.

עַל־הַמַּרְאֶה וְאֵין מֵבִין:

א בִּשְׁנַת אַחַת לְדָרְיָוֶשׁ בֶּן־אֲחַשְׁוֵרוֹשׁ מִזֶּרַע מָדָי אֲשֶׁר הָמְלַךְ עַל מַלְכוּת

ב כַּשְׂדִּים: בִּשְׁנַת אַחַת לְמָלְכוֹ אֲנִי דָנִיֵּאל בִּינֹתִי בַּסְּפָרִים מִסְפַּר הַשָּׁנִים אֲשֶׁר הָיָה

Daniel henceforth devoted himself to the work of God — i.e., the rebuilding of the Temple in Jerusalem, a task which commenced in the first year of Cyrus. Sheshbazzar in *Ezra* (1:8 and 5:15) is identified as Daniel. 'Why is he called Sheshbazzar? — Because he lived through שֵׁשׁ בַּצַּר, *six tribulations.*'

וָאֶשְׁתּוֹמֵם עַל־הַמַּרְאֶה — [*And*] *I was confounded by the vision.*

The translation follows *Rashi.*

Malbim refers this to the sight of the writing on the wall (see above). Thus, *I was amazed (See Radak in Shorashim* s.v. שמם) *at the sight.*

Daniel was amazed at the swiftness with which events were proceeding. He had just seen the vision foretelling the advent of the Persian empire, and it was already happening.

וְאֵין מֵבִין — *But no one perceived.*

No one discerned my dismay. In public Daniel kept his composure (*Rashi*).

No one but Daniel was able to decipher the writing. Because of his knowledge of things to come, Daniel was able to read in the writing the message that Persia would conquer the kingdom of Babylon (*Malbim*).

IX

1. Daniel Prays for Redemption

לְדָרְיָוֶשׁ בֶּן־אֲחַשְׁוֵרוֹשׁ — *Of Darius, the son of Ahasuerus.*

See *commentary* to 6:1 that this is the Darius who, together with Cyrus, conquered Babylon. Therefore he cannot be the son of the Ahasuerus of *Esther*. According to the tradition of the Sages (see *comm.* to *v.* 22), this vision took place in 3390 A.M., the seventieth year from Nebuchadnezzar's subjugation of Yehoyakim — i.e., the year of Babylon's destruction (see *comm.* to 5:2).

In connection with the above it is noteworthy that the Sages hold that

the Darius mentioned in *Ezra* (6:1) in whose reign the Holy Temple was rebuilt was the son of Ahasuerus and Esther (*Midrash Vayikra Rabbah* 13:5; *Esther Rabbah* 8:3 cited in *Rashi* to *Chagai* 1:1; see *Ibn Ezra, Radak,* and *Rav Josef Kara* there; *Tosafos* to *Rosh Hashanah* 3b s.v. שנת). Thus we have two kings named Darius ben Ahasuerus. The first one, Darius the Mede, who reigned for just one year (*Seder Olam* ch. 28; *Megillah* 12a), is the king mentioned here. The second is Darius the Persian, son of Ahasuerus and Esther, who gave the ultimate permission to rebuild the Holy Temple. The

founded by the vision, but no one perceived.

In the first year of Darius, the son of Ahasuerus, of the seed of Media, who was made king over the kingdom of the Chaldeans: ² In the first year of his reign, I, Daniel, contemplated the calculation, the

similarity in names is not totally coincidental. According to *Yossipon*, cited in *comm.* to 6:1, Cyrus was the son-in-law of Darius the Mede. Therefore, if Ahasuerus were a descendant of Cyrus, it is reasonable that both he and his son were given names already in the family.

Moreover, according to some *Midrashim* (*Midrash Avkir* and *Panim Acherim* version II to *Esther* 1:2 and *Targum Sheni* 1:1), Ahasuerus of Purim fame was the son of Darius the Mede.

מִזֶּרַע מָדָי — *Of the seed of Media.*

To distinguish him from the second Darius, who was a Persian (*Malbim*).

אֲשֶׁר הָמְלַךְ עַל מַלְכוּת כַּשְׂדִּים — *Who was made king over the kingdom of the Chaldeans.*

Although Darius was a Mede, he is described as king of the Chaldeans — in effect, as Belshazzer's successor rather than as the founder of a new dynasty This description is best understood in the light of the Sages' statement (*Seder Olam*; See *comm.* to 5:26 and 30) that Darius's one-year reign is reckoned as the seventieth year of the Babylonian empire for purposes of interpreting the various prophecies (see further). Thus, the Sages do not reckon his reign as part of the Persian empire's duration (*Rabbi Yehoshua Leiman*).

2. בִּשְׁנַת אַחַת לְמָלְכוֹ — *In the first year of his reign.*

[This year was the seventieth year counting from Nebuchadnezzar's first subjugation of Yehoyakim (see *comm.* to 5:2). However, it was already the seventy-first year from Nebuchadnezzar's ascension to the throne.]

בִּינֹתִי בַּסְּפָרִים — *I ... contemplated the calculation.*

The translation follows *Rashi* and *Metzudos* (from מִסְפָּר, *number*). *Malbim* renders בַּסְּפָרִים, *in the books. Radak* (*Shorashim* s.v. ספר) considers both renditions possible.

The Sages infer from this phrase that Daniel, too (like Belshazzar), initially erred in the computation of these seventy years:

בִּינֹתִי, *I contemplated,* suggests that upon reflection he realized something that had not been apparent to him at first. While Daniel knew that the count of seventy years began with the year of Nebuchadnezzar's first subjugation of Yehoyakim (in 3319 or 3320), he erred in thinking that the prophesied rebuilding of the Holy Temple would occur then. When Daniel saw that the date set in the prophecy was very close and yet no sign of the impending redemption was to be seen, he was agitated. He thought that the sins of Jewry had caused the date to be delayed or

דְּבַר־יהוה אֶל־יִרְמְיָה הַנָּבִיא לְמַלֹּאות
ג לְחָרְבוֹת יְרוּשָׁלַם שִׁבְעִים שָׁנָה: וָאֶתְּנָה

canceled. This prompted him to fast and pray as related in this chapter. When he ended his prayer, the angel Gabriel revealed himself, explained that Daniel had erred, and clarified the calculation: the Temple would be rebuilt seventy years after the destruction of Jerusalem by Nebuchadnezzar's armies in 3338, eighteen years after the initial subjugation of Jerusalem. Hence the promised redemption was still eighteen years away (*Megillah* 12a).

לְמַלֹּאות לְחָרְבוֹת יְרוּשָׁלַם — *To complete ... from the ruins of Jerusalem.*

After his prayer had been answered through the revelation of the angel Gabriel (*v. 21-7*), Daniel understood that the seventy years prophesied by Jeremiah had commenced with the *destruction* of Jerusalem, not its subjugation, as he had thought previously. This verse is a summary of the chapter. Thus: *I, Daniel, contemplated the calculation* [and I became agitated, fearing that the prophecy would not be fufilled. Thus, the intervention of the angel made me aware that] *the number of years* would be counted *from the ruins of Jerusalem.*

[This rendition is supported by the cantillation which places a disjunctive *esnachta*, pause, under the word בַּסְּפָרִים signaling the ends of this phrase.]

Some commentators interpret the angelic revelation to Daniel as far more comprehensive than that given above. They consider two ambiguous prophecies and show how they were clarified to Daniel. In *Jeremiah* 25:12 we find: *And it shall come to pass when*

seventy years are completed for Babylon [וְהָיָה כִמְלֹאות שִׁבְעִים שָׁנָה לְבָבֶל], *that I will punish the king of Babylon ...* Further on (29:10) Jeremiah prophesied, *after seventy years are completed for Babylon* [לְפִי מְלֹאת לְבָבֶל שִׁבְעִים שָׁנָה] *I will remember you ...* Daniel very reasonably assumed both terms of seventy years to be identical. When he saw that the first prophecy had come to pass with the destruction of Babylon, but the promise to remember Jewry showed no sign of imminent fulfillment, he was saddened by the thought that something had happened to obstruct the fulfillment of this prophecy. Through his prayer, he merited the revelation that he had erred; the starting point of the second prophecy was the subjugation of Jerusalem — referred to as לְחָרְבוֹת יְרוּשָׁלַם, *the ruins of Jerusalem — which took place in the second year of Nebuchadnezzar's reign* (כִּבּוּשׁ יְהוֹיָקִים). This was fulfilled in the next year when Darius the Mede died and Cyrus, upon ascending to the throne, proclaimed (*Ezra* 1:3) *Whoever there is among you ... let him go up to Jerusalem and build the house of HASHEM, the God of Israel.* (*Rav Avraham bar Chiya, Megillas HaMegaleh* p.85-7; *R' Saadiah*).

[An alternative clarification of the ambiguous prophecies and Daniel's error is as follows: Daniel interpreted *Jeremiah* 29:10 as ending in the first year of Darius the Mede, as above. Through his prayer it was revealed to him that reckoning was to begin only a year later, seventy years after the first subjugation of Jerusalem. Furthermore, a detailed meaning of Jeremiah's prophecy was revealed to him.

Daniel was informed of an element not explicitly stated by Jeremiah: לְחָרְבוֹת יְרוּשָׁלַם, *the ruins of Jerusalem.* This implied that destruction, not merely subjugation, was an element of the

9
3
number of years about which the word of HASHEM
had come to the prophet Jeremiah, to complete the
seventy years from the ruins of Jerusalem. ³ *And I set*

reckoning. Thus, he understood that Jeremiah's reference to seventy years of Jerusalem could also be interpreted to mean of the *destruction* of Jerusalem.

Accordingly, we have three different perceptions of seventy years in the prophecy of Jeremiah: 1) Seventy years from the start of Nebuchadnezzar's reign, Babylon would fall *(Jeremiah 25:12)*; 2) Seventy years from Nebuchadnezzar's initial sujugation of Jerusalem, the exiles would be allowed to return *(Jeremiah 29:10)*; 3) Seventy years from the destruction of the Holy Temple and Jerusalem, the Temple would be rebuilt *(Daniel 9:2)*.

This last prophecy, though not explicit in the book of *Jeremiah*, had nevertheless been revealed to Jeremiah and (for reasons unfathomable to us), had been forgotten until it was again revealed to Daniel (see *Malbim*). This conception of Daniel's error is reconcilable with the view of *Megillah* (12a) that Daniel erred in his calculations (See *Megillas Hamegaleh, ibid.*).

Malbim proposes another translation of the word בַּסְפָרִים, and with it a novel interpretation of this verse. When Daniel saw that Babylon's downfall had occurred in the seventieth year, as prophesied, without the promised redemption taking place, he searched for an answer in the books of Jeremiah's prophecies. He found in one of the books a version that was not intended for posterity and therefore has not come down to us. (See *Megillah* 14a where the principle is set forth that prophecies not needed for posterity were not recorded.) Hence, the words לִמְלֹאות לְחָרְבוֹת יְרוּשָׁלַיִם, *to complete the seventy years from the ruins of Jerusalem* were written here in *Daniel*, but not in the record of

Jeremiah's prophecies. To reconcile the discrepancy between the two versions, Daniel assumed that the first appointed time, seventy years from the subjugation, was conditional upon Israel's repentance; the second appointed time, seventy years from the destruction was unconditional, and would remain valid whether or not Israel was worthy. So he set about to hasten the impending redemption [See *Overview*].

Abarbanel (Mayenei HaYeshuah 10:1) connects Daniel's prayer to the previous chapter. Though he had long known of the four kingdoms which would flourish before the final redemption, Daniel had no conception of a Second Temple to be followed by a Third. The Temple about to be built was, in his mind, the ultimate Temple which would usher in the glorious reign of the fifth kingdom, that of the God of heaven, *which will never be harmed* (2:44). Thus, though he knew Jeremiah's prophecy which set a limit of seventy years upon the Babylonian exile, he assumed that these four kingdoms would follow one another within this period. When he was told by the angel in his vision that the redemption would not take place, *until ... two thousand and three hundred ...* (8:14), he concluded that Jewry's sins had caused a deferment of the seventy-year limit foretold by Jeremiah. He then prayed to God to pity the exile and to restore the prophesied redemption. Upon completing his prayer, the angel informed him that no con-

אֶת־פָּנַי אֶל־אֲדֹנָי הָאֱלֹהִים לְבַקֵּשׁ תְּפִלָּה
ד וְתַחֲנוּנִים בְּצוֹם וְשַׂק וָאֵפֶר: וָאֶתְפַּלְלָה
לַיהוָה אֱלֹהַי וָאֶתְוַדֶּה וָאֹמְרָה אָנָּא אֲדֹנָי

tradition existed between the words of the angel and Jeremiah's prophecy, which spoke only of a temporary redemption, after which a second exile would take place (v. 26-27). Only upon the termination of this exile would the fourth kingdom fall, and the promised total redemption (גְּאוּלָה שְׁלֵמָה) take place.[1]

3. וָאֶתְּנָה אֶת־פָּנַי — *And I set my face.*

... Toward the southeast, i.e., Jerusalem (*Ibn Ezra*).

The *Midrash* senses that the term וָאֶתְּנָה אֶת־פָּנַי, *And I set my face*, denotes resolution and strength. A good advocate presents his client's case in a manner acceptable to the judge. 'But two advocates stood up to defend Israel and stood [ready], as it were, to defy the Holy One, Blessed be He (וְהֶעֱמִידוּ פָנִים כִּבְיָכוֹל

(נֶגֶד הקב"ה) ... Daniel [did so] as it says, *And set my face.*'

לְבַקֵּשׁ תְּפִלָּה וְתַחֲנוּנִים — *To request prayer and supplication.*

Besides his actual prayer, he asked God to *grant him* prayer — i.e., to give him the wisdom and eloquence needed to pray. The same sentiment is expressed by David when he prays; *My Lord! Open my lips,* and *my mouth will declare Your praise.* (Psalms 51:17). So important is this introductory prayer, that our Sages have prefaced every daily prayer with David's request, incorporating it into the *Shemoneh Esrei* itself (*Berachos* 9b כִּתְפִילָה אֲרִיכְתָּא דָמְיָא; cf. *Tur Orach Chaim* 111 and *Beis Yosef ibid.*; From *Malbim* and *Mayenei HaYeshuah* 10:2).

In keeping with this tradition, special prefatory prayers were com-

---

1. It must be assumed in this interpretation that Daniel knew, either through רוּחַ הַקֹּדֶשׁ, *Divine Inspiration*, or oral tradition, that the redemption would come gradually, in stages, rather than suddenly. Otherwise he would not have been disturbed, since even according to his erroneous reckoning, the date promised for the erection of the Temple was still a year off. This was unlike the ultimate redemption, which according to the *Talmud* (*Succah* 41a, *Rashi* and *Tosafos* s.v. א"י) will come abruptly (see *Malachi* 3:1 וּפִתְאֹם יָבֹא אֶל הֵיכָלוֹ הָאָדוֹן, *and suddenly the Lord will come to His Temple*).

The exile of Yehoyachin (Yehoyakim's successor who reigned for only three months) took place seven years after the initial conquest of Jerusalem by Nebuchadnezzar. When we find in *Jeremiah* (52:28) in reference to the first exile, *in the seventh year* ... the years are counted from the first conquest of Jerusalem. (See *comm.* to 1:1 and *Overview* to *Esther.*) Zedekiah's rule lasted eleven years (*Jeremiah* 52:1; see *Megillah* 11b and *Rashi*, there; *Seder Olam Rabbah* 25). Thus, eighteen years elapsed from Jerusalem's initial subjugation to the destruction of the Temple. Consequently, eighteen years elapsed from the initial return from exile to the rebuilding of the Temple.

The breakdown of the final eighteen years is as follows:
1) Three years of Cyrus's reign (see *Daniel* 10:1, *In the third year of Cyrus, king of Persia*). In his first year, Cyrus authorized Israel to return to its land. 2) Fourteen years of Ahasuerus' reign. [The casting of the lots occurred *in the twelfth year of King Ahasuerus Esther* 3:7. In the thirteenth of Ahasuerus' rule, the miracle of Purim happened. The following year, Mordechai and Esther sent the second letter of Purim (*Esther* 9:29).] 3) One year of Darius' (II) reign *until the second year of Darius, King of Persia* (*Ezra* 4:24).

(See *Seder Olam Rabbah* 29; *Megillah* 11b; *Rashi* there and to *Chaggai* 1:1).

my face toward my Lord, God, to request prayer and supplication, with fasting, sackcloth, and ashes.
⁴ *I prayed to HASHEM, my God, and I confessed. And I said, 'I beg of You, my Lord the Almighty,*

posed by the *Payetanim* [liturgical poets] to introduce the prayers of the High Holy days.

Alshich adds that Daniel here addresses God with the same Name [אֲדֹנוּת signifying *Lordship*] as David does.

A similar sentiment is read by *Midrash Shocher Tov* (108:1) into the seemingly redundant תְּפִלָּה וְתַחֲנוּנִים *prayer and supplication*. *Prayer*, תְּפִלָּה, refers to the actual prayer. Supplication, תַּחֲנוּנִים, denotes a separate plea that God will listen to and accept the prayer.

בְּצוֹם — *With fasting.*

It has been ordained by the Sages to fast for any misfortune which befalls the community until they find mercy [in the eyes] of heaven (*Rambam Hilchos Ta'anios* 1:4 from *Ta'anis* 10a).

Abarbanel (*Mayenei HaYeshuah* 10:1) sees the fast as a substitute for a sacrifice. The loss of body fat and blood caused by the fast can be a substitute for the fat and blood that ought to have been offered on the altar. This idea is echoed quite often in the Selichos for the High Holy Days.

וְשַׂק וָאֵפֶר — *Sackcloth and ashes.*

As an additional sign of humility (*ibid.*).

In addition to the numerous references in the Bible to sackcloth and ashes as the supreme symbol of grief and humility, we also find in the *Mishnah* (*Taanis* 15a) that it was customary on a fast day to put ashes on the Holy Ark, the Torah Scrolls, and the heads of all those assembled. *Rambam* (*Hilchos Taanios* 4:1) adds, 'and all the people assemble and don sackcloth.' He goes on to explain that the purpose of sackcloth and ashes is 'to increase the weeping and humble the hearts ... that they be ashamed and repent.'

4. Ours is the Shamefacedness

וָאֶתְפַּלְלָה ... וָאֶתְוַדֶּה וָאֹמְרָה — *And I prayed ... and I confessed. And I said.*

We find Daniel referring to his prayer with the same three terms later (*v.* 20), *And more I was speaking, praying, and confessing my sin*. The prayer had three essential components:

1) Praise of God (*v.* 4).
2) Confession (*v.* 8-17);
3) The prayer (request) itself (*vs.* 18-19). Since this is the most important part, it is mentioned first, though in sequence it is last (*Mayenei HaYeshuah* 10:1).[1]

1. [This is in keeping with the dictum: 'A person should praise God, יְסַדֵּר שִׁבְחוֹ שֶׁל מָקוֹם (lit. he should arrange the praise of God) first and then pray (*Berachos* 32a). This is also expressed by the sequence of the *Shemoneh Esrei*, which prefaces the prayer with three benedictions of praise (*Rambam, Hilchos Tefillah* 1:4 from *Berachos* 31a and 34a)].

Repentance, of which confession is an essential component (see *Rambam, Hilchos Teshuvah* 1:1: 'When one repents of his sin, he is required to confess'), is a prerequisite for successful prayer. The prophet Isaiah, in enumerating the evil consequences of sin, exclaims (*Isaiah* 1:15): *Even when you make many prayers I do not hear!* (see *Rambam, op. cit.* 9:7).

ט
ד

הָאֵל הַגָּדוֹל וְהַנּוֹרָא שֹׁמֵר הַבְּרִית
וְהַחֶסֶד לְאֹהֲבָיו וּלְשֹׁמְרֵי מִצְוֹתָיו:

Alshich and *Malbim* understand
וָאֶתְפַּלְלָה וָאֶתְוַדֶּה, *and I prayed ...
and I confessed*, to be separate from
וָאֹמְרָה, *and I said*. First, Daniel
prayed and confessed for himself so
that he would be considered worthy
to pray for the entire Jewish people.
Only after this did he start his
prayer for the Jewish people. [The
esnachta, placed under וָאֶתְוַדֶּה supports this interpretation. See *v.* 20,
וּמִתְוַדֶּה חַטָּאתִי וְחַטַּאת עַמִּי
יִשְׂרָאֵל. [1]

הַגָּדוֹל וְהַנּוֹרָא — *(The) Great and
(the) Awesome.*

This formula, so familiar to us
from *Shemoneh Esrei*, omits הַגִּבּוֹר,
the Mighty. Similarly, Jeremiah
(32:18) uses this formula with the
omission of וְהַנּוֹרָא, *and the
Awesome*. The complete formula
was originated by Moses (*Deut.*
10:17). The Sages say in comment
on this (*Yoma* 69b): 'Jeremiah did
not say וְהַנּוֹרָא [because he
reasoned, if] heathens dance in His
Temple, where is His
awesomeness?'

Maharsha (Chidushei Agados) explains
that Jeremiah did not mean to contradict
Moses ח"ו. His omission of וְהַנּוֹרָא was
meant only to illustrate that God's attribute
of awesomeness, though everpresent, was
not evident in his generation. Only הַגָּדוֹל,
which refers to the greatness of God as
evidenced though the fact of Creation and
nature, is an everpresent and ever-evident attribute, hence it was said by all the prophets.

Similarly, Daniel said, If the
heathens enslave His children,
where is His mightiness?

[Therefore] he did not say הַגִּבּוֹר,
the Mighty.

Jeremiah, at the beginning of the exile, had
not yet witnessed the enslavement of his people (*Maharsha, ibid.*).

Then they [אַנְשֵׁי כְּנֶסֶת הַגְּדוֹלָה, *the
Men of the Great Assembly*] came
and said: On the contrary this is His
mightiness [since] He restrains His
will [as it were] and is slow to vent
anger [שֶׁנּוֹתֵן אֶרֶךְ אַפַּיִם] upon the
evildoers. And this is His awesomeness because were it not for the
awe of the Holy One, Blessed be He,
[which somehow prevents the
destruction of Israel] how could this
one nation exist among the
nations?

They reinstituted the complete
formula הַגָּדוֹל הַגִּבּוֹר וְהַנּוֹרָא
(*Nehemiah* 9:32). For they had
already seen the miracles employed
by God to ensure His people's existence in the exile; they had seen
that even during the concealment of
the Divine Countenance [הֶסְתֵּר פָּנִים]
during the exile, the rays of
God's Providence pierce the
darkness and proclaim His Presence
and Providence to His people. A
classic example is the story of
Purim. The promise: *Yet for all
that, when they are in the land of
their enemies, I will not reject them*
(*Leviticus* 26:44) has always been
kept (*Maharsha, loc. cit.*)

שֹׁמֵר הַבְּרִית וְהַחֶסֶד — *Who
safeguards the covenant and the
lovingkindness.*

This phrase occurs in *Deut.* (7:9).

1. This sentiment is reflected in the ruling of the *Talmud* (*Ta'anis* 16b) that the *chazan*
should be someone 'whose house is empty of sin' (בֵּיתוֹ רֵיקָם מִן הָעֲבֵירָה) and whose reputation
is unblemished (שֶׁלֹּא יָצָא לוֹ שֵׁם רַע בְּיַלְדוּתוֹ). Greater standards of excellence are demanded of
the *chazan* who prays for the people than of the individual (see *Orach Chaim* 53:4).

דָּנִיֵּאל [244]

9
5
Great and Awesome, Who safeguards the covenant
and the lovingkindness to those who love Him and
keep His commandments. ⁵ We have sinned, acted

It probably refers to the covenant with Abraham (*Gen.* 17:7), as indicated a few verses later (*Deut.* 7:12): *And God will safeguard the covenant and the lovingkindness that He swore to your fathers* (see *Ibn Ezra*, there). Thus *the lovingkindness which had been sworn* to the fathers must be the reward promised for keeping the covenant: *And I will give to you and to your seed after you the land of your sojournings, all the land of Canaan, for an everlasting possession* (*Gen.* 17:8; *Ibn Ezra* to *Deut.* 7:12).

This interpretation fits our context very well since Daniel proceeds to confess that Israel's sins had caused them to lose the land of their fathers. How appropriate is it then for him to preface this with a declaration that God has kept His part of the covenant: *Who safeguards the covenant and the lovingkindness.*

Ha'amek Davar (*Deut.* 7:9), interprets the *covenant and the lovingkindness* as referring, not to God's love for Israel, but to Jewry's love for God. Thus, *God safeguards* the account of Israel's deed in order to repay Israel's adherence to the covenant and its love for God. הַבְּרִית, *the covenant*, refers to the keeping of the precepts of the Torah (or in a narrower sense the prohibition against idolatry as suggested by *Netziv*). הַחֶסֶד, *the lovingkindness*, refers to what is done over and above the required (מִדַּת חֲסִידוּת).

לְאֹהֲבָיו וּלְשֹׁמְרֵי מִצְוֹתָיו — *To those who love Him and those who keep His commandments.*

Rashi (*Deut.* 7:9) understands אֹהֲבָיו to refer to those who serve out of love.

Ramban (*Exodus* 20:7), says that אֹהֲבָיו refers to those who, out of love for God, subject themselves to martyrdom rather than transgress His commandments. וְאָהַבְתָּ אֵת ה' אֱלֹקֶיךָ, *And you will love HASHEM, your God* (*Deut.* 6:4) is understood by the Sages (*Sifre ibid.* quoted in *Pesachim* 24a and *Rashi*) as requiring devotion to God אֲפִילוּ הוּא נוֹטֵל אֶת נַפְשֶׁךָ, *even though he may take your life.* Thus, a Jew must be prepared even to face martyrdom if need be.

שֹׁמְרֵי מִצְוֹתָיו, [*those who*] *keep His commandments* refers to those who uphold the Torah without suffering martyrdom.

Netziv (*Deut.* 33:8) sees yet another meaning in these two categories. אֹהֲבָיו, *those who love Him*, are those who, out of love for Him, accept with love the vicissitudes of the fate accorded them by His hand (קַבָּלַת יְסוּרִים בְּאַהֲבָה) as formulated in the *Mishnah* (*Berachos* 9:5): חַיָּיב אָדָם לְבָרֵךְ עַל הָרָעָה כְּשֵׁם שֶׁמְבָרֵךְ עַל הַטוֹבָה, *a person is obligated to give thanks for the bad just as he gives thanks for the good.*

שׁוֹמְרֵי מִצְוֹתָיו, [*those who*] *keep His commandments* are those who try to fulfill the commandments לִפְנִים מִשּׁוּרַת הַדִּין, in the most exemplary manner, beyond the minimum halachic requirement.

ה חָטָאנוּ וְעָוִינוּ °וְהִרְשַׁעְנוּ וּמָרָדְנוּ וְסוֹר
מִמִּצְוֹתֶךָ וּמִמִּשְׁפָּטֶיךָ: וְלֹא שָׁמַעְנוּ אֶל־
עֲבָדֶיךָ הַנְּבִיאִים אֲשֶׁר דִּבְּרוּ בְּשִׁמְךָ אֶל־
מְלָכֵינוּ שָׂרֵינוּ וַאֲבֹתֵינוּ וְאֶל כָּל־עַם
ז הָאָרֶץ: לְךָ אֲדֹנָי הַצְּדָקָה וְלָנוּ בֹּשֶׁת
הַפָּנִים כַּיּוֹם הַזֶּה לְאִישׁ יְהוּדָה וּלְיֹשְׁבֵי
יְרוּשָׁלַם וּלְכָל־יִשְׂרָאֵל הַקְּרֹבִים

5. חָטָאנוּ וְעָוִינוּ וְהִרְשַׁעְנוּ וּמָרָדְנוּ —
*We have sinned, acted wickedly,
done evil, and rebelled.*

Therefore the promised redemption has not taken place, in spite of
the fact that God *safeguards the
covenant and the lovingkindness*
(*Malbim; Alshich*).

The difference between חֵטְא and
עָוֹן is clearly delineated in the
Talmud (*Yoma* 36b). חֵטְא is שׁוֹגֵג,
inadvertent sin. עָוֹן is מֵזִיד, *intentional sin*. The next two categories
are uncertain. *The Talmud (ibid.)*,
lists another category, פֶּשַׁע, which
is defined as *rebelliousness* (אֵלּוּ
הַמֹּרְדִים).

*Maharsha (Chidushei Aggados,
ibid.)* points out that רֶשַׁע (וְהִרְשַׁעְנוּ)
mentioned here cannot be identical
with פֶּשַׁע, *rebelliousness*, since that
is clearly included in וּמָרָדְנוּ, *we
have rebelled*. He suggests that רֶשַׁע
may be an intermediate category
between עָוֹן, *intentional sin*, and
מֶרֶד, *rebellious sin*, but does not
clearly define this. Perhaps, according to the *keri* (pronunciation)
which reads הִרְשַׁעְנוּ without the
connective *vav*, הִרְשַׁעְנוּ could be
coupled with וּמָרָדְנוּ, thus: *We have
done evil rebelliously* — i.e., not
only have we rebelled on an intellectual level, but we have acted out
our rebelliousness in doing evil.

Malbim defines חֵטְא as *lustful*
sin; עָוֹן *philosophical deviation
from God's way;* רֶשַׁע as *sins
against one's fellow man;* and מֶרֶד
as a general description of the three
aforementioned categories — i.e., all
of this was done in a spirit of rebellion.

וְסוֹר מִמִּצְוֹתֶיךָ וּמִמִּשְׁפָּטֶיךָ — *And [we]
deviate from Your commandments
and Your ordinances.*

In addition to the above mentioned sins, we have deviated. It is
possible to sin sporadically yet to
cling generally to a Torah way of
life by adhering to the *mitzvos* in a
dispirited habitual way. But *we
have deviated*, we have not even
kept the Torah out of force of habit
(*Alshich*).

מִמִּצְוֹתֶיךָ — *From Your commandments.*

The precepts pertaining to the
duties one has *vis-a-vis* God are
called מִצְוֹת.

וּמִמִּשְׁפָּטֶיךָ — *And (from) Your ordinances.*

The precepts pertaining to one's
duties toward his fellow man are
called מִשְׁפָּטִים (*Malbim*).

Ralbag suggests that the phrase
וְסוֹר מִמִּצְוֹתֶיךָ, *and we deviate from
Your commandments*, refers to the
sin of idolatry, which, though a
single transgression, constitutes

9

6-7

wickedly, done evil, and rebelled; and we deviate from Your commandments and Your ordinances. 6 Nor have we heeded Your servants the prophets, who spoke in Your Name to our kings, our nobles, and our elders, and to all the people of the land. 7 Yours, O Lord, is the righteousness, and ours is the shamefacedness as of this day: the men of Judah, and the inhabitants of Jerusalem, and all of Israel, the

---

total rejection of God and His Torah.

6. וְלֹא שָׁמַעְנוּ — *Nor have we heeded.*

Our sin has been compounded by the fact that we have been exhorted by God to repent and leave our evil ways, but we refuse to listen (*Alshich*).

וַאֲבֹתֵינוּ — *And our elders.*

The translation follows *Ibn Ezra* and *Ibn Yachya*. Similarly, *Abarbanel (Mayenei HaYeshuah 10:4)* renders it *our priests*. It could hardly be meant in its usual sense, *our fathers*, since they would be included in the next phrase: וְאֶל כָּל עַם הָאָרֶץ, *And to all the people of the land.*

[It could be argued that all the categories mentioned before and after refer to the present, and אֲבֹתֵינוּ could be rendered *our ancestors*, refer to the previous generation. This would be in agreement with *Leviticus* (26:40): *And they shall confess their sins and the sins of their fathers* (see *Ramban* to *Levit.* 26:16, who seems to have understood it this way). The confession of sins committed by previous generations is also found in *Nechemiah* (1:6), *Psalms* (106:6), and other places. It is included in most versions of the *viduy* [the formula of confession said on *Yom Kippur* and in *Selichos* (אֲבָל אֲנַחְנוּ וַאֲבוֹתֵינוּ חָטָאנוּ). However, if this were the case וַאֲבוֹתֵינוּ should have been placed either at the beginning or at the end of this list. Its position between שָׂרֵינוּ, *our nobles*, and עַם הָאָרֶץ, *the people of the land*, indicates that it is another social class.]

7. לְךָ ה' הַצְּדָקָה — *Yours, O Lord, is the righteousness.*

The punishment meted out to is richly deserved.

Abarbanel (Mayenei HaYeshuah 10:4) in his interpretation of *Midrash Tanchuma (Ki Sissa 14; Shemos Rabbah 41:1)* interprets צְדָקָה in the sense of חֶסֶד, *loving-kindness*. God does not desist from his kindness even when Israel has sinned. Even while the Jews were bowing down before the Golden Calf, the *manna* did not cease to fall.

וְלָנוּ בֹּשֶׁת הַפָּנִים — *And ours is the shamefacedness.*

It befits us to be ashamed since we have been the cause of our own misfortunes (*Rashi*).

The *Talmud (Sanhedrin 93a)* relates that when Chananyah and his colleagues were rescued from the fiery furnace, all the gentiles said to sinful Jews, 'You have such a God and you worshiped idols?!' They all spat at the Jewish idolators in derision. At that time the trio exclaimed, *Yours O Lord is righteousness.*

וּלְכָל־יִשְׂרָאֵל — *And (to) all of Israel.*

I.e., even to the ten exiled tribes of Israel (*Mayenei HaYeshuah 10:4; Malbim*).

[It is possible that לְאִישׁ יְהוּדָה, *to the men of Judah*, refers to the peo-

וְהָרְחֹקִים בְּכָל־הָאֲרָצוֹת אֲשֶׁר הִדַּחְתָּם

ח שָׁם בְּמַעֲלָם אֲשֶׁר מָעֲלוּ־בָךְ: יהוה לָנוּ

בֹּשֶׁת הַפָּנִים לִמְלָכֵינוּ לְשָׂרֵינוּ וְלַאֲבֹתֵינוּ

ט אֲשֶׁר חָטָאנוּ לָךְ: לַאדֹנָי אֱלֹהֵינוּ

י הָרַחֲמִים וְהַסְּלִחוֹת כִּי מָרַדְנוּ בּוֹ: וְלֹא

שָׁמַעְנוּ בְּקוֹל יהוה אֱלֹהֵינוּ לָלֶכֶת

בְּתוֹרֹתָיו אֲשֶׁר־נָתַן לְפָנֵינוּ בְּיַד עֲבָדָיו

יא הַנְּבִיאִים: וְכָל־יִשְׂרָאֵל עָבְרוּ אֶת־

תּוֹרָתֶךָ וְסוֹר לְבִלְתִּי שְׁמוֹעַ בְּקֹלֶךָ וַתִּתַּךְ

עָלֵינוּ הָאָלָה וְהַשְּׁבֻעָה אֲשֶׁר כְּתוּבָה

בְּתוֹרַת מֹשֶׁה עֶבֶד־הָאֱלֹהִים כִּי חָטָאנוּ

יב לוֹ: וַיָּקֶם אֶת־°דברריו | אֲשֶׁר־דִּבֶּר עָלֵינוּ

וְעַל־שֹׁפְטֵינוּ אֲשֶׁר שְׁפָטוּנוּ לְהָבִיא עָלֵינוּ

° דְּבָרָו ק'

---

ple left in *Eretz Yisrael* after the exile of Zedekiah (at the time of the Temple's destruction). *II Kings* (25:23) refers to them as: *The people left in the land of Judah.* וּלְיוֹשְׁבֵי יְרוּשָׁלַיִם, *and the inhabitants of Jerusalem,* could refer to the exiles of Yehoyachin and Zedekiah. *All of Israel* would mean the ten tribes of Israel who were exiled and lost. The sequence in the verse matches the chronology of these exiles, moving from the present to the past.]

8. ... לִמְלָכֵינוּ — *Our kings* [lit. *to our kings*]...

Here Daniel clarifies that the shame mentioned in *v.* 7 envelops not only the nation in general, but *all* of its social strata (*Malbim*).

אֲשֶׁר חָטָאנוּ לָךְ — *For we have sinned against You.*

Our shame is not because we have, as part of our punishment, lost our glory. Rather, we now feel deeply ashamed merely because we

dared to sin against You (*Alshich; Malbim*).

9. God Hastened The Calamity

כִּי מָרַדְנוּ בּוֹ — *For we have rebelled against Him.*

We have rebelled, yet we still exist. This must be due to God's forgiveness. Thus, to God belongs *compassion and forgiveness*, the proof of which is that he permits us to survive although *we have rebelled against Him* (*Rashi; Ralbag*).

10. וְלֹא שָׁמַעְנוּ — *Nor did we heed.*

[This continues *v.* 9: *we have rebelled against Him. Nor did we heed* ...]

Even when He sent His prophets to warn us about our evil ways, we did not heed them (*Malbim; Alshich*).

[This verse is similar to *v.* 6, but here the emphasis is on amazement at God's compassion and forgiveness.]

*near and the distant, in all the lands You have driven
them because of betrayal with which they betrayed
You. ⁸ HASHEM, ours is the shamefacedness — our
kings,' our nobles,' and our ancestors' — for we have
sinned against You.*

*⁹ 'My Lord our God's is the compassion and
forgiveness, for we have rebelled against Him. ¹⁰ Nor
did we heed the voice of HASHEM our God to follow
His teachings which He placed before us through His
servants the prophets. ¹¹ All Israel has transgressed
Your teaching and deviated so as not to heed Your
voice; and poured out upon us were the curse and the
oath which is written in the Torah of Moses, servant
of God, for we have sinned against Him. ¹² And He
confirmed His word which He spoke about us and
about our judges who judged us to bring upon us a*

---

11. וְכָל־יִשְׂרָאֵל — *All Israel.*

This is an elaboration on *v.* 5.
Where Daniel says generally חָטָאנוּ,
*We have sinned ... Nor have we
heeded (v. 6),* he goes on to clarify
in *v.* 11 that *all Israel has transgressed ... and deviated so as not to
heed Your voice* [through Your servants the prophets.]

וַתִּתַּךְ — *And poured out.*

The translation follows *Donash
[ben Lavrat]* and *Metzudos* here,
and *Ibn Ezra* and *Rashi's* preferred
rendering to *Exodus* 9:33. It can
also be rendered *and the curse ...
has reached,* as do *Rashi* and
Onkelos to *Exodus ibid.*

הָאָלָה וְהַשְּׁבֻעָה — *The curse and the
oath.*

This is a reference to the תּוֹכָחָה,
admonition, of Moses in *Deuteronomy,* which is characterized as *the
covenant* [=the oath] *and ... curse
(Deut.* 29:11). Therefore, Daniel

here describes it as ... *which is written in the Torah of Moses, servant
of God* — i.e., which Moses wrote in
the capacity of God's servant. The
admonition in *Deuteronomy* is
written by Moses in the first person
(see *Rashi,* to *Lev.* 26:19 and *Abarbanel* in his preface to
Deuteronomy), whereas the admonition in *Leviticus* is written as
spoken by God Himself *(Alshich;
Malbim).*

[*Rashi* understands this phrase to
refer to the *oath* contained in the
admonition, in *Leviticus.]*

12. וְעַל־שֹׁפְטֵינוּ — *And about our
judges.*

[As written in the *admonition,
HASHEM will bring you and the
king whom you will set over
yourself to a nation that you had
not known (Deut.* 28:36). One of
the functions of the king was to act
as a judge, as evidenced from

רָעָה גְדֹלָה אֲשֶׁר לֹא־נֶעֶשְׂתָה תַּחַת כָּל־
הַשָּׁמָיִם כַּאֲשֶׁר נֶעֶשְׂתָה בִּירוּשָׁלָָם:
יג כַּאֲשֶׁר כָּתוּב בְּתוֹרַת מֹשֶׁה אֵת כָּל־
הָרָעָה הַזֹּאת בָּאָה עָלֵינוּ וְלֹא־חִלִּינוּ
אֶת־פְּנֵי | יהוה אֱלֹהֵינוּ לָשׁוּב מֵעֲוֹנֵינוּ
יד וּלְהַשְׂכִּיל בַּאֲמִתֶּךָ: וַיִּשְׁקֹד יהוה עַל־
הָרָעָה וַיְבִיאֶהָ עָלֵינוּ כִּי־צַדִּיק יהוה
אֱלֹהֵינוּ עַל־כָּל־מַעֲשָׂיו אֲשֶׁר עָשָׂה וְלֹא

Samuel I (8:5), *Now make us a king to judge us like all the nations.* Therefore when Daniel speaks about judges, kings are also included. The plural form is used because of the tragic fate which befell the last three kings who reigned before the exile: Yehoyakim, Yehoyachin, and Zedekiah.]

אֲשֶׁר לֹא־נֶעֶשְׂתָה — *There has not been done.*

Sword fighting, murder, burning of the city, the ravishing of the captives (*Rashi*).

[This again is a fulfillment of *Deuteronomy* (29:22-23), *Brimstone and salt, burned is all her land ... and all the nations will say* (in amazement); *'Wherefore has HASHEM done thus to this land?'*]

13. כַּאֲשֶׁר כָּתוּב בְּתוֹרַת מֹשֶׁה — *Just as is written in the Torah of Moses.*

Here Daniel is referring to the *admonition* in *Leviticus* which Moses pronounces in the name of God. That is why he does not refer here to Moses *servant of God* as in *v.* 11 (*Alshich; Malbim*).

וּלְהַשְׂכִּיל בַּאֲמִתֶּךָ — *And to comprehend Your truth.*

To understand that You are the true God (*Metzudos*). [Perhaps אֱמֶת refers to God's revealed truth — i.e., the Torah and the teaching of His prophets.]

פְּנֵי — *The countenance.*

פָּנִים, *countenance*, usually refers to God's smiling, gracious face, so to speak. See *Rashi* to *Numbers* 6:25. Similarly when God's anger is aroused against His people, He is said to conceal His face, or turn it away. See *Deuteronomy* 31:18.

14. וַיִּשְׁקֹד ... כִּי צַדִּיק — *(And) HASHEM hastened the calamity ... for HASHEM is righteous ...*

Because we deserved the punishment meted out to us, HASHEM in His righteousness hurried to punish us (*Rashi*).

[צַדִּיק, *a righteous (one)*, can be derived from either צֶדֶק, *righteousness, justice,* or from צְדָקָה, *charity,* which connotes compassion and almsgiving.]

The Sages say (*Sanhedrin* 38a); 'HASHEM was compassionate when He hastened to begin the exile two years before its assigned time. In warning Israel of the eventual punishment for its future sins, Moses said, וְנוֹשַׁנְתֶּם בָּאָרֶץ וְהִשְׁחַתֶּם

great calamity; for under the entire heaven there has not been as has been done in Jerusalem. [13] *Just as is written in the Torah of Moses, all this calamity has come upon us; yet we have not entreated the countenance of* HASHEM *our God, to repent our sins, and to comprehend Your truth.* [14] HASHEM *hastened the calamity and brought it upon us, for* HASHEM *our God is righteous in all His deeds which he has done,*

כִּי אָבֹד תֹּאבֵדוּן ..., *and you will have been long in the land, and will become corrupt ... you shall soon utterly perish [Deut. 4:25-26].* The numerical value of וְנוֹשַׁנְתֶּם is 852. Had they been in the land for the entire period of 852 years in a corrupt state, the prophesied curse *You will soon utterly perish* would be fulfilled. Therefore they were sent into exile 850 years after their coming to the land so that the ultimate punishment could be softened.

The breakdown of this is as follows: From their entry into *Eretz Yisrael* to the building of the Temple, 440 years elapsed. [See *I Kings* 6:1; *And it came to pass in the four hundred and eightieth year after the children of Israel were come out of the land of Egypt ... that he began to build the house of* HASHEM. The sojourn of the Jews in the desert was forty years ·so we are left with 440 years from the entry into *Eretz Yisrael* to the building of the Temple.] **The Temple stood 410 years.** This number can be approximated by adding together the years of the kings, but for the exact number of years we must rely on the tradition handed down by the Sages (*Yoma* 9a.) For a breakdown of the figures see the chart drawn up by the *Vilna Gaon* printed at the end of *Aderes*

Eliyahu Nevi'im U'Kesuvim and and *Seder Olam Rabbah. (Rashi* from *Sanhedrin* 38a).

'HASHEM was compassionate when He hastened the exile of Zedekiah while the exiles of Yechoniah were still alive. About the exile of Yechaniah it is written: *And the Charash and the Masger one thousand (II Kings* 24:16). The Sages (*Sanhedrin* 38a) interpret *Charash* and *Masger* as a reference to the most gifted *scholars.* God hastened their exile so that a basis for religious life could be established in anticipation of the large exile following the destruction. See *Overview).*

[*Maharsha (Chiddushei Agados ibid.) comments that the Talmud saw fit not to understand Charash and Masger in its literal sense [craftsman and locksmith] because the verse says, The Charash and the Masger ... all of the strong men and fit for war. In its literal meaning this is incomprehensible, since to be a craftsman one does not need to be strong and fit for war. Therefore this is interpreted allegorically as* גּבּוֹרִים בְּמִלְחַמְתָּהּ שֶׁל תּוֹרָה, *heroes in the war of Torah. It should also be added that Daniel and Mordechai are probably counted among these exiled scholars.*

שָׁמַעְנוּ בְּקֹלוֹ: וְעַתָּה | אֲדֹנָי אֱלֹהֵינוּ אֲשֶׁר֩ טו
הוֹצֵ֨אתָ אֶת־עַמְּךָ֜ מֵאֶ֤רֶץ מִצְרַ֙יִם֙ בְּיָ֣ד
חֲזָקָ֔ה וַתַּֽעַשׂ־לְךָ֥ שֵׁ֖ם כַּיּ֣וֹם הַזֶּ֑ה חָטָ֖אנוּ
רָשָׁ֑עְנוּ: אֲדֹנָ֗י כְּכָל־צִדְקֹתֶ֙ךָ֙ יָֽשָׁב־נָ֤א אַפְּךָ֙ טז
וַחֲמָ֣תְךָ֔ מֵעִֽירְךָ֥ יְרוּשָׁלַ֖͏ִם הַר־קָדְשֶׁ֑ךָ כִּ֤י
בַחֲטָאֵ֙ינוּ֙ וּבַעֲוֺנ֣וֹת אֲבֹתֵ֔ינוּ יְרוּשָׁלַ֣͏ִם
וְעַמְּךָ֥ לְחֶרְפָּ֖ה לְכָל־סְבִֽיבֹתֵֽינוּ: וְעַתָּ֣ה | יז
שְׁמַ֣ע אֱלֹהֵ֗ינוּ אֶל־תְּפִלַּ֤ת עַבְדְּךָ֙ וְאֶל־
תַּ֣חֲנוּנָ֔יו וְהָאֵ֣ר פָּנֶ֔יךָ עַל־מִקְדָּשְׁךָ֖ הַשָּׁמֵ֑ם
לְמַ֖עַן אֲדֹנָֽי: הַטֵּ֨ה אֱלֹהַ֥י | אָזְנְךָ֮ וּֽשֲׁמָע֒ יח
°פְּקַחֲ עֵינֶ֗יךָ וּרְאֵה֙ שֹֽׁמְמֹתֵ֔ינוּ וְהָעִ֕יר

° פְּקַח ק׳

---

15. For Your Sake, My God

אֲשֶׁר הוֹצֵאתָ אֶת עַמְּךָ מֵאֶרֶץ מִצְרַיִם בְּיָד חֲזָקָה — *Who has taken Your people out of the land of Egypt with a strong hand.*

You took the Jews out of Egypt even though they did not yet deserve it (*Mayenei HaYeshuah* 10:5).

וַתַּעַשׂ־לְךָ שֵׁם כַּיּוֹם הַזֶּה — *And gained Yourself renown as of this day.*

But you redeemed them nevertheless, not because of their own merit, but to sanctify Your Name (*Mayenei HaYeshuah* 10:5; Malbim*).

חָטָאנוּ רָשָׁעְנוּ — *We have sinned and acted wickedly.*

Though in Egypt, too, we sinned, this did not delay the redemption which was to sanctify the Name. Therefore, we beseech You to overlook our sins now as well (*ibid.*).

Rashi interprets this phrase as referring back to the opening phrase of the verse: *And now ... our God ... we have sinned.* The middle section of the verse, *Who has taken Your people ... this day*, is a parenthetical description of God's goodness to Jewry, meant to show greater contrition, You, *Our God* to Whom we owe everything — instead of repaying Your kindness with good deeds, *we have sinned ...*

16. כְּכָל־צִדְקֹתֶךָ — *In keeping with all Your righteousness.*

Just as in the past Your compassion was with us even when we did not deserve it, so we beg You to let Your compassion turn *Your fury away from ...* (*Mayenei HaYeshuah* 10:5; Malbim).

מֵעִירְךָ יְרוּשָׁלַם הַר־קָדְשֶׁךָ — *From Your city Jerusalem, Your holy mountain.*

If not in our merit, do it for *Your city Jerusalem* and for *Your holy mountain*, the Temple Mount (*ibid.*).

כִּי ... יְרוּשָׁלַם וְעַמְּךָ לְחֶרְפָּה — *Because ... Jerusalem and Your people have become the scorn.*

Even if the merit of Jerusalem and the Temple do not suffice, You

9

15-18

but we heeded not His voice. ¹⁵ And now, my Lord our God, Who has taken Your people out of the land of Egypt with a strong hand, and gained Yourself renown as of this day — we have sinned and acted wickedly. ¹⁶ My Lord, in keeping with all Your right-eousness, please let Your anger and Your fury turn away from Your city Jerusalem, Your holy moun-tain; for because of our sins and the sins of our ancestors, Jerusalem and Your people have become the scorn of all those around us. ¹⁷ And now, pay heed, our God, to the prayer of Your servant and to his supplications, and let Your countenance shine upon Your desolate Sanctuary for my Lord's sake. ¹⁸ Incline, my God, Your ear, and listen, open Your eyes and see the desolation of ourselves and of the

---

must help us because *Jerusalem and Your people have become the scorn.* Therefore, redeem us for the sake of Your Name, so that it not become defiled *(ibid.).*

17. וְהָאֵר פָּנֶיךָ עַל־מִקְדָּשְׁךָ הַשָּׁמֵם לְמַעַן אֲדֹנָי — *And let Your countenance shine upon Your desolate Sanctuary for my Lord's sake.*

This should be understood as if it said: *For Your sake, My Lord* (Ibn Ezra).

For the sake of the Holy Name by which the Sanctuary is called, as written, *The Sanctuary of the Lord, which Your hands have wrought* (Exodus 15:17; (Rashi).

[Obviously, *Rashi* is commenting on the fact that here, and in *Exodus,* the Sanctuary is exalted by identifying it with the Name representing God's Lordship.

[Rashi's reference to *Exodus* 15:17 in-dicates that he translates it as we have given it above. In his commentary to *Exodus,* however, *Rashi* renders: *the*

Sanctuary which Your hands have wrought, O Lord (see *Malbim* ad loc.).]

The *Talmud (Berachos* 7b) states, Daniel was only answered in the merit of Abraham as it is said, *And let Your countenance...for My Lord's sake...*It should have said, לְמַעֲנָךְ, *for Your* [i.e., God's] *sake* ... [But this is the meaning] in the merit of Abraham who called You my Lord [because the *Talmud* had stated previously that Abraham was the first man to address God with the Name אָדוֹן, *Lord,* when he said: אֲדֹנָי ה' בַּמָּה אֵדַע כִּי אִרָשֶׁנָּה, *my Lord, HASHEM/ ELOHIM, whereby shall I know that I am to inherit it? (Genesis* 15:8; see comm. to ArtScroll ed. *loc. cit.).*

18. הַטֵּה אֲדֹנָי אָזְנֶךָ — *Incline, my God, Your ear.*

And listen to my prayer (Metz-udos; Malbim).

פְּקַח עֵינֶיךָ ... אֲשֶׁר־נִקְרָא שִׁמְךָ עָלֶיהָ — *Open Your eyes ... upon which Your Name is proclaimed.*

If my prayer is not enough, act for the sake of Your holy Name which is being desecrated (Malbim).

אֲשֶׁר־נִקְרָא שִׁמְךָ עָלֶיהָ כִּי | לֹא עַל־
צִדְקֹתֵינוּ אֲנַחְנוּ מַפִּילִים תַּחֲנוּנֵינוּ לְפָנֶיךָ
כִּי עַל־רַחֲמֶיךָ הָרַבִּים: אֲדֹנָי | שְׁמָעָה
אֲדֹנָי | סְלָחָה אֲדֹנָי הַקְשִׁיבָה וַעֲשֵׂה אַל־
תְּאַחַר לְמַעֲנְךָ אֱלֹהַי כִּי־שִׁמְךָ נִקְרָא עַל־
עִירְךָ וְעַל־עַמֶּךָ: וְעוֹד אֲנִי מְדַבֵּר
וּמִתְפַּלֵּל וּמִתְוַדֶּה חַטָּאתִי וְחַטַּאת עַמִּי
יִשְׂרָאֵל וּמַפִּיל תְּחִנָּתִי לִפְנֵי יהוה אֱלֹהַי

יט

כ

שִׁמְמֹתֵינוּ וְהָעִיר — *The desolation of ourselves and of the city.*
The word שִׁמְמֹתֵינוּ [=שְׁמָמוֹת שֶׁלָּנוּ] refers also to *the city* as if it said, *our desolation and the desolation of the city* (Rashi).

כִּי לֹא עַל־צִדְקֹתֵינוּ — *For not because of our righteousness.*
[As he had already mentioned in vs.15-16].

אֲנַחְנוּ — *We.*
No doubt the whole Jewish community was now pouring out its heart in prayer in expectance of the impending redemption. אַנְשֵׁי כְּנֶסֶת הַגְּדוֹלָה, *the men of the Great Assembly*, and the prophets Chaggai, Zechariah, and Malachi, as well as Ezra and Nechemiah and other great men were alive in this period, so it is inconceivable that only Daniel prayed for redemption (Alshich).

19. אֲדֹנָי שְׁמָעָה — *O my Lord, heed.*
I.e., heed our prayers.

אֲדֹנָי סְלָחָה — *O my Lord, forgive.*
Forgive the sins to which I have confessed (Rashi; Ibn Ezra).

הַקְשִׁיבָה וַעֲשֵׂה — *Be attentive and act.*
We ask only that God should

listen to our prayers, for if He listens, we are sure He will act (Midrash Shocher Tov 116).

אַל־תְּאַחַר — *Do not delay.*
Do not delay the date set in the prophecy of Jeremiah (see v. 2; Malbim).

כִּי שִׁמְךָ נִקְרָא — *For Your Name is proclaimed.*
Seventy angels are appointed over the seventy nations so that each one should have dominion over his nation and country. But the Holy One, Blessed be He, gave Israel the secret of His holy Name, and He Himself has dominion over Israel and Jerusalem. Thus it is written, *Because Your Name is called upon Your city and Your people* (Tikunei Zohar p.163).

20. וְעוֹד אֲנִי — *And more I.*
Daniel recited additional prayers that are not recorded here.
The translation follows most commentators (Ibn Ezra; Abarbanel; Malbim; Metzudos) who adopt this translation to avoid a redundancy, as verse 21 begins with the same phrase. However, R' Shmuel Masnuth and Ibn Yachya render both this וְעוֹד and the וְעוֹד in verse 21: *while.*

מְדַבֵּר וּמִתְפַּלֵּל וּמִתְוַדֶּה — *Speaking, praying, and confessing.*

city upon which Your Name is proclaimed; for not because of our righteousness do we cast down our supplications before You, rather because of Your great compassion. ¹⁹ *O my Lord, heed; O my Lord, forgive; O my Lord, be attentive and act, do not delay; for Your sake, my God, for Your Name is proclaimed upon Your city and Your people.'*

²⁰ *And more I was speaking, praying, and confessing my sin and the sin of my people, Israel, and casting my supplication before HASHEM, my God,*

These are the same three categories mentioned before in verse 4. מְדַבֵּר here is identical with וָאֹמְרָה before (*Mayenei HaYeshuah* 10:2). After finishing the above-quoted prayer, and not receiving an answer from God, he commenced to pray again in the same manner.

[The prayer followed the sequence just mentioned. In verse 4, וָאֹמְרָה, *And I said*, is mentioned last because it is followed by the actual words of the prayer; it is placed last to introduce them. Here, since the text of the prayer is not recorded, the words describing the three parts are given in their actual sequence.]

חַטָּאתִי וְחַטַּאת עַמִּי יִשְׂרָאֵל — *My sin and the sin of my people, Israel.*

[See *comm.* to *v.* 4 in the name of *Alshich* and *Malbim*.]

וּמַפִּיל תְּחִנָּתִי — *And casting my supplication.*

Malbim interprets the verse thus: מְדַבֵּר וּמִתְפַּלֵּל, *speaking and praying*, are linked together — i.e., speaking in prayer. This is the first category of prayer, which is the outpouring of the soul to God through which דְּבֵקוּת, *intimacy*, with God is reached. [This is probably the same as the first category described above according

to *Abarbanel*, which is the giving of praise to HASHEM.] Then, comes וּמִתְוַדֶּה, *and confessing*. And finally וּמַפִּיל תְּחִנָּתִי, *and casting my supplication* which refers to the prayer itself.

[This interpretation leaves unexplained why a different sequence is adopted here than above (*v.* 4). Moreover the *esnachta, pause*, under יִשְׂרָאֵל signals that the phrase ends here, and consequently that וּמַפִּיל תְּחִנָּתִי is the beginning of a new thought. The coupling of תְּפִלָּה, *prayer*, with תַּחֲנוּן, *supplication*, throughout this chapter (*vs.* 3, 17) is a redundancy which needs explanation (see *comm.* to *v.* 3).

For a plausible explanation, we should define the difference between the *Tefillah* (Shmoneh Esrai) and the *Tachanun* sections of the daily prayers. *Rambam* (Hilchos Tefillah 5:1 and 13), states: 'There are eight things the person who prays should be careful to do ...*prostration.* How [is] prostration [done]? ... He sits upon the ground and falls upon his face and offers any supplication he desires.' It follows therefore that there are some basic differences between תְּפִלָּה and תַּחֲנוּן:

1) תְּפִלָּה is said standing and תַּחֲנוּן is said face down;

2) תְּפִלָּה is basically intended for כְּלָל, *the public*, whereas תַּחֲנוּן can be for private needs.

3) תְּפִלָּה has נוּסַח הַתְּפִלָּה, *a set formula*, to which additions must conform (see above v. 4). תַּחֲנוּן is prayer unfettered by any given form or formula.

Therefore, after Daniel had gone through the whole sequence necessary for תְּפִלָּה, he

כא עַל הַר־קֹדֶשׁ אֱלֹהָי: וְעוֹד אֲנִי מְדַבֵּר
בַּתְּפִלָּה וְהָאִישׁ גַּבְרִיאֵל אֲשֶׁר רָאִיתִי
בֶחָזוֹן בַּתְּחִלָּה מֻעָף בִּיעָף נֹגֵעַ אֵלַי כְּעֵת
כב מִנְחַת־עָרֶב: וַיָּבֶן וַיְדַבֵּר עִמִּי וַיֹּאמֶר

---

was free to present his private תַּחֲנוּן, *sup-plication*, free of any conventions or rules. The language used, וָמַפִּיל תְּחִנָּתִי, *casting my supplication*, is clearly reminiscent of the terminology used by the Sages and by all Jews to this day, נְפִילַת אַפַּיִם, *falling upon one's face*, which suggests the posture to be taken during this prayer as described by *Rambam*.]

עַל הַר־קֹדֶשׁ ... — *For the mountain of the Sanctuary.*

The word עַל is interpreted in the sense of בְּעַד, *for*, inasmuch as Daniel prayed that God answer his prayer for the sake of the mountain upon which the Sanctuary will be built (*Rashi*).

Ralbag suggests that it is possible to render עַל in the usual way, *on*. Daniel traveled to Jerusalem to pray *on* the Temple Mount, because the prayer would more likely be answered there.

הַר קֹדֶשׁ — *The mountain of the Sanctuary.*

I.e., the Temple Mount. The translation follows *Ibn Ezra*. If קֹדֶשׁ were to be understood as an adjective modifying הַר, *the holy mountain*, it should have read הַר הַקֹּדֶשׁ.

21. וְעוֹד אֲנִי מְדַבֵּר בַּתְּפִלָּה — *Still I was speaking in prayer.*

This refers back to the prayer mentioned in the previous verse (20; *Ibn Ezra*).

Malbim intimates from this verse that Daniel started a third round of prayer.

בַּתְּחִלָּה — *In the beginning.*

In the vision (ch. 8) which had

taken place in the third year of Belshazzar [8:1] (*Rashi*).

וְהָאִישׁ גַּבְרִיאֵל — *And the man Gabriel.*

[In 8:15-16, he is referred to similarly as גֶּבֶר, *man*. According to *Abarbanel*, who holds that Daniel's fasting and prayer were a consequence of the vision he had from Gabriel, it is very fitting that Gabriel himself returned to clarify matters for him.]

[Perhaps בַּתְּחִלָּה refers to the vision in chapter 7 where Daniel spoke to an unidentified angel (*vs.* 16-27). Thus we could render, *in the beginning vision*. Similarly, the vision in chapter 7 is referred to in chapter 8 as, *the one which had been revealed* בַּתְּחִלָּה *at first*.]

מִנְחַת־עָרֶב — *The afternoon offering.*

The תָּמִיד שֶׁל בֵּין הָעַרְבַּיִם, *tamid sacrifice of the afternoon*, is called *minchah* as evidenced in II Kings (16:15): אֵת עוֹלַת הַבֹּקֶר, *the morning burnt offering*, וְאֵת מִנְחַת הָעָרֶב, *and the afternoon offering*, and in Psalms 141:2; (*Radak* in *Shorashim* s.v. מנח).

R' Saadiah (according to an emendation by *R' S.A. Keidanover*) also renders מִנְחַת־עָרֶב the *tamid* sacrifice of the afternoon. Thus he narrows down the time Daniel was answered to the third hour of the afternoon, which is the regular time for the *tamid* (see *Pesachim* 58a).

[*R' Aharon Shmuel Keidanover*

9

21-22

for the mountain of the Sanctuary of my God. [21] *Still I was speaking in prayer, and the man Gabriel, whom I saw in the beginning vision, was lifted in flight approaching me about the time of the afternoon offering.*

[22] *He made me understand and spoke to me. And*

(*Rashak*) in his responsa (*Emunas Shmuel* 20) gives an interesting reason why the afternoon *tamid* was called *Minchah*. *Minchah* also means *gift,* as in וַתַּעֲבוֹר הַמִּנְחָה עַל פָּנָיו, *and the gift passed before him* (*Genesis,* 12:22).

The *Midrash* (*Shir HaShirim Rabbah* 1:9; *Tanchuma* to *Pinchas* 13 quoted in *Rashi* to *Isaiah* 1:21) tells us: 'A person never lodged in Jerusalem with unintentional sins to his account. Any sins done at night were atoned for by the morning *tamid,* and the sins of the day, were atoned for by the afternoon *tamid* — i.e., the הַקְטָרַת אֵימוּרִין, the fat of the day's offerings which was burned upon the altar at night (not the offering of the *tamid* itself which was done by day). Therefore, the offering of the afternoon *tamid* itself, since it was not intended to atone for sin, was called a מִנְחָה, *a gift.* This is also the reason why the corresponding afternoon prayer, *Minchah,* is so called.]

Tosafos (*Pesachim* 107a s.v. סמוך) asks why the afternoon prayer is called *Minchah.* One of the answers is that we find that the prophet Elijah's prayer was answered at the time of the *Minchah* offering — i.e., the meal offering which is usually called *Minchah* as is written (*I Kings* 18:36): *And it came to pass* בַּעֲלוֹת הַמִּנְחָה, *at the time of the meal offering.* From this the *Talmud*

(*Berachos* 6) derives that a person should always be careful to pray the *Minchah* prayer because Elijah was answered only at that time. The implication is that this time of the day is propitious for the acceptance of prayers. For this reason the prayer is called *Minchah.* (The correct reading in *Tosafos* seems to be שֶׁאָז הוּא שְׁעַת רָצוֹן not שְׁאָז הָיָה as in our editions. See *Magen Avraham* at the beginning of *Orach Chaim* ch. 232; *Tosafos Yom Tov* to Berachos 4:1; also *Shnos Eliyahu,* there). It is therefore very fitting that Daniel too was answered while praying *Minchah.* The translation should accordingly read, *At the time of the afternoon meal offering.*

However *Ramban* (*Exodus* 12:6) holds that מִנְחַת עָרֶב does not refer to the offering of the *minchah,* rather it is a name given to the *afternoon.* מִנְחָה is from נחה, *to rest,* referring to the 'resting' of the sun, when the great heat of the mid-day sun seems to relent. Similar opinions are stated by *Radak* (*Shorashim* s.v. מנח) and *Abudraham* (*Tefillas Minchah* — quoted in the margin of *Pesachim* 107a).

22. Gabriel Clarifies

וַיָּבֶן — *He made me understand.*

I.e., He made me understand the mistake I had made in my calculations [see *comm.* to *v.* 2] (*Rashi*).

The *Midrash* (*Koheles Rabbah* 9:4) understands וַיָּבֶן as referring to

---

ט
כג-כד

דָּנִיֵּאל עַתָּה יָצָאתִי לְהַשְׂכִּילְךָ בִינָה:
כג בִּתְחִלַּת תַּחֲנוּנֶיךָ יָצָא דָבָר וַאֲנִי בָּאתִי
לְהַגִּיד כִּי חֲמוּדוֹת אָתָּה וּבִין בַּדָּבָר וְהָבֵן
כד בַּמַּרְאֶה: שָׁבֻעִים שִׁבְעִים נֶחְתַּךְ עַל־עַמְּךָ|

God. Daniel said, [God]understood, therefore He has now sent His angel to speak to me.

לְהַשְׂכִּילְךָ בִינָה — To make you skillful in understanding.

The angel corrected the false understanding Daniel had of Jeremiah's prophesied seventy years (Malbim).

23. בִּתְחִלַּת תַּחֲנוּנֶיךָ — At the beginning of your supplications.

As it is written (Isaiah 65:24), Before they call I will answer (R' Saadiah).

But the vision was not revealed to you then, for you are greatly beloved. He [God] desired to hear your prayer (Koheles Rabbah 9:7 according to Radal's emendation). [God left questions in Daniel's mind so that he would pray for their resolution. God treasures the sincere prayers of righteous people.]

יָצָא דָבָר — A word went forth.

The word — i.e., the following vision (Ibn Ezra; Metzudos).

The angel told Daniel that a decree had been promulgated that the Holy Temple be rebuilt (Koheles Rabbah 9:7).

[It seems from this Midrash that if not for Daniel's prayer there was a possibility that the return prophesied by Jeremiah could have been delayed and the prophecy interpreted in some other way. Only through Daniel's prayer was this in-

terpretation adopted (see comm. to 5:26).]

כִּי חֲמוּדוֹת אָתָּה — For beloved are you.

'Three times it is written [that Daniel was] beloved (Daniel 10:11-19). He (the angel) said: 'Your Creator loves you, the heavenly host loves you, and [the people of] your generation love you' (Koheles Rabbah 9:7; see Radal).

וּבִין בַּדָּבָר — Contemplate the matter.

Abarbanel (Mayenei HaYeshuah 10:6), adhering to his theory about Daniel's worry (see comm. to v. 2), has this phrase refer to the prophecy of Jeremiah concerning the seventy years. This prophecy is called דָּבָר, statement or word, in allusion to v. 2: אֲשֶׁר הָיָה דָבָר אֶל יִרְמְיָה הַנָּבִיא, about which the word of HASHEM had come to Jeremiah. It also alludes to Jeremiah 25:3, הַדָּבָר, אֲשֶׁר הָיָה עַל יִרְמִיהוּ, the word which was upon Jeremiah, which is clarified by this prophecy.

וְהָבֵן בַּמַּרְאֶה — And gain understanding in the vision.

This refers to Daniel's vision in chapter 8 in which the part which disturbed him so (v. 14) is characterized in vs. 16-26 as a מַרְאֶה.

The other commentators (Rashi; Ibn Ezra) understand דָּבָר and מַרְאֶה to be synonymous expressions referring to the following vision.

דניאל [258]

9
23-24

he said, 'Daniel, I have just gone to make you skillful in understanding. ²³ At the beginning of your supplications a word went forth, and I have come to relate it, for beloved are you. Contemplate the matter and gain understanding in the vision. ²⁴ Seventy weeks have been decreed upon your people and your

---

24. שִׁבְעִים שָׁבֻעִים — *Seventy weeks.*

Seder Olam (ch. 28) and all the commentators, especially *Ibn Ezra,* interpret the expression to mean 490 years: *seventy weeks of years.*

[Similarly, we find (*Lev.* 25:8), *And you will count seven weeks of years* (שַׁבְּתוֹת) should be translated *weeks* just as שֶׁבַע שַׁבְּתוֹת תְּמִימֹת in *Lev.* 23:15 referring to the seven-year sabbatical cycles, is translated *weeks;* see *Onkelos* and *Yonasan* there). Also מְלֹא שְׁבֻעַ זֹאת, *fulfill the week of this one,* (*Genesis* 30:27), is understood by *Ramban* to mean seven years, a week of years.]

The Sages (*Seder Olam Rabbah* ch. 28) hold that these 490 years commenced with the destruction of the First Temple in the year 3338 from Creation (the word שלח, [=338] is used as a mnemonic device). The beginning of the restoration of the Temple in the second year of Darius the Persian (*Haggai* 1:1-8) took place seventy years later in the year 3408. The Second Temple stood 420 years (see *Yoma* 9a, *Avodah Zarah* 9a, *Arachin* 12b). This adds up to a toal of 490 years, with the destruction of the Second Temple taking place in the year 3828 (see *Avoda Zara* 9b; *Tosafos* s.v. האי).

It follows that his decree had been promulagated not later than the date of the First Temple's destruction and that it preceded Daniel's vision by 51 years (see *comm.* to v. 2; *Seder Olam, ibid.*).

This interpretation is followed by the consensus of commentators (*R' Saadiah Gaon* in *Emunos VeDeos,* 8; *Rashi; Abarbanel*).

Abarbanel and *Malbim* understand the angel's reference to seventy weeks as an additional interpretation of the seventy years of Jeremiah. These seventy years were meant as seventy weeks of years. Malbim adds to this that Jeremiah's prophecy had a dual meaning. The seventy years of exile had been in punishment for the desecration of seventy שְׁמִיטוֹת, *sabbatical years.* In *Leviticus* (26:34) God warned Israel that if they would sin, desolation would be visited upon their land and, *then the land will rest and it will atone for its sabbaths.* Thus the sin of desecrating the sabbatical years had been atoned for by the seventy-year exile in Babylon. This is seen clearly in *II Chronicles* (36:21): *to fulfill the word of HASHEM by the month of Jeremiah ... all the years of its desolation it kept the sabbath to complete seventy years.*

But in addition to the sin of desecrating sabbatical years, the Jews had committed other sins (*Yoma* 96 specifies idolatry, licentiousness, and bloodshed), throughout the period occupied by these sabbatical periods (490 years). For this, seventy years of exile would not suffice, and the full

ט ° וְלַהְתֵּם ק׳   וְעַל־עִיר קָדְשְׁךָ לְכַלֵּא הַפֶּשַׁע °וּלְחַתֵּם
כה ° חַטָּאת ק׳   °חַטָּאות וּלְכַפֵּר עָוֹן וּלְהָבִיא צֶדֶק
עֹלָמִים וְלַחְתֹּם חָזוֹן וְנָבִיא וְלִמְשֹׁחַ קֹדֶשׁ
כה   קָדָשִׁים: וְתֵדַע וְתַשְׂכֵּל מִן־מֹצָא דָבָר

period of 490 was needed as atone- ment. However because the period of the Second Temple, was not a period of גְּאוּלָה שְׁלֵמָה, *complete redemption*, it could conclude this period of atonement. (For elabora- tion of this theme see *Ramban* to *Lev.* 26:16). Had the Jews not sinned again during this period, the complete redemption would have occurred upon its completion.

According to *Abarbanel* (v. 2) that Daniel's consternation was caused by his realization that the total redemption was still far off, and would not be coming at the end of the seventy years, this verse starts the angel's reply to Daniel's request. The redemption will come as promised, but it is not a true redemption. It is part of the process of exile and atonement. The real, complete redemption is still far off in history. According to most of the commentators, who hold that Daniel erred in his calculation this verse is a new revelation not con- nected with the reply to Daniel. The reply comes in v. 25.

[*Ibn Ezra* takes a completely different view of this vision. He finds it in- congruous that the seventy years of ex- ile (punishment) should be bunched together with the 420 years of redemp- tion (see above *Abarbanel* and *Malbim* which removes this difficulty). The 490 years start from the time of Daniel's prayer. This is the meaning of *at the beginning of your supplications, a word went forth (v. 23).* The further ramifica- tions of this interpretation will be given later in the appropriate places.

Needless to say this interpretation contradicts the tradition of the Sages which gives 490 years as the total number of years between the destruc- tion of the First Temple and that of the Second Temple. It is upon this tradition that our calculation of the amount of years from creation rests. This tradition is universally accepted among Jews. Ac- cording to *Ibn Ezra* the amount of years from creation would be increased by fifty-one. Furthermore this interpreta- tion leads *Ibn Ezra* to attribute more years to the Second Temple (and to the rule of the Persians over *Eretz Yisrael*) than are assumed by the Sages according to their tradition.]

לְכַלֵּא הַפֶּשַׁע — *To terminate transgression.*

The *transgression* would be *terminated* through atonement. [See above *v.* 5 for the differences between these synonyms.]

Rashi and *Metzudos* understand this as referring to the period fol- lowing the 490 years — i.e., the exile following the destruction of the Se- cond Temple. Thus, *seventy weeks have been decreed upon your peo- ple and your city* [for relative well- being] after which the Jews will receive the remainder of their punishment in the last exile whose purpose it will be to *terminate* [i.e., *to atone for*] *transgression.*

וּלַהְתֵּם חַטָּאת — *To end* [lit. *to make whole*] *sin.*

[The translation reflects the *keri* (pronunciation). According to the *kesiv* (the spelling) it would be literally, *to seal,* וּלְחָתֵּם, indicating the same general meaning.]

9
25

holy city to terminate transgression, to end sin, to wipe away iniquity, to bring everlasting righteousness, to seal vision and prophet, and to anoint the Holy of Holies.

²⁵ And you should know and comprehend: From the emergence of the word to return and build

וּלְהָבִיא צֶדֶק עֹלָמִים — *To bring everlasting righteousness.*
It will usher in the epoch of the Messianic king.

וְלַחְתֹּם חָזוֹן וְנָבִיא — *And to seal vision and prophet.*
I.e., to fulfill the promised prophecy.

וְלִמְשֹׁחַ קֹדֶשׁ קָדָשִׁים — *And to anoint the Holy of Holies.*
[The expression refers specifically to the chamber containing the ark with the Tablets of the Law. The ark was not present in the Second Temple. The Holy Ark, the altars, and the holy vessels will be revealed through the Messianic king.]
This refers to the Third Temple, which, in contradistinction to the Second Temple, will be anointed. The Sages (*Yoma* 21b) tell us that the Second Temple, which had not been anointed (see *Tosefta Sotah* 13:2) lacked five things, among them *Shechinah*, the evident Presence (as it were) of God. But the Third Temple will be anointed, therefore, in comparison to the second, it will be a *holy of the holies* (*Malbim*).

Another view, taken by some commmentators, is that this verse, (according to *Malbim* and *Abarbanel* only the phrase *to finish the transgression*) refers to the period of the seventy weeks — i.e., the era of the Second Temple. Thus,

seventy weeks ... (during which opportunity is given) *to terminate the transgression.*

וּלְהָבִיא צֶדֶק עֹלָמִים — *To bring everlasting righteousness.*
If the Jews had repented during this period the Messianic king would have come at its termination (*Mayenei HaYeshuah* 10:6; *Malbim*).
Or: to [bring about] *the setting* [as in וּבָא הַשֶּׁמֶשׁ, *when the sun sets* (*Lev.* 22:7)] *of eternal righteousness* — i.e., the destruction of the Second Temple (*Ibn Ezra*).

וְלַחְתֹּם חָזוֹן וְנָבִיא — *And to seal vision and prophet.*
To end the era of visions and prophecy. [See *Sotah* 48b: from the time when Chaggai, Zechariah, and Malachi died, פָּסְקָה רוּחַ הַקֹּדֶשׁ, *prophecy ended.*] The beginning of the Second Temple marks the end of the glorious era of prophecy (*Ibn Ezra; R' Saadiah*).

וְלִמְשֹׁחַ קֹדֶשׁ קָדָשִׁים — *And to anoint the holy of holies.*
I.e., to build the Second Temple (*Ibn Ezra*).

25. מִן־מֹצָא דָבָר — *From the emergence of the word.*
You will now understand that from the starting point of *the word* which went forth in the *beginning of your supplications* (*v.* 23) until *to return and build Jerusalem ... will be seven weeks* (*Rashi*).

[261] *Daniel*

לְהָשִׁיב֙ וְלִבְנ֤וֹת יְרֽוּשָׁלִַ֙ם֙ עַד־מָשִׁ֣יחַ נָגִ֔יד
שָׁבֻעִ֖ים שִׁבְעָ֑ה וְשָׁבֻעִ֞ים שִׁשִּׁ֣ים וּשְׁנַ֗יִם
תָּשׁוּב֙ וְנִבְנְתָ֣ה רְח֣וֹב וְחָר֔וּץ וּבְצ֖וֹק

[The angel told Daniel that the restoration and rebuilding of Jerusalem would take place only *seven weeks* of years (forty-nine years) after the beginning of the *seventy week* (490 years) period mentioned in verse 24. Daniel had erroneously thought that 2,300 years would elapse before the rebuilding. (See *Abarbanel* to v. 2).]

From the destruction of the Temple (the starting point of this calculation) to the advent of Cyrus, fifty-one full years elapsed. [The reign of Cyrus commenced in the fifty-second year.][1] This does not however, contradict the words of the angel in any way. He is referring here to weeks of years of which there were only seven (49 years). The additional years did not add up to a week (*Rashi* and others).

From the beginning of the *word of God to Jeremiah* (v.2) until *to return and build Jerusalem ... will be seven weeks* (*Mayenei HaYeshuah* 10:6).

עַד־מָשִׁיחַ נָגִיד — [And] until *anointing the prince*.

The prince is:

— Cyrus, about whom it is written: *Thus says HASHEM to His anointed Cyrus ... He will build My city and he will let My exiles go free*

(*Isaiah* 45:1 and 13) (*Rashi*).

— Or: Yehoshua ben Yehotzadak, the High Priest who came up to *Eretz Yisrael* with the first returnees, and commenced to build an altar and offer sacrifices (*Ezra* 3:2 and *Haggai* 1:1). [He was permitted to offer sacrifices even though the Temple had not yet been rebuilt; see *Megillah* 10a and *Rashi* there s.v. קלעים] (*Mayenei HaYeshuah* 10:6 in the name of *Yossipon* ch.3).

— Or: Zerubabel ben Shealtiel, a descendant of Yechaniah (Yehoyachin) King of Judah. (For his exact genealogy see *comm.* to *I Chron.* 3:13 and *Sanhedrin* 37b). About him we are told (*Haggai* 1:1) that he was *governor of Judah*. (*Mayenei HaYeshuah* 10:6, *Kisvei HaRamban*, Vol. 1, p. 313, and *Sefer HaGeulah* ch.3 ed. Chavel p.282).

[Thus, *until the anointed prince* should be rendered as [*and*] *until ...*, because the end of the seventy years will bring about both the rebuilding and the anointing.]

These three events all coincide with the time given by the angel. Both Yehoshua ben Yehotzadak and Zerubabel apparently attained their posts upon Cyrus's proclamation. Since the offering of sacrifices commenced with the first returnees to *Eretz Yisrael*, it is reasonable to assume that Yehoshua,

---

1. This can be arrived at very simply. We know from *II Chronicles* 36:21-22 that at the advent of Cyrus seventy years had been completed. From here we see that only forty-nine years had passed. The evident solution is (see above v. 2) that there were seventy years from the first conquest of Jerusalem to the first year of Cyrus. But the completion of the redemption would be when seventy years had passed from *the desolation of Jerusalem* (v.2).

It can be demonstrated from Scripture that the time span from the first conquest of Jerusalem to the destruction of the Temple was eighteen years (See *Megillah* 11b and *comm.* to 1:1). Hence the advent of Cyrus was eighteen years before the rebuilding of the Temple and in the fifty-second year after its destruction (i.e., after fifty-one full years had passed).

9
26

Jerusalem until anointing the prince will be seven weeks, and for sixty-two weeks it will be rebuilt, street and moat, but in troubled times. ²⁶ *And after*

who is mentioned later as the High-Priest, officiated from the beginning in that capacity, same can be said for Zerubabel, who was among the first returnees (*Ezra* 2:2).]

The term מָשִׁיחַ here is not used in its literal sense, of one who is anointed with שֶׁמֶן הַמִּשְׁחָה, *the oil of anointment*, rather it is used to indicate greatness (*Metzudos*).

[*Onkelos'* persistent rendition of all forms of the root מָשַׁח as רְבוּ, *greatness* or *exaltation*, lead one to the conclusion that he considers it to be the primary meaning. See *Radak* (*Shorashim* s.v. משח and *comm.* to 2:46.]

שָׁבְעִים שִׁבְעָה — *Seven weeks.*

Here too (as in *v.* 24) weeks of *years* are meant: forty-nine years.

This phrase contains the angel's answer to Daniel. He made it clear that the year Daniel had thought to be the seventieth was really only part of the eighth week, i.e., — the 52nd year.

Ibn Ezra, in keeping with his concept that the 490 years start with the year of Daniel's vision, interprets this verse differently. The anointed prince is Nechemiah ben Chachaliah who was appointed governor of Judah in the twentieth year of Artachshast (*Nechemiah* 2:1 and 12:26). From Darius the Mede to the second year of Darius the Persian (when he permitted the Temple to be rebuilt) is nineteen years (see note to *v.* 1). Darius the Persian reigned for ten years after this (*Ibn Ezra* offers no Biblical source, but cites Persian chronicles.) Add to this twenty years of Artachshast's rule for a total of forty-nine years. Accordingly, we could

interpret *to return and build Jerusalem* in forty-nine years [*seven weeks*] beginning with the edict of Cyrus and ending with Nechemiah. As described in *Ezra* and *Nechemiah*, the returnees were hampered in their work of restoring Jerusalem until Nechemiah came and completed the walls.

וְשָׁבְעִים שִׁשִּׁים וּשְׁנַיִם — *And for sixty-two weeks.*

Sixty-two weeks come to 434 years, plus the four years remaining from the eighth week of years which had begun before the *anointed prince* reigned. [As discussed above, Cyrus reigned in the fifty-second year which used up seven weeks of years plus an extra three years that were not counted because they did not add up to a week.] We have a remainder of four from this incomplete week giving a total of 438 years. Eighteen of these years passed between Cyrus's edict and the building of the Temple which stood 420 years. The breakdown of the seventy weeks is as follows: seven full weeks before the reign of the anointed prince; sixty-two full weeks from his accession to the throne, and one divided week, part before and part after his accession (*Rashi*).

וְנִבְנְתָה — *It will be rebuilt.*

I.e., Jerusalem.

וּבְצוֹק הָעִתִּים — *But in troubled times.*

They were under the rule of the Persians, then the Greeks, and finally the Romans who oppressed them.

כו הָעִתִּים: וְאַחֲרֵי הַשָּׁבֻעִים שִׁשִּׁים וּשְׁנַיִם
יִכָּרֵת מָשִׁיחַ וְאֵין לוֹ וְהָעִיר וְהַקֹּדֶשׁ
יַשְׁחִית עַם נָגִיד הַבָּא וְקִצּוֹ בַשֶּׁטֶף וְעַד
כז קֵץ מִלְחָמָה נֶחֱרֶצֶת שֹׁמֵמוֹת: וְהִגְבִּיר
בְּרִית לָרַבִּים שָׁבוּעַ אֶחָד וַחֲצִי הַשָּׁבוּעַ
יַשְׁבִּית | זֶבַח וּמִנְחָה וְעַל כְּנַף שִׁקּוּצִים

26. יִכָּרֵת מָשִׁיחַ — *An anointed one will be cut off.*

The offering of sacrifices, represented here by the *anointed* priesthood will stop (*R' Saadiah Gaon* in *Emunos VeDeos* Ch.8).

Or, the *anointed one* may be King Agrippa II (a descendant of Herod), king of Judah at the time of the destruction of the Second Temple, who was killed (*Rashi*; see *Yossipon* ch. 47). [*Ramban* imputes this information to the Sages (וכן אמרו ז"ל יכרת וגו' זה אגריפס): as the editor notes, his source is unknown.]

Other commentators understand this to refer to the High Priest (*Mayenei HaYeshuah* 10:6; *Malbim*).

עַם נָגִיד הַבָּא — *The people of the prince who comes.*

These are the legions of Vespasian and Titus (*Rashi*).

The destruction is ascribed to the legions since Titus desired only the submission of Jerusalem, not its destruction. (*Mayenei HaYeshuah* 10:6 citing *Yossipon*).

[The alleged opposition of Titus to the destruction of Jerusalem seems to be in sharp contrast to what the *Talmud* (*Gittin* 57b) relates about his conduct. However, *Maharal* (*Netzach Yisrael* ch. 5) sees no contradiction in this and distinguishes between the external Titus, who was, as Yossipon relates, a benevolent and compassionate man, who did not wish to destroy the Temple, and the true (perhaps sub-conscious) nature of Titus. The Sages with their inspired intuition pierced the misleading veneer of Titus's disposition and saw the true Titus, whereas Yossipon, with his limited human perception, saw only outward appearances.]

וְקִצּוֹ בַשֶּׁטֶף — *But his end shall come like a flood.*

The end of the Romans who destroyed Jerusalem will be total destruction through the promised Messianic King (*Rashi*).

Alternatively, the end of Jerusalem *will be like a flood* (*Mayenei HaYeshuah* 10:6; *Malbim*)

וְעַד קֵץ מִלְחָמָה — *(And) until the end of war.*

Till after the final wars waged by the Messianic King and the war of Gog and Magog, *desolation is decreed* for the city (*Rashi*).

By the end of Titus's campaign, most of the city was destroyed. Only a small part of the city was allowed to remain (*Ibn Ezra*; *Mayenei Hayeshuah* 10:6).

27. וְהִגְבִּיר בְּרִית לָרַבִּים — *(And) he will strengthen a covenant with the great ones.*

This verse refers back to the last of the sixty-two weeks allotted to Jerusalem. The Roman emperor will

the sixty-two weeks an anointed one will be cut off and will be no more; the people of the prince who comes will destroy the city and the Sanctuary, but his end shall come like a flood. Until the end of a war, desolation is decreed! ²⁷ *He will strengthen a covenant with the great ones one week; and for half of the week he will abolish the sacrifice and offering, and upon soaring heights will the mute abominations be,*

make a firm covenant with the Jewish nation for seven years. לָרַבִּים here means with the *great ones* — the Jewish rulers, rather than its more common usage of *many* (Rashi).

וַחֲצִי הַשָּׁבוּעַ יַשְׁבִּית זֶבַח וּמִנְחָה — *And for half of the week he will abolish the sacrifice and offering.*

The Romans did not abide by their covenant, but broke their promise and *abolished the sacrifice* (Rashi; Ramban, loc. cit.; Mayenei HaYeshuah 10:6; and others).

[A literal reading of the verse implies that the sacrifice stopped three and a half years — *half a week* — before the destruction. Here again there is no clear-cut source for this in the words of the Sages. But *Yossipon* (ch.79 as amended by *Rabbi Chaim Huminer*) implies that the sacrifices stopped before the destruction of the Temple. *Yerushalmi* (*Taanis* 4:5) relates that during the Roman siege two baskets of gold coins were lowered from the city wall every day, and in return two lambs were hoisted up the wall. One day instead of lambs, pigs were given. At that hour the daily sacrifice was stopped (בּוּטַל הַתָּמִיד) and the Temple was destroyed.' The implication is that the destruction followed immediately upon the cessation of the sacrifice — not *half a week* later. The difficulty can be resolved in two ways.

1. Although all other sacrifices had to cease three and a half years before the destruction of the Temple, as foretold to Daniel, the תָּמִיד, *daily sacrifice* , was allowed to go on till the period immediately preceding the destruction of the Temple. This would not contradict our verse which mentions only זֶבַח וּמִנְחָה *sacrifice and offering*, not the *daily sacrifice*.

2. It is logical to assume that the daily payment of two baskets of gold coins could not endure very long even in peacetime, let alone during a siege. The *Talmud* (*Gittin* 56a) gives three years as the duration of the siege. We may assume that the Sages gave an approximate figure that the exact duration of the siege was, as *Yossipon* relates, 1290 days, or three and a half years. But upon closer examination one could say that the passage in *Gittin* refers only to the three years spent by Vespasian *personally* in this campaign. After three years of Vespasian's siege, the Emperor Nero died and Vespasian was apponted to replace him (ibid. 56b; *Josephus, Wars* 5:10; *Yossipon* ch. 75). Vespasian left for Rome to claim his crown and sent his son Titus to carry on the campaign. The seven months Titus required to take the city, plus his father's three years gives us the total of three and a half years mentioned in our verse (see *Josephus, Wars*, subtitles of Books 5/6).

וְעַל כְּנַף — *And upon soaring heights.*

The word כָּנָף, *wing*, is a metaphor for a high place, just as a winged bird flies high (Rashi).

שִׁקּוּצִים מְשֹׁמֵם — *The mute abominations.*

מְשׁוֹמֵם וְעַד־כָּלָה וְנֶחֱרָצָה תִּתַּךְ עַל־
שׁוֹמֵם:

א בִּשְׁנַת שָׁלוֹשׁ לְכוֹרֶשׁ מֶלֶךְ פָּרַס דָּבָר
נִגְלָה לְדָנִיֵּאל אֲשֶׁר־נִקְרָא שְׁמוֹ
בֵּלְטְשַׁאצַּר וֶאֱמֶת הַדָּבָר וְצָבָא גָדוֹל וּבִין

This refers to the temple for idol worship Hadrian erected upon the site of the Sanctuary in the aftermath of Bar-Kochba's ill-fated revolt fifty-two years after the destruction of the Temple.

[This seems to be *Rashi's* interpretation with additions from other commentators.]

Abarbanel (*Mayenei HaYeshuah* 10:6) interprets כְּנַף as *because*, (leaving unexplained the word's derivation): *Because of the abomination of the Jews*, the city and the Temple are מְשׁוֹמֵם, *desolate*.

Radak (*Shorashim* s.v. כנף) interprets עַל כְּנַף שִׁקּוּצִים, *the spread of abominations*, מְשׁוֹמֵם — *will cause people to be astonished*.

R' Avraham bar Chiya (*Megillas HaMegalleh*) renders וְעַל כְּנַף like וְעַד כְּנַף *to the corners* [*of the world*]. No doubt he follows the *Mesorah* mentioned in *Minchas Shai* that this is one of nine places where וְעַל is understood like וְעַד. Thus, *to the corners* [*of the world*] *they* [the nations ruling the world after the destruction of the Temple] *will spread abomination and desolation*.

וְעַד־כָּלָה וְנֶחֱרָצָה — *Until extermination as decreed*.

[The translation follows *Rashi*. *Radak* (*Shorashim* s.v. חרץ) interprets a similar passage in *Isaiah* (10:23) כִּי כָלָה וְנֶחֱרָצָה, *for a decreed destruction*. (חרוץ, *cut off*, is used

in the sense of *decreed* as in מִשְׁפָּטֶךָ אַתָּה חָרָצְתָּ, *you decreed laws*, in *I Kings* 20:40). The *vav*, usually *and*, is then superfluous as are many others.

עַל־שׁוֹמֵם — *Upon the abomination*.

The idols and their worshipers (*Rashi*).

[We have translated שׁוֹמֵם *abomination* even though this is the translation of שֶׁקֶץ, because the English adjective *mute* here needs an object — i.e., the mute abomination.]

Or: *Upon the desolator* — i.e., the Romans (*Ramban loc. cit.*; cf. *Radak to Shorashim* s.v. שמם).

[According to *Ibn Ezra's* interpretation of the seventy weeks, this last week of the seventy was not included in the sixty-two weeks mentioned before. In order to arrive at a total of seventy weeks, the last week spoken of here has to be added to the sum of the seven weeks in *v.* 25 and the sixty-two in *v.* 26. Probably because of the turmoil and the unrest preceeding the destruction, this week is not counted among the weeks where *it will be rebuilt, street and moat* (*v.* 25). One might argue that since, according to *Rashi* (*v.* 26), Agrippa was killed in the years before the destruction, i.e., in the seventieth week, this week is set apart so that it can be said, *And after the sixty-two, an anointed* [Agrippa, according to *Ibn Ezra*]

9   *until extermination as decreed will pour down upon the abomination.*

10   *In the third year of Cyrus, King of Persia, a*
1   *matter was revealed to Daniel, who was named Belteshazzar — the matter was true and a long time*

will be cut off. This adds another seven years to *Ibn Ezra's* calculation of the era of the Second Temple. Thus we get a total of 471 years from the building of the Temple in the second year of Darius the Persian till its destruction, fifty-one years more than allotted in the tradition of the Sages.

The Seleucid system for counting years, which was inaugurated 380 years before the destruction of the Second Temple, was still in use in *Ibn Ezra's* time. *Ibn Ezra* could not argue, therefore, that there were many more years during the last part of the Second Temple period than are indicated by that calendar. The additional fifty-one years could only have been under the earlier Persian rule. Therefore, instead of the fifty-two years allotted to the Persian era by the Sages (eighteen years from the first year of Darius the Mede to the second year of Darius the Persian and thirty-four years after the rebuilding of the Temple; see *Avoda Zara* 10a) we would have approximately 103 years.]

X

The following three chapters comprise one vision. As noted before (*prefatory notes* to 3:31-33), the chapter division is not of Jewish origin and cannot be considered authoritative.

1. Daniel's Fast

בִּשְׁנַת שָׁלוֹשׁ — *In the third year.*

[*Seder Olam* (ch. 28; see *Megillah* 11b; *Rashi* there s.v. שנים) assumes that he reigned only three years. (See note to 9:1.)]

לְכוֹרֶשׁ — *Of Cyrus.*

[This is Cyrus who reigned directly after Darius the Mede (see *comm. ibid.* and to 6:1). He was the Persian king whose proclamation (*Ezra* 1:1-5) opened the way for the first exiles to return to Jerusalem.]

דָּבָר נִגְלָה לְדָנִיֵּאל — *A matter was revealed to Daniel.*

I.e., the vision described below beginning in verse 5 (*Mayenei HaYeshuah* 11:1; *Malbim*; and similarly implied by most commentators).

According to *Ibn Ezra*, however, this vision is *distinct* from that described later in this chapter. We are only told here that a vision — meant exclusively for Daniel — was shown to him, but the vision itself is not further described.

וֶאֱמֶת הַדָּבָר — *(And) the matter was true.*

Because Daniel foresaw many strange and wondrous things in this vision, i.e., the coming of the Messiah and the resurrection of the dead

ב אֶת־הַדָּבָר וּבִינָה לוֹ בַּמַּרְאֶה: בַּיָּמִים **י**
הָהֵם אֲנִי דָנִיֵּאל הָיִיתִי מִתְאַבֵּל שְׁלֹשָׁה **ב-ג**
ג שָׁבֻעִים יָמִים: לֶחֶם חֲמֻדוֹת לֹא אָכַלְתִּי

(12:2), he needed reassurance of the veracity of his vision (*Mayenei HaYeshuah* 11:1).[1]

וְצָבָא גָדוֹל — *And a long time [off].*
The translation follows *Rashi.* There are other instances in Scripture, where the word צָבָא means *time* e.g. (*Job* 7:1) הֲלֹא צָבָא לֶאֱנוֹשׁ, *is there not time [still left to live] to man* (*Radak* to *Shorashim* s.v. צבא).

R' Saadiah Gaon (quoted by *Ibn Ezra*; see *Radak* ibid.) derives צָבָא from the Aramaic צְבָא as in וְדִי הֲוָה צָבֵא (above 5:19) *and whom he wished.* Thus: *and the desire [for the thing foretold in the prophecy] is great.*

Ibn Ezra connects וְצָבָא גָדוֹל to נִגְלָה i.e., *a prophecy and a great multitude* (of angels) *were revealed ...*

It is in this vein that our Sages say (*Yerushalmi Sanhedrin* 1:1 and *Shir HaShirim Rabbah* 1:9): R' Yochanan said: 'The Holy One, Blessed be He, does not do anything in His world until He consults with His 'cabinet' (פַּמַלְיָא שֶׁלוֹ), as it were, as it is said, 'וֶאֱמֶת הַדָּבָר וְצָבָא גָדוֹל, *the matter is "true"* [in the sense of *unchanging*] and [*has been revealed to*] *a great host.*' When is the 'seal' of the Holy One, אֱמֶת, [*unchanging*] (*as noted in Shabbos* 55a: חוֹתָמוֹ שֶׁל הקב"ה אֱמֶת — the 'seal' of the Holy One, Blessed be He, is אֱמֶת)? —When He consults with the heavenly tribunal (See *R' Saadiah*).

וּבִין אֶת הַדָּבָר — *To understand the matter.*

I.e., to understand the earlier vision. Thus, according to *Ralbag* and *Malbim* [and this seems to be the implication in *Rashi* and *Abarbanel* as well] the contextual flow of the passage is: The following matter (beginning in verse 5) was revealed to Daniel in greater detail *to allow him to understand the earlier vision.*

וּבִינָה לוֹ בַּמַּרְאֶה — *And to so explain to him through the vision.* [2]

[I.e., and to so employ the

---

1. [Sometimes a prophet foretells an event, but because of the sins of the people, it is not fulfilled. The prophecy is conditional upon the behavior of the people. See *Shabbos* 55a: Never did a favorable decree go forth from the Holy One's mouth which He retracted for evil; and *Yoma* 73b: Though a decree emanating from a prophet can be retracted, the decree emanating from the *Urim* and the *Tumim* is never retracted. Cf. *Berachos*: Every statement which has come forth from the Holy One, Blessed be He, promising good, even if the promise is conditional, has never been retracted by Him; and *HaKosev* in *Eyn Yaakov*, ibid; *Mizrachi*; *Gur Aryeh*, and *L'vush Ha'orah* to *Genesis* 32:8. *Lechem Mishneh* to *Hilchos Yesodei HaTorah* 10:4 holds that even a prophecy transmitted in the Name of God can be retracted, unless the prophet is charged with relaying the message in God's Own words.

Rambam's opinion on this is not clear. On the one hand he (uncharacteristically) quotes the passage from *Shabbos* 55a. The context, however, shows that there is no exception to this rule, for if there were exceptions no false prophet could ever be prosecuted. This is clearly seen also in his preface to his commentary to *Mishnayos* (p. 106, column 1 in *Shas Vilna*), where he asks why Jacob was afraid that his sins might cause God to alter His promise to him. There is evidence that the statement במסכת שבת ... ולא מצינו in *Rambam's* text is a marginal addition by a later scribe which found its way into the text (see חילופי נוסחאות in *Mishneh Torah*, Shulsinger, ed. and his commentary to *Mishnayos*, Kafich ed., note 2, page 6, in הקדמה).]

דניאל [268]

off — to understand the matter, and to so explain to him through the vision. ² *In those days, I, Daniel, was mourning three weeks of days.* ³ *I ate no*

medium of a vision to clarify the earlier matter entirely.]

This follows the implication of *Rashi* and the commentators cited above who perceive the word וּבִינָה as a transitive verb, synonymous with וּלְהָבֵן, to [so cause] to understand.

As *Abarbanel* explains, the following vision elaborates on the familiar theme of the Four Kingdoms, in that it adds much detail regarding the third and fourth Kingdoms, as well as references to the fifth, Messianic, Kingdom, and the *End.* Thus, earlier allusions thereby became more clear to Daniel.

Malbim develops this further and differentiates between דָּבָר and מַרְאֶה. דָּבָר refers to the words Daniel had heard from the angel (7:17; 23-27; 8:19-27; and 9:22-27); מַרְאֶה refers to the *visions* seen by Daniel (7:2-16, 19-22; 8:2-12). Both the דָּבָר, *matter*, and the מַרְאֶה, *vision*, needed further elaboration and understanding.

Ibn Ezra and *R' Shmuel Masnuth* take וּבִין, *understood*, of the preceding phrase, as imperative (צַוּוּי). Thus: *And (I was told:) 'Understand the matter.'* The word וּבִינָה,

here, is taken to be a noun — *understanding.* Thus: *And he had understanding in the vision.*

2. הָיִיתִי מִתְאַבֵּל — *I ... was mourning.*

Daniel was mourning because of Cyrus' revocation of his permission to build the Temple as told in *Ezra* (4:5; *Rashi* and others).

שְׁלֹשָׁה שָׁבֻעִים יָמִים — *Three weeks of days.*

The translation follows *Ibn Ezra, R' Saadiah,* and *Abarbanel.* Evidence for this translation is also provided by *Ralbag, Ibn Yachya,* and others.

Rashi (probably interpreting יָמִים as *years* as in *Lev.* 25:29 יָמִים תִּהְיֶה גְאֻלָּתוֹ, *its redemption shall be for [two] years*) understands that three weeks of years are meant here, i.e., twenty-one years. Daniel mourned during the eighteen years from the first of Cyrus to the second of Darius, when the Temple construction began. His three additional years of mourning could have taken place *before* Cyrus ascended his throne. Or, perhaps Daniel had vowed (for an unknown reason) to mourn for a total of twenty-one years and therefore continued to

2. R' Berechiah (*Mishnas Rabbi Eliezer Parshah* 6) comments on the nine times Scripture mentions the word מַרְאֶה in connection with Daniel's vision: 'All the prophets see the Presence of God (רָאוּ הַכָּבוֹד) through nine *visions* [i.e., the Presence of God is beyond the grasp of the human intellect. Therefore, the Presence has to be filtered as it were through different אַסְפַּקְלַרִיּוֹת, *lenses,* so as to allow the prophet to grasp whatever is being revealed to him. The Presence may be compared to the sun, which cannot be looked at without first veiling the eye to protect it from the strength of the sun's rays. So are the prophets said to need nine 'veils' to enable them to perceive the Divine Presence.] But our teacher Moses [saw] through one vision [i.e., lens] ... and so it says regarding Daniel: *And, to explain to him through the vision ...* '[He enumerates all the nine passages where מַרְאֶה, *vision,* is mentioned.]

וּבָשָׂר וָיַיִן לֹא־בָא אֶל־פִּי וְסוֹךְ לֹא־סָכְתִּי
עַד־מְלֹאת שְׁלֹשֶׁת שָׁבֻעִים יָמִים:
ד וּבְיוֹם עֶשְׂרִים וְאַרְבָּעָה לַחֹדֶשׁ הָרִאשׁוֹן
וַאֲנִי הָיִיתִי עַל־יַד הַנָּהָר הַגָּדוֹל הוּא
ה חִדָּקֶל: וָאֶשָּׂא אֶת־עֵינַי וָאֵרֶא וְהִנֵּה

mourn even while the Temple was being rebuilt.

[We may conjecture a third alternative. Having already seen that a monarch — Cyrus — could give permission to build, only to revoke his decree, Daniel may have well been unimpressed by the good will later exhibited by Darius. If so, he would have ceased his fasting not when Darius gave permission to build the Temple, but only when its construction was finally completed. If so, we can reconstruct Daniel's twenty-one years as follows: Cyrus allowed construction to begin in the first year of his reign. Presumably, his change of heart came in the next year. That was when Daniel started to fast. Seventeen years later, Darius ordered the building to start anew. Daniel continued fasting until the work was completed four years later — a total of twenty-one years.]

Abarbanel (11:1) adds that these three weeks corresponded to the three nations to which Israel would be subservient to in exile.

3. לֶחֶם חֲמֻדוֹת — *Desirable bread.*

... White (clean) bread. Similarly we find (*Genesis* 27:15) הַחֲמֻדוֹת, which *Onkelos* renders דְּכִיָתָא, *the clean ones* (*Rashi*).

Ibn Ezra and *Abarbanel* assume that the fasting mentioned in verse 2 included the *nights*. *Abarbanel*, therefore, interprets this verse,

[*even*] *desirable bread I did not eat*, i.e., even though bread is desirable (and healthy) to the body, I did not partake of it. The same holds true for meat and wine.

Malbim assumes that he fasted only during the *days*. But even when he broke his fast at night, he refrained from such tempting foods as *desirable bread* ...

[According to *Rashi's* view that this took up a span of 21 years, it is impossible that Daniel fasted continuously. Probably he fasted during the day only and ate at night, but even then, he abstained from certain foods such as white bread, meat, and wine. Or perhaps verse 2 does not mean that he fasted continuously rather, often, during this period.]

4. The Angel

לַחֹדֶשׁ הָרִאשׁוֹן — *Of* [lit. *to*] *the first month.*

According to the Torah which commands us to consider *Nissan* the first month of the year (*Exodus* 12:2) we should identify this month as *Nissan*. *Ibn Ezra* who maintains that Daniel had fasted both night and day for the twenty-one days, points out that if this month were *Nissan*, Daniel would have fasted straight through Passover. But it is difficult to believe that Daniel would not observe the *mitzvos* of matzah and the four cups of wine.

10
4-5

desirable bread, nor did meat or wine enter my mouth, nor did I anoint myself, till the completion of three weeks of days.

⁴ *On the twenty-fourth of the first month, I was on the bank of the great river, which is Chidekel.* ⁵ *I*

Ibn Ezra therefore reasons that not the first month of the *calendar year* is meant, but the year counted from the month of Cyrus' ascension to the throne. A similar instance is found in *Ezekiel* (40:1) where רֹאשׁ הַשָּׁנָה, *the beginning of the year*, refers to the month Av by reason of its being the first month of the exile.

Abarbanel (Mayenei HaYeshuah 11:1) assumes that the fast started on the first of Nissan, from when Daniel fasted continuously excepting the Sabbaths. If we allow for three Sabbaths this brings us up to the twenty fourth of Nissan. Accordingly, it *would* appear that he fasted even on the festival of Passover because he felt that the stopping of the Temple's construction warranted this. [We find a similar instance of a fast taking place on Passover in *Esther* 4:17. See *Megillah* 15a; *comm. ibid).*]

[It is not clear why *Abarbanel* feels that Daniel did not fast on the Sabbath, even though he fasted on Passover. It may be that since a person cannot exist without food for seven days (*Rambam, Hilchos Shevuos*), Daniel arbitrarily picked the Sabbath as the day when he would break his fast.]

וָאֲנִי הָיִיתִי — [*And*] *I was.*

Ralbag suggests that this was part of a prophetic *dream.* Daniel dreamed that he was at the Chidekel and that he saw *a man, but the people who were with me did not see the vision*; all this did not really happen.

Abarbanel (Mayenei HaYeshuah 11:2) objects vigorously to this. If *Ralbag* were right, these particulars would be superfluous. Besides, the Sages (see *comm.* to *v.* 7) even identify the people who were with Daniel!

[*Ralbag* is no doubt led to his opinion under the influence of *Rambam* in *Moreh Nevuchim* 2:41 (see *footnote* to 3:25, *comm.* to 8:18, ArtScroll *comm.* to *Genesis* 18:1) that angels, being noncorporeal, cannot be seen by the eye. All sighting of angels must be visionary. Additionally, *Ralbag* holds that Daniel retired from Darius' service after the miracle of the lions' pit, and settled in *Eretz Yisrael.* Thus he could not have been at the Tigris in the third year of Cyrus' reign. If we accept the first premise, that the angel actually appeared to Daniel, then we must surely assume that he lived in the exile (see note to 1:21).]

הַנָּהָר הַגָּדוֹל — *The great river.*

The *Midrash (Bereishis Rabbah* 2:17) points out that the Euphrates (פְּרָת) is called *the great river (Deut.* 1:7). However, the *Chidekel* is here called *the great* river in comparison to the river Ulai, where Daniel had seen a vision previously (8:2). *Matnos Kehunah (ibid.)* advances the possiblity that הַגָּדוֹל, *the great*, refers not to the river, but to the vision. Thus: *the river of the great [vision].*

'Even though He spoke to them (the prophets) in the exile ... He only spoke to them בְּמָקוֹם טָהוֹר, *in a pure place*, i.e., near water ... *(Mechilta* to *Exodus* 12:4).

אִישׁ־אֶחָד לָבוּשׁ בַּדִּים וּמָתְנָיו חֲגֻרִים
בְּכֶתֶם אוּפָז: וּגְוִיָּתוֹ כְתַרְשִׁישׁ וּפָנָיו
כְּמַרְאֵה בָרָק וְעֵינָיו כְּלַפִּידֵי אֵשׁ
וּזְרֹעֹתָיו וּמַרְגְּלֹתָיו כְּעֵין נְחֹשֶׁת קָלָל
וְקוֹל דְּבָרָיו כְּקוֹל הָמוֹן: וְרָאִיתִי אֲנִי
דָנִיֵּאל לְבַדִּי אֶת־הַמַּרְאָה וְהָאֲנָשִׁים
אֲשֶׁר הָיוּ עִמִּי לֹא רָאוּ אֶת־הַמַּרְאָה אֲבָל
חֲרָדָה גְדֹלָה נָפְלָה עֲלֵיהֶם וַיִּבְרְחוּ
בְּהֵחָבֵא: וַאֲנִי נִשְׁאַרְתִּי לְבַדִּי וָאֶרְאֶה

ז

ח

5. אִישׁ־אֶחָד — *A single man.*

Ralbag and *Abarbanel* identify this "man" as the angel Gabriel, the angel revealed to Daniel in his previous visions (8:16 and 9:21). Support for this view can be found in *Rashi, Tanchuma* and *Zohar Genesis* 37:5 (cf. *comm.* to 2:19) where אִישׁ is identified as the angel Gabriel. *Rashi* to 11:1 also mentions Gabriel as the angel speaking to Daniel. [On the connection between אִישׁ and גַּבְרִיאֵל see *comm.* to 9:21.]

[This view is clearly held by the Sages in the addition to the text of *Yoma* 77a. This addition, which was missing in earlier editions of the *Talmud* and was preserved in *Eyn Ya'akov,* has been reinserted into the text in the Vilna edition. There is strong proof for its veracity. It was in *Rashi's* version as seen from his commentary printed in *Eyn Ya'akov* and from his quotation of this passage in this chapter (10:12). *R' Chananel* had it in his version as did *R' Shmuel Masnuth* (10:12). It was in *Tosafos'* version (*Tosafos Yeshanim* s.v. יהבי). Moreover, the manner in which *Abarbanel* and *Ralbag* take for granted that the angel was Gabriel indicates that they drew on a well-known source, such as the *Talmud.* The entire text is also found in *Yalkut Ezekiel,* 347. Nevertheless, *Ibn Ezra* (*Perush HaKatzer* p. 12), after citing *R' Saadiah Gaon's* opinion that the angel of this chapter is Gabriel, rejects this without giving any reason for his objection.]

Ibn Yachya understands the אִישׁ, *man,* to be an anthropomorphic representation of God, similar to the אָדָם, *man,* described in the *Merkavah* of *Ezekiel* (1:27). The mystery surrounding the meaning of this vision renders it inappropriate to elaborate upon — a vision which even the prophets Chagai, Zechariah, and Malachi did not have the privilege to see. It will suffice here to quote the words of the *Yerushalmi* (*Rosh HaShanah* 2:5) in referring to the angel described here: 'He has five attributes (וְאִית בֵּיהּ חֲמֵשׁ אַפִּין) i.e., the five details described here refer to five different attributes of this angel: 1) *his body like Tarshish;* 2) *his face like the appearance of lightning;* 3) *his eyes like flaming torches;* 4) *his arms and legs like the surface of burnished copper;* 5) *the sound of his words like the sound of a multitude.*

בְּכֶתֶם אוּפָז — *With fine gold.*

The translation follows *Radak* (*Shorashim* s.v. כתם and פזז), *Metzudos,* and *R' Shmuel Masnuth. Ibn Ezra* renders כֶּתֶם as a *girdle.* Thus, *his loins were girded with a girdle of fine gold.* Yet another translation for כֶּתֶם is *pearls* (*Ibn Janach* cited by *Radak, ibid.*). Rashi renders כֶּתֶם as a combination of

10

6-7

*raised my eyes and saw, behold! a single man clothed
in linen, his loins girded with fine gold; ⁶ his body
like Tarshish, his face like the appearance of lightning, his eyes like flaming torches, his arms and legs
like the surface of burnished copper, and the sound
of his words like the sound of a multitude. ⁷ I, Daniel,
alone saw the vision; but the people who were with
me did not see the vision; indeed a great fear fell
upon them, and they fled to concealment.*

⁸ So I remained alone and saw this great vision. No

precious stones and metals; here it would mean a *girdle of fine, be-jeweled, gold.*

6. וּגְוִיָּתוֹ כְתַרְשִׁישׁ — *His body like Tarshish.*

His body was the color of a precious stone called Tarshish (*Exodus* 28:20). *Radak* (Ezekiel 1:16) says it is a bluish stone. This seems to be *Rashi's* opinion, too (see *Chullin* 91b s.v. גוייתו), as well as *Onkelos'* (כְּרוּם יָמָא) in *Exodus*. [The translation תַרְשִׁישׁ, *crystal*, in *Rashi* to *Ezekiel* (ibid) seems to be a later addition]. *R' Yosef Kara* (Ezekiel, ibid.) gives crystal as the translation. *Ibn Ezra* (Genesis 2:11) is skeptical about *R' Saadiah Gaon's* translation of the names of the precious stones. We have therefore left תַּרְשִׁישׁ, *Tarshish*, untranslated.

כְּעֵין — *Like the surface* [lit. *like the appearance*].

— The color and luster of bur-nished copper.

7. וְהָאֲנָשִׁים אֲשֶׁר הָיוּ עִמִּי — *But the people who were with me.*

The Sages maintain that the prophets Chagai, Zechariah, and Malachi were with him (*Rashi* from

Megillah 3a; see footnote to *comm.* 1:5).

אֲבָל חֲרָדָה גְדֹלָה נָפְלָה עֲלֵיהֶם — *Indeed* [lit. *but*] *a great fear fell upon them.*

Even though they did not see the vision, they felt that something awesome was happening. The Sages say (*ibid.*): 'Though they did not see, their souls in heaven saw.'

The *Talmud* (*ibid.*) adds to this: 'They were greater than he, [for] they were prophets where he was not. But he was greater than they, because he saw [the vision] whereas they did not.'

In the matter of being able to see an angel face to face Daniel was greater than they. But being prophets, they could feel the presence of a supernatural being among them (*Malbim*).

בְּהֵחָבֵא — *To concealment.*

R' Shmuel Masnuth renders the word בְּהֵחָבֵא, *in fright*. Though this fits the context very well, there is no precedent for this rendition of the root חבא. [It could be argued that the common rendition, *hiding*, is a secondary meaning evolving from the primary meaning, *fear*, the usual cause of hiding.]

אֶת־הַמַּרְאָה הַגְּדֹלָה הַזֹּאת וְלֹא נִשְׁאַר־
בִּי כֹּחַ וְהוֹדִי נֶהְפַּךְ עָלַי לְמַשְׁחִית וְלֹא
ט עָצַרְתִּי כֹּחַ: וָאֶשְׁמַע אֶת־קוֹל דְּבָרָיו
וּכְשָׁמְעִי אֶת־קוֹל דְּבָרָיו וַאֲנִי הָיִיתִי
י נִרְדָּם עַל־פָּנַי וּפָנַי אָרְצָה: וְהִנֵּה־יָד נָגְעָה
יא בִּי וַתְּנִיעֵנִי עַל־בִּרְכַּי וְכַפּוֹת יָדָי: וַיֹּאמֶר
אֵלַי דָּנִיֵּאל אִישׁ־חֲמֻדוֹת הָבֵן בַּדְּבָרִים
אֲשֶׁר אָנֹכִי דֹבֵר אֵלֶיךָ וַעֲמֹד עַל־עָמְדֶךָ
כִּי עַתָּה שֻׁלַּחְתִּי אֵלֶיךָ וּבְדַבְּרוֹ עִמִּי אֶת־
יב הַדָּבָר הַזֶּה עָמַדְתִּי מַרְעִיד: וַיֹּאמֶר אֵלַי
אַל־תִּירָא דָנִיֵּאל כִּי | מִן־הַיּוֹם הָרִאשׁוֹן
אֲשֶׁר נָתַתָּ אֶת־לִבְּךָ לְהָבִין וּלְהִתְעַנּוֹת
לִפְנֵי אֱלֹהֶיךָ נִשְׁמְעוּ דְבָרֶיךָ וַאֲנִי בָאתִי

8. A Great Vision is Revealed

וְלֹא נִשְׁאַר־בִּי כֹחַ — *No strength
remained in me.*

'When they receive prophecy
their limbs tremble and the strength
of their body weakens, and their
[personal] thoughts become confused so that the mind can be con-
centrated to understand what it will
see ... as is written about Daniel, *No
strength remained in me...*' (Rambam *Yesodei HaTorah* 7:2).

9. וּכְשָׁמְעִי אֶת־קוֹל דְּבָרָיו — *And as I
heard the sound of his words.*

The hearing of this supernaturally strong voice frightened Daniel to
the point where he fell down
prostrate, as if all his strength had
left him, and lay on the ground as if
in a deep sleep (*Malbim*).

נִרְדָּם עַל־פָּנַי — *In deep sleep upon
my face.*

Because of excessive fright
(*Rashi*).

11. The Angel Has Been Delayed

אִישׁ־חֲמֻדוֹת — *Greatly beloved man.*

The translation follows *Metzudos* and *Radak* (*Shorashim s.v.*
חמד) whose rendition is supported
by *Midrash Koheles* 9:7 (see *comm.*
to 9:23).

Rashi interprets חֲמֻדוֹת here
(unlike in 9:23) *pure.* [A similar
rendition of חֲמֻדוֹת is found above
(10:3) where לֶחֶם חֲמֻדוֹת is rendered
(by *Rashi*) clean (i.e., white) bread.
Cf. *Rashi* to Gen. 27:15.]

עָמַדְתִּי מַרְעִיד — *I stood atremble.*

[Though he had regained enough
strength to stand up as the angel
had asked him to, he still stood
trembling in fright.]

12. אֲשֶׁר נָתַתָּ אֶת לִבְּךָ — *That you
set your heart.*

Your prayer was heard even
before you started your fast. 'In the
days of *R' Zeira* [the government]
promulgated a decree that forbade

10
9-12
*strength remained in me, and my robustness changed
to pallor, and I could retain no strength. ⁹ I heard the
sound of his words, and as I heard the sound of his
words, I was in deep sleep upon my face, with my
face earthward. ¹⁰ And behold! a hand touched me
and moved me onto my knees and the palms of my
hands.*

*¹¹ He said to me, 'Daniel, greatly beloved man, un-
derstand the words that I speak to you, and stand in
your place, for now I am sent to you.' As he spoke
this matter to me, I stood atremble. ¹² He said to me,
'Do not fear, Daniel, for from the first day that you
set your heart to understand, and to fast before your
God, your words have been heard, and I came*

the Jews to fast [in time of drought
so as not to give them credit if their
prayers were successful (*Rashi*)]. So
R' Zeira said, 'Let us accept the fast
upon us, and when the decree will
be revoked we will fast [and this
will help as though we had fasted
now (*Rashi*).]'

They said to him, 'How do you
know [this will be effective
(*Rashi*)]? He said to them, 'Because
it is written: *(And) he said to me ...
from the first day that you set your
heart ... your words have been
heard'* (*Ta'anis* 8b).

נִשְׁמְעוּ דְבָרֶיךָ — *Your words have
been heard.*

We do not find the words of his
prayer recorded anywhere in Scripture [though no doubt Daniel
prayed many a prayer during his
long fast]. R' Z'ev Einhorn, in his
commentary to *Midrash Rabbah*
(*Maharzu*, to *Devarim Rabbah*
2:17), suggests a novel approach
based on evidence from the
Midrash): The prayer mentioned
here is Daniel's long prayer in ch. 9.

This vision and the one in ch. 9 are
one and the same.

[The breaking up of the vision into
two parts could be because the first part
is directed to clarifying Daniel's confu-
sion about the period of seventy years
foretold by Jeremiah (see *v.* 2), whereas
the second part (ch. 10-12) contains the
prophecy about the future of the Jews
during the Second Temple and the
promised coming of the Messianic
King. This fits in very well with Rashi's
view that the three weeks were twenty-
one years (*v.* 2). According to this view,
Daniel started his fast in the first year of
Darius the Mede. This coincides with
what Daniel says above (9:3), *with
fasting and sackcloth.* There are,
however, two problems with this. First,
as has already been pointed out above
(*v.* 2), this *midrash* interprets the three
weeks as 21 days. Second, the text upon
which this supposition is based is
questionable (see *Yalkut Yeshayah*
109).]

וַאֲנִי בָאתִי בִדְבָרֶיךָ — *And I came
because of your words.*

'I came to you with this message
because of your words.' However,
our Sages interpret this in *Yoma*

בִּדְבָרֶיךָ: וְשַׂר | מַלְכוּת פָּרַס עֹמֵד לְנֶגְדִּי   יג
עֶשְׂרִים וְאֶחָד יוֹם וְהִנֵּה מִיכָאֵל אַחַד
הַשָּׂרִים הָרִאשֹׁנִים בָּא לְעָזְרֵנִי וַאֲנִי
נוֹתַרְתִּי שָׁם אֵצֶל מַלְכֵי פָרָס: וּבָאתִי   יד
לַהֲבִינְךָ אֵת אֲשֶׁר־יִקְרָה לְעַמְּךָ בְּאַחֲרִית
הַיָּמִים כִּי־עוֹד חָזוֹן לַיָּמִים: וּבְדַבְּרוֹ עִמִּי   טו
כַּדְּבָרִים הָאֵלֶּה נָתַתִּי פָנַי אַרְצָה

(77a; see note to 10:5): *'I have* [been allowed to] *come* into the Divine presence (לְתוֹךְ הַפַּרְגּוֹד) because of your prayers and fasts. Previously I had been banished because of my defense of the Jewish People' (see *ibid.*). Now, in Daniel's merit, he had been recalled to the Divine presence (*Rashi*).

13. וְשַׂר מַלְכוּת פָּרַס — *But the heavenly prince of the Persian kingdom.*

[I.e., the angel appointed as caretaker of the affairs of Persia.]

עֹמֵד לְנֶגְדִּי — *Stood opposed to me* [lit. *was standing against me.*]

The *heavenly prince of the Persian kingdom* had been petitioning for additional longevity for his proteges throughout these 21 days and I have been fighting his petition (*Rashi*).

[It stands to reason that these 21 days, are identical with the 21 days of Daniel's mourning (above v. 2). It follows that here, too, years are meant. Hence, this vision took place not in the third year of Cyrus, but during the rule of Darius the Persian (see above v. 2). The angel was imparting to Daniel that these 21 years (the fall of Babylon, the start of reconstruction of the Temple in the first year of Cyrus's reign, the

subsequent revocation of Cyrus's edict, and the renewed construction of the Temple at the time the angel was speaking) were due to the relative position of the angels assigned to the respective nations, not to the apparent political causes.]

I would have come to you *from the first day that you set your heart* ... but have been delayed these 21 days through the *heavenly prince of the Persian kingdom* (R' Saadiah, *Mayenei HaYeshuah* 11:2).

הַשָּׂרִים הָרִאשֹׁנִים — *Of the foremost heavenly princes.*

I.e., one of the most eminent of the angels (*Rashi*).

[In the heavenly tribunal, Michael is prince of Israel, as seen in v. 21 (מִיכָאֵל שַׂרְכֶם, *Michael your heavenly prince*). *Ramban* (*Lev.* 18:28), however, differentiates between Michael and the other angels cast in the position of *heavenly princes*. Whereas the other angelic princes actually have hegemony over their charges, Israel's prince is different because *HASHEM's portion is His People* (*Deut.* 32:9), unlike the other nations who are under the guidance and rule of their *heavenly prince*. This is what Moses means When he admonishes the Jews: *Take heed unto yourselves ... lest you lift up*

10

13-16 because of your words. ¹³ But the heavenly prince of the Persian kingdom stood opposed to me for twenty-one days, when, behold! Michael, one of the foremost heavenly princes, came to help me, and I remained there beside the kings of Persia. ¹⁴ I have come to make you understand what shall befall your people in the End of Days, for there is yet a vision for the days.'

¹⁵ As he spoke these words to me, I set my face toward the ground, and was dumbfounded. ¹⁶ And

your eyes, and see ... all the host of heaven ... which HASHEM your God has allotted unto all the peoples under the whole heaven. You, however, HASHEM has taken (Deut. 4:15-20). Therefore, Michael's role is only that of an advocate for his People, which role he filled perfectly, as seen in this verse.]

וַאֲנִי נוֹתַרְתִּי שָׁם — And I remained there.

To counteract the petitions of the heavenly prince of the Persian kingdom (Rashi).

[This is a recapitulation of what the angel has told Daniel up to now.]

Malbim sees this as prophetic symbolism representing the welfare of the Jews from that time on in the Persian empire. I remained — i.e., my influence is now acknowledged by the heavenly prince of the Persian kingodm.

14. וּבָאתִי לַהֲבִינְךָ — (And) I have come to make you understand.

Though I have used my influence to insure your well-being under the Persians, do not be lulled into a false sense of security.

אֵת אֲשֶׁר־יִקְרָה — What shall befall.

Other empires will yet rule over the Jews where I have not been able to make my influence felt (Malbim).

כִּי־עוֹד חָזוֹן לַיָּמִים — For there is yet a vision for the days.

There is yet a vision to be revealed to you which will only be fulfilled in the many days allotted till the קֵץ, End (Rashi).

[The יָמִים, days, of our verse are synonymous with the יָמִים רַבִּים, many days, of 8:26. Daniel is being told that there are more visions which will allude to the occurrences that will take place during the years leading up to the final קֵץ End.

The apparent meaning of this is that the יָמִים רַבִּים, many days, mentioned in 8:26 as being indicated by the vision of the night and the morning are contained in the עִדָּן וְעִדָּנִין וּפְלַג עִדָּן, time and times and half a time of 7:25 which is interpreted in 12:7 as מוֹעֵד מוֹעֲדִים וָחֵצִי (see comm. there). Hence, the visions of what is yet to come will be fulfilled in the יָמִים רַבִּים, many days allotted for the מוֹעֵד, term, that precedes the End — i.e., מוֹעֵד מוֹעֲדִים וָחֵצִי.]

There is yet a vision about the suppression of the Jewish people

טז וְנֶאֱלָמְתִּי: וְהִנֵּה כִּדְמוּת בְּנֵי אָדָם נֹגֵעַ
עַל־שְׂפָתָי וָאֶפְתַּח־פִּי וָאֲדַבְּרָה וָאֹמְרָה
אֶל־הָעֹמֵד לְנֶגְדִּי אֲדֹנִי בַּמַּרְאָה נֶהֶפְכוּ
יז צִירַי עָלַי וְלֹא עָצַרְתִּי כֹּחַ: וְהֵיךְ יוּכַל
עֶבֶד אֲדֹנִי זֶה לְדַבֵּר עִם־אֲדֹנִי זֶה וַאֲנִי
מֵעַתָּה לֹא־יַעֲמָד־בִּי כֹחַ וּנְשָׁמָה לֹא
יח נִשְׁאֲרָה־בִי: וַיֹּסֶף וַיִּגַּע־בִּי כְּמַרְאֵה אָדָם
יט וַיְחַזְּקֵנִי: וַיֹּאמֶר אַל־תִּירָא אִישׁ־חֲמֻדוֹת
שָׁלוֹם לָךְ חֲזַק וַחֲזָק וּכְדַבְּרוֹ עִמִּי
הִתְחַזַּקְתִּי וָאֹמְרָה יְדַבֵּר אֲדֹנִי כִּי
כ חִזַּקְתָּנִי: וַיֹּאמֶר הֲיָדַעְתָּ לָמָּה־בָּאתִי
אֵלֶיךָ וְעַתָּה אָשׁוּב לְהִלָּחֵם עִם־שַׂר פָּרָס

which will come to pass in the days yet to come — i.e., under the Greeks and the Romans (Malbim).

16. Daniel's Fright

כִּדְמוּת בְּנֵי אָדָם — *One in human likeness* [lit. *in the likeness of the sons of man*].

The angel was changed from the awesome figure portrayed above into something like a man, so as to comfort Daniel and take away his fright (R' Saadiah, Metzudos).

בַּמַּרְאָה — *In the vision.*

In the previous part of the vision (vs. 5-9); *my joints shuddered* from fright (R' Saadiah; Metzudos).

Malbim takes an opposite view of this verse. Having become accustomed to the previous part of the vision, Daniel's fright was allayed somewhat. But when the angel assumed a new form for this part of the vision, his extreme fright returned.

נֶהֶפְכוּ צִירַי עָלַי — *My joints shuddered.*

I.e., Daniel trembled so much that he felt as though his limbs were being dislocated (Rashi).

R' Shmuel Masnuth derives צִירַי from צִירִים וַחֲבָלִים (Isaiah 13:8), *pangs and throes.*

17. עֶבֶד אֲדֹנִי זֶה — *This servant of my lord.*

He called the angel directly addressing him now: *my lord*, and himself, *servant*, i.e., How can I, *your* servant, speak with you (Rashi)?

R' Saadiah interprets: *How can this servant of my lord* — i.e., Daniel refers to himself as the servant of *the angel whom he saw in the first part of the vision* (5-15) — speak with אֲדֹנִי זֶה *this my lord* — i.e., with the angel now facing him.

וַאֲנִי מֵעַתָּה — *And as for me.*

Even now that I have recovered from my initial shock, I still do not

10

17-20 *behold! one in human likeness was touching my lips. I opened my mouth and spoke, and I said to the one standing opposite me, 'My lord, in the vision my joints shuddered, and I could retain no strength. ¹⁷ How can this servant of my lord speak with this lord of mine? And as for me, from now on my strength shall not remain with me, nor is breath left in me.'*

¹⁸ Then he touched me again — the likeness of a man — and strengthened me. ¹⁹ He said, 'Fear not, greatly beloved man. Peace to you; grow stronger and stronger.'

As he spoke to me, I strengthened myself, and I said, 'Speak, my lord, for you have strengthened me.'

²⁰ He said, 'Do you know why I came to you? Now I will return to battle with the heavenly prince of Per-

---

feel strong enough to talk to you. The previous fright has drained my strength (*Metzudos*).

18. The Angel Strengthens Daniel

כְּמַרְאֵה אָדָם — *The likeness of a man.*

While still in the guise of a man, he touched me again (*Metzudos*).

וַיְחַזְּקֵנִי — *And strengthened me.*

With his encouraging words (v. 19) (*Mayenei HaYeshuah* 11:2; *Metzudos; Malbim*).

19. חֲזַק וַחֲזָק — *Grow stronger and stronger* [lit. *grow strong and grow strong*].

חֲזַק, *grow strong*, in body, וַחֲזָק, *and grow*, in spirit (*Mayenei HaYeshuah* 11:1; *Malbim*).

20. וַיֹּאמֶר הֲיָדַעְתָּ — *(And) he said, Do you know ... ?*

This is a rhetorical question. Now you know that my intentions are

just to help you. Thus: [*Now*] *do you know why I have come to you?* (*Metzudos*).

וְעַתָּה אָשׁוּב — *(And) now I will return.*

Though I have already achieved victory in my first battle with the *heavenly prince of the Persian Kingdom* (v. 13) — the sending up of the exile to *Eretz Yisrael* in the first year of Cyrus — I still have another battle to fight, for the rebuilding of the Temple was stopped in the days of Cyrus (*Mayenei HaYeshuah* 1:2).

[This follows *Abarbanel's* interpretation that the three weeks were weeks of days, hence, this vision occurred in the third year of Cyrus before the rebuilding of the Temple started again. According to *Rashi*, the angel revealed himself to Daniel not before the second year of Darius the Persian (see above v. 2 and 13), after the end of Cyrus's reign. If so, the *heavenly prince of Persia* could refer to the trouble the Jews had over the erection

כא וַאֲנִי יוֹצֵא וְהִנֵּה שַׂר־יָוָן בָּא: אֲבָל אַגִּיד
לְךָ֖ אֶת־הָרָשׁוּם בִּכְתָב אֱמֶת וְאֵין אֶחָד
מִתְחַזֵּק עִמִּי עַל־אֵלֶּה כִּי אִם־מִיכָאֵל
א שַׂרְכֶם: וַאֲנִי בִּשְׁנַת אַחַת
לְדָרְיָוֶשׁ הַמָּדִי עָמְדִי לְמַחֲזִיק וּלְמָעוֹז לוֹ:

of the wall around Jerusalem in the twentieth year of Artachshast as related in *Nechemiah* (ch. 1-2).]

וַאֲנִי יוֹצֵא — *Then* [lit. *and*] *I shall depart.*

Though I was able to exert influence in the favor of the Jews during the hegemony of the Persians, when the time comes for the *heavenly prince of Greece* — i.e., for Greek domination of the Jewish exile — *I must depart*, i.e., my presence will not be able to make its influence felt. Hence, the exile under the Greeks will not be as mild and benevolent as under the Persians (*Rashi; Mayenei HaYeshuah* 11:2; *Malbim*).

21. אֲבָל אַגִּיד לְךָ — *However, I will tell you.*

Though I cannot be of help against the Greeks as I was with the Persians, *I will* at least forewarn and *tell you* what is to befall your nation (*Mayenei HaYeshuah* 11:2; *Malim*).

The repressions will be much easier to bear with the knowledge that they were foreseen and their end had been prophesied (*Mayenei HaYeshuah ibid.*).

אֶת־הָרָשׁוּם — *What is inscribed.*

I.e., those events which are part of the Divine knowledge of the future and which can be changed through repentance and good deeds. These events are considered to be only *inscribed* — not signed and sealed with the Divine seal as ir-

revocable Divine decrees. However, the events the angel is going to tell Daniel about are not only inscribed, but בִּכְתָב אֱמֶת, *in truthful* [in the sense of *unchanging, irrevocable* (See comm. to v. 1)] writing.

I.e., they have been already decreed and irrevocably sealed (from *Mayenei HaYeshuah* 11:2; *R' Shmuel Masnuth*).

The same idea is expressed by the Sages (*Yevamos* 105b quoted in the above) who ask concerning this phrase: 'Is there a [Divine] writing which is not true [i.e., *irrevocable*]? R' Shmuel bar Ami said, ... A decree with an accompanying oath cannot be rescinded' [i.e., even prayer would be of no avail. See *Rosh HaShanah* 18a].

Thus, a decree unaccompanied by an oath, since it can be revoked through repentance and prayer, is not considered absolute אֱמֶת, *truth.*

[*Yerushalmi*, (*Rosh HaShanah* 2:5) answers the same question slightly differently: Before the decree is signed it is not considered אֱמֶת, *true*. Only after it has been signed can it be considered *true. Shir HaShirim Raba* (1:9) adds to this that אֱמֶת, *truth*, is the seal of HASHEM (See *Shabbas* 55b). Thus we read here, *what is inscribed* with [the seal] אֱמֶת, *truth* [affixed to it]. 'Resh Lakish said, Why is [the seal] אֱמֶת? Because *alef* (the first letter of אֱמֶת) is the first letter of the Hebrew alphabet, *mem* the middle letter, and *tav* the final letter, as if to say: I am first and I am last and there is no God other than Me' (*Isaiah* 44). Since everything owes its

sia; then I will depart — but behold! the heavenly prince of Greece approaches. ²¹ However, I will tell you what is inscribed in truthful writing. And no one reinforces me against these, except your heavenly prince, Michael.'

11
1-2

'And I, in the first year of Darius the Mede, I stood up as a support and stronghold for him. ² Now,

origin and existence to God, that which is decreed and sealed by Him must ultimately come true.

[Upon reflection, there is no contradiction between the *Bavli* and the *Yerushalmi*. In *Rosh Hashanah* (18a) we find total agreement that where the public (צבור) is concerned, a decree (גְזַר דין) can be revoked through prayer. Only when an oath accompanies the decree does it become irrevocable. Since this decree concerned the whole of the Jewish nation, it needed an oath to make it irrevocable. Thus, we may conclude that the oath, as the ingredient which gives the decree the stamp of permanency, is synonymous with the seal and signature of HASHEM which is אֱמֶת, *truth*. This is possibly what *Maharasha* in *Chidushei Agados* to *Yevamos* 105 is trying to convey, but the printed version has apparently been corrupted.]

בְּכְתָב אֱמֶת — *In truthful writing.*

[From *Rashi* to *Yevamos* (105 s.v. אבל אגיד) it is evident that בְּכְתָב , *in writing*, should be read together with רְשׁוּם, *inscribed* (רְשׁוּם בְּכְתָב). As much is suggested by the cantillation. Thus, *that which is inscribed with writing [and is]*

true. The language of *Bavli, Yerushalmi*, and *Midrash* (quoted above) suggest this rendition. The question they pose can easily be answered were the Talmud's rendition of the phrase like ours. However, the translation groups בְּכְתָב with אֱמֶת — thus; *with a true writing* — since this rendition fits the context better and is adopted by the commentators.]

וְאֵין אֶחָד — *And no one.*

In the whole heavenly host, representative of all the nations, there is *no one* on whom I can count to help save Jewry from its oppressors except for Michael (*Mayenei HaYeshuah* 11:2).

כִּי אִם־מִיכָאֵל שַׂרְכֶם — *Except your heavenly prince, Michael.*

In his capacity as *heavenly prince* of the Jewish People, he is empowered occasionally to save his people in supernatural ways despite the wishes of the heavenly host (*Malbim*).

XI

This chapter and chapter twelve, are part of the vision begun in 10:5.

1. Three more Persian kings.

וַאֲנִי בִּשְׁנַת אַחַת — *And I, in the first year.*

The speaker is still the angel, Gabriel. He declares that when Darius the Mede became king of the

empire, the Persian and Median nobles wished to oppress the Jews. Then *I stood up as a support and stronghold for him* — i.e., *for Michael*, the previously mentioned *heavenly prince* of the Jews (*Rashi*).

ב וְעַתָּה אֱמֶת אַגִּיד לָךְ הִנֵּה־עוֹד שְׁלֹשָׁה
מְלָכִים עֹמְדִים לְפָרַס וְהָרְבִיעִי יַעֲשִׁיר
עֹשֶׁר־גָּדוֹל מִכֹּל וּכְחֶזְקָתוֹ בְעָשְׁרוֹ יָעִיר
ג הַכֹּל אֵת מַלְכוּת יָוָן: וְעָמַד מֶלֶךְ גִּבּוֹר
ד וּמָשַׁל מִמְשָׁל רַב וְעָשָׂה כִּרְצוֹנוֹ: וּכְעָמְדוֹ

Abarbanel (*Mayenei HaYeshuah* 11:2) construes this in a contrary sense. In his interpretation of our verse, Gabriel describes himself as a supporter of Darius. When Darius ascended to his throne he was favorably disposed toward the Jews. It was then that *I — Gabriel — stood up as a support ... for him —* Darius. *Abarbanel* distinguishes between the situation in 10:20, where toward the end of Cyrus' rule, the edict to rebuild the Temple was revoked, and, — *I will return to fight with the heavenly prince of Persia* ... But in *the first year of Darius the Mede I stood up as a support ...*

2. אֱמֶת אַגִּיד לָךְ — *The truth will I tell you.*

[Obviously, this verse continues from where verse 21 (chapter 10) was interrupted. With the mention of Michael's name, the angel digressed to mention the aid he had rendered Michael. (According to *Abarbanel* the sequence of the verses is left unexplained.) Now the angel goes back *to tell ... what is inscribed in truthful writing* as he promised above (*v.* 20) and recapitulates, *Now the truth will I tell you ...*]

הִנֵּה־עוֹד שְׁלֹשָׁה מְלָכִים — *Behold! three more kings.*

The Sages (*Seder Olam Rabbah* ch. 30) identify the three as Cyrus, Ahasuerus, and Darius [the Per-

sian] who built the Temple. That which is written, *and the fourth,* includes Darius the Mede.

However, *Yossipon* (ch. 3) writes that Cyrus had a son named Cambyses who reigned after him [Thus without counting Darius the Mede we have four kings.] (*Rashi, Rav Saadiah Gaon* quoted by *Ibn Ezra*).

The *Vilna Gaon* (Glosses to *Seder Olam*) holds that *Seder Olam* does not count Cambyses because his reign lasted only one half year. [It follows from this that it was Darius the Persian who was vanquished by Alexander the Great (see *v.* 3). However, there are other Persian kings named in Scripture. In *Ezra* (4:7) we find the enemies of the Jews writing to Artachshasta (mentioned after Ahasuerus in *v.* 6) not to allow the construction of the Temple to proceed. *Rashi (ibid.)* identifies him as Darius. *Ibn Ezra* (here) and *Ralbag* (there) say he is Ahasuerus. *Ibn Ezra* adds that *Ezra* 4:6, written in Hebrew, has the Hebrew version of the name — אחשורוש, Ahasuerus, but 4:7, in Aramaic, uses his Babylonian name, Artachshasta. We find the name Artachshast throughout *Ezra* 4 (also, *Ezra* 6:14; chapters 7-8; *Nechemiah* 2:1, and 5:14, and 13:6). Since the reign of Darius reaches to Alexander's takeover of the Persian empire, we are forced to conclude with *Rashi* that Artachshast is identical with Darius the Persian. This is probably the reasoning behind *Seder Olam* (ch. 30) quoted in *Rosh HaShanah* (2b) that 'Darius is the same as Artachshast (also Artachshasta mentioned in *Ezra* 4:7) because all the kings are named Artachshast,' like the Egyptian kings who were all titled Pharaoh (*Rashi* to *Ezra* 6:14). This view is also brought out in *Yossipon* (ch. 3-4).]

[*Ibn Ezra*, because of the difficulty of counting the three kings from Cyrus and the four kings from Darius the Mede rejects this interpretation. In his opinion, *three more*

11
3

the truth will I tell you. Behold! three more kings will arise for Persia, and the fourth shall acquire the greatest wealth of them all, and when he grows strong with his riches, he will arouse all against the kingdom of Greece. ³ A mighty king shall arise and shall rule with great domination, and shall do as he

---

kings excludes Cyrus, in whose reign this vision took place. This is indicated by the word עוֹד, *more. And the fourth* includes Cyrus as the first. The chronology of the kings is 1. Cyrus; 2. Ahasuerus (the husband of Esther) who is identical with Artachshasta of *Ezra* 4. Darius, under whose rule the Temple was rebuilt; 4. Artachshast (in *Ezra* 6-8, *Nechemiah* 2 and 5), under whose rule Nechemiah rebuilt the walls of Jerusalem. Since he is the last of the Persian kings, and must therefore be the king who was beaten and killed by Alexander, he must also have been named Darius, since this is known to be the name of the Persian king defeated by Alexander. He thus arrives independently at the same conclusion as the Sages (*Rosh HaShanah* 2b) that Artachshast was a generic name used by all the Persian kings. This view is also adopted by *Ralbag, Ibn Yachiah,* and *Malbim.*]

וּכְחֶזְקָתוֹ בְעָשְׁרוֹ — *When he grows strong with his riches.*

The fourth king — according to *Rashi* is Darius the Persian, son of Ahasuerus. According to *Ibn Ezra,* he is Artachshast who reigned after Darius, and is called Darius II.

יָעִיר הַכֹּל — *He will arouse all.*

All the members of his kingdom will be stirred up to fight with the Greeks. *Rashi* interprets אֵת מַלְכוּת יָוָן, 'against' *the kingdom of Greece.* [For the use of אֵת in this sense see *Ibn Ezra* 10:13 who points out that אֵת and עִם, when used together with מִלְחָמָה, *war,* are used in just this way.]

Ibn Ezra renders this in a contrary sense: Because of his ill-gotten riches *he will arouse everyone*

together with the kingdom of Greece against himself.

[Historically, the Persian kings formed alliances with many nations, some of them Greek, in their campaigns against the Greek city-states.]

3. וְעָמַד מֶלֶךְ גִּבּוֹר — *A mighty king shall arise.*

This is Alexander the Great, the Macedonian (*Rashi* and *comm.* from *Seder Olam Rabbah* chapter 30).

[No doubt this was one of the passages in *Daniel* shown to Alexander when he was greeted on the outskirts of Jerusalem by the High Priest dressed in his priestly vestments as related by Josephus in *Antiquities* (11,8,5). Josephus' story parallels (in most of its particulars) the Sages in *Yoma* (69a) citing *Megillas Taanis* (ch. 9). That Alexander was shown the Book of *Daniel* is not related there, but that part of the story is not pertinent to the purpose of the *Talmud,* which is to explain the nature of the holiday commemorating the victory of the Jews over the Samaritans (כּוּתִים) as related in the *Talmud* and by Josephus.]

וְעָשָׂה כִּרְצוֹנוֹ — *And shall do as he pleases.*

He will conquer the nations with such speed and ease that it will seem that once he decides to do

תִּשָּׁבֵר מַלְכוּתוֹ וְתֵחָץ לְאַרְבַּע רוּחוֹת
הַשָּׁמָיִם וְלֹא לְאַחֲרִיתוֹ וְלֹא כְמָשְׁלוֹ
אֲשֶׁר מָשָׁל כִּי תִנָּתֵשׁ מַלְכוּתוֹ וְלַאֲחֵרִים
ה מִלְּבַד־אֵלֶּה: וְיֶחֱזַק מֶלֶךְ־הַנֶּגֶב וּמִן־שָׂרָיו

---

something, no obstacle can stand in his way (Ralbag).

4. וּבְעָמְדוֹ — But when he has arisen.

I.e., when he will reach the peak of his strength (Rashi).

[Alexander died after a nearly unbroken series of victories which had made him master, first over all the Greek city-states, and then over the whole Near East up to India.]

Ibn Ezra seemingly renders וּבְעָמְדוֹ, and as soon as he has risen. This verse then refers to Alexander's extreme youth at his death. He was only 33 years old when he died of a fever in Persia after having been king of Macedonia for twelve years.

תִּשָּׁבֵר מַלְכוּתוֹ — His kingdom shall be broken.

His kingdom shall break of its own accord without being conquered by another king (it does not say יִשָּׁבֵר, he will break, but תִּשָּׁבֵר, will be broken.). Alexander's sudden demise left his huge empire without a proper successor (Ralbag).

וְתֵחָץ לְאַרְבַּע רוּחוֹת הַשָּׁמָיִם — And be divided toward the four directions of the heaven.

The huge empire was broken up by Alexander's generals into four smaller empires. This is the meaning of the leopard with four wings and four heads that Daniel had been shown earlier (7:6). The same meaning is inherent in the vision of

the he-goat whose single horn broke and was replaced by four horns (8:8). These four kingdoms were situated along the four directions of the compass, north, south, east, and west (Rashi).

[These four empires were Macedonia in the west, Egypt in the south, Syria (and Babylon) in the north, and Persia in the east. The prophet uses Eretz Yisrael as the focal point in giving the directions of the four empires. Persia is due east; Syria-Babylon are northern by comparison with Persia. Babylon (Iraq) stretches to the northwest. Elsewhere in Scripture, Babylon is indeed referred to as north: מִצָּפוֹן תִּפָּתַח הָרָעָה, From the north [Babylon] will the evil begin (Jeremiah 1:14). Macedon, although it is to the northwest, is called the western kingdom because it is much further west than north.]

וְלֹא לְאַחֲרִיתוֹ — But not to his posterity.

His children will not inherit his kingdom (Rashi).

אַחֲרִיתוֹ, (lit. his posterity after him) is used as a synonym for children (similar to the English posterity) because that is what a father leaves in this world after himself (Metzudos).

[Alexander left two sons, Heracles, an illegitimate son, and Alexander IV Aegus born posthumously. Both were killed in their childhood during the tumultuous years following Alexander's demise.]

11
4-5

pleases. 4 But when he has arisen, his kingdom shall be broken, and be divided toward the four directions of the heaven — but not to his posterity, nor like his domination with which he ruled, for his kingdom shall be uprooted and for others besides these.

5 'The king of the south shall grow stronger — and than his nobles. And he shall overpower him and

וְלֹא כְמָשְׁלוֹ אֲשֶׁר מָשָׁל — *Nor like his domination with which he ruled.*

None of these kingdoms will have the power of Alexander's original empire *(Rashi, Ibn Ezra).*

כִּי תִנָּתֵשׁ מַלְכוּתוֹ — *For his kingdom shall be uprooted.*

To be divided into these four principal kingdoms.

וְלַאֲחֵרִים — *And for others beside these.*

There will be other, minor, kingdoms besides these four major ones *(Rashi, Ibn Ezra).*

◈§ Prefatory Note to verses 5-39

Since Rashi does not identify the *king of the north,* nor does he discuss the historical particulars of the kingdoms mentioned here, we will here primarily follow the interpretation of *Abarbanel* which is also adopted by *Malbim.* [Although *Rashi* comments in *vs.* 16-19 that the king of the north is Antiochus IV, he refers only to the king mentioned in those verses. *Rashi* does not identify the king elsewhere in the chapter.] *Malbim's* interpretation deals much more with the wording of the text and updates much of *Abarbanel's* historical data. We refer to it as the primary interpretation; therefore, the source need not be mentioned each time. Wherever necessary, more historical data and additonal interpretation have been added in brackets.

Following each complete verse, is given the gist of *Rashi's* interpretation. At *v.* 40 (where the angel switches to the prophecy of *the time of the End*) some of the other interpretations will be summarized. The complexity of the material precludes elaboration on all these interpretations. Wherever dates have been converted from the Seleucid calendar (מִנְיַן שְׁטָרוֹת) the year 3448 has been assumed as the starting point for this calendar (See *Rambam Hilchos Kiddush HaChodesh* 17:16; *Responsa Ralbach,* 143; *Zemach David* 3448).

5. The King of the South

וְיֶחֱזַק מֶלֶךְ הַנֶּגֶב — *The king of the south shall grow stronger.*

Of the four kingdoms mentioned in *v.* 4 only two had any lasting importance — the 'southern' — Egypt, whose ruler, Ptolemy I Soter son of Lagos founded the Ptolemaic dynasty, and the 'northern' — Syria, where Seleucus I Nicator son of Antiochus founded the Seleucid dynasty.

The king of the south, Ptolemy I,

grew very strong.

[In the 20 years following Alexander's death, Ptolemy emerged as a leading force, counting *Eretz Yisrael* among his conquests.]

וּמִן שָׂרָיו — *And than his nobles.*

The translation follows *Rashi, Ibn Ezra,* and *Metzudos.*

Thus: *The king of the south will grow stronger than [his opponent, the king of the north] and than his (the king of the north's) nobles.*

Abarbanel giving other examples

וְיֶחֱזַק עָלָיו וּמָשָׁל מִמְשָׁל רַב מֶמְשַׁלְתּוֹ:
ו וּלְקֵץ שָׁנִים יִתְחַבָּרוּ וּבַת מֶלֶךְ־הַנֶּגֶב
תָּבוֹא אֶל־מֶלֶךְ הַצָּפוֹן לַעֲשׂוֹת מֵישָׁרִים
וְלֹא־תַעְצֹר כּוֹחַ הַזְּרוֹעַ וְלֹא יַעֲמֹד וּזְרֹעוֹ
וְתִנָּתֵן הִיא וּמְבִיאֶיהָ וְהַיֹּלְדָהּ וּמַחֲזִקָהּ

of this usage, renders this as though it were written מִן שָׂרָיו without a *vav*. Thus; *The king of the south, one of his* — i.e., Alexander's — *nobles, will grow strong.*

[Ptolemy, a Macedonian nobleman, had been one of Alexander's most trusted generals and one of his seven 'bodyguards.']

Malbim joins וּמִן שָׂרָיו to the following וְיֶחֱזַק עָלָיו. Thus: *and [one] of his princes will become stronger than he.* Seleucus I had been one of Ptolemy's generals who later defected and threatened his former master's empire. [After he had been established as ruler of Babylonia, Seleucus I had to flee because of the territorial expansionism of the Persian ruler, Antigonus. He took refuge with Ptolemy and actively participated in the latter's campaign against Antigonus. When Antigonus was defeated, Seleucus returned to his kingdom.]

מִמְשָׁל רַב מֶמְשַׁלְתּוֹ — *His dominion shall be a great dominion.*

Malbim renders מֶמְשַׁלְתּוֹ as if it were מִמֶּמְשַׁלְתּוֹ. Thus, *and he will rule [and] his dominion will be greater 'than' his* [the king of the south's] *dominion.*

[After Antigonus' defeat, Seleucus I returned to Babylon. He then proceeded to enlarge his kingdom eastward to India, and westward to Syria, where he built his capital, Antioch, and the Mediterranean. He

continued his expansion until his kingdom included all of Alexander's Asian conquests. He was killed while on a campaign to conquer Macedonia.]

6. וּלְקֵץ שָׁנִים יִתְחַבָּרוּ — *And at the end of years they shall join together.*

After fighting for many years, Antiochus II Theos (son of Antiochus I Soter, son of Seleucus I Nicator) concluded a peace agreement with Ptolemy II Philadelphus (son of Ptolemy I and sponsor of the Greek translation of the Bible, the *Septuagint*).

[Fighting broke out over the dominion of *Eretz Yisrael*, which had originally been under Ptolemy. Seleucus I, however, considered *Eretz Yisrael* as part of his kingdom. After the death of Seleucus I, fighting broke out between Ptolemy I and Antiochus I Soter. Their successors, Ptolemy II Philadelphus and Antiochus II Theos succeeded in forming an alliance.]

וּבַת מֶלֶךְ־הַנֶּגֶב תָּבוֹא אֶל־מֶלֶךְ הַצָּפוֹן — *And the king of the south's daughter shall come to the king of the north.*

Ptolemy II succeeded in influencing Antiochus II to cast aside his wife Laodice [daughter of his uncle Acheus, a brother of Antiochus I] who had already borne him two children, and to marry Berenice, daughter of Ptolemy II.

rule; his dominion shall be a great dominion. ⁶ And at the end of years they shall join together, and the king of the south's daughter shall come to the king of the north to establish uprightness, but she will not restrain the power of the arm, nor will he nor his arm withstand; and surrendered will she be, those who brought her, her governess, and he who supports her

וְלֹא־תַעְצֹר כּוֹחַ הַזְּרוֹעַ — *But she will not restrain the power of the arm.*

After Ptolemy's death, Antiochus II left Berenice and the son she had borne him in Antioch and went to live with his previous wife, Laodice. Laodice, fearing that Antiochus would honor his pledge to name Berenice's son his successor, had Antiochus poisoned, and Berenice, her son, and her whole retinue murdered.

[*Abarbanel* apparently understands *the power of the arm* to refer to the power of the kingdom. He must then translate וְלֹא תַעְצֹר, *it will not restrain.*]

Malbim understands *power of the arm* to refer to the power of Antiochus. He translates וְלֹא תַעְצֹר, *and she will not restrain*, i.e., Berenice could not keep Antiochus from rejoining his former wife.

[Some writers do not consider the story that Laodice poisoned Antiochus historically trustworthy. But all agree that Antiochus died at approximately the same time as Ptolemy, that subsequently Berenice and her son were put to death, and that Laodice's son ascended the throne. This does not cause any difficulty in *Abarbanel's* interpretation. According to *Malbim*, וְלֹא תַעְצֹר, would refer to Berenice's inability to keep Laodice's power from harming her.]

וְלֹא יַעֲמֹד וּזְרֹעוֹ — *Nor will he nor his arm endure.*

He, (Antiochus) will not withstand, i.e, his reign will not be long. Antiochus II died suddenly a few

years after his marriage of convenience with Berenice. וּזְרֹעוֹ, *his arm*, refers to Antiochus' son by Berenice.

[*Abarbanel* does not explain how וּזְרֹעוֹ refers to this son. It may be that וּזְרֹעוֹ refers to the power of the kingdom symbolized by the arm (as in וְלֹא תַעְצֹר כּוֹחַ הַזְּרוֹעַ). If Antiochus had lived to name Berenice's son his successor, this would have united the Ptolemaic and Seleucid empires, and created a very powerful political bloc. But, Antiochus' sudden death caused that this unified powerful *arm* should never *stand up.*]

וְתִנָּתֵן — *And surrendered* [lit. *given*] will she be [into the hands of her enemies].

וּמְבִיאֶיהָ — *Those who brought her.* The nobles who traveled with her from Egypt as part of her retinue.

וְהַיֹּלְדָהּ — [*And*] *her governess.*

[*Abarbanel* and *Malbim* translate, *her governess*, because history does not indicate that Ptolemy II was killed. *Malbim* cites another instance where a foster parent is said to have begotten. אֲשֶׁר יָלְדָה לְעַדְרִיאֵל, *whom she* (Michal) *bore to Adriel* (II Samuel 21:8), means not that Michal was the physical mother of these children, but that she raised them (See *Targum, Rashi* and other *comm.*). *Rashi*, however,

בָּעִתִּים: וְעָמַד מִנֵּצֶר שָׁרָשֶׁיהָ כַּנּוֹ וְיָבֹא ז
אֶל־הַחַיִל וְיָבֹא בְּמָעוֹז מֶלֶךְ הַצָּפוֹן
וְעָשָׂה בָהֶם וְהֶחֱזִיק: וְגַם אֱלֹהֵיהֶם עִם־ ח
נְסִכֵיהֶם עִם־כְּלֵי חֶמְדָּתָם כֶּסֶף וְזָהָב
בַּשְּׁבִי יָבִא מִצְרָיִם וְהוּא שָׁנִים יַעֲמֹד
מִמֶּלֶךְ הַצָּפוֹן: וּבָא בְּמַלְכוּת מֶלֶךְ הַנֶּגֶב ט
וְשָׁב אֶל־אַדְמָתוֹ: וּבָנָו יִתְגָּרוּ וְאָסְפוּ י
הֲמוֹן חֲיָלִים רַבִּים וּבָא בוֹא וְשָׁטַף וְעָבָר

interprets הַיַּלְדָה in the usual way, her sire.

וּמַחֲזִקֶהָ בָּעִתִּים — *And he who supports her in the times.*

Her advisor(s) who supported her with advice in her times of travail.

[Or simply her political supporters of whom there were no doubt quite a few.]

7. וְעָמַד מִנֵּצֶר שָׁרָשֶׁיהָ — *A scion from her family shall arise* [lit. *there shall arise from a branch of her roots*].

Berenice's brother, Ptolemy III Euergetes, will succeed his father Ptolemy II (Philadelphus) on the Egyptian throne. Ptolemy II and Antiochus II died in approximately the same period as mentioned in *v.* 6.

וְיָבֹא אֶל־הַחַיִל — *Will come to the army.*

When Berenice realized that Antiochus was dead and her life was at stake she shut herself up in a fortress (Seleucia) from where she rallied those faithful to her cause. Ptolemy III arrived too late to save his sister but he still found remnants of the army faithful to her (*Malbim*).

[This rendition, however, makes וְיָבֹא בְּמָעוֹז repetitive. It should have been written וְיָבֹא אֶל הַחַיִל

בְּמָעוֹז]. *Abarbanel*, however, renders אֶל הַחַיִל as if it were עִם הַחַיִל — *with the army.*

וְיָבֹא בְּמָעוֹז — *(He will) enter the stronghold.*

Ptolemy III captured the principal cities of the Seleucid kingdom, Seleucia and Antioch.

וְעָשָׂה בָהֶם — *And succeed in them* [lit. *will do in them*].

Ptolemy succeeded in conquering huge parts of the Seleucid kingdom.

[The boundaries of his conquest are not clear, but it is certain that they were tremendous, and that *Eretz Yisrael* was included. *Malbim* relates that he avenged his sister's death by putting Laodice to death. *Abarbanel* notes that he killed Seleucus II Callinicus, Laodice's son and successor to Antiochus' throne. Both these assertions are not reported in the histories.]

8. נְסִכֵיהֶם — *Their princes.*

These are the nobles who are highly placed in the government (*R' Saadiah*).

The 'princes' of the above-mentioned gods, i.e., the high priests (*Ibn Yachyah*).

מִצְרָיִם — *Egypt.*

[Here *the kingdom of the south* is clearly identified as Egypt.]

11

7-10

in the times. 7 A scion from her family shall arise on his foundation, will come to the army, enter the stronghold of the king of the north and succeed in them, and seize them. 8 Also their gods with their princes, with their precious vessels of silver and gold, in captivity will he bring to Egypt; and he will stand secure for years from the king of the north. 9 And he will enter the kingdom of the king of the south, but he will return to his soil. 10 His sons will agitate themselves, and will gather a multitude of great armies, he will come on, inundate, and pass through.

וְהוּא שָׁנִים יַעֲמֹד — *And he will stand secure for years.*

After Ptolemy III returned victorious to Egypt (some historians claim he was forced to return because of a revolt in his country), Seleucus II Callinicus, the son and successor of Antiochus II, swiftly reversed most of Ptolemy's gains. In the war that ensued, Ptolemy held Seleucus II off for many years. [*Malbim* renders the plural שָׁנִים here as two years. But this is far from certain.] 'Southern Syria' — i.e., *Eretz Yisrael* and surrounding territories, remained in Ptolemy's hands.

R' Saadiah and *Metzudos* render: *and he will stand secure more years than the king of the north.* [The Ptolemaic dynasty endured for many years after the Seleucid kingdom had been converted into a Roman province. Demetrius I was the last real king of this dynasty (d. 3610; 150 B.C.E.) whereas Egypt continued under the rule of the Ptolemies till the death of Cleopatra (3730; 30 B.C.E.)].

9. וּבָא בְּמַלְכוּת מֶלֶךְ הַנֶּגֶב — *And he will enter the kingdom of the king of the south.*

Seleucus II Callinicus reconquered for himself the provinces *the king of the south* had annexed (as related above).

וְשָׁב אֶל־אַדְמָתוֹ — *But he will return to his soil.*

Though achieving great victories on land, Seleucus II suffered a disastrous defeat at sea when a storm destroyed his fleet.

10. וּבָנָיו יִתְגָּרוּ — *His sons will agitate themselves.*

The children of Seleucus II, after his death, stirred up wars in which one of the brothers was killed. [Seleucus III Soter, the older son and the successor to the throne, and Antiochus III, his younger brother, went to war to regain Asia Minor for the Seleucid kingdom. *Abarbanel* declares that the war referred to here was a war against Egypt to avenge the death of Seleucus II. (This is not substantiated by other sources). Seleucus III was assassinated during this campaign after reigning for four years. Antiochus III (the Great) then seized the throne.]

וּבָא בוֹא — *He will come on.*

He, i.e., Antiochus III. The

יא   וְיָשֹׁב °וְיִתְגָּרוּ עַד־מָעֻזֹה: וְיִתְמַרְמַר מֶלֶךְ
      הַנֶּגֶב וְיָצָא וְנִלְחַם עִמּוֹ עִם־מֶלֶךְ הַצָּפוֹן
      וְהֶעֱמִיד הָמוֹן רָב וְנִתַּן הֶהָמוֹן בְּיָדוֹ:
יב   וְנִשָּׂא הֶהָמוֹן °יָרוּם לְבָבוֹ וְהִפִּיל רִבֹּאוֹת
      וְלֹא יָעוֹז: וְשָׁב מֶלֶךְ הַצָּפוֹן וְהֶעֱמִיד
יג   הָמוֹן רָב מִן־הָרִאשׁוֹן וּלְקֵץ הָעִתִּים
      שָׁנִים יָבוֹא בוֹא בְּחַיִל גָּדוֹל וּבִרְכוּשׁ רָב:

singular וּבָא, *he will come* is used instead of the plural וּבָאוּ, *they will come*. Seleucus III had died and Antiochus III reigned alone. Approximately four years after ascending the throne, he opened a campaign to recover 'Southern' Syria (including *Eretz Yisrael* and Lebanon). His opponent was Ptolemy IV Philopater (grandson of Ptolemy II Philadelphus and son of Ptolemy III Euergetes) who was not able to muster a vigorous defense. Antiochus concluded a temporary treaty after he had succeeded in penetrating northern *Eretz Yisrael*.

[He advanced as far as Duro (near Haifa) where, misled by reports of a massive Egyptian build-up, he stopped and tried to extend his victories by diplomacy. Egypt dragged out the negotiations long enough to mobilize and train an army. By the time Antiochus III realized the fruitlessness of the talks, Egypt was ready to fight him.]

וְיָשֹׁב — *And he will return.*

After keeping a truce for many months, Antiochus returned again to war. [Having penetrated into *Eretz Yisrael* and stopped there as described above, he left 'Southern' Syria under one of his generals, and withdrew to Seleucia from where he conducted negotiations. Upon realizing the futility of the negotiations, he returned to the scene of the battle.]

וְיִתְגָּרֶה עַד־מָעֻזֹה — *And agitate* [lit., *he will antagonize,*] *till his stronghold.*

[After resuming the war, Antiochus swept southward across *Eretz Yisrael* where he was met at Raffah by an equal force of Egyptians. Hence, מָעֻזֹה, *his stronghold,* could be referring not only to the fact that this stronghold belonged to Egypt, but also to its proximity to Egypt to the point where it could be considered part of Egypt proper.]

11. וְיִתְמַרְמַר מֶלֶךְ הַנֶּגֶב וְיָצָא — *The king of the south will become embittered and go out.*

[Ptolemy IV momentarily shed his usual indolent attitude and rose to the occasion, encouraging his troops, and personally taking part in the battle.]

וְהֶעֱמִיד הָמוֹן רָב — *[And] he will raise a great multitude.*

[Ptolemy IV was successful in raising and training a great army, during a short period. Some give a figure as high as 70,000 men.]

וְנִתַּן הֶהָמוֹן בְּיָדוֹ — *And the multitude will be delivered into his hand.*

11

11-13

And he will return and agitate till his stronghold.
¹¹ *The king of the south will become embittered, and go out and battle with him — with the king of the north; he will raise a great multitude, and the multitude will be delivered into his hand.* ¹² *The multitude will feel uplifted, and its heart will be proud; though he will fell myriads, he will not prevail.*

¹³ *'The king of the north will return and raise a multitude greater than the first; at the end of the times, years, he will come on with a great army and*

[Antiochus' army, at least equal if not superior in numbers, was outmaneuvered by Ptolemy IV. Antiochus retreated hastily to his capital, Antioch, leaving 'Southern' Syria to Ptolemy.]

12. וְנִשָּׂא הֶהָמוֹן — *The multitude will feel uplifted.*

The Egyptian multitude will be elated over its victory. וְרָם לְבָבוֹ, *and its heart will be proud.*

The Egyptians, drunk with success, unjustifiably felt that they had dealt a death blow to Antiochus. Ptolemy IV reverted to his usual indolent and frivolous self, and failed to consolidate his victory by pursuing Antiochus and crushing him.

וְהִפִּיל רִבֹּאוֹת — *Though he will fell myriads.*

Antiochus suffered great losses in the battle.

וְלֹא יָעוֹז — *He will not prevail.*

Though Ptolemy IV won the battle, Antiochus III returned again to harass Egypt.

[Historians portray Ptolemy IV as an indolent, irresponsible king. His courageous stand against Antiochus III during the campaign against Egypt was the exception, not the rule. After his victory, he returned

to his usual life of fun and pleasure. וְלֹא יָעוֹז can be rendered *he will not strengthen (himself),* — i.e., his character did not change to display the same resolve he had shown in the war. This caused him to lose ground in the ensuing peace.]

13. The King of the North Returns

וְהֶעֱמִיד הָמוֹן — *And raise a multitude.*

When Antiochus III returned to Syria he proceeded to raise a great army. In the ensuing years he conducted many military campaigns.

[He conquered Asia Minor and pushed eastward as far as Afghanistan.]

וּלְקֵץ הָעִתִּים שָׁנִים — *At the end of the times, years.*

[קֵץ הָעִתִּים, *the end of the times* refers to the terminus of an unspecified period of time.]

Ibn Ezra suggests that שָׁנִים, *years,* modifies the indefinite עִתִּים, *times.* Thus, וּלְקֵץ הָעִתִּים, *at the end of times* [i.e.,] *years.*

Approximately 14 years after his defeat by Ptolemy IV, Antiochus III felt the time opportune for a new campaign against 'Southern' Syria and Egypt. By this time Ptolemy IV had died leaving the throne to his

יד וּבָעִתִּים הָהֵם רַבִּים יַעַמְדוּ עַל־מֶלֶךְ
הַנֶּגֶב וּבְנֵי | פָּרִיצֵי עַמְּךָ יִנַּשְׂאוּ לְהַעֲמִיד
טו חָזוֹן וְנִכְשָׁלוּ: וְיָבֹא מֶלֶךְ הַצָּפוֹן וְיִשְׁפֹּךְ
סוֹלֲלָה וְלָכַד עִיר מִבְצָרוֹת וּזְרֹעוֹת הַנֶּגֶב
לֹא יַעֲמֹדוּ וְעַם מִבְחָרָיו וְאֵין כֹּחַ לַעֲמֹד:

---

infant son Ptolemy V Epiphanes.
The country was now being ruled in
the king's name by regents.

14. רַבִּים יַעַמְדוּ — *Many will rise
up.*

Antiochus III at this time concluded alliances with other kings,
notably his uneasy alliance with
Philip V of Macedonia.

וּבְנֵי פָּרִיצֵי־עַמְּךָ יִנַּשְׂאוּ לְהַעֲמִיד חָזוֹן —
*And the sons of the lawless of your
people will exalt themselves to set up
a vision.*

To interpret the known visions of
the prophets (*Malbim*).

Or: To pretend to have had
divine, prophetic inspiration themselves (*Mayenei HaYeshuah* 11:4;
Metzudos).

The Jews, having suffered greatly
under the oppressive rule of the
later Ptolemies, pretended that
Divine prophecy had foretold the
demise of the Ptolemaic dynasty at
this point of history. When this
failed to take place, they were dealt
with as revolutionaries and killed.
The authorities naturally saw them
as part of the revolutionary movement against Ptolemy V (cf. *Josephus, Ant. XII 3,3*).

[This bit of information, unlike the rest of
this chapter, cannot be corroborated from
any other scource. This is not surprising,
since such a pseudo-prophetic movement
would, at most, deserve only a fleeting mention in the discussion of world politics of
those days. Given the sporadic nature of the
information available to us from this period
of history it would be surprising if more
mention of it *were* found! The information
therefore rests on the merits of the interpretation of this verse, which in this case
is rather clear.]

Rambam saw this phrase as a strong
allusion to the founder of Christianity
as follows:

Also about Yeshu the Nazarene who
imagined himself to be the Messiah and
was put to death by the court, it has
already been prophesied by Daniel as is
written, וּבְנֵי פָּרִיצֵי עַמְּךָ, *and the sons of
the lawless of your people, will exalt themselves to set up vision and will stumble.* For
is there a greater stumbling-block than
this? All the prophets foretold that the
Messiah will redeem the Jews, help them,
gather in the exiles, and support their
observance of the commandments. But he
caused Jewry to be put to the sword; to
have their remnants scattered; to be de-
graded; changed the Torah; and misled
most o fthe world to serve a god other
than HASHEM. But the thoughts of the
Creator of the world are unfathomable to
humans. . .' (*Rambam, Hilchos Melachim*
11:4). This passage, cited only in part, is
missing in all recent editions. See *Pardes*
edition which contains it as found in
ancient manuscripts. See also *Rambam's
Igeres Teman*. The same interpretation
is held by *R' Saadiah Gaon* (quoted in
Me-gillas HaMegalleh p. 98), *Ibn Ezra*
(*Perush HaKatzer*), and perhaps *Rashi*
(our versions are extremely ambiguous
and have no doubt been tampered with
by censors).

11
14-15 *with much wealth.* ¹⁴ *In those times, many will rise up against the king of the south; and the sons of the lawless of your people will exalt themselves to set up vision and will stumble.* ¹⁵ *The king of the north shall come and throw up siege-works, and will conquer a fortified city, and the arms of the south will not withstand. As for his chosen people, there is be no strength to withstand.*

[Though this verse belongs to the Greek era according to *R' Saadiah* and *Rashi*, this does not preclude the above interpretation (*Megillas HaMegalleh* already touches upon this apparent contradiction). It is likely that the Nazarene apostasy had its roots in the Hasmonean era. The *Talmud* tells about Yeshua, a disciple of Yehoshua ben Prachiah, in the Hasmonean era (*Sanhedrin* 107b; cf. *Chesronos HaShas*). *Tosafos* (*Shabbas* 104b, s.v. בן סטדא) raises this possiblity. This historical probability was used many times by rabbis in their disputes with Christians (see *Otzar Havikuchim*).]

15. וְיָבֹא מֶלֶךְ הַצָּפוֹן — *The king of the north shall come.*

The vision resumes here from where it was interrupted in *v.* 13 בֹּא יָבֹא, *he will come on. Verse* 14 was a parenthetical digression foretelling the alliances Antiochus formed.

וְיִשְׁפֹּךְ סוֹלְלָה — *And throw up siege-works.*

[This probably refers to Antiochus' almost uncontested sweep through 'Southern' Syria (*Eretz Yisrael*), where he was finally stopped through the stubborn resistance of Gaza. After a lengthy siege, Antiochus finally took the city, fulfilling the prophecy וְלָכַד עִיר מִבְצָרוֹת, *and will conquer a fortified city*, but in the meantime the Egyptians had time to mobilize.]

וּזְרֹעוֹת הַנֶּגֶב לֹא יַעֲמֹדוּ — *And the arms of the south will not withstand.*

[*The arms of the south,* — i.e., its military force. See above *v.* 6].

[At one point the tide shifted in favor of the Egyptians. They hired Scopas, a very able Greek general — for an exorbitant fee — to head their force. Scopas proceeded to reconquer *Eretz Yisrael*. But at the battle of Panian (probably the Talmudical פמייס) he suffered a decisive defeat. His army decimated, Scopas retreated with the remaining 10,000 men of his once mighty army to the seaport of Sidon, where he was besieged on land and sea by Antiochus.]

וְעַם מִבְחָרָיו — *(And) as for his chosen people.*

[Egypt then sent an army to try and lift the siege of Sidon. But they, too, were defeated by Antiochus, who then starved Scopas into surrender.]

וְאֵין כֹּחַ לַעֲמֹד — *There is no strength to withstand.*

[The angel, from his vantage point, is foretelling the future in the present tense as if he is actually seeing it happen prophetically.]

The *vav* in וְאֵין is superfluous (*R' Shmuel Masnuth*).

וַיַּעַשׂ הַבָּא אֵלָיו כִּרְצוֹנוֹ וְאֵין עוֹמֵד טז
לְפָנָיו וְיַעֲמֹד בְּאֶרֶץ־הַצְּבִי וְכָלָה בְיָדוֹ:
וְיָשֵׂם | פָּנָיו לָבוֹא בְּתֹקֶף כָּל־מַלְכוּתוֹ יז
וִישָׁרִים עִמּוֹ וְעָשָׂה וּבַת הַנָּשִׁים יִתֶּן־לוֹ
לְהַשְׁחִיתָהּ וְלֹא תַעֲמֹד וְלֹא־לוֹ תִהְיֶה:
°וְיָשֵׂב פָּנָיו לְאִיִּים וְלָכַד רַבִּים וְהִשְׁבִּית יח

° וְיָשֶׂם ק'

16. The Lawless of Your People

וַיַּעַשׂ הַבָּא אֵלָיו — *The one who will come to him will do.*

Antiochus IV who *will come to him,* (to Ptolemy's domain) *will do* …

כִּרְצוֹנוֹ — *As he pleases.*

Antiochus III proceeded to retake 'Southern' Syria uncontested.

וְיַעֲמֹד בְּאֶרֶץ־הַצְּבִי — *He will stand in the coveted land.*

Eretz Yisrael is called אֶרֶץ הַצְּבִי, *the coveted land,* elsewhere (see *Ezekiel* 20:6 and 15; *Jeremiah* 13:19; *Daniel* 11:41). *Radak* to *Ezekiel* 20:6 and in *Sefer HaShorashim, s.v.* צבי, derives it from the Aramaic צְבָא, *desire, covet. Targum Yonasan* (to *Ezekiel* and *Jeremiah, loc. cit.*) renders תּוּשְׁבַּחְתָּא, *the praised* land.

After consolidating his victory in 'Southern' Syria, Antiochus penetrated *Eretz Yisrael,* where he captured Jerusalem and the rest of the land as far as the Sinai desert.

וְכָלָה בְיָדוֹ — *With annihilation in his hand.*

Had he been so inclined, Antiochus could now have destroyed the land and its inhabitants. His purpose, however, was to keep these lands as permanent additions to his kingdom. Accordingly, destruction would hardly fit his purpose (*Mayenei HaYeshuah* 11:4).

Rashi and other commentators understand this phrase to indicate that Antiochus actually wrought havoc in *Eretz Yisrael.* Nevertheless, *Rashi* seems to have understood *vs.* 16 through 18 to refer to Antiochus IV, the villain of Chanukah (see *Rashi* to *vs.* 17-18). From *Josephus (Ant.* 12:3) we see that Antiochus III was favorably disposed toward the Jews.

Malbim renders וְכָלָה as if it read וְכֻלָּהּ, *and all of it,* or וְכִלָּהּ, *and he completed her,* i.e., he completed his conquest of the land.]

17. לָבוֹא בְּתֹקֶף כָּל־מַלְכוּתוֹ — *To penetrate the strength of his whole kingdom.*

Having conquered all of *Eretz Yisrael,* Antiochus III now stood at the gates of Egypt, where he would *penetrate* Ptolemy's *whole kingdom.*

וִישָׁרִים עִמּוֹ וְעָשָׂה — *And he will reach an agreement with him* [lit., *and upright ways with him] and succeed* [lit, *do*].

The Romans, fearing Antiochus's growing power, and suspicious of his intentions, intervened and took Egypt under their protection. [An emissary, Cornelius Lentulus, was sent from Rome to conduct negotiations with Antiochus on behalf of Ptolemy IV.] Antiochus, feeling the time was not ripe to risk a confrontation with the powerful Romans,

¹⁶ *'The one who will come to him will do as he pleases, and none will withstand him; he will stand in the coveted land, with annihilation in his hand. ¹⁷ He will set his face to penetrate the strength of his whole kingdom, and he will reach an agreement with him and succeed, and the daughter of the women he will give him to destroy it, but it will not abide, and she will not be his. ¹⁸ Then he will turn his face toward isles and will conquer many, but an officer will cause*

responded with a brilliant diplomatic maneuver. Antiochus concluded a peace with Egypt and cemented this peace by joining the two royal houses in marriage. Cleopatra, Antiochus' daughter, would be given in marriage to Ptolemy V Epiphanes. Depending on his daughter to create a fifth column within Egypt, he hoped to gain by treachery what he did not dare attempt to gain on the battlefield.

[The translation treats וְיִשָׁרִים עִמּוֹ *and he will reach an agreement with him*, and וְעָשָׂה, *and he will succeed*, as two separate phrases connected by the conjuctive ו, *and*. Thus: *He* (Antiochus) *will reach an agreement* (the proposal of marriage) *with him* (Ptolemy) *and succeed* (in completing the marriage arrangements).]

Malbim seems to ignore the implication of the conjuctive ו, *and*, and renders the whole as one phrase translating עָשָׂה as *make*. Thus: *He will make an agreement with him.*

וּבַת הַנָּשִׁים — *And the daughter of the women.*

I.e., *the daughter of* [one of his] *women.*

לְהַשְׁחִיתָהּ — *To destroy it.*

[To destroy the kingdom of Egypt. The feminine suffix הָ

refers to the implicit object, מַלְכוּת, the *kingdom* of the south.]

וְלֹא תַעֲמֹד — *But it will not abide* [lit., *stand*].

[*It*, this devious scheme of conquering Egypt from within, *will not abide*, i.e., it will fail.]

וְלֹא־לוֹ תִהְיֶה — *And she will not be his.*

Cleopatra did not play the role her father wanted her to play; rather she was loyal to her husband.

Rashi maintains that these verses (16-18; see above v. 16) refer to Antiochus IV against whom the Hasmoneans revolted. Thus: וְיִשָׁרִים *and the righteous*, i.e., the Hasmoneans, עִמּוֹ, *will be with him* (the king of the south). וּבַת הַנָּשִׁים, *the daughter of women*, is a metaphoric reference to Israel which is represented in the allegory of *Shir HaShirim* as a beautiful woman. *And he* (Antiochus) *will give him* (his general) *the daughter of the women* (the loyal Jewish People who openly profess Judaism) *to destroy her*. וְלֹא תַעֲמֹד, *But it* [his plan] *will not stand up.*

The Hasmoneans will revolt and successfully throw off Antiochus' yoke.

18. וְיָשֵׂם פָּנָיו לְאִיִּים — *Then he will turn his face toward isles.*

קָצִין חֶרְפָּתוֹ לוֹ בִּלְתִּי חֶרְפָּתוֹ יָשִׁיב לוֹ:
יט וְיָשֵׁב פָּנָיו לְמָעוּזֵּי אַרְצוֹ וְנִכְשַׁל וְנָפַל
כ וְלֹא יִמָּצֵא: וְעָמַד עַל־כַּנּוֹ מַעֲבִיר נוֹגֵשׂ
הֶדֶר מַלְכוּת וּבְיָמִים אֲחָדִים יִשָּׁבֵר וְלֹא
כא בְאַפַּיִם וְלֹא בְמִלְחָמָה: וְעָמַד עַל־כַּנּוֹ

Antiochus now proceeded to wage war against *the islands* in the Mediterranean, many of which had been under Roman protection. He concluded an alliance with Hannibal of Carthage, Rome's archenemy, and invaded Greece, thus menacing Rome itself.

[After marrying his daughter to Ptolemy V, Antiochus III crossed the Dardanelles and conquered Thrace (roughly corresponding to modern European Turkey). Finally, fortified by his alliance with Hannibal, and counting on many Grecian forces who were eager to throw off Roman domination, he proceeded to Greece.]

וְהִשְׁבִּית קָצִין חֶרְפָּתוֹ לוֹ — But an officer will cause his insolence to cease.

[The Roman consul, Acilius Glabrio, sent by the Senate to stop Antiochus, soundly defeated him at Thermopylae, which was followed by a decisive defeat of the king's fleet at Corycus. Antiochus then recrossed the Dardanelles to defend his Asian possessions.

The Romans, under the leadership of Lucius Cornelius Scipio and his brother Publius Cornelius Scipio (Africanus), met him in battle at Magnesia (near Smyrna) and crushed him. Antiochus is said to have lost 70,000 men.]

בִּלְתִּי חֶרְפָּתוֹ יָשִׁיב לוֹ — For his in-

solence alone will he punish [lit., return to] him.

[The territories taken from Antiochus as a result of his defeat were purely the price of his insolent lack of respect for Roman power and its imperial interests. When Antiochus sued for peace, the Scipios demanded that he give up all his possessions in Europe, plus a great part of Asia, and pay an exorbitant amount of money in war reparations. The angel here clearly indicates that Antiochus' misfortunes were visited upon him as a consequence of his rash and impudent conduct toward the Romans.]

Rashi understands this verse to refer to the horrible death of Antiochus IV.

19. וְיָשֵׁב פָּנָיו — And he will turn his face.

[Antiochus returned to his native Syria to raise the heavy fine that had been imposed upon him.]

וְנִכְשַׁל וְנָפַל — And he will stumble and fall.

[Impelled no doubt by the necessity to pay his war debt, Antiochus made the mistake of plundering a temple of Bel, holy to the inhabitants of Elymais (Elam). This stirred up the rage of the populace and Antiochus was assassinated.]

וְלֹא יִמָּצֵא — And not be found.

[His remains disappeared.]

11
19-21 *his insolence to cease, for his insolence alone will he punish him.* ¹⁹ *And he will turn his face toward the strongholds of his homeland, and he will stumble and fall, and not be found.*

²⁰ *'There will arise in his place one whose glory of kingship is the passing through of the tax dun. But in a few years, he will be broken, though not through anger, not through war.* ²¹ *There will arise in his*

---

20. The Contemptible One

וְעָמַד עַל־כַּנּוֹ — *There will arise in* [lit. *on*] *his place.*

Antiochus III was succeeded by his elder son Seleucus IV Philopater. His short reign was relatively peaceful, but the treasury was so depleted by the heavy tribute he was forced to pay the Romans, and by the war debts accumulated by his father Antiochus, that the main occupation of his government became the collection of taxes. On account of this, he is described here as: *one whose glory of kingship is the passing through of the tax-dun.*

מַעֲבִיר נוֹגֵשׂ — *The passing through of the tax-dun.*

[נוֹגֵשׂ from לֹא יִגֹּשׂ, *He may not exact (Deut.* 15:2).] The *tax-dun* is the collector who mercilessly forced payment of the exorbitant taxes.]

הֶדֶר מַלְכוּת — *Glory of kingship.*

It was said sarcastically by his contemporaries that the entire glory of his reign lay in the exacting of taxes.

וּבְיָמִים אֲחָדִים יִשָּׁבֵר — *But in a few years, he will be broken.*

After a 12-year reign, Seleucus IV was assassinated by his chief minister, Heliodorus.

וְלֹא בְאַפַּיִם — *Though not through anger.*

The assassination was not the result of anything Selecus did to provoke the anger of a rival monarch against himself (*Metzudos*).

R' Shmuel Masnuth thinks that אַפַּיִם can be synonymous with פָּנִים, *face.* Thus, *not in confrontation.*

Rashi interprets this phrase as following the previous verse, which (according to his view) deals with Antiochus IV of Chanukah infamy. Thus, *One* (Mattisyahu the Hasmonean) *will arise on his place* (מַעֲבִיר נוֹגֵשׂ) *who will depose the oppressor* (Antiochus IV Epiphanes) [*which is the*] *glory of kingship* (of the Hasmonean dynasty for Jewry). But *in a few years it* (the Hasmonean dynasty) *will be broken, but not through anger of,* or *confrontation with, nor through war* (with another nation, but through the internecine quarrels of Hyrcanos and Aristobulus over the throne which will bring the downfall of their dynasty).

21. וְעָמַד עַל כַּנּוֹ נִבְזֶה — *There will arise in his place a contemptible one.*

Antiochus IV Epiphanes, in-

נִבְזֶה וְלֹא־נָתְנוּ עָלָיו הוֹד מַלְכוּת וּבָא
בְשַׁלְוָה וְהֶחֱזִיק מַלְכוּת בַּחֲלַקְלַקּוֹת:
כב וּזְרֹעוֹת הַשֶּׁטֶף יִשָּׁטְפוּ מִלְּפָנָיו וְיִשָּׁבֵרוּ
כג וְגַם נְגִיד בְּרִית: וּמִן־הִתְחַבְּרוּת אֵלָיו
יַעֲשֶׂה מִרְמָה וְעָלָה וְעָצַם בִּמְעַט־גּוֹי:

---

famous for his oppression of the Jews, ascended the throne.

וְלֹא־נָתְנוּ עָלָיו הוֹד מַלְכוּת — *Upon whom they did not confer the glory of kingship.*

Seleucus IV died leaving a teenage son, Demetrius, who was held a hostage in Rome at the time of his father's death, and a baby son Antiochus. Their uncle, Antiochus IV, was not the legitimate heir to the throne.

וְהֶחֱזִיק מַלְכוּת בַּחֲלַקְלַקּוֹת — *And will possess kingship though glibnes.*

[Antiochus IV, at the time of his brother's death, was serving as a general of the Roman forces at Athens. He had been away from Syria for most of his adult life, having been a hostage in Rome from the time of his father's defeat at Magnesia. Thus he could not count on native Syrian forces to support him. But he was able to convince the king of Pergamum (a city near the Dardanelles) to lend him the support of his troops.

When he entered Antioch, the capital, he was able to take over the government of the country. Some historians conjecture, on the evidence of contemporary coins and records, that Antiochus IV did not openly declare himself king at first. He assumed the stance of a caretaker regent, ruling for his underage nephew, Antiochus. Six years after Antiochus Epiphanes's

ascension to the throne, Antiochus son of Seleucus IV, the young heir to the throne, was killed while Antiochus IV was away putting down an insurgency. Upon his return, he had the murderers put to death.]

Rashi interprets this verse as well as the rest of the vision as referring to the fourth kingdom — the Romans.

22. וּזְרֹעוֹת הַשֶּׁטֶף יִשָּׁטְפוּ מִלְּפָנָיו — *The arms that sweep away will be swept away before him.*

[This is a metaphor referring to the power of his opponents. See above *v.* 6 and 15 for a similar use of זְרוֹעַ and *v.* 10 for this use of שֶׁטֶף.]

וְגַם נְגִיד בְּרִית — *And the prince of the covenant as well.*

Ptolemy VI Philometor, the son of Antiochus' sister Cleopatra (see *v.* 17) who was bound by a peace agreement with him.

Ptolemy V had died and Cleopatra ruled on behalf of her minor sons.

Antiochus used his kinship to the queen regent, his sister, (see *v.* 17) to gain entry to Egypt. Once in the country he used the opportunity to plunder and pillage as told in *vs.* 23-24.

[Another version has it that Antiochus did not attempt any action against Egypt during Cleopatra's regency. But when she died and the actual rule passed into the hands of

11
22-24 *place a contemptible one upon whom they did not confer the glory of kingship. He will come in peace and will possess kingship through glibness. ²² The arms that sweep away will be swept away before him and will be broken, and the prince of the covenant as well.*

²³ *'Through alliance with him he will work deceit, and rise up and grow strong with a small nation. ²⁴ In*

two advisors, Eulaeus and Lanceus, Antiochus IV charged, and carried his argument before the Roman senate, that the Egyptians were massing troops on the borders of *Eretz Yisrael* in preparation for a massive attack. The Romans, busy with a war in Macedonia, did not intervene. Antiochus seized the opportunity and struck at Egypt.]

Rashi understands נְגִיד בְּרִית here to refer to the Hasmonean kings who had concluded an alliance with the Romans. The Romans broke their pact after 26 years as related in *Avodah Zarah* (10a).

23. The King's Deceit

וּמִן־הִתְחַבְּרוּת אֵלָיו יַעֲשֶׂה מִרְמָה — *Through alliance with him he will work deceit.*

Antiochus came to Egypt on the pretext of visiting his sister, the queen regent Cleopatra, and was thus able to get into the country and *grow strong* with a small number of people loyal to him.

[*Abarbanel* and *Malbim* evidently place the date of Antiochus' attempt in Egypt during Cleopatra's regency. The particulars of his attempted *coup d'etat* according to their sources are different from the version given in verse 22.

A contemporary historian relates that Antiochus took over the fortress of Pelasium (at the Egyp-

tian border in Sinai) by trickery. It is possible that Antiochus used his family ties with the rulers of Egypt as proof of his peaceful intentions. In those days of poor communications, the townspeople could have been ignorant of Antiochus' complaint before the Roman senate.

Another possible interpetation: Antiochus, after penetrating Egypt, crowned the young Ptolemy VI Philometor. The people of Alexandria, resisting Antiochus, declared the younger brother (later Ptolemy VII Euergetes) king. Antiochus was able to exploit his relationship to the king by acting as a protector of the older brother's legitimate claim to the crown. This enabled him, without the help of a great army, to sweep down the Nile to Memphis, plundering and pillaging without encountering any serious opposition.]

Rashi interprets this verse as referring to the period preceding the state of war between Rome and Israel where there was a treaty of friendship between them. The Roman relying on the pact, were able to conquer the countries surrounding *Eretz Yisrael* without fear of intervention from the Hasmonean kingship (see *Yossipon*).

בִּמְעַט־גּוֹי — *With a small nation.*

I.e., with a small group of men.

כד בְּשַׁלְוָ֤ה וּבְמִשְׁמַנֵּי֙ מְדִינָה֙ יָב֔וֹא וְעָשָׂ֗ה
אֲשֶׁ֨ר לֹא־עָשׂ֤וּ אֲבֹתָיו֙ וַאֲב֣וֹת אֲבֹתָ֔יו בִּזָּ֤ה
וְשָׁלָ֤ל וּרְכ֤וּשׁ לָהֶ֣ם יִבְז֔וֹר וְעַ֥ל מִבְצָרִ֖ים
כה יְחַשֵּׁ֣ב מַחְשְׁבֹתָ֑יו וְעַד־עֵֽת: וְיָעֵר֩ כֹּח֨וֹ
וּלְבָב֜וֹ עַל־מֶ֣לֶךְ הַנֶּ֗גֶב בְּחַ֣יִל גָּד֔וֹל וּמֶ֣לֶךְ
הַנֶּ֗גֶב יִתְגָּרֶה֙ לַמִּלְחָמָ֔ה בְּחַֽיִל־גָּד֥וֹל
וְעָצ֖וּם עַד־מְאֹ֑ד וְלֹ֣א יַעֲמֹ֔ד כִּי־יַחְשְׁב֥וּ
כו עָלָ֖יו מַחֲשָׁבֽוֹת: וְאֹכְלֵ֨י פַת־בָּג֤וֹ יִשְׁבְּר֔וּהוּ
וְחֵיל֖וֹ יִשְׁט֑וֹף וְנָפְל֖וּ חֲלָלִ֥ים רַבִּֽים:

24. וְעָשָׂה אֲשֶׁר לֹא עָשׂוּ אֲבֹתָיו —
*And do what his fathers ... did not
do.*

[Since Alexander no one had
been able to penetrate the fortifica-
tions at the border separating Egypt
from Asia.]

בִּזָּה וְשָׁלָל — *Booty, spoils.*

Rashi (Numbers 31:11) differen-
tiates between בִּזָּה (בָּז) and שָׁלָל: שָׁלָל
refers specifically to clothing and
jewelry plundered in war, whereas
בִּזָּה includes any other looted
movables.

A similar definition is given by
Vilna Gaon (Aderes Eliyahu to
Isaiah 10:6). שָׁלָל is the valuable
booty taken initially. בִּזָּה refers to
the things taken in the second wave
of looting, when in the absence of
real valuables, things of secondary
or negligible value are also taken
(from בִּזָּיוֹן, shame).

לָהֶם יִבְזוֹר — *He will spread among
them.*

He will give lavish bribes to those
who cooperate with him (*Rashi*).

[*Josephus* (Ant. XII 7, 2) reports
that Antiochus' extravagance depleted his treasury.]

וְעַל מִבְצָרִים יְחַשֵּׁב מַחְשְׁבֹתָיו — *And

against fortresses will he concentrate his thoughts.*

All this time [under the guise of
the infant Ptolemy's protector], Antiochus IV was in reality scheming
to conquer Egypt's fortresses.

וְעַד־עֵת — *Until [the] time.*

Antiochus did not think this time
opportune for the ultimate attack.
He waited for the *time* most
propitious for his plan. Thus, but
[he waited] *until a time.*

Abarbanel and *Malbim*, holding
to their interpretation that *vs.* 22-25
refer to Antiochus' actions in Egypt
during Cleopatra's regency, interpret וְעַד עֵת, *until the time*, to
mean that Antiochus, feeling that
the time was not yet ripe, returned
to Syria. Verse 25 refers to his attack on Egypt after Cleopatra's
death.

[According to the view that *vs.*
22-25 already refer to Antiochus'
invasion of Egypt after Cleopatra's
death, וְעַד עֵת does not mean that
Antiochus waited a long period of
time or returned home. Where this
is indicated it is clearly said — in
verse 28. He merely waited for *a
time* he deemed appropriate for a
massive attack. V. 23 states that *he*

11
25-27   *peace and into the richest parts of the country will he come, and do what his fathers and forefathers did not do; he will spread among them booty, spoils, and wealth; and against fortresses will he concentrate his thoughts, until the time.*

25 *'He will arouse his strength and his heart against the king of the south with a great army; and the king of the south will be provoked with an exceedingly great and powerful army, but he will not withstand, for they will devise plans against him,* 26 *and those who eat his food will break him, and he will sweep away his army, and many corpses will fall.* 27 *And as*

---

will rise up and grow strong with a small nation. Now that massive manpower was needed, as clearly stated in *v.* 25, time was needed to organize and transport the huge army he needed.]

25. The Kings Battle Again

וְיָעֵר כֹּחוֹ — *He will arouse his strength.*

Antiochus returned to Egypt a second time after the death of the queen regent Cleopatra.

[The people of Alexandria resisted Antiochus IV, rejecting his pretense of protecting the Egyptian crown, and crowning Ptolemy VII Euergetes king. Antiochus then marched in with a Syrian army and besieged Alexandria.]

עַל מֶלֶךְ הַנֶּגֶב — *Against the king of the south.*

Ptolemy VI Philometor [or: Ptolemy VII Euergetes whom the Alexandrians had acknowledged as king.]

כִּי יַחְשְׁבוּ עָלָיו מַחֲשָׁבוֹת — *For they will devise plans against him.*

Ptolemy VI was betrayed by his own generals whom Antiochus bribed.

[According to the line followed above, this phrase (starting from וְלֹא יַעֲמֹד, *but he will not withstand*) to *v.* 27 is a parenthetic remark foretelling the eventual defeat of the Alexandrians at the hands of Antiochus. This did not take place until Antiochus had returned to Syria as told in *vs.* 28-29.

[The Alexandrian resistance was doomed when the governor of Cyprus (which belonged to Egypt) defected to Antiochus.]

According to *Rashi, vs.* 25-27 refer to a Roman campaign against Egypt during the days of the Hasmonean king Hyrcanos.

26. וְאֹכְלֵי פַת־בָּגוֹ יִשְׁבְּרוּהוּ — *And those who eat his food will break him.*

[This is a further elaboration of what was hinted at the end of *v.* 25.] The subordinates of the Egyptian king betrayed their master and caused his defeat.

וְחֵילוֹ יִשְׁטוֹף — *And he will sweep away his army.*

[The Egyptian army will be so overwhelmed by overpowering numbers that they will be swept

כז וּשְׁנֵיהֶם הַמְּלָכִים לְבָבָם לְמֵרָע וְעַל־
שֻׁלְחָן אֶחָד כָּזָב יְדַבֵּרוּ וְלֹא תִצְלָח כִּי־
כח עוֹד קֵץ לַמּוֹעֵד: וְיָשָׁב אַרְצוֹ בִּרְכוּשׁ
גָּדוֹל וּלְבָבוֹ עַל־בְּרִית קֹדֶשׁ וְעָשָׂה וְשָׁב
כט לְאַרְצוֹ: לַמּוֹעֵד יָשׁוּב וּבָא בַנֶּגֶב וְלֹא־

away as in a flood. *And he*, Antiochus, *will sweep away his*, the Egyptian monarch's, *army*.]

27. וּשְׁנֵיהֶם הַמְּלָכִים — *And as for the two kings*.

Antiochus had the good fortune to capture Ptolemy VI, the heir to the throne, alive. He now assumed the guise of a protective uncle who had just come to protect the interest of his underage nephew. The Alexandrians had meanwhile crowned the younger brother, Ptolemy VII. Antiochus besieged them, all the time maintaining that if the Alexandrians would recognize the older Ptolemy as king he would withdraw.

לְבָבָם לְמֵרָע — *Their hearts will be to do harm …*

[I.e., … to each other.] Antiochus' probable aim was to provoke a civil war between the two brothers, so that, in the absence of a strong central government, he might gain control of the country. Ptolemy VI, in spite of his youth, seems to have understood Antiochus' devious intentions and though he ostensibly cooperated with his uncle, he intended to do him harm.

[The narrative here returns to the point where Antiochus, in league with the elder Ptolemy, besieged Alexandria.]

וְלֹא תִצְלָח — *But it will not succeed*.
[I.e., the plan.]

Antiochus' scheme did not succeed. No sooner had he turned his back to return home (as told in *v.* 28) than the two Ptolemy brothers joined forces against their uncle.

כִּי־עוֹד קֵץ לַמּוֹעֵד — *For there is yet an end for the allotted time*.

[The end was coming to the time allotted for Antiochus' kingship. An alternative interpretation: מוֹעֵד, *the allotted time*, refers to the time allotted to the hegemony of the Greeks over *Eretz Yisrael;* the domination of the third kingdom was coming to an end. Antiochus Epiphanes' reign signaled the beginning of the end of Greek rule.]

According to *Rashi, the two kings* were Hyrcanos and Pompeius. Hyrcanos was the Hasmonean king who, in his struggle with his brother Aristobulus, asked the help of the Romans; and, Pompeius was the Roman general who represented the Roman republic in this alliance. He is called 'king' here in spite of his being only a general because he represented the mighty Roman Empire. The hearts of both will be set *to do harm* to the Jewish nation. But their designs will fail: *For there is yet an end to the allotted time*. The sixty-two weeks of years allotted the Temple (see 9:25) had yet to come to an end.

28. וְיָשָׁב אַרְצוֹ — *And he will return [to] his land*.

During the siege of Alexandria,

11
28-29   *for the two kings, their hearts will be to do harm; at
one table they will speak falsehood, but it will not
succeed, for there is yet an end for the allotted time.
²⁸ He will return to his land with great wealth with
his heart against the covenant of sanctity he will accomplish and return to his land.*

*²⁹ 'At the appointed time he will return and come
to the south; but it will not be like the first, nor like*

Antiochus, returned to Syria for reasons not clear now.

וּלְבָבוֹ עַל בְּרִית קֹדֶשׁ — *With his heart against the covenant of sanctity.*

I.e., the Jewish nation which is identified with its religion, the *covenant of sancity* with God.

[Before Antiochus' campaign against Egypt, there had been turmoil in Jerusalem concerning the office of the high priest. *Josephus (Ant. XII 5, 1)* tells us that when Onias (the Hellenized form of חוֹנִיוֹ, *Chonio*) the High Priest died, his son was too young to succeed him. Yeshua, brother of Onias, who changed his name to the Greek 'Jason' was appointed to the post. The king, because of his anger (*Josephus* does not give the reason for his anger) against Jason, appointed his younger brother, also (strangely) named Onias, who then changed his name to Menelaus.

[Other sources are more explicit about this affair. Yeshua (Jason) offered Antiochus an exorbitant bribe to appoint him high priest. After having served in this post for some time, Menelaus (according to this source not a brother of Yeshua, nor even a *kohen* of the priestly family) promised the king an even greater sum, and was promptly given the post. Both these nominees had promised the king their utmost

cooperation to enforce the king's pet project of Hellenizing the country, by forcibly spreading Greek culture.]

While Antiochus was in Egypt waging war, a rumor spread that the king had died. Jason, the High Priest who had been removed by Antiochus, seized the opportunity to return from his exile, raise a small army and besiege Jerusalem. Antiochus, upon his return, put down this insurrection with a great deal of bloodshed.

Rashi understands this verse to refer to the Romans. בְּרִית קֹדֶשׁ, *covenant of sanctity*, refers to the pact they had made with the Hasmoneans. Thus: *his heart* (Roman intentions) *will be against the covenant of sanctity.* They did not intend to keep the pact for long.

29. The Kittim

לְמוֹעֵד יָשׁוּב — *At the appointed time he will return.*

Antiochus heard that his nephew Ptolemy VI had betrayed him and joined forces against him together with his younger brother Ptolemy VII. He promptly returned to Egypt with a great army and proceeded to conquer the land.

וְלֹא תִהְיֶה — *But it will not be.*

Though initially Antiochus succeeded in subjugating the whole

לא תִהְיֶה כָרִאשֹׁנָה וְכָאַחֲרֹנָה: וּבָאוּ בוֹ
לְ צִיִּים כִּתִּים וְנִכְאָה וְשָׁב וְזָעַם עַל־בְּרִית־
קוֹדֶשׁ וְעָשָׂה וְשָׁב וְיָבֵן עַל־עֹזְבֵי בְּרִית

country, this success was not as durable as his previous successes.

כָרִאשֹׁנָה וְכָאַחֲרֹנָה — *Like the first nor like the last.*

This third invasion of Egypt by Antiochus IV was not successful like the *first* (during the regency of Cleopatra, see *vs.* 22-25) *nor* will it be as successful as the last time (*vs.* 25-29) when he invaded at the beginning of Ptolemy VI's rule. The reason for Antiochus's setback is given in the next verse.

[According to the interpretation followed above only one invasion of Egypt took place before this last onslaught by Antiochus. However, the first campaign can be divided into two phases. The first, where Antiochus entered Egypt almost furtively: *with a small nation (v. 23)*. The second phase was when Antiochus waged full-scale war against Alexandria: *with a great army (v. 25)*. This second invasion, when Antiochus returned from Syria, *will not be like the first, nor like the last.*]

30. צִיִּים — *Ships.*

The translation follows *Rashi* (*Numbers* 24:24), *Ibn Ezra*, and *Radak* (*Shorashim* s.v. ציה). The *Aruch* (s.v. אספר, quoting a reponsum of the *Gaonim*) renders it *legions.* Thus: For legions of Kittim. This seems to be the opinion of *Onkelos* (*Numbers* 24:24) who renders וְצִים as וְסִיעָן, *bands.* *Targum Yonasan* and *Targum Yerushalmi*, strangely, seem to give both translations. *Rashi* here

renders צִיִּים as סִיעוֹת, *bands!*]

כִּתִּים — *Kittim.*

Onkelos (*Numbers* 24:24) identifies כִּתִּים as the *Romans.* So do *Yerushalmi* and *Yonasan.* Though *Yonasan* gives קוֹסְטַנְטִינָא, *Constantinople*, as the translation, it is obvious that Constantinople as the seat of the eastern Roman empire is meant. *Rashi* concurs. Though our editions read אֲרָמִים, *the Arameans*, that is an improbable translation put in our editions by censors (see Berliner's edition of *Rashi* where רוֹמָאֵי, *Roman*, is given).

In *Genesis* (10:4) *Kittim* are the descendants of *Yavan.* *Midrash Rabbah* identifies them as אִיטַלְיָה, *Italy.* The same is true for *Yossipon* (ch. 1), and *Ibn Ezra* (to 10:4). (See *Sanhedrin* 106a and *Rashi* there; *Aruch, s.v.* אספיר).

וְנִכְאָה — *And he will be cowed.*

The Romans under the leadership of Popillius Laenas landed a force in Egypt and forced Antiochus to retreat.

[The story goes that Popillius met Antiochus face-to-face in an Alexandrian suburb. When Antiochus tried to stall, Popillius drew a circle around him, daring him to step out of the circle before submitting to Rome. Antiochus, humiliated, had no choice but to submit.]

וְשָׁב וְזָעַם עַל־בְּרִית־קוֹדֶשׁ — *He will return, and vent his fury at the covenant of sanctity.*

Upon his defeat in Egypt he will return through *Eretz Yisrael.* He will then *vent his anger upon the*

the last. [30] *For ships of Kittim will come against him and he will be cowed; he will return; and vent his fury at the covenant of sanctity, and will accomplish; he will return and have understanding for those who foresake the covenant of sanctity.*

covenant of sanctity (see *v.* 28).

וְעָשָׂה — *And he will accomplish* [lit. *do*].

[*Josephus (Ant. XII* 5, 3) relates that the king, helped by accomplices within Jerusalem, gained entry into the city without a fight. Once inside, he massacred many of his opponents (those who opposed his policy of Hellenization) and plundered the city.]

וְשָׁב — *He will return.*

[Two years later, Antiochus again returned to besiege Jerusalem. The gold and silver of the Temple had attracted his eye and he was determined to take possession of its riches. He left the Temple bare, carrying away with him the golden *menorah*, the golden incense altar, the golden table, and all other vessels of gold and silver. He forbade the Jews to bring קָרְבַּן הַתָּמִיד, *the daily sacrifice,* and declared the death sentence for anyone found adhering to the Torah. Many thousands were killed and carried off as captives (*Josephus, Ant. XII* 5, 4).]

וְיָבֵן עַל־עֹזְבֵי בְּרִית קֹדֶשׁ — *And have understanding for those who forsake the covenant of sanctity.*

Antiochus' policy was not motivated by greed alone. Part of his policy was to hellenize all his subjects. To accomplish this he set out to crush every vestige of Judaism. Those who went along with the king's policy, and forsook the covenant of sanctity found favor in the king's eyes.

Abarbanel interprets this phrase in a contrary sense. Even those who cooperated with the king did not, ultimately, escape their fate. וְיָבֵן, (The king) *contemplated,* eventually to annihilate even *those who forsake the covenant of sanctity.* This is a sad lesson which history has repeated many times.

Rashi interprets this verse as referring to the Roman attacks against *Eretz Yisrael* at the time of the Temple's destruction. The Romans did not honor their pact with the Hasmoneans, and oppressed the Jews. They came and seized the opportunity made available to them through the sins of the Jews וְזָעַם עַל־בְּרִית־קוֹדֶשׁ, *and* [he will] *vent his fury at the covenant of sanctity.* At the end of the Second Temple there was שִׂנְאַת חִנָּם, *indefensible enmity,* between factions of Jews as told in the *Talmud* (*Yoma* 9b) and *Yossipon* (ch. 45).

◆§**Prefatory Note to verses 31-36**

A *barbanel* gives us two basic approaches to these verses. In the first, these verses refer to the kingdom of the fourth beast (ch. 7) — i.e., the Romans (*Mayenei HaYeshuah* 11:8). This approach is adopted by *Malbim* and parallels *Rashi* who interprets the verses from verse 21 as referring to this era. We will give this interpretation first. As this approach is held by a number of commentators who differ in particulars, a source will be given for every comment.

Abarbanel's alternative interpretation (*Mayenei HaYeshuah* 11:4) will be presented in the

לא קֹדֶשׁ: וּזְרֹעִים מִמֶּנּוּ יַעֲמֹדוּ וְחִלְּלוּ
הַמִּקְדָּשׁ הַמָּעוֹז וְהֵסִירוּ הַתָּמִיד וְנָתְנוּ
לב הַשִּׁקּוּץ מְשֹׁמֵם: וּמַרְשִׁיעֵי בְרִית יַחֲנִיף
בַּחֲלַקּוֹת וְעַם יֹדְעֵי אֱלֹהָיו יַחֲזִקוּ וְעָשׂוּ:

lower part of the page. Since *Abarbanel is alone in this second interpretation, we will label it Abarbanel's Interpretation.* (Surprisingly, *Abarbanel* does not state that he is offering two basically divergent interpretations!).

Malbim notes that the angel does not tell us about the outcome of the Hasmonean struggle against the Greeks. The angel evidently felt that more elaboration was not needed here as Daniel had already heard the outcome in the previous vision (8:11-12; see *comm.*). [The period of the Hasmoneans itself did not need elaboration since the purpose of the vision was to explain and add detail to the vision of the four kingdoms. The Hasmonean kingdom, the bridge between the third and fourth kingdoms, did not merit much detail.]

31. The Sanctuary Profaned

וּזְרֹעִים מִמֶּנּוּ יַעֲמֹדוּ — *And arms will arise from him.*

The Romans will send their generals to conquer Jerusalem (*Rashi*).

[*Abarbanel* and *Malbim* interpret וּזְרֹעִים, *arms*, as a metaphor for force: they will send forces. See v. 6 for similar uses of זְרוֹעַ.]

וּזְרֹעִים מִמֶּנּוּ, [the Romans] *will be more powerful than him* [Antiochus].

הַמִּקְדָּשׁ הַמָּעוֹז — *The fortified Sanctuary.*

When Herod rebuilt the Temple,

he built it resembling a fortress (*Malbim; cf. Josephus, Wars V 5, 8*).

[*Josephus (Ant. XV 11, 4)* relates that Herod, when he rebuilt the Temple, also fortified the citadel which had been built to the north of the Temple by the Hasmoneans. This citadel, called Antonia, was fortified to such a degree that it held the key to the defense of the city and the Temple. He relates (*Wars VI 1, 4*) that Titus realized that he must at all cost conquer the citadel in order to conquer the city. Perhaps it is this fortress which is alluded to here.]

ABARBANEL'S INTERPRETATION

31. וּזְרֹעִים מִמֶּנּוּ יַעֲמֹדוּ — *And arms will arise from him.*

Antiochus will leave the administration of *Eretz Yisrael* to his officials.

[Antiochus left the government of his kingdom to a caretaker, Lysias, while he left for the east. *Josephus (Ant. XII 7, 2)* relates that Antiochus, enraged at the revolt fomented by Mattisyahu the Hasmonean at Modi'in, prepared to head his army himself against Judea. But when he realized that his treasury was depleted, he left for Persia to raise money by collecting taxes owed. Other

historians claim he had to put down insurgencies in that part of his kingdom in 3695-165 B.C.E.]

וְחִלְּלוּ הַמִּקְדָּשׁ הַמָּעוֹז — *And will profane the fortified Sanctuary.*

[This evidently refers back to verse 30 where Antiochus *will return and vent his fury at the covenant of sanctity and will accomplish.* The nature of his accomplishment is left unsaid. The angel here returns to give more particulars about this.]

וְהֵסִירוּ הַתָּמִיד — *And they will remove*

³¹ 'And arms will arise from him and will profane the fortified Sanctuary, and will remove the daily sacrifice, and will install the mute abomination. ³² The corrupters of the covenant he will flatter glibly, and the people who know their God will persevere and will accomplish. ³³ The wise among the

וְהֵסִירוּ הַתָּמִיד — *And will remove the daily sacrifice.*

[The קָרְבָּן הַתָּמִיד, *daily sacrifices,* ceased to be offered three and one-half years before the destruction of the Temple (see 9:27).]

וְנָתְנוּ הַשִּׁקוּץ מְשֹׁמֵם — *And (they) will install the mute abomination.*

Hadrian, after putting down Bar Kochba's revolution fifty-two years after the destruction (*Seder Olam* ch. 30), had a temple for idol worship constructed on the site of the Holy Temple (*Malbim*).

[The similarity of the wording here and in 9:27, *he will abolish the sacrifice and offering and upon soaring heights will the mute abomination be* is striking. Perhaps this is one of the reasons why the commentators feel that this verse refers to the Roman era.]

32. וּמַרְשִׁיעֵי בְרִית יַחֲנִיף בַּחֲלַקוֹת — *The corrupters of the covenant he will flatter glibly.*

This is an elaboration of the angel's statement (9:27), וְהִגְבִּיר בְּרִית לָרַבִּים, *and he will strengthen a covenant with the great ones* (Mayenei HaYeshuah; Malbim).

[Since this covenant was made לָרַבִּים, *with the great ones,* no doubt Agrippa II was among them. The derogatory term וּמַרְשִׁיעֵי בְרִית, *the corruptors of the covenant,* surely then applies to him also. From *Sotah* (41a) one gets the impression that Agrippa was one who adhered to the Torah. This is the expressed opinion of *Rashbam (Pesachim* 107b s.v. אגריפס). According to this interpretation one has to assume that the references in the *Talmud* refer only to Agrippa I (the elder), Herod's grandson and father of

---

ABARBANEL'S INTERPRETATION

the daily sacrifice.

[The קָרְבָּן הַתָּמִיד, *daily sacrifice,* was discontinued for three years (3693-6 A.M. — 167-4 B.C.E.; *Josephus, Ant. XII* 5, 4).]

וְנָתְנוּ הַשִּׁקוּץ מְשֹׁמֵם — *And (they) will install the mute abomination.*

[The king set up an altar to his idols on the place of the holy altar and had swine offered upon it (*ibid.*).]

32. וּמַרְשִׁיעֵי בְרִית יַחֲנִיף — *The corrupters of the covenant he will flatter glibly.*

[*Josephus (Ant.* XII, 5, 1) relates that

during the controversy between Jason and Menelaus over the office of high priest (see above *v.* 28) Menelaus' party sent a delegation to the king to state that they were ready to leave their faith and live like Greeks. They also asked for permission to build a gymnasium in Jerusalem. It is also known that the king reinstated Menelaus as high priest. We also see from verse 24 that Antiochus was wont to favor his followers with monetary rewards. This verse may also refer to the defection of the כּוּתִים, Samaritans, to Antiochus as told by *Josephus (Ant.* XII, 5, 5 and XII, 7, 1).]

לג וּמַשְׂכִּילֵי עָם יָבִינוּ לָרַבִּים וְנִכְשְׁלוּ בְּחֶרֶב
לד וּבְלֶהָבָה בִּשְׁבִי וּבְבִזָּה יָמִים: וּבְהִכָּשְׁלָם
יֵעָזְרוּ עֵזֶר מְעָט וְנִלְווּ עֲלֵיהֶם רַבִּים

Agrippa II. In *Yossipon* (ch. 63) we find Agrippa II painted in very dark colors (see glosses to ed. Huminer; the text does not warrant the editor's emendation. *Josephus* says nothing about this).]

וְעַם יֹדְעֵי אֱלֹהָיו — *And the people who know their God.*
I.e., the righteous Jews.

יַחֲזִקוּ — *Will persevere.*
With the Torah and the fear of God *(Rashi).*
[*Rashi* seems to translate יַחֲזִקוּ, *will hold on* — i.e., to the (implied) Torah.]
The wise ... refers to R'

Yochanan ben Zakkai, who interceded successfully with Vespasian to spare Yavneh and its Sages, as related in *Gittin* (56b).

33. וּמַשְׂכִּילֵי עָם — *The wise among the people.*
I.e., the Sages of every generation, like the family of *Rabbi* (Rabbi Yehudah the Prince).

יָבִינוּ לָרַבִּים — *Will make the multitudes understand.*
They will preach the Torah to the people and exhort them to adhere to it.
[They will make it clear to the people that though the Temple is

---

ABARBANEL'S INTERPRETATION

וְעַם יֹדְעֵי אֱלֹהָיו — *And the people who know their God ...*
... Mattisyahu the Hasmonean, his sons, and their compatriots.

יַחֲזִקוּ וְעָשׂוּ — *Will persevere and will accomplish.*
[Mattisyahu started a revolt at Modi'in and destroyed many of the altars which had been set up to idolatry. He reinstituted the *mitzvah* of circumcision which many had abandoned because of the king's decree. When Mattisyahu died a year after the beginning of the revolt (3594 A.M. — 166 B.C.E.), his son Yehudah took over command of the revolt. He met and defeated, first, Appolonius with his army of Samaritans, and then Seron, general of Antiochus' forces in 'Southern' Syria, at בֵּית חוֹרוֹן, *Beth-Choron.* Upon hearing of this, Lysias, the caretaker governor, sent a great force, commanded by Nicanor and Gorgias. Yehudah, with a much smaller force decisively defeated them at Em-

maus and won much booty. Lysias then got together an even greater army (60,000 men) and personally led it in battle. He met Yehudah's army, which he outnumbered six to one, at בֵּית צוּר, *Beth Tzur*, near Jerusalem. Yehudah forced Lysias to flee to Syria. Yehudah then entered the Temple, purified it, reinstituted the daily sacrifices, and *lit the lights.* This is when the miracle of *Chanukah* took place (3696 A.M. — 164 B.C.E.). יַחֲזִקוּ — [They will fortify themselves, probably refers to the initial stage of the revolt when Mattisyahu and his sons fortified themselves in the mountains and caves of Judea. וְעָשׂוּ, *and they will accomplish*, refers to their subsequent victories and their ultimate re-entry into the Temple and its reconsecration.]

33. יָבִינוּ לָרַבִּים — *Will make the multitudes understand.*
The Sages of the generation made the multitudes understand the gravity of the events and exhorted them to stand fast in their conviction.

people will make the multitudes understand; and they will stumble by the sword, by flame, through captivity and plunder, for years. 34 When they stumble, they will be helped with a little help, and many

desolate the Torah has not lost its meaning.] They will also strengthen the hope and resolution of the Jewish People in this dark hour (*Rashi*).

וְנִכְשְׁלוּ בְּחֶרֶב — *And they will stumble by the sword.*

Their steadfast adherence to the Torah caused them to be martyred during the long and bitter exile. *Malbim* finds in this a reference to the ten famous *tannaim* (Mishnaic Sages) who were martyred by the Romans during the period of the destruction of the Temple and the persecutions which followed it during the reign of Hadrian.

בְּשְׁבִי — *Through captivity.*

[Josephus (*Ant.* XII, 5, 4) tells us that Antiochus took 10,000 captives.]

34. יֵעָזְרוּ עֵזֶר מְעָט — *They will be helped with a little help.*

They will be able to bribe their enemies and thus help themselves (*Rashi*).

[Evidently *Rashi* interprets וּבְהִכָּשְׁלָם, *when they will stumble,* in a more general way than the וְנִכְשְׁלוּ in *v.* 33 which meant martyrdom. Here stumbling refers to any and all difficulties that will beset them in their long and bitter exile. They will still have this one avenue of exit open to themselves.]

This refers to the revolt of Bar Kochba (approximately 50 years after the *Churban* 3878-118 C.E. See *Seder Olam* ch. 30) (*Malbim*).

[וּבְהִכָּשְׁלָם, *when they will stumble.* This refers back to *v.* 33, וְנִכְשְׁלוּ בְּחֶרֶב, *and they will stumble by the sword.* This was interpreted as referring to the martyrs during the persecutions under Hadrian (during the revolt). יֵעָזְרוּ עֵזֶר מְעָט, *they will be helped with a little help.* [This probably means the revolt lasted 2½ years (*Seder Olam, ibid.*). One can interpret רַבִּים, *great ones,*

ABARBANEL'S INTERPRETATION

וְנִכְשְׁלוּ בְּחֶרֶב — *And they will stumble by the sword.*

The *wise* will give up their lives in martyrdom. They will be put to *the sword* and thrown into *the flames.*[1]

34. וּבְהִכָּשְׁלָם — *When they stumble.*

During the persecutions of the Greeks.

יֵעָזְרוּ עֵזֶר מְעָט — *They will be helped with a little help.*

The Hasmoneans were able to prevail in spite of their numerical disadvantage.

---

1. [The *Midrash* (*Bereishis Rabbah* 65:22) relates that the famed Sage Yose ben Yoezer (see *Avos* 1) was martyred in this period. His nephew, Yakim, evidently a Hellenist, taunted him, 'See what kind of horse your God gave you to ride upon.'

Yose retorted, 'If this is the fate reserved for those who do His will, imagine what awaits those who transgress His will.'

Overwhelmed by the uncle's straightforward answer and the strength of his conviction, he went and took his own life. While Yose was being led to the gallows he looked up and saw the angels leading the soul of his nephew to גַּן עֵדֶן, *Paradise.* He remarked, 'He has proceeded me into Heaven by a few minutes.'

לה בְּחֲלַקְלַקּוֹת: וּמִן־הַמַּשְׂכִּילִים יִכָּשְׁלוּ
לִצְרוֹף בָּהֶם וּלְבָרֵר וְלַלְבֵּן עַד־עֵת קֵץ
לו כִּי־עוֹד לַמּוֹעֵד: וְעָשָׂה כִרְצֹנוֹ הַמֶּלֶךְ
וְיִתְרוֹמֵם וְיִתְגַּדֵּל עַל־כָּל־אֵל וְעַל אֵל
אֵלִים יְדַבֵּר נִפְלָאוֹת וְהִצְלִיחַ עַד־כָּלָה
לז זַעַם כִּי נֶחֱרָצָה נֶעֱשָׂתָה: וְעַל־אֱלֹהֵי

(as in 9:27) referring to people like Rabbi Akiva who supported Bar Kochba.]

בְּחֲלַקְלַקּוֹת — *With glibness.*

Though God will provide limited help to Israel, many Jews will be taken in by the glibness of the enemy and join them (*Metzudos*).

35. יִכָּשְׁלוּ לִצְרוֹף — *Will stumble to refine.*

Some of the wise will err in trying to calculate the promised deliverance. They will try *to refine,* i.e., to arrive at the pure truth. But they will be mistaken; for *it is not yet the appointed time* (*Rashi*).

Here the angel returns to explain the martyrdom of the *wise among the people* (v. 33). *Some of the wise will stumble to refine*

among *them* — i.e., to atone for the sins of their nation so that they will become refined through this atonement and to *select and cleanse* — i.e., to purify from sin. This pattern will repeat itself throughout the exile עַד עֵת קֵץ, *till the time of the End* (*Malbim*).

'If he (the purported Messiah) will not succeed this far or will be killed, then it is certain that he was not the one that the Torah promised but he is like all the perfect and righteous kings of the house of David who have died, and the Holy One, Blessed be He, has set him up only to test the multitudes, as is written *some of the wise will stumble* (*Rambam, Hilchos Melachim* 12:4, censored out of our editions. See Shulsinger and some of the Israeli editions).

The wise refers to those who, in the face of the trials and tribulations of the

---

ABARBANEL'S INTERPRETATION

בְּחֲלַקְלַקּוֹת — *With glibness.*

[When the Hasmoneans are victorious, *many will join them with glibness.* There were those who during Antiochus's reign had been sympathetic to his policy of Hellenization. But no sooner did they realize that the Hasmoneans were victorious, than they rushed to join the winning side and become pious Jews. *Josephus* (*Ant.* XII, 7, 4 and XII, 8, 1) tells us that Shimon, Mattisyahu's son and eventual successor, was killed by his own son-in-law Ptolemy, who also killed his mother-in-

law and her two sons. Ptolemy also attempted to kill his brother-in-law, Yochanan Hyrkanos, Shimon's heir, but was unsuccessful. No doubt his goal had been to seize the government (see also *Wars* I, 2, 1-5).]

35. וּמִן־הַמַּשְׂכִּלִים — *Some of the wise.*

This refers to Mattisyahu's sons. Of his five sons, four died during the wars against Syria. The cause of this tragedy was the sin of the Jewish nation. לִצְרוֹף בָּהֶם, *to refine among them,* as noted above.

will join them with glibness. ³⁵ *Some of the wise will stumble to refine through them, and to select and cleanse till the time of the End, for it is not yet the appointed time.*

³⁶ *'The king will do as he pleases, and he will exalt himself and make himself greater than any god, and about the God of gods he will speak fantastic things; he will succeed until the wrath is terminated, for that which was decreed was executed.* ³⁷ *About the God of*

---

bitter exile, will remain steadfast in their faith. The angel declared to Daniel (12:10), *Many will become purified, whitened, and refined; but the wicked will do wickedly and they will not understand; but they who are wise will understand.*

Thus, even some of the wise — who have withstood the trial — when faced with even greater trials and hardships, some of them will not be able to hold fast and they too will 'stumble' (*Rambam, Iggeres Teman*).

כִּי עוֹד לַמּוֹעֵד — *For it is not yet the appointed time* [lit. *for there is yet to the appointed time*].

36. 'Fantastic Things'

וְעָשָׂה כִרְצֹנוֹ הַמֶּלֶךְ — *The king will do as he pleases.*

The angel here again skips an entire period. As stated before, his objective was not to give a summary of history but to elaborate on the previous prophecies. This verse refers to 8:23, *And in the latter time their kingdom ... there will stand up a brazen-faced king, an understander of riddles ...*

This refers to the Roman emperor Constantine I (the Great, 4548 A.M. — 308 C.E. to 4577 A.M. — 337 C.E.), the first Roman emperor to convert to Christianity. *The king will do as he pleases* in that ...

וְיִתְרוֹמֵם וְיִתְגַּדֵּל עַל־כָּל־אֵל — *And he*

will exalt himself and make himself greater than any god.

He will endeavor to further the Christian religion and to establish it as the state religion (*Abarbanel; Ibn Ezra; Malbim* without going into detail).

יְדַבֵּר נִפְלָאוֹת — *He will speak fantastic things.*

He will establish principles about the nature of God which will be wondrous — i.e., unfathomable to the rational mind, passing them off as wonders or mysteries (*Malbim*).

This refers to the dogmas of the trinity, the virgin birth, the incarnation of God and transubstantiation (*Mayenei HaYeshuah* 11:8).

These doctrines received their final formulation and acceptance at the council of Nicaea (325 C.E.) which was convoked and influenced by Constantine. The emperor, for political reasons, needed a church united in its beliefs.]

וְהִצְלִיחַ עַד כָּלָה זַעַם — *He will succeed until the wrath is terminated.*

The religion furthered by him will succeed until *the wrath* of God against His people *is terminated by* the coming of the Messiah (*Mayenei HaYeshuah* 11:8; *Malbim*).

כִּי נֶחֱרָצָה נֶעֱשָׂתָה — *For that which was decreed was executed.*

אֲבֹתָיו לֹא יָבִין וְעַל־חֶמְדַּת נָשִׁים וְעַל־
כָּל־אֱלוֹהַּ לֹא יָבִין כִּי עַל־כֹּל יִתְגַּדָּל:
לח וְלֶאֱלֹהַּ מָעֻזִּים עַל־כַּנּוֹ יְכַבֵּד וְלֶאֱלוֹהַּ
אֲשֶׁר לֹא־יְדָעֻהוּ אֲבֹתָיו יְכַבֵּד בְּזָהָב
לט וּבְכֶסֶף וּבְאֶבֶן יְקָרָה וּבַחֲמֻדוֹת: וְעָשָׂה
לְמִבְצְרֵי מָעֻזִּים עִם־אֱלוֹהַּ נֵכָר אֲשֶׁר

The fate which is to befall Jewry has already been decreed and will come to pass (Malbim).

37. וְעַל אֱלֹהֵי אֲבֹתָיו לֹא יָבִין — *About the God of his ancestors he will not understand.*

The Roman emperor will show no regard for the God of Israel's ancestors, Abraham, Isaac, and Jacob (Rashi).

Or: His—Constantine's—ancestors. He will show no regard for the pagan gods his ancestors worshipped (Mayenei HaYeshuah 11:8 Malbim).

וְעַל־חֶמְדַּת נָשִׁים — *Nor about the most desirable of women.*

[The phrase is connected to לֹא יָבִין which appears later in the sentence. Thus, *nor about the most desirable of women ... will he understand.*]

The allusion is to the Jewish People which is metaphorically represented as a beautiful woman [as in *Shir HaShirim;*] (Rashi).

[This phrase can also be understood as a reference to the faith of the Jews. The context seems to imply this. The angel here pithily summarizes the centuries of religious persecution of the Jews by the Christian church.]

He will show no regard for *the desiring* חֶמְדַּת *of women.* The church adopted a policy of celibacy for its priests (Mayenei HaYeshuah 11:8).

וְעַל כָּל־אֱלוֹהַּ לֹא יָבִין — *Nor about any god will he understand.*

The Christian religion will basically adopt the worship of the one God (Mayenei HaYeshuah 11:1 Malbim).

Metzudos understands this phrase otherwise: They will not show understanding even for the one true God. Their monotheism will be tainted by the paradox of trinity.

These opposing views about the nature of Christianity mirror a Halachic dispute. The *Talmud (Bechoros* 2b) prohibits a Jew to form a partnership with an idolater because the latter may some day have to back up his credibility with an oath (שְׁבוּעָה) where he will naturally invoke the name of his god. As a result the Jew would be transgressing a law of the Torah which says (in reference to the names of heathen gods) לֹא יִשָּׁמַע עַל פִּיךָ, *it shall not be heard through you (Exodus* 23:13). *Tosafos (Bechoros* 2b, *s.v.* שמע) comments that this prohibition does not apply to an oath of the gentiles among whom we live. 'Their intent is to the Creator of heaven and earth, although they accompany the name of God with something else [דָּבָר אַחֵר] ... Gentiles are not prohibited from doing this ... ' Some Halachic authorities, however, hold that the ruling of *Tosafos* excluding Christians from the category of idolaters applies only to their oaths: Since gentiles swear by the name of God, there is no transgression of the law if they mention other names in addition, but insofar as the prohibition of idolatry is concerned, *Tosafos'* ruling does not apply (see *Pischei T'shuvah* to *Yoreh Deah* 147:2; *Darkei T'shuvah,* there, 72;

his ancestors he will not understand, nor about the most desirable of women, nor about any god will he understand, for he will aggrandize himself above all. ³⁸ *But he will honor the God of the fortress in His place; and a god whom his ancestors knew not, he will honor with gold, silver, precious stones, and desirable things.* ³⁹ *He will develop strong fortresses*

Machatzis HaShekel and *Pri M'gadim* to *Orach Chayim* 156).

However, *Pischei T'shuvah* correctly points out (ibid.) that *Rama* clearly held that only a Jew was forbidden to include other beings or concepts with his worship of God. Gentiles, however, are not forbidden such 'partnership', hence Christians would not be considered idolaters.

Rambam (*Hilchos Avodah Zarah* 9:4) explicitly states, 'The Nazarenes (נוֹצְרִים) are idolaters ... '(Our versions have Canaanites (כְּנַעֲנִים), but this is clearly an emendation by the censors as seen from the context and old editions and manuscripts, see Shulsinger ed. *Rambam's* ostensible source is *Avodah Zarah* 6a (where the censors' heavy hand has also been felt; See *Chesronos HaShas*).

Even *Rambam* finds a compensating virtue in the advent of Christianity (and Islam). These are his words on this topic (*Hilchos M'lachim* 11:4 *Pardes* ed. from early prints and manuscripts. Parts of this passage are missing in all later editions. The reason is self-evident. *Ramban* quotes this passage in his *D'rush Toras Hashem T'mimah Kisvei HaRamban*, v. 1, p. 144): 'All these doings of Yeshu the Nazarene and of this Ishmaelite (Muhammad) who came after him, are only to pave the way for the Messianic king and to prepare the world to serve HASHEM together ... The world has already been filled about the Messiah and about the Torah and about the *Mitzvos* ... Some say these commandments were true but have been rendered unneccessary in our times and others say ... So when the true Messianic king comes, and succeeds ... they will all repent and know that their ancestors had inherited a falsehood.' Similiar sentiments are expressed by Rav Yaakov Emden (*Lechem Shamayim* to *Avos* 4, *s.v.* כל כנסיה שהיא לשם שמים).

38. וְלֶאֱלֹהַּ מָעֻזִּים — *But ... the God of the fortress.*

[See *v.* 31 where the Holy Temple is referred to as מָעוֹז.]

They will give *honor* to the one true God (*Mayenei HaYeshua* 11:8).

עַל כַּנּוֹ — *In His place.*

[They will give God his honor *in His place* — i.e., in the appropriate manner. They will admit that He is the Prime Cause.]

וְלֶאֱלֹהַ אֲשֶׁר לֹא־יְדָעֻהוּ אֲבֹתָיו — *And a god whom his ancestors knew not.*

And (i.e., but also) *a god* — Yeshu the Nazarene — whom *his ancestors knew not, he will honor* (*Mayenei HaYeshuah* 11:8; *Malbim*).

Ibn Ezra (*Perush HaKatzar*) interprets this as referring to the Christian practice of saint worship.

39. וְעָשָׂה לְמִבְצְרֵי מָעֻזִּים — *[And] he will develop (for) strong fortresses.*

[He shall help to build and maintain them. The phrase עִם אֱלוֹהַּ נֵכָר, *with a strange god*, is a parenthetic identification of these fortresses — i.e., *those with a strange god* ...]

This is an allusion to the churches which are built with towers like fortresses. The *strange god* in these fortresses refers to the statues and icons placed in them (*Mayenei HaYeshuah* 11:8).

[It is possible to understand this verse as a reference to the establishment of the church as an autonomous body. *He will accomplish* —

מ ° יַכִּיר ק' °הִכִּיר יַרְבֶּה כָבוֹד וְהִמְשִׁילָם בָּרַבִּים וַאֲדָמָה יְחַלֵּק בִּמְחִיר: וּבְעֵת קֵץ יִתְנַגַּח

i.e., Constantine's action will ultimately lead to the establishment of the church as a strong fortress. This interpretation allows us to understand the next phrase אֲשֶׁר יַכִּיר יַרְבֶּה כָבוֹד, to whomever he acknowledges he will increase honor, as well as the rest of the verse, as Rashi understands it. Abarbanel and Malbim leave most of the verse without comment.]

אֲשֶׁר יַכִּיר יַרְבֶּה כָבוֹד — To whomever he acknowledges he will increase honor.

Those nobles whom he will choose to flatter and empower he will shower with honor (Rashi).

[The church will dispense its ecclesiastical offices not on the basis of merit, but on the basis of political power.]

וְהִמְשִׁילָם בָּרַבִּים — He will empower them over the multitudes.

The church shall have the power to levy taxes upon the principalities around it (Abarbanel 11:8; Malbim).

[The establishment of the church shall ultimately have as its result that the church shall become the political ruler of many. As is well-known, the church was a great political power in the Middle Ages.]

וַאֲדָמָה יְחַלֵּק בִּמְחִיר — And he will apportion land at a price.

He will distribute land for a pittance to whomever he acknowledges (Rashi).

[The church of the Middle Ages owned a great deal of land. The bishops became, in essence, great feudal lords. Thus: to whomever he acknowledges (the appointed priests) he will apportion land for a price — i.e. for a mere pittance.]

◄§Epilogue

We will mention here highlights from some of the other commentators to this vision.

R' Saadiah Gaon (Emunos Vedeos, 7) gives us an outline to these verses without a running commentary (only fragments of his commentary to Daniel survive in manuscript). Verses 3-15 refer to the Greek kingdom(s). Verses 16-36 are devoted to the Roman empire. Verses 36-12:1 refer to the Arab Empire. R' Saadiah Gaon is here true to his view (see Ibn Ezra to 2:39) that the fourth animal in the vision includes both the Roman and Arab empires.

[A strong case can be made for interpreting verses 40-41 as referring to the attempts of the Christian kingdoms to wrest the Middle East from the Arabs during the Crusades. Verses 43-12:1 can be understood as referring to more recent events. וברוך היודע, Blessed is He Who knows!]

Another interpretation, differing considerably from those given above is that of R' Avraham bar Chiya (Megillas HaMegalleh. pp. 93-98; see Mayenei HaYeshuah 11:5):

The expression king of the north is used interchangeably for the Greek monarchs in Macedonia, and the Romans. Verses 6-10 refer to the vicissitudes of the Ptolemaic kingdom during the reign of Cleopatra (49-30 B.C.E.) up to its annexation by the Romans in 30 B.C.E. (Much of the historical data used in this interpertation cannot be corroborated). The king of the south in verses 11-15 is the Seleucid rulers of the Middle East which is south in relation to Rome. Verse 15 describes the destruction of the Temple and Jerusalem by Vespasian. Verses 16-17 describe the events immediately following the destruction. Verse 18 refers to Constantine the Great's establishment of Constantinople as the capital of the empire (וְיָשֵׂם פָּנָיו לְאִיִּים) and his adoption of the Christian religion (308-337 C.E.). Verse 20 (probably) refers to the division of the empire by Constantine's sons (Constans I, Constantine II, Constantius III).

with the strange god to whomever he acknowledges
he will increase honor; and he will empower them
over the multitudes, and he will apportion land at a
price.

Verse 21 refers to the ascendancy of Mohammed (died 632 C.E.). Verses 22-3 describes his conquest of the Arabian peninsula and his subsequent massacre of the Jews living there (וְגֵם נְגִיד בְּרִית). Verses 24-26 describe Arab expansion under Abu Bakr (632-34) and Omar (634-44). *The king of the south* in verse 25 refers to the conquest of Syria. The two kings in verse 27 are the embodiment of the Arabian and Roman kingdoms. The Arabs, having conquered Egypt and Syria, now deserve the epitaph *king of the south*. Both kings will have their share in the oppression of the Jewish nation (לְבָבָם לְמֵרַע). Verse 29 tells about the establishment of the Arab caliphate in Damascus by the Ummayad dynasty (661-750). Verse 30 tells of the successes of Islam in distant countries (e.g. Afghanistan etc.). This marks the beginning of decline (וְנִכְאָה) and with it an upsurge of anti-semitism (וְזָעַם עַל בְּרִית קֹדֶשׁ), under the Abbasid dynasty (750-1055). עֹזְבֵי בְּרִית קֹדֶשׁ describes the Christian countries. Verse 31 describes the conquest of Jerusalem by the Crusaders (1099 C.E.; in the lifetime of R' Abraham Bar Chiya). וְהֵסִירוּ תָּמִיד refers to the Crusaders prohibiting the Jews from praying at the site of the Temple and from living in Jerusalem. Verses 32-39 are a general description of the deportment of the Jews and their leaders during the long and dark exile. The description of events occuring during and preceding the redemption (בב"א) are contained in the verses from 40 to the end of the book. It must be said that many of the historical facts used (especially up to the Arabian period) are questionable. This interpretation, because it departs radically from the line followed by the commentators given above, has simply been summarized. It opens up many new avenues of thought which we leave for the interested reader. Many other variant interpretations are found in other commentators, but they fall outside the scope of this *commentary*.

⊷§Prefatory Notes to 11:40-12:5
Reading History into the Vision

The following verses describe the events immediately preceding, during, and after the promised redemption בב"א. Up to this point we have at least had the guiding hand of history to aid us in understanding some of the obscure verses. From here on we stumble in darkness. *Ibn Ezra* prefaces his comments to Chapter 11 with the following comment (11:4 *s.v.* ולא כמשלו): 'I will now give you a basic rule. From the beginning of *v*. 5 till the end of *v*. 30, which is clearly about the destruction of the Second Temple, it is futile to search in the ancient books [such as] the book of Joseph ben Gorion *(Yossipon)* — even if we had all his words to learn the details of the wars which occurred then. (*Yossipon* has very little information about the Greek period. Evidently *Ibn Ezra* did not know of *Josephus Flavius*.) I will therefore [only] explain the words and the meanings (of the sentences) in a general way.'

If this is true concerning the nebulous past, how much more truer is it with regard to the unfathomable future!

Rambam admonishes (Hilchos M'lachim 12:2):

All these things, and their like, we will not know how they will be till they happen, for these things were obscured by the prophets [a paraphrase of 12:4 וְאַתָּה דָנִיֵּאל סְתֹם הַדְּבָרִים]. Also the Sages do not have a clear tradition concerning these matters, rather [they follow] the probable meanings of the Scriptures [הכרע הפסוקים] ... At any rate neither the sequence of these occurrences, nor their details, are a principle of the faith [עיקר בדת]. [Therefore] a person should not occupy himself with the *Aggados* [homiletical passages], nor study at length the *Midrashim* dealing with these matters or their like, nor should he consider them as fundamentals (ולא ישימם עיקר). For they lead to neither love nor fear [of God]. Nor should [a person] calculate the *End* [the date of the Redemption] ... Rather one should await and believe in this matter in a general way.

Some commentators, notably *Abarbanel* in *Mayenei HaYeshuah* 11:8, have adopted a dif-

עַמּוֹ מֶלֶךְ הַנֶּגֶב וְיִשְׂתָּעֵר עָלָיו מֶלֶךְ
הַצָּפוֹן בְּרֶכֶב וּבְפָרָשִׁים וּבָאֳנִיּוֹת רַבּוֹת
מא וּבָא בָאֲרָצוֹת וְשָׁטַף וְעָבָר: וּבָא בְּאֶרֶץ
הַצְּבִי וְרַבּוֹת יִכָּשֵׁלוּ וְאֵלֶּה יִמָּלְטוּ מִיָּדוֹ
מב אֱדוֹם וּמוֹאָב וְרֵאשִׁית בְּנֵי עַמּוֹן: וְיִשְׁלַח
יָדוֹ בַּאֲרָצוֹת וְאֶרֶץ מִצְרַיִם, לֹא תִהְיֶה
מג לִפְלֵיטָה: וּמָשַׁל בְּמִכְמַנֵּי הַזָּהָב וְהַכֶּסֶף
וּבְכֹל חֲמֻדוֹת מִצְרָיִם וְלֻבִים וְכֻשִׁים
מד בְּמִצְעָדָיו: וּשְׁמֻעוֹת יְבַהֲלֻהוּ מִמִּזְרָח
וּמִצָּפוֹן וְיָצָא בְּחֵמָא גְדֹלָה לְהַשְׁמִיד

ferent approach. They interpret the angelic prophecy to refer to the historical and political phenomena of their own periods. Such an approach can allow for a wide variety of interpretations, all of them plausible. However, experience teaches that the fortunes of nations can change radically. Thus, an interpretation that once seemed obvious may later be rendered untenable. The history of Ishmael is a striking example. After many centuries of Arab obscurity, Islam became a world power only to fade, but then to rise again as an economic force. The *ultimate* interpretation, therefore, must await the *End of Days*.

It should be added that the terms *the king of the south* and *the king of the north* in the verses do not have counterparts in past history. Indeed, in some of the interpretations (e.g. *Ibn Ezra*) the identity of *the king of the north* shifts from the king of Macedonia to that of the Roman Empire (the Romans did not have a king at the time so even the term *king* has to be interpreted loosely). When the long awaited *Messianic king* will come, בב״א, the real meaning of these verses will shine through plainly and unequivocably so that *all flesh shall see together that the mouth of HASHEM has [already] spoken* (Isaiah 40:5; see *Radak*).

40. At The Time Of The End

יִתְנַגַּח עִמּוֹ — *Shall clash with* [lit. *shall involve himself in goring*] *him.*

[I.e. with the king of the north mentioned in previous verses and in those immediately following.]

Malbim points out the similarities between this prophecy and that of *Ezekiel* (38-39) where the king of Magog will come from *his place in the ends of the north* (38:15) and fall *on the mountains of Yisrael* (ibid. 39:2).

וְיִשְׂתָּעֵר — *Shall storm.*

The translation follows *Radak* (Shorashim *s.v.* סער) and *Metzudos.*

R' *Shmuel Masnuth* adds another

two translations: *shall move; shall become enraged.*

This latter translation is derived from the Arabic.

בָאֲרָצוֹת — *(Into the) countries ...*
... of the south (*Malbim*).

41. בְּאֶרֶץ הַצְּבִי — *The coveted land.*
[*Eretz Yisrael* (see 11:16).]

וְרַבּוֹת — *(And) many ...*
Many lands of the south (*Malbim*).

[The feminine suffix ות indicates a feminine *plural.* Therefore the feminine אֲרָצוֹת, lands, is indicated as the noun modified by the adjective רַבּוֹת, *many.*]

אֱדוֹם וּמוֹאָב וְרֵאשִׁית בְּנֵי עַמּוֹן — *Edom, Moab, and the forward-dwelling people of Ammon.*

⁴⁰ 'And at the time of the End, the king of the south shall clash with him, and the king of the north shall storm at him with chariots, horsemen, and many ships, and he will enter countries, and shall flood and pass through. ⁴¹ And he will enter the coveted land. Many will stumble, but these shall be saved from his hand: Edom, Moab, and the forward-dwelling people of Ammon. ⁴² And he will stretch forth his hand into lands, and Egypt will not be a survivor. ⁴³ And he will gain control of the caches of the gold, and the silver, and all of the desirable goods of Egypt, and the Lubians and Kushim in his footsteps. ⁴⁴ But news from the east and the north will alarm him, and he will set

[The land of Ammon (the vicinity of modern Amman, the capital of Jordan) is north of Moab. The king of the north will conquer *Eretz Yisrael*, but will stop at its southern borders and not enter Edom which lies south of it. However, to the east of the Jordan, he will penetrate southward far enough to conquer most of Ammon, leaving just *the forward-dwelling people*, i.e., the people who live toward the forward edges of its southern border. Moab, lying south of Ammon will escape unscathed (see *Kaftor VaFerach* ch. 47, and *Rashi* to *Numbers* 34:3).

The angel here does not mean the *ancient* Edomites, Moabites, and Ammonites. The people living in those ancestral homelands of nations are meant *(Ibn Ezra)*.

42. וְיִשְׁלַח יָדוֹ — *He will stretch forth his hand ...*

... To kill and destroy *(Metzudos)*.

... To plunder *(Malbim)*.

[It is possible to interpret the previous verse as referring to the Middle East: *many* (countries) in the area of the *coveted land* will stumble (among the eastern nations) but these, *shall be saved: Edom ...* Then the king of the north shall advance upon Africa. He shall stretch forth *his hand into the* (African) *lands, and the land of Egypt shall not escape.*]

43. בְּמִכְמַנֵּי — *The caches.*

The translation follows *Ibn Ezra*, *Radak (Shorashim, s.v.* כמן*)* and *R' Shmuel Masnuth*. The latter gives an alternative translation, *the mines of gold ...*

בְּמִצְעָדָיו — *In his footsteps.*

The king of the north shall conquer the countries beyond Egypt, too *(Ibn Ezra)*.

The translation follows *Ibn Ezra*, who comments that *Lubians* and *Kushim* will be subject to his authority.

Metzudos renders, *will be trampled under his feet.*

Malbim points out that the fall of Egypt in this period was also prophesied by *Ezekiel* 32:15.

44. מִמִּזְרָח וּמִצָּפוֹן — *From the east and the north.*

East and north of Egypt (where

מה וְלְהַחֲרִים רַבִּים: וְיִטַּע אָהֳלֵי אַפַּדְנוֹ בֵּין
יַמִּים לְהַר־צְבִי־קֹדֶשׁ וּבָא עַד־קִצּוֹ וְאֵין
א עוֹזֵר לוֹ: וּבָעֵת הַהִיא יַעֲמֹד
מִיכָאֵל הַשַּׂר הַגָּדוֹל הָעֹמֵד עַל־בְּנֵי עַמֶּךָ
וְהָיְתָה עֵת צָרָה אֲשֶׁר לֹא־נִהְיְתָה מִהְיוֹת
גּוֹי עַד הָעֵת הַהִיא וּבָעֵת הַהִיא יִמָּלֵט

יא מה

יב א

---

the king of the north will then be), the rulers of (Persia) the *east*, and (Babylon) the *north*, will rise up to help their brethren in the south. This is an elaboration on the vision of the small horn in 7:8 (*Ibn Ezra; Metzudos*).

[*Ibn Ezra's* interpretation here is in keeping with his view (7:7) that the animal with the ten horns refers to the kingdom of the Arab nations].

45. אָהֳלֵי אַפַּדְנוֹ — *His palatial tent.*

אַפַּדְנָה is an Aramaic word for *palace* and is used often in the Talmud. It is a great square tent with many rooms, which kings use as a palace (*R' Shmuel Masnuth*).

לְהַר צְבִי קֹדֶשׁ — *And the holy, coveted mountain.*

This refers to Mount Zion (*R' Shmuel Masnuth*).

Metzudos has צְבִי קֹדֶשׁ referring to *Eretz Yisrael* as above (*vs.* 16 and 41). Thus, *the mountain of the holy coveted* [land].

Here again *Malbim* points out the striking similarity between Daniel's vision and that of Ezekiel. There, too, the king of Magog (the north; see *v.* 40) fights his last battle in *the valley of those who pass through on the east of the sea* ... (Ezekiel 39:11), and on *the mountains of Yisrael* (39:2).

XII

1. Your People Will Escape

יַעֲמֹד — *Will stand.*

I.e., Michael will as usual stand up to defend the Jews (*Ibn Ezra; Metzudos; Malbim*).

[The translation follows this interpretation since it appears to fit the literal meaning (פְּשׁוּטוֹ שֶׁל מִקְרָא) best.]

Ibn Ezra adds that this verse is an elaboration of 7:9 where he translates כָּרְסָוָן רְמִיו, *thrones were thrown down* — i.e., the heavenly thrones appointed for the patron angels of the four kingdoms *were*

overturned. Michael in his role of protector of his people will finally succeed in overthrowing the kingdoms.

He will desist from speaking on behalf of Israel when he sees the Holy One, Blessed be He, deliberating on whether to destroy this great nation (the kingdom of the north) because of Israel (*Rashi*).

[The role of Michael is to defend Israel against its detractors. (See *Shmos Rabbah* 18:5; *R' R. Margulies, Malachei Elyon*).

'Michael and Samael (Satan) stand before the Divine Presence.

11

45

12

1

11	*out in great anger to destroy and exterminate many.*
45	[45] *And he will pitch his palatial tent between the seas and the holy, coveted mountain, and he shall come to*
12	*his end, and none shall help him.* [1] *And at that time*
1	*there will stand, Michael, the great heavenly prince, who stands in support of the children of your people, and there shall be a time of trouble such as never was since there was a nation till that time. At that time your people will escape; everything that is found*

Satan slanders [Israel] and Michael defends Israel. Though Satan tries to slander, Michael silences him' (*Shmos Rabbah* 18:5).

[*Radal (ibid.)* explains that the Midrash treats יַעֲמֹד as a transitive verb — i.e. Michael *will silence* the unmentioned Satan who will try at the last moment to obstruct the redemption.]

[Other instances of עָמַד meaning to desist are כִּי עָמְדוּ וְלֹא עָנוּ עוֹד, *because they stand still and answer no more (Job* 32:16; from *p'sichta of Ruth Rabbah* 1) and וּכְפִתְחוֹ עָמְדוּ כָל הָעָם, *and when be opened it* [the Torah Scroll] *all the people fell silent (Nechemiah* 8:5; *Rashi* from *Sotah* 39a notes that this verse indicates that the people kept quiet while Ezra read the Torah. See also *Bais Yosef* to *Orach Chaim,* beginning of 141, s.v. וצריך; *Tur* 146, and *Shulchan Aruch* 146:4 on whether one is obligated to stand during the reading of the Torah.]

The *Midrash* continues: 'The Holy One, Blessed be He, said to [Michael], "You are silent? You do not defend my childen? I swear that I will speak about justice and rescue My children ... Because you have (made) My world, for you have accepted My Torah; however, had you not accepted My Torah I would have returned [the world] to a state of void and disorder." '

הָעֹמֵד עַל־בְּנֵי עַמֶּךְ — *Who stands in support of the children of your people.*

'For he [Michael] insists upon

Israel's needs' (*Shmos Rabbah* 18:5).

וְהָיְתָה עֵת צָרָה — *And there shall be a time of trouble.*

'There will be trouble for the Jewish people in the Heavenly tribunal [See *Midrashim* quoted above. Satan will argue and probably with considerable justice: These (the gentiles) are idolaters and these (the Jews) are idolaters ... Why should these be (treated) differently from these?]

There will be accusatory enmity (קַטֵיגוֹרְיָא) toward Torah scholars and extreme lawlessness (*Rashi* interpolating the signs given in *Kesubos* 112b for the generation of the Messiah into this verse.)

This generation will see the (חֶבְלֵי מָשִׁיחַ), '*pangs of the Messiah*' — the tribulations of the generation of the Messiah described in *Sanhedrin* 97b (*R' Shmuel Masnuth*).

R' Yochanan, speaking about these 'pangs of the Messiah' exclaimed: Let [the Messiah] come, but may I not see it! (*Sanhedrin* 98b).

יִמָּלֵט עַמֶּךְ — *Your people will escape.*

The fourth kingdom, Rome, will be destroyed and Israel will be saved

עַמְּךָ כָּל־הַנִּמְצָא כָּתוּב בַּסֵּפֶר: וְרַבִּים מִיְּשֵׁנֵי אַדְמַת־עָפָר יָקִיצוּ אֵלֶּה לְחַיֵּי

(Rashi). [There are other versions but this seems to be the correct one. Other texts that refer this prophecy to some other nation are undoubtedly the products of censorship.]

כָּל הַנִּמְצָא כָּתוּב בַּסֵּפֶר — *Everything that is found written in the book* [*will occur*].

Everything that is written in this Book — the visions and dreams: *till the beast* (the fourth kingdom) *was killed ... (7:11,18) and the high holy ones shall receive the kingdom ...* — all of this will be fulfilled (Rashi).

Other commentators render this phrase, *everyone who is found written in the book* — i.e., the righteous, who have been inscribed into the *book* of the righteous as is written (Malachi 3:161): *and a book of remembrance was written before Him, for those who fear HASHEM ...* (Ibn Ezra; Metzudos; Malbim).

— All those who have been written into the ledger books of the collectors of charity (R' Shmuel Masnuth).

[The *Talmud* (Sanhedrin 98b) mentions that the giving of charity is one of the things that help one avert the 'pangs of the Messiah'.]

2. Resurrection

וְרַבִּים מִיְּשֵׁנֵי — *Many of those who sleep.*

'He does not say *all ... who sleep ...* because *all ...* would include all of mankind, and He made this promise only to Israel. Therefore he says, *many ...*

'And when He says: *these for everlasting life and others for shame*

... His intent is not that among those who are resurrected some will be rewarded and some punished, for those who deserve punishment will not be resurrected at the time of the redemption. Rather He means that those who will awaken will have everlasting life, and those who will not awaken will be for *shame and* for *everlasting abhorrence.* For all the righteous, [including] those who repented, will live; only the unbelieving and those who died without repentance will remain. All this will happen at the time of the redemption' (R' Saadiah Gaon in *Emunos V'Deos* ch. 7. See *Ibn Ezra*).

Rambam (Perush haMishnah to *Sanhedrin* 10) agrees with R' Saadiah Gaon that the resurrection is destined only for the righteous, and bases his belief on the *Midrash.* This is also the view of *Ramban* and R' Chisdai Crescas (cited by *Abarbanel*); *Sha'ar haG'mul* in *Kisvei HaRamban,* v. 1, p. 52 where the wording is ambiguous; see *Or Hashem* 3, 4:4, p. 77).

Abarbanel (Mayenei HaYeshuah 11a) disagrees with the above and believes that the resurrection will include all of mankind. He notes two purposes in this: 1) It would be most unfair to all the generations who hoped for the Messiah if only those who incidentally had the good fortune to be alive at the time of the redemption would be privileged to enjoy the benefits of his coming. Therefore *all* the dead will be resurrected: the righteous to enjoy the benefits they merited; and the

enemies of Israel will also come alive in order to witness their ultimate downfall. 2) The nations of mankind that will be resurrected will realize the folly of their beliefs and will all come to acknowledge the one true belief, as seen from the words of *Zephaniah* (3:9): *For then I will turn to the nations a clear language that they will all call upon the Name of HASHEM to serve Him, in unison,* and many other prophecies.

An opinion which falls between these two approaches is adopted by *R' Chisdai Crescas (Or Hashem 3, 4, 4, p. 77).* Only the righteous (צַדִּיקִים,), and the wicked (רְשָׁעִים) will be resurrected in order to bring to its culmination the process of Divine retribution (שָׂכָר וָעוֹנֶשׁ).

For many people however, the rewards of the world of the soul גַּן עֵדֶן, *Paradise,* and whatever material benefits they have attained in their lifetimes suffice for their merits.[1]

[This short summary of views in no way pretends to exhaust this topic which deserves a volume in itself. The reader inclined to pursue this topic should study *Ma'amar haT'chiyah* (Rambam); *Sha'ar haGemul* (Ramban); *Chidushei haRamah* to *Sanhedrin Perek Chelek; Igrot Ramah,* etc. See also footnote to 7:10.]

This controversy is closely connected to a larger question basic to the fundamental tenet of retribution.

Rambam (Hilchos Teshuvah, ch. 8) maintains that the principal place of retribution is the World of Souls (עוֹלָם הַנְּשָׁמוֹת) which every person enters following his death. To this *Rambam* applies the term עוֹלָם הַבָּא, *World to Come.* It is therefore not necessary for everyone to be resurrected, since even without being resurrected they collect their reward (or punishment) in the World of Souls. The resurrection is then a *special reward for those singled out for it* by virtue of their righteous conduct.

Many rabbis disagree with this view and cite the words of the Sages to the effect that the main period of reward for the righteous will be after they are resurrected *(Sha'ar Ha'Gemul* quoted by *Perush* on *Hilchos Teshuvah* 9:2; *Yad Ramah* beginning of *Perek Chelek).*

יָקִיצוּ — *Shall awaken.*

1. Since the body, too, plays a role in earning the reward or punishment, Divine Providence demands that the body too, receive its just reward: hence resurrection. A *Talmudic* parable illustrates this.

A blind man and a lame man both desired to raid a certain orchard, but their physical limitations precluded this. The lame man met the blind man and they formed a partnership. The blind man took the lame man upon his back, and the lame man directed him to the orchard. They then shared the fruits of their 'labors'.

When they were caught by the owner of the orchard, the lame man protested that he himself could not have plundered the orchard. The blind man defended himself in the same manner. The owner then took the lame man, set him upon the blind man and administered punishment to them together *(Sanhedrin* 91b).

Man is composed of two 'partners,' body and soul, which collaborate for good or ꞏor ill. The righteous will arise to collect the material good due them for having utilized the bod   or good. The evil will stand up *for shame* and *for everlasting abhorrence* for having turned ꞏe soul to the service of evil.

עוֹלָם וְאֵ֫לֶּה לַחֲרָפ֖וֹת לְדִרְא֥וֹן עוֹלָֽם: ג וְהַמַּשְׂכִּלִים יַזְהִ֖רוּ כְּזֹ֣הַר הָרָקִ֑יעַ וּמַצְדִּיקֵי֙ הָֽרַבִּ֔ים כַּכּֽוֹכָבִ֖ים לְעוֹלָ֣ם וָעֶֽד: ד וְאַתָּ֣ה דָֽנִיֵּ֗אל סְתֹ֧ם הַדְּבָרִ֛ים וַחֲתֹ֥ם הַסֵּ֖פֶר עַד־עֵ֣ת קֵ֑ץ ה יְשֹׁטְט֥וּ רַבִּ֖ים וְתִרְבֶּ֥ה הַדָּֽעַת: וְרָאִ֙יתִי֙ אֲנִ֣י דָֽנִיֵּ֔אל וְהִנֵּ֛ה שְׁנַ֥יִם אֲחֵרִ֖ים עֹמְדִ֑ים אֶחָ֥ד

The dead will be resurrected (Rashi).

Ravina said, [We know the tenet of resurrection] from this verse, *many of those who sleep in the dusty earth shall awaken* (Sanhedrin 92b).

This verse is the most explicit of any in Scripture about the tenet of the resurrection of the dead (Mayenei HaYeshuah 11:9, citing Rambam).

3. וְהַמַּשְׂכִּלִים — *And the wise.*

[It should be borne in mind that a מַשְׂכִּיל, *wise man*, is not only he who has been blessed with an abundance of intelligence. We find וַיְהִי דָוִד לְכָל דְּרָכָיו מַשְׂכִּיל, *David was successful in all his ways* (I Samuel, 18:14). *Radak* (Shorashim s.v. שכל) points out that success is usually due to the ordering of one's life acording to the dictates of reason. Thus a מַשְׂכִּיל should be understood as one who lives his life true to the rules of ultimate wisdom, the Torah.]

— Those who have occupied themselves with Torah and *mitzvos* (Rashi).

— These are the judges who adjudicate their cases with absolute truth (*Bava Basra* 8b).

— These are the rabbis (*Pesichta* of *Eichah Rabbasi* 23).

כְּזֹהַר הָרָקִיעַ — *Like the radiance of the firmament.*

רָקִיעַ denotes the firmament above the heads of the *chayos* which is described by Ezekiel as *awesome ice spread out from above upon their heads* in his description of the *Merkavah* (Ezekiel 1:22). *Radak* (there) comments that the רָקִיעַ, *firmament,* is *awesome* in its brilliance [see ArtScroll *comm.* there]. (From *Pirkei D'Rabbi Eliezer* ch. 4. See *Tosafos Bava Basra* 8b, s.v. ומצדיקי).

וּמַצְדִּיקֵי הָרַבִּים — *And those who make the many righteous.*

These are the collectors of charity, and teachers of children (*Bava Basra* 8b).

[*Maharsha* (*Chidushei Aggados*) points out the appropriateness of the comparison of these people to stars. Just as the stars are forever present, but are visible only during the night, so the collectors of charity are visible only during the collection of charity, but should not be seen by the recipients of their largesse. The teachers of children too, are visible during the actual teaching process, but the conscientious teacher does not relinquish his supervision even when the pupil is not actually in front of him. It should also be added that the influence of the successful teacher follows the pupil throughout his life.]

Sifre [to *Deut.* 1:10] and *Midrash* [*VaYikra, Rabbah* 30:2; see also

12
3-5

everlasting life, and these for shame, for everlasting abhorrence. ³ *And the wise will shine like the radiance of the firmament, and those who make the many righteous, like the stars, forever and ever.*

⁴ *'As for you Daniel obscure the matters and seal the book until the time of the End, let many muse and let knowledge increase.'*

⁵ *'And I, Daniel, saw, and behold! two others are*

Yerushalmi Nedarim 3:8] say, in general terms, that this verse includes all the righteous.

4. The End

סְתֹם הַדְּבָרִים וַחֲתֹם הַסֵּפֶר — *Obscure the matters and seal the book.*

Write down what you know of the *End* in veiled and obscure language — in the form we now have it *(Ralbag; Ibn Yachya; Metzudos).*

Seal the book so that none but the worthy should see it *(Ibn Ezra).*

Two people had the *End* revealed to them but it was later hidden from them — Jacob and Daniel. Daniel, as it is written, *As for you Daniel obscure the matters ... (Bereishis Rabbah* 98:2; see *Overview).*

[See *Rashash* (ibid.) who explains that this verse shows that Daniel originally knew. Had he not known, the angel's admonition *to obscure the matters* would have been superfluous. The proof that Daniel had the *End* hidden from him is from *v.* 8, where Daniel, after hearing the angel giving a precise prediction about the *End*, says: *And I heard but did not understand ...*

[Possibly the command to *obscure the matters and seal the book* means to delete the *words* (דְּבָרִים can be rendered *words)* which explicitly reveal the *End*, and *seal the*

book means that the wording in the book should tend to conceal (סְתֹם, *seal*) the true *End.*]

יְשֹׁטְטוּ רַבִּים — *Let many muse.*

Many people will attempt to unravel the mystery of the *End.*

וְתִרְבֶּה הַדָּעַת — *And let knowledge increase.*

Many theories about the nature and time of the *End* shall be put forth *(Rambam in Iggeres Teman; Ralbag* and others).

'First, it is incumbent upon you to know that the true *End* is impossible for any man ever to know. As Daniel explains (12:9), *For these matters are obscured and sealed till the time of the End.* But the elaborate descriptions of some scholars in this matter, and that some of them have thought they have grasped it (the *End*), has already been foretold by the prophet who said, *Many muse...'* (*Rambam in Iggeres Teman).*

5. שְׁנַיִם אֲחֵרִים — *Two others.*

These are two angels besides the one who had been speaking to Daniel till now *(Ibn Ezra).*

Abarbanel (Mayenei HaYeshuah 11:10) interprets additional angels as referring to the two new religions, Christianity and Islam, speaking to Gabriel, who is representing Israel. Both angels in-

הֵנָּה לִשְׂפַת הַיְאֹר וְאֶחָד הֵנָּה לִשְׂפַת
הַיְאֹר: וַיֹּאמֶר לָאִישׁ לְבוּשׁ הַבַּדִּים אֲשֶׁר ו
מִמַּעַל לְמֵימֵי הַיְאֹר עַד־מָתַי קֵץ
הַפְּלָאוֹת: וָאֶשְׁמַע אֶת־הָאִישׁ | לְבוּשׁ ז
הַבַּדִּים אֲשֶׁר מִמַּעַל לְמֵימֵי הַיְאֹר וַיָּרֶם
יְמִינוֹ וּשְׂמֹאלוֹ אֶל־הַשָּׁמַיִם וַיִּשָּׁבַע בְּחֵי
הָעוֹלָם כִּי לְמוֹעֵד מוֹעֲדִים וָחֵצִי וּכְכַלּוֹת
נַפֵּץ יַד־עַם־קֹדֶשׁ תִּכְלֶינָה כָל־אֵלֶּה: וַאֲנִי ח

quire, 'How long to the hidden
End?' (v. 6) — to the resurrection of
the dead, a tenet admitted by both
these faiths.

הַיְאֹר — The river.
The Chidekel (Metzudos).
[See above 10:4, I was on the
bank of the great river, which is
Chidekel.]

6. לָאִישׁ לְבוּשׁ הַבַּדִּים — To the man
clothed in linen.
The angel who had been speaking to Daniel till now. See 10:5
(Metzudos).

אֲשֶׁר מִמַּעַל לְמֵימֵי הַיְאֹר — Who was
above the waters of the river.
The angel had appeared to Daniel
as though suspended between
heaven and earth. This symbolized
Gabriel's superiority over the two
other angels (Ralbag).

קֵץ הַפְּלָאוֹת — The hidden End.
[The translation follows Metzudos and R' Shmuel Masnuth's
preferred rendition. See Radak
(Shorashim s.v. פלא). R' Shmuel
Masnuth suggests that it could also
be rendered wonders. This seems to
have been followed by Abarbanel
(see v. 5).
[Both renditions are derived from
פלא which embraces both concepts.

Wonders are those phenomena
which are not readily understood by
— i.e., hidden from — human intelligence.]

7. וַיָּרֶם יְמִינוֹ — And he lifted his
right hand.
The gesture is customary during
swearing as in Gen. (14:22) where
Abraham says to the king of
Sodom, I have lifted my hand to
HASHEM ... (see Rashi and Ramban
there; Metzudos).

וּשְׂמֹאלוֹ — And his left hand.
To swear to the two angels
standing on either side of him (v. 5)
who had addressed this question to
him (Mayenei HaYeshuah 11:10).

וַיִּשָּׁבַע — And swore.
The promised redemption could
come in one of two ways. Should
Israel merit it, HASHEM will speed
up the coming of the Messiah. If
(ח"ו) this is not the case, the Messiah will nevertheless come in his appointed time (Sanhedrin 98a; see
Overview). There could even be
more than one appointed time
(Ramban in Sefer Ha'Geulah, ch.
4). The angel wanted to dispel any
notions of the others that, given this
flexibility, the redemption could be
delayed indefinitely (ח"ו).

standing, one on this side of the riverbank and one on that side of the riverbank. ⁶ And he said to the man clothed in linen, who was above the waters of the river, 'How long to the hidden End?'

⁷ And I heard the man clothed in linen, who was above the waters of the river, and he lifted his right hand and his left hand heavenward and swore by the Life of the world, that in a time, times, and a half, and upon completion of the fragmenting of the hand of the holy people, all these shall be finished. ⁸ And I

Therefore, he swore that there was an ultimate point in time which could not pass without the promised redemption *(Malbim)*.

בְּחֵי הָעוֹלָם — *By the Life of the world.*

The translation follows *Ibn Ezra, R' Shmuel Masnuth,* and *Metzudos* who render עוֹלָם, *world. Rambam, (Moreh Nevuchim* 1:72); and *Kuzari* 4:3 render חֵי as *the Life.* Thus, God is described as the One Who gives life to the entire universe.

A similar phrase, presumably based on our verse, is found in the *Baruch She'Amar* prayer. According to the above commentary, there, too the translation חֵי הָעוֹלָמִים would be *Life of the world(s).* Other commentators to *Baruch She'Amar* render differently. The translations there would apply to our verse as well:

R' Yaakov Emden (Sheilos Yavetz 1:14) interprets חֵי *the live One —* God is the epitome of perfect life since His life is intrinsic in Himself and is not dependent on outside sources (see *Rambam, Yesodei HaTorah* 2:10). Hence חֵי הָעוֹלָמִים, God is *the live One of the world(s).*

Many authorities (notably *Abudraham* in his interpretation of

בָּרוּךְ שֶׁאָמַר) render הָעוֹלָמִים as *forever.* their reading is חַי (not חֵי), which means *Who lives: the One Who lives forever.* (See *Otzar HaTefillos* vol. 1 p.189).

[See *Tosafos Yom Tov* to *Tamid* 7:4; *Magen Avraham* 207; *Beur Hagra* after ch. 241; and *Ma'asseh Rav* 32 who all concur that חַי is the correct reading (see *Ba'er Hetev* 207). Many authorities cited in *Iyun Tefillah* (*Otzar haTefillos* v. 1, p. 189) read חֵי. Since all our versions have read חֵי this should resolve the controversy. However, *R' Yaakov Emden* holds חַי and חֵי to be equally acceptable as the construct form, even though there is a slightly different meaning.]

לְמוֹעֵד מוֹעֲדִים וָחֵצִי — *[That] in a time, times, and a half.*

[The same *End* is stated by the angel in 7:25.]

וּכְכַלּוֹת נַפֵּץ יַד־עַם־קֹדֶשׁ — *And upon completion of the fragmenting of the hand of the holy people.*

When Israel's power (יָד, *hand,* is a metaphor for power) has been dissipated, then the redeemer will come, as it is written, *For HASHEM will judge His people ... when He sees that their supporting power is gone ...* (Deut. 32:36; *Rashi*).

Or: נַפֵּץ, *the dispersal,* as in וּמֵאֵלֶּה נָפְצָה כָל הָאָרֶץ, *from these the whole earth was dispersed* (Gen. 9:19). Both renditions, *fragmenting*

שָׁמַעְתִּי וְלֹא אָבִין וָאֹמְרָה אֲדֹנִי מָה
אַחֲרִית אֵלֶּה: וַיֹּאמֶר לֵךְ דָּנִיֵּאל כִּי־ ט
סְתֻמִים וַחֲתֻמִים הַדְּבָרִים עַד־עֵת קֵץ:
יִתְבָּרְרוּ וְיִתְלַבְּנוּ וְיִצָּרְפוּ רַבִּים וְהִרְשִׁיעוּ י
רְשָׁעִים וְלֹא יָבִינוּ כָּל־רְשָׁעִים

and *dispersion* are different manners of dispersion and come from the same root (*Shorashim* s.v. נפץ; *R' Shmuel Masnuth*).

Mayenei HaYeshuah 11:10 and *Malbim* combine these two interpretations and render it thus, *And when the dispersal of the hand — i.e., the shattering of Israel's power — [and of] the holy people — i.e., the Jewish diaspora — will cease.*

The *Talmud (Sanhedrin* 97a) relates that in the era of the Messiah there will be no Torah scholars, 'the penny *perutah* will have gone from the pocket,' and Israel will have given up hope for redemption.

תִּכְלֶינָה כָל־אֵלֶּה — *All these shall be finished.*

All the nations and kingdoms which had been prophesied about in these visions will have found their end (*Mayenei HaYeshuah* 11:10; *Metzudos*).

8. וְלֹא אָבִין — *But (I) did not understand.*

The angels who had inquired readily understood the *End* when it was told them. *But I,* [Daniel] *did not understand (R' Shmuel Masnuth).*

He did not know the extent of these *times (Rashi).*

When he heard this *End* previously (7:25) he said merely, *I kept the matter in my heart* (7:28). Probably he assumed that the *times*

would end together with the seventy years prophesied by Jeremiah (see above 9:2). But when he heard in his second vision (8:14), *till nightfall, morning, two thousand three hundred.* He understood that the complete redemption (גְּאוּלָה שְׁלֵמָה בב״א) was still far off. He realized by now that the Second Temple would be destroyed (see 9:26), and realized that he *did not understand* (*Mayenei HaYeshuah* 11:10).

מָה אַחֲרִית אֵלֶּה — *What is the end of these?*

When will the end of these times come? (*Rashi*).

Or: When will the end of these kingdoms come about? (*Mayenei HaYeshuah* 11:10).

9. These Matters Are Sealed

לֵךְ דָּנִיֵּאל — *Go Daniel.*

Leave this topic. Do not inquire further (*Ibn Ezra; R' Shmuel Masnuth; Metzudos*).

כִּי־סְתֻמִים וַחֲתֻמִים הַדְּבָרִים — *For these matters are obscured and sealed.*

[See above v. 4.]

עַד־עֵת קֵץ — *Till the time of the End.*

Until the time of the redemption draws near (*Rashi*).

[It seems that as the promised time approaches, *the wise ones* will perceive the approach of the *End* before its actual occurence. As

heard but did not understand, so I said, 'My lord, what is the end of these?'

⁹ *And he said, 'Go Daniel! For the matters are obscured and sealed till the time of the End.* ¹⁰ *They will be selected and clarified, and many will be refined; and the wicked will act wickedly, and none of wicked shall understand, but the wise shall understand.*

---

much is intimated by *Ramban* in *Sefer HaGeulah* (ch. 4, p. 290 Chavel ed.)..

R' Berechiah and *R' Simon* said: Three clues were provided about Moses' burial site, *in the valley, in the land of Moab, opposite Beis Peor* (Deut. 34:6) and still, *no man knows his burial site* (ibid). The *End* about which it is written, *For the day of vengeance is in My heart and the year of redemption is come* (Isaiah 63:4), all the more so! *The matters are obscured and sealed till the time of the End.* The heart (in which the day of vengeance is sealed) does not disclose to the mouth (*Midrash Shocher Tov* 9:2).

10. יִתְבָּרְרוּ וְיִתְלַבְּנוּ — *They will be selected and clarified, and...refined.*

The reference is to the calculations about the *End* (*Rashi*).

[וְיִתְלַבְּנוּ from לָבָן, *white*. When the *Talmud* wants to express approval it says מִיחוור or מִיחוורתא, *white* — i.e., it is as free of blemish as something pure white.]

The matter of the *End* will be clarified through the numerous attempts to understand them (*Metzudos*).

[What is probably meant is that among the many calculations about the time of the *End*, there will also be found the right approach. But this will not be known at the time,

for *those matters* have to remain obscured and sealed till the time of the *End.*]

וְיִצָּרְפוּ רַבִּים — *And many will be refined.*

Many will be deluded into thinking that their calculation of the *End* is absolutely *pure* and free from error (*Metzudos*).

[*Rashi's* interpretation is not clear. Perhaps the meaning is that many shall resort to a regime of extreme purification in order to be considered worthy of grasping the secret of the *End.*]

וְהִרְשִׁיעוּ רְשָׁעִים — *And the wicked will act wickedly.*

The wicked will fail in their attempts to find the *End.* But when the time which they have erroneously ascribed to be the appointed time comes without the redemption taking place, they will erroneously come to the conclusion that there will (ח"ו), *God forbid,* be no redemption (*Rashi*).

וְלֹא יָבִינוּ — *And [none] ... shall understand.*

They will not be capable of understanding the קֵץ, *End* (*Rashi*).

They will not have the [humility and] understanding to ascribe the not coming of the Messiah to errors in their conception of the *End* (*Metzudos*).

יא וְהַמַּשְׂכִּלִים יָבִינוּ: וּמֵעֵת הוּסַר הַתָּמִיד
וְלָתֵת שִׁקּוּץ שֹׁמֵם יָמִים אֶלֶף מָאתַיִם
יב וְתִשְׁעִים: אַשְׁרֵי הַמְחַכֶּה וְיַגִּיעַ לְיָמִים
אֶלֶף שְׁלֹשׁ מֵאוֹת שְׁלֹשִׁים וַחֲמִשָּׁה:
יג וְאַתָּה לֵךְ לַקֵּץ וְתָנוּחַ וְתַעֲמֹד לְגֹרָלְךָ
לְקֵץ הַיָּמִין:

וְהַמַּשְׂכִּלִים יָבִינוּ — *But the wise shall understand.*

When the *time of the End* comes (or close to it; see above v. 9), the wise will understand to interpret the calculations of the *End (Rashi).*

[Perhaps even after the *End*, the interpretation of the verses in Daniel pointing to it shall remain *sealed,* except to *the wise.*]

The wise will understand not to trust their intellect. When the Messiah will not have come in the time designated by them they will remain steadfast in their trust *(Metzudos).*

Rambam (his words are quoted above 11:35) interprets this verse as referring to the many trials and tribulations of the bitter Exile. The many will become purified as a result of their steadfast trust during the great trial.

Abarbanel (Mayenei HaYeshuah 11:10) and *Malbim* understand this as referring to the nations of the world. In the period immediately preceding the complete redemption when the *light of the Messiah* will already show its signs on the horizon, many will recognize the true religion and walk in the light of HASHEM. But many will stubbornly cling to their convictions and wage war upon Israel with Gog, King of Magog.

11. וּמֵעֵת הוּסַר הַתָּמִיד — *And from the time the daily sacrifice was removed.*

This took place six years before the destruction of the Temple *(Rashi).*

יָמִים אֶלֶף מָאתַיִם וְתִשְׁעִים — *One thousand two hundred and ninety years.*

The translation follows *R' Saadiah Gaon (Emunos Vedeos* 8), *Rashi,* and the consensus of *commentators.* There are other instances where יָמִים is used for years, e.g. יָמִים תִּהְיֶה גְאֻלָּתוֹ, *its redemption period shall be years* (Lev. 25:29) and many others (See *Radak* in *Shorashim,* s.v. יום).

The daily sacrifice will be removed (i.e., remain removed) and the mute abomination will stay in its place for 1290 years until the Messiah comes. This number of years from the removal of the daily sacrifice coincides with the calculation give above (8:14) which starts from the sojourn in Egypt (see *comm. Rashi).*

Ibn Ezra (9:24) renders יָמִים, *days.* The daily sacrifice will be removed for 1290 days before the destruction of the Temple. This prophecy is the same as above (9:27) where the angel tells Daniel that the daily sacrifice will be abolished half a week [of years]) — i.e., three-and-a-half years (365x

¹¹ *And from the time the daily sacrifice was removed and the mute abomination was emplaced, one thousand two hundred and ninety years. ¹² Praiseworthy is he who awaits and reaches to one thousand three hundred thirty-five years. ¹³ And as for you, go to the end; you will rest and arise to your lot at the End of the Days.'*

3.5=1277.5). Here the angel was more specific and gave the exact duration, 1290 days.

12. לְיָמִים אֶלֶף שְׁלֹשׁ מֵאוֹת שְׁלֹשִׁים וַחֲמִשָּׁה — *To one thousand three hundred thirty-five years.*

Here we have forty-five more years than in the previous verse (1335-1290=45). After the advent of the Messiah there will be forty-five years when the Messiah will again be hidden. Evidence for this is found in *Midrash Ruth Rabbah* and in the *piyutim* of R' Elazar Hakalir for *Parshas Hachodesh* (s.v. וראה ויתכסה מהם. See *Siddur Otzar HaTefillos; Rashi*).

R' Berachia said in the name of R' Levi: The last redeemer (Messiah) will be like the first redeemer (Moses). Just as the first redeemer revealed himself and then was hidden for three months (from when he went to Pharaoh at first until the first plague; cf. *Ramban to Exodus* 5:22) so the last redeemer will reveal himself and then be hidden. How

long will he be hidden? Rav Tanchuma said in the name of the Rabbis: Forty-five years as is written, *And from when the daily sacrifice was removed* ... and as is written, *Happy is he who waits and attains one thousand three hundred forty-five years* ... (*Ruth Rabbah* 5:6 and elsewhere).

Ramban (Sefer HaGeulah ch. 4) holds that after 1290 years the Messiah from the tribe of Ephraim will come. It will be his job to gather the dispersed Jews and to wage war with Gog, King of Magog. He will die in this war. Then the Messiah of the seed of David will come and complete the redemption. His source for this is *Pirkei Heichalos. Ramban* adds that the verse also suggests that all those who hoped for the Messiah (*Praiseworthy is he who waits*) during the Exile shall be repaid in that they *will reach* (i.e., be resurrected) at the end of 1335 years.[1]

According to *Ibn Ezra*, there is no contradiction at all. The 1290 days

1.	*Ramban (ibid.)* draws a striking parallel. If we add together all the years the Jews lived in *Eretz Yisrael* they will add up to the number given here for the years of the Exile. From their entry into the land till the erection of the First Temple, 440 years passed. The First Temple stood 410 years. From their second entry (from the edict of Cyrus) till the destruction of the Second Temple, 439 years passed (the Temple stood 420 years, and nineteen years elapsed between Cyrus' edict and the building of the Temple). This gives us a total of 1289. It seems that the 1290 years of Exile mentioned in *Daniel* exceed by one, and atone for, the total numbers of years Israel lived sinfully in the land. The forty years of war under the leadership of the Messiah ben Ephraim correspond to the forty years of Israel's sojourn in the desert (see *Midrash Ruth Rabbah loc. cit.* which bears this out). The last five of the forty-five years, are the time from the revelation of the Messiah until the completion of his mission.

in *v.* 11 refer to the length of time that the daily sacrifice was removed before the destruction of the Second Temple. Verse 12 refers to the length of time allowed for *the time of trouble* mentioned above (*v.* 1). This would endure for approximately three-and-a-half years as told above (7:25 and 12:7). Here the angel was more precise and gave the exact amount of days.

13. לֵךְ לַקֵּץ — *Go to the end.*

You will pass from this world to collect your reward in the next world (*Rashi*).

[The angel tells Daniel he will die before all this comes to pass.]

וְתָנוּחַ *(And) you will rest.*

Together with the other righteous in the World to Come (*Metzudos*).

[The World to Come is appropriately described as an interlude of rest. *For there is no work ... in the grave where you are going* (*Ecclas.* 9:10). The impression created by this verse is that the עוֹלָם הַנְּשָׁמוֹת, *world of the souls,* is but an interlude between this life and the resurrection of the dead. See above *v.* 2.]

וְתַעֲמֹד לְגֹרָלְךָ — *And (you will) arise to your lot.*

You will receive your portion with the righteous (*Rashi*).

[In contrast to the wicked who will stand up *to shame* and to *everlasting abhorrence* (12:2), you will wake up to the righteous everlasting life.]

לְקֵץ הַיָּמִין — *At the End of the Days.*

The word יוֹם, *day,* is a masculine word; therefore, its proper plural form is יָמִים. The *Mesorah* lists this among the words which should end with a *mem,* but end with a *nun* instead. לְקֵץ הַיָּמִים=לְקֵץ הַיָּמִין (*Rashi*).

The *Midrash* interprets יָמִין homiletically as *right,* a reference to God's *right arm.* His power to work miracles is called *His right arm* (*Midrash Shocher Tov* 137:7). His attribute of kindness is also called *His right arm* (see *Rashi* to *Exodus* 15:6 s.v. יְמִינֶךָ). From the time the Second Temple was destroyed, *God withdrew His right hand in the presence of the enemy* (*Eichah* 2:3. See ArtScroll *comm.* there). God has not revealed the full measure of His miracles and kindness to His people. When the time for the redemption comes (בב״א) He will return *His right arm* to its place. This too, is the intent of the verse (*Psalms* 60:7), הוֹשִׁיעָה יְמִינְךָ וַעֲנֵנִי, *save [with] Your right hand and answer me* (*Eichah Rabbah* 2:6).

In the merit of Israel's unswerving faith during the long, dark night of exile, may the prophecies of the *End* be realized speedily in our time אמן.

תֵּם תִּשְׁלַם שֶׁבַח לְאֵל בּוֹרֵא עוֹלָם

Appendices

⇜ Appendix: Nebuchadnezzar's Arrogance and Punishment

The story of Nebuchadnezzar's dream as related in his letter, though having no apparent connection with the preceding chapter is in reality a sequel to the previous chapter. As explained in the preface to chapter 3, the purpose of the golden image was to circumvent the will of God as expressed in the king's dream (chapter 2). The erection of an image made totally of gold symbolized the supremacy of Babylon over the three empires destined to follow it, thereby foiling the ultimate ascendancy of the kingdom of God. For his arrogance Nebuchadnezzar was punished in a way fitting his sin. Instead of rising to heights not predestined for him, he lost even what rightfully was reserved for him as king of Babylon — his empire — and even what was rightfully his as a human being — his sanctity. This episode fulfills the prophecy of Isaiah (14:13-15) who in reference to Nebuchadnezzar exclaims; "And you said in your heart ... 'I will ascend above the heights of the clouds; I will be like the Supreme [one]! Yet you shall be brought down to Sheol, to the uttermost part of the pit (Mayenei Hayeshuah 4:5; Alshich; Malbim).

This also explains Nebuchadnezzar's motive for publishing his experience throughout his whole kingdom. In order to atone for his brazen, public defiance of God (חילול השם) the sanctification of God (קידוש השם) resulting from his penance had to equal the desecration caused by his previous actions. Just as the event of the golden image had been publicized throughout Nebuchadnezzar's empire, so did his subsequent recognition of God's supreme power and his submission to it have to receive the same amount of publicity (Mayenei Hayeshuah 4:5, Alshich, Malbim).

This also explains the seemingly excessive importance given to Nebuchadnezzar. God not only punishes him for his arrogance but also notifies him before the fact and has him know that the purpose of his punishment is: 'that the living may know that the Supreme [one] rules human government.' Nebuchadnezzar's affliction would last until he was ready to acknowledge the supremacy of God. God's extraordinary divine preoccupation (כביכול) with a vain monarch's arrogance is a reaction to an unprecedented flouting of God's will. When Nebuchadnezzar — having learned in an extraordinary revelation what God's will was concerning not just a small detail in Nebuchadnezzar's life or in that of his empire, but concerning the whole purpose of God's plan in history — went ahead and tried to circumvent this Divine master plan in a blatant, overt manner publicized throughout his empire, this was arrogance par excellence and had to be penalized in a manner commensurate with the sin (Mayenei Hayeshuah 4:6).

Another point about this story is puzzling. The failure of the Babylonian sages to decipher the message of the dream is hard to understand. Upon studying this chapter and Daniel's interpretation of the dream one is tempted to ask why was someone of Daniel's stature needed when the solution is seemingly so transparent. Probably the sages were stymied by the apparent contradictions in the dream (see comm. to vs. 19 and 21). Perhaps they could not envision that this dream pertained to Nebuchadnezzar personally and felt that the king's dream must refer to the fortunes of his whole empire. As much is hinted at in Nebuchadnezzar's own words when he — at the end of his recital of the dream — refers to himself as: 'I King Nebuchadnezzar,' an aggrandizement unusual in private conversation even for him (see e.g. 2:3). It seems that Nebuchadnezzar was trying to stress that the dream had to be tied not to Nebuchadnezzar the man, but to the king. Lechem Sesarim adds that the astrologers knew that no calamity was destined for the Babylonian empire in the near future; on the contrary the stars showed that the glory of Babylon was still to grow.

TABLE I ❧ Chronology of the Period

Year from Creation	B.C.E.	Event	Year of Reigning Monarchy	Parallel time in history of Judah
3320	[440]	Nebuchadnezzar ascends to throne of Babylon	1	Yehoyakim's 4th year
3321	[439]	Nebuchadnezzar conquers Yehoyakim	2	Yehoyakim's 5th year
3325	[435]		6	Yehoyakim rebels (1st year of independence)
3327	[433]	Nebuchadnezzar's reconquers Judah	8	Yehoyakim dies (3rd year of independence)
3328-30	[432-30]	Daniel, Chananyah, Mishael, and Azaryah receive training in Babylonian court		Yehoyachin reigns 3 months; Zedekiahu becomes king
3338	[422]	Nebuchadnezzar destroys Temple	19	
3339	[421]	The events of 'Daniel', chapters 2-4		
3364	[396]	Evil Merodach succeeds Nebuchadnezzar	45	
3387	[373]	Belshazzar succeeds Evil Merodach	68	
3389	[371]	Belshazzar assassinated; Darius the Mede becomes king	70	
3391	[369]	Darius dies; Cyrus succeeds him and proclaims right of Jews to return to Eretz Yisrael; Daniel leaves royal service	1	
3393	[367]	Cyrus dies; Cambyses reigns	3	
3394	[366]	Ahasuerus reigns	4	
3405	[355]	Miracle of Purim	15	
3407	[353]	Darius succeeds Ahasuerus	17	
3408	[352]	Darius permits building of Temple	18	

TABLE II   ·s§ The Chronology of Yehoyakim

	Rashi	Ibn Ezra	Josephus
1*	Yehoyakim reigns	Yehoyakim reigns	Yehoyakim reigns
4	Nebuchadnezzar ascends the Babylonian throne	Nebuchadnezzar ascends the Babylonian throne; conquers Jerusalem and captures Yehoyakim (Daniel 1:1)	Nebuchadnezzar ascends the Babylonian throne
5	Nebuchadnezzar conquers Jerusalem and subjugates Yehoyakim (II Kings 23-24, II Chronicles 36)		
7		Yehoyakim rebels after serving Nebuchadnezzar for 3 years (II Kings 23-4 and II Chron. 36) and rules independently	
9	Yehoyakim rebels		Nebuchadnezzar conquers Jerusalem and subjugates Yehoyakim (II Kings 23-4; II Chron. 36)
11	Nebuchadnezzar reconquers Jerusalem and captures Yehoyakim in the third year of his revolt (Daniel 1:1) after the latter had reigned 11 years and puts him to death	Nebuchadnezzar reconquers Jerusalem; captures Yehoyakim and puts him to death (II Kings 23-4; II Chron. 36)	Yehoyakim rebels (II Kings 23-4; II Chron. 36); Nebuchadnezzar reconquers Jerusalem, captures Yehoyakim (Daniel 1:1) and puts him to death

* All years are counted from Yehoyakim's ascendancy to the throne.

TABLE III
◄§ Seleucid and Ptolemaic Dynasties

SELEUCID DYNASTY	320	300	280	260	240	220	200	180	160	140	120
Seleucus I Nicator			312-281								
Antiochus I Soter				281-262							
Antiochus II Theos					262-246						
Seleucus II Callinicus						246-226					
Seleucus III Soter							226-223				
Antiochus III (The Great; Son of Seleucus II)								223-187			
Seleucus IV Philopater									187-175		
Antiochus IV Epiphanes (Son of Antiochus III)										175-163	
Antiochus V										164-162	
Demetrius I (son of Seleucus IV)										162-150	
PTOLEMAIC DYNASTY											
Ptolemy I		323-285									
Ptolemy II Philadelphus				285-246							
Ptolemy III Euergetes					246-221						
Ptolemy IV Philopator						221-205					
Ptolemy V Epiphanes							205-180				
Ptolemy VI Philometor							180-145				
Ptolemy VII (son of Ptolemy V) co-ruler with his brother Ptolemy VI									170-164		
Ptolemy VII Sole ruler of Egypt								145-116			

* The dates given are the beginning and end of each king's rule. Wherever no indication is given to the contrary, that king is the son of the preceding king.

Bibliography/
Biographical Sketches

Partial Bibliography
of Authorities Cited in the Commentary

Italics are used to denote the name of a work. ***Bold italics*** within the biography indicate the *specific book of that particular author* cited in the commentary.
Works cited only in passing have generally not been included in this listing.

Abarbanel, R' Yitzchak

The title 'Don' *(HaSar)* was conferred on him when he served as a minister of finance in the Spanish government.

Celebrated philosopher and Biblical commentator at the time of the Spanish expulsion (5252, 1492).

A scion of the House of Judah royal family, he was born in Lisbon 5197 (1437). He was a disciple of R' Yosef Chayun.

Alfonso V of Portugal recognized his great capabilities and appointed him minister of the treasury. He fled Portugal for Castile when the king suspected him of complicity in an insurrection against him. King Ferdinand of Castile appointed him minister of finance, a post which he held until the Jews of Spain were expelled from that country (9 Av 5252, 1492). Abarbanel joined the refugees, despite the entreaties of the king and queen that he stay on.

In addition to his major work, a commentary to Torah and Prophets, he composed a commentary on *Daniel*, ***Mayenei HaYeshuah***, and two books about the advent of the Messiah (***Mashmia Yeshuah*** and ***Yeshuas Meshicho***).These and his many other works rank him among the classical Jewish Bible commentators and thinkers. Abarbanel attacks Christian theology in his writings, a feat which in his days was very dangerous. He died in Padua, Italy in 5268 (1508).

Albo, R' Yosef

Spanish philosopher of the fifteenth century.

Little is known about his life, and the dates of his birth 5140 (1380) and death 5204 (1444) can only be conjectured. He was a disciple of R' Chisdai Crescas and, according to some historians, also of R' Nissim Gerondi ('Ran').

His most famous work, ***Sefer HaIk-karim*** ('Book of Principles'), is a major treatise on Jewish philosophy and faith. The book is divided into four parts, the first of which was originally intended to be an independent work. The other three parts, which elaborate upon the first part, were added later. Completed in Castile in 5185 (1425), the work was first printed in 5245 (1485). It achieved great popularity, and has been reprinted many times since.

Alkabetz, R' Shlomo HaLevi

[b. 5265 (1505) Salonica; d. 5336 (1576) — Tz'fas (Safed).]

One of the greatest kabbalists and mystical poets of his day, and author of the *piyyut* 'L'cha Dodi' recited every Friday evening. He was a contemporary and friend of R' Yosef Karo, author of *Shulchan Aruch.*

He is often cited by early commentators, by whom he is referred to as 'Rashba HaLevi'; 'R' Shlomo HaLevi'; 'Harav ibn Alkabetz HaLevi.'

He wrote commentaries on most of the Bible, the Passover *Haggadah*, on *Kabbalah*, and was a noted *paytan*. He wrote ***Menos HaLevi*** on *Megillas Esther* and *Shoresh Yishai* on *Megillas Ruth.* His kabbalistic commentary on *Shir HaShirim* is entitled *Ayeles Ahavim.* It was first published in Venice, in 5312.

In his *piyyut,* 'L'cha Dodi,' he speaks of the sufferings of the Jewish people and their aspirations for Redemption. Probably no other *Piyyut* has reached the popularity of 'L'cha Dodi'; it is recited every Friday evening by all Jewish congregations throughout the world.

Alshich, R' Moshe

[Also spelled Alsheich]

Rav, *Halachic* authority, and Bible commentator, born in Adrianople in 5268 (1508). He studied Torah there in the Yeshiva of R' Yosef Karo. He settled in Safed where he spent most of his life

and was ordained there by R' Yosef Karo with the full *semichah* reintroduced by R' Yaakov Berav. Among his pupils was R' Chaim Vital, whom he ordained in 5350 (1590).

He died while traveling in Damascus before 5360 (1600).

He wrote commentaries on most of the Bible. A collection of 140 of his *halachic* responsa was published posthumously.

His commentary on *Daniel*, **Chavatzeles HaSharon**, the first of his works, was published in his lifetime (Constantinople 5328 — 1568).

R' Moshe Alshich was known in his generation as the *darshan* par excellence. Through the ages he became known as the Alshich HaKadosh, the holy Alshich.

Altschuller, R' Yechiel Hillel ben David

Bible commentator of the 18th century.

In order to promote the study of the Bible, R' Yechiel Hillel's father, R' David, planned an easy-to-read commentary of *Nevi'im* and *Kesuvim* (Prophets and Hagiographa) based on earlier commentators.

R' Yechiel edited his father's unpublished manuscripts and completed the missing books himself. By 5530 (1770), the entire commentary was published. It consisted of two parts: **Metzudas Zion**, which explains individual words; and **Metzudas David**, which provides a running commentary to the text. Due to their simple and concise language, the dual commentaries have become almost indispensable aids in Bible-study. They have attained great popularity and have been reprinted in nearly every edition of Prophets and Hagiographa.

Azulai, R' Chaim Yosef David

Known by his Hebrew acronym CHIDA.

Born in Jerusalem in 5484 (1724), he died in Livorno (Leghorn) in 5564 (1806). *Halachist, kabbalist*, and bibliographer-historian, he possessed great intellectual powers and many-faceted talents. He went abroad as an emissary and he would send large sums of money back to Hebron and Jerusalem. He ended his mission in 1778 in Livorno

(Leghorn) where he spent the rest of his life.

His fame as a *halachist* rests on his glosses to *Shulchan Aruch*, contained in his *Birkei Yosef* and *Machazik B'racha*, works constantly cited by later authorities.

He wrote the famous bibliographic work, *Shem HaGedolim*. Among his many works was the homiletical *Nachal Eshkol* on the *Five Megillos;* **Pesach Einayim** on the *Aggados* of the *Talmud;* and numerous other works.

Antiquities

See *Josephus Flavius.*

Beer HaGolah

See *R' Yehudah Loewe ben R' Bezalel.*

Berlin, R' Naftali Zvi Yehudah

[5577-5653 (1817-1893)]

Known by the acronym of his name: N'tziv.

One of the leading rabbis of his generation and Rosh Yeshivah of Volozhin for some 40 years.

He was born at Mir, and was already known as a great *Talmudic* scholar in his early youth. In 1831 he married the daughter of R' Yitzchak of Volozhin — son of R' Chaim of Volozhin who was the head of the important yeshivah in that town.

Under him, the Yeshivah grew to over 400 students.

His refusal to reduce the number of students at the Yeshivah and to introduce secular subjects into the curriculum, resulted in a government decree to close the Yeshiva in 1892, and N'tziv and his family were exiled. His health was so seriously affected by the closing, that he died in Warsaw about 18 months after his departure from Volozhin. His sons were R' Chaim Berlin and R' Meir Berlin (Bar-Ilan).

Among N'tziv's major works are a comprehensive commentary to the *She'iltos* of R' Achai Gaon entitled **Ha'amek She'elah** (Vilna 5621 — 1861); **Ha'amek Davar** a commentary on the Torah (Vilna 5639 — 1879); *his responsa Meishiv Davar* (2 vols.) *M'romei Sadeh* on the *Talmud;* and a commentary on *Sifre.*

R' Chanoch Zundel ben Yosef

[d. 5627 (1867)]

R' Chanoch lived in Bialystok, Poland, where he devoted his life to writing commentaries on the *Midrash* and the *Ein Yaakov.*

He published two commentaries which appear side-by-side in a special edition of the *Midrash Rabbah* and *Ein Yaakov: Etz Yosef,* in which he strives to give the plain meaning of the text; and *Anaf Yosef* which is largely homiletical.

R' Chanoch also published a commentary to *Pirkei Avos,* but his commentaries to *Yalkut Shimoni* and the *Mechilta* are still in manuscript.

Chazon Ish

See *Karelitz, R' Avraham Yeshayah.*

Chidushei Aggados Maharsha

See *R' Shmuel Eliezer ben Yehudah HaLevi.*

Daas Tevunos

See *Luzatto, R' Moshe Chaim.*

Derech Mitzvosecha

See *Rabbi Menachem Mendel of Lubavitch.*

Dessler, R' Eliyahu Eliezer

[5651-5714 (1891-1954)]

One of the outstanding personalities of the *Mussar* movement.

In 5689 (1929) he settled in London whre he exercised a profound influence on the teaching of *Mussar,* not only because of the profundity of his ideas, but also on account of his personal ethical conduct.

In 5701 (1941), he became director of the Kollel of Gateshead Yeshiva in England.

In 5707 (1947), he became *mashgiach* of Ponievez Yeshivah in Bnei Brak, and remained there until his death.

His teachings reflect a harmonious mixture of *Mussar, Kabbalah,* and *Chassidus.* His writings have been collected and published by his disciples under the title *Michtav MeEliyahu.*

Eidels, R' Shmuel Eliezer ben Yehudah HaLevi

[5315-5392 (1555-1631)]

Known as Maharsha — *Moreinu HaRav Shmuel Eliezer,* he is also known as R' Shmuel Eidels.

One of the foremost *Talmud* commentators, whose **commentary** is included in almost every edition of the *Talmud.* His commentary is divided into two parts. The first deals with the *Halachic* elements and the latter with the *Aggadah.*

Born in Cracow, he moved to Posen in his youth. In 5374 (1614) he became Rav of Lublin, and in 5385 (1625) of Ostrog, where he founded a large Yeshivah.

Einhorn, R' Zev Wolf

Rav in Vilna, end of 19th century.

Author of **Peirush Maharzu,** (*Maharzav*), comprehensive and well-detailed commentary to *Midrash Rabbah* appearing in the Rom edition, and since reprinted in the U.S. and in Israel.

HaBachur

See *Levitas, R' Eliyahu.*

Hirsch, R' Samson ben Raphael

[5568-5648 (1808-1888)]

The father of modern German Orthodoxy, he was a fiery leader, brilliant writer, and profound educator. His greatness as a *talmudic* scholar was obscured by his other monumental accomplishments. After becoming Chief Rabbi and Member of Parliament in Bohemia and Moravia, he left to revitalize Torah Judaism in Frankfort-am-Main which he transformed into a Torah bastion.

His classical works are a six-volume **Commentary on Chumash,** noted for its profound and brilliant philosophical approach to Biblical commentary; his **Commentary to Psalms;** and **Horeb,** a philosophical analysis of the *mitzvos.*

Ibn Chabib, R' Levi ben R' Yaakov

Born in Spain to his famous father R' Yaakov (the author of *Ein Yaakov*) before the expulsion of Jews from that country in 5252 (1492).

R' Levi and his father settled in Turkey. R' Levi finally settled in Jerusalem where

he served as Rav. R' Levi is famous for his opposition R' Yaakov Berav, the Rav of Safed, in the latter's attempt to renew the *Semichah*. The only work we have from Ralbach is a volume of his responsa. The commentary on Rambam, *Hilchos Kiddush HaChodesh*, that bears his name was taken from his responsa.

Ibn Ezra, R' Avraham ben Meir

[b. 4849 (1089) in Toledo; d. 4924 (1164)]

Famous poet, philosopher, grammarian, astronomer. In his Bible commentary he emphasizes the literal meaning of the verse. His commentary on the Torah is most widely studied, and appears in almost all large editions of the Bible.

His short commentary on Daniel, **Perush HaKatzer**, was published in London 5637 (1897). His longer commentary appears in most Hebrew Bibles with commentaries.

Ibn Janach, R' Yonah

[Born in Cordova c. 4750 (990 C.E.).]

Nothing more is known of his life except that he left Cordova in 4772 (1012) for Saragossa.

He published one of the first Biblical grammar books and dictionaries, the earliest to have come down to us in its entirety. It was originally written in Arabic and later translated into Hebrew by R' Yehudah Ibn Tibbon. It is divided into two parts: *Sefer HaRikmah*, and *Sefer HaShorashim*.

He is often quoted by later Bible commentators, and Hebraists such as: Ibn Ezra; Ibn Daud; Radak; Mizrachi.

The notable exception is Rashi, who seems to have been unacquainted with his work.

Ibn Janach was also a physician. He published several treatises on medicine which have been lost. Ibn Ezra also refers to him by the name "R' Merinus".

Ibn Yachya, Rav Joseph ben David

[5244-5294 (1494-1534)]

Commentator to the Bible and philosopher. R' Joseph studied under R' Yehudah Mintz in Padua. His commentary on *Kesuvim* and the *Five Megillos* was printed shortly after his death. *Daniel* was later printed separately in *Tanach Kehillas Moshe* and with a Latin translation (Amsterdam 5493).

Itinerary of R' Pesachiah

See *R' Pesachiah of Regensburg.*

Josephus Flavius

[c. 3800-3860 (40-100 C.E.)]

The earliest Jewish historian whose works have reached us. Born into an aristocratic family of *kohanim*, he entered public life at a young age. When the war against Rome broke out, Josephus was appointed commander in the Galilee. According to his own account, it was the *Tanna* R' Shimon ben Gamliel who recommended him for this appointment. After he was captured by the Romans following the siege of Jotapata, he managed to gain the favor of Vespasian (later emperor) at whose instruction he would go before the walls of Jerusalem, exhorting the inhabitants to surrender. When Vespasian was proclaimed emperor, he freed Josephus. In gratitude, Josephus assumed Vespasian's family name Flavius. Having been an eyewitness and an active participant in the war against Rome, he proceeded to write an account of it, **Wars of the Jews**, which has come down to us in Greek and has been translated into many languages. His other work, **Antiquities**, deals with Jewish History from the Creation to the destruction of the Second Temple.

[See also *Yosippon.*]

Karelitz, R' Avraham Yeshayah

[5638-5754 (1878-1953)]

Also known as *Chazon Ish*, after his works. The foremost Torah scholar and leader, following World War II, in his generation. He was a disciple of his father who was Rav of Kossow (Lithuania).

At an early age, R' Avraham Yeshayah decided to devote himself to learning Torah *Lishmah*, for its own sake; he never sought recognition. Even when he started publishing the first parts of his voluminous **Chazon Ish**, he remained virtually unknown, since he published all his works anonymously. When he settled in *Eretz Yisrael* in 5693 (1933), he was immediately recognized as one of the Torah greats of his genera-

tion. From then on, virtually nothing of importance was done in the religious community without consulting him.

His works, all entitled *Chazon Ish*, deal mainly with *Halacha*. He also wrote a work (incomplete) on ethics: *Al Inyanei Emunah Ubitachon Veod.*

Kimchi, R' David

French grammarian and commentator known by his acronym RADAK.

Born in Narbonne, c. 4920 (1160); died there in 4995 (1235)

His father, R' Yosef, also a grammarian, died when Radak was a child, and he studied under his brother, R' Moshe, who had also published several volumes on grammar.

Radak's *commentary to Prophets* is profound, and is included in most large editions of the Bible.

Many have applied to him the saying from *Pirkei Avos: Without* kemach *[flour i.e., — Kimchi], there is no Torah;* such was his great influence.

His main work was the **Michlol**, the second part of which came to be known independently as the **Sefer HaShorashim** (not to be confused with a work of the same name by Ibn Janach).

At the end of the **Sefer HaShorashim**, he lists the difficult Aramaic words in Scripture. This appendix to the **Shorashim** has been reprinted in the *Kehilos Moshe* Bible (Amsterdam 5484-7) under the name **Perush HaRadak.**

R' Levi ben Gershom

Known by his acronym RALBAG, he is also referred to as Gersonides.

[b. in Bangols, France 5048 (1288); d. 5104 (1344).]

One of the most important Bible commentators of his time, he was a mathematician, astronomer, philosopher, and physician.

He wrote commentaries to the Torah, *Job, The Five Megillos, Prophets, Proverbs,* **Daniel**, and *Nechemiah.*

His commentaries to **Daniel** and *Job* were among the first books printed in Hebrew (Ferrara, 5237 (1477).

To each unit of Scripture, he appended a list of **toaliyos** [lit. benefits] —

the moral, ethical, legal, and practical lessons that could be derived from that unit.

Levitas, R' Eliyahu ben R' Asher HaLevi

[b. Neustadt (Bavaria) 5228 (1468) — d. Venice (1549) 5320.]

Called *R' Eliyahu HaBachur*, from the name of his book **HaBachur**, he is also known as Elijah Levitas.

Grammarian and expert on the *Mesorah*, he left his birthplace and settled in Italy, where he spent most of his adult life. In 5264 (1504) he was in Padua, sustaining himself by teaching children.

When Padua was sacked five years later, R' Eliyahu fled to Rome, where he was hired by Cardinal Egedio di Viterbo to be his Hebrew tutor. R' Eliyahu stayed at the cardinal's house for thirteen years writing many treatises, among them his *Sefer Ha-Bachur*. He also copied many Hebrew manuscripts for the Cardinal, many of which are still extant.

Among his many works are **Tishbi**, a short dictionary on the Aramaic in the *Talmud* and the *Midrashim*; *Meturgeman*, a concordance and dictionary on the Aramaic in Scripture and the *Targum*: **Mesoras HaMesorah** on the *Mesorah*.

R' Levi Yitzchak of Berditchev

[b. 5500 (1740) — d. 5571 (1810)]

Chassidic *tzaddik* and rebbe, he is one of the most famous personalities of the chassidic movement.

Born into a distinguished rabbinic family — his father, R' Meir, was Rav in Hoshakov, Galicia.

He was drawn to *Chassidus* by R' Shmelke of Nikolsburg, and became one of the foremost disciples of R' Dov Ber, the Maggid of Mezeritch.

He succeeded R' Shmelke Horowitz in Richwal, and later became Rav in Zelechov; and in Pinsk.

He ultimately moved to Berditchev in 5545 (1785), and served as *Rav* and *Rebbe* there until his death.

Under him, Berditchev became a great chassidic center and many — including great Torah sages — flocked to consult with him.

In his writings, he noted that 'only he who admonishes Jewish people gently, elevates their souls, and always extols them righteously, is worthy of being their leader.'

Although he did not found a dynasty, he had many pupils and left an indelible mark on *Chassidus*.

His most famous work is **Kedushas Levi** — a commentary on some of the holidays — published during his lifetime in 5558 (1798). A second part — on the Torah — was published posthumously in 5571 (1811).

Likkutei Torah

Shneur Zalman of Liady

Luria, R' David

[b. 5558 (1798) — d. 5615 (1855)]

Lithuanian Rav and *posek*. Student of R' Shaul Katzenellenbogen of Vilna.

Radal was considered one of the Torah leaders of his generation. His scholarly writings embrace almost all of Torah literature. Among his works is his commentary to the *Midrash*, **Chiddushei Radal**, printed in the Rom edition of the *Midrash Rabbah*, and his comprehensive work on *Pirkei D'Rabbi Eliezer* called **Beur HaRadal.**

Luzatto, R' Moshe Chaim

[b. 5467 (1707) — d. 5506 (1746)]

Born in Padua, Italy, R' Moshe Chaim was regarded as a genius from childhood, having mastered *Tanach, Midrash*, and *Talmud* at an early age. He later went on to delve into *kabbalistic* and ethical studies.

He is most famous for his profound ethical treatise, *Mesillas Yesharim* ('The Path of the Upright'), which, alongside the *Chovos HaLevavos* of R' Bachya ibn Paquada, and *Shaarei Teshuvah* of Rabbeinu Yonah, became a standard ethical-*Mussar* work.

Among his *kabbalistic* works are: *Razin Genizin, Megillas Sesarim, Maamar HaGeulah,* and *Derech Hashem;* **Da'as Tevunos** examines the aim of Creation, the nature of Divinity, sin, justice, etc.

He is also known by the acronym RAMCHAL.

In 1743, he emigrated to *Eretz Yisrael.* He lived a short time in Acre, and died there with his family in a plague.

Maharal of Prague

See *R' Yehudah ben R' Bezalel.*

Malbim, R' Meir Leibush

[b. 5569 (1809) — d. 5639 (1879)]

Rav, Darshan, and Bible commentator, his name is an acronym of Meir Leibush ben Yechiel Michel.

Born in Volhynia, studied in his native town until the age of 13 when he went to Warsaw to study. He was Rav in several cities but he suffered much persecution because of his uncompromising stand against Reform, including brief imprisonment on a false accusation. He wandered much of his life, serving as Rav in a given city for several years and then moving on to another community.

His fame and immense popularity rest upon his commentary to the Bible which is widely esteemed. His first published commentary was on *Megillas Esther* 5605 (1845). His commentaries to the remaining books of the Bible were published between then and 5636 (1876). His commentary on **Daniel** is entitled **Yefe'ach LaKetz.**

Masnuth, R' Shmuel ben Nissim

Very little is known with certainty about him. Some wish to identify him with the R' Shmuel ben Nissim of Allepo (Aram Zova) lavishly praised by R' Yehudah Al Charizi in his poetical work *Tachkemoni.*

Since Al Charizi visited the Middle East in 4978 (1218) this would place R' Shmuel Masnuth in the period between 4950-5000 (1190-1240). However, this identification is far from certain. His commentary to **Daniel** was printed in Jerusalem (together with his commentary on *Ezra and Nechemiah*), (1968) by I.S. Lange and S. Schwartz under the name **Midrash Daniel.** Other known works by R' Shmuel are: *Midrash Bereishis Zuta* (the name was given by S. Buber); *Mayan Ganim* on *Iyov;* and *Midrash Divrei HaYamim.*

Rabbi Menachem Mendel of Lubavitch

(1789-1866).

A grandson of Rabbi Shneur Zalman of Liady, he became the third leader

of the *Chabad* movement, a position he held for nearly forty years. He was one of the leading figures of his time — a great halachic scholar, a chassidic thinker, and a Jewish leader who won the recognition and esteem of the Russian government. He is generally known as the *Tzemach Tzeddek* after his posthumously published halachic responsa. His *Derech Mitzvosecha* is a wide-ranging exposition on the commandments which blends virtually all areas of Torah thought.

Midrash Rabbah

[Lit. 'The Great Midrash.]

Amoraic classical *Midrash* on the Torah (Pentateuch) and on the Megillos.

R' Moshe ben Maimon

(b. 5895 (1135) — d. 5964 (1204).]

Known by his acronym, RAMBAM, and as Maimonides, he was one of the most illustrious figures in Judaism in the post-Talmudic era, and among the greatest of all time. He was a rabbinic authority, codifier, philosopher, and royal physician.

Born in Cordova; he wandered through West Africa and settled in Fostat, the old city of Cairo, Egypt.

At the age of 23 he began his *Commentary on the Mishnah*, which he wrote during his wanderings. Recently R' Y. Kafich has prepared a new translation of the commentary on the *Mishnah* based partly on manuscripts assumed to be in Rambam's own handwriting. His main work was **Mishneh-Torah, (Yad HaChazakah)**, his codification of the spectrum of *Halachah* up to his day. This was the only work he wrote in Hebrew; all his other works he composed in Arabic, a fact he is said to have regretted later in life.

He is also known for his profound and philosophic **Moreh Nevuchim ('Guide to the Perplexed')**, and for his many works in the field of medicine, hygiene, astronomy, etc.

Rambam also wrote many short treatises in the form of letters, among them his famed **Iggeres Teman,** *(Letter or Epistle to Yemen)*, in which Rambam endeavors to encourage the Yemenite Jews, who were having serious doubts

about pseudo-Messiah, and were subject to serious persecution on his account.

R' Moshe ben Nachman

[b. 5944 (1194) — d.c. 5030 (1270).]

Known by his acronym, RAMBAN, and as Nachmanides.

The leading Bible and Talmud scholar in the generation following Rambam; also a renowned philosopher, poet, and physician.

Born in Gerona to a famous rabbinic family, he is sometimes referred to as R' Moshe Gerondi, after his native town. He spent most of his life in Gerona, supporting himself as a physician. He exercised extensive influence over Jewish life. Even King James I consulted him on occasion.

By the age of 16, he had published works on *Talmud* and *Halachah*.

Among his works are: *Milchamos Hashem*, in defense of Alfasi (Rif) against the arguments of R' Zerachiah HaLevi in his *Sefer HaMaor*; *Sefer HaZechus*, in response to the arguments of the Ravad against Alfasi (Rif); *Sefer HaMitzvos*; *Iggeres HaRamban*; *Iggeres HaKodesh*; and his profound and encyclopedic **Commentary on the Torah**, which is printed in all major editions of the Torah. His **Sefer HaGeulah**, which treats the topic of the redemption and the *End* is included in *Kisvei HaRambam* ed. by Rabbi Ch. Chavel.

R' Pesachyah of Regensburg

(Bavaria)

Chiefly noted for the **Itinerary** of his voyage from Prague, through Poland and Southern Russia, the Crimea, Turkey, Iraq and *Eretz Yisrael*. He reported faithfully on all that he saw, and his *Itinerary* is a sourcebook for historians. Speculation places the time of his voyage between the years 4930-45 (1170-85). The Hebrew name of his book is **Sibuv R' Pesachya**. The *Tosafist* R' Yitzchak ben R' Yaakov (Ri HaLavan) of Prague was his brother.

Pirkei D'Rabbi Eliezer

An early *Midrash* attributed to the *tanna* Rabbi Eliezer ben Hyrkanos. Many of the early commentators cite him, notably Rambam.

Rabinowitz, R' Tzadok HaKohen

[b. 5583 (1823) — 5560 (1900)]

Born in Kreisburg, Latvia, young Tzadok attracted attention as a phenomenal genius. Orphaned at the age of six, he was raised by his uncle near Bialystock. Such was the child's reputation, that R' Yitzchak Elchanan Spektor of Kovno made a point of testing him when he happened to be nearby. He prophesied that the boy would light a great torch of knowledge in Israel.

In later years, he lived in Lublin where he became a disciple of both R' Liebele Eiger, and his *rebbe*, R' Mordechai Yosef of Izbica. With their passing, R' Tzadok became Rebbe of the Chassidim of Izbica. He became known far and wide as the *Kohen of Lublin*. Many considered him the greatest Torah scholar in all of Poland.

He was a very prolific writer. The breadth and depth of his thought is astonishing. Although many of his works have been published, he left many unpublished manuscripts that were destroyed during World War II.

Pri Tzaddik is a collection of his discourses on the weekly portion and festival. Among his other works are Responsa *Tiferes Zvi; Meishiv Tzeddek;* **Resisei Laylah**; and **Sichos Malachei Hashares.**

Radak

See *Kimchi, R' David.*

Ralbach

See *R' Levi ben Yaakov (Ibn Chabib).*

Ralbag

See *R' Levi ben Gershom.*

Rambam

See *R' Moshe ben Maimon.*

Ramban

See *R' Moshe ben Nachman.*

Rashi

See *R' Shlomo ben Yitzchak.*

RI HaZaken

See *R' Yitzchak ben R' Simcha.*

R' Saadiah (ben Yosef) Gaon

(b. 4652 (892) — d. 4702 (942).

Rosh Yeshivah of Sura and one of the most important figures of the illustrious Gaonic period, R' Saadiah was made Gaon by the Resh Gelusa (Exilarch) David ben Zakkai in 928. The ancient academy in Sura, founded by Rav, then entered upon a new period of brilliancy.

A sage in every sphere of Torah knowledge, he had a full grasp of the secular knowledge of his time. A dynamic leader, he fought a valiant battle against the growing influence of Karaism.

He published in many areas: *Halachah*, responsa, philosophy, grammar, but most of his works are lost or scattered among the *genizos*, waiting to be published.

Among the most important of R' Saadiah's works to have come down to us are parts of his commentary to the Bible and his **Tafsir**, a translation of the Bible, which was the first translation of the Bible from Hebrew into Arabic, and has remained the standard Bible for Yemenite Jews; his *Siddur; Sefer Ha-Agron*, on grammar; and his profound **Sefer Emunos V'Deos**, (Book of Beliefs and Doctrines), originally written in Arabic and translated into Hebrew by R' Yehudah ibn Tibbon. This major philosophical work is the earliest such work to have survived intact. Recently R' Y. Kafich has retranslated this book from manuscripts, showing that R' Saadiah later made many changes which are not found in the standard editions.

The commentary attributed to him in our editions of *Daniel* was probably not compiled by him. R' Yaakov Emden (*Mitpachas Sefarim*) maintains that the Gaon was not the author of this commentary. Its style betrays its author to be from the French-German school. Some attribute this work to R' Saadiah ben Nachmani, a commentator and *payetan* who lived in Rashi's time, who is thought by many to be the author of the commentary on *Chronicles* attributed to Rashi.

In order to differentiate between what is attributed to the Gaon by the early commentators (e.g. *Ibn Ezra*) and the commentary bearing his name, we

have called the latter *R' Saadiah* (without the suffix Gaon).

R' Saadiah Gaon's **Tafsir** to *Daniel* has been recently reproduced in Israel (without translation). Parts of his commentary on *Daniel* have been found in the Genizah but have not, as yet, been published.

Sefer HaIkkarim

See *Albo, R' Yosef.*

Sefer HaYashar

An early Hebrew work in *Midrashic* form which retells and elaborates upon Biblical narratives, especially on the Pentateuch. Its origins are obscure.

Though Ramban and Ibn Ezra quote this book, they express doubt as to its reliability. Nevertheless, it is of great antiquity.

R' Shlomo ben Yitzchak

[b. 4800 (1040) — d. 29 Tamuz 4865 (1105)]

Known by his acronym RASHI, he is the leading commentator on the Bible and the *Talmud.*

He was born in Troyes, France in 1040 — the year Rabbeinu Gershom M'or HaGolah died. According to tradition, Rashi's ancestry goes back to R' Yochanan HaSandlar and to King David.

Rashi's commentary on the *Talmud* — an encyclopaedic and brilliant undertaking has no peer in the impact it has had upon all who study *Talmud.* Rashi's commentary opened to all what otherwise would have been a sealed book. Without his commentary, no one would dare navigate the 'Sea of Talmud.' Every word is precise and laden with inner meaning. Rashi's corrections of the *Talmud* text were so generally accepted that, for the most part, they were introduced into the standard editions and became the accepted text.

Rashi's **Commentary to the Bible**, too, made a similar impact — and virtually every printed Bible contains his commentary which is distinguished by its conciseness and clarity.

Many *Halachic* works from the 'School of Rashi' have come down to us: *Sefer HaOrah; Sefer HaPardes; Machzor Vitry; Siddur Rashi;* and responsa.

Shmoneh Prakim

[Lit. *Eight Chapters*]

Rambam's preface to his commentary on Tractate *Avos.* It contains eight chapters, hence its name.

See *R' Moshe ben Maimon.*

R' Shmuel ben Meir

[B. 5840 (1080)]

Known by his acronym RASHBAM, he was a Bible and *Talmud* commentator and *Tosafist.* Born in Northern France, he was the son of R' Meir, one of the first *Tosafists* and disciples of Rashi, whose daughter Yocheved, R' Meir married.

A grandson of Rashi, Rashbam was also the brother of the prominent Rabbeinu Tam, and a colleague of R' Yosef Kara.

Rashbam studied under his father, but was most influenced by his grandfather. They spent much time together in legal and exegetical discussions. In many instances, it is noted that Rashi accepted his grandson's opinion in exegesis.

Rashbam lived a simple life, always praying that he might be privileged to perceive the Truth and to love peace.

He is most famous for his commentary to the Bible which is characterized by his extreme devotion to *p'shat.* He constantly refers to 'the profound literal meaning' of the text. In many ways, he considered his commentary as complementing that of Rashi. His commentary is often exactly identical with his grandfather's.

He is also known as a *Talmudic* commentator. His commentary to portions of *Pesachim* and *Bava Basra* were intended to complete unfinished works of Rashi.

Rabbi Shneur Zalman of Liady

(1745-1813)

Also known as the *Rav,* and the *Baal HaTanyah,* he was one of the outstanding scholars and leaders of his century, and the founder of the Lubavitch dynasty. He became one of the leading disciples of Rabbi Dov Ber, the *Maggid* of Mezritch. The Maggid assigned him to compose an updated *Shulchan Aruch,* code of law. His *Rav's Shulchan*

Aruch remains one of the major contributions to the field. As a Chassidic leader, he was subject to vicious attack and, as a result of slanderous accusations, was twice arrested by the Czarist government which later exonerated him. He developed a rigorous intellectual-philosophical exposition of *Chassidism* which came to be known as *Chabad*. The principle *Chassidic* text he published in his lifetime is the classic *Likkutei Amarim*, known as *Tanya*, a masterly exposition of *Chabad*. His **Likkutei Torah** and *Torah Ohr*, both profound Kabblistic commentaries on the Torah, were published posthumously.

Sifri

Name of the *Tannaitic Midrashim* on *Numbers* and *Deuteronomy*. It differs from *Midrash Rabbah* in that it concentrates almost exclusively on the *Halachic* aspect of the Torah.

Rabbeinu Tam

See *R' Yaakov ben Meir Tam.*

Targum

The ancient, authoritative translation of the Bible into Aramaic. The *Targum* on Bible was compiled by Onkelos while the *Targum* on Prophets is by Yonasan ben Uziel. The *Targumim* **Yonasan** and **Yerushalmi** are really variant versions of a Jerusalemite *(Eretz Yisrael)* *Targum*. The *Targumim* on the books of *Kesuvim* are of uncertain origin. It is assumed that they originated in *Eretz Yisrael*.

Toaliyos

See *R' Levi ben Gershon.*

Tosafos Yom Tov

Classic commentary to *Mishnah*. See *R' Yom Tov Lipman Heller.*

R' Tzadok HaKohen

See *Rabinowitz.*

Wars of the Jews

See *Josephus Flavius*, and *Yossipon.*

R' Yaakov ben Meir Tam

Usually called Rabbeinu Tam (a nickname for *Yaakov* from *Genesis* 25:27.

One of the greatest *Tosafists*. His father R' Meir ben Simcha was Rashi's son-in-law. Was disciple of his father and of his elder brother, R' Shmuel (Rashbam). His comments on the *Talmud* were collected by him and his disciples in *Sefer HaYashar* which also contains some of his responsa. Many of the greatest *Tosafists* were his disciples. He also wrote on Hebrew grammar and there is evidence that he wrote commentaries on the Bible. R' Tam also wrote *Piyutim* and *Selichos* (Liturgy). Died Tamus 4, 4931 (1171).

Rav Yaakov ben Asher:

(1270-1340)

Posek and codifier.

Son of Rav Asher ben Yechiel (the 'ROSH') under whom he studied. He was born in Germany. He followed his father to Toledo, where he lived in great poverty and devoted his life to Torah.

Rav Yaakov's enduring fame rests on his encyclopedic Halachic codification *Arbaah Turim* which is the forerunner of our *Shulchan Aruch* today. As a result, he is referred to as the "Baal haTurim."

The arrangement and wealth of content made it a basic work in halachah and it was disseminated widely through the Jewish world. It became so widely accepted that when Rav Yosef Caro wrote his major work, *Bais Yosef,* he decided to base it upon the *Turim* "because it contains most of the views of the *Poskim.*"

Rav Yaakov also wrote a comprehensive commentary on the Chumash anthologizing the literal explanations *(p'shat)* by earlier Bible commentators. To the beginning of each section he added "as a little appetizer, *gemmatrios* and explanations of the *Masorah,* in order to attract the mind." Ironically, the whole work was printed only twice. It was just these "appetizers" that were popularly published alongside most editions of the Bible under the title **Ba'al HaTurim.**

Among Rav Yaakov's students was Rav David Abudraham.

According to *Shem haGedolim*, Rav Yaakov died en route to *Eretz Yisrael*.

Yaffe (Ashkenazi), Rav Shmuel

16th Century Rav in Constantinople.

Not being satisfied with any commentary to the *Midrash*, Rav Shmuel devoted himself to writing a comprehensive commentary to *Midrash Rabbah* and to the *Aggados* in the *Talmud*.

His first published work was *Yefe Mar'eh* on the *Aggados* in the Jerusalem *Talmud* (5347); *Yefe To'ar* to *Midrash Rabbah*; *Genesis* (5357-66); *Exodus* (5417); *Leviticus* (5408); *Yefe Anaf* to *Ruth, Esther,* and *Eichah* (5451); and *Yefe Kol* to *Song of Songs* (5499).

His commentary to *Ecclesiastes,* and his *halachic* writing are still in manuscript form.

Yalkut Shimoni

The best known and most comprehensive Midrashic anthology covering the entire Bible.

It is attributed to Rav Shimon haDarshan of Frankfort who lived in the 13th century.

The author collected *Midrashim* from more than 50 works, arranging them into more than 10,000 statements of *Aggadah* and *Halachah* according to the verses of the Bible.

Rav Yedidiah Shlomo Raphael of Norzi

Rav and Commentator.

Became Rav in Mantua in 1585.

Rav Yedidiah consecrated the greater part of his life to studying the *Masorah* of the Bible — and by studying every previously printed *Masorah* text, comparing the various readings scattered through *Talmudic* and *Midrashic* literature, as well as in published and unpublished manuscripts.

The resulting work was entitled *Goder Peretz,* but was published under the name **Minchas Shai.**

This work, which was as perfect as thorough learning and conscientious industry could make it, has become the most accepted work in establishing the *Masorah*. The **Minchas Shai** is printed as an appendix to most large Bibles.

Rav Yehudah Loewe ben Bezalel

Known as the MAHARAL of Prague.

One of the seminal figures in the last 500 years of Jewish thought. The year of Rav Yehudah's birth is not known with certainty. He died in Prague in 1609. His genealogy can be traced to King David.

Although he was universally acknowledged as one of the rabbinic greats of the era, his life was not an easy one. He delayed his marriage for many years due to financial difficulties. He was Chief Rabbi of Moravia, residing in Nikolsburg for 20 years. Then, in 1573, he transferred his yeshiva to Prague, the Torah metropolis of Europe. Upon two different occasions, he accepted the rabbinate of Posen. He was elected Chief Rabbi of Prague in 1598 as a very old man. It appears that the position had been denied him up to then because of his outspokenness in attacking social evils and religious laxity.

Though commonly known as a folk hero and miracle worker, his greatest contribution was his formulation of a self-contained system of Jewish thought. His many books and lengthy sermons formed the basis for much of the significant writing of succeeding centuries.

Among his many erudite works were: *Novellae* on *Shulchan Aruch Yoreh Deah;* **Gur Aryeh** on the Torah; *M'er haGolah* **Derech Chaim;** *Netzach Yisrael; Nesivos Olam,* etc. Many of his works are extant and were recently republished in an 18-volume set: *Sifrei Maharal.*.

R' Yeshayah (b. Mali) of Trani

Great Talmudist and Biblical commentator in Southern Italy. Is also called R' Yeshayah Harishon or Hazaken to differentiate between him and his grandson, R' Yeshayah b. Elijah of Trani. Was a disciple of R' Simchah of Verona who in turn was a disciple of Ri Hazaken. In spite of his great reverence for Rashi, whom he calls *Hamoreh*, the teacher, he does not hesitate to disprove Rashi's and other great commentators' views. Many unique views are to be found in his writings. Wrote voluminously on the *Talmud* (*Tosafos Rid* and *Piskei Rid*).

He also wrote a commentary on Torah,

mainly dealing with Rashi's commentary (printed in Chida's Pnei David), and commentaries to most of the Prophets and Kesuvim. Recently, R' S.A. Wertheimer has collected the commentaries on Prophets and Kesuvim (both printed and manuscript) and printed them in 3 volumes. The commentary to Daniel appeared in Jerusalem 5738. There is a controversy as to whether R' Yeshayah ben Mali is actually the author of the commentaries on Prophets and Kesuvim. Some ascribe these to his grandson, R' Yeshayyah b. Elijah. Flourished approximately 4980-5030 (1220-1270).

R' Yissachar Berman haKoken:

Known as R' Berman Ashkenzai.

16-17th Century commentator on the Midrash.

Very little is known about him except that he was born in Sczebrzesyn, Poland, and that he was a student of the Rama (R' Moshe Isserles).

He is the author of the famous commentary to the Midrash Rabbah, **Matenos Kehunah,** first published in 1587 and appearing subsequently, in nearly every edition of the Midrash.

R' Yissachar makes it very clear in his introduction that he was very concerned with establishing the correct text for the Midrashim, basing his text upon all the various printed editions up to his time and on various manuscripts.

R' Yitzchak (ben Simcha)

Usually called **RI** (acronym for R' Yitzchak) **Hazaken** (the elder, probably to differentiate between him and RI Habachur, the younger).

Celebrated French Tosafist. His father, R' Simcha, was a grandson of R' Simcha of Vitri the famed disciple of Rashi and son-in-law of R' Meir, Rashi's son-in-law. Was a disciple of his illustrious uncles, R' Shmuel (Rashbam) and R' Yaakov (R' Tam).

His comments collected and recorded by his disciples serve, together with R' Tam's comments, the basis of Tosafos. Died approximately 1140 (1380).

Rabbeinu Yonah of Gerona

Spanish Rav and Moralist of the thirteenth century.

Rabbeinu Yonah was a cousin of Ramban (Nachmanides). He was one of the most prominent students of Rav Shlomo ben Avraham of Montpellier (Min haHar).

Rabbeinu Yonah was one of the people who banned the Rambam's Moreh Nevuchim out of fear that philosophical influences — rampant at the time — would cause untold harm to the religiosity of the people. But when he saw that this anti-Rambam controversy was getting out of hand — and even resulted in the public burning of the Talmud in the same place where the philosophical writings of Rambam had been destroyed — Rabbeinu Yonah publicly admitted that he was wrong in all his acts against the works of Rambam. In his repentance, he vowed to travel to Eretz Yisrael and prostrate himself over the grave of the great teacher and implore his pardon in the presence of ten men for seven consecutive days.

He left France with that intention, but was detained. He died in 5024 (1263) before he was able to fulfill his plan.

Rabbeinu Yonah wrote many works, among them commentaries on portions of Scripture; commentary of Avos; Chiddushim on several tractates of the Talmud many of which were compiled by his disciples (see Shem HaGedolim) and his famous Mussar works, Iggers HaTeshuva; Shaarei Teshuvah; and Sefer haYirah.

Rabbeinu Yonah established Yeshivos. Among his most prominent pupils was Rav Shlomo ibn Adret (Rashba).

He stayed in close contact with his cousin, Ramban, and Ramban's daughter married Rabbeinu Yonah's son. When Rabbeinu Yonah died, his daughter was pregnant. When she gave birth to a son, Ramban told her to name the child Yonah so that he would assuredly excel in Torah and piety.

R' Yom Tov Lipman (ben R' Nosson) Halevi Heller

Famous mainly for his commentary to Mishnah entitled **Tosafos Yom Tov.**

Born 5339 (1579) in Wallerstein (Bavaria).

Studied under Maharal of Prague and R' Ephraim Lunshitz. Eventually he was elected Rav of Prague. After a short while, he was accused of making anti-Christian statements in his books and was condemned to die. However, the king was moved to pardon him. R' Yom Tov then left Austria and spent the rest of his life as Rav of various cities in Poland.

He also composed a commentary to *Rosh* which has been partly printed, and many other books. R' Yom Tov died in Cracow 5414 (1654).

Yosippon

The name given to an ancient Jewish history quoted often by Rashi and other early writers. The author gives his name as Joseph ben Gorion and mentions that he wrote a parallel history for the Romans. His account of the destruction of the Temple is written in eye-witness style and resembles Josephus very much. All this raises speculation whether this book is Josephus' Hebrew version of his history. [See also *Josephus.*]